D0933731

"Asylum for Mankind"

"Asylum for Mankind"

America, 1607–1800

MARILYN C. BASELER

Cornell University Press

ITHACA AND LONDON

First published 1998 by Cornell University Press

Library of Congress Cataloging-in-Publication Data

Baseler, Marilyn C.
    "Asylum for mankind" : America, 1607–1800 / Marilyn C. Baseler.
      p. cm.
    Includes bibliographical references (p.) and index.
    ISBN 0-8014-3481-5 (cloth : alk. paper)
      1. United States—Emigration and immigration—History.
    2. Immigrants—United States—History.   I. Title.
    JV6451. B37   1998
    325.73′09′032—dc21   97-53079

Printed in the United States of America

Cornell University Press strives to use environmentally responsible suppliers and materials to the fullest extent possible in the publishing of its books. Such materials include vegetable-based, low-VOC inks and acid-free papers that are recycled, totally chlorine-free, or partly composed of nonwood fibers.

Cloth printing   10 9 8 7 6 5 4 3 2 1

*For my family
and in memory of
David Nelson Case*

Contents

Preface

M Y INTEREST in American immigration began in my first year of graduate school while searching for a paper topic for Bernard Bailyn's seminar in early American history. After unsuccessfully lobbying for a study of poor relief in revolutionary America, I accepted Professor Bailyn's recommendation that I examine, instead, the impact of the American Revolution on immigration. Professor Bailyn was absolutely correct in arguing that this project would lead me into fertile and untilled soil, but he was overly optimistic in claiming that post-Revolutionary immigration was a more "manageable" topic than poor relief—in terms of producing a seminar paper in the nine weeks that remained of our thirteen-week semester. That semester was long enough, however, to reveal many unanswered, and often unasked, questions about America's immigrants—their numbers and experiences in the early republic and the ways in which these newcomers helped define not only the American people but also the nation itself. That semester was also long enough for me to catch a glimpse of a well-hidden, but incredibly rich, treasure trove of information about the American republic's first immigrant generation: naturalization records stored in the dusty attics and basements of courthouses scattered across the eastern states. As I uncovered more and more information on America's republican immigrants, I found that each country and city had its own distinctive migration pattern, ethnic profile, and immigrant experiences. It was soon obvious that more than one book was needed to do justice to the stories that were waiting to be told.

"*Asylum for Mankind*" analyzes the promise of America that attracted so many voluntary immigrants both before and after the American Revolution and the disabilities and opportunity they experienced; it also examines that extent to which Africans arriving in chains subsidized the improved living standards of European immigrants. In focusing on the migration patterns, immigrant policies, and naturalization procedures that emerged in the seventeenth and eighteenth centuries, this book provides the context necessary for understanding the experiences and impact of the men, women, and children who emigrated to America in the first decades of independence. In the process individual immigrants were submerged, especially women and children—dependents who had no legal identity of their own and whose eligibility for "the rights of Englishmen" depended on the naturalization of their husbands and fathers. They will, however, be the focus of my next book on America's immigrants.

My research and the writing of this book were made possible by the help and support of dozens of people in the academic community. Bernàrd Bailyn can always be counted on to ask the tough questions and to force me to aim ever higher. Stephan Thernstrom and Pauline Maier have provided me with moral support and sound advice for longer than I can remember. On my arrival in Texas, I discovered and enjoyed the support of many official and unofficial mentors and colleagues. Denise Spellberg, Ann Ramsey, Janet Meisel, Susan Burns, Aline Helg, Michael Hall, and Howard Miller all deserve special thanks for helping me through the rough spots. Both Harvard University and the University of Texas at Austin have provided generous financial support. A grant from the Artemas Ward Foundation at Harvard funded my initial research; the University of Texas facilitated the writing of this book by awarding me a summer research fellowship in 1992 and a Dean's Fellowship in the fall of 1996.

During my research trips I encountered many individuals who went far beyond the call of duty on my behalf. James Owens, director of the National Archives and Record Center in Waltham, not only helped me track down elusive records, but also was there with a set of jumper cables when my car battery went dead. Robert Plowman, former director of the National Archives and Record Center in Philadelphia, went out of his way to accommodate my needs, as did the wonderful people at Maryland's Hall of Records and State Library in Annapolis and at the Virginia State Library in Richmond. The clerks of Monroe and St. Lawrence County in New York were especially helpful in opening up their records to me. I must also thank the interlibrary loan librarians at Widener Library, who somehow managed to fill all my requests; Janice Donald Andersen of the Groton Public Library, who performed similar feats when I moved to Connecticut; and the people at the Connecticut College library, who have been so generous in granting me library privileges.

My family also deserves recognition and thanks for allowing me to pursue my academic dreams. Although my husband and children often wished I had stayed at home, they always took up the slack during my absence and periods of mental abstraction—successfully handling domestic crises that ranged from grocery shopping to my son's broken jaw. I have especially enjoyed the enthusiastic and compassionate support of my daughter, Anne, who has always listened to me talk about "my immigrants" and whose common sense and computer savvy have helped me out of some incredible messes. My mother has been another able and enthusiastic supporter. She not only accompanied me on some tedious road trips, but was also willing to be put to work once we arrived. My thanks also go to my father and his green thumb; Beverly and Chuck, for their hospitality (and Chuck's expertise); my brother for his occasionally wise advice; Karin, who always knew what I was going through; Torbjørn, who has promised to promote my book in Norway; my *barnebarn*, Danny, Fallon, Emily, Sarah, and Jack; and Pat and Ray.

MARILYN C. BASELER

Austin, Texas

"Asylum for Mankind"

Introduction

IN THE 1870s a group of French citizens celebrated the centennial of the American Revolution by commissioning a statue of "Liberty Enlightening the World." The statue was presented to the United States to commemorate the success of the American Revolution, but its primary purpose was to remind the French of the links between the two nations and to promote the reestablishment of republican government in France. In America, promotional tours and contests were organized to raise the $300,000 needed to build a pedestal for the huge French statue. During these fund-raising campaigns, Emma Lazarus, the daughter of a prominent Jewish family in New York City, wrote the poem "The New Colossus," which transformed the French statue of "Liberty Enlightening the World" into the American Statue of Liberty welcoming the oppressed. By the middle of the twentieth century, Americans believed that their statue was indeed crying,

> Give me your tired, your poor,
> Your huddled masses yearning to breathe free,
> The wretched refuse of your teeming shore.
> Send these, the homeless, tempest-tost to me.[1]

The commitment of the United States to serve as an asylum for the oppressed and a land of opportunity for the world's "huddled masses" has recently come under attack from two different directions. Americans who fear the consequences of serving as a refuge and place of new beginnings for those who have suffered from economic as well as political and religious repression have worked to narrow the parameters of the American asylum. Policies have evolved that

---

[1] *Liberty Enlightening the World* (New York: Illustrative Press Bureau, 1886); John Higham, "The Transformation of the Statue of Liberty," in *Send These to Me: Jews and Other Immigrants in Urban America* (New York: Atheneum, 1975), 78–87, "The New Colossus," in *Send These to Me*, 78.

I

require foreigners seeking sanctuary to prove narrowly defined political harassment, rather than generalized misery produced by an oppressive government or a failing economy. Excluded from the right of asylum are foreigners who hope simply to end generations of poverty and fear for themselves and their children. More recently, laws have been passed that limit the rights of immigrants, most notably by denying legal immigrants access to the social services that are funded, in part, by the taxes they pay.

As some Americans are questioning their obligation to serve as an asylum, very different groups are arguing that the United States has never been a land of opportunity for the oppressed. Modern historians are reexamining the filiopietistic myths that have obscured and misrepresented the roots of the American republic. Efforts are being made to rescue previously hidden victims from historical oblivion—the men, women, and children whose enslavement or exploitation generated American prosperity and underwrote the political liberty enjoyed by propertied white males. However, these studies have often tipped the scale too far in the opposite direction. Too narrow a focus on the suffering and immiseration of America's victims distorts their lives as well as those of their putative oppressors. So, too, does the tendency to accept, with little question, the charges made by or on behalf of the "underclasses" while rejecting as self-seeking and spurious evidence generated by the "better sort." Difficulty in comprehending the context in which these events and experiences took place compounds the problem. Actions that violate twentieth-century sensibilities were not necessarily repugnant to the men and women of the seventeenth and eighteenth centuries; the ideas and ideals that shape possible courses of action available to people separated by more than two centuries are just as divergent.

This book analyzes the genesis and eighteenth-century definition of the United States as an asylum for liberty and land of opportunity and the extent to which immigrants were able to realize the promise of America.

Emma Lazarus transformed the meaning and purpose of the French statue of "Liberty Enlightening the World"; her words also distorted and oversimplified American immigration policy. After declaring independence Americans were forced to define the status of aliens and their place in a republican society. The regulations and policies that were hammered out in the quarter century that followed were compromises that ended often bitter battles among Americans holding different political beliefs and priorities. Compromises reached during the first decades of independence remain at the heart of America's immigration and naturalization policies today. The debates and conflict that shaped alien policies in the 1780s and 1790s reveal not only the different republican visions of the revolutionary generation but also the contradictory principles and impulses embodied in the American asylum.

America's obligation to serve as a refuge is deeply rooted in European history. The Protestant Reformation was a major force in formulating the American asylum, as it set in motion the people, ideas, events, and rivalries that generated the concept of the newfound lands as a refuge. French Huguenots were the most persistent, and the English Puritans who settled Massachusetts Bay the most successful, in establishing Protestant sanctuaries in the New World. The willingness of victims of religious persecution to search out a new home in the American wilderness is evidence of the severity of their treatment in the Old World and the steadfastness of their faith. The willingness of European governments to sanction such undertakings is far more complex.

Martin Luther's actions triggered almost two centuries of warfare in Europe, as Protestants and Catholics battled for the right to define the one true faith. In the second half of the sixteenth century Philip II of Spain used American treasure to finance his dream of a universal Christendom, united once again under God's vicar at Rome. A century later, French monarchs embarked on a similar program. The Catholic counteroffensive increased the number of religious refugees and transformed several European countries into asylums for persecuted Protestants. Offers to serve as a refuge for the victims of "papist" oppression were, at the official level, largely pragmatic. Believing that people, and especially skilled workers and men of property, were the true wealth of a nation, European governments had been recruiting valuable subjects from rival countries for centuries. The militance of the counter-Reformation increased the attractive power of countries that offered asylum to the victims of religious persecution.

Europe's religious refugees also looked to the New World for sanctuary. During the sixteenth century, French Protestants were powerful enough to win the official and financial backing necessary to send out several Huguenot expeditions. These attempts to create a Franco-American refuge failed, victims of the New World environment, Spanish and English hostility, and the waning of Huguenot influence in France. Ultimately France would join Spain in restricting emigration to prevent the creation of overseas centers of dissent. Religious and political dissidents in seventeenth-century England were more successful. In the first half of the century, while English Puritans were preparing sanctuaries in America that would shield them from the wrath of God and the Stuart kings, Charles I chartered a Catholic refuge in Maryland. This new colony was designed not only to protect English Catholics from their intolerant Protestant brethren, but also to assert the prerogative power of the English monarch against his Puritan parliament. Throughout the seventeenth century, Stuart kings increased religious toleration in their American colonies to exercise disputed royal rights, to protect their dissenting and Catholic supporters from parliamentary persecution, and to increase the demographic base of English wealth and power.

As European colonizers adopted different imperial strategies, the role of the New World as a refuge for the victims of religious, political, and economic oppression gradually devolved on the British colonies of North America. As heretics, political dissidents, and ne'er-do-wells were excluded from the Spanish and French empires, England increasingly relied on its American colonies to relieve various social, demographic, and political pressures in the British Isles.

The early promoters of English colonization had promised that their new settlements would both siphon off and rehabilitate England's "redundant" and nonproductive population. Orphans were gathered off the streets of London and sent to Virginia; "vagabonds and beggars" were similarly transported to the New World to be transformed, in Gregory King's words, from those "Decreasing the Wealth of the Kingdom" into productive subjects.[2] Subversive elements of British society also were encouraged or forced to emigrate to America. Jacobites and prisoners of war were exiled to the colonies under various conditions of servitude; British convicts were given the option of escaping the hangman's noose by agreeing to labor in America. The American colonies also became part of England's imperial labor market, a place of last resort, where men unable to find employment at home could indenture themselves to labor-hungry colonists.

At the end of the seventeenth century, England also began to promote its American colonies as a refuge and land of opportunity for the oppressed and discontented subjects of European rivals. While England continued to underwrite the emigration of social liabilities, growing fears of depopulation led officials to formulate policies designed to settle British North America with "people not her own."[3] English officials seduced Protestant settlers from rival nations by promises of free land, economic opportunity, religious toleration, easy naturalization, and the "rights of Englishmen" as guaranteed by the British Constitution. To fill the expanding colonial labor market with non-English subjects, the crown also granted charters to slavers and financed the transportation of foreign-born Protestants to New York, Carolina, and Georgia, while encouraging colonial proprietors and officials to do likewise. In advertising its American colonies as a refuge for both foreign and domestic malcontents and misfits, England hoped to build a prosperous and powerful empire without expending its own human capital. By offering America as a refuge for "those whom bigots chase from foreign lands"[4] and Europe's "huddled masses," England also could enhance its

[2]Gregory King, *Natural and Politicall Observations and Conclusions upon the State & Condition of England*, 1st publ. 1696, in George E. Barnett, ed., *Two Tracts by Gregory King* (Baltimore: Johns Hopkins University Press, 1936), 31.

[3]The phrase is by William Penn and is quoted in Walter Allen Knittle, *Early Eighteenth-Century Palatine Emigration: A British Government Redemptioner Project to Manufacture Naval Stores* (Philadelphia: Dorrance & Company, 1937), 27.

[4]Quote, from the English poet James Thomson's 1735 description of British America, in Richard Koebner, *Empire* (Cambridge: Cambridge University Press, 1961), 95.

own status as an asylum without having to incorporate hordes of impoverished refugees into English society.

Policies that promoted the removal of England's social and political liabilities to the New World and the settlement of foreign-born Protestants were presented in terms that gave British America a regenerative gloss. Indentured servitude and emigration were depicted as mechanisms that gave the unfortunate and the depraved an opportunity to better themselves. The Transportation Act of 1717, which set up the machinery for transferring convicts from England to America, often was described as a humanitarian reform that would rehabilitate the vicious while transforming England's social liabilities into productive colonial subjects. This image of British North America received its ultimate definition at the hands of St. John de Crèvecœur, an adventurer who settled in New York after serving with the French army in North America. Crèvecœur's manuscript was not published until the 1780s, but the America he celebrated was the British colonial asylum, that magical place where Europe's dispossessed, "mowed down by want, hunger, and war," took "root and flourished."[5]

American settlers were less euphoric about some of the immigrant policies devised by British officials and colonizers, especially those that saddled them with Europe's outcasts and increased their dependence on slave labor. From the beginning, settlers often pleaded with their English backers to substitute industrious workers for the "scum of the earth" they had been sending. Although most colonists deplored the arrival of worthless or dangerous immigrants, their demographic needs and definition of "worthless" differed. Chesapeake planters wanted impecunious laborers who, after turning over their land headrights, could be forced into the tobacco fields; Virginia's Governor William Berkeley, on the other hand, yearned for "men of . . . good families" to impose order. Similar differences emerged in the north. Most seventeenth-century New Englanders placed a premium on economic independence, wanting only settlers who came "well provided, and . . . but few servants and those useful ones." At the same time, however, Puritans such as Emanuel Downing were arguing that Massachusetts could not "thrive untill wee get in a stock of slaves sufficient to doe all our business."[6] Colonial religious preferences were just as varied. The seventeenth-century proprietors of Maryland would have peopled their colony with Catholics had sufficient numbers been available for transplantation, but were forced to recruit troublesome Puritans who eventually overturned Maryland's Catholic regime and the colony's policy of religious toleration. In Massachusetts Bay, the

[5] J. Hector St. John de Crèvecœur, *Letters from an American Farmer*, 1782 (London: J. M. Dent & Sons, 1971), Letter III, 42.

[6] Quotes from *Calendar of State Papers, Colonial Series, 1574–1660* (London: Longman et al., 1860), 155; William Berkeley, *A Discourse and View of Virginia* (London, 1663), 3; John Winthrop to John Winthrop, Jr., July 23, 1630, *Winthrop Papers*, ed. Stewart Mitchell, 5 vols. (Boston: Massachusetts Historical Society, 1929–1947), II, 306; Emanuel Downing to John Winthrop, 1645, in Elizabeth Donnan, ed., *Documents Illustrative of the History of the Slave Trade to America*, 4 vols. (Washington, D.C.: Carnegie Institution of Washington, 1930–1935), III, 8.

colonists hoped to establish exclusive enclaves of Puritan saints while Virginians preferred Anglicans.

Colonial status limited the settlers' ability to define the immigration policies that shaped their communities. American laws that abrogated unpopular policies were often vetoed in England or by colonial governors. However, conflict over American immigration policy was not a simple contest that pitted colonists against imperial agents and proprietors. It embodied not only the divergent goals and priorities of different colonies, but also divisions within communities and individuals themselves. Americans often used their dependent status to assuage personal misgivings and to exonerate themselves from complicity in the exploitation of enslaved and dangerous immigrants who threatened to undermine public safety and communal harmony. Colonists in labor-short America promoted, by their actions, the arrival of those whose presence they officially deplored. During the eighteenth century American assemblies passed laws that prohibited, taxed, or otherwise discouraged the immigration of Catholics, British convicts, the dissolute dregs of the Old World, and African slaves. Yet the same colonists who condemned British officials for vetoing these proscriptive measures ensured the continuing arrival of "undesirable"immigrants by purchasing the labor contracts of Catholic and profligate servants; the colonists did not exercise their power to destroy the slave and convict trades by the simple expedient of refusing to purchase those workers. American protests against transported convicts and African slaves may have been little more than rituals to absolve colonists for placing private profit ahead of public good, and they reveal some of the inner contradictions that shaped American immigration policy and the colonial asylum.

By the middle of the eighteenth century, British North America had become a pragmatic refuge for European Protestants, an asylum designed to promote English power, rather than to relieve the world's "huddled masses yearning to breathe free." Promises of religious toleration, political liberty, free land, and economic opportunity were made to lure valued foreigners to England and her American colonies. Whatever their origin, these promises seem to have been fulfilled for Europeans who emigrated to British North America in the eighteenth century. Virtually every modern study has found that these emigrants enjoyed more political rights, greater religious liberty, and a higher standard of living than their Old World counterparts. The opposite was true for African slaves.

The appropriation of the fruits of slave labor was one of the factors that made Euro-Americans richer, taller, healthier, and better fed than those they had left behind. It is no accident that Southern planters, who profited most from slavery, were the richest and tallest of all eighteenth-century Americans. African slavery also subsidized the emigration of Europe's "downtrodden masses." Because colonial legislatures were prohibited from passing laws that banned or placed prohibitive duties on the African slave trade, Americans developed other strategies to reduce the dangers of slavery, while continuing to reap its benefits. The vigorous recruitment of Europeans was, in part, an attempt to dilute and control America's servile work force. In the South, the nonprohibitive customs duties that were levied on new slave arrivals often were used to fund the transportation of indentured servants, redemptioners, and "persecuted Protestants"; fear of a black majority led Chesapeake planters to purchase the service contracts of thousands of transported British convicts, despite their strong aversion to "gaol birds." Colonial policies that expanded the political rights and economic opportunity of Europeans thus created a cruel legacy, as the American refuge and land of opportunity became inextricably intertwined with African slavery.

Although the promise of British North America was real for most eighteenth-century European immigrants and their progeny, it also was transitory. Built to enhance England's stature, all offers of asylum could be revoked at will, when they no longer served the interests of the mother country. As tensions rose in the colonies at the end of the Seven Years' War, British promises of free land to foreign-born Protestants were rescinded, colonial naturalization procedures were closed down, and in 1776, English convicts were denied access to America's supposed regenerative haven. During these same years, American patriots came to believe that England was also reneging on its promise of political liberty, religious freedom, and economic opportunity for its colonial subjects.

The war that was fought to secure independence from England altered the contours of the American refuge in many ways. The American Revolution expanded the commitment of the thirteen colonies to serve as an asylum for liberty. In the 1770s, American revolutionaries repudiated England's claim to possess the world's freest government and arrogated to themselves the title of guardian of liberty. American patriots rallied to the ringing rhetoric of Thomas Paine, responding to his challenge to preserve freedom and to "prepare in time an asylum for mankind."[7] The republican and religious ideals that imbued America's patriotic aspirations envisioned the independent states leading the way to a utopian future and creating a nation governed by the needs of the people rather than the ambitions of princes. Both secular and religious millenarians anticipated that republican America would be an irresistible magnet, drawing "mankind" into their "Glorious Cause."

Preserving liberty on behalf of humanity required more than independence from England; only by winning the battle against tyranny, at home and abroad, could the American states offer a refuge for the oppressed. Therefore, although wartime Americans recruited men willing to fight for republican liberty, they also

---

[7] Quote from Thomas Paine, *Common Sense*, 1st publ. 1776, in Philip S. Foner, ed., *The Life and Major Writings of Thomas Paine* (New York: Citadel Press, 1945), 31.

banished those who clung to monarchist principles and erected barriers to keep out newcomers whose personal characteristics and political principles would subvert their new republics. The exigencies of war prompted America's rebel governments to adopt some extraordinary restrictions on the rights of resident aliens, whether newly arrived immigrants or colonists who refused to acknowledge the legitimacy of the new state governments. The extralegal bodies and institutions that had propelled the colonists into war relied on the voluntary support of the people. Successful government and the winning of independence depended on a similarly shared commitment to the rebel cause. Therefore steps were taken to educate and convert the hesitant or uncommitted and to exclude men of treasonous or subversive principles from the body politic. Quaker pacifists from Pennsylvania who refused to contribute to the war effort were interned in Virginia; overt loyalists and those who refused to subscribe to test oaths were disenfranchised and often driven into exile.

The wartime demand for ideological conformity was mitigated by the patriots' belief that freedom lovers from all over the globe would support their cause once they realized that the American battle against tyranny was being waged on behalf of humanity. Acting on this belief, Virginia rebels in 1776 pondered the ways in which Scottish Highlander Regulars, captured off Newfoundland, might be "reconcile[d] . . . to prosecute their different Occupations in this Country"; political education and offers of land and republican citizenship were likewise employed in the 1780s to win over the Hessian troops transported by England to quell the American rebellion.[8]

During the war confidence that America's revolutionary ideals would strike a responsive chord in the hearts of all was severely tested. The subjects of Old World governments largely ignored the invitation to join in America's struggle for liberty. Instead, the English people rallied around George III and the Irish parliament voted to fund British regiments to be used against the American rebels. Newly arrived immigrants, especially those from Scotland, exhibited a distressing preference for monarchical rule; even America's French allies seemed, at times, to have their own, nonrepublican, agenda. These troubling developments produced wartime laws that increased alien disabilities and naturalization requirements and barred certain categories of immigrants.[9]

After winning independence, Americans embarked on the weighty task of securing the foundations of their republican governments. During this process patriots who had been united by Paine's stirring call to action revealed differing conceptions of the American republic and its role as an "asylum for mankind." The immigrant policies that were formulated in the early years of the republic

---

[8] Quote from Edmund Randolph, Williamsburg, June 23, 1776, to Thomas Jefferson, *The Papers of Thomas Jefferson*, ed. Julian P. Boyd (Princeton: Princeton University Press, 1950–), I, 407.

[9] For example, Georgia's naturalization laws prohibited the entry of immigrants from Scotland and required a longer period of residence for ethnic groups believed to harbor anti-republican tendencies.

were part of a long and often acrimonious debate over the proper definition of the American republic and people. The political battles of the 1790s possessed a savagery that seems surprising to modern observers. But hyperbole and rancor were the natural consequences of a struggle that was perceived as a battle to define the soul and fundamental principles of the new republic. The decisions and compromises that were made were seen as deciding the future not only of America, but also of liberty, free government, and humanity.[10]

Americans who disagreed on the essential characteristics of republican government naturally held different beliefs on the social and political attributes required for those who sought republican citizenship. The Federalists were the first to overcome the doubts and animosities engendered by the war. In the early republic, Americans who envisioned a government firmly controlled by an acknowledged elite backed policies that promoted the nation's economic and demographic development and increased America's international standing. These hierarchical Americans tended to see most loyalists as true, if previously deluded, republicans and urged their repatriation. They argued that, by allowing loyalists to return, Americans would prove their humanity, increase their economic and human capital, and demonstrate America's national honor by fulfilling its treaty obligations. In the 1780s, Americans who would become Federalists believed that foreign-born immigrants, as well as returning loyalists, held hierarchical values and would therefore be properly deferential to their natural superiors. Such Americans therefore encouraged immigration and backed liberal naturalization policies in the hope that immigrants would expand the republic's population and work force, promote prosperity, and increase the international clout of the United States.[11]

Americans who lined up against the Federalists in the 1790s were far more ambivalent about population growth, fearing that it would promote social stratification and an aristocratic government more concerned with increasing state power than with serving the people. In the early postwar years, it seemed obvious that banished loyalists opposed the principles and goals of patriot republicanism; acquiescing in their return would reward the seditious, at the expense of true patriots, and destroy republican liberty. Those who became Jeffersonian Republicans also were wary of the social, economic, and political consequences of large-scale immigration.

[10] See, for example, President Washington's assertion that "the preservation of the sacred fire of liberty and the destiny of the republican model of government" depended "on the experiment intrusted to the hands of the American people." First Inaugural Address, April 30, 1789, in *The Washington Papers: Basic Selections from the Public and Private Writings of George Washington*, ed. Saul K. Padover (New York: Grosset & Dunlap, 1955), 265; and Nathan O. Hatch, *The Sacred Cause of Liberty: Republican Thought and the Millennium in Revolutionary New England* (New Haven: Yale University Press, 1979).

[11] The Federalists' hierarchical principles also facilitated their antislavery activities. It was far easier to envision the emancipation of slaves in a hierarchical society, where all knew and accepted their place and were firmly controlled by a powerful government, than in a democratic republic, where freed slaves, untutored in self-government, would enjoy unrestrained liberty.

America's revolutionaries initially shared the widespread belief in the beneficial nature of population growth. According to the Radical Whig canon, "Countries are generally peopled in Proportion as they are free. . . . Liberty naturally draws new People to it, as well as increases the Old Stock; and Men as naturally run when they dare from Slavery and Wretchedness."[12] While America's Federalists to a large extent retained a mercantilist faith in the blessings of a large population, those who joined the Republican opposition were more ambivalent. Republican leaders developed a "Malthusian" attitude toward population growth even before the publication of Thomas Malthus's influential tract. By 1786, James Madison had concluded that "A certain degree of misery seems inseparable from a high degree of populousness." While rejecting the pessimism of Malthus and the relevance of his theory for America, the political principles of the Republican opposition led them away from the demographic optimism of their Radical Whig forebears and America's Federalists.[13]

Republicans both feared the consequences of a rapidly expanding population and worried that immigrants who lacked the training, inclination, or experience necessary to become independent, politically virtuous, and vigilant self-governing republican citizens might promote the development of a decadent and stratified Old World society in America and occupy land that should be reserved for future generations of independent American farmers. Republicans joined Federalists in assuming that foreigners would find it difficult to shake off Old World values and the habit of deferring to a ruling elite. Although doubtful about the benefits of large-scale immigration, Jeffersonian Republicans sought not to close the American door, but to develop policies that would acculturate immigrants untutored in republican ways and to deny citizenship to those who would destroy the American republic and the liberty it guarded.

The naturalization policies that were hammered out in the 1790s were shaped by America's wartime experiences and differing republican visions. While most loyalists were allowed to return, doubts about the political principles of foreign immigrants continued. In the debate over the Naturalization Act of 1790, Congress rejected the extreme open-door proposals of mercantilists who argued that every immigrant, "rich or poor, must add to our wealth and strength" and of democratic idealists who maintained that "we shall be inconsistent with ourselves if, after boasting of having opened an asylum for the oppressed of all

---

[12] Quote from "Cato's Letters," No. 62 (1721), in David L. Jacobson, ed., *The English Libertarian Heritage* (New York: Bobbs-Merrill, 1965), 134. See also David Hume's dictum that "if every thing else be equal, it seems natural to expect that where there are the wisest institutions, and the most happiness, there will also be the most people." *New York Gazette and Weekly Mercury*, August 11, 1783.

[13] James Madison to Thomas Jefferson, June 19, 1786, in *The Papers of James Madison*, ed. William T. Hutchinson et al. (Chicago: University of Chicago Press; and Charlottesville: University of Virginia Press, 1962–), IX, 247. See also Drew R. McCoy, "Jefferson and Madison on Malthus: Population Growth in Jeffersonian Political Economy," *The Virginia Magazine of History and Biography*, 88 (1980), 259–76; and J. J. Spengler, "Malthusianism in Late Eighteenth-Century America," *American Economic Review*, 25 (1935), 697–707.

nations . . . we make the terms of admission to the full enjoyment of that asylum so hard as is now proposed."[14] The law that was passed, and that was labeled "illiberal," required a two-year residence, along with evidence of good character and an oath to support the new Constitution. In the decade that followed, the prerequisites for naturalization increased, as Americans of all political persuasions became wary of the principles of different immigrant groups. Hierarchical Federalists identified the radical virus infecting the American electorate as a foreign import carried by Jacobin immigrants from all parts of the Old World. The Republican opposition, on the other hand, believed that the refugee planters from St. Domingo brought with them not only the aristocratic ethos that would strengthen the Federalists' hierarchical proclivities, but also radicalized slaves who would foment race war in the states. Consequently, the Naturalization Act of 1795 increased the residency requirement to five years and aliens were now required to declare, in advance, their intent to apply for citizenship. In 1798, the now-fearful Federalists secured a provision requiring all aliens to register their arrival in the United States, with lists transmitted to the Secretary of State. All of these changes were incorporated in the Naturalization Act of 1802, which became the nucleus of America's naturalization policy for more than a century.

When postwar Americans redefined immigrant policies and the republic's obligation to serve as a refuge and land of opportunity, they repudiated many elements of the colonial asylum and the principles on which it was built. Americans who wrestled with the problem of formulating naturalization policies that would safeguard republican government while fulfilling America's commitment to serve as a refuge for liberty and humanity rejected the British precedent of creating different classes of citizenship. In England, denization removed some of an alien's disabilities; naturalization through an act of Parliament removed still more, but did not confer the full rights of natural-born Englishmen. While permanent limitations on the political power of foreigners would have been an easy solution to the dilemma faced by American legislators, it was rejected as unrepublican.

Republican America also eschewed, for many different reasons, the colonial practice of subsidizing immigration. American economic developments made indentured servitude, the mechanism that financed the transportation of impoverished Europeans, obsolete. A postwar recession and surge in immigration combined with the northern trend toward free labor reduced the market for bound workers in most states. The recruitment of Europeans, through indentured servitude and bounties, was no longer a necessary expedient to dilute the dangers of

---

[14] Quotes from John Lawrence, the future Federalist from New York, and John Page of Virginia, who would join the Republican opposition, during the Congressional debate of February 3, 1790, in Joseph Gales, ed., *Annals of the Congress of the United States*, 42 vols. (Washington, D.C.: Gales and Seaton, 1834–1856), I, 1115, 1110.

slavery once Americans were free to regulate the African slave trade directly. Northerners used their new authority to cleanse themselves of slavery; southern planters who used their power to limit the number of new arrivals from Africa had no need to resume their previous practice of transforming duties generated by the slave trade into bounties for Europeans. In addition, Americans who wanted to circumscribe governmental authority and limit economic competition and stratification lobbied against proposals to subsidize immigration. These opponents of government subsidies argued that freedom lovers, the immigrants Americans valued most, needed no such enticements, but would be naturally drawn to the American land of liberty when their efforts to establish freedom in Europe proved futile.

Most postwar Americans, while celebrating the bounty of their land, also rejected their previous obligation to serve as a dumping ground and regenerative haven for Europe's "wretched refuse." Dependent and unprincipled immigrants posed a special threat to noncoercive republican governments in which a single class of citizens governed themselves. Republican policymakers therefore did their best to exclude foreigners who were likely to become the tools of demagogues and tyrants. American laws were passed, and now enforced, that banned the landing of Old World convicts. Colonial statutes that had placed proscriptive fines on the landing of destitute and dissolute foreigners were continued, but with less success. Laws restricting the entry of the poor and infirm were rarely enforced, as ship captains landed impoverished passengers in hundreds of obscure inlets. Americans were even less successful in dealing with their most dependent and politically dangerous immigrants, African slaves. While northern states repudiated slavery as incompatible with republican liberty, the South simply regulated the African slave trade to maximize profits and minimize risk. State and federal naturalization laws that required applicants to be both free and white neutralized the political threat posed by these clearly unrepublican immigrants. Postwar measures that accommodated slavery meant that the most oppressed victims of tyranny would continue to underwrite American liberty and economic opportunity for European immigrants.

Americans committed themselves to providing a refuge for liberty and the European victims of tyranny, but they assumed no obligation to succor those beaten down by the equally oppressive hand of poverty. Nonetheless, pride in the blessings conferred by their new republican governments prompted Americans to extend a welcome to the Old World's victimized whites, regardless of their political principles and economic status. Ultimately, the new republic became a haven for Irish revolutionaries, French and British radicals, exiled royalty, Haitian planters, and thousands of ordinary Europeans who emigrated each year in search of economic opportunity. The welcome extended to this motley assortment of Old World subjects was a consequence of American humanitarianism and pride. Believing that the superiority of their republic would soon become obvious to the victims of oppressive regimes, Americans were willing to share the blessings of liberty with a wide variety of newcomers who, if not committed republicans, could be converted into supporters of the American asylum of liberty.

The postwar American asylum bore a superficial resemblance to the earlier British model, but it embodied fundamental differences. England's colonial asylum was designed primarily by mercantilists to increase the power of the state. British promises of free land, political liberty, and religious toleration for Europe's oppressed Protestants had been politically inspired, the work of English monarchs and statesmen who believed that a large population enhanced state power, whether by supporting the royal prerogative of the Stuart kings or by increasing England's ability to win additional wealth—and people—from Old World rivals. Although some British officials were moved by humanitarian ideals, the regenerative function of their New World asylum was also a largely self-serving device that justified the transportation of people who drained England's economy and threatened its stability.

America's republican asylum was constructed on very different principles. Republican policies that welcomed foreigners who cherished liberty differed qualitatively from the mercantilist recruitment of Old World subjects to increase state power. The obligation Americans assumed to serve as an asylum for liberty and the victims of Old World oppression was an expression of republican ideals that could not be easily revoked. American revolutionaries defined their objective as a battle against tyranny on behalf of all humanity; to deny the blessings of liberty to the victims of tyranny would repudiate these revolutionary ideals and the principals that helped to define the American republic. The Constitution of 1787 was shaped, in part, by delegates who balanced America's obligation to serve as an asylum against the threats posed by nonrepublican immigrants. Federalist attempts in 1798 to deny sanctuary to European radicals and to revoke the political rights of aliens were depicted by Republicans as part of a larger plot to subvert American liberty. The fears generated by the Alien, Sedition, and Naturalization Acts of 1798 played a large role in the Federalists' downfall and ensured that the hopes, fears, and principles of the Republican opposition would define not only the new nation, but also the American "asylum for mankind." The coeval formulation of immigrant policies and American republicanism make a redefinition of the American asylum especially difficult. Unlike the heirs of mercantilist asylums, Americans cannot simply rescind the offer of sanctuary and repudiate immigrant policies that have become inconvenient. Such changes must be reconciled with America's fundamental principles.

I *The Demographic Roots of Empire*

THE TRADITION OF THE UNITED STATES as a nation of immigrants—where citizens are linked not by ethnicity but by volitional allegiance to a common government—has roots that extend to the fifteenth century. During the Age of Discovery, Old World rivalries spawned the conviction that colonial acquisitions and a large domestic population were essential components of a powerful state. Attempts to reconcile these often incompatible goals led European imperialists to develop divergent modes of colonization. Most European states sacrificed the peopling of their New World colonies to the need to protect and nurture their domestic population; England, rather reluctantly, devised a different strategy. In its first century of colonization, England settled its "vacant" American lands with thousands of its own subjects. However, at the end of the seventeenth century escalating fears of domestic depopulation produced an increasing reliance on non-English settlers and workers. Recruitment campaigns, which magnified the liberal aspects of colonial society, were launched to entice non-English Protestants to emigrate to England's colonies; mechanisms also were devised to ensure a continuous flow of convict and enslaved workers. Although both procedures often ran roughshod over colonial preferences, ideals, and prejudices, the recruitment of non-English settlers allowed British officials to maintain their American empire without draining England of its valuable subjects.

Planting the Newfound Land

Western Europe's discovery of America triggered a demographic revolution. In the century after the arrival of the Europeans and their microbes the indigenous population of the New World plummeted to about 10 per cent of its pre-Columbian total, primarily through infectious disease. The resulting demographic void was filled by the more than 10 million voluntary, coerced, and enslaved

Africans and Europeans who crossed the Atlantic between 1492 and 1820.[1] Both the devastation and repopulation of America were accidental. European discoverers had intended to exploit, not kill, New World natives. The initial goals of European explorers were to reap the treasure of the Indies, while expanding the bounds of Christendom and the temporal power of their kings. Neither explorers nor their sponsors anticipated the wholesale deaths and trans-Atlantic migrations that followed.

Europeans who ventured across the Atlantic at the end of the fifteenth century had no intention of repopulating the lands they discovered. They hoped simply to establish new trade routes to channel exotic commodities back to Europe. The discovery of a new continent and new peoples, instead of a route to the Indies, did little to alter European aspirations and expectations. Early explorers from all nations tried to establish trade with the newfound natives by creating "factories" similar to those used to facilitate commerce in Europe. Such trading stations required neither conquest nor colonization. European factories were national enclaves, where *factors*, or traders, gathered and stored imports and arranged for the sale of their country's exports. The factors governed themselves according to the laws of their native land, but the continuation of their activity depended on the ruler of the territory that surrounded them. When, however, American natives refused, or were unable, to provide the support services essential to European-style commerce, the traditional European trading enclave was redesigned and transformed into a colonial possession.[2]

Columbus learned that New World outposts had to be built around a substantial nucleus of Europeans on his first voyage to the New World. Prior to returning to America, Columbus petitioned Ferdinand and Isabella for two thousand settlers who would create a town and farms on the island of Hispaniola in return for the right to trade with the Indians and prospect for gold.[3] A century later, northern explorers also learned the futility of attempting to establish a

---

[1] Alfred W. Crosby, Jr., *The Columbian Exchange: Biological and Cultural Consequences of 1492* (Westport, Conn.: Greenwood, 1972), chap. 2; Woodrow Borah, "America as Model: The Demographic Impact of European Expansion upon the Non-European World," *Actas y Memorias del XXX Congresso Internacional de Americanistas*, 3 (1964), 379–87; Sherburne F. Cook, "The Incidence and Significance of Disease among the Aztecs and Related Tribes," *Hispanic American Historical Review*, 26 (1946), 320–25; David Eltis, "Free and Coerced Trans-atlantic Migrations: Some Comparisons," *American Historical Review*, 88 (1983), 251–80; Paul E. Lovejoy, "The Volume of the Atlantic Slave Trade: A Synthesis," *Journal of African History*, 23 (1982), 473–501.

[2] D. W. Meinig argues the prior existence of an Iberian model of colonization that was adopted in the New World in *Atlantic America, 1492–1800*, vol. 1 of *The Shaping of America: A Geographic Perspective on 500 Years of History* (New Haven: Yale University Press, 1986), 4–24. It does seem likely that the techniques used during the *reconquista* did indeed shape Spain's colonization in America. Both Spain and Portugal certainly gained experience in settling workers on various Atlantic islands in the fifteenth century. Nonetheless, the early European explorers had much more limited goals, hoping to trade with the natives, not repopulate and rule the lands they discovered. New World colonization policies gradually evolved to fill American exigencies and were not a simple adoption of a pre-Columbian model.

[3] J. H. Parry, *The Age of Reconnaissance* (New York: New American Library, 1963), 57–58; Angus Calder, *Revolutionary Empire: The Rise of the English-Speaking Empires from the Fifteenth Century to the 1780s*

"factory" in the New World. In 1607 Englishmen set up a trading post at Sagadahoc on the coast of Maine and awaited the arrival of natives bearing furs and other valuable commodities. After a year of fruitless waiting and squabbling, Sagadahoc was abandoned.[4]

The Old World soon realized that a successful American colony had to contain a fully articulated European society with its own commercial and political infrastructure, but adventurers still hoped to exploit, not destroy, native populations. Early settlers expected to be supported by an indigenous work force. The desire to convert heathens to Christianity also mandated the survival of New World natives. But biology made this scenario impossible. Military operations and brutality killed thousands of American natives, but European diseases destroyed millions. As a result, each European claimant faced the problem of repopulating its American lands. The various expedients that were devised to solve this problem shaped the empires that were established in America in unexpected ways and gave the term "colonization" a host of new meanings.

Spain's empire builders were the first to resolve their demographic problems. Their swift success was aided by two fortuitous circumstances. First, the relative sophistication of the Aztecs and Incans made them easier to exploit than either the Arawaks of Hispaniola or the natives encountered by other European colonizers. Because Aztec and Incan emperors already had trained their subjects to produce exotic commodities and to serve autocratic rulers, Spanish conquistadors could simply replace the indigenous ruling class at the top of a productive Indian hierarchy. In addition, Spanish monarchs were able to draw on recent experience in conquering, controlling, and exploiting alien peoples during the *reconquista* and the settlement of the Canary Islands. In 1502 Nicholas de Ovando, who had formerly governed conquered Muslims in Spain, was chosen to create order on Hispaniola. The encomienda and township systems that he devised were then transferred to Spain's mainland colonies. When native workers died off, Spain again drew on her experiences in the Canary Islands and authorized the transportation of enslaved Africans to her American colonies via the Portuguese slave trade network that had evolved in the fifteenth century to supply Portugal's uninhabited Atlantic islands with workers.[5]

(New York: E. P. Dutton, 1981), 10–11; Samuel Eliot Morison, *The European Discovery of America: The Southern Voyages, A.D. 1492–1616* (New York: Oxford University Press, 1974), 26, 43, 93, 99–101, 117–121, 160.

[4]Charles M. Andrews, *The Colonial Period of American History: The Settlements*, 3 vols. (New Haven: Yale University Press, 1934–1937), I, 91–95 (hereafter Andrews, *Settlements*); Samuel Eliot Morison, *The European Discovery of America: The Northern Voyages, A.D. 500–1600* (New York: Oxford University Press, 1971), 430–37 (hereafter Morison, *Northern Voyages*).

[5]Charles Gibson, *The Aztecs under Spanish Rule* (Stanford, Calif.: Stanford University Press, 1964), chap. 9; Charles Verlinden, *The Beginnings of Modern Colonization*, trans. Yvonne Frecerro (Ithaca: Cornell University Press, 1970), 124–27; Meinig, *Atlantic America*, 9–16.

Comparative studies of European imperialism usually stress Spain's national unity as the key to its success. Spanish monarchs were both able and willing to take a vigorous role in exploration and colonization. However, this factor explains only the timing, not the end result. The early-seventeenth-century Englishmen who went to Virginia represented a nation united in its Protestantism and enmity of Spain. Although English settlers had the same aspirations and advantages as their Iberian predecessors, they failed to duplicate Spain's achievements, for reasons that had little to do with the amount of governmental support they received. The natives encountered by Englishmen proved to be unexploitable—too few in number, too mobile, and unaccustomed to laboring for a master class. And, when Virginians faced a labor shortage after 1660, the Chesapeake economy was too weak to tempt significant numbers of slave traders to alter their well-established and lucrative trading routes between Africa and South and Central America.[6]

Northern Europe's lack of unity and consequent delay in entering the race for American land had a far greater impact in dictating the demographic bases of later empires than in determining their "success."[7] By the end of the sixteenth century Spain had laid claim to the regions with the most abundant natural resources—strategically located areas that would allow Spain to control trade routes, extract valuable minerals, and exploit large numbers of natives organized into sophisticated societies. Later claimants were forced to develop new techniques to produce profitable colonies in less obviously lucrative regions, each adopting different solutions to the problem of creating a viable economy and labor force. Mercantilist theories, with their increasing emphasis on guarding a nation's demographic resources, compounded the problems facing northern European colonizers.

Mercantilism

The economic principles that Adam Smith would label the "mercantile system" were formulated largely in response to the development of trade with the New

[6] *Captain John Smith's America: Selections from His Writings*, ed. John Lankford (New York: Harper & Row, 1967), 104; Edmund S. Morgan, *American Slavery, American Freedom: The Ordeal of Colonial Virginia* (New York: W. W. Norton, 1975), chap. 4.

[7] There are many ways to assess the "success" of the different variants of European imperialism. In *Atlantic America* Meinig equates success with rapid colonization and the conquest of millions of native Americans and tons of valuable minerals. However, it could be argued that Spain's need to colonize—to transport Old World subjects to the New—was a necessary expedient undertaken after its original plan had failed. Therefore, the speed with which European nations embarked on the transplantation of Old World settlers could be construed as an index of failure. The British Empire in North America also can be seen as far more successful than anything Spain achieved, as American treasure undermined Spain's domestic economy and its status as a world power, while the British colonies quietly contributed to a steady expansion of England's prosperity, power, and international standing.

World. Mercantilists believed that the world contained a fixed amount of wealth. Therefore, a nation could increase its wealth only at the expense of another. At first, mercantilists simply tried to augment their nation's supply of bullion, the most obvious manifestation of wealth. But they soon devised a more sophisticated approach. Mercantilist governments worked to capture a preponderant share of the world's wealth by establishing a favorable balance of trade with rival nations. To forge a prosperous national economy that could compete successfully in the world market, the state took the regulation of the economy out of the hands of the localities and legislated measures to promote vital export-producing industries. The mercantilist state also set up protective barriers to nurture, protect, and enhance the elements deemed essential to achieving a favorable balance of trade. High on the list of essential components to be protected and nurtured was the state's people.[8]

Europe had a long tradition of glorifying a large population, dating back to the time of the prophets of the Old Testament who enjoined their followers "to be fruitful and multiply" and proclaimed that "In the multitude of people is a king's glory: But in the want of people is the destruction of the prince."[9] While also recognizing that large populations could be a source of weakness, seventeenth-century mercantilists became increasingly staunch proponents of the belief that people were "the real Strength and Riches of a Country," a resource to be jealously guarded and nurtured.[10] Skilled craftsmen were obviously essential to the increased production of a nation's exports and were accordingly protected. Laws were passed that prohibited the emigration of artisans, and policies were devised to entice skilled workers from rival kingdoms.

Colonizing nations also tried to guard their demographic resources by limiting emigration to worthless or dangerous subjects. Initially, French, Spanish, and English monarchs all acquiesced in the use of convicts for exploration and colonization. In the sixteenth century convicts accompanied Jacques Cartier of France and Martin Frobisher of England on their voyages to North America. In 1598 the French government authorized the creation of a colony of convicts on Sable Island, off the coast of Acadia. In the seventeenth century Irish malcontents and rebels were transported to the English colony at Virginia; Irish, Scottish, and

---

[8] Adam Smith, *An Inquiry into the Nature and Causes of the Wealth of Nations*, 1st publ. 1776 (New York: Modern Library, 1937), Book IV; D. C. Coleman, ed., *Revisions in Mercantilism* (London: Methuen & Co., 1969); Eli F. Heckscher, *Mercantilism*, rev. ed., trans. E. F. Soderlund, 2 vols. (New York: Macmillan, 1955), I, introduction, 128–36; II, 175–81, 238–61.

[9] Genesis, i, 28 (quote); Proverbs, xiv, 28 (quote); R. H. Tawney and Eileen Power, eds., *Tudor Economic Documents*, 3 vols. (London: Longmans, Green, 1924), III, 311–45.

[10] Charles Emil Stangeland, *Pre-Malthusian Doctrines of Population: A Study in the History of Economic Theory* (New York: Columbia University Press, 1904), 103 (quote); Niccolo dei Machiavelli, *History of Florence* Book I, chap. 1; in *Machiavelli: The Chief Works and Others*, trans. Allan Gilbert, 3 vols. (Durham, N.C.: Duke University Press, 1965), E. P. Hutchinson, *The Population Debate: The Development of Conflicting Theories up to 1900* (Boston: Houghton Mifflin, 1967), chap. 2.

English prisoners of war were sent to the British West Indies.[11] But theorists who categorized unskilled workers as national assets criticized the emigration of even "worthless" subjects. Political economists cited Machiavelli to prove that sheer numbers increased a nation's power. Mercantilists who aimed at more commercial goals also came to believe that the greater the population, the lower the cost of labor, and therefore the greater the quantity of goods that could be produced for export.[12]

Mercantilist nations with imperial aspirations could conserve their domestic populations by securing settlers from foreign countries. In the sixteenth and seventeenth centuries about 1.5 million Africans were enslaved and settled on New World lands.[13] But most Old World governments rejected the option of recruiting unenslaved Europeans who owed allegiance to rival powers. The transportation of convicts, malcontents, rebels, African slaves, and European aliens created many problems. Colonies were valued for the riches they added to the colonizing nation and simultaneously excluded from their rivals. It was therefore essential to establish settlements strong enough to repel rival claimants.[14] Each nation needed *reliable* settlers to defend its territorial claims and to produce markets and resources for its national economy.

"No Peace Beyond the Line"

In the sixteenth and seventeenth centuries, the New World was a brutally competitive place. Relying on foreign or recalcitrant recruits to settle and defend infant colonies in this hostile environment was a risky business. The dictum of Grotius that "bellum aliud est privatum, aliud publicum, aliud mixtum," gave a gloss of legitimacy to the lawlessness of Europeans in the New World, as it was reformulated into the phrase, "no peace beyond the line." By this maxim, "private war" in America could be overlooked by European officials because

[11] Abbot Emerson Smith, *Colonists in Bondage: White Servitude and Convict Labor in America, 1607–1776* (Chapel Hill: University of North Carolina Press, 1947), 91–95; Theodore G. Corbett, "Migration to the Spanish Imperial Frontier in the Seventeenth and Eighteenth Centuries: St. Augustine," *Hispanic American Historical Review*, 54 (1974), 420–21; Morison, *Northern Voyages*, 433–37, 517; *Calendar of State Papers, Domestic Series, 1547–1580* (London: His Majesty's Stationary Office, 1856), 545; Meinig, *Atlantic America*, 33, 35; Aidan Clarke, "Pacification, Plantation, and the Catholic Question, 1603–1623," in T. W. Moody et al., eds., *A New History of Ireland*, 9 vols. (Oxford: Clarendon Press, 1976), III, 219; Patrick J. Corish, "The Cromwellian Regime, 1650–1660," in *New History of Ireland*, III, 362–64, 383–84.

[12] Heckscher, *Mercantilism*, II, 159–64. According to Machiavelli, powerful princes were those who had the demographic and fiscal resources necessary to gather "an army sufficient to fight . . . whoever comes to attack," *The Prince* (chap. 10), in *Machiavelli: The Chief Works*, I, 42.

[13] Woodrow Borah, "The Mixing of Populations," in Fredi Chiappelli, ed., *First Images of America: The Impact of the New World on the Old*, 2 vols. (Berkeley: University of California Press, 1976), II, 709–10.

[14] George Louis Beer, *The Origins of the British Colonial System, 1578–1660*, 1st publ. 1908 (New York: Peter Smith, 1933), 53–77.

there were no provisions for public justice to arbitrate differences by peaceful means.[15] European adventurers took full advantage of this legal void in their quest for personal gain and national glory. Englishmen attacked Spanish treasure ships and burned three fledgling French colonies to the ground. In the sixteenth century both Portugal and Spain destroyed French Huguenot colonies, one off the coast of Brazil and one at Terra Florida (now Port Royal Island, South Carolina). Seventeenth-century Spaniards also plotted an attack on the English settlement at Jamestown and drove English colonists off Association and Providence Islands.[16] Under these conditions, it was obviously hazardous to settle New World colonies with men who owed allegiance to rival powers or had seditious tendencies.[17]

Spain minimized its risks by limiting immigration. Jews, infidels, heretics, and most foreign subjects were banned from Spain's New World empire. The only aliens officially allowed in Spanish America in significant numbers were Africans, whose potential for subversion was circumscribed by the institution of slavery. Spain also chose to conserve its domestic population by regulating Spanish emigration. Licensing procedures winnowed out the schismatically inclined, and the cost of obtaining the documents necessary for emigration prevented impoverished Spaniards from using the New World as a place of new beginnings. Spain's restrictive immigration policies resulted in the transplantation of approximately 750,000 Spaniards to the New World between 1492 and 1700, an annual average of 3,750 emigrants out of a population of 8 million. These numbers were insufficient to control the vast territories claimed by Spain. Therefore Spain focused on areas with the greatest concentration of Indian manpower and riches and forfeited less promising regions of South America to the Portuguese and almost the entire continent of North America to later claimants from northern Europe.[18]

[15] *Origins*, 7–8.

[16] Ibid.; "Letter of Father Pierre Baird, 1614," in Lyon Gardiner Tyler, ed., *Narratives of Early Virginia, 1606–1625* (New York: Charles Scribner's Sons, 1907), 227–34; "Letter of Don Diego de Molina, 1613," in ibid., 217–24; *Calendar of State Papers, Colonial Series, 1574–1660* (London: Longman et al., 1860), 147–48; Meinig, *Atlantic America*, 26.

[17] The Dutch experience in New Netherlands illustrates the danger. Initially the Dutch were content with trading posts along the Hudson River. But in the 1630s, Dutch investors tried to establish plantations to provide provisions for their trading ships and settlers. Ineffective attempts to attract immigrants from Holland forced the Dutch West India Company to recruit foreigners and allow the settlement of New Englanders who agitated for self-government and against autocratic Dutch governors. When, during the Second Anglo-Dutch War, English warships appeared in the harbor of New Amsterdam, the Dutch colony capitulated without a fight. Michael Kammen, *Colonial New York: A History* (Millwood, N.Y.: Kraus-Thomson Organization, 1975), 26–63.

[18] Auke Pieter Jacobs, "Legal and Illegal Emigration from Seville, 1550–1650," in Ida Altman and James Horn, eds. *"To Make America": European Emigration in the Early Modern Period* (Berkeley: University of California Press, 1991), 59–84; Morison, *Southern Voyages*, 93; Charles Gibson, *Spain in America* (New York: Harper & Row, 1966), 112; Borah, "The Mixing of Populations," 708. Approved foreigners who paid the *composicion* or were naturalized in Spain prior to their departure, were allowed to settle in Spanish America. Magnus Morner, "Spanish Migration to the New World prior to 1810: A Report on the State of Research," in Chiappelli, ed., *First Images of America*, II, 738.

The French government also developed cautious demographic strategies. France's exclusion of potential subversives began when Francis I allowed the explorer Jacques Cartier to recruit French convicts, excepting those incarcerated for heresy and "lèse-majesté divine et humaine." In the second half of the sixteenth century France experimented with using the New World as a religious refuge for French protestants. However, the Huguenot colonies that were established soon fell victim to international rivalries, the waning of Huguenot influence in France, and French preoccupation with domestic problems during the final round of its Wars of Religion. When French interest in colonization resumed, both Protestants and foreigners were excluded as permanent settlers and colonizers focused their recruitment efforts on the nonseditious portion of France's expendable population. Unfortunately, as the first Intendant of New France pointed out in 1663, "there [were] not enough supernumeraries and useless subjects in old France to people the new one."[19]

The decision to exclude religious dissenters from its empire cost France dearly when, in the century following the Revocation of the Edict of Nantes, thousands of French Huguenots were forced to seek refuge in the lands and colonies of rival powers. Denied the right to recruit either foreign subjects or the most mobile segment of the French population, France's colonizers resorted to a wide variety of expedients to populate their American lands. In the seventeenth century cargoes of marriageable French women were sent to Canada, along with instructions to Quebec's Intendants to produce "a yearly [natural] increase of at least 200 families" through tax incentives for large families and fines on fathers who refused to marry off their children at an early age. Jesuits published pamphlets chastising the "many strong and robust peasants in France who have no bread to put in their mouths" yet preferred to "languish in their misery and poverty" at home rather than "place themselves someday at their ease among the inhabitants of New France." Royal edicts ordered ships trading with the French colonies to carry indentured servants or petty criminals in proportion to their tonnage. Despite these efforts, Canada's population stagnated.[20]

In the seventeenth century about 45,000 Frenchmen emigrated to France's American colonies, an average of 600 per year; most settled in the French West Indies, with about 20 per cent going to Canada. Because a large proportion of the emigrants to the North American mainland were military and naval

[19]John Duncan Brite, "The Attitude of European States toward Emigration to the American Colonies and the United States, 1607–1820" (Ph.D. diss., University of Chicago, 1937), 200 (quote); Leslie Choquette, "Recruitment of French Emigrants to Canada, 1600–1760," in Altman and Horn, eds., *To Make America*, 131–71, quote on 132; Christian Huetz de Lemps, "Indentured Servants Bound for the French Antilles in the Seventeenth and Eighteenth Centuries," in ibid., 172–203.

[20]Heckscher, *Mercantilism*, II, 160–61 (quote); Choquette, "Recruitment of French Emigrants," 133–62, quotes on 149; Kenneth D. McRae, "The Structure of Canadian History," in Louis Hartz, ed., *The Founding of New Societies* (New York: Harcourt, Brace and World, 1964), chap. 7.

personnel who soon returned to France, Canada remained an insecure, under-populated imperial appendage, a frozen wasteland that few other than the conquest-minded British Americans found attractive.[21]

England's Dilemma

England, with a population one half the size of Spain's and a quarter of France's, had every reason to limit its demographic investment in America. But domestic and international considerations led Elizabethan and Stuart England to authorize the wholesale emigration of its subjects, including religious and political dissidents. To some extent England had no choice. By the time England entered the race for American lands, the most promising regions, those with a native population capable of sustaining a colony without large infusions of Old World immigrants, had been claimed. Initially, the hostility of Europe's Catholic powers made it impossible for Protestant England to recruit foreign subjects to settle its American lands.[22] But even more important in the decision to transplant English subjects was Queen Elizabeth's use of private enterprise to achieve official ends and to solve the "Irish problem." These factors combined to create the unique demographic contours of England's American colonies.

The accession of the Protestant Queen Elizabeth in 1558 precipitated a crisis that threatened the premature extinction of England's Tudor dynasty. Europe's Catholic powers, led by Philip II of Spain, were determined to replace Elizabeth with a legitimate Catholic monarch. They fomented discord in England and plotted military coups against the new queen. In 1570, Pope Pius V excommunicated Elizabeth, absolved English subjects of their allegiance, and encouraged them to rebel against their heretic monarch. The Queen's survival is a tribute to her statecraft, her ability to postpone a showdown with Spain while accumulating the resources needed to win that battle. In fending off her enemies, Elizabeth was often forced to adopt policies that she found expedient but repugnant. Although she feared the precedents she was setting, Elizabeth encouraged Continental subjects to rebel against their Catholic rulers, allowed her restless gentry to join Protestant campaigns in Europe, and acquiesced in the execution of Mary Queen of Scots. A similar mixture of motives shaped Elizabeth's New World policies.

Queen Elizabeth had many compelling reasons for remaining aloof from the competition for the American continent. Her preeminent concern was to build up England's treasury and arsenal for the inevitable confrontation with Spain,

---

[21] Borah, "The Mixing of Populations," 709; Choquette, "Recruitment of French Emigrants," 161–62.

[22] Foreigners who appeared in England's colonies in the first half of the seventeenth century often were expelled or executed as spies. "Letter of Don Diego de Molina, 1613," in Tyler, ed., *Narratives of Early Virginia*, 217–24; Andrews, *Settlements*, I, 143–47.

while postponing the eruption of that conflict. Elizabeth had no wish to squander royal treasure or manpower by establishing outposts in distant lands; she also feared that the activities of English adventurers might precipitate a premature war with Spain. But many ardent Englishmen were impatient with Elizabeth's temporizing policies. They craved vengeance, not appeasement; bold action, not cautious diplomacy. These restless men urged the Queen to challenge Spain's cruel and haughty dominion in Europe and the New World and to build up the might of Protestant England.[23] Although Elizabeth was not completely immune to such arguments her interest in overseas voyages and colonies was determined by the role they would play in her struggle with Spain. The Queen backed privateering ventures that poured Spanish gold into England's coffers and her private purse—but only when they avoided blatant violations of international law that might precipitate war with Spain.[24]

Transplanting Englishmen

The Elizabethan colonization of Ireland was shaped by the same international and dynastic considerations. It was undertaken to secure England's flank and to deny Spain a Catholic foothold in the British Isles. While English kings had long claimed suzerainty over the neighboring island, sporadic attempts to enforce their claims were ineffectual. With the accession of Elizabeth, traditional Irish unrest gained a dangerous religious dimension, as the Queen's Continental foes offered aid to ambitious Gaelic chieftains and discontented Catholics. But England lacked the resources for a military conquest and occupation of Ireland. So the Queen authorized the same type of private enterprise that had challenged Spain at sea. Elizabeth offered Irish lands to private groups of adventurers who would settle the island and secure Irish allegiance.[25]

Elizabethan England was filled with men who were willing to risk their lives and fortunes in Ireland for the chance of winning military glory and wealth, especially after the temporary truce with Spain in 1574 removed the Spanish Netherlands as a field of battle and honor. The original plan was for private expeditionary forces to displace "tyrannical" Irish chieftains while allowing native Irish laborers to remain on the lands distributed to their English "liberators." The soldiers who settled in Ireland would establish outposts of English

---

[23] Wallace T. MacCaffrey, *The Shaping of the Elizabethan Regime* (Princeton: Princeton University Press, 1968), and *Queen Elizabeth and the Making of Policy, 1572–1588* (Princeton: Princeton University Press, 1981).

[24] Andrew, *Settlements*, I, 25–45; David Beers Quinn, *Raleigh and the British Empire* (New York: Macmillan, 1949), chap. 2; Calder, *Revolutionary Empire*, 69–71, 78–79.

[25] David Beers Quinn, "Ireland and Sixteenth-Century European Expansion," *Historical Studies* I (1958), 20–32; Karl S. Bottigheimer, "Kingdom and Colony: Ireland in the Westward Enterprise, 1536–1660," in K. R. Andrews et al., eds., *The Westward Enterprise* (Detroit: Wayne State University Press, 1979), 45–56.

civilization and gradually lead the Irish churls up the cultural ladder, much as Roman soldier-colonists had done in first-century Britain. In this way Ireland would be converted from a barbarous and underdeveloped liability into a valuable economic appendage.[26]

While attempting to establish private estates in Ireland and attacking Spanish treasure ships, Elizabethan adventurers also carried their crusade to America. Colonizing enthusiasts waxed poetic in their descriptions of the "manifolde comodyties that are like to growe to this Realme of Englande by the Westerne discoveries." They predicted that American colonies would lead to "thinlargement of the gospell of Christe whereunto the Princes of the refourmed relligion are chefely bounde," "bridle" the wealth and power of the King of Spain, enlarge royal revenues, increase English shipping, repair England's "decayed trades," and provide for the "imploymente of nombers of idle men." Again, Queen Elizabeth authorized private ventures that promised royal profits and the opportunity to undermine Spain.[27]

England's initial ventures in America overlapped its efforts in Ireland and suffered from the same problems. The lands the English were attempting to colonize on both sides of the Atlantic, lacked the wealth and social structure necessary to meet the goals of colonizers. The men who led England's expeditions were gentlemen with relatively minor prospects at home. They embraced military adventure to "win control over land and men." In America, as well as Ireland, these gentlemen adventurers hoped to replace an indigenous ruling elite and live off the rents and tribute of conquered natives, as Spanish conquistadors had done before them. The soldiers who manned their expeditions would share in the spoils and be settled on conquered lands as personal retainers, owing military service and rents. But this "tributary" mode of colonization failed.[28] Englishmen gradually learned that the natural resources of Ireland and North America would not support purely extractive ventures. In England's colonies, land had to be cultivated and a labor force imported to produce subsistence crops and salable commodities. When the native Irish proved intractable, England embarked on a massive program of removal and replacement. Private individuals and groups, such as the Corporation of London, agreed to replant huge segments of Irish land

[26] David Beers Quinn, "Sir Thomas Smith (1513–1577) and the Beginnings of English Colonial Theory," in American Philosophical Society, *Proceedings*, 89 (1945), 550–56; Quinn, "Ireland and Sixteenth-Century European Expansion," 27; Cyril Falls, *Elizabeth's Irish Wars* (London: Methuen, 1950), 114–17.

[27] Carole Shammas, "English Commercial Development and American Colonization, 1560–1620," in Andrews et al., eds., *Westward Enterprise*, 162–74; Richard Hakluyt the Younger, "Discourse of Western Planting," in Eva G. R. Taylor, ed., *The Original Writings and Correspondence of the Two Richard Hakluyts*, 2 vols. (London: Hakluyt Society, 1935), II, 211–13, 313–19, quotes on 211; Theodore K. Rabb, *Enterprise and Empire: Merchant and Gentry Investment in the Expansion of England, 1575–1630* (Cambridge: Harvard University Press, 1967), 35–52.

[28] Quinn, "Sir Thomas Smith," 552–54; Shammas, "English Commercial Development," 152–59, 170 (quote); Andrews, *Settlements*, I, 69–72; Quinn, *Raleigh and the British Empire*, chap. 7; Sigmund Diamond, "From Organization to Society: Virginia in the Seventeenth Century," *American Journal of Sociology*, 63 (1958), 457–75.

with English subjects after the natives had been "removed." When similar problems occurred in America, the same devices of removal and transplantation were adopted.

Queen Elizabeth's belief that colonizing projects undertaken by the crown would tie up resources needed in the duel with Spain led her to entrust such activities to private individuals and joint stock companies. The pressing need to secure Irish allegiance and provide an outlet for her gentry led Elizabeth to authorize the use of English subjects to resettle Ireland. Since the same personnel were involved in American ventures, the devices used in Ireland were, rather unthinkingly, carried over to the New World. And so, England adopted a mode of American colonization eschewed by other European nations, the wholesale transplantation of its own subjects. After the death of Elizabeth, James I continued the pattern of authorizing private plantations, issuing the charters and orders in council needed to establish substantial English enclaves in Ireland and the New World.[29]

The Demographic Debate

The problems involved with relocating thousands of British subjects were myriad, beginning with the rationale required to undertake such a program. The decision that barbarians incapable of imbibing English civility had to be removed from lands that could be cultivated more productively by the English was made in Ireland following Irish rebellions in the 1570s, 1598, 1606, and 1641, and in Virginia after the Indian massacres of 1622 and 1641. Although continuing efforts would be made to convert the natives in America, the policy of removal and its justification would henceforth be invoked against tribes that failed to acculturate.[30] The decision to settle Englishmen on lands "vacated" by savages was not taken as easily or as irrevocably as the decision for removal.

Ever since the 1560s English colonizers had contended that their projects would benefit the nation by ridding England of its dangerous surplus population. At the end of the sixteenth century Sir Walter Raleigh asserted that "When any country is overlaid by a multitude which live upon it, there is a natural necessity compelling it to disburden itself and lay the load upon others." Both Raleigh and

[29] Shammas, "English Commercial Development," 162–74; Rabb, *Enterprise and Empire*, 26–29; M. Perceval-Maxwell, *The Scottish Migration to Ulster in the Reign of James I* (London: Routledge & Kegan Paul, 1973), 74–77.

[30] Nicholas P. Canny, "The Ideology of English Colonization: From Ireland to America," *William and Mary Quarterly*, 3rd ser., 30 (1973), 595–97; Perceval-Maxwell, *Scottish Migration to Ulster*; G. A. Hayes-McCoy, "The Completion of the Tudor Conquest and the Advance of the Counter-Reformation, 1571–1603," in Moody et al., eds., *A New History of Ireland*, III, 94–115; Aidan Clarke, "Pacification, Plantation, and the Catholic Question, 1603–1623," in ibid., 219–24; Patrick J. Corish, "The Cromwellian Conquest, 1649–53," in ibid., 357–75; Edmund S. Morgan, *American Slavery, American Freedom* (New York: Norton, 1975), chaps. 3, 11, 13.

Sir Francis Bacon maintained that national welfare made it necessary "to remove by all means possible, that material cause of sedition . . . which is, want and poverty in the state." These arguments provided the theoretical foundation of English colonization through transplantation. Colonizing enthusiasts claimed that overseas settlements in both Ireland and America would provide a home for "needy people of our countrey, which now trouble the commonwealth." By increasing English trade, colonies would give employment to England's poor who "doe now live here idly to the common annoy of the whole state." Such predictions struck responsive chords in a society concerned by the rootlessness of its growing number of poor people who could be exploited by England's Catholic enemies.[31]

But many Englishmen questioned such claims. England's population rose dramatically in the second half of the sixteenth century, increasing by a third between 1560 and 1600, from three to four million. This population growth was concentrated in London, which almost doubled in size between 1600 and 1650 as it drew in about half of the nation's natural increase. While London, the center of England's colonizing activity, was becoming obviously congested, other parts of England were suffering population losses, as residents moved on in search of economic opportunity or succumbed to epidemics such as the plague of 1625. During the first half of the seventeenth century many Englishmen expressed concern over the "decay" of population in English villages and towns. In 1607, Parliament launched an inquiry into the causes of "the rural depopulation" of Lincolnshire.[32]

England, in truth, had no absolute demographic surplus. But some aspects of its population growth worried England's rulers. Enclosures and other changes in agrarian organization produced an alarming mobility, as those pushed off the land wandered the countryside and congregated in London in search of employment. Poor harvests and "a breakdown in the distribution of food" at the end of the sixteenth century produced acute grain shortages. The Elizabethan poor laws and apprentice regulations were designed to control this potentially dangerous "surplus," as colonizers proposed transporting that debilitating element to Ireland and America.[33]

[31] Walter Raleigh, "A Discourse of the Original and Fundamental Cause of Natural, Arbitrary, Necessary, and Unnatural War," in *The Works of Sir Walter Ralegh, Kt.*, ed. William Oldys and Thomas Birch, 8 vols. (Oxford: Oxford University Press, 1829), VIII, 256; Francis Bacon, "Essay of Seditions and Troubles," in *The Works of Francis Bacon*, ed. James Spedding et al., 15 vols. (St. Clair Shores, Mich.: Scholarly Press, 1969), XII, quote on 127; Beer, *Origins*, George Peckham and Humphrey Gilbert quoted on 37.

[32] E. A. Wrigley and R. S. Schofield, *The Population History of England, 1541–1871: A Reconstruction* (Cambridge: Harvard University Press, 1981), 531, 532; Bernard Bailyn, *The Peopling of British North America: An Introduction* (New York: Alfred A. Knopf, 1986), 24–25; Mildred Campbell, "'Of People Either Too Few or Too Many': The Conflict of Opinion on Population and Its Relation to Emigration," in William Appleton Aiken and Basil Duke Henning, eds., *Conflict in Stuart England: Essays in Honour of Wallace Notestein* (London: Jonathan Cape, 1960), 172–82.

[33] Shammas, "English Commercial Development," 167–68; Peter Clark, "The Migrant in Kentish Towns, 1580–1640," in Peter Clark and Paul Slack, eds., *Crisis and Order in English Towns, 1500–1700* (Toronto:

The claims of England's colonizers to be acting for the nation's good by ridding the country of its "lewd vagrants" could be plausible to Londoners and magistrates involved in controlling England's mobile poor. They were, however, unconvincing to English people who were worried about the economic, social, and political consequences of rural depopulation. The demographic arguments of English colonizers also contradicted the growing mercantilist belief that population growth was a national blessing and that the idle poor would become industrious and low-paid laborers producing goods for export that would enhance England's wealth and power. But these differences were glossed over by promoters who emphasized the mercantilist benefits of colonization. Publicists argued that colonies would prevent England's surplus population from being seduced into the service of a rival nation. In the colonies idle Englishmen would be transformed into economic assets—as producers and consumers, and as defenders of England's territorial claims.[34]

The Ambivalent Solution

The arguments that England had a dangerous surplus population and that the survival of the nation depended on fending off the Spanish threat allowed England to experiment with a form of colonization that required the emigration and settlement of its own subjects, in both Ireland and America. During its first century of colonization, England's rulers authorized, by ad hoc measures, the transplantation of about 500,000 English subjects, from a population that rarely exceeded five million. Between 1630 and 1642 alone, more than 200,000 emigrated from Great Britain to Ireland and British America.[35] But, during these years, England failed to develop a coherent emigration policy that coordinated the demographic needs of England and those of its British dependencies and American colonies. The English government never completely accepted mercantilist arguments that claimed unalloyed benefits from unlimited population growth and the beneficent role of colonies in strengthening a nation's demographic resources. During the same years that England's mobile population was being defined as a dangerous surplus, English rulers proved reluctant to let their

University of Toronto Press, 1972), 117–63; Joyce Oldham Appleby, *Economic Thought and Ideology in Seventeenth-Century England* (Princeton: Princeton University Press, 1978), 129–35, quote on 131.

[34] Beer, *Origins*, 35–42. In Richard Eburne's 1624 tract promoting the colonization of Newfoundland, a farmer voiced the anticolonization arguments that were triumphantly refuted by the more knowledgeable merchant. Louis B. Wright, ed. *A Plain Pathway to Plantations*, 1st publ. 1624 (Ithaca: Cornell University Press, 1962).

[35] Figures derived from Russell R. Menard, "British Migration to the Chesapeake Colonies in the Seventeenth Century," in Lois Green Carr et al., eds., *Colonial Chesapeake Society* (Chapel Hill: University of North Carolina Press, 1988), 103–5; Henry A. Gemery, "Emigration from the British Isles to the New World, 1630–1700: Inferences from Colonial Populations," *Research in Economic History*, 5 (1980), 197–98; Wrigley and Schofield, *Population History of England*, 219–24; Bailyn, *Peopling*, 25–26.

people go. Emigration policy was inconsistent, as English monarchs succumbed to the logic of first one interest group and then another and consequently alternated between promoting and inhibiting colonization.

According to English political thought, the primary duty of Englishmen was "to attend at all times, the Service and Defence of their King and Native Country, when they shall be thereunto required."[36] This gave English monarchs the right to regulate the movements of their subjects, which they often invoked. A statute passed in 1381 prohibited "the Passage utterly of all Manner of People . . . except only the Lords and other Great Men of the Realm, and true and notable Merchants, and the King's Soldiers . . . out of the said Realm without the King's special Licence." Prior to 1606, the Act of 1381 was the legal foundation for prohibiting the emigration of English subjects whose services were needed by their king. Under the authority of this statute Elizabeth and James I routinely regulated the movements of Catholics, who might be plotting with England's enemies.[37]

Colonizing charters exempted some English subjects from the provisions of the Act of 1381. The 1578 patent granted to Sir Humphrey Gilbert gave him permission to "goe and travell thither [Newfoundland], to inhabite or remaine there, to build and fortifie at the discretion of the sayde Sir Humfrey . . . the statutes of or actes of Parliament made against Fugitives, or against such as shall depart, remaine or continue out of our Realme of England without licence, or any other acte, statute, lawe or matter whatsoever to the contrary in any wise notwithstanding." Gilbert was further authorized to "have, take and lead in the same voyages . . . and to inhabite there with him . . . such and so many of our subjects as shall willingly accompany him," as long as "none of the same persons, nor any of them be such as hereafter shall be specially restrained by us."[38] Although Queen Elizabeth thus licensed the emigration of her subjects, she also displayed some doubts about colonization. A pamphlet published in 1571 to promote Sir Thomas Smith's Irish colony promised volunteers land and "farmers out of the Ile of Man and othere poore men out of England, so they may be ayded at the

---

[36] Quote from Proclamation of 1635 restraining the "King's Subjects Departing out of the Realm without License" into "the Kingdom, or Country of Any Foreign Prince, State or Potentate," in John Rushworth, ed., *Historical Collections, The Second Part, Containing the Principal Matters Which Happened from the Dissolution of the Parliament on the 10th of March 4 Car. I 1628/9 until the Summoning of Another Parliament, Which Met at Westminster, April 13, 1640* (London: John Wright and Richard Chiswell, 1680), 298.

[37] Statute of 1381 (5 Ric. II, St. 1, c. 2), in Owen Ruffhead, ed., *Statutes at Large, from Magna Charta to the Twenty-fifth Year of the Reign of King George the Third, inclusive*, 10 vols. (London: Charles Eyre and Andrew Strahan, Printers, 1786), I, 330–332. For restrictions on Catholic emigration, see "An Acte for the Due Execution of the Statutes against Jesuits, Seminarie Priestes Recusants &c.," in Clarence S. Brigham, ed., "British Royal Proclamations Relating to America, 1603–1783," in American Antiquarian Society, *Transactions and Collections*, 12 (1911), 3–4.

[38] Gilbert's patent is found in Francis Newton Thorpe, ed., *The Federal and State Constitutions, Colonial Charters, and other Organic Laws of the States, Territories, and Colonies Now or Heretofore Forming the United States of America*, 7 vols. (Washington, D.C.: Government Printing Office, 1909), I, 49–52, quote on 49.

firste with some stock of Corn and Cattel." The Queen, in turn, promised to punish those responsible for presuming to publish the book "without our knowledge or allowance." It is unclear whether Elizabeth's ire was produced by Smith's "presumption," his encouragement of the emigration of England's gentry, "farmers and othere poore men," or the complaints of English officials in Ireland who feared that Smith intended to "expel or destroy the Irish race." It is clear that Smith's colonization project did not enjoy the Queen's wholehearted support.[39]

In 1606, after James VI of Scotland became James I of England, an Act of Parliament repealed the Scottish and English laws that restricted movements between those two kingdoms. One of the statutes thus repealed was the Act of 1381. Although the English law of 1606 was designed to regularize relations between two countries that now shared a common king, it also, incidentally, removed a legal impediment to colonization.[40] More important in giving a new impetus to English colonization was James I's enthusiasm for planting Ireland with his English and Scottish subjects. As in the reign of Elizabeth, the resettlement of Ireland by more "civilized" and loyal peoples seemed the most economical and effective solution to the "Irish problem." Gaelic plantations also promised domestic benefits. As king of England, James was finally able to offer Irish land to his Scottish subjects, who had coveted it for so long. Scottish settlements in Ireland would also reduce the discordant element that occupied the border between England and Scotland. During the reign of James I more than 14,000 Scots, many of them former "Borderers," settled in the Irish province of Ulster.[41]

James I also continued the practice of designating convicted felons as an expendable surplus suitable for emigration. In 1603 the king ordered his Privy Council to implement the provisions of an Elizabethan act "for punyshment of Rogues Vagabonds and Sturdy Beggars" by transporting them to "parts beyond the Seas." The Privy Council complied by designating "The Newfound Land, the East and West Indies, France, Germanie, Spaine, and the Low-countries, or any of them" as the "places and partes beyond the Seas to which any such incorrigible or dangerous Rogues shall be banished." But nothing came of this plan until 1611, when Virginia's governor proposed sending English convicts under sentence of death to the colony for three years, "as do the Spaniards." In January 1615, James I issued the necessary commissions "to reprive and stay from execucon such and soe many persons as nowe stand attaynted

[39] Quinn, "Sir Thomas Smith," 550–54.

[40] 1606 Act "for the Utter Abolition of All Memory of Hostility, and the Dependence thereof, between *England* and *Scotland*" (4 Jac. I, c. 1), in Ruffhead, ed., *Statutes at Large*, III, 62–64; William Cobbett and John Wright, eds., *The Parliamentary History of England from the Earliest Period to the Year 1803*, 36 vols. (London: T. C. Hansard, 1806–1820), I, 1071–1119; David Harris Willson, "King James I and Anglo-Scottish Unity," in Aiken and Henning, eds., *Conflict in Stuart England*, 44–51.

[41] Perceval-Maxwell, *Scottish Migration to Ulster*, 20–29; 286–89.

or convicted of or for any robberie or felonie, (wilful murder rape witchcraft or Burglarie onlie excepted) whoe for strength of bodie or other abilities shall be thought fitt to be ymploied in forraine discoveries or other services beyond the Seas."[42]

The transportation of English convicts began immediately. Felons were sent to America throughout the seventeenth and eighteenth centuries, but the practice was suspended in 1622 when James instructed his commissioners to consider, as an alternative to transportation, setting convicts to work in England. He suggested that reprieves be issued on condition the convicts be "constrayned to toyle in some such heavie and painefull manuall workes and labors here at home, and be kept in chaynes in the houses of correction or other places . . . which servitude, as it is conceived, wilbe a greater terror than death itself."[43] Thus, it would seem, the king had changed his mind concerning the absolute expendability of able-bodied convicts, and had decided they might serve the English interest best by remaining at home.

The promotion of Irish colonization diminished the supply of men and money available for the New World.[44] And, while Stuart kings were the driving force behind the colonization of Ireland, they showed less enthusiasm for American plantations. During the reign of Charles I, several barriers were erected that, in effect, reinstituted the Act of 1381, by prohibiting all unlicensed emigration to America. In February 1633, passengers sailing for America were required to take the oath of allegiance and have their "names certified to the Exchequer yearly." In 1636 a royal proclamation prohibited the embarkation of "all passengers, but under six of the hands of the Privy Council." In 1637 Charles I expressed his concern that "great numbers of His Subjects have bin, and are every yeare transported into those parts of America, which have been granted by Patent to severall persons, and there settle themselves, some of them with their families and estates: amongst which numbers there are also many idle and refractory humors, whose onely or principall end is to live as much as they can without the reach of authority." The king therefore issued a proclamation "against the disorderly transporting His Majesty's subjects to the plantations within the parts of America." This proclamation ordered English officials to prevent "any persons being Subsidie men, or of the value of Subsidie men, to embarque themselves . . . for any of the said Plantations, without License from His Majesties Commissioners for Plantations." Licenses required each prospective emigrant to take "the Oaths of supremacie, and Allegiance" and provide "Testimony from

---

[42] Perceval-Maxwell, *Scottish Migration to Ulster*, 285; Brigham, ed., "British Royal Proclamations," 1–2; Smith, *Colonists in Bondage*, 91–95, quotes on 92, 93.

[43] Ibid., 94.

[44] Perceval-Maxwell, *Scottish Migration to Ulster*, 14, 46; T. W. Moody, *The Londonderry Plantation, 1609–41: The City of London and the Plantation in Ulster* (Belfast: William Mullan and Son, 1939), 31.

the Minister of the Parish of his conversation and conformity to the Orders and discipline of the Church of England."[45]

Stuart restrictions on emigration were shaped, primarily, by the fear that religious dissenters would join the nation's enemies in attacking the Church of England. In 1603 licensing procedures were devised to prevent English Catholics from fleeing to the Continent; in the 1630s they were part of Archbishop Laud's campaign to revoke the charter granted to English Puritans by Charles I. Laud, whose attempts to wipe out nonconformity in England had provided much of the impetus for the Puritan migration to New England, feared the domestic consequences of an American colony of dissenters. From 1634 Archbishop Laud was the head of the newly established Commission for Regulating Plantations. His policies were designed to enervate the colony at Massachusetts Bay by cutting off its supplies and reinforcements. To achieve this goal, ship captains were denied licenses to sail until they had presented affidavits that their passengers had taken the oaths of supremacy and allegiance. But these licensing procedures applied to all vessels sailing with passengers to any part of America and reflected a more general concern over the effects of emigration on the mother country.[46]

Arguments formulated to oppose the Puritan migration were translated into indictments against the transplantation of all English subjects beyond the seas. In 1638 a letter from William Lord Maynard called Laud's attention to the dangers of allowing the sailing of the fourteen ships for America then in the Thames, with "So much corn . . . that there will be hardly enough left in this great scarcity, to last until harvest." He was also alarmed by the proposed emigration of "numbers of persons of very good abilities" and of "divers clothiers of great trading." The danger of "divers parishes being impoverished" by such departures was clearly a universal risk of any large-scale emigration, not just that of the "schismatically inclined." Rules regulating the emigration of the English people caused delays and added to the expense of all trans-Atlantic voyages throughout the reign of Charles I.[47]

The failure of American settlements to produce the benefits promised by colonial publicists made them susceptible to the charges leveled against "schismatic" colonies. Although some of the arguments advanced by colonizers had been

[45] *Journals of the House of Lords* (London: His Majesty's Stationery Office, 1888–), IV (1628–1642), 188; Brigham, ed., "British Royal Proclamations," 80–82 (quotes); *Calendar of State Papers, Colonial Series, 1574–1660,* 261.

[46] Everett Emerson, ed., *Letters from New England: The Massachusetts Bay Colony, 1629–1638* (Amherst: University of Massachusetts Press, 1976), 120–23; Andrews, *Settlements,* I, 408–24; Edmund S. Morgan, *The Puritan Dilemma: The Story of John Winthrop* (Boston: Little, Brown, 1958), 18–33.

[47] *Calendar of State Papers, Colonial Series, 1574–1660,* 174, 192, 266 (quote), 276. For petitions to embark, see ibid., 176, 214, 281, 287, 303, 306 for Virginia; 273, 274 for Guinea; 281 for Providence Island; 307 for Newfoundland; 192, 226, 292, 273, 274, 275, 284, 286, 307 for New England.

merely self-serving obfuscations, their initial plans did involve relieving England of its poor and troublesome subjects. In this, the English government had been happy to cooperate. In 1622 and 1623 the Council for New England successfully solicited "poor children of 14 years and upwards" from the City of London, obtained a letter "from the King to the Lieut. of every shire for sending their poorer sort of people to New England," and proposed that "A statute of Queen Elizabeth for binding poor children apprentices . . . be made use of for the benefit of the plantation."[48] Similar means were used to populate the colony of Virginia. In 1618 and 1619 the City of London spent about £500 to transport two hundred of its poor children to Virginia. In 1619 a joint stock was formed to send young women to Virginia, with their passages to be paid by the planters who selected them as wives. By the following year the institution of indentured servitude had emerged in Virginia to facilitate the transplantation of England's poor to her labor-hungry settlements.[49]

But there also was disquieting evidence that the New World colonies were not content with providing a home for England's dangerous classes. Colonizers were recruiting people the nation could ill afford to lose. The New England colony, which had promised to lower England's poor rates by transplanting some of those on parish relief in 1622, was soon disillusioned with the performance of such settlers. By 1632 New Englanders were demanding "skilful artificers," rather than "the very scum of the earth sent over" earlier. Other English colonies experienced the same disillusionment with "rogues and vagabonds," blaming their early failures on the quality of such settlers and recruiting men who were more industrious, wholesome, and propertied. Furthermore, the drawing off of England's discontented subjects had not aided the political situation in the mother country; rather, it seemed to have concentrated and enhanced the dissenters' political power and grievances.[50]

The English Civil War brought to power the Puritan lords who had been active colonizers and the Puritan merchants who later dominated the Commonwealth Parliament that developed the English Navigation system. England's primary concern now became controlling its colonies, not questioning their peopling procedures. Nevertheless Interregnum officials displayed a surprising ambivalence about the emigration of Englishmen to the American colonies.[51] Oliver Cromwell's "Western Design" was an attempt to challenge Spanish claims in the West Indies through the government-backed colonization of Jamaica. Cromwell

---

[48] Minutes of the Council for New England, *Calendar of State Papers, Colonial Series, 1574–1660*, 31 (July 5, 1622); 35 (Jan. 15, 1623); 37 (Feb. 18, 1623).

[49] Smith, *Colonists in Bondage*, 8–16; Beer, *Origins*, 46–48.

[50] Campbell, "Of People Too Few," 188; *Calendar of State Papers, Colonial Series, 1574–1660*, 155. See also ibid., 30 (1622); 36 (1623); 110 (1630); 112–13 (1630); *Winthrop Papers*, ed. Stewart Mitchell, 5 vols. (Boston: Massachusetts Historical Society, 1929–1947), II, 273n, 304, 306; III, 422–26, 463–76; William Berkeley, *A Discourse and View of Virginia* (London: 1663), 3.

[51] Beer, *Origins*, 380–83, 410–13.

was willing to colonize with English subjects if necessary. But he also tried to obtain settlers "from other parts," by encouraging the emigration of New England Puritans and Irish Protestants to Jamaica and by transporting political and military prisoners to America.[52] In 1657 the Council of State revoked commissions granted to carry Irish vagrants to American plantations, because agents had been luring English residents as well as the Irish poor "by false pretences either by getting them aboard the ships, or in other by-places into their power, and forcing them away, the person so employed having so much apiece for all they so delude." Emigration from England to the New World continued to be licensed.[53]

All of the measures inhibiting emigration from England to the American colonies during the first century of colonization can be explained as special cases that transcended normal English policy. Elizabeth's anger at Smith's unauthorized recruitment pamphlet could have had a number of different causes. The measures taken in the 1630s are usually ascribed "to a desire to control the Puritan exodus to Massachusetts, which it was feared would become a centre of religious and political dissension," and not the result of any general opposition to emigration.[54] Restrictions during the Interregnum were designed to prevent abuses and protect the credulous. Although these actions can thus be explained as the product of special circumstances, taken together they present a picture of an English officialdom skeptical, from the very beginning, of the wisdom of settling colonies with transplanted English subjects.

Elizabethan England had embarked on empire building in response to domestic and international imperatives and under the assumption that the emigration of a few adventurers would suffice to conquer, control, and exploit overseas civilizations. The steadily escalating need to transplant more and more English subjects was justified by the plausible arguments of promoters of various colonization schemes. But seventeenth-century England never developed the theoretical principles necessary to vindicate the wholesale emigration of English subjects whose duty it was "to attend at all times, the Service and Defence of their King" and increase their nation's wealth.[55]

Regulating Emigration

The failure of the seventeenth-century colonies to pay their promised social and political dividends and their recruitment of English people who were not

---

[52] Andrews, *Settlements*, III, 30–31; Christopher Hill, *God's Englishman: Oliver Cromwell and the English Revolution* (New York: Harper & Row, 1970), 157–60, quote on 158; John Winthrop, *Winthrop's Journal*, ed. James Kendall Hosmer, 2 vols. (New York: Charles Scribner's Sons, 1908), II, 82–84.

[53] Smith, *Colonists in Bondage*, 152–70, quote on 168; *Calendar of State Papers, Colonial Series, 1574–1660*, 341, 398, 400, 401.

[54] Beer, *Origins*, 43n.

[55] Quote from 1635 Proclamation, in Rushworth, ed., *Historical Collections*, 298.

members of the expendable "dangerous class" helped the English government to resolve its ambivalence over creating colonies by the transplantation of English subjects. During the 1660s, vague and intermittent concern over the transfer of large numbers of English subjects to America grew into an official resolve to control and limit emigration from England. By the beginning of the eighteenth century government officials had decided that it was "the interest of England to improve and thicken her colonys with people not her own."[56] The English government then tried to assume a more active role in the colonization process, defining which subjects were available for transportation, restricting the mobility of valued workers, and subsidizing the recruitment of foreign subjects for its American colonies.

After the Restoration Charles II was bombarded with suggestions by his advisors and political economists about the steps to be taken to make England great and its monarchy strong. Although the proposals of these would-be policymakers were various, virtually all agreed with Samuel Fortrey that "Two things . . . appear to be chiefly necessary, to make a nation great, and powerfull; which is to be rich and populous."[57] Far from advocating the strengthening of the British colonies through the emigration of English subjects, the king's advisors urged him to promote immigration *into* England and to "Stopp the draine, that carry's away the Natiues from us." In 1679, the Commissioners of Customs went even further when asked to consider the proposed transportation of Huguenot refugees, at government expense, to Carolina. The Commissioners replied,

> We cannot advise that his ma[jes]tie should give any Incouragement to any People who are settled in this Kingdome whether Natives or fforeigners to transport themselves from hence to any of his Ma[jes]ties Plantacons or Ireland. On the contrary, we are of opinion that there are too many ffamilyes that do daylye Transport themselves both to the Plantacons & to Ireland to the unpeopling & ruine of this Kingdome. And we are of opinion that means are rather to be used for the hindring then the promoting thereof.[58]

England's Restoration governments tried to develop policies that would fulfill their simultaneous commitment to empire and to increasing the nation's domestic resources. All parts of the British empire would benefit by building colonial populations from people whose presence in England, rather than adding to its strength, constituted an economic drain or threat to its security. Policies were

[56] William Penn, quoted in Walter Allen Knittle, *Early Eighteenth-Century Palatine Emigration: A British Government Redemptioner Project to Manufacture Naval Stores* (Philadelphia: Dorrance & Company, 1937), 27; Campbell, "Of People Too Few," 188–94.

[57] Samuel Fortrey, *England's Interest and Improvement*, 1st publ. 1663 (Baltimore: Johns Hopkins University Press, 1907), 12.

[58] George Louis Beer, *The Old Colonial System, 1660–1754*, 1st publ. 1913, 2 vols. (New York: Peter Smith, 1933), I, 20–28; quotes on 28; Campbell, "Of People Too Few," 190 (quote).

therefore formulated to facilitate the emigration of English people of problematic loyalty and value. Steps also were taken to prevent the emigration of individuals who could serve the empire best by remaining home.

Charles II continued the tradition of transporting "Rogues and Vagabonds" to America. He ordered English officials to implement the Elizabethan Act that banished, beyond the seas, "such as will not be reformed of their rogish kinde of lyfe by the former Provisions of this Acte." In May 1662, Charles gave his assent to a statute "for preventing the mischiefs and dangers that may arise by certain persons called Quakers, and others, refusing to take lawful oaths" that punished the third refusal to take an oath "by abjuration of the realm or transportation to the plantations." Two weeks later the king approved yet another bill authorizing the transportation of rogues, vagabonds and beggars found in the cities of London and Westminster who were "duly convicted and adjudged to be incorrigible."[59]

While designating rogues, vagabonds, and schismatics as suitable colonists, British officials worked to restrict the emigration of English indentured servants to those whose value was limited at home. In 1660 complaints were made that "diuerse Children from their Parents, and Seruants from their Masters, are daylie inticed away, taken upp, and kept from their said Parents and Masters against their Wills, by Merchants, Planters, Commanders of Shipps, and Seamen trading to Virginia, Barbados, Charibee Islands and other parts of the West Indies, and their Factors and Agents, and shipped away to make Sale and Merchandize of." Such accusations led to the creation in 1664 of an office to register the contracts of those going to the colonies as servants. At the same time the newly established Council for Foreign Plantations was instructed "to take into yor consideracon how our severall Plantacons may be best supplied with servants, that neither our Collonies, especially such as are imediately under our comissions, may be unprovided in so essentiall an assistance, nor any of our good subjects may be forced or inticed away by any unlawfull or indirect way; and that such as are willing to be transported thither to seeke better fortunes than they can meete with at home, may be encouraged thereunto." Although these actions were aimed at preventing abuses in transporting English servants to America, they also were seen as inhibiting such traffic. In the early 1680s, settlers in Jamaica accused the government of cutting off the servant trade to their island. They claimed that "my Lord Chief Justice will permit none to come, though they are willing and go to acknowledge it before the Magistrate as the law directs."[60] Other factors were largely responsible for the drying up of the supply of English servants at the end of the

---

[59] Leo F. Stock, ed., *Proceedings and Debates of the British Parliaments Respecting North America, 1452–1754*, 5 vols. (Washington, D.C.: Carnegie Institution of Washington, 1924–1941), I, 288–90, 293, 305; Beer, *Old Colonial System*, I, 33.

[60] Ibid., I, 33, 32n "Instructions for the Councill appointed for forraigne Plantacons 1 Dec. 1660," in John Romeyn Brodhead, *Documents Relative to the Colonial History of the State of New-York*, ed. E. B. O'Callaghan, 11 vols. (Albany, N.Y.: Weed, Parsons and Company, 1853–1861), III, 35.

seventeenth century. But the registration procedures were indeed designed to regulate the traffic in English servants, allowing the emigration of only those seeking "better fortunes than they can meete with at home." Such ambitious English subjects could add more wealth to the empire by emigrating than by remaining in straitened circumstances in England.

The government of Charles II also resurrected the idea of peopling the colonies with convicts. Petitions from Jamaican merchants prodded English officials into resuming that practice in 1661. Although approximately 4,500 English felons were transported to the American plantations between 1661 and 1700, the British government was not sufficiently committed to the project to oversee its workings or to underwrite its cost.[61] The wholesale transportation of convicts did not develop until 1717, when the English government created the machinery and procedures necessary to ensure the continuous flow of English convicts to its American empire. By that time, many colonists were disillusioned with the project and attempted to veto or tax the trade out of existence. The English government had, however, finally decided that its convicts could serve the empire best by laboring in America and thus persevered. Once that decision had been made, all obstacles were removed. Parliament rewrote its penal code, designating offenses for which transportation to the colonies would henceforth be the penalty. The English government provided subsidies for transporting convicts overseas and disallowed colonial legislation that threatened that traffic.[62]

The laws governing convict transportation were part of the program to regulate emigration. Indeed the deportation of convicts promised England a double benefit: first, by ridding the country of a dangerous and nonproductive class of subjects; and second, by the convict's theoretical regeneration in the American environment, which could turn an English deficit into an imperial asset. Similarly, the Act of 1718 "to prevent the inconvenience arising from seducing artificers in the manufactures of Great Britain to foreign parts" retained those individuals in England whose value could not be enhanced by emigration.[63] These measures became the nucleus of England's eighteenth-century domestic emigration policy.

The steps taken to restrict English emigration reveal the divergence of interests that had developed between England and its colonies. By 1670 Roger Coke was arguing that "Ireland and our Plantations Rob us of all the growing Youth and Industry of the Nation, whereby it becomes week [*sic*] and feeble, and the Strength, as well as Trade, becomes decayed and diminished." Claiming that

---

[61] Smith, *Colonists in Bondage*, 96.

[62] Ibid., 96–117; A. Roger Ekirch, *Bound for America: The Transportation of British Convicts to the Colonies, 1718–1775* (Oxford: Clarendon Press, 1987), esp. chaps. 1 and 3.

[63] Smith, *Colonists in Bondage*, 92–93, 128; 15 Geo. II, c. 27 (1718), in Ruffhead, ed., *Statutes at Large*, V, 157–58.

"England's existing military inferiority to France was due to this emigration," Coke pointed to the superiority of the Spanish mode of colonization that gained it new, conquered subjects, while "we in our Plantations wholly people them from ourselves." Two years earlier Josiah Child had maintained "That colonies have not decreased the population of England, as some say they have of Spain." Child was not, however, claiming that colonizing with English subjects increased the nation's demographic base, but rather, that the colonies minimized a population loss that was undesirable but inevitable. He argued, "New England was originally inhabited, and hath since successively been replenished, by a sort of people called Puritans . . . and had there not been a New England found for some of them, Germany and Holland probably had received the rest; but Old England, to be sure, had lost them all." Similarly, the original settlers of Virginia and Barbados were "a sort of loose, vagrant people . . . who probably could never have lived at home to do service for their country" and would probably have been "hanged, or starved, or died untimely of some of those miserable diseases that proceed from want or vice."[64]

An apparent decline in England's demographic surplus also fueled the movement to restrict emigration. In the second half of the seventeenth century, England's rate of population growth decreased. At the same time, London was relieved of some of her dangerous congestion by the Plague of 1665 and the employment opportunities resulting from the fire of 1666.[65] England's high unemployment and rising poor rates continued, but a new group of political economists transformed those demographic facts from a weakness into an asset. Colonizing tracts that had promised to rid England of its debilitating population surplus were replaced by the writings of men whose fascination with statistics or "political arithmetic" led them to focus on people, rather than territorial expansion, as the root of national greatness.

At the end of the seventeenth century, England's political economists no longer characterized the nation's poor as dangerous, but as idle—people "undisposed for labour" who could be trained in habits of industry by public works projects and workhouses. William Petyt's 1680 argument that "the odds in population must also produce the like odds in manufacture; plenty of people must also cause cheapness in wages, which cause cheapness of the manufacture" left no people who must inevitably be "hanged, or starved, or died untimely." Similarly, William Petty's assertion that "tythes increase within any territory, as the labor of that country increases, and labor does, or ought to, increase as the people do" left no room for a population surplus that could benefit England only by consignment

---

[64] Roger Coke, *A Discourse of Trade* (1670), quoted in Beer, *Old Colonial System*, I, 22; Josiah Child, *New Discourse of Trade* (1668), quoted in Stangeland, *Pre-Malthusian Doctrines*, 157.

[65] According to Wrigley and Schofield, England's seventeenth-century population peaked in the 1650s at about 5,300,000 and then declined. At the end of the century England's population was just under 5,000,000, *Population History of England*, 208–209, table 7.8.

to the colonies.[66] Even London's congestion was turned into an asset by political economists who cited Holland as evidence of the prosperity produced by a dense population. In 1690 Nicholas Barbon argued that "Enlarging of Cities" was a "great Advantage to *Trade*" as "Man being Naturally Ambitious, the Living together, occasion Emulation, which is seen by Out-Vying one another in Apparel, Equipage, and Furniture of the House; whereas, if a Man lived Solitary alone, his chiefest Expence, would be Food."[67] Thus, "The unwelcome hordes of masterless men at the beginning of the century appeared to the most concerned of their betters seventy years later as a pool of badly managed labor . . . the free laborer was but a potential resource."[68] The decline of the apparent need to export an unruly population facilitated the decision to control and restrict English emigration to the New World. To make these decisions more palatable to British imperialists, the government undertook to provide a replacement for the English people they now wished to keep at home.

Colonizing with "People Not Our Own"

The second half of England's colonization program was identifying and facilitating the emigration of acceptable alternative settlers from non-English populations. By the 1660s, as the American colonies themselves had become a source to be tapped to provide settlers for new or underpopulated colonies, the government of Charles II continued Cromwell's policy of encouraging intercolonial migration.[69] The Restoration government also tried to provide settlers from the non-English regions of the British Isles. At the same time that the emigration of English servants was being regulated and restrained, the 1663 "Act for the Encouragement of Trade" authorized the shipment of locally grown provisions and "Servants or Horses" from Ireland and Scotland to England's colonies, while otherwise excluding those countries from the colonial trade.[70]

Protests from American, Scottish, and Irish officials testify to the efficacy of England's attempt to shift at least part of the burden of populating its colonies to other parts of its empire. In 1698 the Scots Privy Council decreed that those

[66] Stangeland, *Pre-Malthusian Doctrines*, 155 (Petyt quote), 144 (Petty quote). Even in the anti-emigration climate of Restoration England promoters of colonization such as William Penn continued to argue that "colonies are the Seeds of Nations, begun and nourish'd by the Care of wise and populous Countries" and "best for the Increase of humane Stock, and beneficial for Commerce." Beer, *Old Colonial System*, I, 19–20 (quote).

[67] Campbell, "Of People Too Few," 186–87; Nicholas Barbon, *A Discourse of Trade*, 1st publ. 1690 (Baltimore: Johns Hopkins University Press, 1905), 34.

[68] Appleby, *Economic Thought*, chap. 6, 142 (quote), 152.

[69] "Instructions to the Council for Foreign Plantations, 1670," in Campbell, "Of People Too Few," 195; *Calendar of State Papers, Colonial Series, 1661–1668* (London: Longman et al., 1880), 764, 904, 912.

[70] 15 Car. 2, c. 7 (1663), in Ruffhead, ed., *Statutes at Large*, III, 267–71.

aiding emigration be punished as man-stealers. In 1729 Irish authorities, alarmed by the loss of the Protestant (and loyal) element of their population and by the prospect of lower rents, proposed a bill to restrict Irish emigration. This was turned down by the British Privy Council as an "unreasonable restraint" on His Majesty's subjects and as a measure that would give too much power to Irish officials.[71]

Data on the eighteenth-century servant trade to British North America demonstrate England's success in replacing English servants in its American colonies with Irish, Scottish, and foreign-born recruits. Although the statistics on indentured servants are scattered and incomplete, those compiled by A. E. Smith show a decline in the number emigrating from London from over 800 a year in 1684 to an annual average of about 300 in 1720–1732. A recent survey of the literature concludes that between 1700 and 1775, 25,000 servants emigrated from England to British North America, compared with 70,000 from Ireland and Scotland and 35,000 from Germany.[72]

The decline in the supply of English servants at the end of the seventeenth century forced the Chesapeake planters to rely more heavily on slave labor that became available to them for the first time. Prior to the 1660s, the Dutch supplied most of the slaves carried to England's colonies. With the slave trade centered on Brazil, virtually no slave shipments were sent to mainland colonies where the demand was not great enough to justify an extension of the voyage from Africa. Barbados, on the northern perimeter of the Dutch slave circuit, was the only English colony to receive slaves in significant numbers before the middle of the seventeenth century. However, in the 1660s England's Navigation Acts decimated Dutch trade to the British West Indies and left the Barbadians to the mercy of maverick English slavers, at the precise time that English indentured servants were becoming increasingly scarce.[73]

In 1663 Charles II responded to the arguments of "London merchants and Westminsters officials . . . that such a major and vital trade needed promotion and protection" by chartering the Company of Royal Adventurers into Africa with a monopoly on the English slave trade. Problems encountered by the company led in 1672 to its reorganization into the Royal African Company with a new charter and an obligation "to deliver slaves to the English colonies on a large scale." During the next forty years the Royal African Company provided the English West Indies with about 120,000 slaves. However, the company continued

---

[71] Ian Charles Cargill Graham, *Colonists from Scotland: Emigration to North America, 1707–1783* (Ithaca: Cornell University Press, 1956), 90; R. J. Dickson, *Ulster Emigration to Colonial America, 1718–1775* (London: Routledge and Kegan Paul, 1966), 181–89, quote on 188; Campbell, "Of People Too Few," 200.

[72] Smith, *Colonists in Bondage*, Appendix, 308–11.

[73] Richard S. Dunn, "Servants and Slaves: The Recruitment and Employment of Labor," in Jack P. Green and J. R. Pole, eds., *Colonial British America: Essays in the New History of the Early Modern Era* (Baltimore: Johns Hopkins University Press, 1984), 159; Russell Menard, "From Servants to Slaves: The Transformation of the Chesapeake Labor System," *Southern Studies*, 16 (1977), 355–90.

to ignore marginal markets on the North American continent. It was only with the loss of the Royal African Company's monopoly, after the Glorious Revolution, that the slave trade to the English mainland colonies became significant. As soon as Parliament agreed in 1698 to allow the participation of private slavers in the African trade, the English slave trade soared "fantastically" and direct shipments to the Chesapeake began.[74]

While the English government was promoting the transplantation of colonial subjects, Irish and Scottish servants, English convicts, and African slaves, it also began recruiting the Protestant subjects of Continental rivals.[75] In 1679 the English government urged the Proprietors of Carolina to transport French Huguenots who could produce in America products that England then imported from southern Europe. When the Proprietors declared themselves satisfied with their current method of obtaining settlers, which did not require subsidies, the English government paid to transport two shiploads of Huguenots to the colony. After the collapse of Carolina's proprietary government in 1719, English officials ensured the flow of non-English immigrants by granting lands directly to foreigners, on condition that they be settled by Protestants.[76] In the 1710s the English government spent thousands of pounds to transport and subsidize Germans who would produce naval stores in New York. George I instructed his German agent to offer "all Germans and Swiss who are not Catholics" a transportation subsidy and lands

> west of the Allegheny Mountains, usually considered a part of Pennsylvania, but not yet belonging to it. Each family shall have fifty acres of land in fee simple, and for the first ten years the use, without charge, of as much as they shall want, subject only to the stipulation that after that time the yearly rent of one hundred acres shall be two shillings. There is enough for 100,000 families, and they shall have permission to live there, not as foreigners, but on their engagement, under oath, to be true and obedient to the King, . . . to have the same rights as his natural-born subjects.[77]

[74] Richard S. Dunn, *Sugar and Slaves: The Rise of the Planter Class in the English West Indies, 1624–1713* (New York: W. W. Norton, 1973), 226–33, quote on 231; Dunn, "Servants and Slaves," 164–68, quotes on 167.

[75] Foreign-born Protestants also were recruited for Ireland. Flemish tanners were settled there in the 1570s and "Dutch linen workers in the 1630s," Clarke, "The Irish Economy, 1600–60," 181. For the later recruitment of French Huguenots for Ireland, see Chap. 2, note 15.

[76] Beer, *Old Colonial System*, I, 27–28; Peter [Pury], *A Description of the Province of South Carolina, Drawn Up at Charles Town, in September 1731*, in Peter Force, comp., *Tracts and Other Papers, Relating Principally to the Origin, Settlement, and Progress of the Colonies of North America, from the Discovery of the Country to the Year 1776*, 1st publ. 1836, 4 vols. (New York: Peter Smith, 1947), II, document XI, 4; M. Eugene Sirmans, *Colonial South Carolina: A Political History, 1663–1763* (Chapel Hill: University of North Carolina Press, 1966), 167–68.

[77] Knittle, *Early Eighteenth-Century Palatine Emigration*, 143–44, 160–70; Lowell Colton Bennion, "Flight from the Reich: A Geographic Exposition of Southwest German Emigration, 1683–1815" (Ph.D. diss., Syracuse University, 1971), 193; Emberson Edward Proper, *Colonial Immigration Laws: A Study of the Regulation of Immigration by the English Colonies in America* (New York: Columbia University Press, 1900), quote on 47.

In addition, the English parliament passed the General Naturalization Act of 1709, which gave foreigners a cheap and easy avenue to English citizenship. Parliament believed that such a law would promote emigration since only citizenship could secure alien land titles in America.[78]

England's struggle to devise a colonization program that coordinated its commitment to empire with domestic demographic needs created the unique ethnic mixture that would henceforth distinguish the American states. International conditions and the absence of an abundant and sophisticated native American work force led English rulers to experiment with methods eschewed by other European states—transplanting large contingents of voluntary, involuntary, and enslaved Old World subjects. In the early decades of colonization, English rulers acquiesced, somewhat reluctantly, in the transportation of their own subjects to settle "vacant" American lands. When English migrations seemed to threaten domestic depopulation and political instability, British officials turned to alternative, non-English sources. English laws, policies, and institutions were designed to ensure colonial vitality without enervating the mother country. By the middle of the eighteenth century British officials had devised the immigration policies necessary to safeguard England's domestic population while ensuring a continuous supply of English dissenters and outcasts, foreign Protestants, and enslaved Africans for their American colonies. Although English subjects continued to emigrate in significant numbers, it seemed to many observers that England's daring approach to colonization had succeeded, allowing England to win the mercantilist battle of expanding its own power at the expense of its rivals.

---

[78] Knittle, *Early Eighteenth-Century Palatine Emigration*, 28; James Kettner, *The Development of American Citizenship, 1608–1870* (Chapel Hill: University of North Carolina Press, 1978), 70–75.

2   The Creation of the Colonial Asylum

ENGLAND'S DECISION to repopulate its New World lands with Old World peoples originated not only America's tradition as a nation of immigrants but also its obligation to serve as an asylum for the oppressed. In early modern Europe many states offered a refuge to the persecuted and discontented subjects of their rivals. Some of these offers reflected a humanitarian concern for the victims of religious persecution, but most were motivated by mercantilist goals—the hope of winning a larger proportion of the world's wealth by seducing the subjects of rival powers. According to mercantilist theory, foreign immigrants and refugees could strengthen a nation in many ways. Wealthy immigrants brought property with them; skilled immigrants expanded a nation's industrial capacity and promised to improve its balance of trade; more people meant larger armies and navies, more workers, and settlers for undeveloped or newly conquered lands. The belief that these gains were matched by a corresponding debilitation of the state abandoned by refugees made such prospects even more alluring.[1]

Operating on these assumptions, English monarchs created the asylum role that would be reprised by their colonists. From the reign of Queen Elizabeth, England laid claim to the title of Protector of persecuted Protestants; by the eighteenth century England also claimed to be the paragon of enlightened government, offering the subjects of oppressive rulers the prospect of sharing in the rights of Englishmen. England's rulers consistently strove to reap the rewards of asylum providers, but popular prejudice and political struggles limited the attractive power of the English refuge and led to the designation of America as an

[1] Lowell Colton Bennion, "Flight from the Reich: A Geographic Exposition of Southwest German Emigration, 1683–1815" (Ph.D. diss., Syracuse University, 1971); Warren C. Scoville, *The Persecution of Huguenots and French Economic Development, 1680–1720* (Berkeley: University of California Press, 1960); Jon Butler, *The Huguenots in America: A Refugee People in New World Society* (Cambridge: Harvard University Press, 1983); Mack Walker, *The Salzburg Transaction: Expulsion and Redemption in Eighteenth-Century Germany* (Ithaca: Cornell University Press, 1992).

adjunct asylum, a place to settle refugees who aroused the xenophobia of the English people. The decision to shift part of England's obligation to its colonies was facilitated by the evident American need for settlers; it was justified by officials and colonizers who stressed America's regenerative possibilities and exaggerated the willingness of the colonists to serve as an asylum for Europe's "downtrodden masses."

The English Asylum

Seventeenth-century England had a long tradition of encouraging the immigration of skilled and propertied foreigners, which was matched by an equally long tradition of revoking special privileges and expelling aliens when their activities stirred up the resentment of the English people. Medieval Jews who received royal protection in return for the financial support they gave the monarchy were expelled in 1290 at the instigation of English aristocrats who hoped for more control over the king once his financial backers were removed. In the fourteenth century, Edward III extended commercial privileges to Flemings and Gascons in the hope that they would support his claim to the French crown. These privileges were gradually whittled away on the demand of English merchants who saw no reason to remove the handicaps of foreign competitors or to diminish national revenues by waiving the special customs and taxes paid by resident aliens.[2]

During the Middle Ages, England was also a haven for "divers persons . . . from parts beyond the sea" who sought "shelter and refuge, by reasons of banishment out of their own country, or who for great offence or other misdeeds have fled from their own country." After the Reformation England hosted increasing numbers of refugees whose "great offence" was religious dissent.[3] When Queen Elizabeth became the sixteenth-century Protector of Protestants, foreign and domestic policy mandated at least a modicum of support for Protestant regimes against the Catholic powers and an English welcome for victims of "papist" tyranny. There was no clear dichotomy between England's religious refugees and immigrants seeking economic opportunity; both groups aroused English xenophobia. Often the two groups of immigrants overlapped, as was the case with the

---

[2] W. Cunningham, *Alien Immigrants to England*, 1st publ. 1897, 2d ed. (London: Frank Cass and Co., 1969), 70–89.

[3] Quote from 13 Ed. I, Stat. Civitatis London in ibid., 92n. The transformation of England into a Protestant country did not produce an immediate influx of religious refugees. Henry VIII did not welcome Lutherans, although Thomas Cromwell and other officials "were ready to give them protection for a time." Under Henry VIII, laws were passed "to deter, not encourage, the advent of foreign artisans" and the Proclamation of 1544 expelled all "Frenchmen, not denizens." Under Edward VI, Walloons and Germans were given refuge, became exiles under Mary, and then returned with the accession of Elizabeth. Ibid., 140–41, 146–48.

sixteenth-century Walloons and Flemings, who, after fleeing Spanish persecution, introduced the "new draperies" in England and Holland.[4]

England relied primarily on offers of naturalization and religious toleration to entice aliens to its shores. Prior to the Glorious Revolution, English sovereigns claimed the right to control both of those processes. It was the monarch's right to decide which foreigners to accept as subjects and on what terms. Naturalization removed disabilities on an alien's right to own land, practice a trade, and participate in commerce on an equal footing with English subjects. Therefore, in granting citizenship an English monarch diminished his revenues, as he no longer received the double taxes and customs duties usually assessed on foreigners and no longer fell heir to the real estate of deceased aliens. After the Reformation the English monarch, as head of the Church of England, gained additional authority to determine the extent to which exceptions should be made to laws that imposed disabilities on non-Anglicans. However, English people who resented foreign competition and interlopers often forced their rulers to rescind or modify the welcome extended to aliens. Additional constraints were placed on royal largesse when, during the seventeenth century, Parliamentarians challenged the king's right to confer English citizenship and to suspend alien and religious disabilities.

Naturalization

Initially, England's king and Parliament worked together to naturalize. Foreigners first petitioned Parliament for citizenship. That body would then recommend that the king adhere to certain guidelines when he issued his letters patent. Parliament's recommendations could, however, be overridden by the royal prerogative. Thus, an Act of Parliament in 1431 recommended that Henry Hansford, a Prussian, be given "full rights and that he should pay scot and lot and all customs, taxes, etc. like natives." In this instance, Henry VI ignored Parliament's advice and assented to the naturalization only "on condition that the suppliant pay customs, subsidies and other dues to the king like strangers."[5]

By the seventeenth century, the English naturalization procedure had split into two separate channels that could lead to identical ends: a grant of full or partial naturalization or endenization by act of Parliament (to which the king gave his assent) or by royal letters patent. But the accession of James VI of Scotland to

[4]Cunningham, *Alien Immigrants to England*, introduction, 156, 168–76, 205–06; London's 1563 "Return of Strangers" reported that 1,647 foreigners had arrived in the city since the accession of Elizabeth. Of this number, 712 had emigrated for "reasons of religion." Ibid., 149n.

[5]William A. Shaw, ed., *Letters of Denization and Acts of Naturalization for Aliens in England and Ireland, 1603–1700*, Huguenot Society of London, *Publications*, 18 (1911), iii–viii, quotes on v; Clive Parry, *British Nationality Law and the History of Naturalisation* (Milan: Guiffre, 1954), 33–41; James H. Kettner, *The Development of American Citizenship, 1608–1870* (Chapel Hill: University of North Carolina Press, 1978), 29–34.

the English throne in 1603 produced a reexamination of citizenship and naturalization procedures. The English parliament rebuffed James's efforts to create a single consolidated kingdom of Great Britain in which all his subjects would be equally citizens. This turmoil over the political relationship between the two countries ruled by James I, and later struggles between the king and Parliament, hardened and magnified the differences between the two modes of naturalization.[6]

In deciding the case of James's Scottish subjects, Edward Coke, the champion of English common law against the royal prerogative, claimed that, although the king could "by his letters patent . . . make a denizen," he could not "naturalize . . . to all purposes, as an act of parliament may do; neither can letters patent make any inheritable in this case, that by the common law can." After further confrontations with the Stuart kings, Coke would state that only Parliament, whose jurisdiction was "so transcendant and absolute, as it cannot be confined either for causes or persons within any bounds," had the power to "naturalize a meere alien, and make him a subject borne." But it would take the Glorious Revolution to validate Coke's claims. In the meantime, James I continued to exercise his royal prerogative to naturalize his Scottish subjects, free of all fees and to promote immigration, farming block grants of endenization to recruiters, who awarded them to valuable aliens they introduced into England.[7]

Religious Toleration

The religious toleration seventeenth-century England used to recruit immigrants also was shaped by struggles between king and Parliament. Through most of the century, the religious liberty envisioned by England's rulers was far ahead of public opinion, forcing them to use executive powers to circumvent political and popular opposition. The early Stuarts could not prevent Parliament from passing anti-Catholic legislation, but they could mitigate its impact. Under both James I and Charles I, penal laws "were enforced only fitfully and intermittently," as royal proclamations commanding their enforcement were generally issued only in years when Parliament was in session.[8] The English king also had the power to

[6] Shaw, ed., *Letters of Denization, 1603–1700*, vi–viii; David Harris Willson, "King James I and Anglo-Scottish Unity," in William Appleton Aiken and Basil Duke Henning, eds., *Conflict in Stuart England: Essays in Honour of Wallace Notestein* (London: Jonathan Cape, 1960), 44–51.

[7] Willson, "King James I"; Kettner, *Development of American Citizenship*, 16–30, quote on 27n. By the 1760s denization was defined by William Blackstone as a product of the royal prerogative that created an inferior status, "a kind of middle state between an alien and natural-born subject," whereas naturalization was attainable only through an act of parliament and placed the petitioner in "exactly the same state as if he had been born in the king's ligeance," ibid., 30. Parry, *British Nationality Law*, 59–60; Shaw, ed., *Letters of Denization, 1603–1700*, xxxiii–xxxiv, 1–37.

[8] Godfrey Davies, *The Early Stuarts, 1603–1660* (Oxford: Clarendon Press, 1937), 202–08, quote on 205; W. K. Jordan, *The Development of Religious Toleration in England*, 4 vols. (Cambridge: Harvard University Press, 1932–1940), II, 61–108.

remit recusancy fines and, by letters of grace, protect individual dissenters. This allowed the early Stuarts to offer immunity from religious disabilities to alien immigrants, as well as British Catholics and Protestant dissenters. But the political cost of exercising these royal powers limited their use.[9]

As English rulers were cautiously offering individual exemptions from religious persecution, a coherent theory of religious toleration gradually evolved in seventeenth-century England. Experiences during the Interregnum convinced many English people of the need to tolerate religious differences, to license and control rather than extirpate and expel religious dissidents.[10] England's political economists expedited the process by expounding on the economic benefits of religious toleration. As early as 1614, a Baptist tract cited the social and economic gains to be reaped in a kingdom based on liberty of conscience, where "no man need to flee out of his native country and fatherland, for persecution sake." In the 1640s, Henry Robinson temporarily diverted his attention from economic theorizing to fight Presbyterian intolerance. In 1643, he pointed out the absurdity of destroying one oppressive national church only to replace it with another, which would continue to drive English subjects out of their native land, carrying "with them their gifts, arts, and manufactures into other countries, to the greatest detriment of this commonwealth."[11]

Oliver Cromwell's interest in protecting Jews from persecution was a natural extension of his belief in freedom of conscience. But he also was influenced by "an exaggerated conviction that the Jews, if they were given a tolerable legal status in England would greatly assist in the economic rehabilitation of the nation and in the expansion of its trade."[12] Cromwell's duality mirrored that of other Englishmen whose messianic and mercantilist dreams led to negotiations, in 1655, to legalize the admission of Jewish immigrants for the first time since 1290. Millenarianists believed that the return of Christ would be preceded by the conversion of the Jews. As long as Jews were excluded from their country, the English would be unable to hasten that glorious day through proselytizing. For this reason, the Nominated Parliament considered the resolution that "the Jews should be called into this Commonwealth, and have places alloted

[9] Jordan, *Development of Religious Toleration*, II, 61–108. By 1621 promises of royal protection had helped to expand London's alien population to about 10,000 foreigners. Ibid., II, 33, 52n.

[10] Richard Burgess Barlow, *Citizenship and Conscience: A Study in the Theory and Practice of Religious Toleration in England during the Eighteenth Century* (Philadelphia: University of Pennsylvania Press, 1962), 28–32.

[11] Jordan, *Development of Religious Toleration*, II, 284–98, quote on 295; IV, 140–76, Robinson quote on 146. In 1652 Roger Williams argued that Englishmen would "outshoot and teach their neighbours" by establishing complete religious freedom. Such a policy would divert from Holland the "confluence of the persecuted" that drew "boats, drew trade, drew shipping, and that so mightily in so short a time, that shipping, trading, wealth, greatnesse, honour . . . have appeared to fall as out of heaven in a crown or garland upon the head of that poor fisher town." Ibid., III, 498–515, quote on 503.

[12] During the Protectorate Oliver Cromwell adopted strategies similar to those of the early Stuart kings to protect both English and alien dissenters. His manipulation of Parliament and personal intervention created an unprecedented measure of religious freedom in England. Ibid., III, 160–253, quote on 209.

to them to inhabit in, and exercise their lyberty, for there tyme is neere at hand." Backers of this motion buttressed religious arguments with claims that the admission of Jews would produce great economic benefits, since those prosperous Iberian merchants would undoubtedly be accompanied by the large stores of bullion they had garnered in the American trade. But parliamentary negotiations came to naught; it was Charles II who finally, in 1664, accorded Jews the official right to live and trade in England.[13] Although the English Commonwealth failed to establish the political stability and economic prosperity promised by the promoters of religious freedom, the theories had been developed that would allow England to lay claim to the title of asylum for the victims of religious persecution.

Restoration Policies

With the restoration of the monarchy in 1660, the English tradition of encouraging immigration by executive dispensation reached full flower. The fervor with which England sought to restore order and stability by returning to a traditional monarchical form of government resuscitated some royal powers that had been challenged in the years preceding the Civil War. Charles II used these revived powers to promote immigration by royal fiat, adding thousands of propertied and industrious foreigners to England's population. However, Charles's determination to claim and exercise traditional royal rights revived parliamentary distaste for the prerogative power. As Parliamentarians circumscribed monarchical rights, they also undermined royal efforts to expand the English asylum.

The mercantilists who advised Charles II on the ways to increase England's wealth and power urged him to extend religious freedom to all Protestants. Samuel Fortrey, in a pamphlet addressed "To The most High and mighty MONARCH, CHARLES the II," advocated the removal of the "impediments" that restrained "the free liberty of mens consciences" of those who "profess the Protestant Religion" to attract "wealthy and industrious people, from all parts of *Europe*." In 1677, the Irish pamphleteer Thomas Sheridan expanded this mercantilist argument. Instead of requiring aliens to pay special duties, Sheridan proposed that immigrants be exempted from *all* taxes for a period of seven years. He also pointed out that the removal of religious impediments would prevent the emigration of valuable English dissenters.[14]

---

[13] Ibid., quote at III, 212; Cecil Roth, *A History of the Jews in England*, 1st publ. 1941, 3d ed. (Oxford: Clarendon Press, 1964), chap. 7; Abram Vossen Goodman, *American Overture: Jewish Rights in Colonial Times* (Philadelphia: Jewish Publication Society of America, 1947), 6.

[14] Samuel Fortrey, *Englands Interest and Improvement*, 1st publ. 1663 (Baltimore: Johns Hopkins University Press, 1907), quotes on 14; Caroline Robbins, "A Note on General Naturalization under the Later Stuarts and a Speech in the House of Commons on the Subject in 1664," *Journal of Modern History*, 34 (1962), 170–71 (Sheridan quote), 177; Jordan, *Development of Religious Toleration*, IV, 344.

Charles II heeded this advice. He began his reign by instructing the Duke of Ormonde, the Lord Deputy of Ireland, to recruit immigrants to repair the devastating consequences of the Cromwellian wars. Ormonde promptly embarked on a program to expand Ireland's population and to reconstitute the Irish linen industry. Five hundred skilled textile workers and their families were imported from Brabant, La Rochelle, and the islands of Ré and Jersey, along with additional French Protestants to settle Ormonde's own Irish estates. A tract entitled "Memoire pour encourager les Protestans de venir habiter en Hirland," written and published at Ormonde's behest, promised industrious Protestant immigrants religious freedom, aid in escaping from France, and a pledge that the Duke "would borrow their idle funds (up to 15,000 écus per person) at 10 per cent interest until they found other investment opportunities." In 1662, an Act of the Irish parliament offered free naturalization to all foreign Protestants who settled in Ireland with their families and took the oath of allegiance.[15]

Similar steps were taken to enhance England's population and industrial capacity. In 1663 the English parliament passed the same law providing for the naturalization of Protestant linen and tapestry workers who transported their families and stock into England and took an oath of allegiance. In 1666 Charles II issued a declaration promising to "protect the property and person of any Frenchman—especially one of the 'Religion Reputedly Reformed'—who sought refuge in England." In 1672 the king continued his campaign by extending an invitation to all Dutch immigrants and by introducing a bill in Parliament to provide for the general naturalization of Protestant immigrants.[16] However, Charles overstepped the bounds of his royal power by promising aliens legislative naturalization. While the compliant Irish parliament acceded to royal commands to recruit and naturalize foreigners, its English counterpart balked.

Parliament Versus the Prerogative

In Restoration England, parliamentary naturalization was a difficult and costly process. Aliens had to secure the passage of special legislative acts, which required multiple readings of private bills, the payment of £50 to £60 in fees, and typically demanded oaths that could not be taken by Catholics and Jews. In 1664, a bill was introduced to make parliamentary naturalization cheaper and easier. This bill proposed granting citizenship to any alien petitioner, except Jews, who took the oaths of supremacy and allegiance and paid a small fee of 1 or 2 shillings.

---

[15] Scoville, *Persecution of Huguenots*, 335–37, quote on 336; Caroline Robbins, "A Note on General Naturalization," 168.

[16] Scoville, *Persecution of Huguenots*, 321–22, quote on 322; E. Lipson, *The Economic History of England*, 3 vols. (London: A. & C. Black, 1915–1931), III, 60; Robbins, "A Note on General Naturalization," 168–69.

Although initially they were attracted to this measure as a way to expand England's demographic resources, members of Parliament ultimately rejected the bill for political reasons.[17]

Parliamentary opposition to the naturalization bill of 1664 was twofold. It was shaped by popular prejudice—the "loud outcries . . . of the poore Artificers of London" who protested setting the "Door soe wide open that all persons of all Nations and occupations shall have liberty to come in amongst us and the first Comer be as free to trade as the Natives are after seven years service [i.e., apprenticeship]." London's workers predicted that the passage of this act would allow aliens to take the "very bread out of their mouths." Members of Parliament also opposed the bill because it threatened to upset the Restoration settlement. As Sir John Holland pointed out, the new law would require the "repeal of two Acts already passed this Parliament, one whereof I think you cannot, the other I believe you will not. That which you cannot is the Act for the Settlement of the Customs and book of Rates. . . . That which I think you will not, is the Act of Uniformity . . . [which] you seem to judge . . . necessary for the preservation of the peace of the church and state." With the defeat of the general naturalization bill of 1664, Charles II was forced to rely on the royal prerogative to recruit and endenize valuable aliens.[18]

Parliament's refusal to pass the general naturalization bill promised by Charles II in 1672 was part of the struggle between king and Parliament for political control of the nation. Growing parliamentary opposition to royal measures was the natural result of the furor caused by the 1672 Declaration of Indulgence, the Stop of the Exchequer, and a foreign policy that produced war against the Dutch in alliance with French Catholics at a time when most English people would have preferred a war against the French in alliance with Dutch Protestants. Since foreign policy was clearly within the scope of the English royal prerogative, Parliament could use only indirect means to try to change the king's mind. Parliament did, however, flatly deny to the king that part of the prerogative power that allowed him to dispense with statutory law. In doing so, parliamentarians decreased the king's ability to attract foreign refugees.

In May 1662, when Charles was at the height of his popularity, English parliamentarians and bishops combined to defeat his attempt to suspend the operation of the Act of Uniformity for three months. In December 1662, Charles issued his first Declaration of Indulgence and lobbied for an act of Parliament that would confirm his right to do so. Again he was rebuffed, as even a Parliament filled with royalists jealously upheld its rights. The king's second suspension of

[17] Robbins, "A Note on General Naturalization," 168–69.

[18] Ibid.; all quotes from Holland's Speech of May 4, 1664, are reprinted on 176–77. For the hundreds of foreigners endenized during the reign of Charles II, see Shaw, ed., *Letters of Denization, 1603–1700*, 79–167. It should be emphasized that, although it opposed the passage of a general naturalization statute, Parliament did in 1663 aid the king's recruitment efforts by passing a special act to naturalize Protestant linen and tapestry workers who transported their families and stock into England. See note 16.

the penal laws against dissenters and recusants occurred in 1672 after the prorogation of Parliament. When Parliament reconvened in 1673, the House of Commons seized its first opportunity to claim that only an act of Parliament could suspend the operation of ecclesiastical penal statutes. The Commons threatened to deny the king money until he rescinded his action. Within a month, Charles recalled his Declaration and never again claimed the right to suspend parliamentary law.[19] Parliament then refused the king his general naturalization act. The bill of 1673 was defeated because it would undermine the power of Parliament and prevent that body from winnowing out undesirable aliens.[20]

The Huguenot Sweepstakes

Although Parliament refused to encourage immigration by liberalizing naturalization procedure, most of England joined Charles II in welcoming Huguenot refugees. The English readily joined in the Protestant scramble to provide the most attractive refuge for these victims of Catholic absolutism—and their property. Waves of French Protestants fleeing persecution occurred periodically in the years following the first French War of Religion in 1562. But the largest Huguenot emigration came in the 1680s as Louis XIV authorized increasingly drastic measures to force all of his subjects into the Catholic church. Despite the draconian penalties decreed for French Protestants caught emigrating, the number of Huguenot refugees increased along with the severity of the king's campaign. Untold thousands would flee before French Protestants secured their legal right to worship in 1803, with more than 200,000 emigrating between 1680 and 1720.[21]

In 1681 Charles II, hoping to capitalize on the Huguenot exodus, renewed his 1666 invitation to foreign Protestants. He promised all Protestant refugees the freedom "to follow commerce, arts, and trades as permitted by the laws of the realm" and to educate their children, along with exemption from special levies on aliens.[22] Other Protestant nations were even more generous in the terms they

[19] J. R. Tanner, *English Constitutional Conflicts of the Seventeenth Century, 1603–1689* (Cambridge: Cambridge University Press, 1928), chap. 14.

[20] Attorney General Finch hinted at a possible solution whereby "a good bill may come out of this," by contrasting the English practice of naturalization that "makes any man equal in privilege to original birth" with the Roman practice, where aliens were "admitted a long time to the first degree, and some good distance of time before they were capable of offices." However, since the defense of Parliament against royal absolutism was rooted in its claim to be protecting time-honored custom and the English Constitution from encroachment and corruption, the House of Commons was effectively precluded from changing the terms on which they had traditionally naturalized aliens. Debate in House of Commons, March 24, 1673, in William Cobbett and John Wright, eds., *The Parliamentary History of England from the Earliest Period to the Year 1803*, 36 vols. (London: T. C. Hansard, 1806–1820), IV, cols. 577–79.

[21] Scoville, *Persecution of Huguenots*, 6, 73, 98–99, 118–22.

[22] Ibid., 322 (quote). In 1681 Charles II invited into all his dominions "such afflicted Protestants, who, by reasons of the rigours and severitys which are used towards them upon the account of their religion, shall

offered. The Elector of Brandenburg's invitation, in 1685, paralleled England's, but also offered the emigrants financial aid in establishing homes and businesses, a special legal system to adjudicate problems encountered by French refugees, and subsidies on voyages from France to any Prussian city. The United Provinces won the asylum sweepstakes, presumably by offering a "unique liberalism in commerce and religion," which garnered that nation over 25 per cent of the Huguenot emigrants, including the wealthiest. England came in second as she provided a refuge for an estimated 40,000 to 50,000 French Protestants.[23]

The English political community responded generously to appeals for funds to aid needy Huguenot refugees. Nonetheless, in the next three decades, Parliament refused its assent to seven bills that would have eased their naturalization.[24] Parliament's intransigence was more the product of political fear than distaste for the refugees—the fear of providing a means by which any foreigner could automatically gain the full rights of Englishmen and the fear that French Catholics were entering the kingdom in the guise of "oppressed Protestants." Indeed, after the death of King Charles II the pro-refugee sentiments of England's Whigs forced a reluctant James II to continue his brother's immigration policies.[25]

Parliamentary Politics

The success of England's Whigs in emasculating the royal prerogative in the years following the Glorious Revolution vested the formulation of immigrant policy in Parliament. Ironically, the victory of the Whigs, traditional champions of religious toleration and easy naturalization, diminished the welcome England offered future immigrants. In seventeenth-century England, it had been the executive who had protected religious dissenters and aliens from English xenophobia, whether political or popular. With parliamentary supremacy secured, no more royal indulgences could be granted to mitigate the penalties imposed by ecclesiastical statutes; no longer could the king offer full grants of citizenship by letters patent. Foreigners would have to depend on Parliament for protection or on the diminished power of the crown to circumvent alien and religious disabilities.

The particular circumstances of the Glorious Revolution and its aftermath confirmed Parliament's traditionally narrow immigrant policies. The victory of the Whig party of toleration and the arrival of a king dedicated to defending the

---

be forced to quitt their native country, and shall desire to shelter themselves under his Majestys Royall protection for the preservacon and free exercise of their religion," quoted in Kettner, *Development of American Citizenship*, 68–69.

[23] Scoville, *Persecution of Huguenots*, 321–58, quote on 341; Walker, *Salzburg Transaction*, 70–72.

[24] Robbins, "A Note on General Naturalization," 168–77.

[25] Scoville, *Persecution of Huguenots*, 116–17.

Protestant cause in Europe produced party strife rather than an enhanced welcome for aliens. In 1690, an order in council prohibited English monarchs from exempting denizens from alien duties when they issued letters patent. In 1694 a general naturalization bill was defeated as a party measure, when Tory rhetoric turned mercantilist arguments in favor of immigration into an indictment of Whig policies. The resentment of Dutch "strangers" who accompanied William of Orange produced a provision in the Act of Settlement of 1701 that prohibited all aliens, whether naturalized or not, from holding great offices under the crown, sitting in Parliament, or receiving royal land grants. This provision was renewed when the Hanoverian succession brought yet another wave of foreigners to take their places in England's councils and was inscribed in all future naturalization bills.[26]

In 1709, the Whigs finally won their campaign to liberalize England's naturalization law by passing a statute that conferred citizenship on all aliens who took the sacrament in any Protestant church and paid a one-shilling fee. But their success was also their undoing. Tories had opposed the Whig bill by arguing that the "conflux of aliens" that "would probably be the effect of such a law" would undermine the English constitution, church, economy, and domestic tranquillity. Whig backers of the bill countered these predictions with data showing how Huguenot refugees had enhanced England's wealth "to the prejudice of France," been firm supporters of the English Constitution, and had, for the most part, become members of the Church of England. So, argued Whig orators, it was crucial that England enact the measures necessary to retain such valuable foreigners and encourage them to "bring over such of their friends and relations as might hope to inherit their estates."[27] But the "conflux" of Palatines in the months following the law's passage demolished the Whig position and seemed to validate Tory fears.

The Palatines

England's new Naturalization Act was not responsible for the Palatine migration of 1709. The English government had recruited these immigrants and subsidized their transportation to provide settlers for the American colonies; London was simply the first stop on their journey. Government recruiters had, however, assumed that the German emigrants would be similar to the propertied Huguenot refugees of the 1680s. Instead London was inundated with what a parliamentary committee described as "a parcel of vagabonds, who might have lived

---

[26] Thomas W. Perry, *Public Opinion, Propaganda, and Politics in Eighteenth-Century England: A Study of the Jew Bill of 1753* (Cambridge: Harvard University Press, 1962), 16; Cobbett and Wright, eds., *Parliamentary History*, V, 849–57; for the Act of Settlement (12 & 13 Wm. III, c. 2) and its 1714 renewal (1 Geo. I, Sess. 2, c. 4) see Parry, *British Nationality Law*, 90.

[27] Cobbett and Wright, eds., *Parliamentary History*, V, 780–84.

comfortably enough in their native country, had not the laziness of their dispo-sitions and the report of our well-known generosity drawn them out of it." Included among the 13,500 Palatine immigrants were more than 3,000 Catholics, who were immediately returned to the Continent.[28]

The Palatine emigration of 1709 resulted in the repeal of England's general naturalization law and the discrediting of its theoretical foundation. To English public opinion, the influx of destitute opportunists in 1709 demonstrated the dangers of expanding the boundaries of the English asylum. According to Jonathan Swift, the lesson to be learned from the Palatine experience was that

> The maxim, "That people are the riches of a nation," hath been but crudely under-stood by many writers and reasoners upon that subject . . . to invite helpless families, by thousands, into a kingdom inhabited like ours without lands to give them, and where the laws will not allow that they should be part of the property as servants, is a wrong application of the maxim. . . . The true way of multiplying mankind to public advantage, in such a country as England, . . . is to invite from abroad only able handicraftsmen and artificers, or such who bring over a sufficient share of property to secure them from want. . . . Whether bringing over the Palatines were a mere consequence of this law for a general naturalization; or whether as many surmised, it had some other meaning, it appeared manifestly, by the issue, that the public was a loser . . . a kingdom can no more be the richer by such an importation, than a man can be fatter by a wen, which is unsightly and troublesome, at best, and intercepts that nourishment, which would otherwise diffuse itself through the whole body.[29]

Queen Anne reacted very differently. In good mercantilist fashion, the English monarch tried to redirect the Palatine emigrants to underpopulated regions within the British Isles. The Palatines had been transported to London in the belief and hope that they would continue on to the New World. Instead, Queen Anne attempted to scatter them around the English countryside, believing "that it would be much more advantageous to Her Kingdom, if these people could be settled comfortably here instead of sending them to the West Indies [the American colonies]." Of the approximately 13,500 Palatines who landed in England in 1709, over 3,000 were sent to Ireland "to strengthen the Protestant cause there," where they were distributed as tenants to forty-three Irish land-lords. Such attempts to relocate the Palatines in England and Ireland were largely thwarted by the determination of the German emigrants to settle in America. Nonetheless, fewer than 3,000 Palatines reached the New World. Most who did

---

[28]Walter Allen Knittle, *Early Eighteenth-Century Palatine Emigration: A British Government Redemptioner Project to Manufacture Naval Stores* (Philadelphia: Dorrance, 1937), chaps. 1–2; Hugh Hastings, ed., *Ecclesiastical Records of the State of New York*, 7 vols. (Albany: J. B. Lyon, 1901–1916), III, 1754 (quote).

[29]Swift, quoted in Cobbett and Wright, eds., *Parliamentary History*, VI, 1089–90.

were sent to New York to undertake, unsuccessfully, a project designed to relieve England of its dependence on foreign powers for naval stores.[30]

England's Asylum for the Oppressed

England's Whigs shared more of the Queen's enthusiasm for the Palatine emigrants than Swift's pessimism. Nevertheless, they were forced to acquiesce in the repeal of the Naturalization Act of 1709 that had encouraged such migrations to remove it as a political issue after their disastrous losses in the election of 1710.[31] Despite these setbacks, England's reputation as an asylum grew to its apogee in the decades following the Glorious Revolution. When William of Orange, the Protestant champion against Catholic absolutism, was placed on the English throne, the nation committed its resources to his cause and reclaimed the mantle of Protector of Protestantism. English opposition to Catholic principles was cemented as the Bourbon kings harbored and promoted the pretensions of the deposed James II and his Catholic heirs. As the French monarchy continued its domestic and international tyranny, the number of its opponents looking to England for aid increased. An idealized portrait of the English polity was drawn by the foes of political absolutism, in England and abroad. Frenchmen longing to reform their own government created the Enlightenment gloss of England as the home of liberal, rational, and balanced government. In their eyes, the English Constitution became the mechanism that ensured good government and freedom of conscience, protected property, safeguarded the rights of the subject against both king and the lower classes, and promoted economic prosperity.[32]

While the Glorious Revolution perfected the British Constitution and England's reputation as "asylum to the oppressed," its consequences restricted alien access to the vaunted "rights of Englishmen."[33] England's eighteenth-century treatment of aliens clearly demonstrates the constraints of the refuge it offered. England's Act of Uniformity continued to circumscribe the rights of

---

[30] Knittle, *Early Eighteenth-Century Palatine Emigration*, 51–91, 98–110, 128–73, quotes on 73, 82.

[31] Geoffrey Holmes, *British Politics in the Age of Anne* (London: Macmillan, 1967), 69, 105–6; Perry, *Public Opinion, Propaganda, and Politics*, 34.

[32] For the *philosophes*' view of England, see Chapter 4; Henry Steele Commager, *The Empire of Reason: How Europe Imagined and America Realized the Enlightenment* (New York: Anchor Press, 1977), 1–6; Arthur M. Wilson, "The Enlightenment Came First to England," in Stephen B. Baxter, ed., *England's Rise to Greatness, 1660–1763* (Berkeley: University of California Press, 1983), 1–28. Eighteenth-century England's claim to be the preeminent defender of Protestantism did not go unchallenged. Other European princes who offered succor to oppressed Protestants had similar aspirations and made similar claims. See, for example, Walker, *Salzburg Transaction*, chaps. 2 and 5 for Frederick William of Prussia's dramatic championing of Salzburg exiles in the 1730s, which led Baron Pollnitz (pp. 142–43) to liken the Polish king to Moses and proclaim that, although "France is the asylum of unhappy Kings [James Stuart and Stanislav Lesczynski], the States of Prussia are the asylum of oppressed peoples."

[33] Reference to England as "asylum to the oppressed" in debate on the 1824 Alien Bill in the House of Commons in T. C. Hansard et al., eds., *The Parliamentary Debates* (London: T. C. Hansard, 1825), New Series, 10, 1334.

those who did not embrace the established church; Catholics and Jews were denied political rights throughout the century. Prospective students at English universities were required to take the oath of supremacy before matriculating; no degree could be conferred until they subscribed to the Church of England's Thirty-nine Articles.[34] In eighteenth-century England foreigners continued to pay special taxes and were excluded from trading under the Navigation Acts. After 1701 even naturalized aliens were unable to hold military commissions, sit in Parliament, or receive land grants from the king.

The Colonial Asylum

Eighteenth-century England bolstered its image as an asylum by providing a haven for Europe's discontented and oppressed subjects in its American colonies. The successful incorporation of Huguenot refugees, at the end of the seventeenth century, led Parliament to experiment with measures that expanded the contours of the English asylum. While the unexpected arrival of thousands of destitute Germans forced Parliament to rescind measures that fostered indiscriminate immigration, there was a positive lesson to be learned from the Palatine experience. According to Jonathan Swift's analysis, even if England could not benefit from the importation of "helpless families," other societies could. Swift had argued that unpropertied immigrants benefited "those countries where the lord of the soil is master of the labour and liberty of his tenants, or of slaves bought by his money. . . . And sometimes, in governments newly instituted, where there are not people to till the ground . . . in all these cases, the new comers have other lands allotted them, or are slaves to the proprietors."[35] England's American colonies, with their vacant lands and slaveholders, clearly fit the description of countries that would be enriched by the immigration of the unpropertied, the helpless, and the enslaved. By directing impoverished foreigners and refugees to its colonies, England could maintain its reputation as the Protector of Protestants and asylum for the oppressed, without jeopardizing its own society. Creating an expansive refuge in its colonies would increase England's reputation and national power while insulating its domestic population from alien competition and its religious and political establishments from contamination.

The designation of British North America as an adjunct asylum also was part of England's decision to conserve its domestic population. In making only a small portion of their people available to colonizers, British officials left a large deficit to be filled from non-English sources. The English government and colonial proprietors therefore employed all the techniques England had developed to seduce the subjects of Old World rivals to recruit American settlers. Prospective

---

[34] Roth, *History of the Jews in England*, 246–47, 289; Goodman, *American Overture*, 23, 62.

[35] Swift quoted in Cobbett and Wright, eds., *Parliamentary History*, VI, 1089–90.

colonists were promised religious toleration, easy naturalization, and the benefits that came from living under the "glorious" British Constitution. Colonial recruiters also offered foreigners the land grants and tax exemptions that were unavailable to them if they emigrated to England. The result was the creation of an American refuge far more expansive than England's, where Europe's oppressed and downtrodden subjects were promised an unprecedented measure of freedom.

Although Americans, with their chronic need for labor, usually collaborated with English recruitment efforts, they often attempted to undermine policies that were imposed on them by frustrated Englishmen, who, unable to reform their native land, experimented with the social structure in America. The colonists were especially chary of measures that saddled them with Old World outcasts and aliens who threatened to destroy or pervert the Anglo-American societies they were constructing in the wilderness. Nonetheless, by the middle of the eighteenth century, the interplay of English and American ideals, prejudices, and fears had, both accidentally and deliberately, transformed the British mainland colonies into a society that expanded the rights of most voluntary European immigrants.

Religious Freedom

Colonial liberty of conscience was largely a byproduct of English politics and did not necessarily reflect a strong commitment by America's early settlers to the principles of religious freedom. By granting favors and exemptions to English nonconformists and Catholics and to foreign Protestants, the Stuart kings also were asserting the powers they claimed to be inherent in the crown against the counterclaim of parliamentary supremacy. As Parliament steadily whittled away the royal prerogative in England, the colonies became the place where royal ideals could be implemented, religious dissenters protected, and kingly power exercised. Although the promise of religious toleration became an important element in recruiting American settlers, it was often undermined in America, as innovative idealists and politicians were forced to compromise with the traditional forces of bigotry and conservatism. Nonetheless, by the middle of the eighteenth century, these colonial struggles had produced a greater level of religious freedom than could be found in the Old World.

The Stuarts initiated England's tradition of using its American lands as a religious refuge. In 1632 Charles I conveyed to the Catholic Lord Baltimore a princely grant of land in America and powers of governance denied to the king himself—all this for a man who had been forced to resign as secretary of state after his 1625 conversion to Catholicism and was openly seeking New World land as an asylum for his new coreligionists.[36] After the Restoration, Charles II continued his father's practice of providing in America a measure of religious freedom that was unobtainable in England. The charter granted to the Carolina Proprietors produced a religious haven for Protestants who would have received short shrift in England; William Penn's enabled him to build a Quaker colony while that sect was the most despised, feared, and persecuted in England.[37]

After receiving their charters, the proprietors of Maryland, Pennsylvania, and Carolina wrote religious toleration into the fundamental laws of their colonies. The proprietary motives were twofold, to create an oasis of religious freedom and to lure settlers from groups fleeing persecution in the Old World or the New.[38] But the Whiggish or paternalistic determination of the proprietors to establish liberty of conscience often was sabotaged in America. The urgent need for people to establish viable settlements forced colonizers to introduce discordant elements that worked against their ideals. Settlers, whose traditional intolerance and xenophobia were not diminished by a voyage across the Atlantic, often undermined the rights of dissenters in the New World that had been created by legal instruments in England.

The most extreme forms of official intolerance in America occurred during the seventeenth century with the proscription of settlers whose beliefs differed from those of established churches. In Massachusetts Bay, the persecution of non-Puritans led to the founding of Rhode Island and the execution of Quakers who returned after banishment. In Maryland, the need to protect Roman Catholics from their ascendant Puritan neighbors led to the 1649 Act Concerning Religion that made those who should "blaspheme God . . . or deny our Saviour Jesus Christ to be the sonne of God, or shall deny the Holy Trinity" or use "reproachful words and speeches" against Mary or the apostles, liable to fines, whippings, banishment, death, or confiscation of all lands and goods. Dale's Laws in Virginia and the Massachusetts code of 1648 also established the death penalty for blasphemy. Religious persecution during the English Civil War forced

[36] Aubrey C. Land, "Provincial Maryland," in Richard Walsh and William Lloyd Fox, eds., *Maryland: A History* (Annapolis: Hall of Records Commission, 1983), 3; Charles M. Andrews, *The Colonial Period of American History: The Settlements*, 3 vols. (New Haven: Yale University Press, 1934–1937), II, 291.

[37] Andrews, *Settlements*, III, 45n, 143n; II, chap. 2, 192, 272–78; Frank Hayden Miller, "Legal Qualifications for Office in America, 1619–1899," in American Historical Association, *Annual Report for 1899*, 2 vols., I, 100; Perry Miller, *The New England Mind: From Colony to Province* (Cambridge: Harvard University Press, 1953), 126–27.

[38] Land, "Provincial Maryland," 13; Sally Schwartz, *"A Mixed Multitude": The Struggle for Toleration in Colonial Pennsylvania* (New York: New York University Press, 1987), 22–26; colonial charters in Francis Newton Thorpe, ed., *The Federal and State Constitutions, Colonial Charters, and other Organic Laws of the States, Territories, and Colonies Now or Heretofore Forming the United States of America*, 7 vols. (Washington, D.C.: Government Printing Office, 1909).

Maryland's Jesuits to flee to Virginia while Virginia's Puritans sought refuge in Maryland.[39]

As some American settlers tried to nullify the efforts of the king and proprietors to establish religious freedom in the colonies, others backed such efforts, either from conviction or as a necessary way to increase the strength and prosperity of their New World communities. Most of the colonies in British North America enacted legislation offering a measure of religious freedom and, in practice, tolerated even more. The laws of South Carolina were the most overt in promising religious freedom as an inducement to immigration, beginning with the 1696 "Act for making aliens free of this part of this province, and for granting liberty of conscience to all Protestants." Promotional tracts for Pennsylvania and Carolina emphasized their liberal religious policy toward Protestants; in 1750 even Massachusetts Bay, so long notorious for her bigotry, advertised that German immigrants to that colony "will have as free an exercise of their Religion here as in any part of the British Dominions." In 1753 a similar claim was made by the Ohio Company of Virginia. Hoping to dispel "the Prejudices that have been artfully propagated" and to convince Germans intending to emigrate that "they may on equal if not better terms settle in this Colony than in Pensylvania [sic] or the other adjoining provinces," these land speculators prepared a list of Virginia's liberal policies. First on the list was the claim "That with regard to their religious Liberties, all foreign protestants may depend on enjoying in this Government the Advantage of the Acts of Toleration in as full and ample manner as in any other of his Majesties plantations whatsoever."[40]

Although religious freedom was promised to foreign-born Protestants, anti-Catholicism remained a salient feature of eighteenth-century America. England's decision to recruit persecuted Protestant for its colonies ensured a continuous reinforcement of anti-Catholic sentiment. In addition, colonial Americans were surrounded by Spanish and French Catholics, who, accompanied by their Indian allies, periodically decimated frontier settlements. The fear that Catholic immigrants might cooperate in such designs perpetuated and fanned traditional prejudices and produced anti-Catholic legislation. Instructions issued to Governor Robert Hunter of New York in 1709 altered the traditional royal command "to permitt a liberty of conscience in matters of religion to all persons . . . contented with a quiet and peaceable enjoymt of it" by excepting "Papists."[41] In 1717

---

[39] Miller, *New England Mind: From Colony to Province*, 119–29; Goodman, *American Overture*, 17, 136–39, quote on 136–37; Frederic Cople Jaher, *A Scapegoat in the New Wilderness: The Origins and Rise of Anti-Semitism in America* (Cambridge: Harvard University Press, 1994), 87–89.

[40] Emberson Edward Proper, *Colonial Immigration Laws: A Study of the Regulation of Immigration by the English Colonies in America* (New York: Columbia University Press, 1900), 46–47; Erna Risch, "Joseph Crellius, Immigrant Broker," *New England Quarterly*, 12 (1939), 241–67, quote on 248; "Proposal to Settle Foreign Protestants on Ohio Company Lands" (1753), *The Papers of George Mason, 1725–1792*, ed. Robert A. Rutland, 3 vols. (Chapel Hill: University of North Carolina Press, 1970), I, 28–31, quotes on 28.

[41] John Romeyn Brodhead, *Documents Relative to the Colonial History of the State of New-York*, ed. E. B. O'Callaghan, 11 vols. (Albany: Weed, Parsons, 1853–1861), III, 373, 546 (quote), V, 132 (quote).

Maryland levied a special head tax on Irish Catholic servants entering the colony. Maryland's upper house defeated an assembly bill of 1756 that would have required the payment of £5 by all German or French Catholic immigrants (or £200 if they were priests or Jesuits), but the forty-shilling tax on Catholic servants remained in force until the Revolution. Pennsylvania's attempts to restrict immigration through taxation in the 1720s also were aimed, in large measure, against Catholics.[42]

Traditional Old World anti-Semitism also was transmitted to America. However, on the mainland, it was not reinforced by strategic considerations or by large enclaves of Jewish settlers. In America, most anti-Semitic measures were nullified by the intervention of English authority or nonenforcement. In 1685, New York City denied Jews the right to public worship or to engage in retail trade. However, in 1686 the instructions of James II to New York Governor Dongan ordered freedom of worship for all men "of what Religion soever." Within a decade, New York City's Jews had established the first synagogue in England's colonies. Although there was no formal revocation of the occupational ban, by the 1720s Jewish merchants were again active in New York's retail trade.[43] In the British West Indies, sizable Jewish merchant communities faced far greater discrimination. In Jamaica, a special tax on Jews of £1,000 a year was repealed by the assembly only after the intercession of George II in 1741. In both Barbados and Jamaica, colonial assemblies passed laws forbidding Jewish ownership of slaves or indentured servants.[44]

Although the religious freedom established in British North America did not live up to the hopes of idealistic proprietors, the colonies generally eschewed the civil penalties imposed on religious minorities in the Old World. The colonists did not adopt the practice of English universities that banned the matriculation of Jewish and Catholic students; colonial colleges were open to students of all religious beliefs. In Rhode Island, Jewish students were allowed, "if they choose it . . . a Tutor of their own Religion, who may have the immediate Care of their Education."[45] While Americans usually invoked religious tests for the professors and officers of their sectarian colleges, few other colonial occupations were closed off by reason of religion.

The experiences of the English Civil War discredited the use of militant measures to enforce religious uniformity in England and its American colonies. In the eighteenth century, more subtle tactics were used to promote religious homogeneity and to deny power to those outside the official orthodoxy. During the eighteenth century, the religious rights of dissenters remained curtailed in both England and its colonies as established churches retained their favored status,

---

[42] Goodman, *American Overture*, 146–47; for Pennsylvania's restrictions, see Chapter 1.
[43] Jaher, *Scapegoat in the New Wilderness*, 87–96; Goodman, *American Overture*, 102–7.
[44] Goodman, *American Overture*, 8–10; Jaher, *Scapegoat in the New Wilderness*, 85–86.
[45] Jaher, *Scapegoat in the New Wilderness*, 21–23, 59–68, quote on 65.

supported by taxes assessed on members and nonmembers alike. The ability of some colonial sects to win exemptions from tithes did not constitute religious freedom since these were not rights to be claimed, but favors granted by the state.[46]

The measure of religious freedom established in the New World was a product of the interaction of English politics, the need to recruit settlers, and the ability of American colonists to evade the intent of trans-Atlantic policymakers when it conflicted with their own assessment of the public good. Variations in the degree of religious liberty offered in the different colonies belied the expansive promises of American recruiters. But the legal and de facto religious freedom of British North America generally exceeded that found in the Old World. Similar factors worked to expand and constrain the political rights offered to America's immigrants and produced the same colonial diversity.

Colonial Naturalization

Although most colonists worked to recreate England's political institutions, circumstances in the New World expanded the political power of British subjects in America. The availability of American land increased the number of colonists who owned the traditional forty-shilling freehold needed to vote. The weakness of the colonial governor, an ocean away from his powerbase, allowed the popularly elected assembly to usurp powers usually reserved to the representative of the crown. The ability of non-British immigrants to share in these expanded "rights of Englishmen" depended on their acceptance as full members of their adopted communities, through formal naturalization or an informal disregard of alien disabilities. Although most colonial legislatures supported attempts to recruit alien subjects with offers of citizenship, some settlers fought against the naturalization policies imposed on them by English idealists and politicians. The result was a wide variety of colonial naturalization procedures that embodied a broad spectrum of political principles.

The primitive state of colonial society in the seventeenth century initiated the confusion that would characterize naturalization in America. Royal charters that gave patentees the powers of governance necessary to protect their property rights also guaranteed transplanted British subjects and all born within the

---

[46] And exceptions were contingent on membership in an approved church, which discriminated against Catholics, Jews, and atheists. William G. McLoughlin, *New England Dissent, 1630–1833: The Baptists and the Separation of Church and State*, 2 vols. (Cambridge: Harvard University Press, 1971), I, 216–43, 440–53; Richard L. Bushman, *From Puritan to Yankee: Character and the Social Order in Connecticut, 1690–1765* (New York: Norton, 1970), 221–30; Rhys Isaac, "Religion and Authority: Problems of the Anglican Establishment in the Era of the Great Awakening and the Parsons' Cause," *William and Mary Quarterly*, 3d ser., 30 (1973), 3–36.

province "all Privileges, Franchises and Liberties of this our Kingdom of England, freely, quietly, and peacefully to have and possess."[47] However, no mention was made of the rights and duties of aliens. Once foreigners began settling in the American colonies, provincial officials turned to the nearest means at hand to ensure the allegiance of non-English immigrants.

During the seventeenth century pragmatic considerations prompted colonial governments to ignore Old World precedent and to devise liberal procedures to transform "strangers" into law-abiding citizens. In 1641 the colony of Massachusetts Bay guaranteed "every person within this Jurisdiction, whether Inhabitant or forreiner . . . the same justice and law, that is general for the plantation" and allowed aliens to participate in town meetings. A Massachusetts law of 1652 required only an oath for admission of the "divers strangers of foreign parts [who] do repair to us of whose fidelity we have not that Assurance which is Commonly required of all Governments."[48] The Carolina Proprietors, pressured by Charles II to settle their grant with foreign-born Protestants, provided for naturalization in their Fundamental Orders. Pennsylvania's first assembly, held two months after Penn's arrival, naturalized all of the non-British residents within the boundaries of his grant.[49]

The naturalizations that were performed in seventeenth-century America were based on the assumption that the power to confer citizenship was inherent in the rights granted by colonial charters. The power of American governments to naturalize remained unchallenged until 1682 when the first of several test cases appeared in English courts. The timing and circumstances of these challenges made it impossible for the colonies to maintain their assumed power. The test cases involved the admission of foreigners into the English Navigation system and thus the issue of allowing aliens into a monopoly reserved for Englishmen. Arguments against such measures had been instrumental in defeating England's general naturalization bills and were therefore readily available to demolish colonial presumption. Even more potent was the issue of parliamentary supremacy. There was no way that Parliament, so jealous of its power to naturalize that it denied that right to the king, would allow the American colonists to determine who became English citizens. Consequently, in 1700 the Board of Trade rescinded the power of royal governors to endenize and claimed that the power to confer English citizenship had never been delegated to colonial patentees. The temporary spotlight on colonial affairs also resulted in the English veto of an Act of the Pennsylvania legislature that had naturalized a group of unnamed aliens. This veto ended further colonial experimentation with procedures that admitted foreigners to citizenship indiscriminately without scrutinizing the

[47] Quote from Maryland's Charter of 1632, in Thorpe, ed., *Federal and State Constitutions*, III, 1680–81.
[48] Kettner, *Development of American Citizenship*, 111.
[49] Ibid., 66, 78–85; Parry, *British Nationality Law*, 69–71.

qualifications of each alien.[50] After 1700, the only colonial naturalization procedure recognized by the English government was the denization of individuals by
provincial legislatures that conferred local rights valid only within the colony that
endenized.[51]

English politics, which constrained colonial naturalization at the end of the seventeenth century, had the opposite effect a few decades later. After the repeal of
England's General Naturalization Act in 1712, Whig politicians were unable to
liberalize domestic policy. They were, however, able to achieve in the colonies
many of the reforms sought so unsuccessfully at home. London's inundation by
unpropertied Palatines in 1709 seemed to indicate that easy naturalization was
inappropriate for England. But the arguments used to secure the repeal of the
English Act of 1709 suggested that the American colonies might well benefit from
such laws and inundations. Therefore when, after a thirty-year moratorium,
England's Whigs revived their campaign to liberalize British naturalization
policy, they began with colonial reform. The Plantation Act of 1740 created a
mechanism that would automatically confer English citizenship, upon payment
of a two-shilling fee, on all non-Catholic aliens who had resided for seven years
in any American colony, received the sacrament in any Protestant church, swore
allegiance to the English king, and professed their belief in Christianity. Additional provisions allowed colonial Quakers and Jews to omit the sacramental
requirement and tailor oaths to suit their religious beliefs. A bill introduced by
Georgia's General Oglethorpe in 1747 amended the Act of 1740 to allow "foreign
Protestants who conscientiously scruple the taking of an oath" to affirm rather
than swear.[52]

In 1748, emboldened by their success, English Whigs resumed their battle
for naturalization reform in England. The result was a resounding failure, in the
same Parliament that had, less than a year before, reformed the already liberal
Plantation Act. This defeat was followed by an attack on the laws governing
colonial naturalization by Englishmen who professed to fear that undesirables

---

[50] Parry, *British Nationality Law*, 69–71. Kettner, *Development of American Citizenship*, 93–97; Shaw,
Letters of Denization, 1603–1700, xxviii–xxx.

[51] The English government had never opposed the naturalization of alien subjects who settled in the
colonies as long as citizenship was conferred by the proper English authorities. After the Restoration the
promise of enjoying the rights of Englishmen in the colonies was held up as an inducement to the subjects
of rival nations by English officials as well as private recruiters. When in 1710 the English government subsidized the transportation of a group of Palatines to New York, it also promised free denization. England's
General Naturalization Act of 1709 was itself believed to have originated as a recruitment measure designed
to encourage Palatine immigration by providing a cheap and easy way to secure New World land titles.
Knittle, *Early Eighteenth-Century Palatine Emigration*, 28; Kettner, *Development of American Citizenship*,
66–71, 101.

[52] 13 Geo. II, c. 7 (1740) and 20 Geo. II, c. 44 (1747), in Owen Ruffhead, ed., *Statutes at Large, from Magna
Charta, to the Twenty-fifth Year of the Reign of King George the Third, inclusive*, 10 vols. (London: Charles
Eyre and Andrew Strahan, Printers, 1786), VI, 384, and VII, 68; Leo Francis Stock, ed., *Proceedings and
Debates of the British Parliaments Respecting North America*, 5 vols. (Washington, D.C.: Carnegie Institu-
tion of Washington, 1924–1941), V, 15, 17, 21–22, 29, 249.

who obtained citizenship in the colonies would then return to England to use their new rights to subvert the English government, church, and economy. England's Whigs were again forced to sacrifice naturalization reform at home to the exigencies of party politics, but their determination to maintain the independence of Parliament prevented the mutilation or repeal of colonial naturalization laws. The Whigs refused to repeal the Plantation Act of 1740 to prevent a Tory revival of "church spirit" and to maintain the dignity and stature of Parliament, which they believed would be undermined if Parliament rescinded the rights previously granted to those who had settled in America on the strength of their promised naturalization. In 1762, Parliament created an additional general naturalization procedure that offered citizenship, valid throughout the empire, to foreign Protestants who served for two years in the Royal American Regiment.[53]

Colonial naturalization laws that were formulated in England by government officials and proprietors were thus derived from the mixed motives of England's political community and were shaped primarily by domestic power struggles, first between Parliament and king, then among parliamentary factions. However, the ability of the colonists to ignore, evade, and reshape English regulations vitiated many policy decisions and generated a chaotic array of citizenship procedures.

Colonies that were displeased with liberal English mandates regularly exercised their capacity to evade them. In 1710, the English Lords of Trade directed New York's Governor Hunter to secure the naturalization of the Palatine immigrants "without Fee or Reward" under the provisions of England's Naturalization Act of 1709. The New York assembly refused to comply with the governor's request, "for no reason that I can guess but that it was recommended to them." In Maryland, the anti-Catholicism of the lower house prevented the passage of a liberal naturalization bill backed by the proprietor, after a controversy that included differences over land tenure for aliens and the need to uphold the honor of the Maryland assembly and "the rights of the People." With the bill's defeat, the proprietary interest was forced to circumvent colonial law and prejudice to secure land titles for unnaturalized Catholics—which it accomplished by routinely regranting titles to the heirs of deceased aliens.[54]

---

[53] Cobbett and Wright, eds., *Parliamentary History*, XIV, 133–48; Perry, *Public Opinion, Propaganda, and Politics*, chaps. 5 and 8; provisions of 22 Geo. II, c. 45 (1749) and 2 Geo. III, c. 25 (1762), in Parry, *British Nationality Law*, 87; Shaw, ed., *Letters of Denization, 1603–1700*, xxxi. Although colonial interests were involved in creating naturalization policy for America, colonial concerns appeared only as secondary arguments against the repeal of the Act of 1740. (See, for example, Cobbett and Wright, eds., *Parliamentary History*, XV, 102; Horace Walpole, *Memoirs of King George II*, ed. John Brooke, 3 vols. (New Haven: Yale University Press, 1985), I, 243. The statute of 1762 was derived from the same imperial motives that produced the Act of 1749, which promised naturalization to aliens willing to serve for three years on a British whaler.

[54] Governor Hunter to Lords of Trade, Nov. 28, 1710, in Brodhead, *Documents Relative to the Colonial History of the State of New-York*, V, 184 (quote); Kettner, *Development of American Citizenship*, 120–21, quote on 120. In South Carolina, the Dissenter Assembly party challenged the political rights and

The imperial naturalization statutes of 1740 and 1747 were predicated on the assumption that the American provinces differed from England in their ability to benefit from the introduction of all who wished to immigrate. Although the need for labor and a vast supply of undeveloped land allowed Americans to accommodate newcomers more easily than England, many colonists shared the bitterness of Pennsylvania's James Hamilton toward "that unhappy Act of Parliament which invested [German settlers] with the rights of Englishmen before they knew how to use them."[55]

Disgruntled Americans were well situated to override policies imposed on them from England. The Plantation Act of 1740 endowed colonial courts with the responsibility of deciding when alien petitioners had fulfilled the statutory requirements for imperial citizenship. In noncorporate colonies, judges were appointed by colonial governors and thus represented the royal or proprietary interest. Colonial secretaries, also appointees of the governor, were charged with registering all naturalizations under the Act of 1740 within their provinces, by remitting lists to the English Board of Trade. However, by delegating authority to colonial officials, Parliament subjected naturalization to the pressure of the same local interest groups that defied the governor's efforts to implement royal and proprietary instructions relating to such issues as paper money emissions, salaries for colonial officials, and smuggling.[56]

In the 1760s, Rhode Island refused naturalization to two Jewish merchants who petitioned for citizenship under the Act of 1740, using the specious argument that the preamble of the Act exempted the colony from abiding by its provisions. Since the stated purpose of the act was to encourage population growth, Rhode Island's judges claimed that the colony could not "come within the intention of the said act" as it was already so full of people that many of his Majesty's good subjects born within the same have removed." These two petitioners were eventually naturalized in New York and Massachusetts under the Act of 1740.[57]

While some colonists resisted the expansive citizenship policies imposed by England, others embraced them. American politicians in several colonies made effective use of the naturalization procedures instituted by the Act of 1740 for local ends. This was especially true in Pennsylvania, where more than 6,000 aliens

---

naturalizations of French Huguenots, who were supported by the Proprietors in England and the Church of England party in the colony. Arthur Henry Hirsch, *The Huguenots of Colonial South Carolina* (Durham, N.C.: Duke University Press, 1928), 103–52.

[55] Schwartz, "*Mixed Multitude*," 204 (Hamilton quote), 258; Benjamin Franklin to Peter Collinson, May 9, 1753, *The Papers of Benjamin Franklin*, ed. Leonard W. Labaree et al., (New Haven: Yale University Press, 1959–), IV, 479–86.

[56] 13 Geo. II, c. 7 (1740), in Ruffhead, ed., *Statutes at Large*, VI, 134–36; Bernard Bailyn, *The Origins of American Politics* (New York: Random House, 1968), chaps. 2–3.

[57] Kettner, *Development of American Citizenship*, 116–17, quote on 116; Goodman, *American Overture*, 53–58.

were naturalized under the provisions of the Plantation Act between 1740 and 1773.[58] American advocates of easy naturalization also succeeded in perpetuating the remarkably liberal tradition of the seventeenth century by running roughshod over imperial attempts to restrict their power to endenize. Foreigners who were willing to settle for local denization, which was more expensive than naturalization under the Plantation Act of 1740 and did not confer full English citizenship, had little trouble meeting colonial requirements. In 1715 New York's colonial assembly offered local citizenship to all foreigners who took the required oaths within nine months of registering as aliens. New York's law of 1715 was passed over the objections of the colony's governor. Similarly liberal denization procedures were adopted in Virginia and Delaware.[59]

Alien Disabilities

Uncertainty as to the disabilities on colonial aliens and their consequent need for formal naturalization added to the confusion surrounding colonial citizenship. In the mother country, naturalization was needed to obtain political rights, remove commercial duties, and secure land titles. In England, all Jews were disfranchised until the middle of the nineteenth century, while laws prohibiting Catholics from voting and officeholding remained in force until the end of the eighteenth century. Similar prohibitions against political activity by English dissenters remained on the books until 1828, even though "occasional conformity" allowed them to hold local office.[60] Not all of these restrictions obtained in the American colonies.

In America, the political rights of aliens varied from colony to colony, and all deviated from the English model. A Georgia law of 1761 gave unnaturalized aliens who had resided in the colony for six months the right to vote if they were free, white, male, twenty-one years old, and owned fifty acres of land. In New England's corporate colonies, admission to freemanship seems to have conferred full rights, obviating the need for formal naturalization under the Act of 1740 or endenization by provincial assemblies. In other colonies, unnaturalized foreigners voted, although they lacked the legal right to do so, through the connivance or ignorance of local officials. The English Act of Settlement of 1701 also inaugurated a period of uncertainty over the ability of naturalized aliens to hold office

[58] Kettner, *Development of American Citizenship*, 103; M. S. Giuseppi, ed., *Naturalizations of Foreign Protestants in the American Colonies Pursuant to Statute 13 George II, c. 7*, Huguenot Society of London, *Publications*, 24 (1921), xii–xv. Of these, almost 5,000 were naturalized in a single decade, between 1760 and 1769. Edward A. Hoyt, "Naturalization under the American Colonies: Signs of a New Community," *Political Science Quarterly*, 67 (1952), 249; James T. Mitchell and Henry Flanders, eds., *The Statutes at Large of Pennsylvania from 1682 to 1801*, 16 vols. (Harrisburg: Clarence M. Busch, 1896–1908), IV, 57, 148, 219, 283–84, 327–28.

[59] Kettner, *Development of American Citizenship*, 98–99; "The Oath of Abjuration, 1715–1716," New York Historical Society, *Quarterly Bulletin*, 3 (1919), 35–40; Hoyt, "Naturalization under the American Colonies."

[60] Barlow, *Citizenship and Conscience*, 62–77.

in the colonies. In 1773 Parliament finally ruled that the provisions of the Act of 1701 pertained only to Great Britain and Ireland.[61]

The American colonies emulated English models most closely in restricting the political power of non-Christians and Catholics. Colonial laws were passed to discourage non-Protestants from immigrating and to keep those already settled from subverting public policy and the English Constitution. In 1729, Rhode Island's assembly approved a law limiting freemanship to "Men Professing Christianity and of competent estates, and of Civil Conversation . . . (Roman Catholicks only excepted)," which disfranchised Jews, Catholics, and nonbelievers. However, in colonies controlled by an intolerant religious establishment, persecuted minorities fought for the opposite result—increased political rights for dissenters. So it was in the Massachusetts power struggle that pitted newcomers against the Puritan polity established by the Charter of 1629. In the northern colony, the franchise was restricted to members of the Puritan church until Anglican and sectarian agitation in Massachusetts and England secured the franchise for all male inhabitants with a forty-shilling freehold or other property worth £40 sterling in the royal charter of 1691.[62]

Colonies that did not pass laws restricting the political rights of religious dissidents could achieve the same ends by requiring oaths of voters and officeholders that could not, in good conscience, be taken by Catholics, Jews, or atheists. In addition, the requirement of any oath automatically disfranchised those with religious scruples against swearing, unless provisions were made to substitute affirmation for the oath. Maryland's Puritans used such techniques to strip Catholics of their political rights by requiring that all officeholders and voters take the oath of supremacy. Similar oaths removed the right of Catholics to elective office in Pennsylvania after 1706.[63]

The American colonies also emulated England in the evasion and nonenforcement of political disabilities. In England, occasional conformity mitigated the political proscription of dissenters; in the colonies, simple evasion produced the same result. Laws disfranchising Jews in New York and South Carolina were ignored. In Pennsylvania unnaturalized voters were so numerous that the proprietary interest, in 1765, publicized their intent "to come well armed to the Election," to "thrash the Sheriff, every Inspector, Quaker & Minonist [Mennonite] to Jelly," to ensure "that not a Menonist nor German should be

---

[61] Robert Francis Seybolt, *The Colonial Citizen of New York City: A Comparative Study of Certain Aspects of Citizenship Practice in Fourteenth Century England and Colonial New York City* (Madison: University of Wisconsin Press, 1918); Kettner, *Development of American Citizenship*, 86–88, 100–103, 111, 122–26; Schwartz, "*Mixed Multitude*," 185.

[62] Goodman, *American Overture*, 43–46, quote on 43–44; Andrews, *Settlements*, II, 61; Benjamin W. Labaree, *Colonial Massachusetts: A History* (Millwood, N.Y.: Kraus-Thomson, 1979), 119.

[63] Land, "Provincial Maryland," 6–8, 11–13, 20–31; Schwartz, "*Mixed Multitude*," 32–34, 42–46, 104, 160–62.

admitted to give in a Ticket without being Sworn that he is naturalized & worth £50 & that he has not voted already."[64]

The economic rights of foreigners in America also were ill defined. Alien duties were less common in the colonies than in England, as most assemblies offered special benefits, not disabilities, to encourage the immigration of foreign merchants and skilled workers. Colonial occupational regulations were applicable to native citizens and aliens alike. Admission to the rights of a craft or trade also implied a loss of all alien impediments and apparently constituted a de facto naturalization in some colonies. Local procedures and custom could, however, do nothing to lift the restrictions on aliens trading within the English Navigation system. Americans were unable to protect endenized aliens who traded outside their adopted colony from seizures by zealous customs officers. These foreigners would be forced to secure forged papers or naturalization under the Plantation Act of 1740. However, aliens involved in intercolonial trade, whose need for imperial citizenship was the greatest, also were the most injured by the mandatory seven-year residence, without being "absent out of . . . the said Colonies for a longer Space than two Months at any one Time during the said seven Years." The ability of the colonists to influence British officials charged with enforcing imperial, as opposed to local, disabilities on aliens also was limited. There is, however, abundant evidence of the American practice of frustrating the prosecution of local violators of the trade and navigation acts by packing juries, suborning witnesses, and intimidating prosecutors. Colonial communities also used these techniques to shield non-English traders.[65]

Land ownership was the most cogent reason for America's aliens to seek naturalization. Although there is no evidence that the English restriction on the king's right to grant lands to naturalized foreigners extended to the colonies, impediments on alien land titles clearly did. In virtually all of the American provinces, lands owned by unnaturalized aliens escheated to the king, proprietor, or charter government on their demise. Since colonial assemblies usually shared the desire of alien purchasers for clear land titles to facilitate subsequent real estate transactions, they readily legislated toward that end. Because most colonial attempts to vest aliens with full land titles were disallowed in England, as infringements on the rights and dignity of the king or proprietor, naturalization became the only effective remedy. The assemblies of New York in 1715 and North Carolina in 1764 went to the extreme of naturalizing dead aliens to secure their estates. The more common solution was the naturalization

[64] Schwartz, "*Mixed Multitude*," 211–36, quote on 235; William Thomas Johnson, "Some Aspects of the Relations of the Government and German Settlers in Colonial Pennsylvania, 1683–1754," *Pennsylvania History*, 11 (1944), 81–102, 200–207; Butler, *Huguenots in America*, esp. chap. 4.

[65] 13 Geo. II, c. 7 (1740), in Ruffhead, ed., *Statutes at Large*, VI, 134 (quote); Carl Ubbelohde, *Vice-Admiralty Courts and the American Revolution* (Chapel Hill: University of North Carolina Press, 1960); Goodman, *American Overture*, 39; Jaher, *Scapegoat in the New Wilderness*, 95.

of living foreigners under the provisions of local laws or the English statute of 1740.[66]

Colonial naturalization policies were shaped by a diverse and confusing amalgam of contradictory principles. Political power struggles at all levels, in England and America, led to the adoption of policies that were both purposefully and incidentally liberal. Ultimately, the colonists remained the arbiters of their own societies through their power to define and enforce alien disabilities. When an alien was denied, for example, the right to vote or to inherit land, he would also be informed of the necessary remedy, whether naturalization under the Act of 1740, denization by a colonial legislature, or an application for freemanship. By directing foreigners to provincial assemblies for endenization or to colonial judges for naturalization under the Act of 1740 Americans could enforce community standards. The colonists had the final say in delineating their citizenship procedures and the rights of aliens and naturalized immigrants. American conviction, prejudice, expediency, and circumstances thus shaped policies that extended more of "the rights of Englishmen" to aliens than refugees could find in England. And during the eighteenth century colonial officials naturalized far more foreigners than their counterparts in England.[67]

During the colonial period English priorities and attempts to resolve *domestic* problems produced an expansive British American asylum for Old World victims of religious and political oppression. The need to repopulate its New World lands combined with mercantilist theories that placed a premium on demographic resources led England to open up its American colonies to religious and political dissidents from all European nations. The contours of England's colonial refuge were then accidentally expanded by a wide variety of serendipitous factors. New World conditions generated some of the liberal mutations that expanded the freedoms enjoyed by settlers of all nationalities. The vast expanses of American land allowed an unprecedented proportion of the colonial population to acquire the forty-shilling freehold that endowed them with the political rights of Englishmen. The width of the Atlantic Ocean, which separated the large American electorate from imperial authority, gave the colonists the ability to expand their political power, by ignoring or defying uncongenial edicts. Even more important in expanding the contours of the colonial asylum was the ten-

---

[66] Kettner, *Development of American Citizenship*, 111–12, 119–21; Erna Risch, "Encouragement of Immigration as Revealed in Colonial Legislation," *Virginia Magazine of History and Biography*, 45 (1937), 10.

[67] Although eighteenth-century naturalization records for both England and the colonies are scattered and incomplete, published sources show more than 8,000 aliens naturalized in the Thirteen Colonies under the provisions of the Plantation Act of 1740 between 1740 and 1774. Giuseppi, ed., *Naturalizations in the American Colonies*; Jeffrey A. Wyand and Florence L. Wyand, *Colonial Maryland Naturalizations* (Baltimore: Genealogical Publishing Co., 1975); Lorena Shell Eaker, "The Germans in North Carolina," *The Palatine Immigrant*, 6 (1980), 5–8. During the same period just over 500 aliens were naturalized by the British parliament and another 174 endenized by the king. William A. Shaw, ed., *Letters of Denization and Acts of Naturalization for Aliens in England and Ireland, 1701–1800* in Huguenot Society of London, *Publications*, 27 (1923), 143–80.

dency of frustrated Englishmen to see their American colonies as a tabula rasa on which they could inscribe their dreams. Beginning early in the seventeenth century, British North America became a place where men who lacked the political power to implement their visions in England could experiment. Only in the colonies could the English king use his prerogative power to offer a refuge to Catholics and sectarians and grant lands to aliens. Only in the colonies could British mercantilists experiment with devices that fostered the mass migrations that, they argued, increased the power of the state. Only in America could England's Whigs implement the naturalization reforms that had fallen victim to party strife at home.

While American settlers modified or sabotaged many British visions, the pragmatic and idealistic experiments of English politicians and reformers, combined with the liberating influence of the American environment, generated a colonial asylum in which transplanted Europeans and their children enjoyed a greater measure of political and religious liberty than could be found in any Old World country. By the middle of the eighteenth century, foreign subjects who emigrated to Britain's thirteen mainland colonies were more likely to receive bounties and free land than be shackled with alien disabilities. The few local restrictions on the rights of aliens that existed could be quickly removed through denization in the colonies. Although naturalization under the Plantation Act of 1740, which was needed to remove imperial handicaps, was a lengthier process, requiring a seven-year residence, it conferred more of the "rights of Englishmen" and was open to more non-Catholics aliens than the English version.

3   *The Best Poor Man's Country*

DURING THE EIGHTEENTH CENTURY ENGLAND'S AMERICAN ASYLUM for the oppressed gained its reputation as the best "poor man's country," a place where "every man that had industry became opulent" and Europe's failures were rehabilitated. Critical observers, from the eighteenth century to the present, have found it easy to demonstrate the flawed nature of America's asylum of liberty and land of opportunity, citing among other impediments colonial laws that proscribed Catholic, Jewish, Irish, impoverished, infirm, and felonious immigrants; the absence of opportunity for enslaved Africans and native Americans; the brutal exploitation of servants indentured to unscrupulous masters; and the premature deaths of immigrants who fell victim to the New World's disease climate.[1]

Mercantilist arguments, British officials, and English reformers did indeed foster more than liberal mutations of "the rights of Englishmen" for eighteenth-century immigrants. The settlers who repopulated England's North American lands were selected by a wide array of men scattered throughout the British empire whose perception of American, English, and imperial needs, as well as their own personal interests, changed over time. The interaction of the needs, fears, prejudices, and ideals of these myriad interest groups generated contradictory impulses that shaped the experience of various immigrant groups in very different, and often unexpected, ways. During the eighteenth century the

---

[1] Robert Beverly, *The History and Present State of Virginia*, 1st publ. 1705, ed. Louis B. Wright (Chapel Hill: University of North Carolina Press, 1947), 275 (quote); William Moraley, *The Infortunate: or, The Voyage and Adventures of William Moraley, of Moraley, in the County of Northumberland, Gent.*, 1st publ. 1743, eds. Susan E. Klepp and Billy G. Smith (University Park: Pennsylvania State University Press, 1992), 89; William Smith, Jr., *Information to Emigrants, Being a Copy of a LETTER from a Gentleman in North-America: Containing a Full and Particular Account of the Terms on Which Settlers May Procure Lands in North-America, Particularly in the Provinces of New-York and Pensilvania* (Glasgow, 1774), 5; Barbara DeWolfe, ed., "Discoveries of America: Letters of British Emigrants to America on the Eve of the Revolution," *Perspectives in American History*, new ser., 3 (1987), 40–41; see also Chapter 2.

mainland colonies of British North America became a forced labor camp for British convicts, a land of slavery for kidnapped Africans, a haven for European victims of religious and political oppression, and "the best poor man's country" for industrious Protestants who were seduced by promises of bounties, transportation subsidies, free or cheap land, tax abatements, and unparalleled economic opportunity. As a result, both by accident and design, British North America simultaneously became a liberal refuge and land of opportunity for Europe's persecuted Protestants and "downtrodden masses," and the home of thousands of involuntary immigrants—people who were not drawn by the promise of the New World but were forcibly transported and sold into servitude or slavery.[2]

Winnowing Out Undesirables

During the seventeenth century British colonizers resorted to many expedient solutions to the problem of establishing viable footholds in the New World, such as recruiting social misfits, convicts, and men who were driven by desperation to take a chance in the wilds of America. The colonists often were dismayed by such recruits and denied their obligation to serve as a regenerative haven for Europe's depraved subjects and social liabilities. Laws passed by colonial legislators attempted to erect barriers that would keep out undesirable immigrants and restrict their ability to violate social norms.

By the end of the seventeenth century American colonists were especially reluctant to extend a welcome to impoverished foreigners and the "Rogues and vagabonds" that England had so graciously decided she could spare. In Massachusetts statutes were passed, beginning in 1701, to prevent the landing of the "poor, vicious and infirm," laws that required the master of each vessel to post a bond that towns receiving any "lame, impotent, or infirm persons, incapable of maintaining themselves . . . would not be charged with their support." In the absence of this security, the captain was to return such passengers to their port of embarkation. A Rhode Island law of 1700, reenacted in 1729, ordered shipmasters bringing in foreigners from outside "Great Britain, Ireland, Jersey and

---

[2]For an overview of involuntary immigration to British North America, see David Eltis, "Free and Coerced Transatlantic Migrations: Some Comparisons," *American Historical Review* 88 (1983), 251–80; Richard S. Dunn, "Servants and Slaves: The Recruitment and Employment of Labor," in Jack P. Greene and J. R. Pole, eds., *Colonial British America: Essays in the New History of the Early Modern Era* (Baltimore: Johns Hopkins University Press, 1984), 157–94; Philip D. Curtin, *The Atlantic Slave Trade: A Census* (Madison: University of Wisconsin Press, 1969); Barbara L. Solow, ed., *Slavery and the Rise of the Atlantic System* (New York: Cambridge University Press, 1991); Abbot Emerson Smith, *Colonists in Bondage: White Servitude and Convict Labor in America, 1607–1776* (Chapel Hill: University of North Carolina Press, 1947); A. Roger Ekirch, *Bound for America: The Transportation of British Convicts to the Colonies, 1718–1775* (Oxford: Clarendon, 1990).

Guernsey" to post a £50 bond as a guarantee that their passengers would not become public charges.[3]

The unexpected arrival of thousands of foreigners in Pennsylvania produced similar restrictive measures. In 1717 Pennsylvanians were startled by an unprecedented surge of immigration. The hope that these Irish and German settlers would prove to be "Industrious" additions to the colony's population quickly gave way to "uneasiness" over the arrival of an "unlimited Number of Foreigners . . . without any Licence from the King, or Leave of this government." At the request of the governor, Pennsylvania's council ordered that henceforth ships would not be allowed to enter until their masters had submitted a list of the passengers they carried and their "Characters." The 1727 arrival of 1,300 Germans in a single month led to renewed fears and attempts to limit the immigration of "Strangers" who "pretended at first that they fly hither on the Score of their religious Liberties, and come under the Protection of His Majesty." Pennsylvanians feared that the newcomers, "ignorant of our Language & Laws," would create foreign enclaves, squat on lands they did not intend to purchase, and stir up the Indians by their presence on the frontier. These fears were exacerbated by rumors that many of the immigrants spoke French and were therefore identified as "papists."[4]

While appealing to England for aid, Pennsylvanians embarked on their own program to control alien arrivals. The Provincial Council ordered that shipmasters' lists now include each passenger's name, occupation, place of residence, and reason for emigrating. Each immigrant would also be required to sign a declaration of allegiance. In 1728, Lieutenant Governor Patrick Gordon informed the Pennsylvania assembly of "positive Orders" he had received from "Britain . . . to provide, by a proper Law, against those Crouds of Foreigners who are yearly pour'd in upon us." According to Gordon, these orders did not arise "from any Dislike to the People themselves, many of whom we know are peaceable, industrious, and well affected, but it seems principally intended to prevent an *English* Plantation from being turned into a Colony of Aliens. It may also require our Thoughts to prevent the Importation of Irish Papists and Convicts, of whom some of the most notorious, Im [sic] credibly informed, have of late been landed in this River."[5] The result was Pennsylvania's law of 1729 that levied a duty of forty

[3] "An Act Directing the Admission of Town Inhabitants," in *The Acts and Resolves, Public and Private, of the Province of Massachusetts Bay*, 21 vols. (Boston: Wright and Potter, 1869–1922), I, chap. 23 (1701), 451–53, quotes on 452; renewals in 1723, ibid., II, 244–45; 1725, ibid., II, 336–37; and 1757, ibid., III, 982; Emberson Edward Proper, *Colonial Immigration Laws: A Study of the Regulation of Immigration by the English Colonies in America* (New York: Columbia University Press, 1900), 35.

[4] Sally Schwartz, "*A Mixed Multitude*": *The Struggle for Toleration in Colonial Pennsylvania* (New York: New York University Press, 1987), 81–90, quotes on 85, 86, 87, 90.

[5] William Thomas Johnson, "Some Aspects of the Relations of the Government and German Settlers in Colonial Pennsylvania, 1683–1754," *Pennsylvania History*, 11 (1944), 92; Governor Gordon's message quoted in Gertrude MacKinney and Charles F. Hoban, eds., *Pennsylvania Archives*, 8th ser., 8 vols. (Harrisburg, Penn., 1931–1935), III, 1911–1912.

shillings on "every person being an alien born out of the allegiance of the King of Great Britain ... coming into this province by land or water" and twenty shillings on "any Irish servant or passenger upon redemption." It was hoped that these fees would "discourage the great importation and coming in of numbers of foreigners and of lewd, idle and ill-affected persons into this province, as well from parts beyond the seas as from the neighboring colonies, by reason whereof not only the quiet and safety of the peaceable people of this province is very much endangered, but great numbers of the persons so imported and coming into this government, either through age, impotency or idleness, have become a heavy burden and charge upon the inhabitants of this province and is daily increasing." The Pennsylvania assembly repealed this draconian measure at its next session, for reasons that are unclear, and replaced it with a law requiring shipmasters to return all "poor and impotent" immigrants to their ports of origin or to post a bond against their becoming public charges. Those importing "persons convicted of heinous crimes" would be fined £5 a head.[6]

As eighteenth-century Americans displayed an intermittent reluctance to serve as a haven for Europe's downtrodden masses, their opposition to Catholic immigrants was more vehement and constant. The colonial fear of "papists" was rooted in the internecine struggle between Elizabethan England and the Catholic powers of Europe and perpetuated by Puritan intolerance and a general Protestant abhorrence of the "pernicious" doctrines of Catholicism. The arrival of the victims of religious persecution in British North America, from German Palatines to French Huguenots, fanned colonial anti-Catholicism; so did the power struggles between Protestants and Catholics in the Chesapeake, especially in Maryland, where the Calverts continued to fill the colony's most lucrative posts with Catholics. American anti-Catholicism was further intensified by the imperial wars of the eighteenth century, during which Catholic powers and their Indian allies decimated frontier settlements, and by the efforts of Spaniards in Florida to incite slaves to rebel or run away from their masters in Carolina and Georgia.[7] Under these circumstances, measures to discourage Catholic immigrants seemed prudent.[8]

[6] Schwartz, "*Mixed Multitude*," 91–92; chap. CCCVII (1729) and chap. CCCXIV (1730), James T. Mitchell and Henry Flanders, eds., *The Statutes at Large of Pennsylvania from 1682 to 1801*, 16 vols. (Harrisburg, Penn.: Clarence M. Busch, State Printer, 1896–1908), IV, 135–40, 164–71, quotes on 136, 164, 165; "Votes and Proceedings of the House of Representatives of the Province of Pennsylvania Beginning the Fourteenth Day of October, 1726," in MacKinney and Hoban, eds., *Pennsylvania Archives*, 8th ser., III, 1909–1912, 1915–1916, 1951–1952, 1956–1963, 1977, 1984.

[7] Aubrey C. Land, "Provincial Maryland," in Richard Walsh and William Lloyd Fox, eds., *Maryland: A History* (Annapolis: Hall of Records Commission, 1983), 1–50.

[8] See, for example, Virginia's law of 1643 that prohibited popish recusants from holding public office and ordered Catholic priests to be deported within five days of their arrival. Act LI, 1643, in William Waller Hening, ed., *Statutes at Large of Virginia: Being a Collection of All the Laws of Virginia from ... 1619*, 13 vols. (Richmond: George Cochran, 1809–1823), I, 268–69. For the special inducements held out to Protestant immigrants, see below.

The Meridian of Slavery

While rejecting the obligation to serve as a haven for Europe's failures and Catholic immigrants, the American colonists also opposed less laudable British visions that attempted to transform their settlements into penal colonies, dependent on the involuntary servitude of transported felons and African slaves. The men who defined British North America included not only idealistic visionaries who hoped to create a humanitarian refuge for the oppressed but also pragmatic mercantilists determined to enhance the wealth and power of England. In their quest for greatness, England's political nation condoned and promoted colonial practices that were repudiated in the mother country. While zealously guarding English liberty and the domestic English population from the "badges of Slavery," policymakers promoted and subsidized the involuntary servitude of English felons and African slaves in America, overriding the protests of settlers who were increasingly fearful of the social, economic, and political consequences of overreliance on a servile labor force.

English explorers and colonizers had, from the very beginning, employed convict labor, but that practice peaked after the revision of England's criminal code in 1717–1718. England's eighteenth-century decision to deport convicted felons to the colonies was seen as crucial to reducing crime in the mother country in a way that did not violate the political and humanitarian sensibilities of the English people. The arguments of reformers who hoped to reduce England's reliance on the death penalty were more acceptable when paired with the promise to exile reprieved felons. Sentencing convicts to forced labor in the colonies would obviate the need to increase England's "standing army" of law enforcement personnel that would be needed to guard convict workers at home. Transportation also neutralized the opposition of Englishmen who asserted that involuntary servitude was "not calculated for this *meridian of liberty*" and that it would be dangerous for English people who lived under the protection of the British Constitution to become "accustomed to the sight of Chains which are the badges of Slavery." Once a way had been found to drain England "of its offensive Rubbish without taking away their lives," convict transportation was widely touted as a liberal and humane alternative to execution—one that afforded transportees a chance for moral and economic rehabilitation.[9] Eighteenth-century English officials had few qualms about exposing their colonial subjects to "the sight of Chains" and impatiently brushed aside colonial objections and legal barriers to convict transportation.[10] American measures that

[9] Ekirch, *Bound for America*, chap. 1, quotes on 20.

[10] An exception to England's disregard of colonial protests can be found in Lord Bacon's statement, "It is a shameful and unblessed thing to take the scum of people, and the wicked condemned men to be the people with whom you plant," quoted in Basil Sollers, "Transported Convict Laborers in Maryland during the Colonial Period," *Maryland Historical Magazine*, 2 (1907), 39n.

taxed or prohibited the landing of transported felons were routinely disallowed in England.[11]

The slavery that Englishmen deemed inappropriate for themselves soon became a hallmark of the colonial societies they created in North America. The 250,000 Africans transported to England's mainland colonies during the eighteenth century and thousands of enslaved native Americans vividly embodied the status that Englishmen found too repugnant to observe at home but were willing to promote in their colonies.[12] Special interest groups, political economists, British officials, and colonizers all developed theories that rationalized slavery as essential to successful colonization. As with convict labor, different standards were developed to determine the constitutionality of English and colonial institutions. And once again, British officials ignored American protests and hampered efforts to limit the proliferation of slave labor.

The chartering of England's Company of Royal Adventurers in January 1663 was a significant step in the development of slavery in British North America as it created a powerful interest group determined to wrest control of the international slave trade from European rivals and to ensure an expansive colonial market for their human cargoes. In March 1663, Charles II responded to the Royal Adventurers' assertion "that the very being of the Plantations depends upon the supply of negro servants for their works," by decreeing that all "Negro Slaves" transported directly to the American colonies would be free from "any Duty or Imposition whatsoever to Us or Our Successors."[13] From 1664 on, colonial governors were instructed "to give all due encouragement & invitation to Merchants & others who shall bring Trade unto Our said Province. . . . And in particular to ye Royal African Company of England." They were also ordered to withhold their "assent to . . . any act imposing duties upon Negroes imported into the . . . province under your government, payable by the importer" or on their reexport. Colonial laws that attempted to tax or restrict England's slave trade were consistently challenged; those that levied duties payable by the importer were usually disallowed.[14]

[11] Ekirch, *Bound for America*, 133–40; James Davie Butler, "British Convicts Shipped to American Colonies," *American Historical Review*, 2 (1896), 12–33; Sollers, "Transported Convict Laborers," 17–47. Colonial laws prohibiting or impeding convict transportation can be found in Bernard Bush, ed., *Laws of the Royal Colony of New Jersey, 1703–1745* (Trenton: New Jersey State Library, Archives and History Bureau, 1977), 423 (1730); Mitchell and Flanders, eds., *Statutes at Large of Pennsylvania*, III, 265–67 (1722); IV, 164–67 (1729); and IV, 360–67 (1743); William Hand Browne, ed., *Archives of Maryland*, 72 vols. (Baltimore: Maryland Historical Society, 1883–), II, 540–41 (1676), XXXI, 300 (1728); Hening, ed., *Statutes at Large of Virginia*, II, 509–10 (1670). For the disallowance of such laws, see Browne, ed., *Archives of Maryland*, XXXV, 212 (1724), XXXI, 118 (1756); Leonard Woods Labaree, ed. *Royal Instructions to British Colonial Governors*, 2 vols. (New York: D. Appleton-Century, 1935), II, 673.

[12] For Indian slavery in North America, see Almon Wheeler Lauber, *Indian Slavery in Colonial Times within the Present Limits of the United States* (New York: Columbia University Press, 1913).

[13] Elizabeth Donnan, ed., *Documents Illustrative of the History of the Slave Trade to America*, 4 vols. (Washington, D.C.: Carnegie Institution of Washington, 1930–1935), I, 87–92, 160–72, 194–95, quotes on 164, 163.

[14] John Romeyn Brodhead, *Documents Relative to the Colonial History of the State of New-York*, ed. E. B. O'Callaghan, 11 vols. (Albany: Weed, Parsons and Company, 1853–1861), III, 374 (quote), 547; V, 136;

Theorists who transformed the involuntary servitude of transported English felons into their opportunity for redemption in the New World had a more difficult time justifying the practice of enslaving Africans and native Americans. That tortuous process began when the English identified the slave trade as a source of profit, power, and national greatness. Mercantilists argued that winning control of the African slave trade would generate profits for English shipowners and investors, provide a vent for manufactures, serve as "a nursery for seamen," and deny those benefits to other nations. The successful planting of English colonies in the New World magnified the perceived benefits of slavery as political economists promoted African slavery in the colonies as a way to prevent the depopulation of the mother country. They also argued that slavery increased the productivity of transplanted subjects, as an Englishman overseeing slave workers produced more profit for England than he could, by his own labor, at home.[15] For more than a century settlers from Massachusetts to Georgia declared that they could not "thrive untill wee get in a stock of slaves sufficient to doe all our business" because servants "desire freedome to plant for themselves, and [would] not stay but for verie great wages." Southern planters added the argument that only Africans could labor in their miasmic swamps and enervating heat,[16] while racists and cultural chauvinists rationalized slavery as an opportunity for backward and savage peoples to imbibe Christianity and a superior civilization.[17] In

---

VI, 32–34, 37–38; Labaree, ed., *Royal Instructions*, II, 673–74, quote on 674; Donnan, ed., *Documents Illustrative of the Slave Trade*, III, 38, 77n, 409, 450–56; IV, 9, 55–56, 94–95, 102–17, 122–27, 262–64, 276n, 315; W. E. Burghardt Du Bois, *The Suppression of the African Slave Trade to the United States of America, 1638–1870* (Cambridge: Harvard University Press, 1896), 11, 219.

[15] David Brion Davis, *The Problem of Slavery in Western Culture* (Ithaca: Cornell University Press, 1966), 129–34; William Postlethwaite, *The African Trade the Great Pillar and Support of the British Plantation Trade in America* (London, 1745); Donnan, ed., *Documents Illustrative of the Slave Trade*, I, 164–65, 177–78, 421; II, 44–45, 67, 96–99, 107–9; IV, 587–611; *Calendar of State Papers, Colonial Series, 1661–1668* (London: Longman and Co., 1880), 229; *Calendar of State Papers, Colonial Series, 1681–1685* (London: Eyre and Spottiswood, 1898), 317–18.

[16] Davis, *Problem of Slavery in Western Culture*, 147–48; Emanuel Downing to John Winthrop, 1645, in Donnan, ed., *Documents Illustrative of the Slave Trade*, III, 8 (quote); Preamble of South Carolina's "Act for the better Ordering and Governing Negroes and other Slaves," in ibid., IV, 257n; Patrick Talifer, *A True and Historical Narrative of the Colony of Georgia . . . with Comments by the Earl of Egmont*, ed. Clarence L. Ver Steeg (Athens: University of Georgia Press, 1960); John Percival, *The Journal of the Earl of Egmont: Abstract of the Trustees Proceedings for Establishing the Colony of Georgia*, ed. Robert G. McPherson (Athens: University of Georgia Press, 1962); William Stephens, *The Journal of William Stephens, 1741–1745*, 2 vols., ed. E. Merton Coulter (Athens: University of Georgia Press, 1958–1959).

[17] William M. Wiecek, *The Sources of Antislavery Constitutionalism in America, 1760–1848* (Ithaca: Cornell University Press, 1977), 23; "The African Slave Trade Defended," *London Magazine*, 9 (1740), 493–94; "Considerations on the Present Peace, 1763," in Donnan, ed., *Documents Illustrative of the Slave Trade*, II, 516; Winthrop Jordan, *White over Black: American Attitudes toward the Negro, 1550–1812* (Chapel Hill: University of North Carolina Press, 1968), 179–92; Davis, *Problem of Slavery in Western Culture*, 148; Lorenzo Johnston Greene, *The Negro in Colonial New England, 1620–1776* (New York: Columbia University Press, 1942), 61–63; Edmund S. Morgan, *American Slavery, American Freedom: The Ordeal of Colonial Virginia* (New York: Norton, 1975), 97–100; Gary B. Nash, "The Image of the Indian in the Southern Colonial Mind," *William and Mary Quarterly*, 3d ser., 29 (1972), 197–230; Lauber, *Indian Slavery in Colonial Times*, 48–50.

this way, the 1663 dictum of the Company of Royal Adventurers, that "the very being of the Plantations depends upon the supply of negro servants for their works," became a pillar of British imperialism.

The decision to promote slavery in colonial America came at the same time that the English were questioning its legitimacy at home. In 1701, just three years after William III authorized the use of private slavers to increase the flow of Africans to British America, England's Chief Justice ruled that "as soon as a negro comes into England, he becomes free; one may be a villein in England, but not a slave." Subsequent decisions muddied the issue, and the English judiciary evaded the problem by differentiating between the institution of slavery in England and in its colonies. In the Somerset case, Lord Mansfield, while recognizing the property rights of Englishmen involved in the slave trade, ruled that a master's dominion over the people thus enslaved depended on the local law codes promulgated in different parts of the British Empire. In this way, Mansfield bowed to the strength of the West Indian and slave trade lobbies while ensuring that courts in England would not be governed by the barbarous provisions of colonial slave codes.[18]

The Protestant Ballast

In subsidizing the African slave trade, English policymakers did more than promote colonial slavery; they also unintentionally increased the welcome Americans extended to Europe's "downtrodden masses," as eighteenth-century colonists scrambled to recruit white Protestants to dilute and guard their slave labor force. Although British officialdom clung to the belief that an unfettered slave trade was "highly beneficial and advantagious to this kingdom, and to the Plantations and Colonies thereunto belonging," American settlers became increasingly worried about its consequences.[19] Early opposition to a labor system built on slavery came from a handful of humanitarians, New Englanders who thought African slaves unprofitable in northern climes, colonists involved in the Indian trade, and free whites whose wages and prospects were undermined by slave workers.[20] Indian wars, slave insurrections, and economic hardships were,

[18] Edward Raymond Turner, *The Negro in Pennsylvania: Slavery—Servitude—Freedom, 1639–1861* (Washington, D.C.: American Historical Association, 1911), 25n; Wiecek, *Sources of Antislavery Constitutionalism*, chap. 1, quote on 23; A. Leon Higginbotham, Jr., *In the Matter of Color: Race and the American Legal Process, The Colonial Period* (New York: Oxford University Press, 1978), chaps. 8–10. As Davis points out, the English were not alone in promoting colonial slavery while repudiating the institution at home. In 1688 Louis XIV authorized shipments of slaves to Canada, for mercantilist reasons, long after slavery had been eradicated in France. In 1709 slavery was legally established in Canada and the French government began paying bounties on new slaves brought in from Africa. Davis, *Problem of Slavery in Western Culture*, chap. 4.

[19] Quote from preamble to 1698 "Act to Settle the Trade to Africa," in Donnan, ed., *Documents Illustrative of the Slave Trade*, I, 421.

[20] Governor Dudley to Board of Trade, 1708, *Calendar of State Papers, Colonial Series, 1708–1709* (London: His Majesty's Stationery Office, 1922), 110; Edgar J. McManus, *A History of Negro Slavery in*

however, more important in prompting settlers from Massachusetts to South Carolina to seek ways to prevent the creation of a dangerous servile majority in their midst.

By the beginning of the eighteenth century a preference for white workers was apparent in most of England's mainland colonies. In 1708 Rhode Island's Governor Samuel Cranston informed the Board of Trade of his colony's "general dislike" for slaves currently supplied from Barbados, and of "the inclination of our people in general . . . to employ white servants before negroes."[21] Similar sentiments prevailed in Massachusetts, where an article in the Boston *News Letter* in 1706 argued "That the Importing of Negroes into this or the Neighbouring Provinces is not so beneficial either to the Crown or Country, as White Servants would be" as "They do not People our Country as Whites would do whereby we should be strengthened against an Enemy." White servants, because they were cheaper than African slaves, could be more easily acquired by farmers; they also could serve as substitutes in the local militia the way negroes could not. Consequently this correspondent urged his neighbors to subsidize "the importing of White Men Servants." In 1711 Governor Gibbes also recommended that Carolina assemblymen direct their attention to "the introduction of white immigrants on account of the large increase of negroes, who were beginning to exhibit a malicious disposition."[22]

Slave conspiracies and Indian wars generated myriad schemes to reduce colonial dependence on slave labor. New York's insurrection of 1712, in particular, spread ripples of fear throughout British North America. Governor Robert Hunter citing "the Late Hellish Attempt of yor Slaves," urged the New York assembly to recognize "the necessity of Putting that Sort of men under better regulation by Some good Law for that purpose, and[,] to take away the Root of that Evill, to Encourage the Importation of White Servants." Legislators responded by enacting a new black code that prescribed more severe punishments for slaves, made manumission almost impossible, and circumscribed the rights of free blacks. New Yorkers, however, refused to subsidize white immigration. In 1734 Governor William Cosby was still "earnestly" recommending the passage of laws to deal with "the disadvantages that attend the too great Impor-

---

New York (Syracuse, N.Y.: Syracuse University Press, 1970), 48; *Journal of the Legislative Council of the Colony of New-York . . . 1691–1775*, 2 vols. (Albany: Weed, Parsons, 1861), I, 676; W. E. Burghardt Du Bois, *The Philadelphia Negro: A Social Study*, 1st publ. 1899 (New York: Benjamin Bloom, 1967), 412–14; Leila Sellers, *Charleston Business on the Eve of the American Revolution* (Chapel Hill: University of North Carolina Press, 1934), 102–5.

[21] Governor Cranston to the Board of Trade, Newport, Dec. 5, 1708, in Donnan, ed., *Documents Illustrative of the Slave Trade*, III, 109–10, quote on 110. In 1708 Governor Dudley of Massachusetts reported the same preference for white servants in the Bay Colony, *Calendar of State Papers, Colonial Series, 1708–1709*, 110.

[22] (Boston) *News Letter*, June 10, 1706, in Donnan, ed., *Documents Illustrative of the Slave Trade*, III, 21–23, quotes on 21, 22; Governor Gibbes quoted in ibid., IV, 257n.

tation of Negroes and Convicts" and to promote the peopling of the colony "with honest usefull & laborious white people, the truest riches and Surest Strength of a Country." Just as ineffectual was a 1737 editorial in the *New York Weekly Journal* that lobbied for high duties on the African slave trade to fund bounties for white servants.[23]

New York's slave conspiracy and Carolina's Tuscarora War prompted other colonies to take more vigorous action. Restrictive duties were levied on new slave arrivals in several colonies, primarily by settlers who worried about the social and economic consequences of slavery but did not question its legitimacy.[24] Fearing the complicity of Indian and African slaves, Massachusetts in 1712 and Rhode Island in 1714 prohibited the importation of all Indian slaves and servants. In 1715 Connecticut, the recipient of Indians captured during Carolina's Tuscarora War, decreed that any Indian slave "hereafter imported" would be forfeit and the importer fined fifty pounds. In 1713 and 1714 New Jersey placed a duty of ten pounds on all "imported" Africans, and in 1712 Pennsylvania's assembly increased the impost on negro and Indian slaves to a prohibitive twenty pounds.[25] In 1714 Carolina legislators placed an additional duty of two pounds on "all negro slaves from twelve years old and upwards, imported . . . from any part of Africa." In 1717 this surcharge was increased to "forty pounds current money" and was applied to "all negro slaves of any age or condition whatsoever, imported or otherwise brought into this Province, from any part of the world" for the next four years. In 1740, following the Stono Rebellion, South Carolina's "Act for the better strengthening of this Province" placed a tax of £100 on all slaves from Africa and £150 on those brought in from other American colonies.[26]

Colonial slave imposts often were designed to serve the dual purpose of limiting slavery while promoting white immigration. In New England and the Deep South, funds raised by duties on new slaves subsidized the immigration of European Protestants, who, it was hoped, would forestall the creation of a servile majority, promote economic development, and provide reliable white manpower

---

[23] Arthur Zilversmit, *The First Emancipation: The Abolition of Slavery in the North* (Chicago: University of Chicago Press, 1967), 15–18; Brodhead, *Documents Relative to the Colonial History of New-York*, V, 460–61; *Journal of the Legislative Council of New-York*, I, 333 (1712 quote), 631 (1734 quote), 652; McManus, *History of Negro Slavery in New York*, 151.

[24] Nonrestrictive duties on slaves also were legislated by colonists who saw such taxes as a convenient way to raise revenue; see, for example, Browne, ed. *Archives of Maryland*, XXXVIII, 51–52 (1695); XXXVIII, 198 (1716); Hening, ed., *Statutes at Large of Virginia*, III, 193–95 (1699), 229–35 (1705), 482 (1710); IV, 30 (1712). In some colonies duties also were placed on the African trade by Americans who hoped to increase their share of the slave trade. See Donnan, ed., *Documents Illustrative of the Slave Trade*, III, 113–15 (Rhode Island's Act of 1715); Browne, ed., *Archives of Maryland*, XXVI, 349–50 (1704).

[25] *Acts and Resolves of Massachusetts Bay*, I, 698; Butler, "British Convicts," 24; Barnard C. Steiner, *History of Slavery in Connecticut* (Baltimore: Johns Hopkins University Studies in Historical and Political Science, 11th series, 1893), 10–16; Donnan, ed., *Documents Illustrative of the Slave Trade*, III, 408, 450n; Mitchell and Flanders, eds., *Statutes at Large of Pennsylvania*, II, 433–36; Du Bois, *Suppression of the Slave Trade*, 206.

[26] Donnan, ed., *Documents Illustrative of the Slave Trade*, IV, 257 (Act of 1714, quotes); Du Bois, *Suppression of the Slave Trade*, 211 (Act of 1717, quotes); 215 (Act of 1740).

to protect the colony from slave insurrections and external attack. In 1709 the General Court of Massachusetts Bay placed a duty on Indian slaves brought into the province, with the proceeds to be used to pay a bounty of forty shillings per head to persons transporting white male servants between the ages of eight and twenty-five years. In Carolina, slave duties often were combined with "deficiency laws," laws designed to reduce the imbalance of "negroes [who] do extremely increase in this Province" and "white persons" who, "through the afflicting providence of God . . . do not proportionably multiply" by requiring planters to maintain a certain proportion of white men among their slaves.[27]

In 1698 Carolinians, already worried about the dangers posed by "the great number of negroes which of late have been imported into this colony," offered a bounty of thirteen pounds to shipmasters for each white male servant they "brought into the Ashley river," while requiring that "owners of every plantation to which doth belong six men negro slaves above sixteen years old, shall take from the Receiver one servant." In 1716, Carolina assemblymen, having learned through "sad experience . . . that the small number of white inhabitants of this Province, is not sufficient to defend the same even against our Indian enemies," required one white servant for every ten slaves, "young or old" and, in 1717, increased the bounty for each white servant brought into the province to twenty-five pounds.[28] Carolina's Act of 1751 "for the better strengthening of this Province" provided that three-fifths of the revenue raised by slave duties during the next five years be used to subsidize white immigration at the rate of "six pounds proclamation to every poor foreign protestant whatever from Europe, or other poor protestant (his Majesty's subject)," between twelve and fifty years of age, whose "good character" was certified by "the minister and elders of any church, meeting or congregation in Great Britain or Ireland;" those between two and twelve years would receive three pounds; an additional fifth of the slave duty was set aside to recruit shipbuilders and subsidize the colony's shipbuilding industry.[29] Subsequent acts, with minor alterations, extended South

---

[27] "Act to Encourage the Importation of White Servants" (1709), in *Acts and Resolves of Massachusetts Bay*, I, 634; Du Bois, *Suppression of the Slave Trade*, 209 (quotes). Deficiency laws originated in Spanish America early in the sixteenth century when King Ferdinand decreed that there should always be one Spaniard for every three Negroes. They were widely adopted, and flouted, by the plantation colonies in the British West Indies during the seventeenth century. Davis, *Problem of Slavery in Western Culture*, 128–29.

[28] Thomas Cooper, ed., *The Statutes at Large of South Carolina*, 4 vols. (Columbia, S.C.: A. S. Johnston, 1836–1838), II, 153 (Act of 1698, quotes), 646–49; Donnan, ed., *Documents Illustrative of the Slave Trade*, IV, 257n–258n (Act of 1716, quotes).

[29] Act of 1751, in Cooper, ed., *Statutes at Large of South Carolina*, III, 739–43 (quotes). In 1754, after the fund created to subsidize shipbuilding had failed to answer "the intention of the Legislature, as it hath not proved any encouragement, either to the building of ships, or for shipwrights and caulkers to become settlers in this Province," South Carolina's assembly ordered that 4772 pounds of the unexpended money be "applied toward . . . surveying and running out lands, and the passing of grants to such poor Protestants as have settled in this Province" since 1751. Ibid., IV, 11.

Carolina's bounty to poor Protestants until the Act of 1751 was finally repealed in August 1769.[30]

The slave labor system developed in South Carolina was far too profitable for plantation owners even to consider altering their work force. It was widely believed that only African slaves could be forced to perform, and survive, the labor required for rice and indigo cultivation. When the Stono Rebellion of 1739 made the dangers of a "black majority" too obvious for even the most myopic planters to ignore, prohibitive duties were placed on newly arriving Africans. The result was a precipitous decline in the number of slaves brought into South Carolina in the 1740s. By the 1750s, however, the profits of slavery again overrode planters' fears, prompting Carolinians to buy Africans in record numbers while enacting new deficiency laws and expending thousands of pounds to subsidize white immigration.[31]

Although desperate for European immigrants to control their "black majority," South Carolinians firmly excluded potential white troublemakers. Both convicts and Catholics were seen as more likely to foment than inhibit slave rebellions. Consequently the planters of South Carolina, unlike their neighbors in the Chesapeake, honored their colonial fiat against transported felons. Carolinians did not succumb to the temptation to procure cheap white convict labor because they believed that Europeans could not survive in the rice fields and that amoral convicts would incite their slaves into committing all sorts of atrocities. Henry Laurens, writing in 1768, advised an English mercantile house to send only "White Passengers healthy People, artificers, ploughmen, &c. not convicts, gaolbirds."[32] Catholic immigrants were seen as posing a similar hazard. Until the founding of Georgia, Carolina was the most vulnerable of England's mainland colonies to depredations by Spanish forces in Florida. From the colony's inception, settlers were forced to contend with Spanish and French intrigues that encouraged Carolinian slaves to run away or revolt. Therefore South Carolina limited its recruitment efforts to Protestants, who would not be tempted to join forces with England's Catholic foes; placed special disabilities on

---

[30] *The Papers of Henry Laurens*, ed. Philip M. Hamer et al., 7 vols. (Columbia: University of South Carolina Press, 1968–), IV, 464n; Cooper, ed., *Statutes at Large of South Carolina*, IV, 309–10. The Act of 1761, for example, set the bounty at four pounds sterling for each "poor Protestant" transported to South Carolina.

[31] Peter H. Wood, *Black Majority: Negroes in Colonial South Carolina from 1670 through the Stono Rebellion* (New York: Knopf, 1974), 320–26; Cooper, ed., *Statutes at Large of South Carolina*, III, 556; IV, 6; Donnan, ed., *Documents Illustrative of the Slave Trade*, IV, 303, 303n; Bounty Act of June 14, 1747, in Cooper, ed., *Statutes at Large of South Carolina*, IV, 6; "Act for the better strengthening of this Province," June 14, 1751, in ibid., III, 739–43.

[32] Warren B. Smith, *White Servitude in Colonial South Carolina* (Columbia: University of South Carolina Press, 1961), 39; Laurens to William Cowles & Co., Feb. 18, 1768, in Hamer, ed., *Papers of Henry Laurens*, V, 597 (quote). Assembly Journals and modern studies of convict transportation provide evidence that South Carolina's Act of 1712 that banned the importation of convicts was enforced. Roger Ekirch, in *Bound for America*, 113, estimates that fewer than 200 English convicts were transported to South Carolina in the eighteenth century.

Catholic immigrants; and, in the 1750s, tried desperately to rid itself of the Acadian exiles foisted on them by the British government.[33]

The planters of South Carolina went to great lengths to recruit reliable white immigrants. Promises of free land, expansive political rights, and religious toleration lured propertied Protestants from France, Germany, and the British Isles, while cash payments and travel subsidies facilitated the immigration of the poor. Deficiency laws that ordered slaveholders to acquire white servants promoted the emigration of poor Europeans by ensuring a good market for ships carrying servants. Even more efficacious were the thousands of pounds, raised by duties placed on the African trade, paid to "poor Protestants" of good character as well as to the shipmasters who carried them to South Carolina. In a single two-month period, between December 25, 1767, and February 12, 1768, Charleston mercantile firms received £2,362 sterling for transporting 689 immigrants from northern Ireland and £68 for 18 English servants from Bristol. In addition the South Carolina treasurer paid 20s. sterling to each Protestant immigrant who produced a certificate of good character. In 1768 a hostile Anglican observer reported that "above 30,000£ Sterling have lately been expended to bring over 5 or 6,000 Ignorant, mean, worthless, beggarly Irish Presbyterians."[34] South Carolina's vigorous recruitment efforts were not a repudiation of slave labor. Except for a brief period in the 1740s, most Carolinians never contemplated altering the nature of their lucrative labor force. Immigrant subsidies, along with black codes and slave patrols, allowed white Carolinians to exploit slave labor without unacceptable risk.

Carolina planters reaped immense profits from colonial slavery. By the middle of the eighteenth century the province was the richest of the mainland colonies. Although prosperous planters had few complaints about England's determination to ensure an expansive market and profits for British slavers, there were occasions when imperial policy threatened to destroy the precarious balance between black slaves and white masters in South Carolina. Parliamentary statutes and royal instructions that sent potentially subversive convicts and Catholics to the colony raised the specter of a horrific race war between Carolina's slaves and its outnumbered master class. English officials also caused consternation when they threatened to veto laws that placed duties on African slaves, as slave imposts

[33] Wood, *Black Majority*, 303–14; Cooper, ed., *Statutes at Large of South Carolina*, II, 131–33, 251–53; Laurens to John Pagan, Mar. 16, 1768, Hamer, ed., *Papers of Henry Laurens*, V, 631; Ruth Allison Hudnut and Hayes Baker-Crothers, "Acadian Transients in South Carolina," *American Historical Review* 43 (1938), 500–513. The creation of Georgia as a buffer colony between British and Spanish America mandated a similar exclusion of Catholics. Georgia settlers who struggled to overturn their colony's ban on slavery proposed schemes similar to those adopted by South Carolina—deficiency laws and bounties on white immigrants—so that they, too, could reap the profits of slavery while reducing its dangerous consequences. See sources cited in note 16.

[34] Hamer, ed., *Papers of Henry Laurens*, V, 504–5, 505n, 603n; Charles Woodmason, "Journal of C. W. Clerk, Itinerant Minister in South Carolina 1766, 1767, 1768," in *The Carolina Backcountry on the Eve of the Revolution* (Chapel Hill: University of North Carolina Press, 1953), 60–61 (quote).

subsidized the immigration of the European Protestants needed to maintain white control. Even though the colonists of South Carolina never achieved a white majority, they were successful in fending off the threats posed by English policymakers and black Carolinians and in molding a labor force that made them very rich indeed.

During the eighteenth century most Chesapeake planters had goals similar to those of their counterparts in South Carolina, hoping to maximize their profits while minimizing the danger of an enslaved work force. Prior to the 1760s, Maryland and Virginia levied few restrictive duties on the slave trade. Imposts occasionally attempted to exclude "refuse" slaves, Negroes transported from other colonies "for Crimes or Infected with Diseases," but most slave duties were simply economic measures—designed to raise revenue, limit the tobacco crop, or reduce planter indebtedness. Chesapeake colonists were, nonetheless, well aware of the "many bad consequences of multiplying these Ethiopians amongst us," fearing that the excessive importation of Africans slaves would transform the region into a "New Guinea, . . . blow up the pride, and ruin the Industry of our White People," promote "Inhumanity," and create a potentially explosive human reservoir that could be used by any "Cataline" to "kindle a Servile War."[35] The absence of formal deficiency laws and restrictive duties on slaves in the Chesapeake is evidence, not of complacency, but of the adoption of other means to prevent the creation of a dangerous African majority.

After initially pleading for enough warm bodies to perpetuate their precarious foothold on the coast of North America, the settlers of Maryland and Virginia soon began experimenting with ways to create a safe and profitable work force. By the end of the seventeenth century, Chesapeake legislators had at various times barred potentially subversive Quakers, separatists, popish priests, and transported "jaile birds" from landing on their shores. More subtle means also were used to discourage the immigration of dangerous men and to attract reliable Protestants. Thus, whereas Chesapeake legislators levied special fines on popish recusants and Quakers and mandated extended terms of service for Irish servants arriving without indentures, Virginia's Burgesses ordered shipmasters carrying immigrants from England to make sure their passengers and "poor servants" were well provided with food, clothing, and bedding. Virginia's 1753 decision to deny freedom dues to transported felons was based, in part, on the belief that "Putting Volunteers and Convicts on the same Footing as to Rewards and Punishments" discouraged voluntary servants, since "what honest Man would chuse to serve in a Country where no Distinction is made?"[36]

---

[35] Browne, ed., *Archives of Maryland*, XXXIV, 269; Donnan, ed., *Documents Illustrative of the Slave Trade*, IV, 24n, 91–92 (quotes), 131–32 (William Byrd to Earl of Egmont, July 12, 1736, quotes).

[36] Ekirch, *Bound for America*, 155; Hening, ed., *Statutes at Large of Virginia*, VI, 359 (Act of 1753, quotes). In 1660 the Burgesses rescinded the longer term for Irish servants on realizing that it was being applied to all aliens, thereby discouraging some of the foreigners they hoped to recruit.

Southern legislatures used positive incentives, as well as preferential treatment for Protestant servants, to recruit European immigrants. A moratorium on debt collection proceedings was promised to prospective settlers who owed money in England; Virginia offered lower tonnage duties to non-British "seafaring men" who took up residence in the colony for one year and exempted artisans from public taxes for periods ranging from three to five years. British and foreign-born Protestants willing to settle the frontier lands of Maryland and Virginia were offered rent and tax exemptions for periods ranging from three to fifteen years. Chesapeake legislators, "for the better encouragement of aliens," also facilitated the naturalization of hundreds of foreign-born settlers by requiring simply an oath of allegiance.[37]

Variable duties, placed on new arrivals, also were used to shape immigration in the Chesapeake by reducing the profits of shippers who transported unwanted passengers, servants, convicts, and slaves. In 1699 the Virginia legislature placed a fifteen-shilling tax on all servants not born in England or Wales. In the same year, Maryland required immigrants from Ireland to pay a twenty-shilling duty and in 1732 exempted Protestant immigrants from the impost paid by new arrivals. Maryland's Act of 1754, which placed a duty of five shillings on all servants, including Protestants, levied a twenty-shilling tax on "seven-year passengers," a sobriquet for transported convicts.[38]

Chesapeake planters also hoped that variable duties would limit the expansion of their slave population by making indentured servants much cheaper than slaves. Maryland's revenue act of 1695 required "All Masters of Shipps & other Vessells importing servants into this Province" to pay "the sum of two shillings & sixpence sterling" for each servant; ten shillings sterling "for every Negro imported into this Province either by land or by water & exposed for sale within three months after arrival." In 1704 Maryland legislators increased the duty on negroes to twenty shillings and, while eliminating the general impost on servants, required the masters of vessels "or others importing Irish Servants into this Province by Land or by Water" to pay twenty shillings sterling "per poll." The purpose of this law, according to the act's title, was to raise "a Supply to defray the Public Charge . . . and . . . to prevent the Importing too great a number of Irish Papists into this Province."[39] Similar steps were taken by Virginia's legislature. When in 1699 the burgesses laid a duty of fifteen shillings on "every servant not born in England or Wales," they required a payment of twenty shillings "for

[37] Hening, ed., *Statutes at Large of Virginia*, I, 256–57; William L. Saunders, ed., *The Colonial Records* of *North Carolina* (Goldsboro, N.C.: 1886–1907), I, 674–75; Cooper, ed., *Statutes at Large of South Carolina*, II, 124.

[38] Hening, ed., *Statutes at Large of Virginia*, III, 193–95; Browne, ed., *Archives of Maryland*, XXVII, 496; XXVIII, 470; XLVI, 616.

[39] Browne, ed., *Archives of Maryland*, XXXVIII, 51–52 (Act of 1695, quotes); XXVI, 289 (Act of 1704, quotes). The imposts levied in Maryland's Act of 1695 were renewed in 1696 and 1699; those in the Act of 1704 were continued in 1708, 1712, 1715, 1717, 1728, and 1735.

every negro or other slave" brought into Virginia. The provisions of Virginia's Act of 1699 were continued in 1701 and 1704. A major change was made, however, in the Act's 1705 renewal. Whereas the preamble to Virginia's Act of 1705 cited the benefits gained from "Impositions upon liquors and upon servants and slaves imported into this colony," this new law taxed only liquor and slaves, not servants.[40]

The Chesapeake's variable duty acts were primarily revenue measures that also made non-Irish, Protestant servants a more attractive investment by raising the price of slaves. The increased cost differential between slaves and servants was deliberate, designed to persuade the colonists, especially small or indebted planters, to rely more heavily on indentured Europeans than on enslaved Africans. The strongest evidence of the determination of the Chesapeake planters to maintain a white majority can be seen in their decision to purchase convict labor. The tobacco planters of Maryland and Virginia often expressed their distaste for transported felons, who, they feared, would "do great Mischiefs, commit Robbery and Murder, and spoil Servants, that were before very good." Both legislatures, from the 1670s on, banned or placed prohibitive import duties on transported convicts. Laws also were passed to protect society from the felons who ended up in the Chesapeake. Virginia, in 1677, declared all men "convicted in England or elsewhere . . . forever incapable of bearing office, civil or military" and in the eighteenth century denied convicts the right to vote during their term of transportation. Both Virginia and Maryland also prohibited felons from testifying in court, except against other convicts.[41]

Americans often blamed England for saddling them with transported convicts. In disallowing colonial prohibitions, British officials did indeed place a tempting supply of cheap workers in the ports of labor-hungry Americans. English promotion of the African slave trade also increased the attractiveness of white convict labor as a way to prevent the creation of an African majority. Yet, ultimately it was the decision of the colonists themselves to invest in such workers that perpetuated the practice of convict transportation. As Maryland's governor pointed out in 1725, "While we purchase, they will send them [convicts], and we bring the Evil upon our selves."[42]

[40] Hening, ed., *Statutes at Large of Virginia*, III, 193–95 (Act of 1699, quotes), 212–13, 346 (Act of 1705, quotes), 492. A general tax of six pence per poll was levied on all new arrivals in Virginia, whether fare-paying passengers, servants, or slaves, in 1705, and renewed in 1710. Such laws were indeed revenue measures and, given the minor sum involved, would have had little impact on immigration patterns.

[41] Hugh Jones, *The Present State of Virginia*, 1st publ. 1724, ed. Richard L. Morton (Chapel Hill: University of North Carolina Press, 1956), 53 (quote); Ekirch, *Bound for America*, 153–54 (quotes); Hening, ed., *Statutes at Large of Virginia*, II, 391–92 (Act of 1677, quote); VII, 517–19 (Act of 1762).

[42] Browne, ed., *Archives of Maryland*, XXXV, 212 (quote). In *Bound for America*, Ekirch argues that it was the availability of a lucrative export to fill the holds of returning ships that determined the flow of convicts to the Chesapeake. However, wheat and flax seed from Pennsylvania and rice and indigo from South Carolina could have served as valuable export options had shipmasters found a market for convicts in those colonies.

The tobacco planters of Maryland and Virginia purchased transported felons to dilute their African work force. Unlike South Carolina and Georgia, the Chesapeake colonies did not provide direct subsidies for white servants. The incentives they offered, such as free land, tax abatements, and easy naturalizationm, did little to facilitate the immigration of poor whites. Unable to compete with the largesse of their southern neighbors, the residents of Maryland and Virginia did not attract enough of the voluntary servants they preferred to fill their labor needs. Faced with a choice between convicts and African slaves, the Chesapeake planters purchased felons transported from English, Irish, and Scottish jails.

In the decades following Carolina's Stono Rebellion the number of African slaves brought into the Chesapeake diminished as the number of convicts rose. Maryland's slave trade steadily declined from its peak in the 1720s when "perhaps as many as 500 to 1,000 Africans" arrived each year to an annual average of only 200 new slaves in the 1750s and 1770s. The pattern of convict arrivals in Maryland was the mirror image of the African trade. From 1718 to 1744 approximately 3,700 convicts were transported from London jails to Maryland, an average of 137 a year. In the next three decades, Maryland became the new home of at least 9,423 English convicts, an annual average of 314; the Irish and Scottish convicts clandestinely transported during that same period, raised Maryland's total to at least 400 transported felons each year. The entry books for Annapolis for 1746 to 1775 indicate that convicts made up 38 per cent of the Maryland port's 23,347 new arrivals, whereas Africans accounted for only 14 per cent. Virginia's convict and slave trades exhibit the same temporal patterns and reciprocal relationship. Thus, the determination of Chesapeake planters to prevent the creation of a dangerous black majority made Virginia and Maryland the destination of 97 per cent of the English convicts shipped from London in 1718–1744 and of 78 per cent of the vessels reported as sailing from Ireland with convicts between 1730 and 1774.[43]

England's decision to settle its Americans lands with "people not her own" and to promote the African trade ensured the widespread incidence of colonial slavery. By the 1770s black slavery was an established element of the economies

[43]Slave data from Alan Kulikoff, "'A Prolifick People': Black Population Growth in the Chesapeake Colonies, 1700–1790," *Southern Studies*, 16 (1977), 393–95; *Tobacco and Slaves: The Development of Southern Cultures in the Chesapeake, 1680–1800* (Chapel Hill: University of North Carolina Press, 1986), 65–67. Kulikoff points out that the natural increase of the Chesapeake's slave population, which mandated the recruitment of more white workers, also obviated the need to purchase new Africans and contributed to the growing density of the Chesapeake's slave population despite the efforts of the planters to limit it. Convict figures from: Ekirch, *Bound for America*, 115; A. E. Smith, *Colonists in Bondage*, 325; Sollers, "Transported Convict Laborers," 44; Audrey Lockhart, *Some Aspects of Emigration from Ireland to the North American Colonies between 1660 and 1775* (New York: Arno Press, 1976), 171–208. A breakdown of the 23,347 immigrants entering the port of Annapolis made by Sollers shows 2,142 free passengers (9 per cent), 9,035 indentured servants (39 per cent), 8,846 convicts (38 per cent), and 3,324 African slaves (14 per cent).

of all thirteen mainland colonies, even in areas where African slaves were seen as a marginal investment. The American settlers were not, of course, innocent victims of an English plot to saddle them with a servile work force. Most colonists who hoped to enervate the slave trade were motivated more by strategic, economic, and social considerations than by moral outrage. Still other Americans were part of a powerful pressure group in England who argued, in court and out, the legality of slavery in the New World. Indeed, it was the power of the West Indian planters and the "property" rights guaranteed them by the British Constitution that made it so difficult for English judges to eliminate the institution in England and prompted them to distinguish between the rights guaranteed by the British Constitution at home and those in the colonies.

British proponents of the slave trade found it easy to justify their actions by claiming that they were merely filling the colonists' insatiable demand for labor and to disassociate themselves from the barbarous treatment of servile workers in America. From the middle of the seventeenth century, the English government tried to shield Indian and African slaves from colonial abuse. American governors were instructed not only "to find out the best means to facilitate & encourage the Conversion of Negros & Indians to the Christian Religion," but also to secure the passage of "a Law for the Restraining of Unhuman Severitys which by all masters or overseers may bee used toward their Christian servants, or slaves, wherein provision is to be made that ye wilful killing of Indians & Negros may bee punished with death, And that a fit penalty bee imposed for the maiming of them." During the eighteenth century Pennsylvania and New Jersey laws that decreed castration for negroes who attempted to rape white women were disallowed in England as excessively barbaric.[44]

Colonial laws that taxed the African slave trade were vetoed in England for a wide variety of reasons—because they challenged royal and parliamentary authority, violated the chartered rights of slave traders, undermined the British Navigation system, and threatened the livelihood of English workers and colonial prosperity. These vetoes handicapped Americans who questioned the wisdom, if not the morality, of slavery and tried to reduce the social cost of slave labor. England's promotion of the slave trade also had less predictable consequences. Slavery, combined with the threats posed by England's Catholic rivals, heightened the colonists' distaste for "pernicious Catholick principles" and led Americans to erect barriers against "papist" immigrants. On the other hand, slavery and foreign intrigue also led the colonists to subsidize the transportation of "downtrodden" Protestants. The dangers of slavery even convinced Chesa-

[44]Brodhead, *Documents Relative to the Colonial History of New-York*, III, 374 (quotes), 547; V, 138, 356; Henry Scofield Cooley, *A Study of Slavery in New Jersey* (Baltimore: Johns Hopkins University Studies in Historical and Political Science, 14th ser., 1896), 39, 50; Du Bois, *Philadelphia Negro*, 411; Turner, *Negro in Pennsylvania*, 29n; John Spencer Bassett, *Slavery and Servitude in the Colony of North Carolina* (Baltimore: Johns Hopkins University Studies in Historical and Political Science, 14th ser., 1896), 42–44.

peake planters to accept the uncongenial role thrust on them by Parliament—of serving as a regenerative haven for the transported felons they feared and despised. Ultimately, the colonists would be accorded sole responsibility for the vicious forms of slavery and exploitation that emerged in the New World. By the time of the American Revolution, British writers had become fond of vilifying the colonists as a "race of convicts" and barbaric "drivers of slaves," hypocritically yelping for liberty.[45]

Spiriting

Critics who excoriated the colonists for their brutal exploitation of African slaves often challenged America's claim to be "the best poor man's country," accusing Americans of virtually enslaving the European immigrants that they had kidnapped or seduced with false promises. Europeans concerned about the loss of valuable subjects joined disillusioned immigrants in publishing exposés of the deceptive advertising of recruiters, the rapacious practices of the shipping trade, and the bleak conditions that greeted the credulous once they landed in America. Such allegations limited the ability of Americans to recruit the white Protestants who were increasingly needed to contain their servile population, cast a shadow over the system of indentured servitude that served as a vehicle to transport impoverished Europeans to the New World, and challenged America's reputation as a land of liberty and economic opportunity. This controversy over the degree of exploitation and opportunity Europe's oppressed masses experienced in America, continues today.

Denunciations of the methods used to recruit indentured workers as kidnapping and of the servant's virtual enslavement emerged from England's first permanent American colony. Early in the seventeenth century letters from Englishmen serving in Virginia told piteous tales of being sold and worked "like a damnd slave." By mid-century similar stories were surfacing in all parts of British America. In 1661 two Irish servants testified in a Massachusetts court that they had been "brought out of o'r owne country, contrary to our owne Wills and mindes" and sold to masters who saddled them with exorbitant years of service. In 1670 a convicted "spirit" told of individual Englishmen who sent between 500 and 840 kidnapped victims to the colonies each year.[46]

[45] James Boswell, *Boswell's Life of Johnson, together with Boswell's Journal of a Tour to the Hebrides and Johnson's Diary of a Journey into North Wales*, rev. ed., ed. George Birkbeck Hill, 6 vols. (Oxford: Clarendon, 1934), III, 201 (quotes).

[46] Extracts of 23 letters written by Virginia colonists that arrived in England on the *Abigail* in June 1623, in Susan Myra Kingsbury, ed., *The Records of the Virginia Company of London*, 4 vols. (Washington, D.C.: Government Printing Office, 1906–1935), IV, 228–39, "like a damnd slave" on 235; George F. Dow and Mary G. Thresher, eds., *Records and Files of the Quarterly Courts of Essex County, Massachusetts*, 9 vols. (Salem, Mass.: Essex Institute, 1911–1975), II, 293 (quote); A. E. Smith, *Colonists in Bondage*, 74.

Old World publicists turned the tales of kidnapping and misery that trickled back from America into popular melodrama. By the eighteenth century, lurid tales of disillusioned and abused servants and redemptioners[47] were commonplace—the theme of books, plays, doggerel, ballads, and human interest stories in European newspapers and periodicals.[48] English people who were moved by the plight of the innocent victims of American rapacity or feared the depopulation of England petitioned king and Parliament to intervene and provide the safeguards necessary "to prevent stealing and transporting children, and other persons . . . to the plantacions" and the enslavement of those "spirited on board" vessels bound for America.[49]

Men involved in transporting servants to America refuted charges of kidnapping, often accusing unscrupulous servants of fabricating tales. In July 1664 a group of British "merchants, planters, and masters of ships trading to the Plantations" announced that they too "abominate[d]" the "wicked custom" of spiriting "young people to go as servants to the plantations" as such activities gave "the opportunity to many evil-minded persons to enlist themselves voluntarily to go the voyage, and having received money, clothes, diet, &c. to pretend they were betrayed or carried away without their consents."[50] In 1691 English and colonial merchants petitioned the king and Parliament for protection from "malicious persons [who], after having voluntarily offered themselves to go servants to the plantations, and bound themselves to that purpose, and received money and cloaths for their several voyages, have pretended themselves spirited away, contrary to their wills; and have caused the merchants entertaining them to be prosecuted as trepanners." These and other petitioners argued that "The generality of volunteers for transportation are the scum of the world, brought to volunteer by their own prodigality; if they do not go to the Colonies they will

---

[47] For the difference between indentured servants and redemptioners, see Farley Grubb, "Redemptioner Immigration to Pennsylvania: Evidence on Contract Choice and Profitability," *Journal of Economic History*, 46 (1986), 407–18; David Galenson, *White Servitude in Colonial America: An Economic Assessment* (New York: Cambridge University Press, 1981), 10–15.

[48] An overview of the literature on kidnapping may be found in A. E. Smith, *Colonists in Bondage*, chap. 4; Richard B. Morris, *Government and Labor in Early America* (New York: Columbia University Press, 1946), 337–45; Bernard Bailyn, *Voyagers to the West: A Passage in the Peopling of America on the Eve of the Revolution* (New York: Knopf, 1986), 307–12. Contemporary accounts include John Melville Jennings, ed., "'The Poor Unhappy Transported Felon's Sorrowful Account of His Fourteen Years Transportation at Virginia in America'," *Virginia Magazine of History and Biography*, 56 (1948), 180–94; William Moraley, *The Infortunate; Gottlieb Mittelberger's Journey to Pennsylvania in the Year 1750 and Return to Germany in the Year 1754*, 1st publ. 1756, ed. and trans. Oscar Handlin and John Clive (Cambridge: Harvard University Press, 1960); James Annesley, *Memoirs of an Unfortunate Young Nobleman . . .* (London, 1763); William Eddis, *Letters from America, Historical and Descriptive; Comprising Occurrences from 1769 to 1777 Inclusive* (London, 1792); *Look before You Leap; or A Few Hints to Such Artizans, Mechanics, Labourers, Farmers, and Husbandmen, as Are Desirous of Emigrating to America* (London, 1796).

[49] Leo F. Stock, ed., *Proceedings and Debates of the British Parliaments Respecting North America*, 5 vols. (Washington, DC: Carnegie Institution of Washington, 1924–1941), I, 400 (quotes); *Calendar of State Papers, Colonial Series, 1661–1668* (London: Longman and Co., 1880), 770, 771, 1720; *Calendar of State Papers, Colonial Series, 1675–1676*, 827.

[50] *Calendar of State Papers, Colonial Series, 1661–1668*, 769.

probably go to Tyburn." Furthermore, the American colonies required "a considerable number of white servants, as well to keep the blacks in awe, as for bearing arms in case of an invasion." Thus justice, national interest, and colonial security demanded that those trading in servants be protected from malicious harassment by scoundrels whose transportation to America would save them from the gallows and increase England's wealth.[51]

Logic and fragmentary evidence suggest that not all servants and redemptioners were guileless innocents suffering at the hands of cruel and greedy spirits and shipmasters. Marcus Rediker's study has shown that Anglo-American seamen regularly abrogated the articles of agreement that bound them to serve for the duration of a voyage. These maritime workers, whether impressed by crimps or voluntary recruits, frequently took advantage of American labor shortages to "renegotiate" their service contract through desertion. Rediker argues that, although cruel or unfit shipmasters may have precipitated such action, common seamen considered it part of their "social wage" and a legitimate way to equalize the distribution of profits earned by their labor.[52] There is abundant evidence that indentured servants also absconded after receiving a recruiter's "farthing." In 1728 a group of indentured passengers ran off soon after landing in Philadelphia; William Moraley reported that on his voyage to America in 1729 one servant jumped ship before it sailed from England. Maritime desertion and the well-documented tendency of transported convicts to refuse to serve any master lend credence to complaints that servants often signed indentures simply to receive free passage across the Atlantic, with no intention of serving time in America.[53]

There can be no doubt that "spiriting" did occur and that many shipping agents indulged in dubious recruiting practices. However, recent studies suggest that various legal safeguards made outright kidnapping increasingly difficult and unprofitable. In 1645, the English parliament instituted a program to apprehend and bring "to condigne punishment, all such lewd persons as shall steale, sell, buy, inveigle, purloyne, convey, or receive any little Children" and ordered "the Marshals of the Admiralty, and the Cinque-Ports" to "make strict and diligent search in all Ships and Vessels upon the River, and at the Downes, for all such Children." In the following decades, various English municipalities and the Privy Council established registration procedures to prevent "the Inveigling, purloining, carrying and Stealing away Boyes[,] Maides and other persons and transporting them beyond Seas and selling or otherwise disposeing them for private

---

[51] Ibid., 220 (quote); *Calendar of State Papers, Colonial Series, 1681–1685*, 318 (quote); Stock, ed., *Proceedings and Debates*, II, 36 (quote).

[52] Marcus Rediker, *Between the Devil and the Deep Blue Sea: Merchants, Seamen, Pirates, and the Anglo-American Maritime World, 1700–1750* (Cambridge: Cambridge University Press, 1987), 100–106. See also Henry Laurens to William Cowles & Co., Charleston, S.C., February 18, 1768, *Papers of Henry Laurens*, V, 596–99.

[53] Moraley, *The Infortunate*, 59, 64n; Ekirch, *Bound for America*, 194–212.

gaine and proffitt." Such ordinances required that indentures be signed in the presence of magistrates, that minors be bound only with the consent of their parents or master, and that the "clerk of the Peace . . . keep a fair book, wherin the name of the Person so bound, and the Magistrats name . . . and the time and place of doing thereof, and the number of the file shalbe entred, and for the more easy finding the same, the Entries are to be made alphabetically according to the first letter of the Surname." Bristol's Ordinance of 1654 levied a fine of twenty pounds on any shipmaster found guilty of transporting an unregistered servant.[54] Scottish and Irish officials enacted similar regulations, and Continental authorities erected even more rigorous barriers to prevent the emigration, voluntary or otherwise, of valuable subjects.[55]

Servant registration programs and the penalties faced by kidnappers seem to have reduced the number of European immigrants sent to America against their will. Eighteenth-century merchants seeking cargoes of indentured workers in England found crimps and spirits unreliable and unable to deliver servants with the skills and character needed to bring high prices in the colonies. They consequently relied primarily on recruiting unemployed transients who congregated at Gravesend and other major ports.[56] Such developments did not, however, end the lurid tales of the kidnapping of helpless children and incredulous peasants. In 1752 the St. Andrews Society of Philadelphia awarded 50 shillings to a Scottish woman who said "she was born in Glasgow of reputable parents, but seduced and decoyed thence to America at the age of nine yers, . . . was in want." Irish servants arriving at Charleston aboard the ship *Pearl* in 1767, were ordered set free after claiming "that they were kidnapped . . . & inhumanly treated besides." In the 1770s men like the Earl of Seaforth, proprietor of the Scottish Isle of Lewis, still seethed with righteous indignation on hearing that American recruiters were "ensnaring & seducing the inhabitants [of his island] to emigrate to America, and not only carry off persons who are lessees and under engagements for a future tract of time . . . but also apprentices and infants under the age of 21 years without

---

[54] These ordinances are reprinted in Galenson, *White Servitude in Colonial America*, 188–92.

[55] Ian Charles Cargill Graham, *Colonists from Scotland: Emigration to North America, 1707–1783* (Ithaca: Cornell University Press, 1956), 90; R. J. Dickson, *Ulster Emigration to Colonial America, 1718–1775* (London: Routledge and Kegan Paul, 1966), 181–89; John Duncan Brite, "The Attitude of European States toward Emigration to the American Colonies and the United States, 1607–1820" (Ph.D. diss., University of Chicago, 1937), 195–223; Lowell Colton Bennion, "Flight from the Reich: A Geographic Exposition of Southwest German Emigration, 1683–1815" (Ph.D. diss., Syracuse University, 1971), 190, 207–8, 218–20; Marianne Sophia Wokeck, "A Tide of Alien Tongues: The Flow and Ebb of German Immigration to Pennsylvania, 1683–1776" (Ph.D. diss., Temple University, 1983), 48–52; Agnes Bretting, "Organizing German Immigration: The Role of State Authorities in Germany and the United States," in Frank Trommler and Joseph McVeigh, eds., *America and the Germans: An Assessment of a Three-Hundred-Year History*, 2 vols. (Philadelphia: University of Pennsylvania Press, 1985), I, 25–32.

[56] Bailyn, *Voyagers to the West*, chap. 9; James Horn, "Servant Emigration to the Chesapeake in the Seventeenth Century," in Thad W. Tate and David L. Ammerman, eds., *The Chesapeake in the Seventeenth Century: Essays on Anglo-American Society and Politics* (Chapel Hill: University of North Carolina Press, 1979), 92–94.

the consent of their masters and parents." According to the Earl's steward, once abducted, young boys were "lock[ed] up on board of the vessel, and the poor parents and masters are debarred from ever seeing them." Ignored by the irate Earl were the rack-renting practices that made his tenants susceptible to the blandishments of American recruiters.[57]

Charges of unscrupulous chicanery by recruiters who stopped just short of kidnapping while assembling their "human cargoes" also persisted. Gottlieb Mittelberger's eloquent denunciation of the "nasty tricks" used by "the great Dutch traffickers in human souls" and "their man-stealing emissaries," first published in 1756, continues to color modern accounts of indentured servitude. Equally long-lived is Mittelberger's charge that bound workers were sent not where they "want[ed] to go but to another place in America," where shippers "calculate they can sell their human cargo for a better price."[58]

The variable contracts negotiated by indentured servants and redemptioners of all nationalities are evidence that, even though recruiters may have exaggerated the promise of America, most bound Europeans were not kidnapped, but were voluntary immigrants who had some control over their future. David Galenson's research shows "that merchants adjusted the term of service for minors, and the size of cash payments for adults, in view of the cost of transportation to America and the price the servant was expected to bring in the colonies. If coercion had played an important part in the recruiting process, merchants would have had no need to give more valuable servants preferable bargains in the form of wages or shorter terms." Russell Menard's study of British migration patterns to the Chesapeake has uncovered additional evidence that indentured servants played an important role in choosing their own destiny. Finding that servants emigrated from seventeenth-century Bristol "in greater numbers when [English] wages were low," Menard concluded that the servants themselves "made the decision to move. . . . If, on the other hand, the choices of merchants and planters regulated the volume of migration, there should be little relationship between real wages and the number of migrants."[59]

[57] Erna Risch, "Immigrant Aid Societies before 1820," *Pennsylvania Magazine of History and Biography*, 60 (1936), 18n (quote); *Papers of Henry Laurens*, V, 504–5, 625–31, quote on 629; Bailyn, *Voyagers to the West*, 307–12, quotes on 309–10.

[58] Mittelberger, *Journey to Pennsylvania*, quotes on 9, 28. For the persistence of such charges, see John van der Zee, *Bound Over: Indentured Servitude and American Conscience* (New York: Simon & Schuster, 1985); Horn, "Servant Emigration to the Chesapeake," 92; Gary Nash, *The Urban Crucible: Social Change, Political Consciousness, and the Origins of the American Revolution* (Cambridge: Harvard University Press, 1979), 111.

[59] Galenson, *White Servitude in Colonial America*, chap. 7, quote on 112; David Galenson "The Market Evaluation of Human Capital: The Case of Indentured Servitude," *Journal of Political Economy*, 89 (1981), 446–67; Farley Grubb, "The Market for Indentured Immigrants: Evidence on the Efficiency of Forward-Labor Contracting in Philadelphia, 1745–1773," *Journal of Economic History* 45 (1985), 855–68; idem, "Redemptioner Immigration to Pennsylvania: Evidence on Contract Choice and Profitability," *Journal of Economic History*, 46 (1986), 407–18; Russell R. Menard, "British Migration to the Chesapeake Colonies in the Seventeenth Century," in Lois Green Carr et al., eds., *Colonial Chesapeake Society* (Chapel Hill: University of North Carolina Press, 1988), quotes on 108–9.

Death at Sea

Publicists who hoped to reduce the flow of European immigrants to British North America stressed the abuse and high mortality rates endured by trans-Atlantic passengers.[60] Clearly America could not be a land of opportunity for those who did not survive the voyage. Disillusioned immigrants charged rapacious ship-owners with skimping on provisions and overcrowding their vessels to increase profits and brutal masters and crews with plundering and abusing debilitated passengers. According to William Moraley, he and his fellow servants were placed on a daily diet of "Three Biscuits ... and a small Piece of Salt Beef, no bigger then [sic] a Penny Chop of Mutton. Some Days we had Stockfish, when every Man was obliged to beat his Share with a Maul to make it tender, with a little stinking Butter for Sauce." Their "scanty Allowance of Water, not above three Quarts" to be divided among five men, prompted the servants "to drink the Salt Water," which only "increased [their] Thirst." German passengers aboard the ill-fated *Love and Unity*, which sailed from Rotterdam to Philadelphia in 1731, described their captain as "a wicked murderer of souls, [who] thought to starve us, not having provided provisions enough according to agreement; and thus got possession of our goods. ... To keep from starving we had to eat rats and mice. We paid from eight pence to two shillings for a mouse; four pence for a quart of water. ... In one night several persons miserably perished and were thrown naked overboard; no sand was allowed to be used to sink the bodies but they floated." Then, after enduring such horrors, the survivors were forced "*to pay the whole freight of the dead and living*." Gottlieb Mittelberger told of passengers whimpering for "a piece of good bread or a good fresh drop of water," of a German immigrant robbed at sea of 1800 florins, and of conditions so deplorable that "Children between the ages of one and seven seldom survive the sea voyage."[61]

[60]Colonial publicists painted a very different picture. George Alsop, writing in 1666, told prospective servants that, after committing "themselves unto the care of the Merchant ... they need not trouble themselves with any inquisitive search touching their Voyage; for there is such an honest care and provision made for them all the time they remain aboard the Ship, and are sailing over, that they want for nothing that is necessary and convenient." Alsop, who had served a four-year term in Maryland, also execrated those who claimed that servants were "sold in open Market for Slaves, and drawn in Carts like Horses; which is so damnable an untruth, that if they should search to the very Center of Hell, and enquire for a Lye of the most antient and damned stamp, I confidently believe they could not find one to parallel this." George Alsop, *A Character of the Province of Maryland*, 1st publ. 1666, in Clayton Colman Hall, ed., *Narratives of Early Maryland, 1633–1684* (New York: Charles Scribner's Sons, 1910), quotes on 356–57. Alsop's credibility is undermined by many implausible or inflated claims, such as his statement that in Maryland, "the Roman Catholick, and the Protestant Episcopal (whom the world would perswade have proclaimed open Wars irrevocably against each other) contrarywise concur in an unanimous parallel of friendship, and inseparable love intayled unto one another." Ibid., 349.

[61]Moraley, *The Infortunate*, 59–60 (quotes); *Gentleman's Magazine*, April 1732, 727 (quote); Mittelberger, *Journey to Pennsylvania*, 14 (quotes), 22. The most evocative depiction of the horrors facing European immigrants comes from Henry Fearon's description of his early-nineteenth-century voyage to America: "As we ascended the side of this hulk, a most revolting scene of want and misery presented itself. The eye involuntarily turned for some relief from the horrible picture of human suffering, which living sepulchre

Charges that profit-hungry shippers killed off their passengers by skimping on provisions and packing them more tightly than slaves into squalid holds persist despite evidence to the contrary. During the eighteenth century many mainland colonies, hoping to attract industrious Protestant immigrants, passed laws to curb the excesses of rapacious shipmasters who transported both passengers and servants. In 1750 Massachusetts hired an agent to recruit and transport foreign-born Protestants to strengthen its frontier counties. As part of this recruitment program, the Massachusetts General Court passed an Act to prevent overcrowding on vessels carrying immigrants and to ensure that "Germans and other passengers coming to settle in this province . . . be well provided with good and wholesome meat, drink and other necessaries . . . during the whole voyage."[62]

The Pennsylvania assembly passed similar passenger acts to ensure the safe arrival of healthy immigrants and their property. Pennsylvania's Act of 1750 ordered shipmasters to provide their passengers with "good and wholesome meat, drink and other necessaries" and established minimum space requirements for each passenger. Ship captains also were required to tender "a true and perfect inventory" of the effects of any passenger "who in their passage hither or soon after may happen to die, leaving goods, chattels, money or other effects on board." The protections afforded Pennsylvania's immigrants were increased by an Act of 1765 that required vessels carrying fifty or more "full freights" to provide "an able and well recommended surgeon and a chest with a complete assortment of medicines . . . at the charge of the owner or owners of the vessel." Medicines were to be "administered by the said surgeon to any passenger . . . as often as occasion may require, without his demanding any pay or satisfaction." Passenger ships were also to be "thoroughly smokcd by burning tar between the decks" and "well washed with vinegar" twice a week. The Statute of 1765 also ordered shipmasters carrying German passengers to Pennsylvania to provide each with "a bill of lading" for all "chests, trunks, crates, bales, casks and other packages" put in the ship's hold; restricted the profit margin on food, liquor, and "other necessaries" sold on shipboard; limited the years of service of children orphaned during the voyage; and prohibited the separation of married couples "by disposing of them to different masters or mistresses but by mutual consent of such husband and wife." On the arrival of passenger vessels from Germany, Pennsylvania officials, accompanied by "a reputable German inhabitant . . . well versed in the English

---

afforded. . . . The captain . . . is an American, tall, determined, and with an eye that flashes with Algerine cruelty. . . . The deck was filthy. The cooking, washing and necessary departments were close together. Such is the mercenary barbarity of the Americans who are engaged in this trade, that they crammed into one of those vessels 500 passengers, 80 of whom died in the passage." Henry Bradshaw Fearon, *Sketches of America: A Narrative of a Journey of Five Thousand Miles through the Eastern and Western States*, 1st publ. 1818, 2d ed. (New York: Benjamin Blom, 1969), 149–50.

[62] Erna Risch, "Joseph Crellius, Immigrant Broker," *New England Quarterly*, 12 (1939), 247–48; *Acts and Resolves of Massachusetts Bay*, III, chap. 12 (1751), 536–37, quotes on 536; Schwartz, "*Mixed Multitude*," 202.

and German languages," were to "call together the passengers and in a loud and audible voice in the German language" and inform them of the provisions of the Acts of 1750 and 1765 and of the presence of the official charged with hearing complaints and enforcing their rights. Half of the fines, which ranged from £10 to £100 for each violation, were set aside to aid sick immigrants.[63]

Politicians, ethnic leaders, immigrant aid societies, and "ship-chasing" lawyers placed additional pressure on shippers by helping aggrieved immigrants win redress even in colonies with no passenger acts. Petitions of the surviving Irish passengers on board the *Nancy*, which arrived at Charleston in June 1767, led South Carolina's Assembly to excoriate the ship's owners as "covetous and avaricious" and lacking "Humanity and Principle of Justice"; the Assembly also denied them payment of the colony's bounty money.[64]

Skimpy data have prevented modern researchers from calculating precise mortality rates for eighteenth-century trans-Atlantic passengers. Anecdotal evidence abounds for voyages that ended in disaster as newspapers on both sides of the Atlantic regaled their readers with horrific accounts of shiploads of passengers virtually wiped out by "Fever & flux," smallpox, starvation, shipwrecks, pirates, and privateers.[65] Stories of ship captains who deliberately stinted on the necessities of life and sadistically tortured their helpless passengers also were prominent in the writings of disillusioned immigrants and anti-emigrationists.[66] Surviving pockets of data on specific subsets of seventeenth- and eighteenth-century passengers have been used to amplify the impressionistic evidence found in these literary sources. These data generate death rates that range from 15.8 per cent for 2,814 Palatines transported to New York by the British government in 1709–1710, to 11 per cent for fourteen regiments (8,347 men) sent to British America between 1776 and 1780, and 10 to 15 per cent for English convicts transported to Maryland in 1718–1775. Similar analyses of British slave trade records yield mortality rates of 23.6 per cent for 60,783 Africans sent to America between 1680 and 1688, 8.7 per cent for 15,754 slaves transported in 1791, 17 per cent for 1792 (31,554 slaves), and 9.1 per cent for the late 1810s through the 1840s.[67]

---

[63] Mitchell and Flanders, eds., *Statutes at Large of Pennsylvania*, V, 94–97 (Act of 1750, quotes); VI, 432–40 (Act of 1765, quotes).

[64] Risch, "Immigrant Aid Societies before 1820"; W. B. Smith, *White Servitude in Colonial South Carolina*, 21; Hamer, ed., *Papers of Henry Laurens*, V, 505n (quotes); VI, 148–50.

[65] Frequently cited accounts of disastrous voyages include: a ship landing at Boston with 14 survivors out of 123 passengers and crew, (Boston) *Weekly News-Letter*, May 1, 1729; a vessel carrying Irish immigrants, 100 of 190 dead of starvation, ibid., Nov. 6, 1729; a vessel with 50 survivors from original 150 German immigrants, ibid., Mar. 2, 1732; a ship carrying 400 Palatines, ibid., Jan. 25, 1739; a vessel carrying 300 Irish immigrants to Charleston, *South Carolina Gazette*, June 29, 1767, all cited by John Duffy, "The Passage to the Colonies," *Mississippi Valley Historical Review*, 58 (1951), 27–28, 31–32. The *Good Intent*, *Maryland Gazette*, July 2, 1752; and a vessel carrying 280 Scots to New York, 80 dead from starvation and overcrowding, *Rivington's New York Gazetteer*, Jan. 13, 1774 cited in A. E. Smith, *Colonists in Bondage*, 214.

[66] See Mittelberger, *Journey to Pennsylvania*; Moraley, *The Infortunate*.

[67] Walter Allen Knittle, *Early Eighteenth-Century Palatine Emigration: A British Government Redemptioner Project to Manufacture Naval Stores* (Philadelphia: Dorrance & Co., 1937), 146–47; Henry A. Gemery,

Studies of surviving data runs and published reports of disasters at sea have produced wildly divergent conclusions about trans-Atlantic mortality, and its causes. According to Richard Morris, vessels carrying servants "were overcrowded; passengers were at times packed like herrings in a box. . . . A mortality of more than 50 per cent of the passengers was not an unusual experience on the 'White Guineamen,' as the ships engaged in this trade were called." Another historian cites the 25 per cent death rate on ten passenger vessels that arrived in Philadelphia in 1710 and other "quite small samples of early eighteenth-century north Atlantic shipping" as evidence that "the indentured servant and immigrant trade" experienced "very high epidemic rates." Billy G. Smith has given a similar reading of Philadelphia data, stating that "Sickness and disease were recurrent themes of the long journey . . . German redemptioners, indentured servants, and poor immigrants, who collectively comprised the bulk of Philadelphia's new arrivals, frequently experienced appalling voyages across the Atlantic, at times equaling even the horrors of the African 'middle passage.' . . . Because of the harsh ordeal of the North Atlantic passage, the mortality level of the newly arrived immigrants must have been exorbitant."[68]

Other researchers have given the same data a more optimistic gloss. Marianne Wokeck, in her study of German immigration into colonial Philadelphia, concluded that, although "too few" health reports survived (for 35 vessels out of 348 known arrivals) "to suggest even a rough estimate of mortality . . . they do indicate that a substantial proportion of immigrant ships arrived with most of their passengers in good or at least acceptable health."[69] The economist Farley Grubb goes further, arguing that it is misleading to deduce immigrant mortality rates from the experiences of the Palatines of 1709–1710, convicts or troops, since all of those groups were transported by governments that may have been less "sensitive to mortality-producing conditions" than competitive entrepreneurs. Grubb also points to "seldom cited" sources that postulate relatively low death rates for both voluntary immigrants and convicts—rates that range from 0.17 per cent (1 death) for 600 Moravians who immigrated between 1736 and 1762 and 0.4 per cent (6 deaths) for the 1,500 who emigrated to Georgia in 1741, to a revised estimated death rate of 4 per cent for British convicts transported to America

---

"Emigration from the British Isles to the New World, 1630–1700," *Research in Economic History*, 5 (1980), 187; Herbert S. Klein, *The Middle Passage: Comparative Studies in the Atlantic Slave Trade* (New Haven: Yale University Press, 1978), 64–65.

[68] Morris, *Government and Labor in Early America*, 321 (quote); Klein, *Middle Passage*, 70 (quote); Billy G. Smith, "Death and Life in a Colonial Immigrant City: A Demographic Analysis of Philadelphia," *Journal of Economic History* 37 (1977), 872–73 (quote); Marcus Wilson Jernegan, *Laboring and Dependent Classes in Colonial America, 1607–1783*, 1st publ. 1931 (New York: Frederick Ungar, 1960), 50–51; Duffy, "Passage to the Colonies," 21; Billy G. Smith, *The "Lower Sort": Philadelphia's Laboring People, 1750–1800* (Ithaca: Cornell University Press, 1990), 42–44.

[69] Wokeck, "Tide of Alien Tongues," 204–5 (quotes). Wokeck also states that, "Upon reading many individual accounts about the voyage, the impression is clearly that the majority of commentators attest to much genuine concern that captains showed for their charges," ibid., 201, n84.

between 1718 and 1775. Grubb's own analysis of 1,566 German passengers arriving in Philadelphia between 1727 and 1805 produced an average mortality rate of 3.83 per cent, or 5.5 per cent if the German immigrants who died in shipwrecks during that period were included.[70]

However, most statistical studies of trans-Atlantic death rates lead to the conclusion that African slaves, convicts, military recruits, bound laborers, and fare-paying passengers all experienced similar levels of mortality during the eighteenth century, in the neighborhood of 10 to 15 per cent.[71] Yet even those who agree on these figures can interpret them in very different ways. Shipboard mortality figures are sometimes translated into a standard "crude death rate" (CDR) form that measures the annual number of deaths per thousand members of a given population. Because in the eighteenth century trans-Atlantic voyages lasted approximately two months, the crude death rate of a vessel on which 12 per cent of the passengers died would be 720 ($12 \times 10 \times 6$). This is an astronomical figure in a time when Europe's deadliest cities had CDRs that rarely exceeded 60. A crude death rate of 720 strongly suggests that immigrants who crossed the Atlantic would have improved their life chances dramatically by remaining in the Old World.[72]

Studies that find similar death rates among European passengers and African slaves also seem to support the argument that America's immigrants often were treated like slaves, as avaricious shippers with a callous disregard for human life sacrificed the health and lives of their passengers in their single-minded pursuit of profit. This scenario ignores the fact that it was counterproductive for profit-minded shippers to abuse or starve servants since the dead generated no return on their investment and healthy servants brought higher prices in the American labor market. It also is built on the assumption that passenger survival rates were determined by decisions made by a vessel's owner and crew, whereas surviving data suggest that trans-Atlantic mortality rates were a function of factors over which shippers, and passengers, had little control.[73]

No available evidence supports the charge that shippers killed off their passengers by packing them too tightly. Studies of the African slave trade to Rio de Janeiro from 1794 to 1811 and of European immigrants arriving in Quebec between 1833 and 1850 show that the mortality rates of crowded ships were no

[70] Farley Grubb, "Morbidity and Mortality on the North Atlantic Passage: Eighteenth-Century German Immigration," *Journal of Interdisciplinary History*, 17 (1987), 565–85.

[71] Klein, *Middle Passage*; Eltis, "Free and Coerced Transatlantic Migrations"; Gemery, "Emigration from the British Isles," 187. Some of these estimates include "seasoning" deaths, those that occurred soon after landing.

[72] For the translation of voyage deaths into CDRs, see Grubb, "Morbidity and Mortality," 571–72. Grubb, after estimating passage mortality at a relatively low 5.5 per cent, with a CDR of 264, states (572n) that "The relative hazards of transatlantic travel were even greater than suggested, since immigrants were concentrated in the low mortality ages of the late teens and early twenties relative to nonimmigrant populations. Thus age-specific differences in crude death rates would be even higher."

[73] Mittelberger, *Journey to Philadelphia*, 16–17; Grubb, "Morbidity and Mortality," 567, 572.

higher than for those carrying a handful of passengers. Indeed, Herbert Klein found that the death rate of vessels with smaller complements of slaves was "slightly higher" than on more crowded vessels. A study of 7,192 adult male Germans who immigrated to Pennsylvania between 1727 and 1754 reveals a similar reverse correlation between crowding and the number of men too ill to disembark on their arrival at Philadelphia. In this sample, the vessels carrying the largest number of passengers had the lowest level of "debarkation morbidity."[74] Consequently, David Eltis and others have concluded that shipboard mortality was "quite likely, a function of the diseases on board ship when it left port. . . . The lack of correlation between deaths and size of cargo suggests that even half-empty ships generated pathogenic conditions." Unfortunately, as Eltis points out, "the state of medical knowledge at the time was such that the treatment accorded" European immigrants and African slaves "during the voyage should have had little or no influence over mortality. What was not known could scarcely have been influential."[75] Burning tar between the decks, disinfecting with vinegar, or the presence of a doctor and medical supplies could do little to save children and adults who lacked immunities to smallpox and other infectious diseases that passengers brought on board with them. Equally ineffective were colonial laws that established minimum space requirements for passengers.[76]

Many exposés of the horrors and abuses of the trans-Atlantic passage and the shipboard sales of "white slaves" were written to reduce the flow of servants and Europeans to England's American colonies.[77] Although largely unsuccessful in their primary purpose, these accounts have challenged the image of colonial America as a land of opportunity for Europe's oppressed.[78] As few contemporary sources document the lives of "the powerless," modern accounts have relied heavily on published exposés, newspapers accounts of catastrophic voyages, and legal action brought against brutal ship captains to reconstruct the lives of immigrants who responded to the lure of America. Consequently, shipwrecks, epidemics, abuse, death, and the auctioning off of pathetic survivors have played an exaggerated role in America's immigration history.[79] In the seventeenth and

[74] Klein, *Middle Passage*, 51–72. In his study of the African slave trade in Rio de Janeiro, 1795–1811, Klein discovered (p. 66) "no significant correlation between the number of slaves carried and the rate of mortality. If anything, the smaller vessels have slightly higher rates of mortality"; Grubb, "Morbidity and Mortality," 573–76.

[75] David Eltis, "Free and Coerced Transatlantic Migrations," 269.

[76] Mittelberger made the same observation in 1756 in *Journey to Pennsylvania*.

[77] Firms involved in the passenger trade also denounced the avaricious practices of their rivals while exonerating their own shipmasters. See W. B. Smith, *White Servitude in Colonial South Carolina*, 42; Hamer, ed., *Papers of Henry Laurens*, VI, 150; V, 625, 628.

[78] Farley Grubb has speculated that negative reports of trans-Atlantic voyages may have reduced emigration to eighteenth-century America and thereby "altered the growth path of world output and the growth in the personal wealth of prospective emigrants, by postponing the movement of labor from low-productivity employment in Europe to high-productivity employment in America." Grubb, "Morbidity and Mortality," 566–67. Nonetheless, the high rate of immigration to the mainland colonies and the United States throughout the eighteenth century must be construed as evidence of the failure of those who hoped to destroy the lure of America.

[79] Modern works that focus on the horror and abuses of the immigrant voyage include: Cheesman A.

eighteenth centuries ocean travel was dangerous. Vessels blown off course or becalmed did run out of provisions; epidemics and shipwrecks occasionally left few surviving passengers; and greedy men of all nationalities were ever anxious to turn a profit at the expense of the naive. Yet such events seem to have been the exception rather than the rule.

"A Worse than Egyptian Bondage"

As involuntary servitude for slaves and transported felons became an increasingly salient feature of British North America, the colonists became vulnerable to the charge of enslaving unwary Europeans. According to the German immigrant Gottlieb Mittelberger, the "poor defrauded" immigrants who were forced to sell themselves into servitude upon their arrival in America were "beaten like cattle until they . . . learned hard labor"; those who ran away from harsh masters were "quickly recaptured" and sentenced to additional weeks and months of forced labor.[80] This claim that bound workers were ruthlessly exploited and treated little better than African slaves is a recurrent theme in modern accounts of American indentured servitude. Once again horror stories of death, degradation, and cruelty resonate more vividly than a balanced assessment of fragmentary evidence. Most modern indictments of indentured servitude are based on the writings of victims who charged that avaricious merchants and colonists, after seducing naive Europeans with visions of streets paved with gold, abused and exploited them in ways that denied servants access to the bounty of America. However, studies that focus on the poverty, distress, and cruel exploitation of immigrants too often ignore or minimize contrary evidence.[81]

The factors that determined the fate of America's servants were so numerous that it is impossible either to condemn indentured servitude as simply an exploitive institution that transformed people into commodities or to defend it as a regenerative mechanism that extended opportunity and freedom to the victims of the Old World. A servant's future was shaped by the timing of his

Herrick, *White Servitude in Pennsylvania: Indentured and Redemptioner Labor in Colony and Commonwealth* (Philadelphia: J. J. McVey, 1926), 178–94; Knittle, *Early Eighteenth-Century Palatine Emigration,* 146–49; Sharon V. Salinger, *"To Serve Well and Faithfully": Labor and Indentured Servants in Pennsylvania, 1682–1800* (New York: Cambridge University Press, 1987), 87–97; B. G. Smith, "Death and Life," 872; idem, "*Lower Sort,*" 42–45.

[80] Mittelberger, *Journey to Pennsylvania,* 29, 28, 19.

[81] For modern studies that emphasize the exploitative brutality of indentured servitude, see van der Zee, *Bound Over;* A. E. Smith, *Colonists in Bondage;* Edmund S. Morgan, *American Slavery, American Freedom;* Salinger, "*To Serve Faithfully and Well*"; B. G. Smith, "*Lower Sort.*" Among the largely ignored writings of contemporaries who defended or praised indentured servitude are: William Wood, *New England's Prospects* (1635), cited in Galenson, *White Servitude in Colonial America,* 10; Anonymous, *A Brief Description of the Province of Carolina on the Coasts of Floreda* (1666), cited in ibid.; John Hammond, *Leah and Rachel* (London: Printed by Mabb, 1656); George Alsop, *Character of the Province of Maryland,* 1st publ. 1666, (Cleveland: Burrows Brothers, 1902); Peter Kalm, *Travels into North America,* 1st publ. 1748, trans. John Reinhold Forster, ed. Ralph M. Sargent (Barre, Mass.: The Imprint Society, 1972).

emigration, the disease climate and demographic conditions he encountered, the character of his master, and myriad vagaries of fate. Studies of the seventeenth-century Chesapeake have produced a vivid picture of the horrors awaiting bound labor, when almost half of all servants succumbed to disease, malnutrition, or overwork before completing their term of service.[82] Court records of seventeenth-century Massachusetts Bay also contain reports of abusive masters beating servants and, in one instance, hanging a flogged servant "by the heels as butchers do beasts for the slaughter."[83]

Colonial law codes can be seen as additional evidence that, once in America, indentured servants and redemptioners were denied the traditional rights of Englishmen and virtually enslaved.[84] Laws governing the rights and obligations of voluntary servants often were combined with those of slaves and transported convicts into a single code. This practice conflated the status of all three groups in the minds of some colonists and most critics of indentured servitude, from the seventeenth century to the present. Laws that subjected runaway servants to whippings and "moderate" corporal punishment and authorized gaol keepers to hire out unclaimed runaways after placing "a strong iron collar" around their necks, smacked of enslavement. So did statutes that required runaways to serve one to ten days for each day of their absence and sentenced servants who laid violent hands on their master, mistress, or overseer to an additional two years of servitude.[85] One Dutch Labadist described the Chesapeake's "hundreds of thousands" of servants as "poor slaves" whose "bloody sweat" supported the "insatiable avarice" of their masters. One "sick and languishing" servant was even forced to "dig his own grave, in which he was to be laid a few days afterwards, in order not to busy any of the others with it, they having their hands full in attending to the tobacco." Some eighteenth-century observers claimed that servants were treated even more harshly than valuable African slaves. In 1774 William Eddis argued that

> Negroes being a property for life, the death of slaves, in the prime of youth or strength, is a material loss to the proprietor; they are, therefore, almost in every

[82] Morgan, *American Slavery, American Freedom*; Russell R. Menard, "From Servant to Freeholder: Status, Mobility, and Property Accumulation in Seventeenth-century Maryland," *William and Mary Quarterly*, 3d. ser., 30 (1973), 37–64; Russell R. Menard, P. M. G. Harris, and Lois G. Carr, "Opportunity and Inequality: The Distribution of Wealth on the Lower Western Shore of Maryland, 1638–1705," *Maryland Historical Magazine*, 69 (1974), 169–84.

[83] Dow and Thresher, eds., *Records . . . of the Quarterly Courts of Essex County, Massachusetts*, II, 222–23, 302–3 (quote).

[84] Nash, *Urban Crucible*, 15, argues that indentured servants "sold at dockside to the highest bidder . . . were circumscribed so thoroughly by the law that most rights regarded as basic to the English heritage were held in abeyance until their terms of service were up."

[85] Hening, ed., *Statutes at Large of Virginia*, I, 538; II, 114–18, 266; IV, 106, 168–75, quote on 171; VI, 360–68; Waverly K. Winfree, comp., *The Laws of Virginia, being a Supplement to Hening's, The Statutes at Large, 1700–1750* (Richmond: Virginia State Library, 1971), 212–22; Morris, *Government and Labor in Early America*, 434–503.

instance, under more comfortable circumstances than the miserable European, over whom the rigid planter exercises an inflexible severity. They are strained to utmost to perform their allotted labour; and, from a prepossession in many cases too justly founded, they are supposed to be receiving only the just reward which is due to repeated offences. There are, doubtless many exceptions to this observation, yet, generally speaking, they groan beneath a worse than Egyptian bondage.[86]

Such accounts of the horrific nature of white servitude have all but obliterated the words of contemporaries who defended the institution. According to the ex-servant George Alsop, writing in 1666,

the Servants here in Mary-Land of all Colonies, distant or remote Plantations, have the least cause to complain, either for strictness of Servitude, want of Provisions, or need of Apparel. Five dayes and a half in the Summer weeks is the alotted time that they work in; and for two months, when the Sun predominates in the highest pitch of his heat, they claim an antient and customary Priviledge, to repose themselves three hours in the day within the house, and this is undeniably granted to them that work in the fields. In the Winter time . . . they do little or no work or imployment, save cutting of wood to make good fires to sit by.

Furthermore,

those Servants which come over into this Province, being Artificers . . . never (during their Servitude) work in the fields, or do any other imployment save that which their Handicraft and Mechanick endeavours are capable of putting them upon, and are esteem'd as well by their Masters, as those that imploy them, above measure. . . . In short, touching the Servants of this Province, they live well in the time of their Service, and by their restrainment in that time, they are made capable of living much better when they come to be free.[87]

Alsop's idyllic account has been dismissed as the writing of a man who, "if not intentionally dissimulating, has at least based [his] conclusions too exclusively on his own treatment by a considerate [master]."[88] But more moderate assessments of indentured servitude also have been ignored or rejected by modern researchers. The Swedish botanist Peter Kalm, who traveled through North America in 1749–1751, saw little difference between American servitude and English servants in husbandry—describing indentured immigrants as the "kind of servants, the *English* call *servings*." The journal kept by John Harrower, a Scottish indentured servant who worked as a tutor in Virginia in the 1770s, reveals a harmonious relationship between Harrower and his master.[89]

---

[86] Quotes from Jaspar Danckaerts, *Journal of Jasper Danckaerts, 1679–1680*, 1st publ. 1867, ed. Bartlett Burleigh James, and J. Franklin Jameson, trans. Henry C. Murphy (New York: Charles Scribner's Sons, 1913), 111–12, 134; Eddis, *Letters from America*, 69–70.

[87] Alsop, *Character of the Province of Maryland*, 357–59.

[88] Van der Zee, *Bound Over*, 103.

[89] Kalm, *Travels into North America*, 197–98; John Harrower, *The Journal of John Harrower, an Indentured Servant in the Colony of Virginia, 1773–1776*, ed. Edward Miles Riley (Williamsburg, Va.: Colonial Williamsburg, 1963).

The ubiquitous advertisements for runaway servants in colonial newspapers also have been construed as evidence of abusive masters or unendurable hardships. Little attention is paid to masters who claimed that servants who ran off were rogues with no intention of fulfilling their contractual obligations or to the repetition of runaway advertisements and their often despairing tone, which suggest that many servants evaded recapture. It is more often assumed that runaway servants were desperately fleeing brutal masters, who inexorably hunted them down and, when apprehended, condemned them to whippings and additional years of servitude and abuse.[90]

There is little evidence to show why servants ran away and how many were recaptured and whipped or forced to serve additional time. A search of the court records of seventeenth-century Massachusetts Bay has uncovered the trials of eighty recaptured fugitive servants; another fourteen cases have been found in the dockets of the Suffolk County Court between 1702 and 1765. According to these records, most seventeenth-century runaways were subjected to corporal punishment, and a few were sentenced to serve additional time; in the eighteenth century, on the other hand, only one servant was whipped, and most were "returned to the master without a specific decree of extra punishment."[91] Runaway servants were more severely punished in the Chesapeake. Between 1668 and 1776, Maryland's county courts inflicted additional service, at the rate of 10 days for each day of absence, on more than 90 per cent of the 267 recaptured fugitives they tried, whereas in Virginia, whippings were usually combined with an extension of servitude at the rate of 2 days for each day of the servant's absence. The severity of these sentences can probably be attributed to the fact that a large proportion of the runaway servants in the Chesapeake were convicts—35 per cent of those advertised in the *Maryland Gazette* in 1745–1748 were transported felons; in 1756–1760 that proportion had climbed to 70 per cent.[92]

For some servants running away seems to have been an effective weapon in renegotiating service contracts. At least two runaways in seventeenth-century Virginia were *not* punished under the colony's statute that made such actions liable to "moderate corporall punishment" and additional service. Rather, one servant, on his return, had his years of service *reduced*; the other won the promise of an additional yearly wage, that would grow from 50 shillings for the first year to £6 for his sixth and final year of service. The eighteenth-century indentured

---

[90] Estimates of the number of eighteenth-century servants who ran away after arriving in America range from less than 3 per cent in Bailyn, *Voyagers to the West*, 350, to more than 6 per cent in Sharon Salinger, "*To Serve Faithfully and Well*," 103–7. For the assumption that runaways were fleeing abusive masters, see Salinger, "*To Serve Faithfully and Well*"; Jernegan, *Laboring and Dependent Classes*, 225, n36; Nash, *Urban Crucible*, 15.

[91] Morris, *Government and Labor in Early America*, 439. Records searched were those of the Massachusetts Court of Assistants (17th century) and the county courts of 17th-century Essex county and 17th- and 18th-century Suffolk county (which include the city of Boston).

[92] Ibid., 450–58.

servant William Moraley adopted similar tactics and won similar concessions. Moraley ran away when his master refused to transfer his indenture to a Philadelphia tradesman; when Morally was apprehended, his master agreed to shorten his term from five to three years.[93]

During the eighteenth century many colonial governments revised their legal codes to protect the rights of white indentured servants in order to recruit more immigrants. Arguing that "The barbarous usage of some servants by cruell masters bring soe much scandall and infamy to the country . . . that people who would willingly adventure themselves hither, are through feare thereof diverted," American legislators passed laws that guaranteed certain freedom dues, limited terms of service and punishments that could be inflicted, and established institutions and redress procedures to protect servants from abusive masters.[94]

Various incidents illustrate the inability of legal proscriptions to protect servants from a sadistic master or mistress. Heart-rending tales have survived from seventeenth-century Virginia, when indentured workers were relatively abundant and protective mechanisms weak or unenforced. Under these circumstances, the Virginia planter Dr. John Pott was able to force a recently bereaved woman, whom he had ransomed from the Indians, into servitude, demanding that she serve out the remainder of her dead husband's term and additional time for the ransom, "two pound of [glass] beades" he had paid her Indian captors. In 1696, Maryland's laws were unable to prevent the mistress of Sarah Gambrell from beating her to death "with an Iron about fourteene Inches Long."[95]

Yet other incidents show the success of individuals and ethnic organizations in enforcing the legal rights of bound Europeans.[96] Redress was possible, even in the early Chesapeake, with masters sitting in judgment on themselves. In the 1630s, the heartless Dr. Pott was ordered by his fellow planters "to either teach his apprentice the art of an apothecary (which he was neglecting to do) or else to pay him wages." The seventeenth-century records of Middlesex county, Virginia, show several servants successfully suing their masters for breach of contract or abuse in the local county court.[97] In 1671 a jury in Suffolk county, Massachusetts, awarded Robert Collins his freedom and court costs

[93] Darrett B. Rutman and Anita H. Rutman, *A Place in Time: Middlesex County, Virginia, 1650–1750* (New York: Norton, 1984), 132–33; Moraley, *The Infortunate.*

[94] Hening, ed., *Statutes at Large of Virginia,* II, 117.

[95] Morgan, *American Slavery, American Freedom,* 117; Kingsbury, ed., *Records of the Virginia Company,* IV, 473; Rutman and Rutman, *A Place in Time,* 134–38; Morris, *Government and Labor in Early America,* 461–500.

[96] A. E. Smith found "that court records reveal a high proportion of cases in which the servant received fair treatment, and a great many in which the humanity displayed by the magistrates did them credit . . . servants could complain to magistrates if they were ill treated . . . and often did so and received justice," *Colonists in Bondage,* 246, 251.

[97] Morgan, *American Slavery, American Freedom,* 126. In the 1620s Jane Dickenson was able to air her grievance against Dr. Pott in London, although the outcome of her appeal is unknown, ibid., 117. Rutman and Rutman, *A Place in Time,* 133–34.

after Collins charged the ship captain who had carried him to America with kidnapping.[98] In 1753 Gottlieb Mittelberger's "intercession" and the humanity of a Dutch sea captain helped a hapless German immigrant, robbed by crew members and fleeced by an "unscrupulous creditor," to retain his freedom. The indentured servants aboard the *Pearl* who denounced the inhumanity of their ship captain to South Carolinian officials won their freedom and bounty money.[99]

The English tradition of servitude was indeed altered by its transplantation into American soil. Colonists dealing with slave and convict workers often resorted to extreme measures to protect their investment in bound workers and to neutralize the dangers inherent in forced labor systems. It is no accident that servant regulations and their enforcement were most lenient in New England, where the number of convict and slave workers was small. The eighteenth-century planters of Maryland and Virginia who used the transported "gaolbirds" they feared and despised to reduce the dangers of slavery enacted more rigorous laws to control indentured workers and were more likely to enforce them.

American servitude evolved along different lines to meet colonial, rather than English, needs. In England employers and lawmakers were not required to redefine servitude to deal with the problems of convict and slave labor, both had been banished to their colonies. By the eighteenth century English labor laws and customs had become mechanisms to control underemployed and masterless English people. With a ready pool of casual labor, employers had no need, or desire, to bind workers to long terms of service. Parliamentary statutes were more concerned with preventing masters from dismissing servants before the expiration of their contracts than with extending the terms of runaways.[100] English magistrates and legislators were no more altruistic in dealing with workers and the poor than their colonial counterparts. In both regions, regulations were designed to reduce a worker's wage and increase his productivity while placing him under the watchful eye of a master who could be held accountable for his conduct. In both regions traditional patriarchal authority

---

[98] Van der Zee tells the story of Robert Collins in *Bound Over*, 128–33, but argues (p. 133) that "Collins's victory was something of an Exception." According to van der Zee, "Though from time to time in Massachusetts and in the other colonies servants were acquitted of charges by the courts, and though occasionally servants even brought suit against their masters and won their freedom, the odds were heavily in favor of the men who owned the ships, stores, plantations, and in many instances the magistrates."

[99] Mittelberger, *Journey to Pennsylvania*, 22–24; Hamer, ed., *Papers of Henry Laurens*, V, 504–5.

[100] S. T. Bindoff, "The Making of the Statute of Artificers," in S. T. Bindoff et al., eds., *Elizabethan Government and Society: Essays Presented to Sir John Neale* (London: Athlone Press, 1961), 56–94; Peter Laslett, *The World We Have Lost: England before the Industrial Age*, 2d ed. (New York: Charles Scribner's Sons, 1971), chap. 1; Ann Kussmaul, *Servants in Husbandry in Early Modern England* (Cambridge: Cambridge University Press, 1981); Robert J. Steinfeld, *The Invention of Free Labor: The Employment Relation in English and American Law and Culture, 1350–1879* (Chapel Hill: University of North Carolina Press, 1991), 25–121; Christopher L. Tomlins, *Law, Labor, and Ideology in the Early American Republic* (Cambridge: Cambridge University Press, 1993), 232–58.

endowed a master with the power to abuse his dependents and to control the institutions that judged his conduct.[101]

The problem of quantifying the treatment of the working poor in England and its colonies makes a comparison difficult. The unemployed who tramped the English countryside looking for work or lived hand-to-mouth in urban squalor may well have preferred bound servitude in the colonies to starvation, a life of crime, or forced labor in English workhouses. The willingness of Old World workers to undertake the known hazards of emigration and to commit themselves to years of servitude in America, despite well-publicized warnings of potential abuse, suggests that the colonial variant of indentured servitude did not violate eighteenth-century expectations or norms.

Vital statistics provide evidence that America's eighteenth-century servants were not treated worse than African slaves. Scanty data make a direct comparison of the physical well-being of the colonial slave and servant populations difficult. Nonetheless, every study undertaken to date has found that African Americans suffered significantly higher levels of mortality than their white neighbors. Infant mortality rates (IMRs), which calculate the number of children who die before their first birthday per 1,000 live births, are considered by demographers to be "one of the best indicators of the general social, economic, and health conditions in a community." In colonial Virginia, the farm record book of Robert Lloyd shows that about 25 per cent of all slave children born in the 1740s and 1750s died before their first birthday, which translates into an IMR of 250. Meanwhile, the infant death rate experienced by Euro-American children born in Charles Parish, Virginia, between 1700 and 1734 was closer to 18 per cent, with IMRs of 183.8 for males and 180.8 for females.[102]

Black and white mortality rates in eighteenth-century Boston diverged even more dramatically. A breakdown of Boston's death rate by race reveals that between 1704 and 1755 the African American population suffered significantly higher mortality levels than the city's Euro-Americans. Black deaths accounted for 15.8 per cent of Boston's total burials for 1704–1752, although Boston's black population made up 8.4 per cent of the city's population in 1742, 9.8 per cent in 1752, and 6.3 per cent in 1755. In 1742 Boston's black population experienced a crude death rate (CDR) of 52.4 per thousand compared to a white CDR of 29.8. In 1752 a small pox epidemic sent death rates soaring for both populations, and the CDRs for Boston's African- and Euro-Americans rose to 117 and 60.7, respectively.[103] Death rates in eighteenth-century Philadelphia reveal a similar

[101] And, as Marcus Jernegan points out, English masters also were charged with inhumane treatment of their servants. Jernegan, *Laboring and Dependent Classes*, 54.

[102] Maris A. Vinovskis, "Mortality Rates and Trends in Massachusetts before 1860," *Journal of Economic History* 32 (1972), 198; Kulikoff, "A Prolifick People," 427; Daniel Blake Smith, "Mortality and Family in the Colonial Chesapeake," *Journal of Interdisciplinary History*, 8 (1978), 413.

[103] John B. Blake, *Public Health in the Town of Boston, 1630–1822* (Cambridge: Harvard University Press, 1959), 247–49; Greene, *Negro in Colonial New England*, 84–85, 338, 348–49. Gary Nash (*Urban Crucible*,

divergence. Between 1730 and 1770, white Philadelphians died at an annual rate of 45 to 50 per thousand, compared with 60 to 77 per thousand for the city's blacks.[104]

Height studies for England's mainland colonies in the eighteenth century also suggest that all white immigrants, including servants, enjoyed a quality of life far superior to that of America's black population. According to Robert Fogel, a "body's ability to generate a surplus for growth" is related to the "accumulated past nutritional experience" of an individual's mother and grandmother, as well as "such factors as age, the climate, the nature of the available food, clothing and shelter, the disease environment, the intensity of work, and the quality of public sanitation." Because a large proportion of colonial immigrants arrived as servants or slaves, the heights attained by native-born Americans in the eighteenth and early nineteenth centuries reflect the living and working conditions of bound populations, as well as the standard of living experienced by free immigrants, creole generations, and the populations actually measured.[105]

During the eighteenth century the average height of the white colonial population soared to unprecedented levels. A study of American-born white males who served in the Seven Years' War shows that those born between 1715 and 1739 reached an average adult height of 67.5"; those born after 1740 averaged 67.9". This upward trend continued throughout the century. The average height of native-born whites who were recruited into the American army between 1775 and 1783 ranged from 67.8" for New Englanders to 68.3" for southern soldiers.[106] The earliest reliable data on heights reached by native-born Americans of African descent emerge only in the nineteenth century. After the ending of the African slave trade in 1808, the masters of coastal vessels transporting slaves from one American port to another were required to record a physical description of each slave they carried. The final adult height of the American slaves recorded on these manifests—all of whom were "residing (but not necessarily born) in the U.S."—averaged 67.1 inches, more than an inch shorter than the eighteenth-century southern white recruits who served during the American Revolution. Analysis of a sample of ex-slaves and free blacks inducted into the Union Army in the 1860s (the vast majority of whom would have been American-born), yields the same average of 67.1 inches, whereas the mean adult height of "contrabands"

445, n25) thinks it "likely" that an undercount of Boston's African-American population in the Census of 1742 artificially inflated the city's black death rate. Although there is no question that colonial data are flawed, all evidence from British North America shows similar differences in the death rates for Euro- and African-Americans.

[104] Susan E. Klepp, *Philadelphia in Transition: A Demographic History of the City and Its Occupational Groups, 1720–1830* (New York: Garland, 1989), 233.

[105] Robert W. Fogel et al., "Secular Changes in American and British Stature and Nutrition," *Journal of Interdisciplinary History*, 14 (1983), quotes on 450.

[106] Ibid., 462–65; Kenneth L. Sokoloff and Georgia C. Villaflor, "The Early Achievement of Modern Stature in America," *Social Science History*, 6 (1982), 453–81.

and runaway slaves who were recorded by Union commanders in Mississippi was 67.4 inches. Virginia's antebellum free black males reached, on average, a final height of 67.9 inches.[107]

The consistent height advantage enjoyed by Euro-Americans over those of African descent documents the extent to which America's eighteenth-century bound Europeans, whether indentured servants, redemptioners, or transported convicts, enjoyed better living and working conditions, and a lesser degree of exploitation, than African slaves. Because they were drawn disproportionately from the lower orders of society, the American soldiers who reached an average height of 68.1 inches were more likely to be the children of impoverished immigrants and freed servants than the sons of propertied immigrants or well-established natives. Therefore the height differential between Euro-American soldiers and African-Americans can be seen as evidence that American masters did *not* provide better care for their more valuable African slaves while forcing their indentured servants into "a worse than Egyptian bondage."[108]

Immigrant Mortality

There is no doubt that Europeans who chose to emigrate, whether rich or poor, free or bound, increased their risk of early death. As epidemiologists have long known, the world is divided into myriad disease environments, and the inhabitants of each region develop complete or partial immunities to the diseases endemic in their region. The introduction of new diseases can produce catastrophic death rates in a newly exposed population; similar demographic crises occur when migrants enter a new environment containing diseases against which they have little or no immunity. In the early modern period, when slow transportation and limited communications prevented the "homogenization" of disease, even domestic migrations, from town to town or from village to city, could be deadly. Consequently, oceanic migrants faced exposure to new health risks simply by gathering in port cities to await shipping. The vessels carrying immigrants to their new homes then became, in effect, another new

[107] Fogel, "Secular Changes," quote on 464; Robert A. Margo and Richard H. Steckel, "The Heights of American Slaves: New Evidence on Slave Nutrition and Health," *Social Science History*, 6 (1982), 516–38; Richard H. Steckel, "Slave Height Profiles from Coastwise Manifests," *Explorations in Economic History*, 16 (1979), 363–80.

[108] John Shy, "Hearts and Minds," in *A People Numerous and Armed: Reflections on the Military Struggle for American Independence*, rev. ed. (Ann Arbor: University of Michigan Press, 1990), 171–73; James Kirby Martin and Mark Edward Lender, *A Respectable Army: The Military Origins of the Republic, 1763–1789* (Arlington Heights, Ill.: Harlan Davidson, 1982), 89–94; Edward C. Papenfuse and Gregory A. Stiverson, "General Smallwood's Recruits: The Peacetime Career of the Revolutionary War Private," *William and Mary Quarterly*, 3d. ser., 30 (1973), 117–32; Mark Edward Lender, "The Social Structure of the New Jersey Brigade: The Continental Line as an American Standing Army," in Peter Karsten, ed., *The Military in America: From the Colonial Era to the Present* (New York: Free Press, 1980), 27–44. Quote from Eddis, *Letters from America*, 38.

and potentially deadly disease environment, as did the foreign soil on which they disembarked.[109]

Most of America's eighteenth-century immigrants landed in one of four port "cities," Boston, New York, Philadelphia, and Charleston. Recent demographic studies have posited extremely high death rates for these ports, with CDRs that approached or surpassed those of Old World cities. Between 1701 and 1774, Boston's average CDR ranged from a low of 31 (1731–1735) to a high of 46 (1721–1725), and Philadelphia's average annual death rate for the 1720s through 1774 fluctuated between 36 and 51 per thousand. Charleston was even unhealthier, with a CDR falling somewhere between 52 to 60 for white inhabitants in 1722–1732.[110] Comparing these colonial mortality rates with those of the Old World highlights the magnitude of American figures. Historical demographers have calculated regional and national CDRs of 17 to 41.7 for Sweden (1691–1750); 20 to 37.5 for Finland (1722–1749); 29.8 to 34.4 for France (1771–1800); and 26.2 to 35 for England (1701–1775).[111] Even more damning are comparisons of American ports and Old World towns of similar size. Some historians have used data from Nottingham, England, to assess the quality of life in colonial America. Between 1700 and 1775 the town of Nottingham grew from approximately 7,000 to 16,510 making it, in the 1770s, comparable in size to Boston, New York, and Philadelphia. During this period

[109] Philip D. Curtin, "Epidemiology and the Slave Trade," *Political Science Quarterly*, 83 (1968), 190–216; Alfred W. Crosby, Jr., *The Columbian Exchange: Biological and Cultural Consequences of 1492* (Westport, Conn.: Greenwood Press, 1972), esp. chaps. 1 and 2; William H. McNeill, "Human Migration: A Historical Overview," in William H. McNeill and Ruth S. Adams, eds., *Human Migration: Patterns and Policies* (Bloomington: Indiana University Press, 1978), 3–8; idem, "Migration Patterns and Infection in Traditional Societies," in N. F. Stanley and R. A. Joske, eds., *Changing Disease Patterns and Human Behaviour* (London: Academic Press, 1980), 27–36; Darret B. Rutman and Anita H. Rutman, "Of Agues and Fevers: Malaria in the Early Chesapeake," *William and Mary Quarterly*, 3d ser., 33 (1976), 31–60; Carville V. Earle, "Environment, Disease, and Mortality in Early Virginia," in Thad W. Tate and David L. Ammerman, eds., *The Chesapeake in the Seventeenth Century: Essays on Anglo-American Society and Politics* (Chapel Hill: University of North Carolina Press, 1979), 96–125. Two studies, in particular, give vivid evidence of the dangers of eighteenth-century migration, even when migrants traveled relatively short distances: Jon Kukla, "Kentish Agues and American Distempers: The Transmission of Malaria from England to Virginia in the Seventeenth Century," *Southern Studies*, 25 (1986), 135–47, and Mack Walker, *The Salzburg Transaction: Expulsion and Redemption in Eighteenth-Century Germany* (Ithaca: Cornell University Press, 1992). In *Salzburg Transaction*, 88–89, Walker found that 40 per cent of the approximately 20,000 Salzburgers who set out for Prussia in 1732 were "lost" along the way; 14 per cent of the children embarked on sixty-four vessels for the final leg of the journey to Konigsberg died during that short voyage.

[110] Blake, *Public Health in the Town of Boston*, 247–49; Klepp, *Philadelphia in Transition*, 233; B. G. Smith, "Death and Life," 888; Peter A. Coclanis, "Death in Early Charleston: An Estimate of the Crude Death Rate for the White Population of Charleston, 1722–1732," *South Carolina Historical Magazine*, 85 (1984), 288–90. Inadequate population and mortality data prevent the calculation of CDRs for colonial New York City.

[111] Gustaf Utterstrom, "Two Essays on Population in Eighteenth-Century Scandinavia," in D. V. Glass and D. E. C. Eversley, eds., *Population in History: Essays in Historical Demography* (London: Edward Arnold, 1965), 538; Eino Jutikkala, "Finland's Population Movement in the Eighteenth Century," in ibid., 564; J. Bourgeois-Pichat, "The General Development of the Population of France since the Eighteenth Century," trans. Peter Jimack, in ibid., 506; E. A. Wrigley and R. S. Schofield, *The Population History of England, 1541–1871: A Reconstruction* (Cambridge: Harvard University Press, 1981), 529.

Nottingham experienced an average CDR of 32.5, with quinquennial rates ranging from 28.3 to 43.9.[112]

Such comparisons seem to substantiate charges that British North America was a deathtrap rather than a land of opportunity and that Europe's oppressed masses could have increased the quality of life for themselves and their children by remaining in the Old World.[113] However, estimated colonial death rates encompass ambiguities that challenge that conclusion. A paucity of reliable data on births, deaths, and population totals and the problem of calculating American mortality rates that do not include the deaths of immigrants who succumbed to shipboard infections soon after their arrival cast doubt about the CDRs calculated for America's eighteenth-century ports.

An examination of Philadelphia's mortality figures shows that its CDR was boosted by two separate phenomena, the deaths of immigrants entering a new disease environment and those of the native-born who succumbed to microbes introduced by immigrants. Because newcomers and native Philadelphians possessed different immunities to the diseases endemic to their formative environment their susceptibility to various epidemics and health conditions also varied. Immigrants weakened by the voyage or shipboard disease were especially vulnerable to Philadelphia's disease climate and died at a rate not replicated in the native-born and previously acclimated immigrant populations. In addition, the death rate of immigrants who died during their seasoning in Philadelphia is magnified by the fact that sick immigrants were disproportionately left behind and buried in the city's cemeteries, whereas the healthy spread into the back-country of Pennsylvania and beyond. On the other hand, immigrants who arrived with immunities to the diseases they brought with them that were not endemic to Philadelphia, such as smallpox, were more likely to survive the diseases they introduced than the city's newly exposed residents. Combining the death rates of Philadelphia's different populations distorts the mortality rate of the city as a whole and magnifies the health hazards faced by permanent residents and new arrivals.

Studies of America's cities suggest that it was their status as ports, rather than population density or squalid living conditions, that made their eighteenth-century death rates so high. Ports, of all sizes, included among their inhabitants seafaring men who suffered higher mortality rates than other occupational groups, transients carrying new diseases, and immigrants entering a new disease climate. These factors could explain part of the difference between the relatively high mortality of the Massachusetts ports of Salem and Boston and the lower

---

[112] Nottingham figures from J. D. Chambers, "Three Essays on the Population and Economy of the Midlands: Enclosure and Labour Supply in the Industrial Revolution," in Glass and Eversley, eds., *Population in History*, 351. Comparisons of colonial ports with Nottingham are made in Klepp, *Philadelphia in Transition*; B. G. Smith, "Death and Life," and "*Lower Sort.*"

[113] B. G. Smith, "*Lower Sort*," 62; Coclanis, "Death in Early Charleston," 290.

rates of the colony's inland communities. They also can explain why the CDRs calculated for eighteenth-century Philadelphia exceed those of Boston, which had a smaller maritime population and received fewer immigrants, and those of the inland city of Nottingham, England.[114]

Historical demographers have long recognized that ports experienced higher death rates than inland communities of similar size, but little attempt has made to integrate that fact into the demographic studies of urban America. Billy Smith, reported that 253 "newly arrived Palatinate redemptioners and indentured servants" were buried in Philadelphia in 1754, but he did not factor that information into his estimated mortality rate for the city.[115] The deaths of immigrants who succumbed to shipboard disease are thus falsely attributed to conditions in Philadelphia. The exclusion of those 253 deaths from Smith's calculations would have lowered his estimated CDR for Philadelphia in 1754 from 50.1 to 34.1. Recognizing the fact that throughout the eighteenth century a large proportion of the burials in at least two of Philadelphia's cemeteries (the Stranger's and Swedish Burying Grounds) were those of immigrants who remained, and died, in Philadelphia only because they were too ill, from shipboard conditions, to move on would greatly reduce the estimated CDRs for Philadelphia's resident population and revise conclusions about living conditions in colonial cities.[116] Distinguishing the deaths of transient "strangers" from the city's overall mortality rate also would provide a more accurate assessment of the hazards faced by eighteenth-century immigrants. The 253 Palatines who were buried in Philadelphia in 1754 are usually included in the estimates of trans-Atlantic mortality; to list them again as victims of Philadelphia's urban environment is to count them twice. The true significance of these 253 deaths emerges when they are analyzed within the context of the more than 6,100 immigrants who landed in Philadelphia in 1754 rather than as a proportion of the city's resident population.[117]

[114] Jan de Vries, "Population and Economy of the Preindustrial Netherlands," *Journal of Interdisciplinary History*, 15 (1985), 667–71; Vinovskis, "Mortality Rates," 189, 196; B. G. Smith, "Death and Life," 887–88. Eli F. Heckscher has also discovered little correlation between population density and crude death rates in early nineteenth-century Swedish cities and towns, "Swedish Population Trends before the Industrial Revolution," *Economic History Review*, 2d ser., 2 (1950), 278.

[115] B. G. Smith, "Death and Life," 871, 873n. Although Smith states that "Perhaps the best estimate ... although admittedly a crude one, is that about one-half of the Strangers' Ground burials, or approximately thirteen per cent of the city's total burials, were accounted for by the deaths of immigrants." He uses total burials divided by Philadelphia's estimated *resident* population to calculate the city's CDR. Ibid., 864–67, 871, 873 (quote). Smith also notes in "*Lower Sort*," 48, n29, that "the death of one hundred immigrants inflated the city's death rate by eight per thousand in 1750."

[116] Smith's figures ("Death and Life," 868) give the following distribution of Philadelphia's deaths/burials: Strangers' Ground: 34 per cent (1738–1744), 29 per cent (1746–1760), 23 per cent (1761–1775); and Swedish Ground: 4 per cent (1738–1744), 3 per cent (1746–1760), 2 per cent (1761–1775). Benjamin Franklin suggests that new immigrants may have been interred in significant numbers in other Philadelphia cemeteries as well, when he reported, in *Poor Richard Improved, 1750*, that "No Account of Burials in the Swedish Ground, was taken in the Year 1743 and those Germans buried in the new Dutch Burying Ground, are numbered among the Strangers, who were chiefly Palatines."

[117] Susan E. Klepp, "*The Swift Progress of Population*": A Documentary and Bibliographic Study of Philadelphia's Growth, 1642–1859 (Philadelphia: American Philosophical Society, 1991), 45–53, 60–83; Wokeck, "Tide of Alien Tongues," 111–11a, 267–67a.

A comparison of the vital rates of eighteenth-century *ports* does not support the description of urban America as a death trap. Crude death rates for the port of London have been variously estimated at 41.4 to 45.5 for 1700–1724, 45.2 to 51.8 for 1725–1749, and 36.3 to 39.9 for 1750–1774; in Stockholm, Sweden, the average death rate was 48.4 per thousand in 1721–1750 and 47.1 for 1751–1800; the Finnish port of Helsinki experienced a CDR of 38 between 1749 and 1773.[118] A similar periodization of colonial mortality data suggests that life in some eighteenth-century American cities could indeed be more hazardous than in European ports. Charleston, South Carolina, at least between 1722 and 1732, was deadlier than London and Stockholm, as the white population (both resident and transient) of that subtropical city experienced an estimated CDR of 52 to 60. On the other hand, figures from the northern port of Boston, Massachusetts, which include all races, generate consistently lower CDRs for all periods of the eighteenth century: 39.2 for 1701–1725; 38.0 for 1726–1750; 34.4 for 1751–1774.[119] Philadelphia data produce less clear-cut conclusions. For most years in the first half of the eighteenth century Philadelphia's death rates were lower than London's. In the 1750s and 1760s the situation was apparently reversed as both white and black Philadelphians died at higher rates than the inhabitants of London and Helsinki. However, in the decades that followed, Philadelphia's overall death rates again fell below those estimated for the ports of London, Stockholm, and Helsinki.[120]

A comparison of the infant mortality rates for American and European port cities suggests that, despite the ambiguous evidence of Philadelphia's CDR, its eighteenth-century residents did indeed experience a higher quality of life than their European counterparts. According to a study by Susan Klepp, the IMR for children born to Philadelphia's Euro-Americans dropped from 253 at the beginning of the eighteenth century to an average of 210 at mid-century. During the same time period, the annual IMR calculated for London ranged from 383 per thousand in 1700–1724 to 334 in the 1760s, and Helsinki's IMR for 1749–1773 was an estimated 341.7.[121]

[118] M. Dorothy George, *London Life in the Eighteenth Century*, 1st publ. 1925, 2d ed. (London: Kegan Paul, Trench, Trubner, 1930), 25; L. D. Schwarz, *London in the Age of Industrialisation: Entrepreneurs, Labour Force and Living Conditions, 1700–1850* (Cambridge: Cambridge University Press, 1992), 131; Oiva Turpeinen, "Infectious Diseases and Regional Differences in Finnish Death Rates, 1749–1773," *Population Studies*, 32 (1978), 536.

[119] Coclanis, "Death in Early Charleston," 288–89; Blake, *Public Health in Boston*, 247–49.

[120] London's CDR ranged from 45.2 to 51.8 per thousand in 1725–1749. Between 1750 and 1774, London and Helsinki CDRs dropped below 40 (36.3 to 39.9 for London; 38.0 for Helsinki), and in Philadelphia that decline occurred later, as the city's CDR fell to 38 in the 1770s and 30 in the 1780s. Schwarz, *London in the Age of Industrialisation*, 131; Turpeinen, "Infectious Diseases," 526; B. G. Smith, "Death and Life," 888, and "Lower Sort," 206; Klepp, *Philadelphia in Transition*, 336; Heckscher, "Swedish Population Trends," 276.

[121] Susan E. Klepp, "Fragmented Knowledge: Questions in Regional Demographic History," American Philosophical Society, *Proceedings*, 133 (1989), 230–31; John Landers and Anastasia Mouzas, "Burial Seasonality and the Causes of Death in London, 1670–1819," *Population Studies*, 42 (1988), 65, n.22; John Landers, "Mortality and Metropolis: The Case of London, 1675–1825," *Population Studies*, 41 (1987), 66; Turpeinen, "Infectious Diseases," 525. So far, no one has been able to calculate the infant mortality rate of Philadelphia's African-American population.

The family reconstitution studies of eighteenth-century Quakers living in both London and Philadelphia permit a direct comparison of the same urban population in the Old and New World. In the first half of the eighteenth century Philadelphia's Quakers could expect to live from 6 to 20 years longer than their coreligionists in London and were far more likely to see their children survive infancy. During the first two-thirds of the eighteenth century the infant mortality rate for Quaker children born in Philadelphia declined from 164 to 131 per 1,000 live births; dramatically lower than the IMR for infants born to Quakers living in London, which ranged from 342 for those born between 1700 and 1724 to 327 for 1750–1774.[122]

The advantages enjoyed by Europeans who survived the voyage and seasoning process are even more apparent in the rural areas of British North America. Although most European immigrants disembarked in colonial port cities, few remained as permanent residents. On the eve of the American Revolution, less than 5 per cent of the entire population resided in towns containing more than 8,000 people.[123] Immigrants who settled in rural regions in the first half of the eighteenth century could expect large numbers of their offspring to survive. In the New England villages of Andover, Ipswich, and Salem[124] the number of infants dying before their first birthday ranged from 112 to 156 per thousand. The IMR of children born in Lancaster county, Pennsylvania, to couples married prior to 1741 was 147.5; in Charles Parish, Virginia, located in what "must have been one of the unhealthiest areas in the colonial Chesapeake," the annual infant death rate in 1700–1734 averaged 184 for males and 181 for females.[125] All of these American infant death rates compare favorably with those of similar rural populations in the Old World, such as the English village of Coylton (IMR of 162–203, 1700–1749); rural parishes in North Shropshire (IMR of 141–194, 1701–1750), the French village of Crulai (IMR of 210–230, 1690–1750); the French parish of Levignac-sur-Save (IMR of 210, 1720–1790); "the rural population of the Paris region" (IMR of 278 for the cohort born 1740–1749); and 51 rural parishes of Finland, 1749–1773 (average IMR, 197, range of 89 to 545).[126] Children born on the mainland of British North America also experienced lower

[122] Schwarz, *London in the Age of Industrialisation*, 138, table 5.9; Robert V. Wells, "The Population of England's Colonies in America: Old English or New Americans?," *Population Studies*, 46 (1992), 94, table 3; Landers, "Mortality and Metropolis," 64; Klepp, "Fragmented Knowledge," 230.

[123] Nash, *Urban Crucible*, 3, 103; Wells, "Population of England's Colonies," 100; Wokeck, "Tide of Alien Tongues," 111, 267; B. G. Smith "Death and Life," 871. More than 91,000 German and Irish immigrants landed in Philadelphia between 1726 and 1775. During that period the city's permanent population increased from 5,300 (in 1722) to 32,000 (in 1775).

[124] Both Salem and Ipswich were ports.

[125] Vinovskis, "Mortality Rates," 198–200; Rodger C. Henderson, *Community Development and the Revolutionary Transition in Eighteenth-Century Lancaster County, Pennsylvania* (New York: Garland, 1989), 87, 90; D. B. Smith, "Mortality and Family in the Colonial Chesapeake," 405 (quote), 413.

[126] E. A. Wrigley, "Mortality in Pre-Industrial England: The Examples of Colyton, Devon, over Three Centuries," *Daedalus*, 97 (1968), 546–80; R. E. Jones, "Infant Mortality in Rural North Shropshire, 1561–1810," *Population Studies*, 30 (1976), 313; Louis Henry, "The Population of France in the Eighteenth Century," trans.

infant death rates than those in French colonies. In French Guyana, the annual death rate for infants born to European colonists between 1700 and 1736 was 267 per thousand, wheres the IMR for French Canadian children in the "first half of the eighteenth century" has been estimated at 246.[127]

Europeans who settled in the rural regions of British North America could also expect their emigration to increase the life expectancy of their children. In the first half of the eighteenth century, the life expectancy at birth for the offspring of married couples in Lancaster county, Pennsylvania, was an estimated 39.4 years. During the same period, the residents of fourteen eighteenth-century German villages, with populations ranging from a few hundred to almost 2,000, had an average life expectancy at birth of 35.5 years; life expectancies in the Dutch town of Eindhoven and five surrounding "entirely agrarian" villages have been calculated as 35 years in 1740, falling to 22 years in 1750 and then rebounding to 36 years in the 1760s.[128] Family reconstitutions of more than a thousand Schwenkfelders who resided in Pennsylvania in during the eighteenth century show that, with a life expectancy at birth of 45.2 years, the children of these German immigrants not only outlasted, by about a decade, rural villagers in Germany, but also lived approximately six years longer than the general population of Lancaster county.[129]

Opportunity

As Gottlieb Mittelberger wrote in his *Journey to Pennsylvania,*

> [T]hings are no better in Pennsylvania. However hard one may have had to work in his native land, conditions are bound to be equally tough or even tougher in the new country . . . the emigrant . . . must spend approximately two hundred florins which no one will refund to him. If he has that much money, he loses it; if he does not have

---

Peter Jimack, in Glass and Eversley, eds., *Population in History*, 434–48; Pierre Goubert, "Legitimate Fertility and Infant Mortality in France during the Eighteenth Century: A Comparison," trans. Marlis Fette, in D. V. Glass and Roger Revelle, eds., *Population and Social Change* (London: Edward Arnold, 1972), 321–30; Turpeinen, "Infectious Diseases," 525. The findings of pre-1981 studies of European infant mortality rates are conveniently summarized in Michael W. Flinn, *The European Demographic System, 1500–1820* (Baltimore: Johns Hopkins University Press, 1981), 130–37.

[127] Louis Henry and Jean Hurault, "Mortalité de la population européenne de Guyane française au début du XVIIIe siècle," *Population*, 34 (1979), 1095; Jacques Henripin and Yves Péron, "The Demographic Transition of the Province of Quebec," in Glass and Revelle, eds., *Population and Social Change*, 225. The infant mortality rate for children born to Sephardi Jews in the Dutch colony of Surinam, 1789–1799, was 225.7. Robert Cohen, *Jews in Another Environment: Surinam in the Second Half of the Eighteenth Century* (Leiden, The Netherlands: E. J. Brill, 1991), 58.

[128] Henderson, *Community Development*, 99–100; John E. Knodel, *Demographic Behavior in the Past: A Study of Fourteen German Village Populations in the Eighteenth and Nineteenth Centuries* (Cambridge: Cambridge University Press, 1988), 25–32, 45, 59; Henk Van Dijk, "Demographic Aspects of Urbanization during the Nineteenth Century," in Richard Lawton and Robert Lee, *Urban Population Development in Western Europe from the Late-Eighteenth to the Early-Twentieth Century* (Liverpool: Liverpool University Press, 1989), 27–50.

[129] Henderson, *Community Development*, 97.

it, he must work off his debt as a slave or as a miserable servant. So let people stay in their own and earn their keep honestly for themselves and their families.[130]

Many recruiters and colonial publicists exaggerated the ease with which aliens could share in the rich abundance of America and the opportunities for the regeneration of the wastrels, scoundrels, and downtrodden masses of the Old World. The writings of misled and disappointed immigrants have led some modern researchers to focus on immigrant exploitation, abuse, and death to debunk filiopietistic myths about America's past. Yet, in the aggregate, most studies suggest that promises of economic betterment were not all hyperbole and that during the eighteenth century the British colonies did indeed serve as a regenerative haven and a land of opportunity for European immigrants and their progeny.

Most indices developed by modern research suggest that rising inequality decreased an immigrant's economic opportunity during the eighteenth century. Colonial tax assessments and probate records have been used to demonstrate an ever-increasing concentration of property into the hands of a few. These records apparently show that by the 1770s America's port towns had evolved into highly stratified societies in which the top 10 per cent of the property owners controlled up to 70 per cent of the city's resources. Similar records for rural counties seem to chronicle the same pattern of increasing stratification, at a somewhat slower pace, during the course of the eighteenth century. As land and resources along the Eastern Seaboard became monopolized by a few large landholders, many free immigrants and recently freed servants were forced to choose between tenancy and the ownership of undeveloped acreage on the often dangerous frontier.[131] However, the level of inequality that existed in the thirteen colonies and the extent to which it hampered the economic betterment of eighteenth-century immigrants are both open to question.

From the earliest settlements, American colonists expected, and promoted, the unequal distribution of property and power. Believing that "in all times some must be rich, some poore, some highe and eminent in power and dignitie; others meane and in subjeccion," most settlers attempted to replicate the social struc-

---

[130]Mittelberger, *Journey to Pennsylvania*, 20–21.

[131]On concentration of property, see Nash, *Urban Crucible*, 396; James T. Lemon, *The Best Poor Man's Country: A Geographical Study of Early Southeastern Pennsylvania* (Baltimore: Johns Hopkins University Press, 1972), 11; and Jackson Turner Main, *The Social Structure of Revolutionary America* (Princeton: Princeton University Press, 1965). On tenancy and frontier issues, see Roland Berthoff and John M. Murrin, "Feudalism, Communalism, and the Yeoman Freeholder: The American Revolution Considered as a Social Accident," in Stephen G. Kurtz and James H. Hutson, eds. *Essays on the American Revolution* (Chapel Hill: University of North Carolina Press, 1973), 256–88; Sung Bok Kim; *Landlord and Tenant in Colonial New York Manorial Society, 1664–1775* (Chapel Hill: University of North Carolina Press, 1978); Gregory A. Stiverson, *Poverty in a Land of Plenty: Tenancy in Eighteenth-Century Maryland* (Baltimore: Johns Hopkins University Press, 1977); Lucy Simler, "Tenancy in Colonial Pennsylvania: The Case of Chester County," *William and Mary Quarterly*, 3d. ser., 43 (1986), 542–69.

tures they had left behind. When colonies and towns were established, ministers, gentlemen, and other men of stature and wealth received the largest land grants. This allocation of wealth according to status was seen as essential to buttress the authority of community leaders and to maintain order in the wilderness.[132] Although designated leaders frequently used their advantages to increase the social distance between themselves and those "meane and in subjeccion," the gulf between the rich and the poor that emerged in colonial America is not an accurate index of the degree of exploitation and immiseration experienced by the lower orders of society.

Colonial inequality cannot be denied, but it is difficult to measure. Tax assessments that have been used to document stratification tell more about who owned real estate than the actual distribution of wealth. During the eighteenth century, taxes fell most heavily on colonists who owned real estate, animals, servants, and slaves; those lacking such capital assets usually paid only a head tax. Studies that label as "poor" any inhabitant who did not appear on an assessment list or who paid only a poll tax exaggerate the incidence of poverty. Those missing from tax rolls include not only the destitute, but also renters and productive workers who lived as "inmates" in the homes of property owners. By law, heads of families in eighteenth-century Pennsylvania were responsible for paying the taxes of those who lived and worked in their households. Although they are often excluded from assessment lists, these "inmates" were taxpayers, as the amount paid by the householder was deducted from their wages.[133] The often meager capital assets of inmates and renters further minimized their perceived economic status. Unassessed workers did indeed tend to be poorer and less rooted in the community than artisans who had amassed taxable property, but there is no precise correlation between income and real wealth. A study by Sharon Salinger and Charles Wetherell has uncovered many instances where Philadelphia artisans owning little or no taxable property "had sufficient income to . . . pay rents that far exceeded the median rent in the city."[134]

America tenantry also was far less pervasive and rigid than in the Old World. During the eighteenth century, European land prices rose and economic opportunity declined. As a result, by 1790, 4,400 families owned 75 per cent of the agricultural acreage of England and Wales and 1 per cent of all Frenchmen engrossed a quarter of France's arable land. In England, tenants had very little

[132] John Winthrop, "A Modell of Christian Charity," in Perry Miller and Thomas H. Johnson, eds., *The Puritans: A Sourcebook of Their Writings*, rev. ed., 2 vols. (New York: Harper & Row, 1963), I, 195 (quote); Philip Greven, *Four Generations: Land, Population and Family in Colonial Andover, Massachusetts* (Ithaca: Cornell University Press, 1970), 45–47; Kenneth A. Lockridge, *A New England Town, the First Hundred Years: Dedham, Massachusetts, 1636–1736* (New York: Norton, 1970), 10–12; Berthoff and Murrin, "Feudalism, Communalism, and the Yeoman Freeholder."

[133] Lucy Simler, "The Landless Worker: An Index of Economic and Social Change in Chester County, Pennsylvania, 1750–1820," *Pennsylvania Magazine of History and Biography*, 114 (1990), 171–72.

[134] Sharon V. Salinger and Charles Wetherell, "Wealth and Renting in Prerevolutionary Philadelphia," *Journal of American History*, 71 (1985), 834.

chance of ever becoming landowners.[135] For many eighteenth-century colonists, on the other hand, tenancy was a rung on the ladder leading to landownership, for the tenant himself or his children. "Developmental leases," in which the owners of undeveloped land charged their tenants little or no rent on condition that they make capital improvements to the property, allowed renters to keep a large proportion of the profits of their labor. A tenant's savings could then be used to purchase his own land. As a result of such mechanisms, it has been estimated that up to 70 per cent of all colonial farmers owned the land they worked.[136]

The fact that many colonial tenants never became landowners is not necessarily evidence of poverty or absence of opportunity. Gregory Stiverson's discovery that many proprietary tenants of eighteenth-century Maryland remained leaseholders for generations led him to describe tenancy as "a permanent condition for an ever-increasing number of Maryland householders . . . trapped in what had once been no more than a transitional stage in the progression to freehold status." These tenants, he argued, "could achieve only minimal economic opportunity for themselves" and "could do little to accumulate sufficient capital to provide their children with greater opportunity."[137] Yet, the work of others suggests that many colonial tenants who had the means *chose* not to become freeholders. A study of eighteenth-century Philadelphia provides several examples of wealthholders, some of whom owned rental property of their own, living in leased dwellings. Such men chose to save or invest their capital accumulations in other ways. Colonial tenant-farmers may have made similar decisions.[138]

The work of Roger Ekirch suggests that eighteenth-century America also made good on its reluctant promise to regenerate British convicts. His examination of Chesapeake court records shows that transported felons were far less likely to be accused or convicted of criminal activity than "more respectable" inhabitants. Ironically, Ekirch argues that the low rate of recidivism among convicts in America was largely a product of the *absence* of economic opportunity in the colonies. Although most English felons had been transported for crimes against property, the underdeveloped American economy had not produced the glittering concentrations of urban wealth necessary to support individual thieves

[135] Christopher Clay, "The Price of Freehold Land in the Later Seventeenth and Eighteenth Centuries," *Economic History Review*, 2d ser., 27 (1974), 173–189; J. V. Beckett, "The Decline of the Small Landowner in England and Wales, 1660–1900," in F. M. L. Thompson, ed., *Landowners, Capitalists, and Entrepreneurs: Essays for Sir John Habakkuk* (Oxford: Clarendon, 1994), 89–112; P. K. O'Brien and D. Heath, "English and French Landowners, 1688–1789," in ibid., 23–62.

[136] Hermann Wellenreuther, "A View of the Socio-Economic Structures of England and the British Colonies on the Eve of the American Revolution," in Erich Angermann, Marie-Luise Frings, and Hermann Wellenreuther, eds., *New Wine in Old Skins: A Comparative View of Socio-Political Structures and Values Affecting the American Revolution* (Stuttgart: Ernst Klett Verlag, 1976), 14–40.

[137] Stiverson, *Poverty in a Land of Plenty*, 28–55, quotes on xiii and 55.

[138] Salinger and Wetherell, "Wealth and Renting," 826–40; James Henretta, "The Study of Social Mobility: Ideological Assumptions and Conceptual Bias," *Labor History*, 18 (1977), 165–79.

or a criminal underworld. Without readily available goods to steal and fences to dispose of stolen property, transported grand larcenists were forced to give up their former avocations; convicts who were determined to continue their life of crime tended to return to England. Upon gaining their freedom, reformed convicts joined former servants and free immigrants in their quest for American prosperity.[139]

Fragmentary data and methodological problems plague demographers who attempt to reconstruct vital statistics for the seventeenth and eighteenth centuries on either side of the Atlantic. Despite these problems, available evidence strongly suggests that during the seventeenth century, British North America was indeed more of a death trap than a land of opportunity for many European immigrants. That situation was, however, reversed in the century that followed. The disease climates in subtropical colonies remained relatively lethal to European migrants and their descendants,[140] but mortality, life expectancy, nutritional, and height data all point to the conclusion that during the eighteenth century the promise of America expanded for Europeans as it was increasingly denied to Africans and that most Euro-American populations increased their life chances by residing in America.

In the eighteenth- century acclimated European immigrants and their children ate better and lived longer and healthier lives than their counterparts in the Old World.[141] A comparative study of the heights of various Old and New World populations provides additional evidence of eighteenth-century America as a land of promise for European immigrants. At 68.1 inches, America's "average" native-born revolutionary soldier was nearly three inches taller than the British-born recruits sent to quell the rebellion; more than two inches taller than enlisted men in eighteenth-century Sweden; 1.5 inches taller than the late-eighteenth-century Germans who were trained at the Duke of Wurttemberg's elite academy, the Stuttgart Carlschule; and, on average, more than an inch taller than the eighteenth-century native-born recruits of the Habsburg army. The heights achieved by America's revolutionary soldiers were also "virtually identical" with those of native-born Americans who served in the Civil War and World War II.[142] The native-born white soldiers who served in America's Continental armies were drawn primarily from the less privileged segments of colonial society, transients,

---

[139] Ekirch, *Bound for America*, chap. 6, quote on 176–77. The apparent low rate of recidivism may, however, have been a function of the tendency of runaway convicts and those who had served out their terms to erase their criminal stigma by migration.

[140] Peter A. Coclanis, *The Shadow of a Dream: Economic Life and Death in the South Carolina Low Country, 1670–1920* (New York: Oxford University Press, 1989), 42–45, 166–74, and "Death in Early Charleston," 280–91; Richard Harrison Shryock, *Medicine in America: Historical Essays* (Baltimore: Johns Hopkins University Press, 1966), 132.

[141] According to Robert Fogel, "The evidence both on stature and on food allotments suggests that Americans achieved an average level of meat consumption by the middle of the eighteenth century that was not achieved in Europe until well into the twentieth century," Fogel, "Secular Changes," 464.

[142] Ibid., 463; Roderick Floud, Kenneth Wachter, and Annabel Gregory, *Height, Health, and History: Nutritional Status in the United Kingdom, 1750–1980* (Cambridge: Cambridge University Press, 1990), table 4.1,

landless laborers, and sons of families who owned little or no taxable property. Since European troops were drawn from similarly disadvantaged social groups, the height differential between Old and New World soldiers is evidence that America's poorest whites were not denied access to the bounty of America and were less exploited than their trans-Atlantic cousins.[143]

The work of Alice Hanson Jones corroborates these findings. Her meticulous study of American probate records shows that, by the 1770s, ordinary, white colonists enjoyed a higher standard of living than their counterparts in Europe and Great Britain. European immigrants who survived seasoning and servants who had served out their time thus became part of the best "middling man's" country.[144] Jones's data also show a strong correlation between opportunity for European immigrants and the colonial slave labor system. The richest colonists in the eighteenth century were southern plantation owners who controlled the labor of large numbers of African slaves. In 1774 the southern colonies, with 47 per cent of the total population and 36 per cent of the free population, possessed 55.2 per cent of the privately owned physical wealth of the thirteen colonies.[145] Chattel slavery obviated the need to share America's profits with enslaved workers; laws that discriminated against free blacks and limited their ability to compete in the marketplace gave further advantages to white entrepreneurs, employers, and workers.

European immigrants also benefited in less obvious ways from American slavery. During the eighteenth century, attempts to limit the spread of African slavery promoted and facilitated the immigration of alternative workers, whether indentured servants, redemptioners, convicted felons, or oppressed Protestants. Although American colonists, in general, preferred prosperous and industrious settlers, their perceived need for white workers to control and dilute the dangers of slavery led them to subsidize the transportation of Europe's "downtrodden masses" through the indenture system as well as promises of free land, cash payments, and tax breaks. Slavery in the Chesapeake even underwrote the regeneration of transported convicts.

During the eighteenth century the interaction of English and colonial needs, prejudices, principles, and goals transformed the British colonies on the conti-

---

148; Lars G. Sandberg and Richard H. Steckel, "Heights and Economic History: The Swedish Case," *Annals of Human Biology*, 14 (1987), 102–6; John Komlos et al., "The Growth of Boys in the Stuttgart Carlschule, 1771–1793," *Annals of Human Biology*, 19 (1992), 139–42; John Komlos, *Nutrition and Economic Development in the Eighteenth-Century Habsburg Monarchy: An Anthropometric History* (Princeton: Princeton University Press, 1989), 55–59, 228–36.

[143] Komlos, *Nutrition*, 54, 226–28; Floud, Wachter, and Gregory, *Height, Health, and History*; Lars G. Sandberg and Richard H. Steckel, "Soldier, Soldier, What Made You Grow So Tall?: A Study of Height, Health, and Nutrition in Sweden, 1720–1881," *Economics and History*, 23 (1980), 93–95.

[144] Alice Hanson Jones, *Wealth of a Nation to Be: The American Colonies on the Eve of the Revolution* (New York: Columbia University Press, 1980), esp. chap. 9.

[145] Ibid., 50–53.

nent of North America into a complex and often ambiguous asylum. The image of the British colonies in North America that reached prospective immigrants was distorted. Promotional literature overlooked the reluctance of the colonists to serve as a refuge for depraved, destitute, and Catholic Europeans. Immigrant recruiters, whether land speculators, ship captains, colonial assemblies, proprietors, or the English government glossed over the continuation of Old World intolerance, painted an idyllic portrait of America as a regenerative haven for all victims of Old World oppression, and idealized the benefits bestowed by the English Constitution in its colonial setting. Eighteenth-century critics responded in kind, pointing out, and exaggerating, the deficiencies of England's colonial asylum and the character flaws of the American "race of convicts" whose experiences as "drivers of slaves" led them to exploit and abuse Europeans who sought refuge, regeneration, and economic opportunity in America.

Although both of these portraits of eighteenth-century America were drawn by biased propagandists, each contains elements of truth. Many colonists were indeed descendants of the 50,000 convicts transported to America; a large proportion enslaved and exploited Africans and Native Americans alike; and some abused and defrauded hapless immigrants and servants. Yet, none of this prevented the colonies from serving as a refuge and land of opportunity for oppressed Europeans. Ironically, slavery was a crucial component of the American refuge. Colonists who lacked the authority to end slavery or limit the slave trade recruited and subsidized the immigration of Europe's "downtrodden masses" to protect themselves from their servile work force, reluctantly accepting even transported convicts as a necessary leaven. Once in America, immigrants continued to profit from the labor of slaves in ways that allowed Euro-Americans and their children to live longer and healthier lives and enjoy a greater measure of wealth than those who had remained in the Old World. The interaction of colonial and English imperatives, and the unexpected consequences they generated, left Americans with a cruel legacy. The Anglo-American societies that emerged on the coast of North America did indeed offer Europeans more economic opportunity and freedom than could be found in the Old World. But the promise of America was built, to a significant extent, on African slavery.

4   Immigration and
the American Revolution

Eɴɢʟᴀɴᴅ's ʀᴇsᴏᴜɴᴅɪɴɢ ᴛʀɪᴜᴍᴘʜ in the Seven Years' War was jubilantly celebrated by her colonists. With France now banished from the mainland, Anglo-Americans would be free to expand into areas previously blocked off by French soldiers and their Indian allies. But colonial dreams were quickly shattered in the decade that followed as English officials attempted to reorganize and rationalize their empire. The imperial reforms that ensued included England's unilateral decision to alter the immigration, naturalization, and land policies that had defined eighteenth-century America as a land of liberty, opportunity, and regeneration.

Although the issues that would trigger the American Revolution were primarily political, England's new demographic policies helped to convince the colonists of the existence of a deeply rooted conspiracy to destroy the rights guaranteed to them by the British constitution. As political tensions intensified, Americans came to believe that the thirteen colonies were the sole repository of English freedom, the asylum where the flame of liberty had to be maintained as it was being extinguished by tyrants in the mother country. As war approached, colonial rebels expanded their mission and the promise of America. The failure of British subjects to rally to their aid prompted Americans to invite all men who loved freedom to join their Glorious Cause. As Europeans of all nationalities responded, for a variety of reasons, American patriots increased their commitment from maintaining the rights of Englishmen to preserving liberty on behalf of "all mankind."

The war years punctured many American illusions. The activities of loyalists, Old World subjects, and recent immigrants led American patriots to question the ability of foreigners to maintain republican liberty and produced restrictions on the rights of men who threatened to destroy or pervert revolutionary ideals. Although American wariness of the political principles of foreigners—who now included British subjects—continued, the restrictive policies produced by the exigencies of war were repealed when peace returned. At war's end, republican America remained committed to its enlarged role as an asylum for liberty and those oppressed by Old World tyranny.

Reevaluating the Empire

In the middle of the eighteenth century there were signs that England's imperial policies needed to be revised. Even though England always had critics who found fault with various aspects of its colonial system, the 1750s produced an increasing number, including those who argued that the demographic costs incurred by England outweighed the benefits of its American possessions. The doubts expressed by a small group of Englishmen about the efficacy of the British colonial system gained widespread support in the decade following the Seven Years' War, as England tried to bring order to its newly expanded empire and was opposed by the increasingly strident American colonists.

By the middle of the eighteenth century, England's long contest with France and continual quest for new overseas possessions had led many Englishmen to question the value of the colonial empire. In 1755 Josiah Tucker, who had earlier expounded on the benefits derived from the American colonies, worried about ways to increase England's population and deplored the "great and continual [demographic] Drains upon us" by "our numerous colonies." Parliamentary debate on the ill-fated Census Bill of 1753 displayed a similar propensity by the English government to reevaluate the country's emigration and colonization policies. Supporters of the census argued that it would produce the statistics necessary for legislators to decide "when to encourage and when to discourage or restrain the people of this island, or of some particular parts of it, from going to settle in our American colonies," and when to forego establishing new colonies except "by means of foreign Protestants, and such of our own people as had never been accustomed to any sort of labour." By 1761 the Duke of Bedford was warning William Pitt that "if we retain the greatest part of our conquests out of Europe we shall be in danger of over-colonizing and undoing ourselves by them as the Spaniards have done." The following year, the author of *Arguments against a Spanish War* contended that "we have . . . more territory than we can people."[1]

At the end of the Seven Years' War, England's perennial concern with the demographic consequences of emigration was compounded by a fear of American population growth. Part of the apprehension of America's rising

[1] Klaus E. Knorr, *British Colonial Theories, 1570–1850*, 1st publ. 1944 (London: Frank Cass, 1963), 105–25, quotes on 119, 109n, 107; Bernard Bailyn, *Voyagers to the West: A Passage in the Peopling of America on the Eve of the Revolution* (New York: Knopf, 1986), 29–36; William Cobbett and John Wright, eds., *Parliamentary History of England, from the Earliest Period to the Year 1803*, 36 vols. (London: T. C. Hansard, 1806–1820), XIV, 1317–65, quotes on 1350, 1351.

strength was economic—the fear that the colonies would replace their imports from England with home manufactures. Malachy Postlethwayt had expressed this concern twenty years earlier when, in a tract in support of the African Company, he opposed "furnishing the colonies with white labor either from the mother country or the Continent on the ground that such emigration would serve to make the colonies manufacturing rivals of England. Instead, he favored slave importations as tending to keep the colonies agricultural." In the mid-1760s the London press published the writings of "Publicola" who reasoned, as had Postlethwayt, that "it cannot be for our Interest to aid their Population . . . [for this] will be hastening them into the very State of Population which will be most dangerous to ourselves, that of peopling large Towns and Cities, which must introduce all Kinds of Manufacturing." In 1768 the English government heard this logic repeated in the reports of General Thomas Gage, the Commander-in-Chief of the British Army in North America. According to Gage, "The Emigrations from Great Britain and Ireland and the Importation of Germans every year from Holland, contribute to the constant increase of Mechanicks and Manufacturers" in Pennsylvania. He recommended that the Ministry discontinue the practice of discharging in America, any British soldier "who has any Trade" as, "Instead of clearing uncultivated Lands, which it was expected they would do, they have for the most part crowded into the Towns to work at Trades, and help to Supply the Inhabitants with Necessarys, which should be imported from the Mother Country."[2]

American expansion into the backcountry was also seen as inimical to England's interest. By settling far from the coast, the colonists severed themselves from the English trade network that they were supposed to serve. Such outposts also were seen as jeopardizing world peace. According to General Gage, Great Britain was "drawn into the War of 1755" when the colonists "ill treated the Savages in various ways," and that war, "which began on the frontiers of Pensilvania and Virginia . . . spread itself over the Globe." The Proclamation of 1763 was designed to keep this situation from recurring, as the English government tried to create a barrier between Indians and whites by closing the trans-Appalachian West to settlement.[3]

The angry reaction of the American colonists to the closing off of their frontier and to the other attempts of the British government to restructure their empire escalated English concern over the increasing American population. The furor over the Stamp Act led "Publicola" and other English writers to argue that, because England would never "be able to controul, by Force, Millions of Men,

[2] Richard B. Morris, *Government and Labor in Early America* (New York: Columbia University Press, 1946), 23 (Postlethwayt quote); James H. Cassedy, *Demography in Early America: Beginnings of the Statistical Mind, 1600–1800* (Cambridge: Harvard University Press, 1969), 183 ("Publicola"); Gage to Shelburne, Jan. 23, 1768, *The Correspondence of General Thomas Gage*, ed. Clarence Edwin Carter, 2 vols. (New Haven: Yale University Press, 1931–1933), I, 160–61 (quote); Gage to Barrington, Dec. 2, 1772, in ibid., II, 627.

[3] Gage to Barrington, Mar. 10, 1768, in ibid., II, 449.

whose Hearts glow with the Flame of Liberty . . . [i]t should . . . be our Policy to let them [the American colonies] go on increasing from their own Numbers, without exterior Aids therein, which we ought rather to obstruct than encourage; while by all Means we should endeavour to increase our Stock of People at home." Again, reports from English officials in the colonies echoed and supported the arguments in London's press. General Gage believed that "It would be well, if the Emigrations from Great Britain, Ireland, and Holland, where the Germans embark for America, were prevented: and our new Settlements should be peopled from the old ones, which would be a means to thin them, and put it less in their power to do Mischief."[4]

In this context, the dramatic surge of emigration from the British Isles in the 1770s was doubly alarming, as it threatened not only the domestic stability of the British Isles, but also the colonial empire itself. It seemed especially dangerous to allow the emigration of the Scots, whose military prowess England might need and certainly wished to deny to rebellious colonists. Indeed, since the confidence in the Americans in their ability to fight English "oppression" grew along with their population, England came to oppose all emigration to its American colonies. These were the circumstances that led to the dramatic changes in English immigration policy in the decade preceding the American Revolution.

The end of the Seven Years' War forced the English government to respond to critics of its imperial policy. William Pitt was driven out of office soon after the accession of George III by a nation and king tired of "this bloody and expensive war." The terms of the 1763 Treaty of Paris did little to mollify Pitt's critics and the English people, who now faced an unprecedented national debt. France's cession of her American possessions to England seemed, to many, a continuing burden rather than a reward. The removal of the Bourbon threat would, by lessening the colonists' dependence on the mother country, merely hasten the Americans' inevitable quest for independence. The cost of organizing the newly conquered regions of North America could hardly be recompensed by the primitive economies of Canada and the Floridas, without vast infusions of money and people from England. And such an investment of English resources in the frozen wastes of Canada, the "pestiferous seacoasts" of the South, "the sunken lagunes of *East-Florida*, and the barren sands of *Mobile* and *Pensacola*" seemed unjustifiable.[5]

[4] Cassedy, *Demography in Early America*, 182 ("Publicola"); Fred Junkin Hinkhouse, *The Preliminaries of the American Revolution as Seen in the English Press, 1763–1775* (New York: Columbia University Press, 1926), 104–8; Gage to Dartmouth, Sept. 20, 1775, *Correspondence of General Thomas Gage*, I, 414–15 (quote).

[5] Howard H. Peckham, *The Colonial Wars, 1689–1762* (Chicago: University of Chicago Press, 1964), chap. 10; Hinkhouse, *Preliminaries of the American Revolution*, 39–42, 104–5; W. A. Speck, *Stability and Strife: England, 1714–1760* (Cambridge: Harvard University Press, 1979), 273 (quote); John Mitchell, *The Present State of Great Britain and North America with Regard to Agriculture, Population, Trade and Manufactures, Impartially Considered*, 1st publ. 1767 (New York: Research Reprints, 1970), quotes on 105.

Men such as Josiah Tucker could see no reason for the periodic decimation of the English population through war, merely to wrest a few West Indian islands from France that would probably not be "worth the cost of governing them." As trade naturally flowed to nations with the best and cheapest manufacturers, and "conquering nations could not manufacture cheaply," it seemed a more enlightened policy to cultivate friendship with populous countries, such as France. According to Tucker, it made no sense to impoverish those you hoped would be customers and to conquer colonies that could not be compelled "to trade with the parent state to any great degree beyond what their own interest would prompt them to," and whose nature it was "to aspire after independence, and to set up for themselves as soon as ever they find that they are able to subsist without being beholden to the mother country."[6]

The reorganization of the British Empire in the 1760s was thus imperative. Governments had to be established in the newly acquired territories in a way that would not increase the English national debt. Anti-imperialists in England had to be silenced by converting the American colonies from an expensive, but prestigious, imperial appendage into an integrated component of English prosperity. British officials involved in the administration of the American colonies who had long advocated reforms to strengthen the empire seized the opportunity to implement their ideas. However, the instability of English politics that produced seven ministries in a single decade wreaked havoc with imperial reform. As men with conflicting, and often ill-defined, imperial visions succeeded each other as designers of the new British colonial system, directives spewed forth from London that exacerbated, rather than relieved, the pressure on the tacit compromises that held the empire together.[7]

Subverting the American Asylum

At the end of the Seven Years' War England began withdrawing the supports that had been used to promote immigration to its New World colonies—policies that had defined British North America as a refuge and land of opportunity. In 1767 the British Privy Council disallowed a Georgia statute that offered free transportation to all Protestants who chose to emigrate from the British Isles. A North Carolina Act of 1771 offering special inducements to Scottish immigrants

---

[6] *Josiah Tucker: A Selection from His Economic and Political Writings*, ed. Robert Livingston Schuyler (New York: Columbia University Press, 1931), 30–39, quotes on 30, 34, 35; Dora Mae Clark, *British Opinion and the American Revolution* (New Haven: Yale University Press, 1930), 278–79; Mario Rodriguez, "The Impact of the American Revolution on the Spanish- and Portuguese-Speaking World," in Library of Congress Symposia on the American Revolution, *The Impact of the American Revolution Abroad* (Washington, D.C.: Library of Congress, 1976), 101.

[7] Bernard Bailyn, "1776: A Year of Challenge—A World Transformed," *Journal of Law and Economics*, 19 (1976), 456–66.

and a land grant for Highlanders from the Isle of Skye were vetoed in England. In 1773 customs officials in England and Scotland were ordered to report the numbers and motives of those sailing from Great Britain to determine a way to end the emigration fever that was sweeping the British Isles. In 1773 instructions were issued to the governors of royal colonies prohibiting all land grants until further notice on the recommendation of the Commissioners of Trade and Plantations. These orders were the result of the Commissioners' belief that such grants encouraged "the emigration of His Majesty's European subjects . . . [which] has for some time past had so great weight with this Board that it has induced us to deny our concurrence to many proposals of grants of land even in those parts of the continent of America where in all other respects we are of opinion that it consists with the true policy of this kingdom to encourage settlements." In February 1774 the ban on land grants was made final. From now on all crown land was to be sold, and then only in small lots and not to land speculators.[8]

The Commissioners' next step was to interdict colonial naturalization. In December 1773 each royal governor was instructed "that you do not upon any pretence whatsoever give your assent to any Bill or Bills that may have been or shall hereafter be passed by the Council and Assembly of the Province under your Government for the naturalization of Aliens . . . nor for establishing a Title in any Person to Lands, Tenements & real estates in our said Province originally granted to, or purchased by Aliens antecedent to Naturalization." The tendency of this measure to inhibit immigration was clearly recognized by British policymakers. Any doubts they might have had would have been removed by the report sent from New York to the Earl of Dartmouth. According to Lieutenant Governor Colden, "His Majestys Instruction, prohibiting his Governors from passing a naturalization Bill, opperates very partially to the prejudice of this Colony surrounded as we are by charter Governments where such Instructions have no effect. Many usefull Foreigners are by this means driven out of this Province where they cannot acquire landed property, and settle in the Charter Governments, where they meet with the greatest encouragement." England's reversal of colonial immigration policy was completed in 1776 when Parliament repealed its 1717 decision to transport convicts to the American colonies. Parliament, claiming that "the transportation of convicts to his Majesty's colonies and plantations in America . . . is found to be attended with various inconveniences, particularly by depriving this kingdom of many subjects whose labour might be useful to the community, and who, by proper care and correction, might be reclaimed from their evil course" passed "An Act to authorize . . . the punishment by hard labour

---

[8]Bernard Bailyn, *The Peopling of British North America: An Introduction* (New York: Knopf, 1986), 39; Bailyn, *Voyagers*, 55–56, 67–70; Commissioners for Trade and Plantations to the Committee of the Privy Council for Plantation Affairs, Apr. 29, 1772, K. G. Davies, *Documents of the American Revolution, 1770–1783*, 21 vols. (Dublin: Irish University Press, 1972–1981), V, 89.

of offenders who, for certain crimes, are or shall become liable to be transported to any of his Majesty's colonies and plantations."[9]

When the American colonists declared their independence from England, the "unnatural" acts of their king and parent country in trying to stunt their demographic growth were prominent on the list of grievances that had driven the colonists "to dissolve the political bands which have connected them with another." The Declaration of Independence indicted George III for trying, inter alia, "to prevent the population of these states; for that purpose obstructing the laws for naturalization of foreigners, refusing to pass others to encourage their immigration thither, & raising the conditions of new appropriations of land.[10] Although the outbreak of hostilities in the aftermath of the Coercive Acts was obviously the reason for Parliament's claim that England should not be deprived of the "useful labour" of her convicts, the confrontations between Americans and the English government in the 1760s and early 1770s did not force the reversal of England's previous immigrant recruitment policies. Rather, the increasing hostility between England and its colonies confirmed and strengthened a continuing uneasiness in the government over the methods adopted by England to people its American lands.

Demographic developments in the 1760s made the English government especially obtuse to colonial sensibilities. An unprecedented surge of emigration from Great Britain at the end of the Seven Years' War panicked English officials and led to their abrogation of the colonial population policies that had been worked out at the beginning of the century. The return of England's fear that the colonies were draining the nation's lifeblood was intensified by the greater maturity of the New World settlements. Seventeenth-century critics of colonization had opposed the depopulation of England to nourish inconsequential settlements; their eighteenth-century counterparts faced the specter of a declining country being challenged by the rising strength of its parasitic and ungrateful offspring. During the Seven Years' War, Americans had given evidence of their perfidy by trading with the enemy. Since the peace, the colonists had continued their unlawful activities by smuggling and refusing to pay the taxes levied on them by Parliament. Colonial agitation over the imperial reforms of the 1760s and 1770s seemed to confirm earlier predictions that on maturity colonies would seek to free themselves from their parent countries.[11] No longer could England allow the

[9] "Instructions to the Royal Governors, 1773," John Romeyn Brodhead, *Documents Relative to the Colonial History of the State of New York*, ed. E. B. O'Callaghan, 11 vols. (Albany: Weed, Parsons and Company, 1853–1861), VIII, 402; Lt. Gov. Colden to Earl of Dartmouth, Apr. 4, 1775, in ibid., VIII, 564; 16 Geo. III, c. 43 (1776), in Owen Ruffhead, ed., *Statutes at Large, from Magna Charta, to the Twenty-fifth Year of the Reign of King George the Third, Inclusive*, 10 vols. (London: Charles Eyre and Andrew Straham, Printers, 1786), VIII, 484.

[10] Declaration of Independence.

[11] Carl Ubbelohde, *Vice-Admiralty Courts and the American Revolution* (Chapel Hill: University of North Carolina Press, 1960), chap. 2; Bailyn, *Voyagers*, 29–50; Clark, *British Opinion*, 25–27, 37–38, 70–71; Hinkhouse, *Preliminaries of the American Revolution*, 105–8; Mitchell, *Present State of Great Britain and North America*, 6–10, 127–63.

free emigration of its subjects; no longer could the mother country underwrite the transportation of alien subjects to strengthen the ability of its colonies to resist its authority; no longer would England encourage immigration to America by offering free land and easy naturalization.

The grievances listed in the Declaration of Independence testify to the opprobrium earned by the English government in its attempts to enervate the rising strength of the American colonies by discouraging population growth. By the early 1770s, many colonists saw an apparent design in the imperial reform measures imposed on them by England—a concerted effort to destroy the colonists' rights as Englishmen and to use their resources to support the growing corruption in England. Americans came to believe that the standing army stationed on their frontier was placed there to cow them into submission and to extend the power of a government whose misrule had forfeited the natural loyalty of its subjects. The new taxes imposed on Americans to support this army of mercenaries and the rest of the oppressive design could only be attempts to confiscate colonial property through taxation to which America's freemen had not given their assent. Changes in England's colonial population policies were additional evidence of the conspiracy afoot to enslave the Americans.[12]

"Every Wise, Just, and Mild Government . . . Will Always Abound Most in People"

In American eyes, English attacks on the demographic strength of the colonies were a two-pronged offensive. The most obvious goal was to limit the ability of the colonists to resist British corruption and, if the discontents were not defused, to achieve independence. Less apparent, but even more insidious, were such policy changes when viewed as an attack on the vitality of the colonial governments that England was now trying to subvert.

The eighteenth-century equation of people and wealth had produced the corollary that a large population was a sign not merely of a successful mercantilist policy, but also of a moral and just government. According to Radical Whig precepts, "Countries are generally peopled in Proportion as they are free . . . upon the same tract of Land that would maintain a Hundred Thousand Freemen in Plenty, Five Thousand Slaves would starve . . . for what they sow and reap is none of their own; and their cruel and greedy Governors, who live by the Labour of their wretched Vassals do not suffer them to eat the Bread of their own Earning." Various writers of the Scottish enlightenment supported David Hume's contention that "every wise, just, and mild government, by rending the condition of its subjects easy and secure, will always abound most in people as

[12] Pauline Maier, *From Resistance to Revolution: Colonial Radicals and the Development of American Opposition to Britain, 1765–76* (New York: Knopf, 1972), chaps. 2 and 6.

well as in commodities and riches." According to Robert Wallace, the Scottish clergyman,

> in a debauched nation, addicted to sensuality and irregular amours, and where luxury and a high taste of delicate living prevails, the number of the people must be proportionally small, as their debauchery will hinder many from marrying, and their luxury and delicacy will render them less able to maintain families.
>
> For the same reason, a nation shall be more populous in proportion as good morals and a simplicity of taste and manners prevail, or as the people are more frugal and virtuous.[13]

The populations of countries enjoying just government grew by immigration as well as natural increase since, "Liberty naturally draws new People to it, as well as increases the Old Stock; and Men as naturally run when they dare from Slavery and Wretchedness." Thus, although it was "more desirable to see a people increase from themselves, by the sole influence of a good internal constitution," foreigners would always "flock to those countries which are well governed, and where they can easily maintain themselves and their families."[14]

The American rebels linked population growth and just government in urging their recalcitrant countrymen on to independence. In February 1776, a contributor to the *Pennsylvania Evening Post* argued that,

> Where encouragement is given to industry, where liberty and property are well secured, where the poor may easily find subsistence, and the middling rank comfortably support their families by labour, there the inhabitants must encrease rapidly; to some of these causes we owe the doubling of our numbers in somewhat more than twenty-five years. If such hath been the progress of population under the former restraints on our trade and manufactures, a population [growth] still more rapid may be reasonably expected when these restraints come to be taken off.

Thus the "probable benefits of independence" would include:

> A free and unlimited trade; a great accession of wealth, and a proportionable rise in the value of land; the establishment, gradual improvement and perfection of manufactures and science; a vast influx of foreigners, encouraged by the mildness of a free, equal, and tolerating government to leave their native countries, and to settle in these Colonies; an astonishing encrease of our people from the present stock.

[13] Quotes from John Trenchard and Thomas Gordon, "Cato's Letters," no. 62 (1721) in David L. Jacobson, ed., *The English Libertarian Heritage* (New York: Bobbs-Merrill, 1965), 134; David Hume, "Of the Populousness of Antient Nations," 1st publ. 1752, in Philip Appleman, ed., *An Essay on the Principle of Population* (New York: Norton, 1976), 3; Robert Wallace, "A Dissertation on the Numbers of Mankind in Antient and Modern Times," 1st publ. 1753, in ibid., 5.

[14] Trenchard and Gordon, "Cato's Letters," no. 62, in Jacobson, ed., *The English Libertarian Heritage*, 134 (quote); Joseph Priestley, "Of the Populousness of Nations," reprinted in *The American Museum*, 10 (1791), 229 (quote).

According to William Gordon, even wartime losses would soon be repaired by the regenerative force of a moral government. Thus he argued that, "Should the country be wasted for a few years, and numbers of its inhabitants be destroyed, ere the wished-for salvation is granted, how soon, after having secured its liberties, will it regain its former prosperity; yea, become far more glorious, wealthy, and populous than ever through the thousands, and ten thousands that will flock to it, with riches, arts, and sciences acquired by them in foreign countries."[15]

Although rebellious colonists identified attempts to restrain their population growth as part of the English conspiracy to deprive them of liberty, others used America's demographic history to argue against separation or to prove the excellence of English rule. In 1773 Benjamin Franklin counseled American moderation, believing that, given their history of rapid population growth, it was only a matter of time and the inevitable renewal of European warfare before the colonies became a crucial element in the defense of the British Empire. At this time the Americans could demand, and win, concessions from the mother country as a price for their support, without resorting to rebellion. Although Franklin's treatment in England would soon turn him into a fiery rebel, other Americans underwent no such conversion experience. James Chalmers, the future Loyalist from Maryland, also subscribed to the belief that the "marks of the best government" were "the encrease, preservation, and prosperity of its members." In his opinion, "Until the present unhappy period, Great Britain has afforded to all mankind, the most perfect proof of her wise, lenient, and magnanimous government of the Colonies . . . viz. our superior felicity and amazing increase." After thus ascribing American prosperity to English, rather than colonial, virtue, Chalmers concluded that it would be fool-hardy to try to secede from the most powerful nation in Europe, even if it were militarily possible. He argued that "it would be most excellent policy in those who wish for TRUE LIBERTY to submit by an advantageous reconciliation to the authority of Great Britain."[16]

In 1776 many American revolutionaries accepted Chalmers's claim that the British government had indeed been the most perfect form known to man. Unfortunately, the events of "the present unhappy period" were evidence of the destruction of English virtue necessary to support liberty and the free government that nurtured prosperity and a burgeoning population. English attempts to reform their empire in the decade following the Seven Years' War were interpreted by many Americans as a design by power-hungry men to subvert their rights as Englishmen. The logic used in resisting this dangerous conspiracy then

---

[15] *Pennsylvania Evening Post*, Feb. 17, 1776, quoted in Philip Davidson, *Propaganda and the American Revolution* (Chapel Hill: University of North Carolina Press, 1941), 133; William Gordon (1774), quoted in ibid., 134.

[16] Bailyn, "1776: A Year of Challenge," 460–61; James Chalmers, *Plain Truth* (1776), in Merrill Jensen, ed., *Tracts of the American Revolution, 1763–1776*, (New York: Bobbs-Merrill, 1967), 447–88, quotes on 451, 469, 488.

led the colonists to believe that only their society possessed the attributes necessary to maintain liberty. Their years of service as an adjunct asylum had groomed the colonies to step in when England faltered. The emphasis placed on the liberal elements of colonial society by promoters of colonization paved the way for the American claim to be the home of enlightened government and the true guardian of liberty. Only by being convinced that their mother country had sunk into irreversible decay could the body of the American people agree on the need for independence. The same reasoning that diagnosed England's political malaise as incurable pointed to colonial vitality. The liberal aspects of colonial society, which were largely the accidental byproduct of English politics, the inability of the colonists to transplant a fully articulated society, and the need to recruit settlers, were now glorified. Colonial deviations were interpreted as the means by which Americans preserved the virtue that the Old World could not sustain and as the foundation of the American asylum for liberty.

Passing the Torch of Liberty

The revolution in the way Americans viewed their society drew on a body of thought developed by groups of reformers and radicals in Great Britain and Europe. During the eighteenth century, Europe's intellectual community had cast up its own, largely mythical, portrait of British North America. Building on the propaganda of Benjamin Furly, French writers transformed the colonial experience into a vindication of their own ideals. William Penn's legislation and John Locke's "Fundamental Constitutions of Carolina" were cited by Voltaire as evidence of enlightened government in America. The prosperity of Pennsylvania then became proof that the principles of religious and political freedom espoused by Voltaire and implemented in America also could work in France. By the middle of the eighteenth century, the writings of men such as Voltaire, Montesquieu, and Louis de Jaucourt had established Pennsylvania "in the minds of French liberals as a land where *bienfaisance*, the spirit of benevolence and humanitarianism, reigned as an operative political principle." The philosophe's image of America spread outside of France along with the dissemination of other Enlightenment ideas.[17]

Across the English Channel the eighteenth-century Commonwealthmen were performing similar feats of legerdemain. Calling themselves Real Whigs, these heirs of seventeenth-century republicanism were becoming increasingly irrelevant to English politics. The growing complexity of British society had rendered

[17] Durand Echeverria, *Mirage in the West: A History of the French Image of American Society to 1815* (Princeton: Princeton University Press, 1957), chap. 1, quote on 18; Henry Steele Commager, *The Empire of Reason: How Europe Imagined and America Realized the Enlightenment* (New York: Doubleday, 1977), chap. 5.

commonwealth precepts outmoded, better suited to the simpler English society that was developing in America. Rather than adapt their thought to changing reality, the Real Whigs explained their deteriorating status through a selective reading of history that chronicled the westward movement of despotism. American success would prove the viability of their principles while failure in England was merely evidence of encroaching corruption. Like frustrated French reformers, these Englishmen transformed the British colonies into the antithesis of their fears.[18]

The idealization of America was not confined to the radical wing of English politics. Politicians, publicists, and reformers of all hues used the American experience to advance their causes and validate their principles. George Berkeley promoted his project to establish a school for Anglican missionaries in the British West Indies by painting a dismal picture of the moral climate in Britain that would vitiate all local attempts at regeneration. Only in America could his plan succeed, where

> the Muse disgusted at an age and clime
> Barren of every glorious theme,
> In distant lands now waits a better time. . . .

In 1735, James Thomson's epic poem *Liberty* promoted the settlement of Georgia, a similar project of regeneration backed by Anglican philanthropists. Accordingly, Thomson celebrated England's "Gay colonies" as:

> . . . the calm retreat
> Of undeserved distress, the better home
> Of those whom bigots chase from foreign lands,
> Not built on rapine, servitude, and woe,
> And in their turn some petty tyrant's prey,
> But, bound by social freedom, firm they rise. . . .

While Thomson saw the settlements "crowding round the charmed Savannah" as a refuge for England's imprisoned debtors and Germans fleeing religious persecution, John Dyer projected a more vigorous destiny on the American continent, one that combined regeneration with economic progress. According to Dyer, the English poet laureate,

[18]Caroline Robbins, *The Eighteenth-Century Commonwealthman: Studies in the Transmission, Development and Circumstance of English Liberal Thought from the Restoration of Charles II until the War with the Thirteen Colonies* (Cambridge: Harvard University Press, 1959); Colin Bonwick, *English Radicals and the American Revolution* (Chapel Hill: University of North Carolina Press, 1977), chaps. 1–3; Bernard Bailyn, *The Ideological Origins of the American Revolution* (Cambridge: Harvard University Press, 1967), chap. 3; Maier, *From Resistance to Revolution*, 161–91; Arthur Sheps, "The American Revolution and the Transformation of English Republicanism," *Historical Reflections*, 2 (1975), 3–6; Oscar and Mary Handlin, "James Burgh and American Revolutionary Theory," Massachusetts Historical Society, *Proceedings*, 73 (1961), 50–52.

No land gives more employment to the loom,
Or kindlier feeds the indigent; no land
With more variety of wealth rewards
The hand of labour: thither, from the wrong
Of lawless rule the freeborn spirit flies;
Thither affliction, thither poverty
And arts and sciences: thrice happy clime,
Which Britain makes the asylum of mankind.[19]

English economists generally eschewed such colonial encomiums, as they worked to maintain control of the British empire and to guide its development to the benefit of the mother country. Britain's imperial bureaucracy had similar motives for minimizing rather than glorifying America's divine destiny while emphasizing the benefits England reaped from its colonies. However, frustrated bureaucrats who saw their proposals drown in Whitehall's sea of inertia and corruption could also cast up an idealized vision of an America that would vindicate the reforms that were so contemptuously tossed aside. So it was, in the 1760s, that Thomas Pownall predicted that the American colonies would "become in some future and perhaps not very distant age an asylum to that liberty of mankind which, as it hath been driven by corruption and the consequent tyranny of government, *hath been constantly retiring westward*."[20]

British entrepreneurs and politicians also were adept at conjuring up idealized colonial images. By the end of 1765, the stoppage in trade by Americans demanding the repeal of the Stamp Act helped to convince British merchants of the righteousness of the colonial cause and the venality or incompetence of the Grenville administration. The weakness of the Rockingham ministry and its need to defuse colonial discontent then led to the alliance of the defenders of parliamentary supremacy and merchants trading to America.[21] The Rockingham Whigs and their merchant allies used American grievances and encouraged colonial defiance to attack their domestic enemies. In 1770 Richard Champion, a Bristol merchant with close ties to the Rockingham Whigs, advised his brother-in-law in South Carolina that, "Your Sentiments are just, and I believe will be for the advantage of both Countries to have them strictly pursued by America, till she has obtained redress for her grievances. While she defends her liberty on legal principles, the

[19] Richard Koebner, *Empire* (Cambridge: Cambridge University Press, 1961), 95–101, quotes on 95 (Berkeley), 97 (Thomson), 101 (Dyer).

[20] Ibid., 101–4; Hinkhouse, *Preliminaries of the American Revolution*, 47–51, 100–104; Bailyn, *Ideological Origins*, 140n–41n (Pownall quote).

[21] G. H. Guttridge, *English Whiggism and the American Revolution*, University of California, *Publications in History*, 28 (1942), 65–70; George Herbert Guttridge, ed., "The American Correspondence of a Bristol Merchant, 1766–1776: Letters of Richard Champion," University of California, *Publications in History*, 22 (1934), 1–72; Michael G. Kammen, *Rope of Sand: The Colonial Agents, British Politics, and the American Revolution* (Ithaca: Cornell University Press, 1968), 117–20; J. H. Plumb, "The Impact of the American Revolution on Great Britain," in Library of Congress Symposia, *Impact of the American Revolution Abroad*, 68–71.

Names of her Defenders will be transmitted with honour to Posterity, as the true friends to their country." David Hartley, one of America's staunchest allies and a member of Parliament from 1774, went even further in his commitment to the cause of "our American fellow subjects . . . driven to resistance in their own defense, and in support of those very claims which we ourselves have success-fully taken up arms in former times, to rescue us from the violence and tyranni-cal pretensions of the House of Stuart." Glowing images of the colonists' valiant fight against corrupt ministers also were employed by members of other Whig groups in their struggle against the King's Friends. Thus Isaac Barré, a member of the Shelburne coterie, countered British critics of American conduct by describing the colonists as planted by British oppression and nourished by British neglect. Barré predicted that the "same spirit of freedom which actuated that people [the colonists] at first, will accompany them still. . . . The people, I believe, are as truly loyal as any subjects the king has, but a people jealous of their lib-erties and who will vindicate them, if ever they should be violated." Reports of such impassioned defense of the American cause were widely disseminated in the colonies and strengthened colonial resolve and conviction.[22]

American agitation in the decade preceding 1776 thus fed into and fed on dif-ferent strands of political discontent in Great Britain. English Whigs who were primarily concerned with protecting parliamentary sovereignty from encroach-ments by the king's ministers were joined in their support for the American cause by imperialists committed more to empire than to parliamentary rights and by English Commonwealthmen who fought to lodge sovereignty in the people rather than in any governmental body. Although English politicians and mer-chants encouraged American defiance of the policies of the corrupt ministry that had gained control of the empire and lauded the colonial defense of English rights, their conception of America's destiny diverged greatly from that imagined by the radical elements of British society. England's political radicals also held up the American example to win the political battle in England and hoped to prevent America's secession from the British empire. But the radical Common-wealthmen, excluded from political power by religious tests, the inequities of parliamentary representation, or poverty, could transfer their millennial hopes to the American continent far more easily than opposition politicians.

By the mid-1770s, England's political radicals were ready to pass on the torch of liberty and urged the Americans to assume, at least temporarily, England's tra-ditional role as asylum of the oppressed. In 1766 Charles Lee, the Englishman who later emigrated to America and served as a general in the rebel army, described Europe as "one continued desert" and expressed his hope that God

[22] Guttridge, ed., "American Correspondence of a Bristol Merchant," 17 (Champion quote); George Herbert Guttridge, "David Hartley, M.P.: An Advocate of Conciliation, 1774–1783," University of California, *Publications in History*, 14 (1926), 249 (Hartley quote); I. R. Christie, *Crisis of Empire: Great Britain and the American Colonies, 1754–1783* (New York: Norton, 1966), 53 (Barré quote).

would "prosper the Americans in their resolution, that there may be one *Asylum* at least on the earth for men, who prefer their natural rights to the fantastical prerogative of a foolish perverted head because it wears a crown." In 1767 Sylas Neville, an obscure Real Whig from London, applauded the emigration of Ulstermen to America and hoped that they would "flourish and set up in due time a glorious free government in that country which may serve as a retreat to those Free men who may survive the final ruin of liberty in this country; an event which I am afraid is at no great distance." In the same year, Neville also recorded a comment by an unnamed stranger who reportedly "wished N. America may become free and independent, that it may be an asylum to those Englishmen who have spirit and virtue enough to leave their country, when it submits to domestic or foreign tyranny." In 1770 a letter from the Supporters of the Bill of Rights Society thanking the assembly of South Carolina for their £1,500 contribution to the defense of John Wilkes declared that "Our cause is one—our enemies are the same." The Society then urged Americans to stand firm against tyranny since "when luxury, misrule, and corruption shall at length, in spite of all resistance, have destroyed this noble Constitution here, our posterity will not, like your gallant ancestors, be driven to an inhospitable shore, but will find a welcome refuge . . . amongst their fellow subjects, the descendants and brothers of Englishmen."[23]

By 1774 the need for American aid and leadership seemed critical. Corruption in England had become so endemic that there was no hope of English people "extricating themselves from that slavery forged for them by the corrupt influence of the Crown." English salvation seemed to lay in the hands of "Our brave American fellow-subjects [who] are not yet corrupted, but gloriously stand up in defence of their undoubted rights and liberties; and whilst they shall maintain them by their public virtue and fortitude, they will defend the freedom of their aged parent country from all the infirmities, evils, and oppression of time, corruption and arbitrary power."[24]

Preserving Liberty

America's patriots responded eagerly to the invitation to assume leadership of the cause of liberty and to prepare an asylum for vanquished freedom fighters. The colonists had, since mid-century, been expressing doubts about the ability of

[23] Quotes from Cecil D. Eby, "America as 'Asylum': A Dual Image," *American Quarterly*, 14 (1962), 484; J. H. Plumb, "British Attitudes to the American Revolution," in *In the Light of History* (Boston: Houghton Mifflin, 1973), 73, 74; Hinkhouse, *Preliminaries of the American Revolution*, 201.

[24] Extract from *Kent Gazette*, Jan. 7, 1775, quoted in Hinkhouse, *Preliminaries of the American Revolution*, 200–201. See also Peter Force, ed., *American Archives: A Documentary History of the English Colonies in North America*, 4th series, 6 vols. (Washington, D.C., 1837–1846), I, 289–90.

the English to uphold liberty in a society riddled with "luxury and corruption," where "People are grown too polite to have an old-fashioned religion, and are too weak to find out a new, from whence follows the most unbounded licentiousness and utter disregard of virtue, which is the unfailing cause of the destruction of all empires." The failure of the English people to halt the ministerial campaign against American liberty seemed to confirm the colonists' forebodings and made them receptive to the fears and hopes of English dissenters and political radicals.

In 1765, Charles Carroll of Carrollton urged a friend to emigrate from England where "the symptoms of a general decay are but too visible" and to settle in Maryland

> where liberty will maintain her empire till a dissoluteness of morals, luxury, and venality shall have prepared the degenerate sons of some future age to prefer their own mean lucre, the bribes, and the smiles of corruption and arbitrary ministers to patriotism, to glory, and to the public weal. No doubt the same causes will produce the same effects, and a period is already set to the reign of American freedom; but that fatal time seems to be at a great distance. The present generation at least, and I hope many succeeding ones, in spite of a corrupt Parliament, will enjoy the blessings and sweets of liberty.

In 1766 Jonathan Mayhew prayed that

> if any miserable people on the continent or isles of Europe, after being weakened by luxury, debauchery, venality, intestine quarrels, or other vices, should, in the rude collisions, or now-uncertain revolutions of kingdoms, be driven in their extremity, to seek a safe retreat from slavery in some far-distant climate; let them find, O let them find one in America under thy brooding, sacred wings; where *our* oppressed fathers once found it.

By the mid-1770s American letters and newspapers were filled with promises that "the Grand *American* Tree of Liberty, planted in the center of the United Colonies of *North America* now flourishes with unrivalled, increasing beauty, and bids fair, in a short time, to afford under its wide-spreading branches a safe and happy retreat for all the sons of Liberty, however numerous and dispersed." They also warned that, "If America is an humble instrument of the salvation of Britain, it will give us the sincerest joy; but, if Britain must lose her liberty, she must lose it alone."[25] Thus, in the eyes of the most militant Americans, the colonies were fast becoming the sole haven of liberty and were destined to assume the English mantle as protector of the oppressed.

[25] Bailyn, *Ideological Origins*, 86–93, quotes on 90, 91; Jonathan Mayhew, *The Snare Broken* (1766), quoted in Davidson, *Propaganda and the American Revolution*, 134; Force, ed., *American Archives*, 4th ser., III, 472 (quote); Maier, *From Resistance to Revolution*, 264–66.

Common Sense

Although American rebels defiantly advertised themselves as guardians of true liberty, comparisons between the population of Great Britain and the colonies and the size of the armies each side could field demonstrated an evident British superiority. By 1776 the apparent impossibility of victory by any army mustered by the colonists over the mightiest military power in Europe led Thomas Paine to change the terms of the debate. By drawing on a developing theory of population that predicted the inevitable decay of nations whose numbers forced them to exchange their simple and virtuous forms of social and economic organization for less egalitarian structures, Paine could argue that American victory was inevitable, that apparent weaknesses were actually strengths. In providing incipient rebels with the optimism necessary to embark on the road to independence, Paine also helped to fix on American thought a duality in its theory of population—one that equated rapid population growth with just government and youthful vigor, while simultaneously fearing the consequences of such growth.[26]

Common Sense marked a turning point in the way Americans interpreted the development of their provincial societies. From the days of the earliest settlements, most colonists had been striving to reach the level of civilization they had left behind. Every colony in British North America established a provincial assembly modeled after, and claiming the rights and powers of, the English House of Commons. The frequency and severity of colonial political disputes were blamed on the incomplete congruence of American institutions with their English counterparts. The most frequently faulted shortcoming was the absence of an aristocracy that could make colonial councils effective mediators between the conflicting powers of the governor and the assembly. The American gentry was well aware of its failure to reach the heights of wealth and gentility of England's ruling oligarchy that would create the social distance between them and their inferiors necessary to win deference. Their efforts to remedy this defect were, however, thwarted by the immaturity of the American economies and the abundance of land. The ease with which settlers acquired land titles deprived the gentry of servile tenants and rents. The lack of secure investment opportunities prevented the husbanding of incipient family fortunes. America's de facto religious freedom also deprived colonial gentry of the support of a strong established church.[27]

---

[26] Stow Persons, "The Cyclical Theory of History in Eighteenth Century America," *American Quarterly,* 6 (1954), 147–63; Drew R. McCoy, *The Elusive Republic: Political Economy in Jeffersonian America* (New York: Norton, 1980), chap. 1.

[27] Bernard Bailyn, *The Origins of American Politics* (New York: Knopf, 1968), 59–66, 131–36; Rowland Berthoff and John M. Murrin, "Feudalism, Communalism, and the Yeoman Freeholder: The American Revolution Considered as a Social Accident," in Stephen G. Kurtz and James H. Hutson, eds., *Essays on the American Revolution* (Chapel Hill: University of North Carolina Press, 1973), 261–62; Rhys Isaac, "Religion

According to Thomas Paine, the Americans had no reason to be defensive about their failure to emulate English models. Their deviations were salutary and would allow the colonists to preserve in America the liberty that was falling prey to corruption in England. The ideal government outlined by Paine incorporated previously deplored features of colonial life. The failure of the Americans to reproduce England's complex mixed constitution gave them the opportunity to adopt a simple model, one "less liable . . . to be disordered, and the easier repaired." What need had the Americans for a king, who "hath little more to do than to make war and give away places; which in plain terms is to empoverish the nation. . . . A pretty business indeed for a man to be allowed eight hundred thousand sterling a year for, and worshipped into the bargain." What need had Americans for a hereditary peerage, the base "remains of Aristocratical tyranny." After lopping off these vestigial and diseased political appendages, the colonial assembly would become the cornerstone of American government. In advocating government by the only republican element in the English constitution and the most powerful political body in the colonies, Paine turned American social defects into assets. He also argued for the beneficial effects of such troublesome colonial developments as widespread landownership that produced a broad electorate, the absence of entail and primogeniture procedures to consolidate and perpetuate inherited power, and religious freedom.[28]

After identifying the factors that produced the decay of virtue and liberty in England and the absence of those elements in America, Thomas Paine presented the colonists with the challenge to do more than sever their ties with a diseased mother country. Although the Americans could never forget the injuries inflicted on them by the English, or restore their lost innocence, "The Almighty hath implanted in us these unextinguishable feelings for good and wise purposes. . . . The social compact would dissolve, and justice be extirpated from the earth, or have only a casual existence were we callous to the touches of affection." Thus, American virtue compelled Paine to issue his call to

> ye that love mankind! Ye that dare oppose not only the tyranny but the tyrant, stand forth! Every spot of the old world is over-run with oppression. Freedom hath been hunted round the Globe. Asia and Africa have long expelled her. Europe regards her like a stranger, and England hath given her warning to depart. O! receive the fugitive, and prepare in time an asylum for mankind.[29]

---

and Authority: Problems of the Anglican Establishment in Virginia in the Era of the Great Awakening and the Parsons' Cause," *William and Mary Quarterly*, 3d ser., 30 (1973), 3–36.

[28] Quotes from Thomas Paine, *Common Sense* (1776), in *The Life and Major Writings of Thomas Paine*, ed. Philip S. Foner, 2 vols. (New York: Citadel Press, 1945), I, 6, 7, 16.

[29] Ibid., I, 30–31.

Recruiting Support for the Glorious Cause

In accepting Paine's reading of history and his challenge to escalate their battle from a local defense of the "rights of Englishmen" to a commitment to preserve liberty for the benefit of all "mankind," the American rebels defied more than England's military power. In proclaiming themselves the sole surviving repository of freedom, the Americans challenged England's national identity as protector of liberty and refuge for the world's fugitives from tyranny. Once hostilities began, the American rebels advertised their asylum to win support. Americans warned the Western world, "If you suffer the iron rod of oppression to reach and scourge you here, remember you have no America to flee to for an asylum."[30] Open letters from the Continental Congress were published throughout the British empire inviting Britons everywhere to participate in the struggle to preserve liberty, either by constitutional agitation or domestic insurrection. New channels of communication were opened between America and Europe.

America's appeal splintered the facade of the Enlightenment community by revealing its wide spectrum of political assumptions, an unwillingness to progress from the safety of theorizing to revolution, and an often expressed belief that the colonists had misunderstood important philosophical nuances. The exigencies of war were just as likely as theoretical principles to determine which Old World groups accepted and actively supported the American claim to be the new asylum of liberty.

In England the American call to arms fell largely on deaf ears. Popular sympathies evoked by America's prewar grievances evaporated in a surge of patriotism as the English people rallied around their constitution and king. The publication of an address from the Continental Congress to the people of Great Britain in English newspapers at the end of 1774 that chronicled "the progression of the ministerial plan for enslaving" the colonists, produced a few subscriptions and a London petition in support of the American cause. *Crisis*, a radical broadsheet published in London, called on the English to prove that they were not "so far degenerated as to TAMELY see a mercenary army of soldiers . . . BUTCHER their BRETHREN and FELLOW-SUBJECTS in America, because they are determined to defend their own rights and the British constitution."[31] However, the more typical response to the American appeal was that of amazement at the colonists' failure to understand the true nature of liberty. "A Gentleman treating on the letter from the American Congress" was astounded that

[30]"Alarum V," *New York Journal*, Nov. 18, 1773, quoted in Maier, *From Resistance to Revolution*, 265n.

[31]Bonwick, *English Radicals*, chap. 4; "LETTER from the GENERAL CONGRESS to the PEOPLE of GREAT BRITAIN," *London Chronicle*, Dec. 20, 22, 1774 (quote); *Crisis* quoted in Maier, *From Resistance to Revolution*, 258; "A LETTER from the GENERAL CONGRESS to the INHABITANTS of CANADA," *London Chronicle*, Dec. 24, 27, 1774.

"this celebrated Congress would advise the people of America to revolt against the Mother Country." Only a people "devoid of understanding and candour" could misread history and English liberty to the extent necessary to express such contempt for "the purity of the [English] constitution." Another Londoner described American grievances as "whimsical." To him it seemed

> very remarkable . . . that when the Congress speaks of the outrages committed by the American patriots . . . it requires every particular charge to be established by legal proof, and treats the most serious as trivial. . . . In the American Bill of Rights particularly, we meet the following declaration from the Congress: "That we hold it essential to English liberty, that no man be condemned unheard, or punished for supposed offenses, without having an opportunity of making his defence." The congressional Demi-gods nevertheless, in opposition to their own principles, condemn the King, Lords, and Commons of Great Britain upon the strength of mere conjecture only, and gravely assert, that the parliamentary claims upon America "are prosecuted with a design, that by having the lives and property of the Colonies in their power, they may with the greater facility enslave the people of England."[32]

After George III declared the colonies to be in a state of rebellion, the position of American sympathizers in England became increasingly untenable. As popular patriotism made support for the rebel cause dangerous, many of the colonists' former friends were even more afraid of the domestic consequences of an American victory. Imperial reformers who had once advocated appeasing the colonists were now determined to defeat American attempts to dismember the empire. The position of parliamentary reformers was even worse since their cause suffered no matter who won the war. A British victory would increase the prestige and power of their domestic opponents and encourage the King's Friends in their attacks on parliamentary supremacy; however, an American victory would also constitute a successful denial of the power of Parliament.[33]

While the pro-American party in England proved unable to provide substantive aid for the colonists, the fears stirred up by the agitation of English radicals increased the conservatism of North Britain. As in England, the initial sympathy of the Scots for American grievances dissipated with the declaration of war. Scottish public opinion believed that the colonies could continue to function as a legitimate asylum for liberty and the oppressed only if they remained within the empire. The formerly impartial *Scots Magazine* responded to the American Declaration of Independence with a series of articles that exposed the colonists' fallacious reasoning. According to one correspondent,

> the opinions of the Americans on Government, like those of their good ancestors on witchcraft, would be too ridiculous to deserve any notice, if, like them too, con-

---

[32] Quotes from ibid., Dec. 29, 31, 1774.
[33] Bonwick, *English Radicals*, 85–102.

temptible and extravagant as they are, they had not led to the most serious evils. In the preamble . . . they attempt to establish a theory of government; a theory as absurd and visionary as the system of conduct in defence of which it is established is nefarious. Here it is that maxims are advanced in justification of their enterprise against the British government. To these maxims, adduced for the purpose, it would be sufficient to say, that they are repugnant to the British constitution. But beyond this, they are subversive of every actual or imaginable kind of government.

The home of the Scottish philosophers, whose works were imbedded in American revolutionary thought, thus became a bastion of government support until mismanagement of the war and the French alliance merged with local grievances to build an opposition party. At that juncture, Scotland's dissidents chose reform over revolution.[34]

The failure of the colonists to win Scottish supporters came as no surprise to the American revolutionaries. From the days of Lord Bute's ministry, Scottish influence throughout the empire had, in the eyes of the colonists, a particularly malevolent tendency. That, combined with the loyalist activities of recent immigrants from the Scottish Highlands, already had led Thomas Jefferson to condemn George III for dispatching "not only soldiers of our common blood, but Scotch & foreign mercenaries to invade & destroy us."[35] The rebels did, however, have higher expectations of Irish patriots. In 1775, the Continental Congress defended the American cause in their "Address to the People of Ireland." After explaining the British tyrannies that had produced turmoil in the American colonies, Congress apologized for having been forced to sever their links with the Irish who "had ever been friendly to the rights of mankind." It consoled the Americans, however, "to reflect, that should it occasion much distress, the fertile regions of America would afford you a safe assylum from poverty, and, in time, from oppression also; an assylum, in which many thousands of your countrymen have found hospitality, peace, and affluence, and become united to us by all the ties of consanguity, mutual interest, and affection."[36]

[34] D. B. Swinfen, "The American Revolution in the Scottish Press," in Owen Dudley Edwards and George Shepperson, eds., *Scotland, Europe and the American Revolution* (New York: St. Martin's Press, 1977), 66–74, quote on 71; C. Duncan Rice, "Scottish Enlightenment, American Revolution and Atlantic Reform," in ibid., 75–82; Dalphy I. Fagerstrom, "Scottish Opinion and the American Revolution," *William and Mary Quarterly*, 3d ser., 11 (1954), 252–75.

[35] Ian Charles Cargill Graham, *Colonists from Scotland: Emigration to North America, 1707–1783* (Ithaca: Cornell University Press, 1956), 128–30, 150–83; Andrew Hook, *Scotland and America: A Study of Cultural Relations, 1750–1835* (Glasgow: Blackie and Son, 1975), chap. 3; Margaret Wheeler Willard, *Letters on the American Revolution, 1774–1776* (Boston: Houghton Mifflin, 1925), 16–17; Force, ed., *American Archives*, 4th ser., I, 293; quote from Jefferson's draft of the Declaration of Independence, a passage deleted by the Continental Congress, *Thomas Jefferson: Writings*, ed. Merrill D. Peterson (New York: Library of America, 1984), 23.

[36] Owen Dudley Edwards, "Ireland and the American Revolution," in Edwards and Shepperson, eds., *Scotland, Europe, and the American Revolution*, 117–26; "Address to the People of Ireland," in *Journals of the Continental Congress, 1774–1789*, ed. Worthington C. Ford et al., 34 vols. (Washington, D.C.: Government Printing Office, 1904–1937), II, 215 (quotes).

America's pleas were, however, unsuccessful in mobilizing the Irish people. Of Ireland's tripartite society, only the Protestant dissenters showed any inclination to support the rebels, and their ardor faded as the colonists moved from resistance to revolution and England's economic and political concessions defused Irish discontent. The hoped-for Irish insurrections that would occupy at least part of the British army never materialized. By the end of 1775, Ireland's parliament had not only censured the American colonists as rebels, but had also voted the British government 4,000 soldiers to be used in America.[37]

Although the American appeal to their fellow subjects throughout the British empire went generally unanswered, other Europeans stepped forward, for a variety of reasons, to support the rebels.[38] The same wartime conditions that dissipated British enthusiasm for the American cause turned England's enemies into America's allies. France, hoping to avenge its defeat by the British in the Seven Years' War and to regain some of its lost stature and territory, secretly encouraged American radicals even before the declaration of war. By 1775 Vergennes, the French Minister of Foreign Affairs, had secret agents gathering intelligence in America. Once assured that there could be no reconciliation between England and the colonists, Vergennes set up a secret, unofficial network to channel money and military supplies to the American rebels. Professional soldiers from France, seeking military action more than republican liberty, began arriving in 1776 to offer their services to the American army. These Frenchmen were joined by other European military men with similar motives, in numbers that threatened to leave few openings for aspiring American officers. By March 1777, the influx was so great that the Continental Congress instructed the Committee of Secret Correspondence "to write all their ministers and agents abroad, to discourage all gentlemen from coming to America with expectation of employment in the service, unless they are masters of our language, and have the best of recommendations." After the signing of the official Franco-American Alliance in 1778, a French army of about 8,000 men arrived on American shores.[39]

The American revolutionaries also enhanced their military position by "encouraging the Hessians, and other foreigners, employed by the King of Great

[37] Edwards, "Ireland and the American Revolution"; Maier, *From Resistance to Revolution*, 255.

[38] George A. Rawlyk, "Nova Scotia and the American Revolution," in Edwards and Shepperson, eds., *Scotland, Europe, and the American Revolution*, 104–10; George Rawlyk, "The 1770s," in J. M. S. Careless, ed., *Colonists and Canadians, 1760–1867* (Toronto: Macmillan of Canada, 1971), 20–40; J. H. Parry and P. M. Sherlock, *A Short History of the West Indies*, 3d ed. (New York: St. Martin's Press, 1971), 134–35; R. R. Palmer, "The Impact of the American Revolution Abroad," in Library of Congress Symposia, *Impact of the American Revolution Abroad*, 6–12.

[39] Claude Fohlen, "The Impact of the American Revolution on France," in Library of Congress Symposia, *The Impact of the American Revolution Abroad*, 21–22, 25; Echeverria, *Mirage in the West*, 80–82; R. R. Palmer, *The Age of the Democratic Revolution: A Political History of Europe and America, 1760–1800*, 2 vols. (Princeton: Princeton University Press, 1959–1964), I, 248–49. Edmund Cody Burnett, *The Continental Congress* (New York: Macmillan, 1941), 241–43, quote on 241; V. G. Kiernan, "Sunrise in the West: American Independence and Europe," in Edwards and Shepperson, eds., *Scotland, Europe, and the American Revolution*, 25–37.

Britain, and sent to America for the purpose of subjugating these states, to quit that iniquitous service." According to the Continental Congress, "such foreigners, if apprised of the practice of these states, would chuse to accept of lands, liberty, safety, and communion of good laws and government, in a country where many of their friends and relations are already happily settled." Thus Congress resolved, on August 14, 1776,

> that these states will receive all such foreigners who shall leave the armies of his Britannic majesty in America, and shall chuse to become members of any of these states; that they shall be protected in the exercise of their respective religions, and be invested with the rights, privileges and immunities of natives, as established by the laws of these states; and, moreover, that this Congress will provide, for every such person, 50 Acres of unappropriated lands in some of these states, to be held by him and his heirs in absolute property.[40]

In 1778 Congress ordered the publication and distribution of a thousand copies of the German translation of its address, "To the officers and soldiers in the service of the King of Great Britain, not subjects of said King." The address pointed out that the Americans were fighting "for the rights of human nature, and therefore merit[ed] the patronage and assistance of all mankind" and promised that an American victory would "secure a refuge from persecution and tyranny to those who wish to pursue the dictates of their own consciences, and to reap the fruits of their own industry." It also reiterated and amplified Congress's earlier offer of land, civil rights, and religious toleration for those who would cease to be "the instruments of avarice and ambition."[41]

Congress was aided in its efforts to subvert the British army by the actions of individual states. In 1781 a proclamation by Virginia's Governor Thomas Jefferson promised fifty acres of land, two cows, and exemptions from wartime taxes and military service to German soldiers who chose to settle in Virginia. Of the 30,000 German soldiers in the British army, over 12,000 failed to return home. It has been estimated that more than 3,000 of these German mercenaries accepted the dual offer of American land and citizenship. An unknown number of British subjects also remained in the new American states after the departure of their regiments, believing that employment opportunities were better in the new states than they would be in postwar England.[42]

---

[40] *Journals of the Continental Congress*, V, 654–55.

[41] Ibid., X, 405–10.

[42] Frank George Franklin, *The Legislative History of Naturalization in the United States* (Chicago: University of Chicago Press, 1906), 5–7; Rodney Atwood, *The Hessians: Mercenaries from Hessen-Kassel in the American Revolution* (Cambridge: Cambridge University Press, 1980); *Belfast News-Letter*, Mar. 3, June 6, July 11, Aug. 8, 1783; *Newcastle Journal*, June 28, 1783.

Neutralizing the Disaffected and Uncommitted

In the 1770s American rebels expanded their mission from maintaining their rights as Englishmen to preserving liberty for all mankind to legitimatize and win support for their struggle with Great Britain. The need for recognition and allies inclined Americans to overlook the weakness of the support they received from their reputed friends in England and Ireland and to ignore the less than lofty motives that placed England's absolutist and Catholic enemies in the American camp. Such diplomatic niceties could not, however, be practiced on the home front. The wartime activities of American-born citizens and immigrants who were not committed to revolution prompted the colonists to harass, intern, or banish English sympathizers and to adopt cautious immigrant policies.

During the war, the American republics were confronted with the problem of how to deal with their loyalists—those Americans who did not believe in the existence of a British conspiracy or did not agree that English policies left them no recourse but revolution. Once the American rebels proceeded to revolution by withdrawing their allegiance to the British king, policies had to be devised to detect and then to neutralize inhabitants who refused to renounce their fidelity to Great Britain and to recognize the legitimacy of the new American governments. Even before the Declaration of Independence officially decreed "That these United Colonies . . . are Absolved from all Allegiance to the British Crown, and that all political connection between them and the State of Great Britain, is and ought to be totally dissolved," the Continental Congress had instituted policies that turned the activities of loyalists into treason. By November 1775, soldiers in the Continental Army could be executed for aiding the enemy. A resolution of the Continental Congress in June 1776 extended the same penalties to civilians, since "all persons residing within any of the United Colonies, and deriving protection from the laws of the same, owe allegiance to the said laws." This and two subsequent resolutions provided the legal foundation for the test laws passed by the new state governments to identify potentially treasonous citizens. Americans who refused to profess their loyalty to the new governments could be fined, disfranchised, or banished; those who actively supported British attempts to return the colonies to their former allegiance could be executed.[43]

Doubts about the loyalty of Americans to their new governments and fear of the consequences of allowing men of dubious political principles to retain their citizenship led to the temporary internment of Pennsylvanian pacifists and the permanent proscription of up to 60,000 tories. These doubts and fears also made American patriots more cautious in welcoming foreigners into their communities. In 1775, two years after his arrival in Virginia from Tuscany, Philip Mazzei

[43]Declaration of Independence (quote); James H. Kettner, *The Development of American Citizenship, 1608–1870* (Chapel Hill: University of North Carolina Press, 1978), 173–84, quote on 179.

was warned by his neighbors that his public service career could be hampered by reports that during his long stay in England he might have come to "an understanding" with the ministerial party. It was also rumored that Mazzei had "spoken and written so well for freedom of religion" in order "to introduce popery among us." Early in 1779, John Patrick Lynch, a "native and Inhabitant of the Kingdom of Ireland . . . wishing to become a Subject and Inhabitant of some one of the United States . . . having seen the Exception contained in the Resolve of Congress of the 23d of March 1774 in favor of Settlers coming to reside in the said States and the property of such Settlers, and reposing full Confidence in the faith of Congress, . . . form'd the design of coming to reside in the City of Philadelphia." The capture of Lynch and his vessel and cargo by a privateer off the coast of Delaware prevented him from becoming an American settler for more than a year. The Irish immigrant remained incarcerated as a prisoner of war even after the Admiralty Court of New Jersey denied the legality of the capture. It was not until the end of August 1780 that the Continental Congress, "satisfied" that the prisoner was "not the John Lynch, who is a Major on halfpay in the corps of the late Roman Catholic Volunteers in the British service," resolved that "John Patrick Lynch, now confined in the States Gaol as a prisoner of war, be enlarged."[44]

A growing awareness of the fragility of the virtue necessary to uphold liberty paralleled the escalation of political tensions in the 1770s. Americans became increasingly convinced that environment was crucial in nurturing people's natural tendency toward virtue and in preventing the corruption of their even stronger instinct for self-preservation into the lust for personal aggrandizement at the expense of the public good. The most favorable environment for cultivating virtue was one that educated men in identifying and upholding their rights. People living under free governments knew their rights and recognized the actions that threatened them. Experience also taught them the steps to be taken to secure their rights and to defeat attempts to subvert liberty. While educated foreigners such as Montesquieu could learn to appreciate a free government, they first had to cast off the attachment to absolutist principles instilled in them from birth. The inability of even Enlightenment thinkers to comprehend all the nuances of the English Constitution made it unlikely that uneducated foreigners, indoctrinated in subordination and superstition under papist or absolute monarchies, could be trusted to uphold republican principles. Given this reasoning, it is not surprising that the wartime conditions that increased American suspicions of the commitment of their fellow citizens to republican principles, made

[44] Ibid., 190–208; Sally Schwartz, *"A Mixed Multitude": The Struggle for Toleration in Colonial Pennsylvania* (New York: New York University Press, 1987), 282–85; Philip Mazzei, *My Life and Wanderings*, ed. Margherita Marchione, trans. S. Eugene Scalia (Morristown, N.J.: American Institute of Italian Studies, 1980), quotes on 219; petition of John Patrick Lynch in *Papers of the Continental Congress*, RG 360, National Archives Microfilm M247, "Petitions Addressed to Congress, 1775–1789," Item 42, vol. 4, 224–26 (quotes).

American patriots hesitant to place the defense of their cause in the hands of foreigners, "unacquainted with our Constitution & Laws."[45]

Wartime Policies

The offers of free land and special privileges made by the Continental Congress during the Revolution to soldiers serving in the British army are traditionally seen as the beginning of the American policy of recruiting immigrants to strengthen their new nation. However, the primary purpose of this program was defensive—to diminish the military strength of the invading British army. The plan was devised by a committee appointed to find a way to encourage "Hessians and other foreigners, to quit the British service." In offering land and naturalization as an inducement to desertion, the Continental Congress employed the traditional method of rewarding British soldiers for their service in America, perhaps reasoning that such an offer would leave foreign mercenaries with no reason to complete their tours of duty. By settling deserters on the land, Congress was also adopting the English method of dealing with disbanded soldiers, whose activities, as they wandered around the countryside, unemployed and lacking a permanent niche in society, had worried Old World governments for centuries. The offer of an exemption from military service for deserters cost the Amcricans nothing, as Congress had already resolved "That no prisoners of war or deserters from the enemy be inlisted, drafted, or returned to serve in the continental army" since "experience hath proved that no confidence can be placed in prisoners of war or deserters . . . who inlist . . . but many losses and great mischiefs have frequently happened by them."[46]

The most significant change in American immigration policies during the 1770s was the Declaration of Independence that transformed British subjects into aliens. The people who had formerly poured into America and served as role models for provincials were now liable to the same disabilities and scrutiny as immigrants from the most despotic Old World governments. The American patriots had appealed to the "native justice and magnamity" of their "British brethren,"

> as well as to the ties of our common kindred to disavow these usurpations which were likely to interrupt our connection and correspondence. They too have been

---

[45] Chilton Williamson, *American Suffrage: From Property to Democracy, 1760–1860* (Princeton: Princeton University Press, 1960), 52 (quote); Glenn Weaver, "Benjamin Franklin and the Pennsylvania Germans," *William and Mary Quarterly*, 3d ser., 14 (1956), 539.

[46] Max J. Kohler, "An Important European Mission to Investigate American Immigration Conditions and John Quincy Adams' Relation thereto (1817–1818)," 1918 reprint from *Deutsch-Amerikanische Geschichtsblätter, Jahrbuch der Deutsch-Amerikanischen Historischen Gessellschaft von Illinois*, 17 (1917), 22; *Journals of the Continental Congress, 1774–1789*, X, 203 (quote).

deaf to the voice of justice & of consanguinity, and when occasions have been given them, by the regular course of their laws, of removing from their councils the disturbers of our harmony, they have, by their free election, re-established them in power. At this very time they too are permitting their chief magistrate to send over not only soldiers of our common blood, but Scotch & foreign mercenaries to invade & destroy us. These facts have given the last stab to agonizing affection, and manly spirit bids us to renounce forever these unfeeling brethren. We must endeavor to forget our former love for them, and hold them as we hold the rest of mankind, enemies in war, in peace friends. We might have been a free and a great people together; but a communication of grandeur & of freedom it seems is below their dignity. Be it so, since they will have it. The road to happiness & to glory is open to us too. We will tread it apart from them, and acquiesce in the necessity which denounces our eternal separation.[47]

The inability of British subjects, raised in a favorable environment, under the English Constitution, to sustain their virtue at home and to support their American kin cast doubt on their value in the new republics. In 1775 the American government decided against holding out exceptional incentives to lure Irishmen to their shores. In its "Address to the People of Ireland" of May 1775, the Continental Congress recognized the special relationship that existed between Ireland and the American colonies, stating that, "*Your* parliament had done us no wrong. *You* had ever been friendly to the rights of mankind; and we acknowledge, with pleasure and gratitude, that *your* nation has produced patriots, who have nobly distinguished themselves in the cause of humanity and America." This Address went on to offer America as an asylum for freedom-loving Irish people who suffered from America's economic sanctions or British oppression. Despite these professions of brotherhood, the American Congress, in October of the same year, rejected a plan devised by its Committee of Trade to encourage Irish immigration. The Committee report stated that,

> As the Cessation of the American Trade with Ireland originated in Policy dictated by Principles of self Preservation and may be attended with Distress to a People who have always manifested a Noble Regard to the Rights of Mankind and have ever been friendly to these much injured Colonies, Your Committee are of opinion that great Kindness and Attention ought to be paid to such of that oppressed Nation as have or may come to settle in America, and that it be earnestly recommended by this Congress to the good People of these Colonies to let them have Lands at a cheap Rate, and on easy Terms, and that the several Conventions and Assemblies and Committees throughout these confederate Countries, afford them Aid and do them every friendly service.

The report that was read in Congress on October 2, 1775, had the Committee's plan for cheap lands and easy terms crossed out. It retained, however, the Com-

---

[47] Jefferson's original draft of the Declaration of Independence, in *Thomas Jefferson: Writings*, ed. Peterson, 22–23 (quotes); Maier, *From Resistance to Revolution*, 255–70.

mittee's recommendation that the guidelines regulating nonimportation be changed to allow the exchange of American flaxseed for Irish woolen yarn and military stores, since "the witholding Flax seed from Ireland will be attended with a much greater Degree of Distress and Ruin to the poor of that Kingdom, than the Congress apprehended."[48]

Doubts as to the wisdom of underwriting the immigration of the Irish to America paled before the determination of the patriots to protect their country from the baleful influence of the Scots. By war's end the state of Georgia had concluded that it was "absolutely necessary for the peace[,] safety and Good Government of this State, that every exertion be used to prevent as much as may be all manner of Persons whose conduct has been inimical to the liberties of AMERICA, and of idle and disorderly Persons emigrating from any of the United States, or else where becoming Citizens of this State." Because "the People of Scotland have in General Manifested a decided inimicallity to the Civil Liberties of America and have contributed Principally to promote and Continue a Ruinous War, for the Purpose of Subjugating this and the other Confederated States," the Georgia legislature decreed, "that no Person a Native of Scotland, shall be permitted or allowed to emigrate into this State with intent to Settle within the same, or to carry on Commerce or other trade, Profession or business, but every such Person, being a Native of Scotland shall within three days after his arrival within this State be apprehended and Committed to Gaol there to remain without bail or mainprize untill an opportunity offers of shipping or Transporting him to some part of the English Kings Dominions."[49]

Although Georgia's Act of 1782 was "not to be construed to extend to such Persons, natives of Scotland, who have exerted themselves in behalf of the freedom and Independence of the United States of America, in the Present contest, and who are now entitled to the Rights of Citizenship in any or either of the United States," it represents in exaggerated form a wartime lesson learned by all the American states. The refusal of Scottish Highlanders to renounce their allegiance to the King of Great Britain tainted the character of all North Britons in America, even those from the Lowlands who tended to side with the rebels. Although distrust of the Scots was highest—and measures against them the most extreme—in New York and the South, where the Highland clans were concentrated, patriots throughout the American states characterized the Scots as supporters of "the cause of slavery and oppression," with "governmental Ideas . . . abhorrent to all Ideas of civil Liberty & . . . full of rigorous tyrannical Superiorities & subordinations."[50]

[48] Address, May 10, 1775, *Journals of the Continental Congress*, II, 214; Report, Oct. 2, 1775, ibid., II, 268.
[49] Act of 1782, Allen D. Candler, ed., *The Colonial Records of the State of Georgia*, 25 vols. (Atlanta: Charles P. Byrd, 1904–1916), XIX, part II, 162–64 (quotes).
[50] Ibid. (quotes); Graham, *Colonists from Scotland*, 150–80.

The failure of British subjects outside the thirteen colonies to rally to the cause of liberty not only led American patriots to expand their mission, but also prompted the belief that they possessed a unique virtue—the virtue necessary to wage a successful war against corruption and to establish and support a purely republican form of government. Given this conclusion, the converse also was true—that men who had refused to take an active role against British tyranny lacked virtue and therefore could not be trusted with the power to uphold or subvert liberty. If Americans extended full political rights to loyalists and aliens, they would jeopardize their liberty and republican future. Test acts were administered to Americans and aliens alike to emasculate the political power of the nonvirtuous.

Because the wartime actions of American loyalists could be construed as treason, they were viewed with more suspicion and endured harsher penalties than foreigners who had not experienced and then rejected the benefits of liberty. This mitigating factor did not, however, remove American doubts about the ability of aliens to support a free republic. British subjects throughout the empire, who should have known better, had failed to recognize and oppose political tyranny in the years preceding 1776 and had forced the American rebels to seek aid from despotic monarchies. The shortcomings of British subjects in the Old World and the New did little to increase American confidence in foreigners who were unacquainted with the liberties they were expected to defend. Americans would cling tenaciously to their belief that, "The good and wise part [of Europe], the lovers of Liberty and human happiness look forward to the establishment of American Freedom and Independence as an event which will secure to them and their Descendants an assylum from the effects and violence of Despotic power." But close contact with their European allies often proved disillusioning. On his arrival in the Netherlands, John Adams doubted "much whether there is any Nation of Europe more estimable than the Dutch" and speculated that he might "yet bring my Family to the Hague and become a Dutchman." After a year of struggling to secure official backing for the American cause, Adams decided that the Dutch nation was "in a melancholy situation; sunk in ease, devoted to the pursuit of gain . . . incumbered with a complicated and perplexed constitution, divided among themselves in interest and sentiment, they seem afraid of every thing." The experiences of the American envoys in Paris produced similar skepticism about the character of their French allies. By November of 1782, John Jay and John Adams were agreed that the French were "intriguing with the English against us" because it was "not their interest that we should become a great and formidable people, and therefore they will not help us become so."[51]

---

[51] Silas Deane to the Secret Committee of the Continental Congress, Paris, Dec. 1, 1776, *Papers of the Continental Congress*, "Letters Addressed to Congress," Item 103, 48 (quote); J. W. Schulte Nordholt, "The Impact of the American Revolution on the Dutch Republic," in Library of Congress Symposia, *Impact of the American Revolution Abroad*, 42, 41, 43 (quotes); Alexander DeConde, "The French Alliance in

Interaction with European "lovers of freedom" in the New World produced similar misgivings about America's foreign allies. As early as 1777, rivalry for command had produced enough friction among American and foreign military men for Congress to seek a moratorium on the recruitment of alien officers. By April 1781 the inability of the French fleet to protect the Chesapeake from Benedict Arnold and his British marauders prompted George Mason to inform Virginia's delegates at the Continental Congress of the "general Opinion prevailing that our Allies are spinning out the War, in order to weaken America, as well as Great Britain; and thereby leave us, at the End of it, as dependent as possible upon themselves." The theoretical doubts of America's revolutionary statesmen were mirrored at the popular level in the less philosophical, but more predictable, clashes between French soldiers and sailors and American civilians.[52]

The wartime activities of foreigners resident in the colonies prior to the Revolution did not assuage colonial doubts about the ability of the subjects of despotic states to support free governments. The character of German sectarians in Pennsylvania who refused to share in the military defense of their adopted land and to abjure their allegiance to George III often was denigrated. The state assembly tried to defuse animosity among its citizens by urging Pennsylvanians to "bear a tender and brotherly Regard" toward those who were "conscientiously scrupulous of bearing arms." The Pennsylvania assembly also urged pacifists to "*Contribute Liberally* in this time of universal calamity" to the war effort and the support of the men who served in the militia. But officers of the Philadelphia Association were not mollified by such exhortations, believing that "People *sincerely* and *religiously* scrupulous are but few in Comparison to those who upon this Occasion, as well as others, make *Conscience a Convenience*."[53]

The wartime need for Americans to present a united front against the British army and to demonstrate their strength and commitment to liberty to Old World spectators limited the role of popular xenophobia in determining public policy. Rebel newspapers omitted or downplayed reports of the brawls between Americans and French soldiers in Boston and New York that were so gleefully chronicled in the loyalist press. American statesmen saved their criticisms of their Bourbon allies for their private correspondence while issuing public statements in praise of America's noble allies. However, many Americans were unconvinced by wartime rhetoric and retained their doubts about the character of foreigners and their value as republican citizens. In 1779, a New Hampshire newspaper criticized an attempt to expand suffrage that would "make possible the outvoting of

Historical Speculation," in Ronald Hoffman and Peter J. Albert, eds., *Diplomacy and Revolution: The Franco-American Alliance of 1778* (Charlottesville: University Press of Virginia, 1981), 22 (quotes).

[52] *The Papers of George Mason, 1725–1792*, ed. Robert A. Rutland, 3 vols. (Chapel Hill: University of North Carolina Press, 1970), II, 680–84, quote on 682; William C. Stinchcombe, "Americans Celebrate the Birth of the Dauphin," in Hoffman and Albert, eds., *Diplomacy and Revolution*, 45–47.

[53] Quotes from Schwartz, "*Mixed Multitude*," 276–77.

property owners by those with no property, so that a number of transients, some Scotch, some Irish, and 'even French peddlers' would be able to vote away the assets of the well-to-do." In August 1776 a group of Maryland militia demanded that all who had borne arms, and had thus demonstrated their republican character, be allowed to vote for delegates to the state's constitutional convention. The freemen from Ann Arundel county, who supported the militia, modified the original demand by instructing their representatives "to secure the vote for all native-born freemen, 'if well-affected' and resident in the colony one year," but to limit the suffrage of foreign-born residents to those "worth 30 pounds currency visible estate or the owners of 50-acre freehold." By December 1781 Thomas Jefferson was voicing his doubts of "the expediency of inviting" the subjects of absolute monarchies "by extraordinary encouragements," since "They will bring with them the principles of the governments they leave, imbibed in their early youth; or, if able to throw them off, it will be in exchange for an unbounded licentiousness, passing, as is usual, from one extreme to another. It would be a miracle were they to stop precisely at the point of temperate liberty."[54]

In the 1770s American patriots united to protect what they defined as their rights as Englishmen. The decade-long attack on those rights produced an intense scrutiny of the nature of liberty and how it was upheld or subverted by various individuals, social developments, and political institutions. The inability of the colonists to convince the British government and people of the validity of their analysis and of the need for reform left Americans with no option but to sever their connection with England and to create an independent nation that would insulate and preserve liberty. The need for moral and military support in severing the link with Old World corruption led American patriots to proclaim themselves leaders in the cause of humanity and to promise a sanctuary for both the spirit of liberty and all who fought on its behalf. But the preservation of America as an asylum depended on both maintaining the virtue of its people and nurturing the elements of American society that supported free government and excluding those people and developments whose moral or social characteristics would introduce in America the decadence and corruption of Europe.

The need for outside support in establishing their revolutionary republic led American leaders to gloss over the defects of their friends and to contrast the noble virtues of their allies with the moral turpitude of those who supported British tyranny. The events leading to the creation of the republic had, however, made Americans increasingly conscious of the disasters awaiting an inert or non-virtuous citizenry and wary of people who lacked the education, experience, and

[54] Stinchcombe, "Americans Celebrate the Birth of the Dauphin," 39–71; Williamson, *American Suffrage*, 106–10, quotes on 106, 109; Thomas Jefferson, *Notes on The State of Virginia*, 1st publ. 1781, ed. Thomas Perkins Abernethy (New York: Harper & Row, 1964), 83–84 (quote).

character needed to be vigilant guardians of liberty. The immigration policies developed in the early years of the republic would be shaped by revolutionary America's dual commitment to serving as a sanctuary for freedom and the victims of Old World tyranny while preserving its own republican liberty.

5 Land of Liberty:
The Republican Challenge

T‍HE A‍MERICAN W‍AR FOR I‍NDEPENDENCE was just one phase of a global struggle for supremacy among Europe's mercantilist empires. In freeing themselves from British control, the Americans forced a realignment of the power structure of the Atlantic basin. During the postwar jockeying for position, the American states tried to do more than merely establish themselves as the newest members of this mercantilist world. They hoped to fulfill their republican vision of an international community built on the free movement of goods and people and where policies were determined by the needs of the people rather than the ambitions of princes.

America's postwar claims and aspirations met with vigorous opposition. Old World leaders saw no reason to dismantle the mercantilist barriers that guarded their trade, their power, and their people. Indeed, in the aftermath of the American Revolution these barriers seemed more necessary than ever before. The final years of the eighteenth century were marked by "a great turbulence of disposition" in the Atlantic community—a time when men, "impatient for a something, they know not what," became "restless in attempting to obtain it." Troubled Old World officials blamed this restless turbulence on the spirit of liberty emanating from America, which infected their subjects with both an "enthusiasm for liberty" and "emigration fever."[1] They used every means they possessed to neutralize that dangerous republican challenge, from erecting ever higher legal barriers around their people to launching propaganda campaigns to puncture American delusions and denigrate their messianic aspirations.

[1] Quotes from *Maryland Gazette or the Baltimore General Advertiser*, Oct. 28, 1785, dateline, London, Sept. 3; and *Leeds Mercury*, Jan. 6, 1784. See also *Newcastle Journal*, May 10, 1783.

Republican Experiments

In the 1770s, American revolutionaries concluded that a world organized around the dynastic needs of monarchs produced unnecessary wars, confusion, and hardships, whereas one linked by the natural economic needs of each country's citizenry would be peaceful, harmonious, and prosperous.[2] During the first heady days of peace, the creation of this enlightened and cosmopolitan world seemed within the grasp of the victorious Americans. Ships from all nations flocked to their ports, carrying goods, people, and congratulatory messages. Americans basked in the praise of Europeans who gloried in the defeat of the British government. The successful rebels invited their friends in the Old World to participate in their exciting republican experiment. Europeans who despaired of establishing liberty in their own nations could emigrate and enjoy the fruits won by their virtuous American colleagues. Those who remained in Europe could advance the Glorious Cause by maintaining their ties with America's republicans, sharing their ideas and offering support through personal friendships and membership in organizations such as the Society of the Cincinnati and the American Philosophical Society.[3]

During the 1780s American statesmen worked to implement their revolutionary ideals. They tried to avoid political alliances and military treaties with dynastic states, hoping to use commercial treaties and the propagation of free trade ideals to enhance the nation's position in the political economy of the Western world.[4] But American diplomatic innovations met with only limited success. Although independence had destroyed Great Britain's exclusive claim to the land and resources of the United States, Europeans continued to define the function of the emancipated states as that of tributaries within the mercantilist system.

To obtain vital French aid during the Revolution, American envoys had, despite their repugnance, been forced to enter into a military alliance with that dynastic state. During the diplomatic maneuvering of the post-treaty years,

[2] Felix Gilbert, *To the Farewell Address: Ideas of Early American Foreign Policy* (Princeton: Princeton University Press, 1961), esp. chaps. 2–3.

[3] *South Carolina Gazette and General Advertiser*, Aug. 2, 1783; *Maryland Gazette*, May 30, Dec. 19, 26, 1783; Thomas Pownall, Feb. 28, 1783, to Benjamin Franklin, in Charles Sumner, *Prophetic Voices Concerning America* (Boston: Lee and Shepard, 1874), 125; Richard Price, *Observations on the Importance of the American Revolution, and the Means of Making It a Benefit to the World* (London: T. Cadell, 1785); Colin Bonwick, *English Radicals and the American Revolution* (Chapel Hill: University of North Carolina Press, 1977), esp. chap. 6; Elizabeth M. Geffen, *Philadelphia Unitarianism, 1796–1861* (Philadelphia: University of Pennsylvania Press, 1961), chaps. 1–4; Caroline Robbins, "Honest Heretic: Joseph Priestley in America, 1794–1804," American Philosophical Society, *Proceedings*, 106 (1962), 60–76; Durand Echeverria, *Mirage in the West: A History of the French Image of American Society to 1815* (Princeton: Princeton University Press, 1957), esp. chaps. 3–4.

[4] Gilbert, *To the Farewell Address*; but see also James H. Hutson, *John Adams and the Diplomacy of the American Revolution* (Lexington: University Press of Kentucky, 1980); and Drew R. McCoy, "The Virginia Port Bill of 1784," *Virginia Magazine of History and Biography*, 83 (1975), 288–303.

French fleets routinely anchored in the harbors of their American allies during voyages to the West Indies. Old World observers assumed that these expeditions were French attempts to strip England of her remaining West Indian possessions. After war broke out between France and England in 1793, the French rattled their 1778 American alliance, hoping to force Great Britain to divert troops to protect Canada from putative American aggression. The French also called on the Americans to furnish more direct military aid by providing ports to outfit and man French warships and privateers and prize courts to condemn captured British vessels. Once again, Indians were called on by Europeans to attack the frontiers and Americans tried to wrest what profits they could from European rivalries, through privateering and the carrying trade. Thus, the colonial pattern of using the New World to fight European battles continued, evidence of the failure of American statesmen to revolutionize international diplomacy.[5]

American commercial policy also was forced into a traditional mold, despite the efforts of iconoclastic Americans and their European friends. The end of hostilities in 1783 signaled the opportunity for governments on both sides of the Atlantic to take advantage of economic changes produced by the war. America's allies and neutrals tried to exploit the independent states, now cut loose from British control. Working primarily on mercantilist assumptions, England's rivals eagerly seized the chance to siphon the strength of the old British empire into their own, while the British government tried to limit the damaging consequences of its territorial dismemberment. By the end of the 1780s, Old World conservatives had forced American statesmen to jettison most of their republican dreams of a world economy driven by the needs of people, rather than the dictates of princes and power politics.

The new American republics may have thrown away the opportunity to apply rigorous pressure for the recognition of the principles of free trade and commercial reciprocity by a precipitate reopening of their ports to British shipping. By 1790 American eagerness to resume trade, plus the willingness of English merchants to assume the risk of shipping to saturated markets, had placed over 40 per cent of the new nation's overseas carrying trade in British hands. Great Britain also captured the American market for manufactured goods, with almost 53 per cent of the tonnage arriving from Europe originating in British ports. All the American states failed, whatever their tactics, to deny Great Britain that disproportionate share of their commerce.[6]

---

[5]Charles R. Ritcheson, *Aftermath of Revolution: British Policy toward the United States, 1783–1795*, 1st publ. 1969 (New York: Norton, 1971), esp. chaps. 1, 9, 13–15.

[6]"Tonnage and Imports for the Year Ending September 30, 1790," *American State Papers: Documents, Legislative and Executive, of the Congress of the United States*, 38 vols. (Washington, D.C.: Gales and Seaton, 1832–1861), VII, 47–63.

In less than a decade, Great Britain had recovered from her military humiliation and had outstripped her Old World rivals in securing the American market for her manufactures and commodities without granting special concessions to the United States. She captured a hefty share of the new republic's carrying trade, without jeopardizing her own Navigation Acts or conceding to American demands for the restoration of their western posts, free trade with the British West Indies, or even a commercial treaty. The completeness of the British commercial and diplomatic victories guaranteed the continuation of international politics based on power, princes, and the principles of mercantilism.

"The Rage for Emigration"

The American states were more successful in eroding barriers that limited the mobility of Old World subjects and insulated Europe from radical republican ideas. The European states that had fought for a share of American commerce were able to secure that trade largely on their own terms. But the price of their commercial success was the transmission of people and ideas along the trade routes carved out in the 1780s.[7]

The legitimacy of the American republics was based on the right of people to remove themselves from both the territory and allegiance of their birth. In the 1780s state laws and constitutions made the American commitment to the right of mobility, expatriation, and volitional citizenship explicit. Once again, the Old World ignored or rejected American claims.[8] After the American Revolution, there was no reason for the Old World to question the mercantilist belief that

[7] In the 1780s, the American population increased by 43.9 per cent, the largest rate of increase in the nation's history. In the 1790s Thomas Malthus used American population figures to demonstrate the inevitability of subsistence crises, as exponential population growth, through natural increase, overtaxed natural resources. Malthus's theory was built on his assumption that America's phenomenal population growth was primarily the result of natural increase. His assumption then became part of the official story of the nation's demographic beginnings. Since the time of Malthus, immigration history has been based on the belief that few foreigners migrated to the United States in the first decades of the republic. But contemporaries told a very different story. The sources cited in the next two chapters tell of high levels of immigration in the 1780s and 1790s. There is no reason to believe that these sources were mistaken. In addition, it is unlikely that the 1780s—a decade of wartime deaths, disruption of family life, and exodus of 60,000 loyalists—would produce an unprecedented and unsurpassed rate of natural increase in the United States. Therefore, this study is built on the assumption that there were indeed surges of immigration in the 1780s and 1790s that were large enough to alarm Old World governments.

[8] Clause XV, "Declaration of Rights of the Inhabitants of the Commonwealth, or State of Pennsylvania" (1776), in Francis Newton Thorpe, ed., *The Federal and State Constitutions, Colonial Charters, and other Organic Laws of the States, Territories, and Colonies Now or Heretofore Forming the United States of America,* 7 vols. (Washington, D.C.: Government Printing Office, 1909), V, 3084; James H. Kettner, *The Development of American Citizenship, 1608–1870* (Chapel Hill: University of North Carolina Press, 1978), 190–209, 267–81; Philip Appleman, ed., *An Essay on the Principle of Population* (New York: Norton, 1976); G. T. Griffith, *Population Problems of the Age of Malthus,* 2d ed. (London: Frank Cass, 1967); Klaus E. Knorr, *British Colonial Theories, 1570–1850* (Toronto: University of Toronto Press, 1944), 219–28, 269–315.

emigration diminished the stature and well-being of a nation and therefore no reason to sanction voluntary expatriation.

In England, the loss of British subjects to the revolted colonies reaffirmed traditional demographic principles. Having already ceded an empire, British patriots were determined to deny America's republicans any more of their patrimony. The departure of wealthy families with their assets clearly diminished British wealth. The emigration of artisans with their tools, or just their skills, seemed prima facie evidence of the extent to which one country's demographic gain was another's loss. In 1785, one Englishman estimated that the 40,000 British subjects who had emigrated to Philadelphia since the Peace would earn, on average, not "less than ten pounds per year each, which is a loss to this nation of four hundred thousand pounds per ann. yearly." He also estimated that these departures reduced British tax revenue by at least £60,000 a year, since each emigrant would have paid no "less than thirty shillings for excise and customs upon the necessaries of life which they consume in a year."[9]

America's seduction of the foreign soldiers who had been sent to subdue them provided Britons with concrete evidence that America's demographic gains came at their expense. Englishmen were outraged by their government's decision to disband British troops in America since so many "have settled in the territories of the United States rather than go to Nova Scotia. . . . Several of these soldiers too had received arrears of pay and dismission money, to the amount of five or six guineas a man; so that by thus disbanding part of the army at New York, America has acquired a considerable number of new subjects, together with some thousands of British guineas which might have been brought to England."[10] The refusal of the Hessians to return to Europe at the end of the Revolution was even more galling. In this instance the American states gained valuable inhabitants and the British people were loaded with additional taxes to pay the fine, estimated at £30 a head, due for all foreign mercenaries not returned to the service of their prince. The American rebels even profited from soldiers who returned to Europe, as their tales of America encouraged postwar emigration.[11]

The emancipation of the American colonies ended all British doubts on the question that had been raised in the decade preceding the Revolution—"whether draining these kingdoms of their most useful hands, for the purpose of peopling the wilds of America, be of advantage to them." The American Revolution had

<hr/>

[9]"Debate in the Commons on the American Intercourse Bill," March 7, 1783, in William Cobbett and John Wright, eds., *Parliamentary History of England, from the Earliest Period to the Year 1803*, 36 vols. (London: T. C. Hansard, 1806–1820), XXIII, 602–15; *Leeds Mercury*, Oct. 25, 1785, dateline London, Oct. 22 (quotes).

[10]*Felix Farley's Bristol Journal*, Nov. 11, 1783, Jan. 10, 1784 (quote); *Newcastle Journal*, May 10, 24, June 28, 1783; *Leeds Mercury*, Jan. 13, 1784.

[11]*Felix Farley's Bristol Journal*, Apr. 26, July 5, Nov. 8, 1783; *Belfast News-Letter*, Mar. 28, Apr. 29, 1783; *Maryland Gazette*, Sept. 20, 1785.

proved "beyond a doubt . . . That every inhabitant taken from us, and added to America, diminishes the strength of this country in a twofold ratio; not only as a simple loss, but as an acquisition to a foreign State, which may turn its arms against us, whenever interest or ambition holds out sufficient inducement."[12] In British North America, a "gentleman in Hallifax" expressed the new, adversarial, relationship between republican America and the British empire. He warned his correspondent in Falmouth (later Portland, Maine) to beware of the settlement of Nova Scotia and New Brunswick by "people flocking in from Great-Britain and Ireland, as well as from the continent" because "the prosperity of these Provinces endanger that of yours, they will become formidable to your liberty."[13]

After the Revolution, it was obvious that Great Britain had nothing to gain and everything to lose by the emigration of its subjects to the independent American states. But in this new, postwar world Great Britian also refused to use native Britons to strengthen its colonies in the East or West. There were many traditional mercantilist reasons for this reluctance to sanction emigration.[14] But the most important was the revival of prerevolutionary fears of depopulation in Ireland and the Scottish Highlands when emigration from those fragile polities resumed with a vengeance at the end of the American Revolution.[15]

In the spring of 1783, British newspapers were filled with descriptions of the "madness of emigration" that prevailed in Ireland, primarily among those "deluded by the false notions of making mountains of gold in America." According to one widely circulated report, "more than 13,000 Emigrants have already gone from the north of Ireland. The Stop that was put to it by the War being removed, they fly thither, with an eagerness never known before." To make matters even worse, these emigrants "were not the profligate, the idle, and dissolute, but the sober, the honest, and industrious country people . . . who all

[12] "Pro Patria," *London Chronicle*, June 28, 1783, (quote); see also the rejoinder by "Ratio," ibid., July 19, 1783.

[13] Halifax letter, dated "Falmouth (in America)," Sept. 3, 1785, *Maryland Gazette*, Sept. 30, 1785.

[14] For the reluctance of Great Britain to settle British North America with its own subjects, see letter from Inverarie, Apr. 29, 1786, predicting that "this country will soon be a desart, if some means are not fallen upon to prevent emigration. No less than four hundred souls go from this little place about the middle of summer. . . . They intend for Canada," *Leeds Mercury*, June 6, 1786; Lord Sheffield, *Observations on the Commerce of the American States*, 2nd ed., 1st publ. 1784 (New York: Augustus M. Kelly, 1970), 239.

[15] British officials resumed their prewar concern over the depopulation of Ireland even before hostilities ended. In a report prepared for the British House of Lords in 1779 Dublin officials observed that "The Temptations to Emigration from this Country to America have always been very great, from the exceeding cheapness of Land there, the high Price of Labour, and the extraordinary Value of every species of Art and Manufacture; to which has gradually been added the Inducement from Relationship and Connection with former settlers." They predicted that "Whenever America shall be in a settled state, let that state be under what Conditions it may, We must expect that the Emigration from this Country will be more numerous than ever; and that our working Hands especially, will carry with them not only the present Wealth of this Country." "Report of the Commissioners of the Revenue . . . Relative to the State and Trade etc. of Ireland," June 26, 1779, *American Papers in the House of Lords Record Office*.

declared that they tore themselves away from their native country, because they could not procure subsistence in it."[16] According to the *Newcastle Journal*, "accounts from different parts of Scotland" told the same story—of "A spirit of emigration . . . spreading fast." In June of 1783 the *Leeds Mercury* worried that if "The rage for emigration to America . . . in Scotland and Ireland" was not "in time opposed by adequate counteraction to the western sides of these countries, the consequences cannot but be fatal."[17]

It was also evident that postwar England was not immune to emigration fever. On March 1, 1783, a report was published of "A considerable society of neighbours and friends from Norfolk and Lincolnshire . . . preparing to emigrate to America." On May 17, 1783, a correspondent from Whitehaven described the "Preparations . . . making by numbers of people in this country for conveying themselves to America. Several families in remote parts of the county, where such emigrations were the most unlikely to take place, are disposing of their property there, and providing for their settlement on that great continent, which is likely in a few months (if this spirit of emigration is equally prevalent in other parts) to have such an innundation of inhabitants as will more than replace the numbers who have fallen in the late unhappy contest."[18] From Liverpool came a report that "there was never known such a concourse of seamen out of employ as at present." As a result, "great numbers are daily making applications for working their passage to America." Other British sailors traveled to Brest "to get a passage to America," where they planned "to enter on board the American fishing vessels at Newfoundland." Sailors serving with the British navy in the West Indies likewise seized every opportunity to desert "to the American continent." A widely reprinted story from London also warned that "A great number of Agents have been for several months past and still are busily employed in London, Birmingham, Sheffield, Manchester, and most of the other great manufacturing towns, in seducing Artificers to emigrate to America."[19]

[16] *Belfast News-Letter*, Apr. 18, 1783 (quote); *New York Gazette*, Sept. 8, 1783, dateline London, June 13, 1783 (quote); *Felix Farley's Bristol Journal*, May 10, 1783; *Newcastle Journal*, May 10, 1783, May 8, 1784 (quote). See also reports of alarming emigration from Munster and Connaught (ibid., Apr. 20, 1784); Belfast (ibid., July 1, 1783, and *Pennsylvania Gazette*, July 28, 1783); Londonderry (*Belfast News-Letter*, May 11, 1784); Dublin (Dublin letter of May 22, 1784, *Pennsylvania Gazette*, Aug. 4, 1784); Sligo ([London] *Daily Universal Register*, Jan. 14, 1784); and Galway (*Pennsylvania Packet*, Nov. 19, 1784).

[17] *Newcastle Journal*, May 10, 1783 (quote); *Leeds Mercury*, June 24 (quote), July 8, 1783, and June 1, 1784; (London) *Daily Universal Register*, July 28, 1785; *Pennsylvania Packet*, Apr. 20, 1784; report presented to the British House of Commons on "the Distress and Famine . . . in Scotland," May 28, 1783, *Parliamentary Papers, Session of 22 January–28 August 1846*, 52 vols. (London: William Clowes and Son, 1846), XXXVII. Letters from Edinburgh stated that, in consequence of the distresses brought upon the "inhabitants of the Highlands, from the bad crops, the failure of the fisheries, and the hurricanes in the year 1782, it has been found . . . that they and their families have emigrated from that part of Scotland and Shetland, for different parts of America, to the amount of 19,000 souls!" *Leeds Mercury*, Sept. 28, 1784.

[18] Quotes from (Dublin) *Public Register*, Mar. 11, 1783, dateline London, March 1; *Felix Farley's Bristol Journal*, May 31, 1783, dateline Whitehaven, May 17.

[19] *Felix Farley's Bristol Journal*, June 10, 1783 (quote); *Leeds Mercury*, July 3, 1783, dateline London, May 29 (quotes); *Felix Farley's Bristol Journal*, May 15, 1784 (quote). Report of agents seducing artificers in *Leeds*

Britain's demographic losses during and after the American Revolution were highly visible and well publicized. But the Republic's friends suffered a similar fate. Active aid or friendly neutrality did not confer immunity from emigration fever on the subjects of allied nations. On the contrary, the more links with the New World, the more at risk a nation became. According to an observer in Altona, Germany, in the summer of 1783, "All Europe seems now to fix its views on the States of America. . . . The emigrations there from all parts of Europe are very considerable, and augment daily; so that this rising republic, situated on a soil favourable in all respects, will, according to all appearance, soon become one of the best peopled and most flourishing countries of the globe. Already the arts and trades are in full vigour by the number of artists and workmen, who continually flock there from all parts."[20]

By the middle of the 1780s, virtually all of the European nations that had established trade with the American states were lamenting the loss of people that their commercial links facilitated and were taking steps to prohibit the emigration of valuable subjects. In the spring of 1784 a Danish edict that ordered "all navigators going to the West-Indies . . . to give security for their return. . . . The ships that have any national passengers on board, without being provided with passports, will be seized as laden with contraband goods; foreign ships even are not excepted from this law, the aim of which is, to prevent the king's subjects from emigrating to the United States of North America, and forming settlements there." Danish subjects who emigrated without permission were to "have their effects confiscated, and their persons imprisoned whenever taken."[21] France instituted a similar program to halt emigration to America. In the spring of 1784, the French government, worried about the number of French emigrating "by means of the passes issued by the American Plenipotentiaries," announced that henceforth none would be allowed to "ship themselves, unless the pass is countersigned by one of the official [French] Ministers." According to one Londoner, the French were

equally as much afraid of many of their most useful mechanics and manufacturers emigrating to America, as we are in this country. This is easily discovered by the care they take at all their ports to prevent any secret embarkations. At Nantes and Bourdeaux they are particularly vigilant, because the American vessels visit those ports more frequently than any other. Not a ship is permitted to go out of those harbours till she has been most scrutinously examined; and though the Government make a shew of granting passports, their fears are evident from the unnecessary delays they make when any passes are solicited for America.[22]

Mercury, Apr. 6, 1784, dateline London, March 30; clock and watchmakers in *Leeds Mercury,* Nov. 11, 1784, dateline London, Nov. 4.

    [20] "Extract of a Letter from Altona," July 17, 1783, in *Leeds Mercury,* Aug. 12, 1783.

    [21] Quotes from *Maryland Gazette,* Aug. 27, 1784, dateline, Copenhagen, May 18; letter from Copenhagen, ibid., Nov. 5, 1784.

    [22] Quotes from: "Extract of Letter from L'Orient," May 7, 1784, in *Virginia Journal,* Aug. 12, 1784; report from London, May 5 in *Belfast News-Letter,* May 16, 1783.

The emigration that alarmed European governments in the 1780s was not directed solely to republican America. European governments also struggled to prevent the seduction of their useful subjects by continental rivals. In 1783 the Genevan government countered a British offer to transport and settle discontented Genevans in Ireland by arresting a leader of the emigration and passing laws to confiscate the property of those who left.[23] Bavarian officials "published restraining laws" and urged their counterparts in Swabia and Franconia to join them in an attempt to nullify campaigns designed to recruit German emigrants for "the deserts" of Russia. In Württemberg, the "rage for emigration" was triggered by "the great encouragement given to agriculture by the King of Prussia in the Western Provinces."[24]

As Old World governments resumed their pre-Revolutionary practice of recruiting skilled aliens, they also continued to sanction or promote the emigration of certain segments of their population. In eighteenth-century Europe, anti-emigration edicts were routinely suspended to allow recruitment by allied or friendly states. This policy was continued after the American Revolution. In 1784, the Duke of Brunswick allowed "a great number of artificers and husbandmen . . . to emigrate to America with their families." In 1785 the French government subsidized the emigration of Frenchmen to South Carolina to establish silk culture in the lands of its American allies. Great Britain, quite naturally, felt no such obligation to facilitate American recruitment. Instead, England used its ties with Hanover to thwart the efforts of the sixty-eight German glass workers, who had emigrated to the United States with their families in 1784, to secure additional workmen from Thuringia and Bohemia for their factory in Maryland.[25]

Although Old World nations tolerated a limited recruitment of their skilled subjects by their friends and allies, they were much more consistent and enthusiastic in promoting the emigration of subjects whose presence undermined rather than strengthened their political economies. American independence did not alter the European perception of the New World as the proper or convenient receptacle for these social liabilities.

In 1783 the Duke of Brunswick, realizing that he could secure employment for only about half of his troops in postwar Europe, ordered his general to discharge in America all soldiers whose physical infirmities or criminal tendencies rendered

[23] *Felix Farley's Bristol Journal*, June 28, Sept. 27, Oct. 4, 1783.

[24] Quotes from "Letter from Frankfurt," Sept. 25, *Felix Farley's Bristol Journal*, Nov. 1, 1783; *Leeds Mercury*, Oct. 12, 1784. Württemberg officials responded with an edict "forbidding any person to depart that dukedom without leave from the reigning Prince, on pain of fine and imprisonment," *Leeds Mercury*, Oct. 12, 1784. A similar order was issued at Mentz, *Felix Farley's Bristol Journal*, July 31, 1784.

[25] *Maryland Gazette*, Dec. 10, 1784 (quote); *Leeds Mercury*, Oct. 25, 1785, March 28, 1786; *Maryland Gazette*, Dec. 16, 1785; Lowell Colton Bennion, "Flight from the Reich: A Geographic Exposition of Southwest German Emigration, 1683–1815" (Ph.D. diss., Syracuse University, 1971), 246; Dieter Cunz, *The Maryland Germans: A History* (Princeton: Princeton University Press, 1948), 163–65.

them unfit for further military service. Other European states also used the American continent to rid themselves of redundant or undesirable subjects. In 1783 the canton of Basel provided an indigent family with the funds necessary to emigrate to America. This project was aborted when the family ran out of money in Holland and was forced to return home. During the 1780s, the county of Nassau suspended sentences and waived the emigration tax of felons willing to settle in the New World. Some German authorities also provided travel funds for paupers who promised never to return. In 1787 an American vessel bound to Philadelphia from Hamburg included among its passengers forty young women "selected from those confined in the [Hamburg] House of Correction." Reportedly, "Upon the rumour of this embarkation, several other young women, of the same calling . . . though not under confinement, offered to undertake the voyage, with a view of gaining a settlement in the above district, where females are said to be wanting."[26]

Great Britain had especially compelling reasons to promote the resumption of America's prewar function as a dumping ground for convicts. English concern over on escalating crime rate and overcrowded jails had been steadily increasing ever since 1776, when Parliament had ended convict transportation to America. With the return of peace, George III and his ministers decided to act on the assumption, born of desperation, that England could resume its earlier practice of "permitting" the Americans, "to obtain Men unworthy to remain in this Island." They assumed that the well-publicized resolve of the "States of America" not to "accept our convicts" could once again be shaken by the need for cheap white labor. British convict contractors tried to ensure this acceptance by disguising their cargoes and their destinations. Stories published in English newspapers of convicts boarding (and escaping from) the vessel *George* bound for Halifax were thus a smoke screen to mask the sailing of that vessel as the *Swift*, carrying "indentured servants" to Baltimore. Even though this subterfuge succeeded in muddying public records, two shipments of English convicts to America in 1783–1784 yielded headaches rather than profits for the contractors and provide evidence that independence had stiffened earlier American resistance to receiving such largess from Great Britain.[27]

---

[26] John Duncan Brite, "The Attitude of European States toward Emigration to the American Colonies and the United States, 1607–1820" (Ph.D. diss., University of Chicago, 1937), 281–84; Albert Bernhardt Faust and Gaius Marcus Brumbaugh, eds., *Lists of Swiss Emigrants in the Eighteenth Century to the American Colonies*, 2 vols. (Baltimore: Genealogical Publishing Company, 1920–1925), II, 201; Bennion, "Flight from the Reich," 245; *Leeds Mercury*, May 8, 1787, dateline Hamburg, Apr. 10 (quotes).

[27] A. Roger Ekirch, *Bound for America: The Transportation of British Convicts to the Colonies, 1718–1775* (Oxford: Clarendon, 1987), chap. 8, quote on 233; Mollie Gillen, "The Botany Bay Decision, 1786: Convicts, not Empire," *American Historical Review*, 97 (1982), 740–66; Eris O'Brien, *The Foundation of Australia, 1786–1800: A Study in English Criminal Practice and Penal Colonisation in the Eighteenth Century*, 1st publ. 1937 (Sydney: Angus and Robertson, 1950); A. G. L. Shaw, *Convicts and the Colonies: A Study of Penal Transportation from Great Britain and Ireland to Australia and other parts of the British Empire* (London: Faber and Faber, 1977). For British awareness of American opposition to receiving convicts, see *Felix Farley's*

The problems incurred in transporting English felons to America in 1783–1784 convinced the British government that their convict problem required new solutions. By early 1787 British felons were embarking on what was hoped to be the first annual fleet to Botany Bay.[28] But doubts over the cost and effectiveness of transportation to Australia led to shipments of British convicts to North America throughout the 1780s. In 1789 the English government, in a cost-cutting move, suspended the use of government ships to carry convicts to Botany Bay. The private contract ships that replaced government transports were allowed to sail "as soon as ready," instead of in annual fleets. This placed the destiny of transported convicts in the hands of individual ship captains whose private interest or judgment led them to unload their cargoes in lands far from New South Wales. So, without official blessing, convicts bound for Botany Bay were in the fall of 1789 landed in Newfoundland.[29]

At least annual shipments of Irish convicts also were dispatched to the New World. In the decade after the American Revolution, the Irish government continued its prewar practice of contracting "with Captains of ships bound to the coast of Africa, the West-Indies, or America, at so much a head for each convict, who generally disposes of them as they can settle it between their humanity and their interest." In the fall of 1785, 109 Irish convicts embarked at Dublin, on board "a vessel bound to Abacco, one of the Bahama-Islands, where a life of frugality and labour may perhaps reclaim the most of them, from being the pest and outcast of society, to be useful members of the community." In December of 1786, the Snow *Anne-Mary* (presumably the same vessel) arrived in the Chesapeake, "where those wretched people were all sold, and disposed of, under the false colour of their being indentured servants from Ireland."[30]

Informal arrangements with individual ship captains minimized the opposition that could be organized to prevent the landing of felons in America and absolved

---

Bristol Journal, Sept. 6, 1783 (quote). False advertising of the vessel *Swift*, Captain Pamp, with convicts for Halifax in 1783, of the *Mercury*, Captain Arnott, and the *Grand Duke of Tuscany* with convicts for Nova Scotia in 1784, *Felix Farley's Bristol Journal*, Sept. 6, 20, Oct. 11, 1783, Apr. 24, May 8, June 6, 12, 1784; *Leeds Mercury*, May 4, 1784; *Maryland Gazette*, Nov. 14, 1783. The plan concocted by George Moore, a British convict contractor, and the Baltimore merchant George Salmon is described in Ekirch, *Bound for America*, 233–35; A. Roger Ekirch, "Great Britain's Secret Convict Trade to America," *American Historical Review*, 89 (1984), 1285–91. English convicts landed at Baltimore in December 1783, and the crimes for which they were transported are listed in "Record of Convicts," Baltimore City Court, Maryland State Archives, Annapolis, Maryland.

[28] Although the sailing of the first convict vessels established the transportation of convicts to Australia as the cornerstone of the British penal system for the next eighty years, its future remained doubtful for two decades. The hope that annual fleets for Botany Bay would clear out English jails proved unfounded at the end of the eighteenth century, as fleets were delayed (*Leeds Mercury*, Apr. 17, 1787): British taxpayers balked at paying £100 a head to transport convicts to a place where the criminal was "equally well provided for . . . as the soldier who guards him" (ibid., Apr. 14, 1789); and the effectiveness of transportation to Botany Bay as a deterrent was questioned (ibid., Apr. 21, 1789).

[29] Ibid., July 21, Dec. 1, 22, 1789; *Pennsylvania Packet*, Oct. 7, 1789.

[30] *Leeds Mercury*, Aug. 28, 1787 (quote); *Maryland Gazette*, Feb. 10, 1786 (quote); *Belfast News-Letter*, Sept. 27, 1785, Feb. 21, 1786 (quote).

Irish officials of responsibility for the eventual disposal of their convicts. Mystery surrounds the identity of the passengers on the Brig *Nancy* that sailed from Dublin in March 1787 for Baltimore with over one hundred persons, described as passengers and redemptioners. After running foul of a sloop on the banks of Newfoundland, the captain of the *Nancy* put his passengers "on such short allowance of provisions that they were compelled by famine to part with their cloathing and other necessaries, to the crew of said vessel, for provisions to keep them from starving." The captain eventually abandoned most of his passengers on the coast of Maine. Two week later, thirty-four of the *Nancy*'s passengers, "in the most wretched and distressed circumstances," were carried to Newburyport, Massachusetts, where they received aid from the overseers of the poor of that town and publicized their ordeal.[31]

While the residents of Newburyport felt an obligation to make "such provision for their necessities as hospitality to strangers, and humanity to our fellow creatures require, until such time as they can find employment," Governor Hancock of Massachusetts felt a different obligation. The governor's letter of August 11, 1787, to the Continental Congress protested the arrival of "a number of persons some probably convicts and all of them people whose manners and conduct will be detrimental to the state."[32] The following year, the Continental Congress received another complaint about the landing of British convicts in American ports, this time in the Chesapeake.[33]

The failure of the Irish administration to fix on "any regular place to transport their convicts" and the clandestine shipments of British felons produced confusion over the ultimate destination of British convicts in the 1780s and fostered an American suspicion that the antecedents of some British immigrants were not what they seemed. By 1788 the Continental Congress felt compelled to act. Congress informed the British Secretary for Foreign Affairs, that "it does not become the court of Great Britain to countenance, nor the United States to tolerate so nefarious a practice." However, since there was no evidence to *prove* that convicts had been landed in the United States "by the orders or desire of the british

[31] Story of the *Nancy* and passengers' deposition in *Maryland Gazette*, Aug. 17, 1787 (quotes).

[32] Ibid. (quote); Governor Hancock's protest in *Journals of the Continental Congress, 1774–1789*, ed. Worthington C. Ford et al., 34 vols. (Washington, D.C.: Government Printing Office, 1904–1937), XXXIII, 511, 533.

[33] According to the *Maryland Gazette*, 131 convicts were shipped from Dublin on the Brig *Chance* in October 1787. Of these, 73 were landed on "a desart Island, called Havango." From there, "they were taken and carried to the Island of New-Providence, where they remained, until 22 of them, 14 men and 8 women were shipped on the 17th July [1788], by permission of Lord Dunmore, for Baltimore-town, together with 5 other persons . . . who, we believe, were convicted in New-Providence, on board the schooner Prince William Henry." When the schooner arrived at Baltimore without a register, the captain "represented her as unfit for sea, wanting a foresail, and jib, and provisions." The vessel was not, however, permitted to land or sell its convicts. Instead, "The vessel, captain, supercargo, and felons, with all the papers, were sent to his Excellency the Governor, to take such orders as may be consistent with the safety of the citizens and the dignity of government, which we think most grossly insulted by Lord Dunmore." *Maryland Gazette*, Aug. 8, 1788.

government," Congress could only ask that Great Britain restrain its subjects from doing "things that are not only disreputable to their own Nation, but also offensive to others." Since no American laws had been violated, the Continental Congress could indeed do little more than protest.[34]

Recognizing the weakness of its position, Congress resolved, on September 16, 1788, "That it be and it is hereby recommended to the several states to pass proper laws for preventing the transportation of convicted malefactors from foreign countries into the United States." The timing of this recommendation suggests that the Continental Congress was seeking a stronger position from which it could act more forcefully in the future. But the compliance of the states was not complete enough to create a national ban on transported convicts. Massachusetts responded to the Congressional recommendation by legislating a £100 fine for landing a convict or "notoriously dissolute person," and requiring the master of each vessel to register the names, nation, age, character, and condition of all foreign passengers with the Overseers of the Poor in the nearest town or district. While similar laws were passed in New York and Virginia, the first Congress under the new federal constitution was still wrestling with the issue. In 1790 Aedanus Burke, the representative from South Carolina, recommended making the importation of British convicts a high misdemeanor.[35]

Independence and the creation of a republican form of government altered many of America's demographic policies. In the years preceding the Revolution, Thomas Paine and other patriots had identified population growth as one of the mechanisms that hastened social maturation and decay. Doubts about the benefits of rapid population growth and the precarious nature of the infant states steeled American determination to keep out Old World outcasts. As colonists, eighteenth-century Americans had often expressed their opposition to the landing of English convicts. Legal barriers were erected in several colonies to prohibit or tax the convict trade out of existence. Although these laws were vetoed in England, the colonists *could* have sabotaged the trade by making it unprofitable—by refusing to purchase convict labor. But this boycott was not attempted until after the colonists had won their independence.

British officials connived to circumvent the American resolve to keep their communities free from disreputable elements. England had a long tradition of ignoring American needs that conflicted with those of its empire. In the 1780s

---

[34] *Leeds Mercury*, Aug. 28, 1787 (quote); Congress to the British Secretary for Foreign Affairs, *Journals of the Continental Congress*, XXXIV, 528–29 (quotes).

[35] *Journals of the Continental Congress*, XXXIV, 528 (quote); *Laws of Massachusetts, 1780 to 1800* (Boston: Wright & Potter, 1886), II, 628–29 (quote); *Laws of the State of New York Passed at the Sessions of the Legislature Held in the Years 1785, 1786, 1787, and 1788, Inclusive* (Albany: Weed Parsons and Company, 1886), 742–43; William Waller Hening, ed., *The Statutes at Large; Being A Collection of All the Laws of Virginia, from the First Session of the Legislature, in the Year 1619*, 13 vols. (Richmond: George Cochran, 1809–1823), XII, 668. Burke's proposal (Feb. 3, 1790), in Joseph Gales, ed., *Annals of the Congress of the United States, First Congress*, 2 vols. (Washington, D.C.: Gales and Seaton, 1834), I, 1117–18.

England was determined to avenge its wartime humiliation and limit its losses. It was only natural that English officials would try to continue the policies that had produced British power and prosperity.[36] Great Britain had special reasons for continuing to treat its former colonists as less than full members of the world community and to sabotage their revolutionary aspirations. But other Old World countries were driven by the same imperatives and also tried to use the New World and its inhabitants as resources to enhance their own stature. They, too, ignored American objections to undesirable immigrants and used the power of government to limit the mobility of their subjects.

Old World Stratagems

Although republican America failed to revolutionize international relations, Old World governments lacked the power and institutions necessary for the strict enforcement of the traditional demographic policies to which they clung so tenaciously. English officials suffered the most severe handicaps in battling postwar emigration. At the end of the American Revolution, Great Britain forfeited the allegiance and human capital of over two million colonial subjects. New demographic losses would be intolerable. But established ties between Great Britain and its former colonies and the long British tradition of emigrating to the New World were too strong to be disrupted easily. By capturing a preponderant share of the American trade, British officials ensured a continuing connection that would perpetuate, rather than eliminate, Anglo-American ties. The British people then exacerbated the problem by challenging their government's right to prohibit emigration.

Unable to prevent the secession of over two million subjects by military force, British officials turned to more subtle stratagems in the years following the Treaty of 1783. The English government retained a tenuous hold on its people by refusing to recognize the right of peaceful expatriation. British subjects who emigrated

---

[36]The fact of American independence did alter some aspects of Britain's demographic policy. It hardened England's determination to end the drain of British subjects to the New World by teaching the apparent lesson that colonial population growth led inexorably to demands for independence. It also taught British officials not to ignore grievances voiced by their remaining colonists lest minor issues escalate into revolution. The American Revolution made British officials more wary not only of taxing without consent but also of shipping convicts to colonies determined not to receive them. General Carleton to Thomas Townshend, Mar. 15, 1783, in K. G. Davies, ed., *Documents of the American Revolution, 1770–1783*, 21 vols. (Dublin: Irish University Press, 1972–1981), XXI, 159–60. For opposition to receiving British convicts in Jamaica, Honduras, the Musquito Shore, and British North America, see Gillen, "The Botany Bay Decision," 747–48; Ekirch, "Great Britain's Secret Convict Trade," 1290–91; O'Brien, *The Foundation of Australia*, 116; (London) *Daily Universal Register*, July 14, 1785; *Virginia Journal*, Jan. 13, 1785; and "First Report from the Committee Appointed to Enquire What Proceedings Had Been Had in the Execution of an Act . . . intituled, 'An Act for the Effectual Transportation of Felons . . .'" (May 9, 1785), in Sheila Lambert, ed., *House of Commons Sessional Papers of the Eighteenth Century* (Wilmington, Del.: Scholarly Resources Inc., 1975), vol. 49, 7, 8–9.

after the Revolution were not recognized as bona fide American citizens because they had not lost their subjectship through treason—by participating in the American Revolution. Officially, postwar emigrants remained British subjects. The refusal to recognize the right of peaceful expatriation would, in the next four decades, provide the legal pretext for impressing native Britons found on American vessels. But it was ineffective in restoring significant numbers of British immigrants to their former allegiance.[37]

Resettling American loyalists in the British empire was more effective in reducing the number permanently lost. After overcoming their surprise at the determination of the republican states to rid themselves of such a large group of valuable citizens, British officials on both sides of the Atlantic schemed to recruit former tories, as well as other disgruntled Americans, as settlers for their remaining colonies.[38] By the end of 1784 British officials had siphoned off thousands of valuable subjects, planted the Canadian wilderness, and congratulated themselves for being more humane and enlightened in their treatment of the loyalists than the vindictive American rebels.[39]

After doing what they could to minimize the demographic losses already sustained, British officials turned to the problem of preventing further defections. The easiest and most obvious solution was to enforce existing anti-emigration

[37] Kettner, *Development of American Citizenship*, 183–87, 269–70; *Belfast News-Letter*, Sept. 5, 1788; Gouverneur Morris (London), Sept. 24, 1790, to Duke of Leeds, "Private Letter Book, July 31, 1789–Aug. 23, 1795," in *The Papers of Gouverneur Morris*, Library of Congress microfilm.

[38] "Extract from a Letter dated New York 2d Decr 1784," British Foreign Office Archives, American Correspondence microfilm, 4/3, folio 143; *Felix Farley's Bristol Journal*, Oct. 18, 1783. Thomas Townshend thought it "impossible to suppose them [the American peace commissioners] so blind to their real interests as wantonly to proscribe so large a number of their fellow citizens whose repossession of their property and reunion to their country is as essential to the prosperity of America as to the honour of Great Britain." Townshend to Henry Strachey, Nov. 19, 1782, in Davies, ed., *Documents of the American Revolution*, XXI, 143. Schemes to settle loyalists in the remaining British colonies are found in Governor Haldimand to Thomas Townshend, Quebec, Oct. 25, 1782, ibid., XXI, 128–31; Governor Tonyn to Earl of Shelburne, St. Augustine, Nov. 14, 1782, ibid., XXI, 136–37; General Carleton to Thomas Townshend, New York, Dec. 20, 1782, ibid., XXI, 144; Hugh Finlay, Quebec, Apr. 4, 1788 to Evan Nepean, in Vincent Harlow and Frederick Madden, eds., *British Colonial Developments, 1774–1834: Select Documents* (Oxford: Clarendon, 1953), 391. Spain launched a similar drive to build up its American colonies by recruiting loyalists. See *Felix Farley's Bristol Journal*, May 1, 1784; *Leeds Mercury*, Aug. 12, Sept. 9, 1783, Feb. 3, May 4, Aug. 10, 1784; Martin de Navarro, "Political Reflections on the Present Condition of the Province of Louisiana" (ca. 1785), in James A. Robertson, ed., *Louisiana under the Rule of Spain, France, and the United States, 1785–1807*, 2 vols. (Cleveland: Arthur H. Clark, 1911), I, 235–61; "Extract from the King of Spain's Proclamation for Settling His New Territory on the Mississippi and Masure," *Maryland Gazette*, Aug. 18, 1789; British consul George Miller, Charleston, Jan. 28, 1790, to Duke of Leeds, British Foreign Office Archives, American Correspondence microfilm, 4/8, folio 60; "Memoir Communicated Secretly to the King by his Excellency the Count Aranda, on the Independence of the English Colonies, after Having Signed the Treaty of Paris of 1783," in Sumner, *Prophetic Voices Concerning America*, 141–45; John G. Clark, *New Orleans, 1718–1812: An Economic History* (Baton Rouge: Louisiana State University Press, 1970), 202–11; Alexander DeConde, *This Affair of Louisiana* (Baton Rouge: Louisiana State University Press, 1976), chap. 3.

[39] For English contempt at the treatment of the loyalists by the perfidious Americans and accounts of their own infinitely more humane conduct, see *Felix Farley's Bristol Journal*, July 5, 1783, Sept. 4, 1784; *Leeds Mercury*, Apr. 22, May 6, July 8, Aug. 12, Sept. 9, Sept. 23, Dec. 9, 1783; *Maryland Gazette*, Aug. 13, 1784, dateline London, May 19.

statutes. By the spring of 1783 the time had come to remind the public of an English law "which inflicted a heavy fine (£500 as this correspondent thinks) and imprisonment upon every person convicted of seducing or being accessary to the seducing any artificer or mechanic to quit this kingdom, in order to exercise his calling abroad." Londoners also called on the Lords of the Admiralty to take action against the "alarming" emigration of shipwrights to America. Those responsible for enticing "these men to leave home and their honour" simply had to "be detected and fined under the act of Parliament."[40]

The British government apparently heeded such advice. Proclamations prohibiting soldiers and sailors from entering foreign service without a license were published in British newspapers and journals, along with extracts from the statutes of 1718 and 1750 that banned the emigration of various artificers from Great Britain and Ireland and penalized those who seduced them into defecting. In 1785 and 1786 the British Parliament reaffirmed its commitment to such measures by extending the prohibitions to the iron and steel trades. The Irish Parliament in 1785 enacted a similar law to prevent the emigration of textile workers and the exportation of their tools.[41] English authorities also breathed new life into these statutes by ordering the arrest of British artisans attempting to carry their tools to America. Reports of these arrests were widely disseminated in the public press, as were the trials of those who "seduced" British subjects and the penalties they suffered.[42]

But British attempts to use the power of government to prohibit emigration proved to be both ineffective and inflammatory. Two manufacturers from Manchester, England who were prevented from emigrating in 1782, succeeded in sailing for Philadelphia in August of 1783. William Leonard, arrested, convicted, and imprisoned for trying to smuggle British machinery from Leeds to the United States, was in 1788 setting up a woolen manufactory in the "neighbourhood" of Boston, Massachusetts. By 1786 the *Birmingham Chronicle* felt compelled to buttress governmental sanctions by advertising "a reward of fifty guineas for such intelligence as will convict any person offering to go to work in foreign countries, to be paid by the commercial committee." In addition to

[40] *Belfast News-Letter*, May 16, 1783, dateline London, May 7 (quote); *Leeds Mercury*, Aug. 31, 1784, dateline London Aug. 24 (quotes).

[41] *Leeds Mercury*, Nov. 30, 1784 (Proclamation of Nov. 19, 1784); reminder of penalties for seducing artisans in ibid., July 27, 1784, and *Belfast News-Letter*, May 16, 1783. 25 Geo. III, c. 67 (1785), and 26 Geo. III, c. 89 (1786), in Owen Ruffhead, ed., *Statutes at Large, from Magna Charta, to the Twenty-fifth Year of the Reign of King George the Third, Inclusive*, 10 vols. (London: Charles Eyre and Andrew Strahan, 1785), IX, 599–601 and 743. For earlier British statutes, see Ruffhead, *Statutes at Large*, V, 157–58 (1718), and VI, 466–68 (1750). The Irish statute of 1785 cited in David Jeremy, "Damming the Flood: British Government Efforts to Check the Outflow of Technicians and Machinery, 1780–1843," *Business History Review*, 51 (1977), 2.

[42] For indictments and arrests see, the customs official who seduced glassworkers, *Felix Farley's Bristol Journal*, Sept. 6, 1783, and his conviction, ibid., Jan. 24, 1784; the arrest of Staffordshire pottery painters, ibid., May 8, 1784; the arrest and conviction of Wm. B. Leonard for trying to smuggle woolen machines to America, *Leeds Mercury*, Mar. 9, 16, 1784; arrest for luring journeymen curriers to France, ibid., Sept. 14, 1784.

funding the reward, the Birmingham commercial committee "applied to Government to outlaw such British subjects who are now, or may in future work at their trades in foreign states."[43]

More important than the ineffectiveness of British attempts to stop emigration by legal fiat was the outcry against the right of the government to restrain the mobility of subjects enjoying the "rights of Englishmen." Although embattled government officials must have found the Birmingham proposal to outlaw British emigrants appealing, they were unable to take such a step. According to British public opinion, the rights of subjects who lived under the protection of the English Constitution included the right to emigrate. "Ratio," writing in the *London Chronicle* in July 1783, argued that while the "Doctrine of *a compulsive Residence*" might be "palatable to the present Ministers," who had lately attempted to govern the American colonies "by *Compulsion* and *Subjugation*," it was as clear a violation "of the Laws and Rights of Nature and Humanity, as of settled Law and Usage of England." It would "be a Piece of unnatural and unhuman Nonsense to compel a Person, starving in a particular Spot, by the Want of Bread and other Necessaries, to remain on that spot, when . . . he desires to get into another Country, where he thinks he may live better, but cannot be worse."[44]

The analysis of the rights of the English people offered by "Ratio" was not idiosyncratic, but was echoed throughout the British Isles and drew on arguments formulated decades earlier.[45] In 1783 the Englishman John King argued that "Nothing consistent with liberty can be done to prevent emigration." According to a correspondent in the *Belfast News-Letter*, "Despotic power . . . (as at this day in Russia) may by edict endeavour to prevent the emigration of its people," but in Ireland, "no such power I trust will ever exist." Alderman Warren, speaking in the Irish House of Commons in 1784, believed that emigration was "an evil that ought to be stopped, not by any coercive measure, but by making the people happy, and finding employment for them at home." In 1786 it was accepted as a truism by those trying to end emigration from the Scottish Highlands that "To prevent people by force from going where they please, particularly if they cannot

---

[43] *New York Gazette*, Oct. 20, 1783; *Leeds Mercury*, Nov. 25, 1788 (William Leonard), Sept. 12, Oct. 3, 1786, (quotes).

[44] *London Chronicle*, July 19, 1783. "Ratio" wrote in response to an assertion made a few weeks earlier by "Pro Patria," that "*Emigration* is worse than a *Pestilence*, and that the Kingdom has an undoubted Right to compel to future Residence Persons intending to emigrate," ibid., June 28, 1783.

[45] In 1728 Hugh Boulter, the archbishop of Armagh, pointed out "the cruelty of forcing people to remain in a country where neither work nor food was to be obtained." In 1730 the British Privy Council rejected an Irish bill that would have banned unlicensed emigration from Ireland on the grounds that it constituted an "unreasonable restraint" on British subjects. R. J. Dickson, *Ulster Emigration to Colonial America, 1718–1775* (London: Routledge and Kegan Paul, 1966), chap. 9. On January 19, 1774, the *Caledonian Mercury* responded to a rumored bill placing a prohibitive tax on British emigrants by labeling it "contrary to all laws, human and divine," Bernard Bailyn, *Voyagers to the West: A Passage in the Peopling of America on the Eve of the Revolution* (New York: Knopf, 1986), 64n.

find employment and subsistance at home, is unconstitutional, and contrary to the principles of natural liberty."[46]

This public outcry forced the British government to explore alternative ways of ending emigration. With the end of the American Revolution, the British government resumed its monitoring of emigration begun in the early 1770s. In June 1783 "Private Orders" were "sent down to all the Custom Houses in England and Scotland, to watch with the greatest attention the Emigration of the People to America, that Administration may immediately know the Extent and the Classes from which it may take Place." Britons who opposed the policy of "compulsive residence" used these and other data to analyze the characteristics of the emigrants to identify and remove the hardships that left British subjects with no recourse but emigration.[47]

In April 1783 a London correspondent suggested that Great Britain emulate the French government, which, "instead of disbanding their seamen when the ships were paid off . . . engaged 15,000 of the most able hands immediately into the King's service, who are now employed in mending and repairing the public roads." While such a step might seem "extraordinary" to the English, the writer believed it "worthy of imitation to adopt any scheme which will prevent our sailors from going into foreign service, to escape starving at home." Other Londoners argued for tax reform since "the lowest orders" naturally left "a country in which they can neither eat, drink, enjoy the light, be born or die, without paying for each article." Emigration from the middling class could be ended by the sale and cultivation of England's wastelands, the equalization of the land tax, and a phasing out of poor rates.[48]

In Scotland reform plans abounded—to build new fishing villages, promote the kelp industry, and introduce manufacturing and scientific farming, as antidotes to emigration fever. In 1786 the members of the Highland Society, believing that "The plan of encouraging fisheries, manufactures, &c. seems to be the only constitutional and effectual method to stop emigrations," subscribed £3000 "for the encouragement of the fisheries in the Highlands." The Society simultaneously appealed to Scottish landowners to improve conditions for their tenants to end

---

[46] John King, *Thoughts on the Difficulties and Distresses in Which the Peace of 1783 Has Involved the People of England; on the Present Disposition of the English, Scots, and Irish, to Emigrate to America. . . .* (London, 1783), in Edith Abbott, ed., *Historical Aspects of the Immigration Problem: Select Documents* (Chicago: University of Chicago Press, 1926), 220; *Belfast News-Letter*, Mar. 28, 1783; Alderman Warren quoted in *Pennsylvania Packet*, July 3, 1784; Scottish quote, *Leeds Mercury*, June 13, 1786. See also Phineas Bond, Philadelphia, Nov. 26, 1788, to Evan Nepean in London, "Letters of Phineas Bond, British Consul at Philadelphia, to the Foreign Office of Great Britain, 1787, 1788, 1789," ed. J. Franklin Jameson, *Annual Report of the American Historical Association for the Year 1896*, 587.

[47] "Private orders," *New York Gazette and Weekly Mercury*, Sept. 8, 1783, dateline London, June 13. John King was one of many who argued that it was "not the barren solitary tracts of America that allure the people to emigration, but the calamities they endure at home." King, *Thoughts on the Difficulties and Distresses*, 220.

[48] *Leeds Mercury*, May 4, 1783 (quotes); *Newcastle Journal*, June 7, 1783 (quote); *Maryland Gazette*, Oct. 31, 1783.

their emigration. In 1795 John Sinclair promoted the creation of the "Company for Preventing Emigrations and Establishing Manufactures and Industry in the Highlands of Scotland."[49]

In Ireland, the need for domestic reform took on a special urgency because of the apparent link between the factors that produced political turbulence and emigration. The need to address Irish grievances was imperative, lest that country go the way of the American colonies. Political agitators in Ireland persistently reminded British authorities of the similarities between their situation and that of the American rebels in the 1770s. Encouraged by American precedent and supported by the now-independent states, the Irish adopted the American techniques of nonimportation, riots, and tarring and feathering to win the "rights of Englishmen." Threats to follow in the footsteps of the American rebels or to emigrate en masse were used to pressure the government for political and economic reform.[50] In his "Address to the Irish People," Napper Tandy cited "undue influence" in the Irish House of Commons as the factor that led to commercial distress and its inevitable consequence, emigration. A warning was issued to Irish officials that, as long as the Irish were "the wretched slaves of a vile, a prostitute aristocracy—denied all share in the constitution . . . sacrificed by the corruption of her Senate" and made "helots to English interest and English monopoly," they would forever "desert a land, where nought but oppression reigns." The solution was to "Give them their rights—protect their manufactures—reform the horrid abuses of representation—then, Irishmen never will forsake, but will fight, will die for Ireland and Liberty."[51]

---

[49] Highland Society activities in *Leeds Mercury*, Nov. 16, 1785; June 13 (quote), 1786; Aug. 17, 1787. Sinclair's project described in J. M. Bumsted, *The People's Clearance: Highland Emigration to British North America, 1770–1815* (Edinburgh: Edinburgh University Press, 1982), 49.

[50] *Felix Farley's Bristol Journal*, July 24, Sept. 4, 1784; *Pennsylvania Packet*, July 1, 1784; *Pennsylvania Gazette*, July 7, 1784; *Virginia Journal*, Dec. 30, 1784; Michael Kraus, "America and the Irish Revolutionary Movement in the Eighteenth Century," in Richard B. Morris, ed., *The Era of the American Revolution: Studies Inscribed to Evarts Boutell Greene* (New York: Columbia University Press, 1939), 331–48. In April 1784 two Dubliners predicted an exodus of Irish manufacturers unless the British government removed restrictions on their country's trade. They reported a request of 50,000 "starving manufacturers in the city of Dublin" for a governmental subsidy to underwrite "their passage to America, as they have been refused the means of subsistence here; they would rather quit their country than rise in insurrection, which must be the consequence if they obtain not relief. They are content to suffer this kind of transportation, if it be refused, they must prowl at large, for they cannot, nor will not peaceably starve." Furthermore, "If the people are forced to emigrate, what becomes of Ireland? There are near one million of souls in the kingdom ready to quit their native soil; should they be forced to put their schemes in execution, England will have a new America to plant and people." Dublin letter, Apr. 9, 1784, *Pennsylvania Packet*, July 3, 1784; Dublin letter, Apr. 14, 1784, *Virginia Journal*, June 24, 1784. Much of the blame for emigration also was placed on Irish landlords whose "extravagant rapacity has long conspired with other circumstances to weigh down this devoted country." "To the LANDLORDS of the NORTH of IRELAND," *Belfast News-Letter*, Mar. 28, 1783 (quote), May 11, 1784, dateline Dublin, May 8. In August 1783, "A Meeting of the Freeholders of the Parish of Dundonald" resolved "That every Landlord, be his rank what it may, who by threats, or any unconstitutional means, attempts to intimidate his tenants from voting according to their conscience, ought to be considered as an enemy to his country, as America stands with outstretched arms, ready to receive the injured and oppressed sons of liberty." *Belfast News-Letter*, Aug. 5, 1783.

[51] Tandy was foreman of a committee appointed to draw up an address and petition to George III. The Address is printed in *Felix Farley's Bristol Journal*, July 3, 1784. A Dublin supporter of the Irish Volunteers

Since attempts to deny the Irish "right" to emigrate would exacerbate an already volatile situation, alternative solutions were explored. Attempts were made to keep the Irish home by resettling distressed tenants within the country. In 1784, the *Belfast News-Letter* publicized a plan to redirect Irish emigrants from Monaghan to Connaught, with terms more generous than any "ever offered by those who wish to transplant us to the wilds of America." In England, Pitt's ministry tried to remove some of Ireland's commercial grievances but was frustrated by English opposition. English merchants and manufacturers emasculated his "commercial propositions," making them completely unacceptable to the Irish parliament. Ireland's absentee landlords used their political power to block land reform.[52]

Some British reform projects were actually implemented. In 1784, the Earl of Lonsdale, "with a truly generous and patriotic zeal, . . . lent the merchants of Whitehaven £10,000, for a term of years, interest free, towards enabling them to establish a Northern and Southern whale fishery," designed to prevent the emigration of "a number of valuable seamen." In Scotland canals were dug to facilitate the movement of natural resources and goods necessary for the full development of the Scottish economy. In 1791 David Dale, the owner of the Glasgow textile mills, offered, on certain conditions, "Employment to all the people [of Argyleshire] who choose to live in their own country."[53] But domestic reform would take time to implement and could do little to prevent emigration triggered by harvest failures such as those that occurred in Scotland and Ireland in the early 1780s. So the British government, hoping for a fast-working, effective, and constitutional antidote to emigration fever, launched its propaganda campaign against republican America.

Anti-American Propaganda

In depicting the United States as a land of social chaos, economic depression, and political licentiousness and as an asylum fit only for scoundrels, British publicists claimed to be performing a public service—protecting the credulous from

---

was even blunter when he recommended that those "gallant asserters of liberty . . . seize the person of his G–ce, as an hostage for the conduct of the enemies towards such persons adhering to the glorious cause as may fall into their hands. May the example of America stimulate Ireland, and may this injured country never relax, until crowned with similar laurels or triumph and independence." *Virginia Journal*, July 1, 1784, dateline, Dublin Apr. 17. See also *Belfast News-Letter*, Apr. 27, 1784, and the description of Ireland's grievous political condition, where "a standing army, the most odious circumstance to a free state, is augmented in the hour of peace, the desires of the people frustrated, and magistrates censured for trying the effect of the civil power to appease an unarmed crowd, in preference to a mercenary band of followers, reeking hot with the blood of the Americans," in *Pennsylvania Packet*, July 3, 1784, dateline Dublin, Apr. 9.

[52] *Belfast News-Letter*, July 30, 1784 (quote); *Leeds Mercury*, Oct. 25, 1785, dateline London, Oct. 22; J. C. Beckett, *The Making of Modern Ireland, 1603–1923* (New York: Knopf, 1966), 236–40.

[53] *Leeds Mercury*, Nov. 2, 1784 (Earl of Lonsdale loan and quotes), June 13, 1786, Dec. 12, 1786 (Dale and quote), Aug. 17, 1787; Bumsted, *People's Clearance*, chap. 2, esp. 42–91.

smooth-talking Americans who stopped at nothing to seduce British subjects from their homeland and natural allegiance. But the negative stories of conditions in the American states that were circulated, and sometimes written, by British officials were part of a desperate attempt to tarnish the American magnet that was drawing away valuable subjects who insisted on retaining the "rights of Englishmen".

The British propaganda campaign against the republican states also was a natural legacy of the American Revolution. In declaring their right to independence, American rebels had denied all hope for the peaceful reclamation of their mother country from the corruption that had engulfed it. Most Britons rejected America's judgment as arrogant and untrue. Even British radicals who had encouraged American agitation in the 1770s in order to save, not condemn, their society were reluctant in the 1780s to relinquish British leadership in the cause of liberty to America. Preferring to continue their battle at home, English radicals pointed out defects in American society and lectured their American friends on the niceties of British liberty.[54] Many of America's friends on the Continent also refused the offer of refuge and expressed concern about the persistence of slavery, the limited power of the state and central governments, and reports of Americans putting private gain before public good, defaulting on debts, and violating treaty provisions.[55]

The gentle rebuffs of America's Old World friends passed virtually unnoticed in the vociferous clamor that accompanied the vehement denial of republican claims by British patriots and officials. British subjects who had rallied to the defense of their king during the American Revolution saw their military defeat as a product of administrative incompetence rather than evidence of the final demise of English liberty. Britons, in office and out, who were determined to regain England's former power and prestige were even more adamant in their rejection of American claims to be heir to the title of asylum for liberty. Conservatives who feared the social and political consequences of the spirit of liberty emanating from America and pragmatists who grasped at any weapon to fight depopulation were united in their determination to remove the aura surrounding the republican experiment taking place in North America in the 1780s.

British predications of the disasters awaiting the colonies if they succeeded in gaining independence began long before the war's end. By 1783 it had become

---

[54] Bernard Peach, *Richard Price and the Ethical Foundations of the American Revolution: Selections from His Pamphlets, with Appendices* (Durham, N.C.: Duke University Press, 1979), 312–42; Robbins, "Honest Heretic," 60–76; Bonwick, *English Radicals*, chap. 8.

[55] Bonwick, *English Radicals*, chap. 6; Dumas Malone, *Jefferson and the Rights of Man* (Boston: Little, Brown, 1951), 96; Lafayette, Cadiz, Feb. 5, 1783, to George Washington, in *The Letters of Lafayette to Washington, 1777–1799*, ed. Louis Gottschalk (Philadelphia: American Philosophical Society, 1944), 260; Nikolai N. Balkhovitinov, *The Beginnings of Russian-American Relations, 1775–1815*, trans. Elena Levin (Cambridge: Harvard University Press, 1975), 46.

an English commonplace that the withdrawal of British troops would usher in American anarchy. According to the British press,

> So long as we keep possession of that place [New York], the rebels will not think their independence fully secured; and therefore, a jealousy of our ultimate designs will, in general, preserve some appearance of unity among themselves.—But the last transport that carries off the troops will be no sooner out of sight, than the spirit of Discord will erect her standard among them. Such a generation of vipers can never live in harmony. They will, in all probability, like the soldiers of *Cadmus*, with whom they seem to have a natural affinity of disposition, quarrel and fight till they have destroyed each other.[56]

It was only natural that British patriots would in the ensuing years select for publication the evidence that vindicated their wartime stance and proved the truth of their prophecies.

Not surprisingly, exiled loyalists were prominent and outspoken critics of the new states, who vigorously denied republican America's right to act as an asylum for liberty or for those oppressed by tyranny. The loyalists had never accepted America's claim to be fighting for liberty against a hopelessly corrupt British nation. With the peace of 1783, Americans who had maintained their allegiance to the British crown had permanent proscription and the confiscation of their property added to their wartime humiliations. Having suffered at patriot hands, American loyalists eagerly joined the British campaign to expose republican shortcomings.

Loyalists who settled in British North America had many incentives to sabotage the aspirations of their neighbors to the south. Believing that commercial concessions to the independent states would hinder their own development and prosperity, British colonists lobbied for the retention of the British Navigation system and their own protected position within it. By securing a permanent ban on republican shipping to the West Indies, the loyalists would gain revenge and a monopoly in supplying those islands with American products. By denying republican ships access to their own ports, the British colonists would protect their shipbuilding industry and promote their own carrying trade.[57]

Canadian loyalists were driven by more than a desire for revenge and the economic prosperity that would provide them a secure existence in an alien land. Many had attained social and political leadership in the thirteen colonies before exile deprived of their cultural identity and material possessions. These loyalist

---

[56] *Connecticut Courant*, Feb. 24, 1784, dateline London, Nov. 18, 1783 (quote).

[57] *Leeds Mercury*, Oct. 12, 1784; "Extract of a letter from a Gentleman at Halifax, Nova Scotia to his friend in Aberdeen, May 31," ibid., Aug. 8, 1786; Edward Winslow to Ward Chipman, Halifax, Apr. 26, 1784, William Obder Raymond, ed., *Winslow Papers, A.D. 1776–1826*, 1st publ. 1901 (Boston: Gregg Press, 1972), 189–91.

leaders were uncomfortable in England, where they were snubbed as uncouth provincials and offered public offices and incomes that they considered demeaning. They therefore strove to create in Canada a distinctively American society, purified of the defects that had produced revolution and anarchy to their south—a society that would allow them to resume their role as natural leaders and would vindicate the stand they had taken during the American Revolution.[58] The exposure of the social and political defects of the United States was an integral part of the promotion of the loyalist settlements in Canada as a superior British-American civilization, where English liberties were secure and where victims of *republican* oppression could find refuge.

The anti-republican campaign of the 1780s also was a natural continuation of the loyalists' prerevolutionary and wartime propagandizing. They had no reason to alter their interpretation of the origins of the United States in a plot by power-hungry, self-interested colonists who had succeeded in their design to replace "the mild, indulgent government (God bless it) of England" with "The *tyranny* of a mob." Postwar loyalists continued to believe that this colonial cabal had opposed unpopular British policies, not on principle, but to secure their personal aggrandizement. "Sensible that in a calm they must grovel in the dirt," the revolutionaries of the 1770s had raised "a storm, by which they hope to be elevated into notice." The military success of the rebel leaders in displacing English rule and America's "natural leaders" did not alter those sordid motives and mistaken political principles. The harassment of loyal Americans by mobs of vindictive republicans during and after the war only confirmed the loyalist reading of American history. At war's end, loyalists still described themselves as "those who from principles of virtuous Loyalty fly from a set of miscreants . . . who have substituted anarchy and misrule in the place of good Government."[59]

The 1770s also had provided the loyalists with experience in the art of antirepublican propaganda. During the Revolution, New York City's *Royal Gazette* was filled with stories, true and false, that discredited revolutionary leaders, exposed the machiavellian schemes of their French allies, and prophesied the imminent defeat of the rebel cause. Although James Rivington, the printer of the *Royal Gazette*, saved himself from proscription by his service to the Continental Army late in the war, other tory publicists continued their careers as British subjects in exile. Included among the latter was William Smith of New York. Possessing an "amazing ability to modify every bit of information to his own

---

[58] Mary Beth Norton, *The British Americans: The Loyalist Exiles in England, 1774–1789* (Boston: Little, Brown, 1972); Ann Gorman Condon, *The Envy of the American States: The Loyalist Dream for New Brunswick* (Fredericton, New Brunswick: New Ireland Press, 1984), esp. chap. 3.

[59] Janice Potter, *The Liberty We Seek: Loyalist Ideology in Colonial New York and Massachusetts* (Cambridge: Harvard University Press, 1983), chap. 1, quotes on 15, 17, 22; Condon, *Envy of the American States*, 43–59; final quote from James A. Cruden, New York, June 23, 1783, to Edward Winslow, *Winslow Papers*, 91.

purposes," Smith first employed his talent in the political battles of provincial New York, in his opposition to the DeLancey clique and "British imperial pretensions." After refusing to renounce his allegiance to Great Britain, Smith used his already established "network of informants" to gather intelligence to aid the British cause.[60]

In the 1780s the loyalist leaders of British North America used William Smith's talents and propaganda techniques to promote their new settlements as the American home of English liberty and asylum for the victims of republican misrule. Glowing accounts and prophesies for the Canadian provinces filled the British press. In occupied New York, Nova Scotia was advertised as "the promised Land, where Freedom and Liberty reign triumphant over every species of Imposition, Oppression, and Persecution." By the fall of 1783, *Felix Farley's Bristol Journal* was filled with stories about the "flourishing" new town of Shelburne, Nova Scotia, which, with 400 houses already built, "bids fair one day to be as populous, if not more so, than any one in America."[61]

While the loyalists who had settled in British North America were vilifying the republican experiment of their neighbors, to prove that their societies would soon become "the envy of the American States," they also provided much of the ammunition used in the larger campaign to discredit the United States in order to prevent emigration from the British Isles. William Smith, the premier propagandist of British North America and the loyalist cause, maintained his contacts in the United States after being forced into exile. This gave Smith the means to provide British officials with the authentic stories of disgruntled residents of the United States, many of whom were probably former loyalists. He also was in a position to pass off as fact any rumor or misinformation that would be useful in Great Britain's campaign to discredit the republican states. The British government paid William Smith £1,000 a year for his services.[62]

The reports Smith forwarded to the British Foreign Office from his American informants painted an incredibly bleak picture of the newly independent states.

[60] Christopher Moore, *The Loyalists: Revolution, Exile, Settlement* (Toronto: Macmillan of Canada, 1984), 96–97, 112; Dorothy Rita Dillon, *The New York Triumvirate* (New York: Columbia University Press, 1949), quote on 83; L. F. S. Upton, *The Loyal Whig: William Smith of New York & Quebec* (Toronto: University of Toronto Press, 1969), 126–40, quote on 140.

[61] Description of Nova Scotia as the promised land from a New York newspaper, reprinted in *Felix Farley's Bristol Journal*, Oct. 18, 1783; Shelburne described, ibid., Sept. 6, Oct. 4, 1783. Acknowledging the fact that "the News-Papers too much abound with Letters dated from America, which are most probably fabricated in England with private Views," the printer of the Bristol paper tried to publish only genuine letters from "candid" gentlemen who actually resided in the New World. These accounts did mention some of the "inconveniences" facing the new settlers, but also predicted that these hardships would soon be overcome, with "God's blessing and a little time, aided by good government and our own industry." Ibid., Sept. 18, Oct. 9, 1784.

[62] *Leeds Mercury*, Sept. 14, 1784, dateline London Sept. 7; *The Diary and Selected Papers of Chief Justice William Smith, 1784–1793*, ed. L. F. S. Upton, 2 vols. (Toronto: The Champlain Society, 1963–1965), I, passim; Upton, *Loyal Whig*, 144. Reports Smith forwarded to British officials in British Foreign Office Archives, American Correspondence, 4/3, folios 142–44, 177–79, 183–85, 189–90, 194–95, 203, 267–68, 289–90.

A letter from New York in December of 1784 reported, "Our Trade is reduced to nothing—Real Estates are sinking—The Jails are filled. . . .—our Merchants clamour—the Farmer complains—private Credit is gone—public Faith a Nonentity—speculators increase, and grow rich on the Spoils of the Public—This is our Situation—Judge you of the consequences." In the following summer, came a report that "The Calamities of America are very sensibly felt, and the Leaders to the Severance of the Empire, find their Principles and conduct reproached as the Cause of them—Themselves admit, that the Condition of the Country is worse than it was; and for their Defence can only insist, that their Miseries would have been greater, if the British Designs had succeeded. Such Suggestions however do not prevent their sinking into Disesteem." Even "Mr. Washington at Mount Vernon—injoying very little of his former Reputation" was despised by ex-soldiers "as a weak man, who could not serve himself but by the army, and who has ruined them by dismissing them [the soldiers] without satisfaction. The Generosity of Great Britain to the Provincial Officers and Loyalists, adds Fuel to their Resentment agt. Washington, the Congress and the Leaders to the Independancy. Many assert without Reserve, that in any future occasion they will list under the Banners of Great Britain." In short, America's republicans were "a ruined People."[63]

British consuls residing in the new American states provided the home government with additional weapons to be used to stop British emigration and to assert English leadership in the cause of liberty. They offered advice on British strategy and provided ammunition for the propaganda campaign. In November 1788 Phineas Bond, the indefatigable consul at Philadelphia, warned that, although "the spirit of migration has of late here remitted exceedingly . . . the phantoms of freedom and happiness under the new Constitution may tempt greater numbers." To prevent this development, Bond supplied his superiors with information on the suffering of "redemptioners and indented servants brought hither from different parts of Europe; numbers crowded in small ships—provisions scarce and bad and the treatment oppressive and cruel." In 1790 he sent proof to London of "the brutal treatment of indented servants," being careful to forward "the original publication because it carries with it the most decided authority." Bond advised British officials to circulate the document widely "as the best means of discouraging a wretched race of [Irish] people from leaving their homes."[64]

[63] Quotes from "Extract from a Letter Dated New York, 2d Decr 1784," ibid., folios 142–43; "Intelligence from NYork 4 June 1785," ibid., folio 185; "Extract of a letter from New York 7th July 1785," ibid., folio 203.

[64] Phineas Bond, Philadelphia, Nov. 16, 1788, to Lord Carmarthen in London, "Bond Letters, 1787–1789," 582; Bond, Philadelphia, Jan. 3, 1790, to Duke of Leeds in London, "Letters of Phineas Bond, British Consul at Philadelphia, to the Foreign Office of Great Britain, 1790–1794," ed. J. Franklin Jameson, *Annual Report of the American Historical Association for the Year 1897*; see also reports from other British consuls in America in British Foreign Office Archives, American Correspondence, 4/4–4/16.

In the 1780s virtually every British newspaper printed "reports from America" that were derived from such official and unofficial sources and thus lent their aid the government's attempt to cut off emigration without infringing on the constitutional rights of the English people. The portrait of the United States that was painted by the British press during the 1780s depicted a country in the throes of social, economic, and political chaos.[65]

Anti-emigration propagandists emphasized the economic hardships that greeted British subjects who were foolish enough to emigrate to the United States. According to a correspondent in Dublin, "Several persons lately returned to this city from America, where they had gone with a view of settling, mention, that such a savageness of manners at present reigns among the Colonists, as render them a most disagreeable people to live with; that their country, in point of commerce, is yet in a very distressful state, and that they cannot find sale for a fifth part of the goods which are crowding in upon them. The consequences, it is to be feared, will speedily be extensively felt." The manufacturers from Birmingham who had emigrated to America in January of 1782 reportedly told the same story as they lamented "their folly in leaving their own country." In letters to their friends in England, they reported that "money is very scarce, provisions very dear; that there are more emigrants than can find employ; and that they shall be obliged either to stay there and starve, or work their way before the mast back to Old England." A gentleman who had just returned from Philadelphia likewise reported that "As Englishmen they were very coldly received" and, although wages were relatively high for some trades, house rent and provisions were "very dear."[66] Personal letters from Americans to their friends and relatives in Great Britain that were published in British newspapers recited the same litany of economic woe. According to the London press, "Few letters arrive from America without informing us of the misery and poverty of the people. Their ports filled with goods which the venders are obliged to sell at a low price, or bring them back to Europe; the price of living exceedingly dear, and considerable discontents prevailing; yet certain persons there are publishing to the world the extreme happiness which the United-states have enjoyed since their separation from Great-Britain, and their union with their most christian ally."[67]

The American states did indeed experience some commercial distress in the 1780s, but the British press exaggerated its extent. In addition, much of this distress was produced by the deliberate flooding of republican markets by British merchants whose determination to regain the American trade was encouraged

---

[65] See *Belfast News-Letter*, Mar. 25, May 6, May 23, 1783; *Newcastle Journal*, May 31, 1783; *Felix Farley's Bristol Journal*, Oct. 9, 1784, dateline London, Oct. 5; *Leeds Mercury*, Oct. 12, 1784, dateline London, Oct. 7.

[66] *Felix Farley's Bristol Journal*, Sept. 25, 1784, dateline Dublin, Sept. 16 (quote); *Leeds Mercury*, Sept. 2, 1783 (quote); *Felix Farley's Bristol Journal*, Sept. 6, 1783, dateline Salisbury, Sept. 1 (quote).

[67] *Belfast News-Letter*, Jan. 25, 1785, dateline London, Jan. 15. See also "Extract of a letter from a merchant at Baltimore, to his brother in Dublin," May 12, 1785, *Maryland Gazette*, Sept. 30, 1785.

by their government. If British mercantile houses were able to control American commerce by extending long credits to republican correspondents, and "await their convenience" for repayment, British officials could continue to deny special concessions to the independent states and thus maintain, intact, the protective barriers around their Navigation system.[68] When, however, American merchants defaulted on their payments or asked for credit extensions, the British press placed the blame squarely on the conduct of the nonvirtuous republicans. The commercial disasters that overtook English merchants in 1784 and 1785 were not blamed on faulty British strategy, but rather on the unscrupulous character of American merchants. Economic problems were attributed to the fact that in America, "every man suspects his neighbour, each province is jealous of that adjoining to it . . . the Southern are in interest diametrically opposite to the Northern States; hence perpetual bickerings are continually happening . . . their ship building is so much cramped, their sailors perishing, their people so oppressed with taxes, and every source of commerce dried up, that it is impossible they can long exist without plundering one another."[69]

American merchants defended themselves by claiming that "the true citizens of these States have notions of equity and honor as nice as those of any commercial man whatever." They asked the British to halt their shipments "till the trade and commerce is brought under some certain regulation between the two countries." But this solution was unacceptable to the English government, which was determined to win the American trade informally, by the risk-taking of merchants, rather than breach their Navigation Acts by entering into a commercial treaty with the United States.[70]

British tales of the hardships faced by hapless immigrants who had been seduced from their homes by the false promises of American recruiters also chronicled the failure of virtue in republican America. Stories abounded of the disillusionment faced by British merchants and "credulous mechanics who had golden dreams" of acquiring "amazing fortunes from their labours." From New Jersey came the report of universal poverty, where inhabitants "with the hardest labour can do little more than earn a decent livelihood, even those who are proprietors of the ground." In Virginia, an unwholesome climate combined with economic hardships to bring an Irish family to the brink of despair. Suffering from "the dumb ague and fever," the immigrant from Belfast hoped only that his family might be "spared through the winter and not seized with sickness in spring, which is equally dangerous as at this season," in order to return home. Condi-

[68] *Leeds Mercury*, Aug. 24, 1784, dateline London, Aug. 19; Mar. 8, 1785 (quote).

[69] "Extract of Letter from Boston, New England, June 11," *Leeds Mercury*, Aug. 17, 24, Sept. 21, Oct. 26, Nov. 2, 1784, July 26 (quote), Sept. 6, 13, Dec. 12, 20, 1785; *Felix Farley's Bristol Journal*, Aug. 14, Sept. 4, 11, Oct. 23, 1784. See also "Extract of a Letter from Philadelphia, July 26," *Leeds Mercury*, Oct. 5, 1784, for report that "Villainy, not necessity" caused the bankruptcies that were convulsing Philadelphia.

[70] "Extract of a letter from Maryland, per ship *Esther*, arrived at Glasgow, May 27," *Maryland Gazette*, Sept. 30, 1785 (quotes); Sheffield, *Observations on the Commerce of the American States*, 198.

tions in the northern states were, reportedly, no better. "In the winter the snows cover the ground, and the cattle are housed, and no manufacture scarcely can proceed; and in summer the heat is so intense, that the verdure is scorched up, and neither man nor beast can well sustain it." Even worse was "the abundance of venemous insects, beasts, and reptiles, that threaten to annoy and sometimes destroy you in this country. In the summer and autumn months, the air, especially near swamps and marshes, is darkened with the musketoes, who sting and torment you night and day. The snakes, and those of the most poisonous kind . . . greatly abound, and sometimes are known to creep into cottages, and crawl into beds." Sad indeed was the plight of British subjects who succumbed to the blandishments of American agents and emigrated from a country, "where many of them could earn a tolerable livelihood," only "to starve in those [republican] provinces."[71]

According to British publicists, America's republicans clearly demonstrated their lack of virtue and illiberal tendencies in their treatment of foreigners. The cold reception of the English after the war seemed to belie the sincerity of the American rebels who had claimed to be fighting a corrupt British government on behalf of "all mankind." At war's end, incidents in New York City demonstrated "the settled dislike that prevails among the lower orders of the people" toward British subjects. Although "disagreeable" frays between "English Tars" and American sailors after eight years at war should not have surprised anyone, the continuation of wartime antipathy was seen as an irrational prejudice and evidence of American shortcomings.[72]

In August 1785 the inhabitants of Charleston battled British merchants who "pour in their goods, and will take nothing but cash in return, which drains the State of specie, whilst their produce lies on hand." Irate Charlestonians posted notices "in every street of the city, warning the English to quit the State in a limited time." They also pressed for passage of a law "prohibiting all British vessels from entering their ports, until an equitable system of commerce is agreed to by the British Government." Letters from Boston told the same story, of an increasing resentment of British merchants, "so great . . . as to make their stay dangerous." An Irish merchant in Philadelphia, who "came to the Continent with the greatest opinion of it and its inhabitants," reported that "Hospitality and friendship, the former characteristics of America, have fled the land."[73]

---

[71] Quotes from: *Belfast News-Letter*, Feb. 22, 1785; "Extract of a Letter from Philadelphia, Dec. 25, 1784," ibid., Feb. 25, 1785; "A Letter of Nov. 7, 1784 from a Person Formerly of This Place, and Now at Falmouth in Virginia," ibid., Feb. 4, 1785; "Extract of a Letter from New York," ibid., Apr. 12, 1784; *Leeds Mercury*, Dec. 13, 1785. See also a false report of plague in Baltimore, *Belfast News-Letter*, Mar. 5, 1784.

[72] *Felix Farley's Bristol Journal*, Sept. 6, 1783 (quote); *Leeds Mercury*, Dec. 16, 1783, dateline London, Dec. 11 (quote); Dec. 23, 1783, dateline London, Dec. 12 (quotes).

[73] "A letter from Charles-Town, South Carolina, Aug. 28, 1785," *Leeds Mercury*, Nov. 15, 1785 (quotes); *Leeds Mercury*, June 28 (quotes), July 5, 1785; "Extract of a Letter from Philadelphia, to a Merchant in Belfast, 24th of Sept. 1783," *Belfast News-Letter.*, Nov. 28, 1783 (quotes).

The Irish, who considered themselves the special friends of the American states, were surprised at not meeting with the "civilities or attention" they had expected. Reports of the hostile reception of Scottish immigrants were less surprising and contained a kernel of truth. Postwar Americans distrusted Scots, believing that their conduct during the Revolution proved "the inveteracy of their national character" and the impossibility of weaning "them from the principles of perfidy, slavery and ingratitude which are native to them." Passengers who arrived in Edinburgh from Philadelphia in March 1786 confirmed and exaggerated "the very bad usage, and the odious light the Scots are held in America." The Reverend Doctor Nisbet, on his return to Scotland from Pennsylvania, reported that "the people who emigrate as indented servants from Scotland are all made slaves, for the Americans declare there are none but Tories in Scotland, and that they deserve not to be freemen." In 1784 a "letter from America" reported that Virginia's naturalization law reflected America's bias against the Scots. According to this [false] account, Irishmen were eligible for citizenship after a two-year residency and Englishmen after five years; but "a Scotchman must reside thirty years to qualify him for enjoying the rights of a free Citizen of Virginia."[74]

According to the British press, the reception faced by impoverished British emigrants who voyaged to America was just as illiberal. Robert Harpur, who emigrated to New York in search of liberty, found instead "the greatest tyranny and cruelty practised, not indeed by one, but by a thousand tyrants; for the mob do as they please; and if any popular leader bears you hatred, he can soon direct the vengeance of the giddy multitude against you, under pretence of your being a public enemy. . . . It grieves me to see so many Irishmen and Scots, who fancied that gold abounded here, wandering pitiless through the streets, for the people, who are chiefly Dutch or Germans, have no compassion for any but of their own language."[75]

The situation of immigrants arriving under indenture was depicted as nothing short of desperate. British newspapers reported that in 1783 over 400 Irish emigrants had gone "across the Atlantic, to the Land of Liberty," only to be "sold at public venue" and enslaved. American newspapers were "full of advertisements of redemptions, servants to be sold, as slaves, for three to five years." These servants, it was claimed, had "no choice in their master, and very often they are treated little better than negroes during their servitude; for a master may, for the smallest offence, put his indented servant into the Workhouse and feed him there

[74] Arthur Lee (Paris) to Richard Price, Apr. 20, 1777, in Peach, *Richard Price*, 308–9 (quotes); "A Letter from Edinburgh, Dated March 10," *Leeds Mercury*, Mar. 21, 1786 (quote); Nisbet letter in *Belfast News-Letter*, Feb. 17, 1786; (inaccurate) report of Virginia's citizenship requirements in "A Recent Letter from America," *Leeds Mercury*, Nov. 9, 1784. See also reports of a growing distaste for the French and Dutch in republican America: *Felix Farley's Bristol Journal*, Nov. 29, 1783; *Leeds Mercury*, June 15, 1784, Mar. 15, 1785.

[75] Robert Harpur, "Extract of letter from New York, Dec. 29, 1784," *Belfast News-Letter*, Apr. 12, 1785.

during his pleasure on bread and water, without the servant having the smallest redress."[76]

In January 1785, London's *Daily Universal Register* reported that during the 1784 season "the number of European white slaves that had been . . . imported at the port of Philadelphia was between ten and twelve thousand! These were all Irish. The Scotch amounted to about three to four thousand!" When the 1785 "live stock traffic" showed no signs of abating, the *Register* resurrected the apocryphal tale of the purchase of "two very handsome" Irish lads by a free negro who "carried [them] home, and . . . although offered his money, he keeps them chained, and treats them with all the savage barbarity natural to his complexion. So much for the land of freedom!" Five months later the paper printed a report from the *Jamaica Royal Gazette* of a Congressional proclamation "forbidding all masters of vessels to bring any more indentured servants, either from Great Britain or Ireland, as, for the want of employment, many of those already arrived are in a starving condition, their indentures not being disposed of." Although untrue, the story was widely reprinted and embroidered upon by the British press. By the end of September, newspapers in Leeds and London were publishing a report from Dublin that, "The miseries, want, and robberies of the Irish emigrants have been such, that proclamations are not only published in America, against the import of any more, but a price set upon the lives of all those called outlaws. Thus, in the very despite of themselves, have the Americans rendered an essential service to this kingdom by a coercion of its deluded people to the native soil."[77]

According to the British press, the hardships immigrants faced were a result of the failure of America's republicans to institute proper governments. The problem lay primarily in "the body of men called the American Congress [who] constitute the Supreme legislature nominally, but not really, substantially, and effectually. They can resolve every thing—but they can execute nothing." In the summer of 1783 it was already clear that this "moonshine Government, the ideal Power, risen in the Western World" was "gradually declining and sinking in its power, authority, and credit, with its own subordinate members, until it has fallen into downright contempt, in its fugitive state begging protection from one of the executive Legislatures against the rude attacks of the enraged soldiery, and begging in vain—seemingly casting an eye ultimately to our [British] army for shelter from the impending storm."[78]

[76] *Leeds Mercury*, May 5 (quotes), Oct. 5, 1784; *Belfast News-Letter*, Nov. 28, 1783 (quote); "Letter from Baltimore, in Maryland, to a gentleman in London," *Belfast News-Letter*, Jan. 4, 1785.

[77] (London) *Daily Universal Register*, Jan. 14 (quotes), Apr. 27 (quote), 1785. For the ubiquitous story of the sale of British subjects to "barbarous" blacks, see *Felix Farley's Bristol Journal*, Aug. 7, 1784; *Leeds Mercury*, Nov. 23, 1784 and May 3, 1785. American "proclamations" against indentured servants and Irish emigrants are reported in *Leeds Mercury*, Sept. 27, 1785; (London) *Daily Universal Register*, Sept. 6 (quote), 20 (quote), 1785; and *Felix Farley's Bristol Journal*, Sept. 10, 1785.

[78] *Felix Farley's Bristol Journal*, Aug. 23, 1783.

Predictions of the imminent demise of American governments, "erected on an insecure foundation" and dependent for their stability on "a riotous populace, a variety of jarring interests, and no public credit," were pervasive. By 1786 the American states were commonly seen as "incapable of settling into a regular, firm, compact system of Government, either to repel foreign invaders, or [to] regulate their own internal policy in peace and tranquillity" and were "sinking deeper and deeper into confusion, anarchy, poverty and wretchedness."[79]

Historical inevitability was occasionally used to explain the anarchy in republican America. To some observers it seemed that independence had simply "come upon them one hundred years too soon, for they are too young to know what use to make of it." To others, the culprit was republicanism itself. During the summer of 1785 events in the Netherlands delineated "the miseries of republicanism." There, "while their existence as a nation is in the most imminent danger, from a formidable and resolute foe," Dutch republicans were "creating such dissentions among themselves as must inevitably" destroy their country. A year later the lesson was even clearer: both the Dutch and American republics had been reduced to "heaps of confusion, strife, animosity, and enmity!—Both under the tuition and guidance of the French Court! . . . Will nothing open the eyes of these infatuated Hollanders or Americans?—even when they are drowning!" Whether through lack of virtue, immaturity, or the inherent tendencies of republicanism, by the end of 1786 it was clear that Americans would never "enjoy a moment's tranquillity till they put themselves under the protection of some foreign power. The only alternative, therefore, is for them to become subjects of France, or return to their former allegiance to England." And given the history of French perfidy and tyranny, there could be no doubt that rational Americans would choose union with England, home of "an enlightened people . . . breathing the very spirit of freedom, under the mildest of all governments" and sole supporter of "the dignity of man."[80]

The Americans' inability to understand or create the necessary underpinnings of stable government obviously prevented them from offering an asylum to those hoping to preserve their liberty or property. Furthermore, even in their weakened state, American governments managed to violate the liberties of their subjects. In the summer of 1783, the English press reported the passage of "several severe laws . . . which, though useful to the community, militate against their boasted liberty, and would be considered in England as highly oppressive to the subject." These included orders "that no man shall have a loaded gun, pistol, or

---

[79] Quotes from *Leeds Mercury*, Aug. 19, 1783, dateline London, Aug. 16; Nov. 11, 1783, dateline London, Nov. 4; and Jan. 16, 1787.

[80] Quotes from ibid., June 21, 1785, dateline London, June 14; Sept. 27, 1785, dateline London, Sept. 24; Jan. 16, 1787, dateline London, Jan. 11; Jan. 2, 1787, dateline, London, Dec. 30, 1786; Dec. 18, 1787; and Nov. 8, 1785, dateline London, Nov. 3. See also ibid., Oct. 18, 1785, for the claim that, "Had America preserved her attachment to England, the people [would] still be rich, powerful, respectable and happy."

any firearms in his house." The British press took special delight in trying to unravel American logic when, after "the clamour first raised by the Americans against the Mother Country . . . in consequence of the Stamp Act, which was represented to be a monster of iniquity . . . the first act of their own legislature, after obtaining their independence, was to lay a Stamp Duty on news-papers, &c." According to the London press, the operation of the Massachusetts Stamp Act was "so odious and irksome . . . that great numbers are said to be emigrating to the new State of Vermont, in quest of a settlement, where those oppressive, though legal stretches of power, may not be necessary." A similar situation obtained in New York, where "the grievous oppression of their taxes and the weakness of government" forced "No less than 2,000 families" to seek refuge in Vermont and led the New York assembly to publish "an edict to restrain settlers from leaving that province." When a printer in Philadelphia was imprisoned "for having published a pamphlet listing the distresses of the country," it was clear that the American states had overstepped the bounds of "oppressive, though legal stretches of power." As one English commentator phrased it, "So much for the freedom of the American press, or rather, so much for that slavery which they prefer to the best government in the world—that of this country."[81]

The selective and distorted reports of conditions in the postwar states clearly questioned the ability of the United States to act as an asylum for the liberty they so dimly comprehended. When "anarchy and insolvency" turned out to be "the only precious effects of their dear-bought independence," the American states became the natural refuge, not of industrious foreigners who sought to secure their property and liberty, but of scoundrels.[82] Therefore it did not seem surprising for disillusioned Americans to turn to England for both in-spiration and succor. Postwar reports of individuals and communities seeking refuge in the British colonies in North America soon escalated to include entire states—including Vermont, Connecticut, and Rhode Island. According to British newspapers, all of these republicans realized that their survival depended on incorporation within the British empire. By 1784 British publicists had discerned "a strong tendency in the majority of the Americans to return to their duty." Having had

> time to reflect that to Britain they first owed their existence; that to her fostering care they are indebted for their prosperity; that their blood and treasure were lav-

[81] Quotes from: *Felix Farley's Bristol Journal*, Aug. 23, 1783, dateline London, Aug. 19; *Leeds Mercury*, July 12, 1785, dateline London, July 6; Sept. 9, 1783, dateline London, Sept. 6; Aug. 17, 1784, dateline London, Aug. 10; Aug. 17, 1784, dateline London, Aug. 14; May 24, 1785, dateline London, May 19.

[82] *Leeds Mercury*, May 3, 1785 (quote). In reporting the defection of two constables who had over £300 that they had collected in taxes, a Bristol newspaper described one of "these *honest tax gatherers*" as "a staunch American in principle," and "supposed he is now on his voyage for the *Land of Promise.*" *Felix Farley's Bristol Journal*, July 31, 1784.

ishly expended in her defence . . . that even when they had commenced open hostilities she put not forth half her strength, and mourned over the wounds she was obliged to inflict . . . they must feel remorse for what they have done and an eager desire to be reconciled to that parent who so tenderly watched over them in their infancy. . . . Loaded with taxes, oppressed by poverty, and groaning under the yoke of a junto of arbitrary despots, who are themselves tools to the Most Christian King, they now look back with regret to those happy times, when, under the wings of Great Britain, they enjoyed peace, plenty, and real freedom.[83]

The inability to the American states to protect their commerce and citizens from Mediterranean pirates taught the same lesson. The weakness of American government made republican vessels the target of Algerian corsairs. Between 1785 and 1790, the British press provided their readers with heart-rending accounts of the suffering endured by the captured and enslaved seamen and passengers who had the misfortune to sail on American vessels and of the humanitarian efforts of British statesmen to relieve these unfortunate victims. The story, later admitted to be a hoax, of the fortitude with which the aged Benjamin Franklin met his fate, was especially poignant.[84] Accounts of the atrocities inflicted by the barbaric infidel on white Christians undoubtedly boosted newspaper readership. But they also were part of the campaign to demonstrate the superiority of British government, promote the British carrying trade, and discourage emigration. It was the weakness of the American states that brought such calamities down on them. There was, however, one European nation that had earned the respect of these pirates who plundered "vessels of every nation that fall in their way, except the British, to which they are extreamly partial." By demanding independence, American sailors and shipowners had foolishly forfeited the protection of the well-respected British flag. Emigrants who took passage and merchants who shipped cargoes on American vessels needlessly shared republican vulnerability.[85]

The failure of American governments to protect and promote their commerce was just one of many symptoms that forecast the imminent failure of the republican experiment. A nation incapable of protecting its sailors could not be expected to stand up against the power of the newly united Indian tribes in America. A national government that rested on the misguided political beliefs

[83] *Leeds Mercury*, Jan. 4 (quotes), 1784; Jan. 25, Feb. 22, Sept. 20, 1785; Jan. 31, Mar. 7, 1786; *Felix Farley's Bristol Journal*, Mar. 18, 1786; Edward Byers, *The Nation of Nantucket: Society and Politics in an Early American Commercial Center, 1660–1820* (Boston: Northeastern University Press, 1987), chap. 11.

[84] *Felix Farley's Bristol Journal*, Oct. 18, 1785; *Belfast News-Letter*, Oct. 18, 1785.

[85] For Algerian attacks on American ships and British immunity, see *Belfast News-Letter*, Aug. 2, Oct. 11, Dec. 6, 13, 1785; *Felix Farley's Bristol Journal*, Oct. 1, Dec. 3, 24, 31, 1785; Jan. 21, 28, Feb. 18, 25, Mar. 25, May 13, 27, June 17, Aug. 5, 1786; *Leeds Mercury*, Dec. 13, 1785 (quote). These reports also warned British seamen that, if they signed on to American vessels they would be liable to the same terrible risks. The higher insurance rates demanded for republican cargoes, combined with shipping advertisements that promised the protection of a "Mediterranean Pass," also made British vessels far more attractive than those flying the thirteen stripes.

of a nonvirtuous and bickering people contained serious structural faults that would, in themselves, destroy or pervert American republicanism. "The debilitated and disorderly state from which America seems unable to raise herself" and American "disgust and disaffection to the present government" would "probably lead to another revolution." If, by some miracle, internal dissension failed to topple the new republics, external attacks—by the Indians, Algerines, Spain, or France—certainly would. In any case, the social, economic, and political chaos in republican America was sufficient to discredit the claim of the United States to be the last refuge of true liberty, or land of opportunity, for industrious immigrants.[86] The American states were the natural asylum only for social outcasts.

In Defense of America

The negative stories and commentaries about America that originated in British newspapers spread throughout the Western world. European editors, who regularly reprinted stories from foreign newspapers, used both British and American accounts to fill their columns, pique their readers, and advance their own domestic agendas. In Europe, as in Britain, government gazettes specialized in anti-American stories to deter emigration and prevent the contagion of liberty. Opposition organs reciprocated by publishing glowing accounts that also distorted conditions in the American states. American attempts to neutralize the hyperbole used by both sides and to inject a note of realism into the controversy did little to set the record straight.

In France and Germany reports of dissension and hardship in the American states were published by royalists who hoped to undermine republican sentiment. The anti-American stories culled from the British press and propagated in the royalist press, found a receptive audience among social conservatives and French merchants who had been burned in their attempt to break into the American trade.[87] This in turn prompted European reformers such as the Marquis de

[86] *Leeds Mercury*, Sept. 7, 1784 (quote); *Felix Farley's Bristol Journal*, Feb. 28, Mar. 13, July 24, 1784; Dec. 31, 1785; *Maryland Gazette*, quoting London sources, Feb. 28, 1784, Nov. 11, 1785. For accounts of Indian depredations and threats, see *Felix Farley's Bristol Journal*, Nov. 5, 12, 19, Dec. 17, 24, 31, 1785. For the inevitable clash between the Americans and Spain, see *Maryland Gazette*, June 28, 1785.

[87] The anti-American campaign in France is described in Echeverria, *Mirage in the West*, chap. 4. According to Horst Deppel, the dissemination of British propaganda in Germany was at once easier and less effective. Throughout the eighteenth century German readers relied on British and French sources for most of their information and myths about America. In the 1770s, these sources had produced a general enthusiasm among the higher bourgeoisie for the American republic, as the embodiment of Enlightenment ideals of liberty and progress. Although the German intelligentsia had little real knowledge or understanding of the principles that animated the American rebels, they were not to be shaken from their conviction that America had replaced England as the land of true liberty. Negative accounts of American conditions in the mid-1780s were embraced only by Germans who had, from the beginning, opposed the Revolution and were now horrified at the "dizziness of liberty" that "seized many brains who do not know that they want or what

Lafayette "to give the lye to false assertions of News papers, and to set to Rights the false ideas of Misinformed people" and to urge Americans to launch their own campaigns to "counteract the Uncandid Accounts" that filled royalist news-papers.[88] But the counteroffensive mounted by Americans and their European friends injected more confusion than light into the war of words.

Americans residing in Europe initially dismissed British allegations as mere slander. Writing in the guise of an officer "lately returned from service and resi-dence in the U.S. of America," where he had "fought and bled for that country," Thomas Jefferson tried to expose both the falsity of British propaganda and its design. Jefferson's mythical European veteran was astonished, on returning to his native country, "to find all the public papers of Europe filled with accounts of the anarchy and destractions [*sic*] supposed to exist in that country." The America he knew was far different, "enjoying all the happiness which easy gov-ernment, order and industry are capable of giving to a people. . . . From the moment of peace to that in which I left it." An inquiry "into the source of all this misinformation," revealed that "every unfavourable account . . . of the transac-tions in America has been taken from the English papers only"—from newspa-pers pervaded by a "deep-rooted hatred" of America and "the fear that their island will be depopulated by the emigration . . . to America."[89]

Other exculpatory letters also found their way into foreign newspapers. In 1784 the *Leeds Mercury* published an "Extract of a letter of a friend, by a gentleman of strict honour and good understanding" from Philadelphia that warned "against receiving unfavourable impressions of the circumstances of these States from any thing you may read in the newspapers, or hear from travelers and adventurers." According to this letter, "The [American] merchant, the farmer, the mechanic, are all busy in their respective vocations, covering, as fast as they can, the marks of British devastation, by new buildings, inclosures, and other improvements, and recovering their former state of happiness and prosperity. Each one anxious in the pursuit of his own, at the same time, without seeming to know or mean it,

---

true liberty is." In Germany, few pro-Americans changed their minds. Horst Dippel, *Germany and the American Revolution, 1770–1800: A Sociohistorical Investigation of Late Eighteenth-Century Political Thinking*, trans. Bernard A. Uhlendorf (Chapel Hill: University of North Carolina Press, 1977), quote on 262. But see also Lafayette to Thomas Jefferson, Sept. 4, 1785, reporting that "the Misrepresentations of Great Britain Have not Been fruitless" in Germany. *The Papers of Thomas Jefferson*, ed. Julian P. Boyd, (Princeton: Princeton University Press, 1950–), VIII, 478–80.

[88] Lafayette to Thomas Jefferson, Sept. 4, 1785, *Papers of Thomas Jefferson*, ed. Boyd, VIII, 478–80.

[89] Jefferson's veteran also pointed out that, although there had been a few disturbances, these incidents were usually limited in scope and bloodless. The American states had witnessed nothing comparable to London's Gordon riots or those that followed the last election in England. In fact, republican America enjoyed more peace and order than the established governments of the Old World. "Where," he asked, "is there any country of equal extent with the U.S. in which fewer disturbances have happened in the same time? Where has there been an instance of an army disbanded . . . without receiving a shilling of the long arrearages due them . . . and yet disbanded peaceably?" Jefferson's "Reply to the Representations of Affairs in America by British Newspapers," published in the *Leyden Gazette* in December 1784, reprinted in ibid., VII, 540–45.

contributing to the public weal." In February 1787 a letter to the editor of the *Leeds Mercury* summarized the contents of a letter from "Dr. Franklin ... to a gentleman of Rank and character" in England, that put a lie to "all the dreadful accounts of mobs, wars, and misunderstandings in America." A letter from Benjamin Rush to Richard Price was forwarded to the printer of the *Belfast News-Letter* to counteract "the animosity and resentment of some disappointed men among us against the inhabitants of the United States, who proclaim their rejoicing at every disastrous event which takes place in that country." The extracts that were published in the *Belfast News-Letter* on May 1, 1787, chronicled "the progress of order, government and knowledge in America." According to Rush, the quarrel between Pennsylvania and Connecticut over the lands in the Wyoming valley had been successfully arbitrated, and "the insurrections in Massachusetts Bay [were] in a fair way of being terminated in favour of the government of that state. The decision and public spirit which have actuated the councils, and arms of those ancient republicans, I hope, will satisfy the world, that the forms of government we have chosen, are agreeable to us, and that we are as ready to risk our lives in defence of *them*, as we were formerly in support of our liberties and independence." In addition, Rush announced the scheduling of a convention, to be "composed of the most respectable characters in the United States," that would meet in Philadelphia in May 1787, "for the purpose of devising a method of strengthening the foederal government."[90]

Although most pro-American pieces denied British allegations, some acknowledged and defended reports of political unrest. Most observers, on both sides of the Atlantic, saw political turbulence in America as evidence of a failure of public virtue and republican government. But Thomas Jefferson turned incidents such as Shays's Rebellion into reassuring signs of Americans' continued vigilance against possible encroachments on their liberty. Jefferson challenged America's critics to search history for "an instance of rebellion so honourably conducted." The motives of the rebels "were founded in ignorance, not wickedness". And, "The people cannot be all, & always, well informed. ... If they remain quiet under such misconceptions, it is a lethargy, the forerunner of death to the public of liberty." In any event, America's thirteen states had produced a single rebellion in their eleven years of independence. According to Jefferson, "That comes to one rebellion in a century & a half for each state. What country before ever existed a century & half without a rebellion? & what country can preserve it's [*sic*] liberties if their rulers are not warned from time to time that their people preserve the spirit of resistance? Let them take arms. The remedy

[90]Quotes from "Extract of a Letter to a Friend, Sept. 23, 1784," *Leeds Mercury*, Nov. 23, 1784; "To the Printer" from "M. M.," ibid., Feb. 27, 1787; "To the Printer" from "Humanity" and Benjamin Rush, Philadelphia, Feb. 14, 1787, to Richard Price in *Belfast News-Letter*, May 1, 1787. On the other hand, I found no evidence that Franklin's "The Retort Courteous," written in 1786 to exonerate America's republicans from charges of defaulting on their debts, was published abroad. *Benjamin Franklin: Writings*, ed. J. A. Leo Lemay (New York: Library of America, 1987), 1123.

is to set them right as to facts, pardon & pacify them. What signify a few lives lost in a century or two? The tree of liberty must be refreshed from time to time with the blood of patriots & tyrants. It is it's [*sic*] natural manure." In short, "a little rebellion now and then is a good thing, & as necessary in the political world as storms in the physical. . . . It is a medicine necessary for the sound health of government."[91]

European reformers were instrumental in securing the publication of the writings of American spokesmen, and also made direct contributions to America's antidefamation campaign. However, such efforts produced mixed results. In 1786 Thomas Jefferson supplied Jean Nicholas Desmeunier with information to be used in an article about the United States in the *Encyclopédie méthodique*. Despite repeated corrections by Jefferson and other knowledgeable Americans, the article that eventually appeared was largely a reworking of the inaccuracies of previous French authors. The four volumes published by Philip Mazzei, a native of Tuscany and former resident of Virginia, provided a more faithful account of America. Mazzei's *Rescherches historiques et politiques sur les Etats-Unis* included the most accurate history of the American states that was published abroad. However, written in Italian and translated into French, *Researches* failed to stir the interest of Europeans who "did not ask to be convinced of the virtues of the Americans, but to be thrilled and moved by them." The book's ponderous repetitions made it even less likely to convert America's critics.[92] Old World reformers who, in their zeal to refute the antirepublican allegations often went too far, produced "Monuments of the complete ignorance of the writers of their subject" and fantastic claims that were easy targets for their ideological opponents. In August 1786 the *Journal politique de Bruxelles* exasperatedly advised "the public, and especially those enthusiasts who write us insulting letters whenever the news from America contradicts their reveries, that this news is not taken from English papers, as they say, but is literally translated from American papers." But the impartial observer had no way to discern the facts that lay behind the writings of the partisans on both sides of the issue. Accurate reports of conditions in America and the reception of immigrants were, in the words of John Adams, "lost in adulatory Panegyricks, and in vituperary Insolence."[93]

[91] Quotes from Thomas Jefferson, Paris, Nov. 13, 1787, to William S. Smith, *Thomas Jefferson: Writings*, ed. Merrill D. Peterson (New York: Library of America, 1984), 911; Jefferson, Paris, Jan. 30, 1787, to James Madison, ibid., 882. See also Jefferson, Paris, Jan. 16, 1787, to Edward Carrington, ibid., 879–81; Jefferson, Paris, Feb. 22, 1787, to Abigail Adams, ibid., 889–90. For Jefferson's similar response to the Whiskey Rebellion in 1794, see Jefferson, Monticello, Dec. 28, 1794, to James Madison, ibid., 1015–17.

[92] Bernard Fay, *The Revolutionary Spirit in France and America* (New York: Harcourt, Brace & World, 1927), 201–3, quote on 203; *Thomas Jefferson: Writings*, ed. Peterson, 575–92; Jefferson to Van Hogendorp, Aug. 25, 1786, *Papers of Thomas Jefferson*, ed. Boyd, X, 299; Philip Mazzei, *Researches on the United States*, 1st publ. 1788, trans. Constance D. Sherman (Charlottesville: University Press of Virginia, 1976).

[93] *Journal politique de Bruxelles*, Aug. 19, 1786, quoted in Echeverria, *Mirage in the West*, 127; John Adams, *Defence of the Constitutions of Government of the United States of America, against the Attack of M. Turgot,*

The Old World campaign to prevent the spread of emigration fever and political radicalism produced a grim picture of life in the American republics. Anti-American publicists apparently succeeded in inhibiting the flow of British emigrants to the United States in the mid-1780s, but this triumph was short-lived.[94] While failing in its primary goal—eradicating the British penchant for emigration in a way that would not violate rights guaranteed by the English Constitution—British propaganda also failed to prevent the spread of the "enthusiasm for liberty" generated by the American Revolution. The support of British radicals for revolutionary France and the Irish Rebellion of 1798 are evidence of the failure of reforms and propaganda to counteract "emigration fever" and people's restless quest for liberty. Governments on the Continent suffered even greater defeats, as they were toppled one by one in the final decades of the eighteenth century.[95]

But Old World conservatives enjoyed some victories. They succeeded in inculcating lasting misperceptions of conditions in America in the 1780s. Postwar propaganda permanently discredited the governments instituted under the Articles of Confederation. Histories of "the critical period" of American history are filled with British exaggerations and myths about the social, economic, and political chaos that reigned in the 1780s until American republicanism was rescued by the Federal Constitution of 1787. The war of words following the Revolution also painted a distorted picture of immigration policies that were developed in the early Republic and muddied America's claim to be *the* asylum for liberty and "mankind".

---

in *The Works of John Adams*, ed. Charles Francis Adams, 10 vols. (Boston: Charles C. Little and James Brown, 1850–1856), V, 494 (quote); Adams (Quincy, Mass.) to Jefferson, May 18, 1817, in Lester J. Cappon, ed., *The Adams–Jefferson Letters: The Complete Correspondence between Thomas Jefferson and Abigail and John Adams*, 2 vols. (Chapel Hill: University of North Carolina Press, 1959), II, 516 (quote).

[94] By 1786 British newspapers and consuls were reporting that "The rage of emigration has from woeful experience pretty well subsided." (London) *Daily Universal Register*, July 13, 1785 (quote); *Felix Farley's Bristol Journal*, Sept. 16, 1786, dateline Dublin, Sept. 9; Phineas Bond, Philadelphia, Nov. 16, 1788, to Lord Carmarthen, "Bond Papers, 1787–1789," 582; Bond to Evan Nepean, Nov. 26, 1788, ibid. But British exultation was short-lived. By 1789 the London press and British officials were reporting the revival of "A dangerous spirit of emigration." *Pennsylvania Packet*, Oct. 6, 1789, dateline London, July 18 (quote); George Miller, the British Consul at Charleston, S.C., Jan. 28, 1790, to Duke of Leeds, British Foreign Office Archives, American Correspondence, 4/8, folios 49–61; John Temple, New York, Oct. 5, 1791, to Lord Grenville, ibid., 4/11, folio 77; Bond, New York, Aug. 15, 1789, to Duke of Leeds, "Bond Papers, 1787–1789," 613.

[95] Palmer, *The Age of the Democratic Revolution*; Library of Congress Symposia, *The Impact of the American Revolution Abroad* (Washington, D.C.: Library of Congress, 1976); Bonwick, *English Radicals*; Albert Goodwin, *The Friends of Liberty: The English Democratic Movement in the Age of the French Revolution* (Cambridge: Harvard University Press, 1979); Marianne Elliott, *Partners in Revolution: The United Irishmen and France* (New Haven: Yale University Press, 1982).

6   *Republican Immigrant Policies*

in the 1780s

THE EVIDENCE MARSHALED by Old World anti-emigration campaigns seriously challenged the ability of republican America to provide a refuge that could secure liberty for either citizens or immigrants; these campaigns also distorted and misrepresented the alien policies that evolved in postwar America. Old World tales of republican perfidy, licentiousness, intolerance, and abuse of immigrants cast a dark cloud on the treatment of aliens and magnified the disabilities they faced. By attributing the 1780s rage for emigration to the seduction of the innocent by unscrupulous recruiters and depicting the American states as the natural resort "of the culprit, and of those who have made themselves the objects of contempt and neglect," Old World propagandists also continued America's colonial image as a regenerative haven for Europe's failures and outcasts—by projecting an American welcome for any gullible or desperate enough to emigrate.[1] America's republicans and their Old World friends vigorously denied the negative image of the new states that was conjured up by those who feared the rage for liberty and emigration that American independence had fostered. However, attempts by the supporters of American republicanism to set the record straight failed, falling victim not only to the clamor of the 1780s but also to political experimentation that made it virtually impossible to describe, with any accuracy, the alien policies that were emerging in the newly independent American states.

In the 1780s Americans were preoccupied with creating laws and institutions that would preserve liberty and establish a secure foundation for their revolutionary republics. Postwar Americans reexamined their political heritage and revised or rewrote state constitutions and legal codes to purge them of nonrepublican elements. Even though the formal development of alien policies was a relatively minor element of this nation-building process, laws relating to aliens and naturalization were subjected to the same scrutiny. During this process, state

[1] Quote from John Lord Sheffield, *Observations on the Commerce of the American States*, 1st publ. 1784, 2d ed. (New York: Augustus M. Kelley, 1970), 193n.

legislators and the Continental Congress validated and reenacted some colonial practices while modifying or rejecting other alien policies as incompatible with republican principles or postwar conditions.

Several factors complicated the reformulation of America's alien policies. During the Revolution American patriots had promised that, once free of British shackles, they would create a new asylum to guard the flame of liberty and succor victims of Old World oppression. The anti-American campaign of the 1780s increased the pressure on Americans to honor this pledge and to adopt strictly republican policies able to withstand the scrutiny of Old World friends and foes alike. While Old World supporters urged their American friends to confound their critics by creating a secure, republican refuge for both liberty and the oppressed, republican lawmakers were hampered by their constituents' doubts about the political and economic consequences of immigration, lingering wartime animosities, and their own divergent republican visions. The result was a confusing amalgam of constantly changing alien policies and naturalization procedures. Nonetheless, by the end of the 1780s, a unique mixture had emerged that, by embodying republican prejudices and principles and mercantilist aspirations, offered European immigrants an unprecedented access, on easy terms, to the political and economic fruits of the American Revolution.

Republican Hubris

Postwar Americans were proud of their ability to attract immigrants and observed, with amusement, the frantic efforts of Old World governments to halt the outpouring of their subjects at the end of the Revolution. This was evidence of the magnitude of their victory—proof that America's military success meant more than merely throwing off British rule. Independence had been a necessary precondition but, to many Americans, it was just the beginning of an international revolution for the betterment of humanity.

The preference of a significant proportion of the invading British army, whether British subjects or foreign mercenaries, for the free air of America over European oppression gave Americans special satisfaction. The *Maryland Gazette* issued regular reports on English dismay at the "desertion of the Hessians" and the British soldiers who refused to leave at war's end and became "subjects of the United States of America." Republican newspapers published reports of the decimated state of British regiments that returned home after the war, telling of 84 survivors of the original 1,000 men in the 21st, and of the 300 of the 71st regiment, "being all that remained of the corps," that "when they embarked at Greenock for America in 1776, was upwards of 2000 strong."[2]

[2] *Maryland Gazette*, June 27, Aug. 15, Oct. 3, 1783; *Pennsylvania Packet*, Apr. 10, 1784.

Americans, who witnessed these desertions and the postwar influx of foreigners into their ports, readily accepted the evidence proffered by European observers that the subjects of the Old World were flocking to their land of liberty to escape oppressive regimes, whose unenlightened policies naturally produced economic and political distress. In August 1783 the *Maryland Gazette* told of reports from Great Britain "that the inhabitants of the isles of Britain and Ireland, are panting earnestly after the milk and honey of this promised land, and that nothing but the want of means prevents them from emigrating in tens of thousands." In April 1784 the *Pennsylvania Packet* printed a letter from London describing the "darkness and confusion" that had engulfed Great Britain and its dependencies and the "swarms of mechanics," who "notwithstanding the strictness of the laws, and the vigilance of the magistrates . . . emigrate to your free, happy country."[3]

The new American states had many reasons to embrace and publicize this evidence of their attractiveness to Old World subjects. The expanding American population provided republican statesmen with what little leverage they had in their campaign to revolutionize international relations. Old World nations that negotiated commercial treaties with the new states, based on the principle of reciprocity, did so to gain access to American markets. Any population growth in the independent states would, by increasing the number of consumers, make those markets even more attractive.[4] Additions to the American population would also allow the United States to secure and defend lands ceded to them by the Treaty of 1783. Thus, by calling attention to their country's irresistible lure to all subjects of the Western world, Americans enhanced their international reputation and increased their ability to deal with traditional statesmen who acted on the assumption that people were the true strength of a nation.

In describing the flight of British emigrants from the desperate conditions that were the inevitable result of tyrannical government, Americans also were documenting England's inability to act as an asylum of liberty and a refuge for the victims of oppression and America's succession to those titles. In the years following the American Revolution, the Western world accepted, virtually without question, the maxim that "Liberty naturally draws new People to it, as well as increases the old Stock."[5] In the 1780s, Americans argued that prospective immigrants were "driven away by the perception of evils" and, because "beneficial

[3] *Maryland Gazette*, Aug. 15, 1783 (quote); "Extract of a Letter from a Merchant in London," Feb. 5, 1784, *Pennsylvania Packet*, Apr. 22, 1784 (quote); "Extract of a Letter from Belfast," *Pennsylvania Gazette*, July 28, 1784.

[4] In 1783 William Bingham warned England against antagonizing the United States with its "three millions of inhabitants, rapidly increasing in numbers, all of whom consume more or less of British manufactures." *A Letter from an American Now Resident in London, to a Member of Parliament . . .* (Philadelphia: Robert Bell, 1784), 13.

[5] David L. Jacobson, ed., *The English Libertarian Heritage: From the Writings of John Trenchard and Thomas Gordon in The Independent Whig and Cato's Letters* (Indianapolis: Bobbs-Merrill, 1965), Letter 62, on 134.

institutions and natural advantages of the country are the substantial encouragements to emigration," no one could "be seduced by the most flattering promises, to exchange the humblest fortunes under a free government, for the turbulence of an Arabian plain or the despotism of modern Greece." An Irish correspondent who reported that his country had "already grown thin by wanton power" based his observation on the same assumptions, as did London's *Daily Universal Register*, when it mocked the efforts of "certain of our political projectors" who "affect to disregard the frequent emigrations of artizans and manufacturers from this country." According to the *Universal Register*, "the wise . . . will ever consider removals of this sort as the effect of weakness or oppression in those who sit at the helm."[6]

American derision of England's futile attempts to limit the mobility and freedom of its subjects also was a response to the British propaganda campaign that tried to prevent emigration by discrediting the republican experiment. American diplomats were naturally anxious to counter the "Exaggerated accounts of the Want of Moderation, Union, Order and Government" that undermined their bargaining position in Europe.[7] The American penchant for filling their newspapers with stories culled from British papers kept the American public abreast of Old World slander and produced similar indignation and denials.

Men like John Miller, the editor of the *South Carolina Gazette*, had special reasons to expose the lies about America that were published in English newspapers. At the end of 1781 Miller, then the printer of the *London Evening Post*, was found guilty of publishing a libel against the Russian ambassador to England and imprisoned. In March 1783 John Miller, now "Printer to the State of South Carolina," published the first issue of his Charleston newspaper. By November Miller was involved in a vigorous campaign to reveal "the scandalous and shameful untruths . . . respecting America" concocted by the English press. An open letter addressed "To the Printers of most of the Daily Papers in London" advised them to discontinue their "present practice of retailing the most improbable, ill-founded, and impudent untruths that ever disgraced the Press," since "All your efforts cannot prevent great emigrations." Miller warned his former colleagues that British officials could neutralize his campaign only by further infringements on the rights of the English because, as long as "the *South*

[6][Tench Coxe], "An Enquiry into the Best Means of Encouraging Emigration from Abroad . . . ," *American Museum*, 10 (1791), 114–17, 165–68, quotes on 116, 168; *Maryland Gazette*, May 31, 1785, dateline Cork, March 31 (quote); (London) *Daily Universal Register*, Sept. 1, 1785 (quote); Gouverneur Morris, *A Diary of the French Revolution*, ed. Beatrix C. Davenport, 2 vols. (Boston: Houghton Mifflin, 1939), II, 3, 19.

[7]John Jay to Egbert Benson, Passy, Sept. 12, 1783, in *John Jay: The Winning of the Peace—Unpublished Papers, 1780–1784*, ed. Richard B. Morris (New York: Harper & Row, 1980), 587 (quote); Benjamin Franklin, "The Retort Courteous" (ca. 1786), in *Benjamin Franklin: Writings*, ed. J. A. Leo Lemay (New York: Library of America, 1987), 1123; *Thomas Jefferson: Writings*, ed. Merrill D. Peterson (New York: Library of America, 1984), 571–74, 821, 831, 835–36, 871, 911–12.

Carolina Gazette . . . is permitted to be read in London," it would expose their "glaring falsehoods."[8]

The American press was especially merciless in unmasking the lies and pretensions of the loyalists who had settled in British North America. According to reports printed in republican newspapers, Canada could never become "the Envy of the American States." Rather, the inhabitants of that unfortunate land looked to the south "with a longing eye. Oppressed with the weight of tyrannic jurisprudence . . . they meditate a revolt . . . and seem determined to add another STAR in the *American constellation*." An anecdote in the *Maryland Gazette* quoted a former resident of Elizabeth-Town, New Jersey, as telling British officials that he had " 'formerly resided in Paradise, but am now bound to Hell'—alluding to that place of penance, Nova Scarcity."[9]

Americans who gloated over the discomfiture of Old World governments at the flight of their subjects to the American land of liberty gave the impression of extending a welcome to all who chose to seek their fortunes in the new states. But that was not the precise message American republicans wished to convey. In the 1770s, American patriots had identified social maturity and decay, which were fostered by population growth and economic development, as key factors in extinguishing liberty in England. While proud of their ability to attract victims of Old World oppression, many Americans feared that demographic growth could lead their infant states to the same end. Others feared the introduction of particular groups of Old World subjects whose presence might jeopardize their republican future. Both groups counseled moderation in inviting aliens to America.

As Minister to France, Thomas Jefferson was active in refuting the anti-American propaganda produced by British publicists, while simultaneously revealing his ambivalence about population growth. In a letter to Gijsbert Karel van Hogendorp, a young Dutch Patriot who had traveled to America in 1783 as part of the entourage of the Dutch ambassador to the United States, Jefferson described the British campaign as producing unintended benefits for the new republics. By destroying American credit, Old World propagandists had "checked" the "disposition to luxury" that undermined the virtue and simplicity necessary to support republican society. As British enmity forced American merchants into new markets, the states expanded their commercial horizons and established links outside the British orbit. Jefferson ended his list of the "most desirable" effects of the anti-American campaign with the fact that British

[8] *Newcastle Journal*, May 31, 1783; Robert R. Rea, *The English Press in Politics, 1760–1774* (Lincoln: University of Nebraska Press, 1963), 182–86, 206–20; Solomon Lutnick, *The American Revolution and the British Press* (Columbia: University of Missouri Press, 1967), 178–79; D. H. Gilpatrick, "Nativism in American Journalism, 1784–1814," South Carolina Historical Association, *Proceedings*, 1948, 8; *South Carolina Gazette*, Nov. 11 (quote), 15 (quotes), 1783; "Another sample of English FABRICATION," *South Carolina Gazette*, Nov. 22, 1783.

[9] *Virginia Journal*, July 8, 1784, dateline Boston, June 12 (quote); "Extract of a letter from a gentleman in Canada, June 14, 1784," ibid., July 15, 1784; *Maryland Gazette*, Aug. 15, 1783 (quote).

slander and commercial barriers also "prevent[ed] foreign emigrations to our country." Jefferson characterized all of these consequences as beneficial to the new republics.[10]

Benjamin Franklin, who had a long career in dispelling British lies about America, also was concerned with setting the record straight to "prevent inconvenient, expensive & fruitless Removals and Voyages of improper Persons" by giving "some clearer & truer Notions of that Part of the world than appear to have hitherto prevailed." In Charleston, home of the crusading editor of the *South Carolina Gazette*, the anonymous author of a pamphlet addressed to the people of South Carolina warned of the danger that their "constitution so equitable and uncommon, will excite the discontented of other countries to swarm in upon us, except some inhibitory measures are taken on our part ... under such inviting circumstances, we ought not to incline indifferently to receive every particular that offers, but to select those, whose reception will be not only consequentially but immediately advantageous to the Republic, as well as to ourselves."[11] Thus, the glowing American descriptions of the glorious future awaiting those fortunate enough to be citizens of the new states were more a celebration of America's victory and its ideals and a denial of British slander than an indiscriminate invitation to Europe's "downtrodden masses."

The postwar propaganda that obscured American attitudes and policies concerning immigration was only partially responsible for the confusion of the 1780s. Just as important in clouding the republican position on immigration were contradictions embodied in American policies. Republican lawmakers, who were often dubious about the wisdom of increasing the nation's population through immigration, were torn by their wartime promise to provide a sanctuary for liberty and the victims of oppression while safeguarding the republic from immigrants who would pervert or destroy its principles and future development.

Throughout the eighteenth century, American colonists had struggled to keep their communities free of undesirable elements. But their efforts to erect barriers against unwelcome immigrants often had been nullified by British or proprietary officials. With independence, the American colonists had won the "right to restrain that influx [of emigrants from abroad], whenever it is found likely to prove hurtful to us." The American states were now able to take direct action

---

[10] Jan Willem Schulte Nordholt, *The Dutch Republic and American Independence*, trans. Herbert H. Rowen, 1st publ. Netherlands, 1979 (Chapel Hill: University of North Carolina Press, 1982), 252–53; Thomas Jefferson, Paris, Oct. 13, 1785, to G. K. van Hogendorp, in *Thomas Jefferson: Writings*, ed. Peterson, 835–836.

[11] Benjamin Franklin, *Information to Those Who Would Remove to America*, Passy, Feb. 1784, *Benjamin Franklin: Writings*, ed. Lemay, quote on 975; Anonymous, "Rudiments of Law and Government Deduced from the Law of Nature," 1st publ. Charleston, S.C., 1783, in Charles S. Hyneman and Donald S. Lutz, eds., *American Political Writing during the Founding Era, 1760–1805*, 2 vols. (Indianapolis: Liberty Press, 1983), I, 597.

to keep out the "ship loads of wretches, too worthless for the old world." States like Pennsylvania would no longer be limited to placing duties on immigrants "she dared not to openly prohibit."[12]

In adopting a republican form of government, Americans made the character of their citizenry even more important than it had been in their colonial past. With government by the people, it was crucial that the people possess the virtue, education, experience, and political principles necessary to produce and select their leaders and to create the laws and institutions that would command respect both at home and abroad.[13] The social characteristics of American citizens were just as important as their political principles because they defined the republic's future development and created the interest groups that would shape and support governmental institutions, policies, and laws. Although American statesmen agreed on the need for citizens possessing the personal characteristics necessary to support republican government and society, they disagreed in their vision of the ideal form that government and society should take. This lack of unanimity over the ends sought naturally produced a variety of opinions on the demographic policies most consistent with those diverse goals.

American positions on population growth ranged from those who retained the traditional mercantilist belief in a large population, as the foundation of national wealth and power, to those who feared that an expanding population accompanied and accelerated the maturation of society as it moved inexorably from youthful vigor and virtue to senile decay and corruption. There also was a splintering of opinion within these two basic positions. If population growth was good, should it be left to natural increase or artificially augmented by the recruitment of foreigners—and if so which ones? If demographic expansion produced social and political decay, was it possible to halt or slow down that process by protecting or artificially perpetuating the mores and institutions of a youthful, virtuous society of independent yeomen farmers and by preventing the growth of luxury, sinful cities, and a landless class of dependent laborers? The conflicting answers to these questions injected ambiguity into America's immigrant policies.[14]

The American Consensus

Whatever their beliefs on the political and social consequences of population growth, Americans agreed that certain types of immigrants could only be

---

[12] Quotes from Coxe, "An Enquiry into the Best Means of Encouraging Emigration," 115, 165.

[13] See, *Mentor's Reply to Phocion's Letter* (Philadelphia: Robert Bell, 1784), 20.

[14] For the spectrum of population theories at the end of the eighteenth century, see Chapter 4 and Drew R. McCoy, *The Elusive Republic: Political Economy in Jeffersonian America* (Chapel Hill: University of North Carolina Press, 1980), chap. 1.

harmful. The new states were unanimous in rejecting the role, thrust on them in their colonial past, of providing a home for Europe's wastrels and convicts. Prior to 1776 the colonies may have had an obligation to serve the British empire as a regenerative haven for men who endangered the security of the mother country. But this obligation clearly ended once independence was secured. Independence also altered the circumstances that had led colonial Americans to purchase convict labor. The postwar surge of immigration filled republican harbors with an abundant supply of the free workers Americans had always preferred. Americans who feared the expansion of slavery and now possessed the power to regulate the slave trade directly no longer viewed transported convicts as a necessary antidote to African slavery. The creation of republican governments also increased the dangers of convict labor. Although transported felons lacked the attributes needed to become virtuous republican citizens, those who served out their time would become part of the self-governing body politic that would determine America's future. Thus, not surprisingly, no postwar arguments emerged for increasing the republic's population and labor supply by importing convicts. After the Revolution, ships carrying transported felons were turned away by indignant Americans.[15]

Postwar Americans retained their colonial reluctance to serve as a regenerative haven for Europe's failures—men who would enervate rather than strengthen the new nation. Benjamin Franklin, America's premier representative abroad, tried to discourage the emigration of French people of "irregular conduct and desperate circumstances, whom we had better be without." He complained of being "pestered continually with numbers of letters from people in different parts of Europe, who would go to settle in America, but who manifest very extravagant expectations, such as I can by no means encourage, and who appear otherwise to be very improper persons."[16]

Postwar governments did their best to staunch the influx of infirm and dissolute immigrants. In 1788 Massachusetts reenacted colonial laws requiring the registration of foreigners and prohibiting the landing of aliens who were likely to need public relief. New Hampshire passed a similar measure in 1791. By Connecticut's law of 1784, all foreigners residing in the state who were likely to become public charges could be sent away, as long as the cost did not exceed "the advantage of such transportation."[17] In 1788 New York's "Act for the better settlement and relief of the poor" required all shipmasters to report "the names

---

[15] For American opposition to transported convicts, see Chapter 5; and Franklin, "On Sending Felons to America" (1787), *Benjamin Franklin: Writings*, ed. Lemay, 1142–44.

[16] Franklin, Passy, Apr. 15, 1783 to Robert R. Livingston, *The Works of Benjamin Franklin*, ed. John Bigelow, 10 vols. (New York: G. P. Putnam's Sons, 1887–1889), X, 107–8; Franklin, Passy, Mar. 9, 1784, to Charles Thomson, *ibid.*, 291.

[17] *The Laws of Massachusetts, 1780 to 1800* (Boston: Wright & Potter, 1886), II, 628–29; Benjamin J. Klebaner, "State and Local Immigration Regulation in the United States Before 1882," *International Review of Social History*, 3 (1958), 271n., 290.

and occupations of every person who shall be brought" into the port of New York City. Ship masters would be fined £20 for each unreported person, and "if any person so neglected to be reported . . . shall be a foreigner," the fine rose to £30 per person. This law also denied admission "to any person who cannot give a good account of himself or herself, to the mayor or recorder" of New York City or "is like to be a charge to the said city." Such persons were to be returned by the master of their vessel "to the place from whence he or she came."[18]

American public opinion firmly supported the actions of their governments in erecting barriers to keep out "improper" strangers. Newspapers routinely applauded the arrival of "valuable" foreigners while denigrating Old World "refuse." In 1784 the *Virginia Gazette* published a report from Ireland stating that not a single redemptioner was included among the "upwards of 300" who were sailing from Cork to Philadelphia, evidence that these immigrants were "not the scum of the people," but had property sufficient to pay passages ranging from four guineas in the hold to ten guineas in the cabin. In 1785 the *Maryland Gazette* reprinted a story from New York that announced the arrival of a ship from Glasgow carrying "about an hundred decent passengers, mostly farmers; amongst whom are several respectable families. Their design is to settle in this country, and have brought considerable property with them—all on board have paid their passages. Decency, sobriety and good education stamp their characters, and their behaviour does honour to the country from whence they have arrived. Such inhabitants are wanted in the United States of America; One cargo of emigrants of this description, is more valuable than twenty of idle miscreants, picked from the streets, or the emptyings of gaols."[19]

However, American attempts to prevent the immigration of Europe's "wretched refuse" were largely ineffectual and unenforced. The records of New York City document the prosecution of scores of shipmasters for failure to comply with the terms of the Act of 1788 and its 1797 revision; these records also show that fines were usually forgiven and that the practice of landing "undesirable" immigrants in obscure inlets around New York City continued unabated.[20]

[18] "Act for the Better Settlement and Relief of the Poor" (1788, chap. 62), *Laws of the State of New York Passed at the Sessions of the Legislature Held in the Years 1785, 1786, 1787, and 1788, Inclusive* (Albany: Weed Parsons and Company, 1886), 731–44 (quotes); "An Act to Amend . . . 'An Act for the Better Settlement and Relief of the Poor'" (1797, chap. 101) *Laws of the State of New York Passed at the Sessions of the Legislature Held in the Years 1797, 1798, 1799, and 1800, Inclusive* (New York: Weed, Parsons and Company, 1887), 134–35.

[19] Quotes from *Virginia Gazette*, Oct. 14, 1784; *Maryland Gazette*, Sept. 27, 1785.

[20] New York City Common Council, *Minutes of the Common Council of the City of New York, 1784–1831*, 19 vols. (New York: M. B. Brown, 1917), II, 446, 450, 454, 465, 478, 484, 485, 490, 491, 634, 635, 641, 646, 652, 702, 711, 715, 717, 724, 727, 734, 736; III, 1, 10, 15, 87, 144, 153, 274–75, 563, 569; IV, 60, 73.

Return of the Loyalists

The American consensus on immigration did not go far beyond a resolve to keep the independent states free from the pernicious influence of transported convicts, the dissolute, and the infirm. The disparity of American opinion on demographic policies first gained prominence in the controversy that surrounded the fate of Americans who had refused to side with the rebels during the Revolution.

In 1783 the American cry for vengeance against the tories was strong and all encompassing. Many postwar American argued that neighbors who had "infamously deserted when their bleeding country demanded their services" by evading wartime service were just as reprehensible as those who had taken up arms against the republic. American collaborators of any stripe were hounded out of several states and examples were made of those attempting to return.[21] While tarring and feathering by mobs of rabid patriots was deplored by many, postwar Americans believed they had legitimate reasons to oppose the return of the loyalists. A meeting of the freemen of Philadelphia pronounced it "inconsistent with the interest and dignity of the good people of this state, that any person who hath voluntarily withdrawn himself from this or any of the United States" and "aided and abetted the measures employed by the king of Great-Britain against this country . . . should be suffered to return to, or reside within the state of Pennsylvania." They also considered "the restoration of the estates forfeited by law, as incompatible with the peace, safety and the dignity of this commonwealth." In New York "Mentor" argued against the return of the loyalists on the ground that since, in a republic, "the people are their own governors . . . government must take its shape from the opinion of the people." To allow loyalists to return would entrench "the tory principle" in America—a principle that encompassed "a moral and irreconcilable hatred of our government." Above all, American patriots feared that the loyalist refugees would "make wretched Republicans."[22]

[21] Quote in letter to the *Newport Mercury* from "An Old Whig," reprinted in *Maryland Gazette*, May 30, 1783; Samuel Harrell, *Loyalism in Virginia: Chapters in the Economic History of the Revolution* (Durham, N.C.: Duke University Press, 1926), 129–38; Carole Watterson Troxler, *The Loyalist Experience in North Carolina* (Raleigh: North Carolina Department of Cultural Resources, Division of Archives and History, 1976), chap. 2; Richard Walsh, *Charleston's Sons of Liberty: A Study of the Artisans, 1763–1789* (Columbia: University of South Carolina Press, 1959), 111–21; David E. Maas, comp., *Divided Hearts: Massachusetts Loyalists, 1765–1790: A Biographical Directory* (Boston: New England Historic Genealogical Society, 1980), introduction; Merrill Jensen, *The New Nation: A History of the United States during the Confederation, 1781–1789* (New York: Knopf, 1950), 266–81.

[22] "PROCEEDINGS of the FREEMEN of the City and Liberties of Philadelphia assembled . . . on the 14th June, 1783," *Maryland Gazette*, June 20, 1783 (quote); *Mentor's Reply to Phocion's Letter*, 20 (quote); *The Papers of Thomas Jefferson*, ed. Julian P. Boyd, et al. (Princeton: Princeton University Press, 1950–), VI, 385 (quote); "Instructions Drawn Up by the Town of Malden," *Maryland Gazette*, June 20, 1783; Carl Van Doren, *Benjamin Franklin* (New York: Viking, 1938), 678–79.

Yet, although Americans in 1783 and 1784 tended to view tories as citizens who had engaged in treason and were therefore liable to the penalties prescribed by the Continental Congress, including death and the forfeiture of their property, an argument for leniency toward all but the most belligerent soon emerged. Goaded by British threats and stung by their portrayal in the foreign press as lawless barbarians, whose "revengeful spirit" was a disgrace to the civilized world, many Americans reexamined their position.[23]

Postwar British patriots and officials concocted numerous schemes to pressure Americans into accepting returning loyalists. Threats were made to continue the British occupation of New York and East Florida until Americans mended their ways and to turn those regions into British asylums for the unfortunate victims of republican oppression. General Carleton ostentatiously delayed the evacuation of New York until every loyalist had been removed beyond the reach of the vindictive rebels. The course England ultimately adopted was to refuse to turn over the western posts until the Americans had fulfilled their treaty obligations to loyalists and other British subjects.[24]

Indigenous arguments soon emerged for moderation in the treatment of loyalists refugees. The roots of the American case for leniency were diverse. Individuals were moved by the pleas of loyalist friends and relatives to save them from the fury of the mob or exile in the frozen wastes of Canada. Virtually every American rebel had links with proscribed men whom they came to characterize as misguided rather than vicious or unprincipled.[25] Many patriots felt compassion for the families of militant tories. This compassion, mingled with a need to uphold property rights and the fear that loyalist families would become public charges, led to the modification of many state confiscation acts to allow the inheritance of estates by the "innocent" wives and children of loyalists. Personal relationships with "harmless" loyalists eventually made Americans receptive to arguments for a more liberal policy—one that discriminated between tories who took up arms against the patriots for "the most dishonorable of human motives" and loyalists who felt it their duty to serve

---

[23] *Felix Farley's Bristol Journal*, July 5, 1783 (quote); *Belfast News-Letter*, June 20, July 15, 1783; *Leeds Mercury*, July 8, Aug. 12, Sept. 9, 23, Dec. 9, 1783, July 27, 1784; Harrell, *Loyalism in Virginia*, 132; John Jay, Passy, Sept. 12, 1783 to Egbert Benson, *John Jay: The Winning of the Peace*, ed. Morris, 586–87.

[24] *Leeds Mercury*, Sept. 9, Nov. 11, 18, Dec. 9, 1783.

[25] Peter Van Schaack, the New York loyalist, received aid from such rebel leaders as Egbert Benson, Gouverneur Morris, Theodore Sedgwick, and John Jay in winning the right to return after being banished in 1777. Eugene R. Fingerhut, *Survivor: Cadwallader Colden II in Revolutionary America* (Washington, D.C.: University Press of America, 1983), 150. Nathanael Greene, the former rebel general, was soon convinced that "it would be the excess of intolerance to persecute men for opinions which, but twenty years before, had been the universal belief of every class of society." Lorenzo Sabine, *Biographical Sketches of Loyalists of the American Revolution*, 2 vols. (Boston: Little, Brown, 1864), I, 89. In 1783 Charles Carroll urged Maryland's legislators to end "odious distinctions" among Americans and unite them all "in the pursuit of the common good." Kate Mason Rowland, *The Life of Charles Carroll of Carrollton, 1737–1832, with His Correspondence and Public Papers*, 2 vols. (New York: G. P. Putnam's Sons, 1898), II, 67–72, quote on 70.

the cause that "Reason, though erroneous, recommended as the most just and virtuous."[26]

Traditional mercantilist arguments also surfaced during the loyalist controversy. In May 1783 General Benjamin Lincoln, then serving as Secretary of War to the Continental Congress, deplored the violence preached by Boston newspapers that was "driving from us many men who might be very useful" and "obliging them to people Nova Scotia." In December 1783 a letter to Virginia's governor warned that a rigorous enforcement of the state's "Citizens Bill" would "render us odious in the opinion of foreigners & greatly diminish the blessings of peace." John Breckinridge also argued against an "exclusive policy" toward loyalists on the grounds that it would not only strip the nation of valuable inhabitants but also subvert America's newly won liberty. Rather than legislate against the return of the loyalists, Breckinridge advised Virginia's legislature to rely on its electorate to keep political subversives out of public office.[27] The "Whig inhabitants" of Berks county, Pennsylvania, although not forgiving "the cowardly desertion and undermining arts of a set of men, unworthy of the name of Americans, who now come out of their hiding places," reached a similar conclusion. They urged that loyalists be allowed to "enjoy the common benefits flowing from a glorious revolution; let them remain to posterity as monuments of the clemency of government . . . but let them never dare to insult the feelings . . . of a free people, so far as to offer themselves as candidates for offices of trust, honour or profit." And so, patriots who were determined to silence British critics and to maintain America's reputation as a land of liberty joined with humanitarians who opposed violence and preached Christian charity and mercantilists who believed that republican America could not afford to lose the human capital of such a large segment of their population to urge a more magnanimous solution to the problem of the American loyalists.[28]

Patrick Henry drew on many of these arguments in urging Virginia to repeal the laws that denied British subjects and American loyalists the right to enter the state and apply for citizenship. He informed his colleagues in Virginia's House of Delegates that

Your great want . . . is the want of men; and these you must have, and will have speedily, if you are wise. Do you ask how you are to get them? Open your doors, sir, and

---

[26] John Jay, Paris, Sept. 17, 1782, to Peter Van Schaack, *John Jay: The Winning of the Peace*, ed. Morris, 467 (quotes); Harrell, *Loyalism in Virginia*, 96–112; Troxler, *Loyalist Experience in North Carolina*, 29–35; Richard D. Brown, "The Confiscation and Disposition of Loyalists' Estates in Suffolk County, Massachusetts," *William and Mary Quarterly*, 3d ser., 21 (1964), 534–50.

[27] General Lincoln quoted in "Ward Chipman Diary: A Loyalist's Return to New England in 1783," Essex Institute of Salem, *Historical Collections*, 87 (1951), 216–217n; J. Banister to Governor Harrison, in William P. Palmer et al., eds., *Calendar of Virginia State Papers and Other Manuscripts Preserved in the Capitol at Richmond*, 11 vols. (Richmond: 1875–1893), III, 551; Lowell H. Harrison, *John Breckinridge: Jeffersonian Republican* (Louisville, Ky.: The Filson Club, 1969), 16.

[28] Resolution of the Whig inhabitants of Berks County in *Maryland Gazette*, May 30, 1783 (quotes); *Belfast News-Letter*, May 20, 1783.

they will come in. The population of the Old World is full to overflowing; that population is ground, too, by the oppressions of the governments under which they live. Sir, they are already standing on tiptoe upon their native shores, and looking to your coasts with a wishful and longing eye. . . . But gentlemen object to any accession from Great Britain, and particularly to the return of the British refugees. Sir, I feel no particular objection to the return of those deluded people. They have, to be sure, mistaken their own interests most wofully, and most wofully have they suffered the punishment due to their offences. But the relations which we bear to them and to their native country are now changed. . . . The quarrel is over. Peace hath returned, and found us a free people. Let us have the magnanimity, sir, to lay aside our antipathies and prejudices, and consider the subject in a political light. Those are an enterprising, moneyed people. They will be serviceable in taking off the surplus produce of our lands, and supplying us with necessaries during the infant state of our manufactures. Even if they be inimical to us in point of feeling and principle, I can see no objection, in a political view, in making them tributary to our advantage. And, as I have no prejudices to prevent my making this use of them, so, sir, I have no fear of any mischief that they can do us. Afraid of them? What, sir, shall we, who have laid the proud British lion at our feet now be afraid of his whelps?[29]

The loyalist solution ultimately adopted by the American states was one that followed the arguments and fears of the Berks county Whigs more than the bold confidence of Patrick Henry and discriminated between the evil miscreants who had espoused the British cause for sordid reasons and the innocent, if deluded, men who felt compelled to honor their oaths of allegiance to Great Britain. By the end of the decade, most of the states had established procedures to readmit all but the most inveterate tories and had responded to the 1787 plea of Continental Congress to repeal any laws that violated the provisions of the Treaty of 1783 regarding the treatment of British subjects and their property.[30] In the South, where the Revolutionary War had produced desperate fratricidal struggles among Americans, the rehabilitation of the loyalists was less swift and complete. South Carolina and Georgia ignored Congress's appeal; Virginia complied in December 1787, but only "with the proviso that the repeal not take effect until Great Britain surrenders the frontier forts and compensates for black slaves seized by Britain."[31]

The Return of the British

Although Americans acquiesced in the quiet return of many former neighbors, to prove their humanity and liberalism and to promote the nation's population

[29] Patrick Henry quoted in Moses Coit Tyler, *Patrick Henry*, 1st publ. 1898 (Ithaca: Cornell University Press, 1962), 290–91.

[30] John Jay, Passy, July 19, 1783, to William Livingston, *John Jay: The Winning of the Peace*, ed. Morris, 564; Maas, comp., *Divided Hearts*, xiv–xxi.

[31] Maas, comp., *Divided Hearts*, xx, n. 59 (quote); John Richard Alden, *The South in the Revolution, 1763–1789* (Baton Rouge: Louisiana State University Press, 1957).

and prosperity, they never formally acknowledged the legitimacy of the British definition of American tories as British aliens, in need, perhaps, of naturalization but not liable to penalties for treason. Two factors made such a definition especially unpalatable to the American people: Article IV of the Treaty of 1783, which called for the payment of debts owed to "real British subjects," and British arguments for the restoration of tory estates that challenged antiloyalist legislation on the ground that treason could be committed only against a sovereign state. According to the British government, the American states were not sovereign until recognized as such in the Treaty of 1783. Therefore American wartime measures against "traitors" were invalid. The Continental Congress officially accepted the British definition of American tories as loyal British subjects by ratifying the treaty and by recommending that the states comply with its terms. But state and local governments were unwilling to increase the debt burden on their patriotic citizens to restore confiscated estates and to repay the debts owed to those who had betrayed the Glorious Cause. As a result, the precise status of American loyalists remained ambiguous. In 1802 the United States government ended, but did not resolve, the controversy over prewar debts owed to "real British subjects" by paying a lump sum to Great Britain to be divided among the claimants, with British officials deciding who was or was not a British citizen.[32]

By evading a precise definition of the legal status of returning loyalists, postwar Americans blurred the line that separated American-born tories, who were generally seen as traitors claiming to be loyal British subjects, from British-born supporters of the crown, whose personal conduct was more defensible, but whose political principles were just as dangerous. The American animus against all who had favored Great Britain during the Revolution merged the grievances against both groups into a generalized indictment of all who espoused British principles. Steps were taken in the early 1780s to banish both groups. Pressure by the British government and the passage of time led to the repeal of the most severe laws aimed against tories and British subjects. But remnants of the American fear of those two groups remained in the form of laws that would limit the rights of all aliens.

After the American victory at Yorktown, British merchants began their campaign to recreate their prewar hegemony over American trade by opening negotiations with rebel governments for the security of their persons and property and the right to continue trading after the withdrawal of British troops. Tory merchants also began returning from exile in New York, Philadelphia, and Florida. The determination of American patriots to control their own commerce merged

---

[32] James H. Kettner, *The Development of American Citizenship, 1608–1870* (Chapel Hill: University of North Carolina Press, 1978), 186–87; John Adams, London, Jan. 19, 1786, to Thomas Jefferson, in Lester J. Cappon, ed., *The Adams–Jefferson Letters: The Complete Correspondence between Thomas Jefferson and Abigail and John Adams*, 2 vols. (Chapel Hill: University of North Carolina Press, 1959), I, 115.

with war-engendered hostility to produce a variety of state laws designed to keep out those British subjects and American tories whose past and present hostility to America's republican aspirations seemed to jeopardize its future and to limit the political power of those who were allowed in. These measures were most extreme in the South, where the memory of wartime atrocities, on both sides, had not yet begun to fade.

As the war wound down, Georgia patriots tried to secure their state's republican future by preventing "all manner of Persons whose conduct has been inimicable to the liberties of AMERICA, and . . . idle and disorderly Persons emigrating from any of the United States, or else where becoming Citizens of this State." Included among those who were banned from the state were disloyal Americans, persons who did not "cultivate a sufficient quantity of land, or follow some trade or Occupation, whereby themselves and families can be supported," and "all idle Persons, who may be found Wandering from place to place of suspicious Character." Georgia's Act of 1782 singled out the natives of Scotland, denying them the right to settle or "carry on commerce or other trade, Profession or business," excepting only such Scots who had demonstrated their virtue by exerting "themselves in behalf of the freedom and Independence of the United States of America, in the Present contest, and who are now entitled to the rights of Citizenship in any or either of the United States."[33]

Georgia also took vigorous steps to neutralize the political power of any tories or British subjects who managed to enter the state. Although the naturalization requirements in colonial Georgia are unclear, the colony's Act of 1761 gave the right to vote to all free white males, aged 21 years or older, if they owned 50 acres of land and had resided for at least six months in Georgia. By this law, naturalized Protestants could be elected to Georgia's assembly if they professed "the christian religion," were 21 years of age, owned 500 acres of land and had lived in the colony for twelve months. Georgia's 1785 "Act for ascertaining the rights of aliens and pointing out a mode for the admission of Citizens" set up a complicated procedure that bestowed the right of "acquiring[,] possessing or holding and Selling[,] devising or otherwise disposing of all kinds of Personal property and renting houses or lands from Year to Year" on all free white persons who enrolled their names with the clerk of their local superior court. After twelve months in Georgia and a certificate from the county's grand jury stating that the applicant was honest and a "friend to the Government of the State," the regis-

---

[33] Quotes from Georgia's "Act for Preventing Improper or Disaffected Persons Emigrating from Other Places, and Becoming Citizens of This State" (1782), in Allen D. Candler, ed., *The State Records of the State of Georgia*, 25 vols. (Atlanta: Charles P. Byrd, 1904–1916), XIX, part II, 162–166. Northern states, whose postwar economies suffered heavily from the British policy decisions of the 1780s, considered similar bans on all British merchants. However, in the North most states decided to tax, rather than banish, British competitors. *Maryland Gazette*, May 6, 27, June 10, July 24, Aug. 16, 30, 1785; Jensen, *The New Nation*, 287–301; Samuel Eliot Morison, *The Maritime History of Massachusetts, 1783–1860* (Boston: Houghton, Mifflin, 1921), 34–40.

tered alien was allowed to take an of oath allegiance to Georgia, entitling him "to all the rights[,] liberties and immunities of a free Citizen" with two exceptions. The adopted citizen was still subject to "such alien duties as have been heretofore or may hereafter be imposed by the Legislature" and could not become a member of the General Assembly, Executive Council, "or hold any office of trust or profit or vote for members of the General Assembly" for another seven years *and* until a special act was passed on his behalf by the state legislature.[34]

Within two weeks of the passage of the Naturalization Act of 1785, Georgia's lawmakers exempted French subjects from the law's most stringent requirements. The 1785 Act in favor of "the subjects of his most Christian Majesty" allowed any French subject "who is properly introduced with a design to become an Inhabitant" of Georgia to be "admitted to all the liberties[,] priviledges and immunities of natural born Citizens of this State" after a three-year residence or, if married to a citizen of Georgia, after one year and the taking of an oath of allegiance to the state, "any Law[,] Usage or custom to the contrary notwithstanding." By easing citizenship for French subjects, Georgia perpetuated the confusion that had surrounded its colonial naturalization code and continued, by default, its wartime discrimination against British immigrants and loyalist refugees.[35]

When South Carolina reopened its borders to chastened tories and British merchants, state lawmakers also devised policies to neutralize their unrepublican political principles. The legislature that assembled in January 1784 granted citizenship to returning loyalists and British subjects only after revising the state's naturalization code. On February 19th, South Carolina's House of Representatives "took into Consideration the Report of the Committee Appointed to Revise the Acts of Assembly making Aliens Citizens of this State." After a brief discussion, the House recommended the repeal of the state's Act of 1704, which provided that no naturalized alien "shall be capable or qualified to be . . . elected a member of the General Assembly," but allowed adult aliens who had sworn an oath of allegiance and abjured "that damnable doctrine . . . that princes excommunicated or deprived by the Pope . . . may be deposed or murdered by their subjects" to vote for members of the legislature if they possessed "fifty Acres of land" or "ten pounds in money, goods, or chattels, or rents" for three months prior to the election.[36]

The preamble and provisions of South Carolina's new Alien Act expressed the state's doubts about the loyalty and political principles of the British subjects and

---

[34] Kettner, *Development of American Citizenship*, 101–3; Erna Risch, "The Encouragement of Immigration as Revealed in Colonial Legislation," *Virginia Magazine of History and Biography*, 45 (1937), 8; Georgia's Naturalization Act of 1785, in Candler, ed., *State Laws of Georgia*, XIX, 375–78 (quotes).

[35] Act of 1785, in Candler, ed., *State Laws of Georgia*, XIX, 448–50 (quotes).

[36] *Journals of the House of Representatives*, ed. Theodora J. Thompson et al. (Columbia: University of South Carolina Press, 1977–), I, 464 (quotes).

American tories who were then petitioning for admission. Beginning with the declaration that "it is expedient that the admission of aliens to the rights of citizenship in this State should be rendered as easy and extensive as may be compatible with the safety thereof," the Act of 1784 granted limited citizenship to "all free white persons (alien enemies, fugitives from justice, and persons banished from either of the United States excepted)" who had resided in South Carolina for a year and produced a certificate showing they had taken an oath of allegiance before a state court of common pleas. Although aliens who fulfilled these requirements were to "be deemed citizens, and entitled to all the rights, privileges and immunities to the character belonging," they were not allowed to vote for "members of the Legislation or of the City corporation" until two years following their admission; naturalized aliens were eligible for high public office (governor, lieutenant governor, Intendant of Charleston, member of the Privy Council and state legislature) only after a special Act of the Legislature was passed on their behalf. The legislature that revised South Carolina's Alien Act in 1786 was even more convinced of the need "to admit aliens to some of the rights and privileges of citizens, and to exclude them from others." By the terms of this Act, naturalized aliens in South Carolina now needed a special legislative act to vote, serve on juries, and to hold an expanded list of public offices.[37]

Virginia adopted a similar course of action in the fall of 1783. At war's end the state launched a double-barreled assault against tories and British merchants. In May of 1779 Virginia had conferred citizenship on "all white persons born within the territory of this commonwealth, and all who have resided therein two years next before the passing of this act." This measure also declared that "all who shall hereafter migrate into the same, other than alien enemies" would be "deemed citizens of this commonwealth" after swearing fidelity to the state and their intention to become permanent residents. However, the ease with which returning loyalist merchants obtained certificates of citizenship merely by taking an oath of allegiance before any justice of the peace, led Virginians to revise their alien code. In October 1782 state legislators denied British merchants the right to enter the state and prescribed penalties for magistrates who administered the oath of allegiance to any British subject. Two months later Governor Benjamin Harrison issued a proclamation barring from the state all persons who had professed loyalty to Great Britain. In the spring of 1783, Virginia's House of Delegates voted to postpone consideration of Patrick Henry's resolution to repeal the Act "to prohibit intercourse with, and the admission of British subjects" into the state. Governor Harrison endorsed this move by issuing a

---

[37]Quotes from Act of 1704, in Cooper, ed., *Statutes at Large of South Carolina*, II, 251–53; "An Act to Confer the Rights of Citizenship on Aliens," Mar. 26, 1784, ibid., IV, 600–1; "An Act to Confer Certain Rights and Privileges on Aliens, and for Repealing the Acts Therein Mentioned," Mar. 22, 1786, ibid., IV, 746–47.

new proclamation, on July 2, 1783, that continued to ban British subjects from migrating into the state.[38]

In October 1783 the Virginia legislature finally repealed its proscription of British subjects and American tories. Although it was now legal for loyalists who had not "actually been in arms, aiding and abetting the common enemy in their endeavours to subvert the rights and liberties of America" to return to Virginia, they were declared forever incapable "of voting for members to either house of assembly, or of holding, or exercising any office of trust or profit, civil or military."[39] At the same time the Virginia legislators revised their citizenship policies. Virginia's Act of 1783 continued the requirements of the Act of 1779, by which any alien who settled in Virginia could be naturalized upon taking an oath of allegiance. However, the new Act was designed to guard "against the introduction of secret enemies" and to keep "the offices of government in the hands of citizens intimately acquainted with the spirit of the constitution and the genius of the people, as well as permanently attached to the common interest." Virginia's Act of 1783 denied naturalized citizens the right to hold "any office, legislative, executive, or judiciary," until they had resided an additional two years in Virginia and had "evinced a permanent attachment to the state," by marrying a citizen of one of the American states or by purchasing lands "to the value of one hundred pounds therein." As the decade progressed, restrictions on the rights of Virginia's adopted citizens increased. Under the Act of 1786, it took five years for a naturalized alien to prove his attachment to Virginia and naturalized merchants were denied "any privilege or bounty which shall hereafter be granted to merchants citizens," until they had married an American citizen or purchased landed property worth £500.[40]

---

[38] Harrell, *Loyalism in Virginia*, 124–40; Tyler, *Patrick Henry*, 288–97; Virginia's Act of 1782 in W. W. Hening, ed., *The Statutes at Large, Being a Collection of All the Laws of Virginia, 1680–1792*, 13 vols. (Richmond: George Cochran, 1809–1823), XI, 136–38.

[39] Hening, ed., *Statutes at Large of Virginia*, XI, 324–25.

[40] Act of 1783, ibid., XI, chap. XVI, 322–23 (quotes); Act of 1786, ibid., XII, chap. X, 261–62 (quote). In colonial Virginia, there had been no residency requirement for voters, whether naturalized or native-born. Chilton Williamson, *American Suffrage: From Property to Democracy, 1760–1860* (Princeton: Princeton University Press, 1960), 15. A comparison of South Carolina's naturalization acts of 1784 and 1786 shows the same pattern of increasing restrictions on the political rights of naturalized aliens: Cooper, ed., *Statutes at Large of South Carolina*, IV, chap. 1214, 600–601, and chap. 1326, 746–47. See also Maryland's Act of 1779, which bestowed "all the immunities, rights, and privileges of a natural born subject of this state," on any foreigner who declared his "belief in the christian religion," and took the oath of allegiance and abjuration. However, such naturalized citizens could not be appointed or elected to any "civic office" until they had lived in the state for seven years, while residence requirements for natural-born citizens ranged from one year (in the county represented) for election to the House of Delegates to three years for Senators and members of the Governor's Council to five years for delegates to the Continental Congress and governor of the state. *Laws of the State of Maryland, Session of 1779*, chap. VI (Annapolis: Maryland General Assembly) in Maryland State Library; Maryland's Constitution of 1776, in Francis Newton Thorpe, ed., *The Federal and State Constitutions, Colonial Charters, and Other Organic Laws of the States, Territories, and Colonies Now or Heretofore Forming the United States of America*, 7 vols. (Washington, D.C.: Government Printing Office, 1909), III, 1691–1712. For naturalization requirements in the other states, see Kettner, *Development of American Citizenship*, 213–21.

The Port Bill of 1784 was Virginia's economic counterpart of the political proscription of British subjects. The Port Bill was designed to thwart the activities of the British "locusts that are crouding here as so many emissaries sent to sound our inclinations and to poison the minds of our people and if possible bring them back to their old destructive paths." By restricting imports carried in non-Virginian ships to a limited number of ports, the bill's backers hoped to prevent the resumption of British control of their tobacco trade and, through it, the state's entire economy. By keeping British factors out of the back-country, the bill would remove Great Britain's competitive advantage and place all foreign merchants on an equal footing in vying for the state's trade. It also offered Virginia the opportunity to gain control of its own commerce by replacing British agents with native-born middlemen and by encouraging the local coasting trade needed to trans-ship tobacco and manufactures from the designated ports.[41]

Mercantilist Dreams

While most Americans discouraged British and tory merchants from settling in their states, Connecticut, New Jersey, and Delaware tried to take advantage of postwar realignments to expand their overseas trade and free themselves of their traditional economic subservience to Boston, New York City, and Philadelphia. As General Carleton was supervising the evacuation of New York, Connecticut encouraged wealthy loyalists to settle, along with their assets, in its port cities. In May 1784 Connecticut's General Court declared New London and New Haven free ports for seven years, where all newcomers who secured "the Major Vote of the Inhabitants or the consent of the Civil Authority" and took an oath of allegiance to the state of Connecticut, would "to all Intents and purposes become free Citizens of this State," paying no more in taxes or customs duties than any other citizen. In addition, those who imported merchandise valued at £3,000 a year from Europe, Asia, or Africa or brought with them into the state £2,000 "in Money," would "be exempted from Assessment for faculty or on account of the Profits arising on such Importation, so far as the Revenue of this or the United States are interested therein." Reports of Connecticut's overtures to propertied British subjects and tories, along with tales of the mis-treatment of loyalists in other states, were immediately disseminated in the

[41] Drew R. McCoy, "The Virginia Port Bill of 1784," *Virginia Magazine of History and Biography*, 83 (1975), 288–303; "locusts," Benjamin Harrison, Sept. 26, 1783, to "The Honorable the Virginia Delegates in Congress," *The Papers of James Madison*, ed. William T. Hutchinson et al., 15 vols. (Chicago: University of Chicago Press and Charlottesville: University of Virginia Press, 1962–), VII, 359. For a similar program by Maryland's merchants to win "the custom" of their country for native-born agents and traders, see Edward C. Papenfuse, *In Pursuit of Profit: The Annapolis Merchants in the Era of the American Revolution, 1763–1805* (Baltimore: Johns Hopkins University Press, 1974), chap. 5.

British press.[42] The states of New Jersey and Delaware adopted, and publicized, similar programs, offering shelter to loyalists who were forced out of New York and Philadelphia.[43]

Many postwar Americans believed that an infusion of British capital was essential to repair the economic and physical structures of their ravaged communities and thus promoted reconciliation. New York City was devastated during the Revolution by fire, battles, and military occupation. With the final withdrawal of British troops in December 1783, American patriots "took possession of a ruined city" with "an heterogeneous set of inhabitants, composed of almost ruined exiles, disbanded soldiery, mixed foreigners, disaffected Tories, and the refuse of a British army."[44] Charleston, South Carolina, suffered the same cycle of wartime casualties and was left in a similar condition when evacuated by the British at the end of 1782. In both cities, the wartime legacy of intense hatred for the British and their American collaborators clashed with the need to rebuild. In both officials who advocated toleration for British subjects and their capital were opposed by former soldiers and fiery patriots.

Alexander Hamilton, believing that "We have already lost too large a number of valuable citizens," tried to end the violence in New York that was driving away British subjects who had hoped to remain, especially "merchants of the second class, characters of no political consequence, each of whom may carry away eight or ten thousand guineas." Hamilton predicted that New York would "feel for twenty years at least, the effects of the popular phrenzy." Robert Livingston also dreaded the consequences of "the violent spirit of persecution which prevails here . . . upon the wealth[,] commerce & future tranquillity of the state."[45] The

[42] Richard L. Bushman, *From Puritan to Yankee: Character and the Social Order in Connecticut, 1690–1765* (New York: Norton, 1970), 124–26; *Maryland Gazette*, June 6, 1783; Connecticut's Act of 1784, in Charles J. Hoadley, et al., eds., *The Public Records of the State of Connecticut, 1776–1803*, 11 vols. (Hartford, 1894–1967), V, 325–26 (quotes); L. F. S. Upton, *The Loyal Whig: William Smith of New York and Quebec* (Toronto: University of Toronto Press, 1969), 143; Robert A. East, *Connecticut's Loyalists* (Chester, Conn.: Pequot Press, 1974), 46–47; Sidney I. Pomerantz, *New York, an American City, 1783–1803: A Study of Urban Life* (New York: Columbia University Press, 1938), 77n. Connecticut's Act of 1784, reported in: *Felix Farley's Bristol Journal*, May 8, July 24, 1784; *Belfast News-Letter*, Sept. 10, 1784; David Macpherson, *Annals of Commerce, Manufactures, Fisheries, and Navigation . . . of the British Empire and Other Countries*, 4 vols. (London: Nichols and Son, 1805), IV, 57.

[43] In New Jersey, Burlington and Perth Amboy were made free ports for twenty-five years so that the state's inhabitants would "no longer be under the necessity of repairing to Philadelphia or New York, either for the disposal of their produce, or for purchasing foreign commodities. . . . All foreigners, whether mariners, manufacturers, or mechanics who . . . plied their usual calling" for a month in either of the free ports "were then to become freemen and citizens." The state of Delaware took similar steps to escape dependence on Philadelphia, declaring Wilmington and Newcastle free ports. *South Carolina Gazette*, July 22 (quote), 1783, and June 17, 1784; Fingerhut, *Survivor*, 99, 104, 123–25; Pomerantz, *New York, an American City*, 77–78; Allan Nevins, *The American States during and after the Revolution, 1775–1789* (New York: Macmillan, 1924), 560–62, 650.

[44] Pomerantz, *New York, an American City*, 76–94; *New York Packet*, Dec. 16, 1784, quoted in ibid., 19.

[45] Alexander Hamilton, Aug. 5, 1783, to James Duane; Hamilton, Aug. 13, 1783, to Robert Livingston; Robert Livingston, Aug. 30, 1783, to Hamilton, in *The Papers of Alexander Hamilton*, ed. Harold C. Syrett, 26 vols. (New York: Columbia University Press, 1961–1979), III, 430, 431, 434.

New York City Sons of Liberty dismissed these calls for moderation, arguing that it was "impossible that Whigs and Tories can ever associate, or be mingled together, or that government can be considered as completely established, while so great a number of Tories, both of wealth and influence, remain in the metropolis." Such men threatened more than the integrity of republican government—they deprived American patriots of their livelihood. "Mentor" also denied Hamilton's arguments, insisting that the expulsion of tories and the exclusion of British merchants would not rob the state of its *real* wealth. According to "Mentor," New York's importance "as a place of trade, is not owing to the quantity of money that is now in it, or that ever was in it." It was the city's geographic location and control of its hinterlands that determined New York's "mercantile consequence," not the wealth of individual merchants. Furthermore, there were, "at present, more adventurers in trade, in America, than there is trade to support." Why then should American patriots allow British and tory merchants to settle among them and "supplant our own traders?"[46]

The debate in Charleston over tories and British merchants followed similar lines. South Carolinian merchants hoped to win the profits of the Anglo-American trade for themselves by ousting the British interlopers who had set up shop during the wartime occupation of Charleston. The city's mechanics and artisans also demanded the expulsion of these "New Adventurers" whose imports denied them a market for their own manufactures. The artisans of Charleston's Marine Anti-Britannic society accused British and tory merchants of monopolizing trade, creating "ruinous competition" and "Artificial Scarcities of the most Necessary articles" and demanded that they be driven from the state. Charleston's Sons of Liberty rioted and tarred and feathered, and the city's Chamber of Commerce restricted its membership to native-born Americans and good Whigs.[47]

The controversy over the "Policy and Consequences of Admitting British Subjects to Engross Our Trade and Become Our Citizens" that rocked Charleston for almost three years cropped up with varying degrees of intensity throughout the new states. Each American community was forced to evaluate the economic and political consequences of continuing the campaign against British subjects and American tories. By forgiving their former neighbors, Americans could silence the critics of republican government who chronicled America's illiberal treatment of returning loyalists and regain the skills and capital lost by their expulsion. By coming to terms with British merchants, Americans could reenter, as junior partners, the familiar and lucrative Anglo-American trade.[48]

[46] Nevins, *American States*, 274 (quote); *Mentor's Reply to Phocion's Letter* (Mar. 1784), quotes on 22, 23.
[47] Walsh, *Charleston's Sons of Liberty*, 107–20, quotes on 113, 114; *South Carolina Gazette*, Jan. 17, 1784.
[48] Quote from Walsh, *Charleston's Sons of Liberty*, 116.

In all the states, the voice of pragmatic moderation triumphed over the passionate cries for vengeance and republican innovation. In March 1783 the Senate of South Carolina voted to naturalize sixty-seven British subjects, while rejecting the citizenship petitions of only twelve. Soon after hostilities ended, Philadelphia extended a de facto toleration to the British merchants who had followed General Howe's army into Philadelphia in 1777. In the mid-1780s, over one-third of the members of New York City's chamber of commerce were British and tory merchants. By the end of the decade anti-tory laws were repealed and loyalists returned home.[49]

The passage of time diluted America's postwar hostility and removed some of the barriers erected to keep the states free of tories and British subjects. But distrust of tory principles and the determination to reserve the economic benefits of the new republics to native-born patriots remained and became permanently enshrined in state codes governing naturalization procedures and alien disabilities.

American Ambivalence

While postwar Americans vigorously opposed the introduction of British merchants, American traitors, convicts, scoundrels, and paupers into their communities, their attitude toward other groups of immigrants was less clearly defined. Immigrants who did not fall into one of these undesirable categories could expect a warmer welcome in republican America. However, eighteenth-century Americans had always been more about cautious receiving strangers than their reputation implied. Prior to the Revolution, agents of land speculators and proprietary and colonial officials had painted a beguiling image of the welcome, rights, and prospects awaiting all who chose to settle in British North America. But the reception proffered by the colonists themselves was more constrained and discriminating, as Americans assessed the probable impact aliens would have on their society. Colonial doubts were intensified by wartime experiences with foreigners and a postwar determination to circumscribe the ability of men of British principles to corrupt America's commercial and political development.

[49] Brent H. Holcomb, comp., *South Carolina Naturalizations, 1783–1850* (Baltimore: Genealogical Publishing Co., 1985), 79–80; *Leeds Mercury*, June 17, 1783; Jensen, *The New Nation*, 265–81; Forrest McDonald, *E Pluribus Unum: The Formation of the American Republic, 1776–1790* (Boston: Houghton Mifflin, 1965), 43–44; Jacob E. Cooke, *Tench Coxe and the Early Republic* (Chapel Hill: University of North Carolina Press, 1978), chap. 2; Pomerantz, *New York, an American City*, 90–91; Fingerhut, *Survivor*, 150; Christopher Moore, *The Loyalists: Revolution, Exile, Settlement* (Toronto: Macmillan of Canada, 1984), 96–97, 112; Wallace Brown, *The Good Americans: The Loyalists in the American Revolution* (New York: William Morrow, 1969), 176–77.

The looseness of the American confederation left each state free to adopt measures most consistent with local needs. The result was a welter of laws and regulations that limited the rights of the foreign-born.

In theory, the American states adopted a positive view of immigration, as "foreigners, and particularly ingenious foreigners, will flock to those countries which are well governed, and where they can easily maintain themselves and their families." In addition to being a testimonial to good government, immigration also gave individual American states additional weight in determining national policy and in arbitrating sectional differences. Pennsylvania's Senator William Maclay boasted in his *Journal* of the wisdom in encouraging immigration that had "set Pennsylvania far ahead of her sister States." In 1784 a New Yorker wrote enviously of "The great number of emigrants from Europe which arrive in Pennsylvania and settle in that State, [who] bid fair to make her, in a short time, the most flourishing in the Union." James Swan of Massachusetts used the same arguments to denounce his state's narrow immigration policy, which produced only a trickle of newcomers, whereas Pennsylvania, "Since the late peace . . . has received above 20,000 good subjects from Germany, Ireland and Scotland." According to Swan, "Every wise government has encouraged mechanics, laborers and new settlers, to emigrate into it: it is particularly the interest of a young country like America, so to do. . . . Pennsylvania, which was settled a long time after the Massachusetts, has increased in agriculture and in numbers, which are the most durable riches, in a much greater ratio, than we have; and this is conceived to arise from the great encouragement given to settlers from every country."[50]

Although many Americans envied Pennsylvania's success in attracting immigrants, others remained dubious about the benefits of foreign migrations. In 1785 New York's Council of Revision vetoed a bill to incorporate a "German Society for encouraging immigration from Germany," arguing that it would be "productive of the most fatal evils to the State to introduce into it a great number of foreigners, differing from the old citizens in language and manners, ignorant of our Constitution, and totally unacquainted with the principles of civil liberty, under such circumstances as will naturally tend to ever keep them a distinct people and prevent their blending with the general mass of citizens with one name and common interest."[51]

Even Pennsylvanians questioned their state's liberality. In 1786 Pennsylvania's

---

[50]Quotes from Joseph Priestley, "Of the Populousness of Nations. . . . From Priestly's [sic] Lectures," *American Museum*, X (1791), 229; William Maclay, *The Journal of William Maclay, 1790*, 1st publ. 1890 (New York: Albert & Charles Boni, 1927), 210; *Pennsylvania Gazette*, Sept. 22, 1784, dateline New York, Sept. 18; James Swan, *National Arithmetick or, Observations on the Finances of the Commonwealth of Massachusetts* (Boston: Adams & Nourse, 1786), 45, 46.

[51]Richard J. Purcell, "Immigration to the Canal Era," in Alexander C. Flick, ed., *History of the State of New York*, 10 vols. (New York: Columbia University Press, 1933–1937), VII, 9 (quote); Pomerantz, *New York, an American City*, 206.

Supreme Executive Council asked the General Assembly to reconsider the 42nd section of their state constitution that decreed "that every foreigner of good character, who comes to settle in this state, having first taken an oath or affirmation of allegiance to the same, may purchase, or by other just means acquire land, &c. &c. and after one year's residence be deemed a free citizen thereof." Charles Biddle, speaking for the Executive Council, believed that "It may be the eventual misfortune of the state that no mode should yet have been adopted for ascertaining the *good character* of such foreigners as have come to settle among us—and exercise the rights of citizens, and we should hold ourselves very deficient in political duty were we not to recommend that some measure should now be devised and adopted, which, while it admitted the industrious and honest, would operate as an effectual bar against the idle and profligate."[52]

National Laissez-Faire

Doubts about the political principles of foreigners and the economic and social consequences of immigration produced ambivalent public policies. In the postwar decade, American governments waived the opportunity to establish immigrant recruitment programs. Instead of re-creating the legal instruments that had promoted immigration in the past, American lawmakers decided to rely primarily on the unofficial actions of their citizens and the nation's natural resources to attract useful foreigners. By the end of the 1780s, republican America would reject the governmental bounties, subsidies, and land grants that had been such successful recruitment devices before the Revolution and were still employed by Old World governments to seduce valuable subjects.

Control of the national domain provided the Continental Congress with its most potent and obvious power to promote immigration. In the 1780s, Congress entertained various suggestions for distributing free land to Americans and foreign immigrants. Thomas Jefferson in his 1784 draft of the Northwest Ordinance proposed that the public lands be given to new settlers to secure the allegiance of those who would otherwise become alienated squatters. At the same time the English Countess of Huntingdon asked the American states for a land grant in or near Indian country, of sufficient magnitude to settle "a considerable Number" of Protestant families who, by "Their more comfortable way of living, their inoffensive and friendly Manners, their modes of Cultivation and their Mechanic Arts," would gradually convert the Indians to Christianity and a "civilized" way of life. This plan would simultaneously "Introduce the benevolent Religion of our Blessed Redeemer among Heathen and Savage Nations," "lead

---

[52] Quotes from "A MESSAGE from the VICE PRESIDENT and the SUPREME EXECUTIVE COUNCIL to the GENERAL ASSEMBLY," *Pennsylvania Packet*, Mar. 1, 1786.

them from Violence and Barbarity," and "provide a refuge for pious, industrious People, who wish to withdraw themselves from scenes of Vice and irreligion [in England], to a Country where they may spend their Days in the pursuits of honest Industry, & in the practice of Religion and Virtue." These noble ends, the Countess believed, would be a fitting sequel to "the Revolution which Providence hath wrought in favour of the American States."[53]

Such visionary plans for the western lands were defeated by America's need for a national revenue and the opposition of land speculators. George Washington, writing as a private citizen, endorsed the Countess of Huntingdon's project, but warned her that free land would be difficult to obtain. Washington had, however, lands that he could sell to the Countess, "as a dernier resort... which lie as convenient to the western Tribes of Indians as any." Jefferson's vision was similarly cast aside when land ordinances, beginning in 1785, arranged for the public domain to be surveyed and sold at public auction in units of 640 acres—a size prejudicial to settlers of limited means. Although Alexander Hamilton would, in the 1790s, advocate populating the western lands by settlers "from abroad rather than at the entire expence of the Atlantic population," the national government, under the Articles of Confederation and the Constitution of 1787, consistently refused to use its power to encourage immigration by offering free or cheap land to aliens.[54]

While the Continental Congress was promoting land policies that would maximize revenue, it also ignored recommendations to offer subsidies to prospective immigrants. In 1783 Elkanah Watson, a Rhode Island merchant who was then residing in London, urged Congress to take advantage of "the spirit of Emigration that so generally prevails throughout England, Ireland, & Scotland, but more particularly in this City." According to Watson, "The enthusiasm is so great, that mechanics of every kind would croud over in a torrent, if the Congress shou'd favor emigrations by allowing a fixed bounty to every Captain who takes over a useful able bodied mechanic incapable of paying his passage, by this means it is difficult to hazard a conjecture, how effectual our principal object of cultivating manufactures, would succeed." Watson also advocated Congressional bounties to facilitate the return of American sailors "now starving in the streets of this city for the want of employment" and to recruit English seamen "who wished to enroll themselves under our stripes."[55] Edward Luttrell, an English "Gentleman bred to the practise of Physic and Surgery" who was interested in buying western

[53] Jensen, *The New Nation*, 353–59; "Letter of the Countess of Huntingdon," Apr. 8, 1784, in *George Washington Papers*, Library of Congress Microfilm, ser. 4, reel 94; "Address of Selina Countess of Huntingdon, to the Friends of Religion and Humanity, in America," Bath, England, Apr. 8, 1784, ibid.

[54] Quotes from George Washington, Mount Vernon, Feb. 27, 1785, to the Countess of Huntingdon, ibid., ser. 2, reel 6; Alexander Hamilton, New York, May 19, 1790, to Arthur St. Clair, *Papers of Alexander Hamilton*, ed. Syrett, VI, 421.

[55] Elkanah Watson, Jr., London, Apr. 30, 1783, to "His Excellency the President of Congress," *Papers of the Continental Congress, 1774–1789*, National Archives Microfilm M247, roll 104, item 78, vol. 24, 363.

lands, made a similar proposal to America's representative in France. Worried that labor shortages would undermine his settlement plans, Luttrell advised Jefferson that

> As the American States are possessed of such a vast unsettled Land to the Westward I should Sir deem it politic in the Federal Commonwealth, or for several States, to hold out such aids, and assistance, as would enable virtuous, and industrious Emigrants from Europe, possessed of some Property, to overcome the first difficulties in settling such as procuring Labourers to clear their Plots of Land, erecting their Log Houses &c. and this to be done at certain stipulated prices; if these aids were made known, and punctually abided by, which would prove a source of accumulated Wealth to America, a number of people possessing a few hundred Pounds, and who depend on a precarious livelihood in England, would gladly embrace the opportunity of settling in America provided the first great risks of settling were overcome.[56]

Members of the Continental Congress decided against promoting immigration through land grants and bounties to aliens for reasons that were largely extraneous to the issue of immigration itself. Men who believed in limiting the power of government, especially at the national level, were joined in opposition to such measures by representatives who did not want to forego revenues from public lands, much less underwrite the transportation of British mechanics and unemployed American sailors. The group opposing land grants and bounties to foreigners also included members of Congress who feared the creation of a manufacturing society in America, men who doubted the wisdom of increasing the population of the states by the introduction of aliens or tories, and those who believed that artificial inducements were either ineffective or unnecessary stimulants to population growth. Whatever their motives, one fact remains clear. Congress adopted none of the techniques used in the past or by the Old World governments in the 1780s to promote immigration.[57]

State Recruitment

State and local governments practiced similar restraint in recruiting foreigners. Most American states, confident of the attractive power of their natural resources

---

[56] Edward Luttrell, Tunbridge, Kent, Jan. 11, 1789, to "Monsieur Jefferson Paris France," *Papers of Thomas Jefferson*, ed. Boyd, XIV, 434–35.

[57] In 1784 Benjamin Franklin publicized the inability of Congress to imitate those "Princes of Europe" who "endeavoured to entice Workmen from other Countries, by high Salaries, Privileges, &c.," Franklin, *Information to Those Who Would Remove to America*, in *Franklin: Writings*, ed. Lemay, 979–80. But the British consul at Charleston was one of very few foreigners who recognized the fact that the American government held "out no particular encouragement" to immigrants. George Miller, Charleston, South Carolina, Jan. 28, 1790, to Duke of Leeds, *British Foreign Office Archives, American Correspondence*, 4/8, folios 59–60.

and liberal governments, saw no need to subsidize immigration. However, as in the colonial period, local practices varied. States with strong demographic needs revived their colonial tradition of offering bounties and land grants and publicized the liberal naturalization procedures and political rights that they hoped would attract reliable, skilled, and propertied foreigners.

The American Revolution had a particularly deleterious effect on the Chesapeake's labor force. Wartime depredations and British confiscations resulted in the loss of thousands of slave workers. Postwar tobacco planters who had traditionally relied on British convicts to fill labor shortages and maintain their white majority had lost that option, first when the British government banned the transportation of English felons in 1776 and then when republican America repulsed British attempts to resume the convict trade at the end of the war. Consequently the Chesapeake states were among the few to offer bounties to immigrants. In 1779 Maryland's wartime legislature, believing that "the encrease of people is a means to advance the wealth and strength of this state," offered a two-year abatement on all taxes to any foreign settler who took an oath of allegiance to the state. To encourage foreign "tradesmen, artificers, and manufacturers, to come and settle in this state," the tax exemption for those groups was extended to four years. Virginia's Citizenship Act of 1786 offered exemptions from duties on the "tools or implements of trade" of "useful artizans, mechanics, and handycraft tradesmen" who emigrated into the commonwealth. Such immigrants would also be free of "all taxes whatsoever, except the land-tax, for the space of five years . . . if he or they shall so long continue the actual exercise of his or their trade or occupation therein." In 1790 North Carolina's legislature passed "An Act to authorize Henry Emanuel Lutterloh to raise by way of Lottery a sum sufficient to enable him to bring into this State foreigners who are Artisans in various Branches of Business."[58]

In the fall of 1783, a group of South Carolinians asked their lawmakers for a similar system of bounties to recruit "the ingenious and industrious brickmaker, bricklayer, carpenter, &c." to rebuild Charleston. Proponents of the bounty system argued that the city's workmen, "taking advantage of the pressing necessity of the moment, by a demand of workmen . . . DEMAND as much for one day's employ, as a carpenter, &c. would in Europe for four." If American workers from the northern states could not be recruited, there were "thousands of industrious, ingenious workmen in France, Holland, Flanders, England, and Ireland—(in Scotland "They're aw Gentlemen") &c. &c. who, with a prospect of procuring their passage, would be happy to make the voyage: and 'twould be a happy voyage to ye poor oppressed, distressed souls."[59] Charleston's artisans indignantly

[58] Maryland's Act of 1779, *Laws of the State of Maryland, Session of 1779*, chap. VII; Virginia's Act of 1786, in Hening, ed., *Statutes at Large of Virginia*, XII, chap. X, 261–65; North Carolina's lottery, in Walter Clark, ed., *The State Records of North Carolina*, 26 vols. (Goldsboro, N.C.: Nash Brothers, 1886–1907), XXV, 94–95.

[59] "Another Patriot," *South Carolina Gazette*, Oct. 18 (quotes), 25, 1783.

denied having taken advantage of their country's distress to extort exorbitant wages and charged the planters, many of whom "came into this country from thirty to fifty years past, emigrants from the lowest classes of mankind in Europe" with using their privileged position to gain private opulence at their expense. Charleston's mechanics argued that it would be better for them to accept the offer of "The wise Empress of Russia" who offers "great privileges, and an exemption of tax, to all artists without exception" willing "to settle in her extensive dominions . . . than tamely to submit to poverty and distress in these unwholesome climes." The city's house carpenters and bricklayers also petitioned the state's legislature for a law prohibiting "Negroes from undertaking Work on their Own Account," complaining "that they have laboured under many inconveniences Since the commencement of the present War, having Scarce had employ Sufficient to Support their families, owing to the Number of Jobbing Negro Tradesmen, who undertake work for little more than the Stuff would Cost, by which it appears they cannot come honestly by the Stuff they work with."[60]

This acrimonious debate generated not the revival of South Carolina's colonial program of immigrant recruitment through bounties and tax exemptions, but increased antipathy toward foreigners. When in March of 1784 the state levied a duty on slaves brought into the state, no funds were set aside to subsidize white immigrants. In 1785 South Carolina legislatures found it "inexpedient" to accede to the governor's recommendation that vessels be chartered "in different Ports of Europe" to transport settlers—"with a Sufficiency of Provision laid in for their passage, free of expence, and on their Arrival here a bounty of Land and a few implements of Husbandry be given them." Although refusing to subsidize European immigrants, the South Carolina legislature gave its assent to "An Act for levying and Collecting an Impost on Transient persons and others not Citizens of the United States." The purpose of this law was to generate revenue for the state and to prevent foreigners "coming into this state to trade," who enjoyed "all the advantages of the citizens thereof, without contributing to the support of the government," from having "greater Advantage than our Citizens."[61]

Although America's state governments generally joined Congress in rejecting the use of bounties and special privileges to recruit immigrants, most found ways to capitalize on the proven allure of their unsettled lands to increase their revenue, population, and reputation abroad. Georgia's need for settlers led her

[60]Walsh, *Charleston's Sons of Liberty*, chap. 5; quotes from: "A MECHANIC," *South Carolina Gazette*, Nov. 4, 1783; petition, *Journals of the [South Carolina] House of Representatives, 1783–1784*, 173–74.

[61]Act of March 26, 1784, in Cooper, ed., *Statutes at Large of South Carolina*, IV, 607. Governor's recommendation (Feb. 1785), *Journals of the [South Carolina] House of Representatives, 1785–1786*, 97–98; duty on transients, ibid., 332, 630, and *South Carolina Gazette and General Advertiser*, Apr. 15, 1784. The House did draw up a bill to provide European immigrants with free land and "Some Implements of Husbandry," but this "passed in the Negative" on its second reading, by a vote of 37 to 46. *Journals of the [South Carolina] House of Representatives, 1785–1786*, 133–34, 150, 164.

assembly to invite "the Connecticut line of the late Continental army, to locate their bounty lands within that State; with other benefits and privileges." Georgia also granted 20,000 acres of land to "his Excellency the Count D'Estaing, to encourage the settlement thereof." The Marquis de Lafayette was the recipient of land grants from several states who wished to reward him for his wartime service. Friedrich Wilhelm von Steuben was the hero New York honored with 16,000 acres of land, for rendering "very essential service to this State." Even Thomas Jefferson, who preferred to see public land held in escrow for future generations of American-born farmers, advocated land grants to foreigners who had distinguished themselves in the American Revolution. Land in western New York was also set aside for the Canadian and Nova Scotia refugees, who had suffered for their adherence to the rebel cause.[62]

Some states adopted more subtle devices to encourage foreigners to settle their "vacant" lands. Pennsylvania was the earliest and most vigorous proponent of "empowering . . . aliens to purchase and hold lands, tenements and hereditaments" in order "to promote the public benefit not only by introducing large sums of money into this state but also by inducing such aliens as may have acquired property to follow their interest and become useful citizens." Thus, the Pennsylvania Constitution of 1776 decreed that "Every foreigner of good character who comes to settle in this state, having first taken an oath or affirmation of allegiance to the same, may purchase, or by other just means acquire, hold, and transfer land or other real estate." When the state's revised constitution failed to offer this privilege to alien landowners, Pennsylvania's legislature conferred the same rights by statutes passed in 1789, 1792, and 1795. During the 1780s the state constitutions of Vermont and North Carolina and the legal codes of Georgia and South Carolina made similar provisions for the full property rights of aliens who were willing to take the state's oath of allegiance.[63]

States that did not waive traditional disabilities on alien landowners encouraged foreign land purchases by providing legal procedures to remove the insecurity of alien land titles. Early in 1784 New York's Governor George Clinton suggested that the state's land office "be so regulated as while it is rendered an object of revenue, it will at the same time, afford the utmost encouragement to

[62] *Maryland Gazette*, June 28 (quote), Aug. 26 (quote), 1785; "Act for the Speedy Sale of the Unappropriated Lands within this State and for Other Purposes Therein Mentioned" (1786), *Laws of the State of New York, 1785–1788*, chap. 67, quote on 342; Thomas Jefferson, Paris, Feb. 8, 1786, to James Madison, *Thomas Jefferson: Writings*, ed. Peterson, 851.

[63] "An Act to Enable Aliens to Purchase and Hold Real Estate within this Commonwealth" (1789), James T. Mitchell and Henry Flanders, eds., *The Statutes at Large of Pennsylvania from 1682 to 1801*, 16 vols. (Harrisburg, Penn.: Clarence M. Busch, State Printer, 1896–1908), XIII, chap. 1387, quote on 179; Section 42 of the Constitution of Pennsylvania of 1776 in Thorpe, ed., *Federal and State Constitutions*, V, quote on 3091; *Development of American Citizenship*, 214–18, 238n; Georgia's "An Act to Enable the Subjects of His Most Christian Majesty to Transfer and Settle Such of Their Estates and Property as Is or Shall Happen to Fall within This State (1785), in Candler, ed. *Colonial Records of the State of Georgia*, XIX, 448–50; Maryland's "Act to Declare and Ascertain the Privileges of the Subjects of France Residing within this State" (1780), *Laws of the State of Maryland, Session of 1780*, chap. VIII.

the speedy settlement of the country ... by facilitating the means of naturalization, and of obtaining and inheriting a portion of the unappropriated lands." The New York legislature responded by passing special acts that, between 1783 and 1789, naturalized 572 aliens.[64] In 1779 Maryland offered "all the immunities, rights, and privileges, of a natural born subject of this state" (except the right to hold office, which required a seven-year residence) to all "who shall hereafter come into this state, from any nation, kingdom, or state," took an oath of allegiance to the state and officially declared their belief in the Christian religion. When alien landowners, "through ignorance of the provisions" of the Act of 1779, failed to seek naturalization, which would secure their land titles, Maryland's legislators gave them a second chance. By an Act of 1789, "foreigners, who, since their settlement in this state" had legally purchased real estate could, by taking the oaths prescribed by the Act of 1779 on or before June 1, 1790, hold their property "as fully and amply ... as the said foreigners would have been entitled to ... if they had respectively naturalized themselves according to the express provisions" of the Act of 1779. In addition, the legislature ordered that the Acts of 1779 and 1789 be published in the state's newspapers "for the space of six weeks, after the end of this session of assembly, in the English, French, and German languages" and the original act published "for the space of two weeks, in the month of May in every year hereafter."[65]

Alien Disabilities

As various states eased alien disabilities and facilitated naturalization to sell and settle their vacant land, most increased restrictions on the rights granted to naturalized citizens. During the eighteenth century colonial Americans had developed denization procedures that conferred local citizenship on non-British immigrants who could not meet the more rigorous requirements of British naturalization law. Denization by colonial statute thus provided a liberal alternative for aliens who did not have the seven-year residence required by the Plantation Act of 1740 for full naturalization. At the same time, colonial Americans also had

[64] "Speech of His Excellency the Governor of New York George Clinton to the Senate and Assembly of New York ... Jan. 21, 1784," in *Connecticut Courant and Weekly Intelligencer*, Feb. 10, 1784 (quote); "The Answer of the Senate of the State of New-York, to the Speech of His Excellence George Clinton ... Jan. 28, 1784," in ibid., Feb. 17, 1784. New York's legislative naturalizations are in *Laws of the State of New York Passed at the Sessions of the Legislature Held in the Years 1777–1800*, 4 vols. (Albany: Weed Parsons and Company, 1886–1887), I, 460, 703; II, 147, 183, 290–91, 556, 592–93, 813–14; III, 83. From 1786 these special acts contained a clause stipulating that real estate acquired by these aliens previous to their naturalization would "rest in such purchaser in the same manner as if such purchaser had been naturalized at the time of such purchase."

[65] Quotes from Maryland's "An Act of Naturalization," *Laws of the State of Maryland, Session of 1779*, chap. VI, and "An Act for the Relief of Certain Foreigners Who Have Settled within This State," *Laws of the State of Maryland, Session of 1789*, chap. XXIV. For the publication of these Acts see *Maryland Gazette*, May 11, 18, 25, June 1, 1790.

tried to increase disabilities for undesirable strangers. Colonial laws that discriminated against transported felons and Irish, Catholic, and Jewish immigrants were, however, usually struck down in England by proprietary officials and the British government. In winning independence, the colonists freed themselves from all British constraints, whether conservative or liberal, in establishing their mode of naturalization and the rights of foreigners. Left to their own devices, America's republicans were thus free to perpetuate the liberal aspects of their colonial past. They also were free to include proscriptive clauses in their laws to discourage the immigration of undesirable aliens and to limit the rights of naturalized citizens.

As state naturalization procedures often left adopted citizens with political and commercial handicaps, other laws encumbered naturalized aliens with special disabilities. The right of the foreign-born to practice law, even after naturalization, was circumscribed in several states. By Pennsylvania's law of 1785, naturalized citizens could not be admitted to the bar until they had completed an additional four-year residence in the state. In Georgia, the right to practice law varied by the nationality of the applicant. By an Act of 1784 citizens of another American state could be licensed to practice law in Georgia after living in the state for six months; subjects of nations allied with the United States could apply one year after receiving Georgia citizenship. However, "no person now a Subject of the Crown of Great Britain [would] be allowed to make any such application until three Years after he shall have become a Citizen of this State and has Actually resided in this or some other of the United States of America."[66]

The commercial and political struggle with Great Britain in the 1780s also placed new handicaps on British traders. The postwar years produced some vindictive attempts to proscribe British competitors. That was the intent of Charleston's Chamber of Commerce when it restricted its membership to "Citizens of America, and . . . subjects of our foreign Allies, now residing in this State." But the tonnage and customs duties that discriminated against British-owned shipping were a more serious burden. By these measures, passed in most states during the 1780s, British aliens involved in commerce were placed at a disadvantage in competing with their American counterparts and other foreigners for a term of years that at least equaled the state's residency requirement.[67]

The most significant change produced by the American Revolution was the altered status of British immigrants. British subjects who felt a special kinship

[66]*Maryland Gazette*, Jan. 28, 1785; Georgia's "Act for Ascertaining the Qualifications Necessary for the Admission of Attorney's [*sic*] Solicitors and Proctors" (1784), in Candler, ed., *State Records of Georgia*, XIX, 284–87. For similar restrictions in Maryland, see Rowland, *Life of Charles Carroll of Carrollton*, II, 67–72.

[67]*South Carolina Gazette*, Jan. 17, 1784 (quote); *Belfast News-Letter*, Oct. 14, 1784; Jensen, *The New Nation*, 179–93, 289–301.

with America and had previously served as role models for the colonists were often surprised and dismayed by the realization that they were now aliens and subject to the disabilities placed on all foreigners. British subjects who resumed after the Revolution their tradition of emigrating to the New World to exchange tenancy for land ownership were now handicapped by alien land laws. British immigrants who settled in America's cities also were liable, for the first time, to the occupational restrictions placed on aliens by municipal charters and by-laws.

Under New York's charter of 1730, which remained in force until its revision in 1827, "no person whatsoever not being a free citizen . . . shall, at any time hereafter use any art, trade, mystery, or occupation within the said city, liberties and precincts thereof; or shall by himself, themselves or others, sell or expose to retail, in any house shop, place, or standing within the said city, or the liberties thereof (save in the times of public fairs) . . . no person or persons shall be made free as aforesaid, but such as are or shall be natural born subjects of us, our heirs or successors, or shall be naturalized, or made Denizens." In 1784 New York City's ship carpenters lodged a complaint with the City Council, charging that George Gar "a shipwright lately (about sixteen or eighteen Months) from Scotland carries on his business in a manner hurtful to the Petitioners and their Brother Shipwrights: And that as the said George is not a Freeman but an Alien they conceive he is not entitled to carry on the said Business therefore they pray that he may [be] fined and prevented for the future from carrying on the said Business, as the Charter directs." In the years that followed, British subjects and other alien residents of New York City were denied licenses as cartmen, butchers, tavernkeepers, and surveyors and were prohibited from serving on juries or as city watchmen.[68]

In the 1780s state laws often denied aliens the right to invest in American corporations. In its 1785 debate over a state bank charter, members of Pennsylvania's General Assembly explained why. These assemblymen opposed alien participation on the grounds that foreign stockholders would gain control of the bank and use it to introduce European politics into their republic and reduce Americans once again "to a state of subordination and dependence upon some one or other of the European powers." By its Constitution of 1787, members of Pennsylvania's Society for the Encouragement of Arts and Domestic Manufactures were required to be United States citizens. Aliens were apparently unable to purchase stock in the Potomac Navigation Company until the 1790 charter

[68] New York's Charter of 1730 in *The Charter of the City of New York. John Montgomerie, Esq. Governor* (New York: L. Nichols & Co., 1801), 40–41; ship carpenters quoted in Richard B. Morris, *Government and Labor in Early America* (New York: Columbia University Press, 1946), 152. For the enforcement of New York's charter restrictions after independence, see, New York City Common Council, *Minutes of the Common Council*: II, 659 (tavern licenses); XV, 545 (butchers); II, 477, 542 (surveyors); II, 631, 633, 636 (city watchmen); Graham Russell Hodges, *New York City Cartmen, 1667–1850* (New York: New York University Press, 1986).

revision gave them the specific right to do so. While other American corporations readily solicited foreign investors, the charters of most banking and insurance companies made American citizenship a prerequisite for election to a company's board of directors.[69]

As the 1780s progressed, so did limitations on the rights of aliens as Americans became increasingly wary of giving untested strangers the ability to shape and subvert their new governments. In the years following the Revolution, many immigrants were not what they seemed. Some undesirable aliens entered the states under false colors, especially British convicts disguised as indentured servants. Others with dangerous political principles, such as tory refugees, tried to slip into the country unnoticed. British merchants arrived with the avowed intent of returning American trade to the English mercantilist orbit. It seemed likely that such men would also try to introduce Old World perversions into America's republican governments.

The disabilities placed on aliens and naturalized citizens in the 1780s were largely the product of wartime animosities and were aimed primarily at British traders and American tories. Hostility to wartime collaborators and the fear that European nations, with "their superiority in wealth, intrigue, and negociation," would "endeavour in their intercourse with us, to acquire an ascendency in American councils" led the states to adopt some Old World techniques for circumscribing the economic and political power of aliens, both before and after their naturalization.[70] Nonetheless, in most states, the postwar years brought an unprecedented opening up of American citizenship, with more rights conveyed on easier terms to more foreigners than anywhere else in the Western world.

In the eighteenth century, there were two avenues to British subjectship for aliens who immigrated to England's North American colonies—naturalization under the Plantation Acts of 1740 and 1747 or denization by colonial legislatures.

[69] (London) *Daily Universal Advertiser*, June 3, 1785 (Pennsylvania Assembly debate); Cooke, *Tench Coxe and the Early Republic*, 103; Joseph Stancliffe Davis, *Essays in the Earlier History of American Corporations*, 2 vols. (Cambridge: Harvard University Press, 1917), II, 105, 246, 299; "An Act to incorporate the Society of Mechanicks and Tradesmen of the City of New York, for charitable purposes," *Laws of the State of New York, 1789–1796*, Session of 1792, chap. 26, 302; "An Act for incorporating the Bank of Virginia (1803), in Samuel Shepherd, ed. *The Statutes at Large of Virginia, 1792–1806*, 3 vols. (Richmond: Samuel Shepherd, 1836), III, chap. 118, 100–108; Virginia's "Act to Amend an Act, Intitled 'An Act for Opening and Extending the Navigation of Patowmack River'" (1790), in Hening, ed., *Statutes at Large of Virginia*, XIII, chap. LVII, 188.

[70] "Instructions to the Delegates of Northumberland County, Virginia," signed by "69 of the most respectable inhabitants" of Northumberland, June 10, 1783, in *South Carolina Gazette*, Sept. 20, 1783. These Virginians also declared that they felt "the most liberal and conciliatory dispositions towards real British subjects; we have especially a generous concern for the redress of many who have suffered by acts of confiscation; but with the utmost scope we can give to these sentiments, we cannot extend them to such natives of these states, as not satisfied with the unnatural election of party they made in the late contest, have superadded the guilt of treachery or paricide. Nor can we exculpate those mercantile persons, who having connections and obligations to the country, that ought to have insured their neutrality, have, nevertheless, retired to British posts in America, and engaged immediately in the war."

Naturalization by British statute conveyed the most rights—granting foreign-born Protestants and Jews who had resided continuously in the colonies for seven years, paid a fee of 40 shillings, and swore (or affirmed) the oaths of allegiance and supremacy, the right to trade within the British Navigation system and political rights, excepting the right to hold high public office. Denization under colonial law varied from colony to colony, but this procedure was usually cheaper (fees ranged from nothing in Georgia to 50 shillings in Virginia) and invariably quicker (in most colonies there was no residence requirement). Although Catholics had been naturalized by colonial governments in the seventeenth century, eighteenth-century denization was open, or limited, to the same religious groups (foreign-born Protestants and Jews) eligible under the Plantation Acts. The rights conveyed by colonial governments were, however, severely circumscribed. Colonial denizens were excluded from trading within the British empire; lost their status and rights when they left the colony; and, although denizens could "usually hold office" in seven colonies, they were permanently banned from all public office in five. In some American colonies, religious restrictions prevented naturalized Protestants and Jews from exercising the political rights granted by either denization or naturalization under Act of Parliament.[71]

After the Declaration of Independence the new states expanded access to American citizenship. In New York, New Jersey, and New England foreigners gained full rights by special legislative act, after meeting minimal requirements. In Massachusetts petitioners who took an oath of allegiance to the state and submitted "sufficient Recommendations and a certifycate setting forth the length of time which such petitioner ... May have resided within this Commonwealth" gained "all the liberties, privileges and immunities of natural born citizens."[72] Article 42 of New York's Constitution of 1777 authorized the state's legislature "to naturalize all such persons, and in such manner, as they shall think proper," stipulating only that the petitioners "settle in and become subjects of this State ... [take] an oath of allegiance to this State, and abjure and renounce all allegiance and subjection to all and every foreign king, prince, potentate, and

[71] See Chapter 2; Edward A. Hoyt, "Naturalization under the American Colonies: Signs of a New Community," *Political Science Quarterly*, 67 (1952), 248–66; Kettner, *Development of American Citizenship*, chaps. 4 and 5.

[72] Ibid., 214–18; quotes from Resolution of October 17, 1787, *Laws of Massachusetts, 1780 to 1800* (Boston: Wright & Potter, 1886), 744; and "An Act for Naturalizing Jonathan Curson and William Oliver," July 7, 1786, in *The Acts and Resolves, Public and Private, of the Province of Massachusetts Bay*, 21 vols. (Boston: Wright & Potter, 1869–1922), vol. 1786–1787, 53–54. Massachusetts law set neither a minimum term of residence nor the number and content of recommendations. Recommenders, who usually stressed a petitioner's good character, industry, admiration for "the Agreeableness of the Country, the goodness of the government, and the manners of the Inhabitants," and fervent desire "to become a Citizen, and here spend the remainder of his days," ranged in number from two to thirty-seven and often included town selectmen. Quotes from petition of James Scobie of Marblehead in Massachusetts State Archives, Legislative Petitions. From 1782 through 1794 the Massachusetts legislature granted naturalization to eighty-seven adult aliens (returning loyalists as well as foreign-born) plus twenty-one children.

State in all manners, ecclesiastical as well as civil."[73] Although New Jersey's naturalization procedure was "obscure," the state's suffrage requirements suggest that even unnaturalized aliens were able to exercise full political rights as its Constitution of 1776 gave the right to vote to all "inhabitants . . . of full age, who are worth fifty Pounds, proclamation money . . . and have resided within the county in which they claim a vote for twelve months immediately preceding the election." Failure to define the word "inhabitant" led to voting by propertied women and free blacks, as well as unnaturalized aliens, until these groups were disfranchised by a law of 1807.[74]

Pennsylvania, Vermont, and the southern states, finding it "expedient to admit aliens to some of the rights and privileges of citizens and to exclude them [temporarily] from others," devised more complicated naturalization procedures that gradually endowed adopted citizens with full political rights after they proved their attachment to republican principles and their new home and had gained experience in the art of self-government.[75] In these states it was common for aliens to be granted a limited form of citizenship very quickly. In North Carolina an alien gained property rights as soon as he took an oath of allegiance and settled in the state; after a year's residence, he was "deemed a free citizen." In Pennsylvania and Vermont, a single year's residence and an oath of allegiance transformed an alien into "a free denizen . . . intitled to all the rights of a natural-born subject of this State; except that he shall not be capable of being elected a representative, until after two years residence." The states of Delaware, Maryland, Virginia, and Georgia granted partial citizenship rights to foreigners within a year or two of their settlement, but delayed full political rights for a period of 5 to 7 years; in South Carolina, after 1786, most political rights required an additional legislative act. Maryland also required alien petitioners to declare their "belief in the christian religion."[76]

---

[73] Thorpe, ed., *Federal and State Constitutions*, V, 2637–38. From 1782 through 1789 the New York legislature naturalized 566 men and women, plus five children, *Laws of the State of New York, 1777–1796*, 3 vols. (Albany: Weed, Parsons and Company, Printers, 1886–1887).

[74] New Jersey's Constitution of 1776, in Thorpe, ed., *Federal and State* Constitutions, V, 2594–98, quote on 2595; Kettner, *Development of American Citizenship*, 217; Carl E. Prince, *New Jersey's Jeffersonian Republicans: The Genesis of an Early Party Machine, 1789–1817* (Chapel Hill: University of North Carolina Press, 1984), 9, 84n., 133–134n.

[75] Quote from preamble of South Carolina's "Act to confer certain Rights and Privileges on Aliens" (1786), Cooper, ed., *Statutes at Large of South Carolina*, IV, chap. 1326, 746–47.

[76] Ibid.; Kettner, *Development of American Citizenship*, 214–16; Constitution of North Carolina, 1776, Art. XL, in Thorpe, ed., *Federal and State Constitutions*, V, 2794 (quote); Constitution of Pennsylvania, 1776, Plan of Government, sec. 42, in ibid., V, 3091; Constitution of Vermont, 1777, chap. II, sec. XXXVIII, in ibid., 3747–48 (quote on 3748). In Vermont's Constitution of 1786, the two-year residence requirement for aliens was extended to the offices of governor, lieutenant-governor, treasurer, and councilor. Constitution of Vermont, 1786, chap. II, sec. XXXVI, in ibid., 3760. Additional residence requirements were also required by Pennsylvania's Constitution of 1790 for the state's governor (seven years "a citizen and inhabitant of this State") and state senators (four years), and residency and citizenship requirements for election as representative to the state legislature were increased to three years. Ibid., V, 3092–93, 3095. Maryland's 1779 "Act for Naturalization," in *Laws of the State of Maryland, Session of 1779*, chap. VI (quote).

In the decade following the Declaration of Independence republican America greatly improved on its previously liberal colonial naturalization policies.[77] With the exception of Maryland, none of the states adopted a religious test to prevent the naturalization of non-Christians. In addition, as religious requirements for suffrage were eliminated, naturalized aliens would no longer be disfranchised for their religious convictions.[78] The gradual whittling away of property requirements for voting in the decades after the Revolution also increased the access of naturalized aliens to the unprecedented political rights of American citizens. Unlike previous colonial and contemporary British practice, adoptive citizens in the new republic suffered no permanent political proscription from public office except, after 1788, from the office of president (and vice-president) of the United States.[79] Article 4 of the Articles of Confederation also ensured that state naturalizations would not confer purely local rights by stipulating that "the free inhabitants of each of these states, paupers, vagabonds, and fugitives from justice excepted, shall be entitled to all privileges and immunities of free citizens in the several states."[80]

Why, given their doubts about the political principles of Old World subjects, did revolutionary Americans develop such expansive citizenship policies? This liberalization was, in part, a natural extension of their colonial heritage. Under British rule, the colonists had made it extremely easy for Protestant aliens to secure local denization. Although British requirements for naturalization in the colonies under Parliamentary statute also were liberal by contemporary standards, they were limited by English imperatives. The denial of citizenship to colonial Catholics and the exclusion of naturalized aliens from high political office had their roots in England's Glorious Revolution and the Hanoverian succes-

[77] For the liberality of citizenship codes in British North America and contemporary practice in French and Spanish colonies, see Chapter 2; James L. Wright, Jr., *Anglo-Spanish Rivalry in North America* (Athens: University of Georgia Press, 1971), 15.

[78] Although most states proclaimed liberty of conscience and eschewed religious tests for naturalization and suffrage, several limited their specific guarantee of rights to Protestants, stipulating, for example, that "no Protestant inhabitant . . . shall be denied the enjoyment of any civil right, merely on account of his religious principles." Sec. XIX of New Jersey's Constitution of 1776, in Thorpe, ed., *Federal and State Constitutions*, V, 2594–98 (quote); Vermont's Constitution of 1777, ibid., VI, 3740. The 1777 and 1786 Constitutions of Vermont also required state representatives, upon assuming office, to take an oath swearing, or affirming, that they "acknowledge[d] the scriptures of the old and new testament to be given by divine inspiration, and own and profess the protestant religion" (chap. II, sec. 11 and chap. II, sec. 12, respectively, in ibid., VI, 3743, 3757). This religious test was omitted when the Constitution was revised in 1793 (see chap. II, sec. 12). The 1793 revision also expanded its guarantee of religious freedom by stating that no man could "be justly deprived or abridged of any civil right as a citizen on account of his religious sentiments, or peculiar mode of religious worship," while adding that "Nevertheless, every sect or denomination of christians ought to observe the sabbath or Lord's day, and keep up some sort of religious worship, which to them shall seem most agreeable to the revealed will of God." Chap. I, Art. 3, Constitution of the State of Vermont, 1793, in ibid., VI, 3762.

[79] New York's Constitution of 1821 also limited the state's governorship to native citizens of the United States. Ibid., V, 2643.

[80] Art. 4, sec. 2 of the U.S. Constitution of 1787 repeated this provision by decreeing that "The citizens of each State shall be entitled to all privileges and immunities of citizens in the several states."

sion. American independence removed at least part of the rationale for these restrictions.

The deletion of religious tests for prospective citizens was primarily the result of the wartime demand for religious freedom by American dissenters and altered geopolitical conditions. Naturalization requirements were affected by the same demand for religious freedom that was expunging religious tests from many of the new state constitutions and legal codes.[81] In 1785 an opponent of "the unchristian unconstitutional bill for support of the Christian Religion," then under consideration in Maryland's House of Delegates, stressed "The dangerous effects this law would have in driving crowds out of the state, and preventing foreigners from venturing into it." Foreigners who had already "removed with their families from different kingdoms of enslaved Europe, and settled among us" would advise their "friends and connexions at home" that they had been "deceived in our expectation of perfect freedom and security against encroachment here." Maryland's citizens were called on to remember the price they had paid before the Revolution for such illiberality, when "lands in Pennsylvania sold fifty per cent. dearer than lands of the same quality in Maryland, where nothing but the partition line divided them—where there was no difference in their fertility or convenience to market. . . . Whence therefore the distinction, so dishonourable and injurious in the latter, but from the religious establishment, which fixed an ignominious stigma, and recognized a principle of extensive and pernicious consequence?" The thought "of living under such a law will hurt ingenuous minds, as it is an opprobrious mark of servility and degradation" and thus "deter the most resolute adventurers from entertaining the most distant thought of becoming citizens with us" and drive recent immigrants into "those enlightened states, where no vestige of religious slavery was ever found." If Maryland's citizens permitted the passage of such a bill they would, once again, pay an economic penalty as the state debt would be paid by reduced numbers of taxpayers, "under the stale plea of preserving religion!"[82]

Similar arguments surfaced in Virginia in "A Memorial and Remonstrance" to the General Assembly listing reasons for opposing "A Bill establishing a Provision for Teachers of the Christian Religion." These memorialists argued, inter alia, that "The proposed establishment is a departure from that generous policy, which offering an asylum to the persecuted and oppressed of every nation and religion, promised a lustre to our country, and an accession to the number of its citizens." The alien victim of religious persecution could only see such a measure

[81] William G. McLoughlin, "The Role of Religion in the Revolution," in Stephen G. Kurtz and James H. Hutson, eds. *Essays on the American Revolution* (Chapel Hill: University of North Carolina Press, 1973); Ronald Hoffman and Peter J. Albert, eds., *Religion in a Revolutionary Age* (Charlottesville: University Press of Virginia, 1994).

[82] For religious toleration as a recruitment tool, see Chapter 3; and *Belfast News-Letter*, July 14, 1786. Quotes from "Philo," "To the Sincere FRIENDS of LIBERTY, and RELIGION of all Denominations," *Maryland Gazette*, Mar. 18, 1785.

"as a beacon on our coast, warning him to seek some other haven, where liberty and philanthropy, in their due extent, may offer a more certain repose from his troubles." Furthermore, the bill under consideration would "have a like tendency to banish our citizens. The allurements presented by other situations are every day thinning their number. To superadd a fresh motive to emigration, by revoking the liberty which they now enjoy, would be the same species of folly, which has dishonored and depopulated flourishing kingdoms." In Virginia, such voices were heeded. State legislators voted down the attempt to create a religious establishment, passed Virginia's "Act for establishing Religious Freedom," and required no religious test for naturalization.[83]

Rescinding colonial discrimination against "papists" was facilitated by the fact that Catholic France was no longer America's mortal enemy. The political proscription of Catholics in the colonies had been one of the consequences of England's Glorious Revolution, as eighteenth-century French monarchs harbored the deposed James II and his heirs, promoted Jacobite plots to topple England's Protestant rulers, and challenged English power in both the Old World and the New. English edicts and the security of the American colonies from French and Spanish depredations mandated restricting the number and political power of their Catholic subjects in America. The aid American rebels received from France in winning their independence and the fervor with which both native and foreign-born Catholics supported the patriot cause changed all this and contributed to the lifting of colonial disabilities on Catholics. The postwar activities of French reformers seemed to confirm America's new assessment of French Catholics. American patriots took great pride in their belief that the wartime exposure of thousands of French soldiers to America's political principles and the fruits of free government had generated the demand for liberty in France and triggered the French Revolution. How in the 1780s could Americans question the political principles of a people who had "spent [their] blood and money to save us" and now carried the torch of American liberty?[84]

Mercantilist aspirations also played a significant role in liberalizing state citizenship policies. Americans who had urged the readmission of the loyalists to promote population growth and economic development used similar arguments

---

[83] "A MEMORIAL and REMONSTRANCE," *Virginia Journal*, Nov. 17, 1785 (quotes); Irving Brant, *James Madison*, 6 vols. (Indianapolis: Bobbs-Merrill, 1941–1961), II, chap. 22; Dumas Malone, *Jefferson the Virginian* (Boston: Little, Brown, 1948), 274–80.

[84] Pauline Maier, "Charles Carroll of Carrollton, Dutiful Son and Revolutionary Politician," in idem, *The Old Revolutionaries: Political Lives in the Age of Samuel Adams* (New York: Knopf, 1980), 201–68; Durand Echeverria, *Mirage in the West: A History of the French Image of American Society to 1815* (Princeton: Princeton University Press, 1957), chap. 3; Charles Downer Hazen, *Contemporary American Opinion of the French Revolution* (Baltimore: Johns Hopkins University Press, 1987), 141–50, quote on 147. In Feb. 1783, Rhode Island, the wartime base of the French forces in America, enacted a law that "fully extended to Roman Catholics . . . all the rights and privileges of the Protestant subjects of this State." *South Carolina Gazette*, June 24, 1783.

to expand the rights of aliens, which, they argued, would attract foreigners, along with their skills and capital. The Pennsylvanians, who in 1789 drafted the state's "Act to Enable Aliens to Purchase and Hold Real Estate within this Commonwealth," anticipated that "the empowering of aliens to purchase and hold lands, tenements and hereditaments . . . would have a tendency to promote the public benefit not only by introducing large sums of money into this state but also by inducing such aliens as may have acquired property to follow their interest and become useful citizens." In New York Governor George Clinton hoped that liberal land ownership policies for aliens would speed up the settlement of his state's frontier lands. The preambles of the naturalization acts passed by Maryland and Virginia were especially explicit in declaring the belief that "the encrease of people is a means to advance the wealth and strength of [a] state" and that "many foreigners, from the lenity of our government, the security afforded by our constitution and laws to civil and religious liberty . . . may be induced to come and settle . . . if they were made partakers of the advantages and privileges which the natural born subjects of this state do enjoy."[85]

Although many economic considerations prompted the adoption of liberal alien policies that could stand up to Old World scrutiny and attract valuable immigrants, the states also felt a need to protect their new republican governments from accidental or deliberate contamination by aliens who had "imbibed in their early youth" the absolutist principles of their native lands. In the 1770s and 1780s, several state legislatures solved this problem by developing a system of "progressive citizenship," which created a temporary, inferior class of citizenship for naturalized aliens who would gain the full rights of native-born Americans after they had proved their attachment to republican principles.[86]

Servitude and Slavery

Although the extension of religious freedom in postwar America increased the nation's appeal to immigrants and enhanced its reputation, the efforts of

[85] Chap. 1387, Mitchell and Flanders, eds., *Statutes at Large of Pennsylvania*, XIII, 179; "Speech of His Excellency the Governor of New York," Jan. 21, 1784, *Connecticut Courant*, Feb. 10, 1784; Maryland's 1779 "Act for Naturalization," *Laws of the State of Maryland, Session of 1779*, chap. VI (quote); Virginia's 1783 "Act for the Admission of Emigrants," in Hening, ed., *Statutes at Large of Virginia*, XI, 322, and 1786 "Act . . . for the Admission of Emigrants to the Rights of Citizenship," ibid., XII, 261.

[86] Thomas Jefferson, "Notes on the State of Virginia," Query VIII, in *Thomas Jefferson: Writings*, ed. Merrill D. Peterson (New York: Library of America, 1984), 211 (quote). Although Georgia allowed the ban on immigrants born in Scotland to expire at the end of the war, peace did not restore its tradition of granting full political rights to immigrants almost immediately on arrival. Neither did Virginia resume her colonial practice of allowing aliens who took an oath of allegiance "the same imunityes and rights" of freeborn Virginians, and "as fully and amply." Virginia's 1680 "Act for Naturalization," in Hening, ed., *Statutes at Large of Virginia*, II, chap. II, 464–65.

American abolitionists to share their freedom with African slaves had the opposite effect. The abolition of the slave trade and gradual emancipation laws in the
north unintentionally reduced American need for Europe's "wretched refuse"
and undermined the institution of indentured servitude that had subsidized
impoverished immigrants. These partial reforms also highlighted the republic's
failure to repudiate slavery and laid Americans open to new charges of treating
servants like slaves.

In the 1780s anti-emigrationists used the existence of republican slavery as a
weapon to ridicule America's claim to be the asylum of liberty. Americans were
described as either hypocrites, securing freedom for themselves while enslaving
both white and African immigrants, or ignorant of the true meaning of liberty.[87]
The link propagandists established between white servitude and black slavery
was reinforcd by gradual emancipation laws in the northern states that transformed the children of slaves into indentured servants and by compromises made
in the Constitutional Convention that semantically conflated white servitude and
black slavery.[88]

Indentured servitude was the mechanism that gave Europe's poor a chance to
become American citizens, by underwriting their passage to the New World
and by providing them with a necessary period of acculturation. Because the
American states denied the right to vote and naturalization to men who were
not free, foreigners who arrived under indenture served a mandatory period of
apprenticeship, during which they learned the responsibilities of republican citizenship.[89] The delay in granting full political rights to naturalized aliens served
the same purpose for foreigners who paid their own fares. Gradual emancipation, which transformed slave children into indentured servants, was the parallel
response by Americans who felt an obligation "to extend a portion of that
freedom to others" but saw Africans, debased by slavery and inexperienced in
the duties and rights of freemen, as dangerous material for citizenship.[90]

[87] *Belfast News-Letter*, Mar. 23, May 4, June 4, 1784, and Chapter 5.

[88] While Vermont and Massachusetts adopted a literal interpretation of the Revolution's declaration that
"all men are created equal," American abolitionists were less successful elsewhere. State laws that provided
for gradual emancipation and the end of the slave trade were seen as inadequate even by America's friends.
David Brion Davis describes the limits of emancipation in postwar America in *The Problem of Slavery in
the Age of Revolution, 1770–1823* (Ithaca: Cornell University Press, 1975), 312–21.

[89] Opinion of Justice Bradford in *Respublica v. Keppele* (1793), in A. J. Dallas, ed., *Reports of Cases Ruled
and Adjudged in the Several Courts of the United States and of Pennsylvania Held at the Seat of the Federal
Government* (Philadelphia: Aurora, 1798), II, 197–99; Thomas Jefferson, "Answers and Observations for
Desmeunier's Article," June 22, 1786, in *Thomas Jefferson: Writings*, ed. Peterson, 579–81.

[90] "Act for the Gradual Abolition of Slavery," 1780, in Mitchell and Flanders, eds., *Statutes at Large of
Pennsylvania*, X, chap. DCCCLXXXI, quote from preamble, drafted by Thomas Paine, on 67. By this Act,
slaves born in Pennsylvania after the law's passage would be freed at the age of 28, after serving the preceding years as indented servants, with all the rights and obligations of a white person serving for a term of
years. Ibid., 67–73. For similar acculturation plans, see Davis, *Problem of Slavery*, 305–6; Lafayette to George
Washington, Feb. 5, 1783, *The Letters of Lafayette to Washington, 1777–99*, ed. Louis Gottschalk (Philadelphia: American Philosophical Society, 1976), 260; James Madison, "Memorandum on an African Colony for
Freed Slaves" (Oct. 1789), in *The Papers of James Madison*, ed. Hutchinson, XII, 437–38; Marvin Meyers,

However, the merger of the institutions that controlled blacks with those that governed white servants left Americans increasingly vulnerable to the charge of treating refugees from Old World tyranny like slaves and made white servitude seem unacceptable in a land of liberty.

The "fugitive slave clause" of the Federal Constitution added fuel to the fire. During the debate over apportioning representatives and taxes among the states, members of the Constitutional Convention replaced the phrase "free Persons . . . bound to servitude" with "free Persons . . . bound to Service" because "servitude" was "thought to express the condition of slaves, and [service] the obligations of free persons." But no such distinction was made between indentured servants and slaves when the Convention acceded to the South Carolinian demand for a provision requiring that "fugitive slaves and servants . . . be delivered up like criminals." The resulting Article IV, section 2 decreed that "No Person held to Service or Labor in one State under the Laws thereof, escaping into another, shall, in Consequence of any Law or Regulation therein, be discharged from such Service or Labour, but shall be delivered up on Claim of the Party to whom such Service or Labor may be due."[91]

These new links between white servitude and black slavery further discredited the system of indentured servitude. Old World propagandists eagerly seized on, and distorted, any evidence they could find to prove that America's republicans actually enslaved white immigrants. Court cases that detailed the suffering of the "white slaves" in America were published in the European press along with stories of the lugubrious fate of servants who succumbed to the blandishments of unscrupulous American recruiters. In 1787 Matthew Carey, an Irish immigrant who had fled to Pennsylvania to escape British oppression in 1783, published his "Prayer of an American Citizen." This poem called on God to help

> . . . this free country ever more
> Prove to th' oppress'd a friendly shore:
> An ASYLUM from TYRANNY,
> And DIRE RELIGIOUS BIGOTRY:
> May they from Hants to Georgia find
> A welcome hearty, warm and kind!
> May servitude abolish'd be,

---

ed. *The Mind of the Founder: Sources of the Political Thought of James Madison*, rev. ed. (Hanover, N.H.: University Press of New England, 1981), 313–36; Winthrop D. Jordan, *White over Black: American Attitudes toward the Negro, 1550–1812* (Chapel Hill: University of North Carolina Press, 1968), 542–69. For similar fears about America's Indians that mandated their isolation on reservations, outside republican society, until they had acculturated, see Bernard W. Sheehan, *Seeds of Extinction: Jeffersonian Philanthropy and the American Indian* (Chapel Hill: University of North Carolina Press, 1973).

[91] Jonathan Elliot, ed., *Debates on the Adoption of the Federal Constitution in the Convention held at Philadelphia*, 2nd ed., 5 vols. (Philadelphia: Lippincott, 1836–1845), V, 540 (quote), 487 (quote), 492.

As well as negro-slavery,
To make *one* LAND OF LIBERTY.[92]

In the postwar years some native-born Americans also began to see white servitude as inconsistent with republican liberty. In January 1784 a group of New Yorkers denounced "the traffick of white people, heretofore countenanced by this State while under the arbitrary control of the British government" as "contrary to the feeling of a number of respectable citizens, and to the idea of liberty this country has so happily established" and proposed "to liberate a cargo of Servants just arrived, by paying their passages and repaying themselves by a small rateable deduction out of the wages of such Servants." A similar proposal was made in December 1783 by "Civis" of Charleston, South Carolina. In an editorial, "Civis" urged "the GENTLEMEN and LADIES of SOUTH-CAROLINA" to display "the genuine lustre of Virtue and Charity, by opening a Subscription for the emancipation of the indigent natives of Ireland, now in our port," who were being offered for sale by the Captain of the *Irish Volunteer* from Waterford. According to "Civis," the time had come for Carolinians to show that they "consider themselves as Stewards of what the ALMIGHTY hath blessed them with; and that every innocent person in bonds, or other distress, is our brother." This was especially true for "these distressed Hibernians (who were mostly forced from their native country, by the cruelty and oppression of rich, and unfeeling *Landlords*)," as the Irish in general "have such a glorious thirst for rational liberty, and . . . have been so remarkably instrumental in promoting our present freedom, happiness, and independence." There is, however, no evidence that either cargo of indentured servants was "liberated." And in 1793 Pennsylvania's Supreme Court ruled that, even though servitude was inappropriate for republican citizens, it was "mutually beneficial" to foreign-born immigrants and the state.[93]

The Problem of Slavery

During the summer of 1787 delegates to the Constitutional Convention worked hard to expunge the shame of slavery from their country and the new Constitu-

[92] *Maryland Gazette*, Aug. 17, 1787; Phineas Bond, Philadelphia, Jan. 3, 1791, to Duke of Leeds, "Letters of Phineas Bond, British Consul at Philadelphia, to the Foreign Office of Great Britain, 1790–1794," ed. J. Franklin Jameson, American Historical Association, *Annual Report for the Year 1897*, 472; *Belfast News-Letter*, Nov. 27, 1787, Feb. 5, 1790. Carey's poem published in *American Museum*, Oct. 1787, "Hants" means New Hampshire.

[93] (New York) *Independent Journal*, Jan. 28, 1784 (quotes); "Civis" in *South Carolina Gazette*, Dec. 6, 1783 (quotes); advertisement for "Sixty-nine Passengers, Tradesmen and Labourers, Indented for 4 years," in ibid., Nov. 29, Dec. 2, 6, 9, 13, 1783. A 1787 proposal to form a society "to alleviate the Sufferings and Distresses of INDENTED SERVANTS of EVERY NATION" was published in the *Maryland Journal and Baltimore Advertiser*, Mar. 20, 1787. Opinion of Justice Bradford in *Respublica v. Keppele* (1793), Dallas, ed., *Reports of Cases, Pennsylvania*, II, 197–99.

tion. But the best they could do was to secure the eventual right of the federal government to prohibit the slave trade and its immediate right to tax it.[94] Antislavery members of the Convention also were successful in withholding a federal sanction for slavery that would come from making direct provisions for its continuance in the new constitution. As a result, Article I, section 9, of the Constitution of 1787 decreed that "The migration or importation of such persons as any of the states now existing shall think proper to admit, shall not be prohibited by the Congress prior to the year 1808, but a tax or duty may be imposed on such importation, not exceeding ten dollars for each person." Part of the ambiguity of this clause was accidental, a necessary consequence of the refusal to sanction slavery by naming it in the Constitution. The use of "words, dark and ambiguous, such as no plain man of common sense would have used" also was dictated by the propaganda battles of the 1780s as American statesmen were indeed anxious "to conceal from Europe, that in this enlightened century, the practice of slavery has its advocates among men in the highest stations." But part of the ambiguity also was deliberate—needed to prevent the Old World from using the new nation as a dumping ground for its social and political liabilities. Members of the Convention recognized that, "as the clause now stands, it implies that the legislature may tax freemen imported." But the obscure wording, dictated by the struggle over slavery, was seen as "necessary for the case of convicts, in order to prevent the introduction of them."[95]

As predicted, both friends and foes of the new constitution did indeed read the document as giving Congress the power to levy a prohibitive duty on voluntary, white immigrants. Thomas Brand Hollis, the English radical, vented his disappointment at this evidence of American inhumanity on John Adams. In a letter to Adams, Hollis expressed his horrified dismay,

> That a person coming to settle in a country should pay a fine . . . in a country which justly glories in being free! Was it St. Marino or Ragusa it might be prudent & necessary, from the few inhabitants & small extent of territory. But represent to your self not only an ingenious poor man—but a worthy honest man & of talents, injured, by the laws delay & insolence of office, who has spent almost his whole substance on resisting oppression;—flatters himself there is still a country an Asylum for the ingenuous tho wretched & where the long hands of Tyrants cannot reach, but when arrived at that happy land, finds at last that he is cruelly disappointed and all his hopes cut of[f] & cannot obtain a landing place for himself and family but at the expence of all his little remaining stock, his necessary pittance, in such a distracted situation, all hope is lost & nothing remains for him abandoned & dejected, but to wait with patiency a speedy admission into that state where truth & liberty reign triumphant & where Tyrants never come &, the wretched at rest. Shall it be possible

[94] Although the antislavery members of the Constitutional Convention attained only limited success, that same summer the Continental Congress outlawed slavery in the Northwest Territory.
[95] Quotes from Art. I, sec. 9, Federal Constitution of 1787; Davis, *Problem of Slavery*, 322; Elliot, ed., *Debates on the Adoption of the Federal Constitution*, V, 478.

for such an instance to be produced against a magnanimous people who having emancipated themselves will not participate that blessing to all the inhabitants of the world! No danger to the publick weal, the gain trifling &, contemptible, whereas universal admission open as heaven would be but just, liberal &, magnificent & worthy of a people the preceptors of mankind.[96]

In state ratifying conventions, supporters of the new Constitution were forced to defend it against those who asked, "Why will the Congress have power . . . to collect by law ten dollars for ever[y] German or Irishman which may come to settle in America?" James Madison tried to dismiss these "Attempts . . . to pervert this clause . . . by representing it on one side as a criminal toleration of an illicit practice, and on another as calculated to prevent voluntary and beneficial emigrations from Europe to America." In Pennsylvania's ratifying convention, James Wilson attempted, unsuccessfully, to prove that the wording of the provision clearly endowed the national legislature with the power "to impose the tax only on those imported," and not all immigrants. Unable to deny that the clause gave Congress the right to regulate nonslave immigration, and specifically convicts, the Federalists were hard pressed to refute the charge that "their darling Constitution . . . has laid newcomers under many legal disabilities and given the discouragement that it durst safely do."[97]

Although the Constitution of 1787 held out no special inducements to immigrants, its supporters asserted that the general thrust of the document did just that. Thus they argued that "Induced by the goodly prospect of a happy and durable government, by which life, religion, freedom, and property would be well secured, America will teem with those who will fly from the slavery, persecution, tyranny and wars of Europe. The civil commotions of Holland will soon open a wide door to let her citizens and those of Germany, into America. The trumpet of war has already sounded in their ears, and we shall soon behold the *industrious laborers* of those countries pouring into our ports and crowding our cities."[98]

Members of the Convention, confident that the natural attractions of republican America would provide the nation with all the immigrants it could handle, negotiated solutions to more crucial issues in ways that inadvertently constricted the welcome extended to foreigners. Control of the western lands was given to the same national body that had rejected proposals to encourage immigration by offering free or cheap land and bounties to foreigners. The new Congress was

[96] Thomas Brand Hollis, The Ilide [Hyde], Nov. 4, 1787, to John Adams in *Adams Papers Microfilm*, reel 371.

[97] James Madison et al., *The Federalist Papers*, ed. Clinton Rossiter, 1st publ. 1787–1788 (New York: New American Library, 1961), No. 42, 267; David Redick, Philadelphia, Sept. 24, 1787, to William Irvine in Merrill Jensen, ed. *Ratification of the Constitution by the States* (Madison: State Historical Society of Wisconsin, 1976–), II, 135 (quote); James Wilson and rebuttal by Robert Whitehill, in ibid., II, 463, 464.

[98] Ibid., III, 147 (quote), 152.

given the power "To regulate Commerce with foreign Nations" that would enable it to establish a navigation system that discriminated against alien merchants. Attempts to free America of the pernicious influence of transported convicts and black slavery produced policies that undermined the institution of indentured servitude as a vehicle to transport poor immigrants, tarnished America's reputation in the Old World, and spread confusion over which immigrants would be taxed, prohibited, or welcomed in the new republic. And, in determining the qualifications for federal office, the Convention followed the practice of the states in setting up additional requirements for naturalized citizens.

Although most of the delegates to the Constitutional Convention wished to avoid giving "the tincture of illiberality to the Constitution," none of them could completely shake the belief that foreigners "bring with them, not only attachments to other countries, but ideas of government so distinct from ours, that in every point of view they are dangerous." The Convention eventually decided that after seven years of citizenship naturalized foreigners could be entrusted with the office of Representative and, after nine years, with that of United States Senator. Aliens who were not naturalized at the time of the ratification of the Constitution were forever barred from the office of president.[99]

The apparent conflation of the status of servants and slaves fostered by gradual emancipation laws and the Constitution of 1787 unintentionally tainted indentured servitude. The Constitutional provision that allowed the federal government to tax new slave arrivals from Africa combined with the ability of the new states to tax or even abolish slavery itself also had unexpected consequences. Americans who hoped to limit the growth of slavery were no longer forced to circumvent British edicts that had prohibited the colonists from regulating the slave trade or even taxing it out of existence.

After achieving independence, northerners who feared the consequences of slavery no longer felt the need to recruit or subsidize the immigration of Europe's "downtrodden masses" to dilute their servile work force; they could now control the number of slaves entering their states directly. In 1769 New Jersey's legislature, having concluded that "Duties on the Importation of Negroes in several of the neighbouring Colonies hath, on Experience, been found beneficial in the Introduction of sober, industrious Foreigners, to settle under His Majesty's Allegiance, and the promoting a Spirit of Industry among the Inhabitants in General," placed a 15 pound duty on "the Purchasers of slaves imported into this colony. After securing independence, New Jersey's legislature in 1786 declared that "the Principles of Justice and Humanity require that the barbarous Custom of bringing the unoffending African from his native Country and Connections into a State of Slavery ought to be discountenanced" and banned the slave trade.

---

[99] Quotes from Art. I, sec. 8 of the Federal Constitution of 1787; Elliot, ed., *Debates on the Adoption of the Federal Constitution*, V, 398 (Madison and Pierce Butler). Qualifications for federal officeholders in Art. I, sec. 2, 3 and Art. II, sec. 1 of the Constitution of 1787.

Although these legislators also decreed "that such as are under Servitude in the State ought to be protected by Law from those Exercises of wanton Cruelty too often practiced upon them; and that every unnecessary Obstruction in the Way of freeing Slaves should be removed," New Jersey did not abolish slavery until 1846—and then, in such a tortuous way that the state's last remaining slaves were not freed until the passage of the 13th Amendment in 1865.[100] In the decades following independence most of the northern states progressed, with somewhat more alacrity, along a similar path—passing laws that not only ended the slave trade and abolished slavery, but also reduced the need to subsidize the white immigrants necessary to oversee, control, and dilute a slave labor force.[101]

While the revolutionary era impetus to abolish slavery in the plantation states was relatively weak and short-lived, southerners eagerly seized the opportunity afforded them by independence to regulate the size, value, and provenance of their enslaved work force. In the South, antislavery forces were strongest in the Chesapeake, where they were supported by the fear of creating a black majority and a shift in agriculture from tobacco to wheat.[102] However, although Maryland, Virginia, and North Carolina all ended the foreign and interstate slave trade by 1786, the relatively high reproductive rates of Chesapeake slaves resulted in a steady increase of the region's black population and the need for white immigrants to decrease the danger of servile insurrections.[103] Slave revolts in St. Domingue in the 1790s, which increased racial fears, and the postwar ban on transported "gaol birds," which decreased the Chesapeake's traditional source of white immigrants, generated the active recruitment of indentured and propertied Europeans.

The states of South Carolina and Georgia banned the African and domestic

[100] W. E. Burghardt Du Bois, *The Suppression of the African Slave-Trade to the United States of America, 1638–1879* (Cambridge: Harvard University Press, 1896), 221, (quote), 227–28 (quote on 227); Arthur Zilversmit, *The First Emancipation: The Abolition of Slavery in the North* (Chicago: University of Chicago Press, 1967), 215–22.

[101] Zilversmit, *The First Emancipation,* Du Bois, *Suppression of the Slave Trade,* 16–38.

[102] Du Bois, *Suppression of the Slave Trade,* 11–15; Jordan, *White over Black,* 319–21; Richard S. Dunn, "Black Society in the Chesapeake," in Ira Berlin and Ronald Hoffman, eds., *Slavery and Freedom in the Age of the American Revolution* (Charlottesville: University of Virginia Press, 1983), 49–82; Allan Kulikoff, "Uprooted Peoples: Black Migrants in the Age of the American Revolution, 1790–1820," in Berlin and Hoffman, eds., *Slavery and Freedom,* 143–71; Madison, *Notes of Debates in the Federal Convention,* 503–4. The charge that Virginia's slaveholders backed the ending of the African slave trade to create a market for, and increase the value of, their own slaves, was made as early as 1787 by Charles Cotesworth Pinckney of South Carolina, at the Constitutional Convention. Madison, *Notes of Debates in the Federal Convention,* 503.

[103] Virginia prohibited "the farther importation of slaves . . . by sea or land" in 1778, in Hening, ed., *Statutes at Large of Virginia,* IX, 471; Maryland passed a similar act in 1783, *Laws of Maryland, Session of 1783,* chap. XXIII. In 1786, North Carolina placed a "prohibitive duty" on "all slaves brought into this state by land or water," £5 on each slave imported from Africa, £10 on each slave from elsewhere, & £50 on a slave from a State licensing manumission," but did not formally prohibit the introduction of slaves into the state, "by land or water" until 1794. Madison, *Notes of Debates in the Federal Convention,* 506; Du Bois, *Suppression of the Slave Trade,* 229, 236.

slave trade after the Revolution at various time for somewhat different reasons. In the Deep South there was neither a slave surplus nor a shift to a less labor-intensive staple. The living and working conditions on rice plantations also prevented a rate of natural increase sufficient to fill the demand for slaves, especially in the backcountry and newly settled regions.[104] Consequently, South Carolinians, at war's end, resumed importing slaves from Africa—and lobbied for subsidies for white immigrants from Europe and the northern states.

In September of 1785 South Carolina's legislature considered a temporary halt to the slave trade, in response to complaints "That a sufficient check has not been put to the Importation of Negro Slaves, although it appears evident that it has always thrown the balance of Trade amazingly against us, has drained us of our Cash, & prevented the increase of population and growth of manufactures."[105] In 1785 the legislature decided against bringing in a bill "for preventing the importation of negroes into this state for the term of three years" by a vote of 51 to 45 on September 28th and 63 to 48 on October 5th. During the debate, proponents of the measure argued that a suspension of the slave trade was essential to reduce the "immense debt" that was "the true cause of all the misfortune . . . by which we were overwhelmed." They maintained that "The great quantity of negroes now pouring in upon us, occasions every planter to wish an increase of his stock, the sight of a negroe yard was to[o] great a temptation for a planter to withstand, he could not leave it without purchasing . . . without any consideration how they were to be paid for." Supporters of the ban characterized the purchase of additional slaves as a luxury they could not, at present, afford and argued that a country's "riches should be estimated by the number of its white inhabitants, for it was upon them that our commerce, our agriculture, and manufacture depended."[106]

These arguments failed to convince representatives such as General Pinckney who portrayed slaves as the essential foundation of the state's strength and riches. Pinckney cited the work of "negroe pioneers" during the war, who had built the "bastions" that scared off British troops; the staple crops African slaves grew in a "country . . . not capable of being cultivated by white men," and the revenues "paid to the state for negroes imported." He then asked whether the state's valiant soldiers who found, "on being released from captivity, their plantations

[104] Du Bois, *Suppression of the Slave Trade*, 7–11, 226, 229, 233, 236–41; Jordan, *White over Black*, 317–19; Philip D. Morgan, "Black Society in the Low Country, 1760–1810," in Berlin and Hoffman, eds., *Slavery and Freedom*, 83–141; Patrick S. Brady, "The Slave Trade and Sectionalism in South Carolina, 1787–1808," *Journal of Southern History*, 38 (1972), 601–20.

[105] "Petition of the Inhabitants of Camden District," Sept. 27, 1785, *Journal of the [South Carolina] House of Representatives, 1785–1786*, 316 (quote); debate of "the Committee of Enquiry into the state of the Republic," *Charleston Evening Gazette*, Sept. 28, 1785, reprinted in Elizabeth Donnan, ed., *Documents Illustrative of the History of the Slave Trade to America*, 4 vols. (Washington, D.C.: Carnegie Institution of Washington, 1930–1935), IV, 483.

[106] Ibid., IV, 480–84; debate of House "Committee of the Whole," *Charleston Evening Gazette*, Oct. 18, 1785, reprinted in ibid., IV, 484–89; quotes on 481 (E. Rutledge), 482 (Bee); 482 (Judge Pendleton).

plundered, and every negroe swept away" should now be denied the ability to purchase the slaves necessary to make their lands productive. John Pringle introduced additional evidence of the extent to which South Carolina's "national welfare" and prosperity depended on a constantly expanding slave labor force. Since the "ballance of trade . . . depended on the cheapness of labour . . . would not a scarcity of necessary labourers tend to enhance the price of labour, and throw the ballance of trade still more against us?" While Pringle "sincerely hoped" that South Carolinians would be more frugal "in the introduction of foreign articles of luxuries . . . negroes were not luxuries; they were a sort of rough journeymen, and from their numbers stimulated our white workmen to a higher degree of exertion than they would otherwise arrive at."[107]

On May 17, 1787 the South Carolina assembly finally agreed, by a vote of 57 to 54 "That no Negroe or other Slave shall be imported or brought into this State either by land or Water within Three years next ensuing." The ban on the introduction of new slaves from overseas would be renewed for the next fifteen years; the restriction on slaves brought in "by land," was lifted in 1788 by the provision "that nothing in this prohibition . . . shall extend to such slaves as are now the property of citizens of the United States, and at the time of passing this act shall be within the limits of the said United States." The interstate slave trade remained legal in South Carolina until an Act of December 1792 decreed that "No slaves, Negroes, Indians, etc., bound for a term of years" could be "brought in from any of the United States or bordering countries," although new settlers could bring their slaves with them.[108]

The reasons for South Carolina's continuation, and hardening, of the slave trade ban in the 1790s are clear, as the radicalism of the French Revolution triggered black revolts in the West Indies and white fears on the continent of North America. These insurrections annihilated the argument that African slaves were the true riches of a state, increasing its security, welfare, and the productivity of "white workmen." By 1805 South Carolina's governor stated that an expansion of the slave population "increases our wickedness, not our strength" and "that in proportion as you add to the number of Slaves you prevent the influx of those men who would increase the means of defence and security."[109] The impetus behind South Carolina's prohibition of the slave trade in 1787 is more ambiguous. The ban was the work of the low-country planters, who, dominating the state's legislature, overrode the wishes of backcountry representatives. With the resumption of the slave trade at war's end, slaves had arrived in numbers sufficient to replenish the low-country work force and increase planter indebt-

---

[107] Ibid., 482–83 (General Pinckney); 487 (Pringle).

[108] *Journals of the [South Carolina] House of Representatives, 1787–1788* (Columbia: University of South Carolina Press, 1981), 231–34, quote on 231; South Carolina's Acts of 1788 and 1792, in Du Bois, *Suppression of the Slave Trade*, 233, 237.

[109] Governor Paul Hamilton quoted in Brady, "Slave Trade and Sectionalism," 616.

edness to alarming proportions. By 1790, slaves outnumbered the low country's white population by a ratio of almost three to one—78,000 slaves for 28,644 whites. The situation was, however, reversed in the upcountry, where by 1790 a dramatically increasing white population outnumbered their slaves by almost four to one, with 29,095 slaves serving 111,988 white inhabitants. The postwar emigration of thousands of Americans and immigrants to Carolina's backcountry generated a demand for slaves and a positive gloss on the benefits of slavery, but the low-country's fiscal fears and stagnating white population, exacerbated by the failure of initiatives to reinstitute the colonial bounty system for European immigrants, led coastal South Carolinians to view slavery in a less sanguine light and to insist on the temporary closing of the African slave trade.[110]

During the 1780s American statesmen adopted a new approach to the issue of immigration and population growth, one that rejected both colonial precedent and the contemporary European practice of using the power of government to seduce the subjects of rival nations. By relying on the nation's natural assets and just government to attract valuable foreigners, republican policy-makers saved money, bowed to the wishes of their constituents who feared foreign competitors, and demonstrated their wariness over the political principles of aliens.

The alien policies developed in the 1780s, which imperfectly reconciled many conflicting demands, defy an easy or simple description. Yet this is exactly what contemporaries tried to do. Old World observers insisted on painting a simplistic picture of republican America. To anti-emigrationists, the American governments and people embraced every defect imaginable; they were no more able to devise wise and liberal immigrant polices than they were to develop effective governments and prosperous economies. Such men readily believed and publicized stories that postwar patriots tarred and feathered every loyalist they could find; that Americans first enslaved and then proscribed white servants; that they lured poor immigrants with promises of gold in the streets so they could victimize them on their arrival; and that Virginia law required Scots to reside in the state for 30 years before being eligible for citizenship. Most of America's Old World friends responded in kind. By doing so, they did not enlighten, but only added misleading white splotches to the black canvas of their adversaries.

Of America's friends, Hector St. John de Crèvecœur went the furthest in distorting the American position on immigration. Crèvecœur's *Letters from an American Farmer* was the most popular and widely read work on America in Great Britain and Europe in the 1780s. Unfortunately, the book, written a decade

---

[110]Brady, "Slave Trade and Sectionalism," 618–19; *Journals of the [South Carolina] House of Representatives, 1787–1788*, 231–34.

before its publication in 1782, was a celebration of the British colonies in the 1760s, not of the American states after independence. Crèvecœur's panegyrics were not an accurate record of life in the British colonies; still less did they describe the postwar republics. The benevolent and free government he described and praised was the very one the Americans had thrown off. The encouragement he offered to Old World emigrants was an anachronistic throw-back to the British view of America as the appropriate home for men who served no useful purpose in their native land. According to Crèvecœur, America was the great asylum where Europe's outcasts would be regenerated, a sanctuary for the "wretch who wanders about, who works and starves, whose life is a continual scene of sore affliction or pinching penury . . . whose fields procured him no harvest, who met with nothing but the frowns of the rich, the severity of the laws, with jails and punishments; who owned not a single foot of the extensive surface of this planet." The salvation of these "wretches" lay in America, where "Every thing has tended to regenerate them; new laws, a new mode of living, a new social system; here they are become men: in Europe they were as so many useful plants, wanting vegetative mould, and refreshing showers; they withered, and were mowed down by want, hunger, and war; but now by the power of transplantation, like all other plants they have taken root and flourished!"[111]

During the 1780s, some American position papers were published in the Old World that contained more accurate descriptions of republican attitudes and poli-cies toward aliens, and contradicted Crèvecœur's rhapsodies. Benjamin Franklin's *Information to Those Who Would Remove to America* was the most widely reprinted statement on America's postwar immigration policy. Written in Febru-ary 1784, it began appearing in the British press the following fall. This tract clearly stated the American preference for immigrants of "mediocre" talents and fortunes—industrious yeomen farmers and artisans with enough capital to buy land and to set themselves up in business and warned against the emigration of idle aristocrats, military men, and "strangers possessing Talents in the Belles-Lettres, fine Arts, &c." Franklin also refuted the prevalent belief that the American governments "to encourage Emigrations from Europe, not only pay the expence of personal Transportation, but give Lands gratis to Strangers, with Negroes to work for them, Utensils of Husbandry, & Stocks of Cattle. These are wild Imaginations; and those who go to America with Expectations founded upon them, will surely find themselves disappointed." The French edition of Thomas Jefferson's *Notes on the State of Virginia*, published in 1785, preached an even

---

[111] J. Hector St. John de Crèvecœur, *Letters from an American Farmer*, 1st publ. 1782 (London: J. M. Dent & Sons, 1971), esp. Letter III, 39–46; quotes on 42; Bernard Fay, *The Revolutionary Spirit in France and America* (New York: Harcourt, Brace & World, 1927), 232–36; Echeverria, *Mirage in the West*, 144–50; Colin Bonwick, *English Radicals and the American Revolution* (Chapel Hill: University of North Carolina Press, 1977), 156.

more restrictive message. Jefferson, with a single exception, could see no reason to encourage the immigration of foreigners from the Old World, whose absolutist principles could only make American society "more turbulent, less happy, [and] less strong." The only immigrants who could improve American society were "useful artificers . . . [who] will after a while go to the plough and the hoe; but, in the mean time, they will teach us something we do not know. It is not so in agriculture. The indifferent state of that among us does not proceed from a want of knowledge merely; it is from our having such quantities of land to waste as we please."[112]

But these publications failed to correct the misperceptions surrounding America's immigration policies. The beguiling imagery of Crèvecœur was too strong to be overcome by pedantic policy statements or warnings that Europeans should not believe everything they read in *Letters from an American Farmer*. In addition, extracts of American letters and essays printed in British and European newspapers often were distorted to reflect the biases of the foreign editors. In March 1787 the *Leeds Mercury* published the paragraph from Franklin's pamphlet on immigration that advised against the emigration of the man "who has no other qualification to recommend him than his birth" and eulogized the husbandman and the mechanic; no mention was made of the hardships, spelled out by Franklin, that awaited immigrants of inadequate means. In January 1788 the same newspaper printed a passage from *Notes on the State of Virginia* in which Jefferson urged Americans to "let our workshops remain in Europe—It is better to carry provisions and materials to workmen there, than to bring them to provisions and materials, and with them their manners and principles." But this extract was published to excoriate Jefferson for his "*shafts* . . . against the morals of this useful class of men . . . [and] against Christianity itself." No attempt was made to reproduce the remainder of Jefferson's thoughts on immigration. The *Belfast News-Letter* also used Franklin's essay on emigration as part of its antiemigration campaign. Their readers were told that

> The rage of emigration which was depopulating this country, and distressing the convenience of the North Americans, induced Doctor Franklin to take up the pen, in consequence of which he produced his late pamphlet, on the nature of emigration to America. He clearly points out in this publication, that all emigrants to that continent are totally useless, except they admit to be employed in the nature of slaves, who are not possessed of a mechanical knowledge, of the knowledge husbandry, and to those attributes must add the labour of their own hands. . . . The Doctor, on the whole, recommends it to every man to stay home, who is not truly *industrious*; for

---

[112] *Information to Those Who Would Emigrate*, in *Benjamin Franklin: Writings*, ed. Lemay, 975–83, quotes on 975; *Notes on the State of Virginia*, in *Thomas Jefferson: Writings*, ed. Peterson, 123–325, quotes on 212. Philip Mazzei's *Rescherches historiques et politiques sur les Etats-Unis* (1788) also reprinted Franklin's tract on emigration and large segments of Jefferson's *Notes on Virginia*.

otherwise America will prove to be to strangers, what people in general little think of—rather a curse than a blessing.[113]

Although this article presents Franklin's views on immigration with relatively few distortions, it was obviously designed to deter emigration. By using Franklin's remarks to tarnish the image of America, the press ensured their rejection by Irish people infatuated with the idea of America, who would see these words as part of the network of lies that had been created to restrain their mobility.

The American position on immigration was thus lost in a cloud of propaganda and rhetoric. America's failure to extend an enthusiastic welcome to all foreigners was overlooked by her friends. The distortion of republican immigration policies by America's foes was more deliberate. British newspapers presented their readers at home and on the Continent with a potpourri of "news" from America that included valid reports, unsubstantiated rumors, and the work of paid anti-American propagandists, all of which were designed, not to reveal the truth about republican America, but to sabotage the new nation and tarnish its image.

In the 1780s the victorious Americans reexamined their political heritage, drafting and revising constitutions and legal codes along republican lines. Colonial laws relating to aliens were subjected to the same scrutiny; some were validated and reenacted by state legislators and others modified or discarded as incompatible with republican principles or postwar conditions. During the Revolution, American patriots had promised that, once free of British tyranny, they would create a New World asylum that would preserve the flame of liberty for themselves and "all mankind." The anti-American campaign of the 1780s increased the pressure on the rebel governments to honor their wartime pledge and to adopt policies that could withstand the scrutiny of the watching world and future generations. Although Americans were well aware that their millenarian destiny could not be fulfilled if their republican experiment failed, they differed in their opinions as to what strengthened and what undermined or perverted a republic. As a result, postwar American governments, at both the state and national levels, gradually developed a vast mosaic of laws, policies, and institutions that were complex compromises between radicals and conservatives, idealistic republicans and pragmatic mercantilists, reformers and bigots.

Liberal pragmatism usually prevailed in America's nation-building process. During the Revolution, American diplomats were forced to accept a traditional military alliance with France. In commerce, the strength of British mercantilism

[113]Philip Mazzei, *Researches on the United States*, 1st publ. 1788, trans. Constance D. Sherman (Charlottesville: University Press of Virginia, 1976), 333–34; *Leeds Mercury*, March 13, 1787 (quote), Jan. 1, 1788 (quote); *Belfast News-Letter*, Oct. 22, 1784 (quote).

also forced Americans to compromise their free trade ideals and adopt measures that discriminated against alien merchants. Similar constraints and compromises shaped America's alien policies. When Old World conservatives tried to discredit and destroy the young states, Americans responded—by trying to insulate themselves from dangerous foreign elements and by limiting the political rights of strangers. The solutions devised in the 1780s to meet America's labor needs reflected the new priorities of postwar America. Both black and white immigrants were seen as elements of risk in a republican society, aliens who lacked both the qualities that constituted the "natural genius" of Americans and experience in self-government. Procedures were devised to admit to full citizenship foreigners with needed skills or attributes after they had been schooled and trained in republican ways. Other procedures were designed to discourage the immigration of those who lacked the moral or physical characteristics that seemed the necessary prerequisites for republican citizenship.

Although republican statesmen constricted access to American commerce and citizenship, they remained committed to the ideal of America as the true asylum for liberty—creating institutions that would preserve liberty for themselves, as well as mankind. The policies that resulted were amazingly liberal. Except for transported convicts, the American door remained open, despite republican doubts, fears, and prejudices, to all white immigrants. Americans who feared the consequences of large-scale immigration did not limit the right of the victims of Old World oppression to seek sanctuary in America; ineffectual laws that failed to keep out Europe's "wretched refuse" were not replaced with more stringent measures. Even after the adoption of discriminatory duties, no American markets were closed to foreign shipping. Even in the most restrictive states, the avenue to full citizenship was never completely closed to aliens as it was in Great Britain. And, in republican America, naturalization could be claimed by all free, white immigrants, including the Jews and Catholics who were denied that right in England.

7 *Immigrants and Politics in the 1790s*

THE FINAL CODIFICATION OF AMERICA'S ALIEN and naturalization policies was an integral part of the political battle in the 1790s to define the republic itself. The policies that evolved were thus the product of the differing hopes and fears of men who eventually coalesced in the Federalist and Republican parties. The divergent demographic principles of Americans who later became Federalists and Jeffersonian Republicans first appeared in the 1780s. Future Federalists revealed their traditional, mercantilist attitudes toward immigration and population growth during the first decade of independence, when they promoted immigration to increase the strength of the new nation and hasten its economic development. In the middle of the 1790s, the ramifications of the French Revolution destroyed Federalist confidence in the benefits to be derived from foreign-born subjects. Denying the nation's obligation to serve as an asylum for European radicals, Federalist lawmakers adopted Old World techniques to keep out undesirable foreigners and to emasculate the political rights of America's aliens.

During the first decade of independence, men who would become Jeffersonian Republicans were far less confident of the beneficial effects of immigration. Future Jeffersonians struggled to reconcile their conception of republican liberty and America's promise to serve as an asylum for the oppressed with doubts about the impact of foreigners on the nation's political, economic, and social development. American laws that delayed full political rights for aliens and naturalized immigrants were shaped by these doubts. Republicans who feared the expansion of governmental power opposed immigrant subsidies because they would extend the power of the government and hasten the economic and demographic developments that could turn their young and virtuous republic into a mature and corrupt state. Yet, despite their fears, Jeffersonians opposed the adoption of Old World measures to deny sanctuary to the victims of oppressive governments. Their opposition to the Alien, Sedition, and Naturalization Acts of 1798 was based not on the desire to augment the republic's population or the need for immigrant votes, but on their fear of Federalist initiatives and their commitment to preserving America as an asylum for both liberty and mankind.

Withholding Official Sanction

The 1790s opened with a sense of cautious optimism, with the hope that the defects in America's central government that had contributed to economic and political malaise in the 1780s would be remedied by the Constitution of 1787. According to its supporters, the benefits to be derived from the new constitution included increased immigration, as foreigners, "Induced by the goodly prospect of a happy and durable government, by which life, religion, freedom, and property would be well secured . . . will fly from the slavery, persecution, tyranny and wars of Europe."[1] Therefore, national lawmakers continued to operate on the assumption that the republic's natural resources and free government would be sufficient to attract all the foreigners the nation needed.

Even though many American statesmen as private citizens promoted the immigration of individual artisans, laborers, or settlers for their own, personal profit, they usually refused, in their official capacities, to extend positive aid to immigrants or special privileges to encourage immigration. As an agent of the Society for Establishing Useful Manufactures, Alexander Hamilton recruited British manufacturers; as the Secretary of the Treasury, he refused to support plans for government subsidies to transport "the Poor, hard wrought, half fed, Inhabitants of Europ.[*sic*]" who were "Utterly unable to pay for a Passage to America." In the 1780s George Washington, in his private capacity as a Virginia planter, recruited indentured servants and an English farm manager. During those years he also participated in negotiations with an English manufacturer who was willing to contravene British statutes against the emigration of artisans and their tools to establish a woolen manufactory in Virginia. However, in 1791 Washington severed his connection with the woolen venture, believing that "it certainly would not carry an aspect very favorable to the dignity of the United States for the president in clandestine manner to entice the subjects of another nation to violate the laws." In 1794 President Washington announced to John Jay, "I have established it as a maxim neither to invite nor to discourage immigrants. My opinion is, that they will come hither as fast as the true interest and policy of the United States will be benefited by foreign population."[2]

---

[1] "A Jerseyman: To the citizens of New Jersey," in Merrill Jensen, ed., *Ratification of the Constitution by the States* (Madison: State Historical Society of Wisconsin, 1976–), III, 147 (quote); Samuel Whitwell, *An Oration Delivered to the Society of the Cincinnati, in . . . Massachusetts, July 4, 1789* (Boston, 1789), 12.

[2] Alexander Hamilton to Samuel Paterson, *Industrial and Commercial Correspondence of Alexander Hamilton, Anticipating His Report on Manufactures,* ed. Arthur Harrison Cole (Chicago: A. W. Shaw Co.,

In the 1790s the new national government also continued to use land sales for public revenue, rather than as subsidies for prospective immigrants. In 1790 federal lawmakers rejected the petition from Hannibal William Dobbyn, an Irishman who asked Congress to "grant him a tract of land on such reasonable terms, as may encourage him to bring settlers to this country." Two months earlier, Pennsylvania's legislators had refused a similar request by Dobbyn, reasoning that "although the settlement of the western lands is an object very desirable, and worthy the attention and encouragement of the General Assembly—yet . . . the terms proposed by the petition are inadmissible." Alexander Hamilton's "Report on Vacant Lands" supported the previous Congressional emphasis on fiscal goals but also recommended the creation of regional land offices to accommodate individual settlers.[3] Even this was enough to alarm Phineas Bond, the British consul in Philadelphia, who warned the London foreign office that "this plan if carried into effect will lead to large speculation in lands which will be held forth for sale by the purchasers, and invite emigrants from Europe and elsewhere:—Many private holders of great tracts of lands are already in Europe endeavoring to dispose of their property." This was indeed Hamilton's intent. Since the settlement of America's western frontier was inevitable, Hamilton thought it "in every view best that it should be in great measure settled from abroad rather than at the entire expence of the Atlantic population." And British officials had no doubt that this latest republican plot to seduce their subjects would succeed. In their view, the American land ordinances were

> a new proposition to be offered to the numerous common rank of mankind in all the Countries of the world, to say that there are in America, fertile soils, & temperate climates, in which an acre of land may be purchased for a trifling value or consideration, which may be possessed in freedom, together with all the natural & civil rights of mankind. The Congress have already proclaimed this, & that no other qualification is necessary but to become *settlers* without distinction of Countries or

---

1928), 110 (quote); Joseph Stancliffe Davis, *Essays in the Earlier History of American Corporations*, 2 vols. (Cambridge: Harvard University Press, 1917), I, 398–401; Marcus Lee Hansen, *The Atlantic Migration, 1607–1860* (Cambridge: Harvard University Press, 1940), 56; Richard B. Morris, *Government and Labor in Early America* (New York: Columbia University Press, 1946), 514n; Herbert Heaton, "The Industrial Immigrant in the United States, 1783–1812," American Philosophical Society *Proceedings*, 95 (1951), 525; Washington to John Jay, Nov. 1, 1794, in *The Washington Papers*, ed. Saul K. Padover (New York: Grosset & Dunlap, 1955), 399 (quote). See also Alan Conway, "Welsh Emigration to the United States," *Perspectives in American History*, 7 (1973), 189–90, for the 1791 refusal of Thomas Pinckney, the American Ambassador to Great Britain, to intercede on behalf of Welshmen who hoped to emigrate to western New York.

[3] (Philadelphia) *Independent Gazetteer*, Nov. 19 (quote), 1789, Jan. 30 (quote), Apr. 24, 1790; Hansen, *Atlantic Migration*, 55–56; Merrill Jensen, *The New Nation: A History of the United States during the Confederation, 1781–1789* (New York: Knopf, 1950), 353–59; Alexander Hamilton, "Report on Vacant Lands," in *The Papers of Alexander Hamilton*, ed. Harold C. Syrett, 26 vols. (New York: Columbia University Press, 1961–1977), VI, 502–6.

persons. The European peasant who toils for his scanty sustenence in penury, wretchedness, & servitude, will eagerly fly to this asylum for free & industrious labour.[4]

Although the district land offices that would facilitate the sale of land in small parcels were not set up until 1800, the system established by American land ordinances was sufficient to attract European immigrants in the 1790s. The republican land sales system compared favorably with that of Canada, where much of the land remained unsurveyed and existing divisions had produced small, irregularly shaped plots that were ill suited to British farming methods. In addition, the inaccuracy of Canadian surveys and complex procedures for receiving crown grants caused tedious delays and litigation. As a result, emigrants to Canada often continued their journey south into the United States.[5] By protecting the political rights of settlers and assuring them of eventual incorporation into the nation, American land ordinances also made western settlement attractive to men of republican principles.

Even more important in promoting immigration were American land speculators. During the 1790s almost every American politician, from John Adams's son-in-law to President Washington, seemed to be involved in land deals in one form or another. In 1789 Gouverneur Morris went to Paris as the agent of Robert Morris, Pennsylvania's premier land speculator and U.S. Senator. Even after his appointment as confidential commissioner to negotiate treaty differences with England, Gouverneur Morris continued to advise prospective emigrants on land purchases. In addition to these political leaders, there were many private citizens and companies eager to enhance the value of their American land holdings. Thus there existed in the national government men with an interest in encouraging immigration, who, in turn, represented an even wider constituency. These were the men who decided not to recruit immigrants with offers of free land, but were anxious to formulate policies that would attract foreign tenants and buyers.[6]

[4]Quotes from Phineas Bond, Philadelphia, Jan. 3, 1791, to Duke of Leeds, in "Letters of Phineas Bond, British Consul at Philadelphia, to the Foreign Office of Great Britain, 1790–1794," ed. J. Franklin Jameson, *Annual Report of the American Historical Society for the Year 1897* (Washington, D.C.: Government Printing Office, 1898), 97; Hamilton, May 19, 1790, to Arthur St. Clair, in *Papers of Alexander Hamilton*, ed. Syrett, VI, 421; D. Hartley, Bath, England, to Marquis of Carmarthen, Jan. 9, 1785, British Foreign Office Archives, American Correspondence (microfilm).

[5]Stanley C. Johnson, *A History of Emigration from the United Kingdom to North America, 1763–1912* (London: George Routledge & Sons, 1913), 179–80, 197–201.

[6]Hansen, *Atlantic Migration*, 62–65; *Papers of Alexander Hamilton*, ed. Syrett, XXII, 178–79, 395–96; William Maclay, *The Journal of William Maclay, 1790*, 1st publ. 1890 (New York: Albert & Charles Boni, 1927), 209–11; Gouverneur Morris, *The Diary and Letters of Gouverneur Morris*, ed. Anne C. Morris, 2 vols. (New York: Charles Scribner's Sons, 1888), I, 18–19, 260–61, 322–24; A. M. Sakolski, *The Great American Land Bubble: The Amazing Story of Land-Grabbing, Speculations, and Booms from Colonial Days to the Present Time* (New York: Harper & Brothers, 1932).

Commercial Restrictions

National lawmakers refused to abandon the laissez-faire immigrant policies that had evolved during the 1780s, but they were more willing to expand the power of the central government to regulate commerce. The laws they devised to enhance the republic's economy added to the disabilities that confronted America's aliens. However, these new restrictions were not intended to deter or regulate immigration, but were the incidental effects of laws designed for other ends.

One of the primary goals of the framers of the Constitution of 1787 was to strengthen the republic's economy. British treatment of the independent states in the years after 1783 forced America's republicans to recognize the strength of mercantilist principles in practical politics. The British, French, and Spanish empires were not willing to be remade in the republican image and were strong enough to enforce their commercial system on the independent American states. The West India islands were seen by Americans as their "natural" trading partners. But these foreign ports were opened to republican shippers only when shortages allowed colonial governors to invoke their emergency power to authorize the importation of scarce commodities regardless of their provenance. Similarly, the opening of a few free ports in France was a French attempt to strengthen commercial ties with its American allies to the detriment of France's British rivals, rather than a rejection of mercantilist principles.[7]

The economic disarray of the American states during the Confederation period, produced largely by their inability to break into or break down the British Navigation system, convinced most American legislators of the futility of trying to implement a brave new international world of commerce and led them to adopt the measures that were being used against them. Acts imposing national tonnage and customs duties were passed at the first meeting of Congress under the 1787 Constitution. These laws were designed to protect and promote the growth of American commerce and manufactures by imposing larger imposts on ships and cargoes owned and produced in foreign countries than those produced or shipped by American citizens.[8]

As the first Congress was encircling the American market with the traditional barriers that conferred advantages on American shippers and manufacturers, it

[7]Felix Gilbert, *To the Farewell Address: Ideas of Early American Foreign Policy* (Princeton: Princeton University Press, 1961), 44–75; Thomas Jefferson, Paris, to G. K. van Hogendorp, Oct. 13, 1785, in *Thomas Jefferson: Writings*, ed. Merrill D. Peterson (New York: Library of America, 1984), 834–37; Henry Blumenthal, *France and the United States: Their Diplomatic Relations, 1789–1914* (New York: Norton, 1970), 3–9.

[8]Charles R. Ritcheson, *Aftermath of Revolution: British Policy toward the United States, 1783–1795* (New York: Norton, 1969), 92–94, 117; Drew R. McCoy, *The Elusive Republic: Political Economy in Jeffersonian America* (New York: Norton, 1980), 136–46, 162–65.

completely closed the nation's coasting trade and fisheries to vessels that were not American-built and wholly owned by American citizens. These commercial regulations were the result of international economic rivalry and were not designed to discriminate against bona fide immigrants who chose to resettle in a republican society, as opposed to the agents of foreign firms who took up temporary residence in the American states to increase their personal wealth and that of their native lands. Nonetheless, these laws did bar aliens from the republic's fisheries and coasting trade and handicap immigrant traders in the American market for at least the period required to attain citizenship, which varied from two years in 1790 to fourteen years in 1798.[9]

Other policy decisions by the national government worked, incidentally, to inhibit the arrival of immigrants on American shores. The Quarantine Act of 1796 was designed to lend the power of the national government to states that were having difficulty enforcing quarantine procedures on vessels that threatened to infect port communities. The issues involved in this legislation were matters of public health and the relative roles of the state and national governments in determining and handling emergency situations. Quarantine procedures worked most harshly and dramatically on immigrants who had been packed into overcrowded ships that lacked proper sanitation facilities and thereby fell prey to infectious disease. But the regulations were not designed to discriminate against immigrants. As public health measures, quarantine acts worked equally on the native-born and foreigners, whether crew members or passengers, and on all cargoes arriving from infected ports or carrying infectious diseases.[10]

The Political Spectrum

Prior to 1798 the republic's official position on immigration was defined in the debates and laws establishing national citizenship requirements. Although the Constitution of 1787 gave Congress the responsibility of creating a uniform naturalization policy for the nation, members of Congress had no mandate or desire to formulate an extensive code governing the rights of aliens and naturalized immigrants. Regulations concerning alien land titles and local occupational restrictions thus remained in the hands of the states and local communities. Individual states also retained the right to set their own franchise requirements and

[9] Stuart Bruchey, *The Roots of American Economic Growth, 1607–1861: An Essay in Social Causation* (New York: Harper & Row, 1965), 112–13; *The Papers of James Madison*, ed. William T. Hutchinson et al. (Charlottesville: University of Virginia Press, 1962–), XV, 424–25.

[10] Joseph Gales, ed., *Annals of the Congress of the United States*, 42 vols. (Washington, D.C.: Gales and Seaton, 1834–1856), 4th Cong., 1347–59, 2916; Hansen, *Atlantic Migration*, 55; J. H. Powell, *Bring Out Your Dead: The Great Plague of Yellow Fever in Philadelphia in 1793* (Philadelphia: University of Pennsylvania Press, 1949), 14–15, 238–44.

could allow aliens to vote or, on the other hand, postpone that right for even naturalized foreigners for a term of years. As a result, it is only in the proceedings of the Constitutional Convention and Congressional debates on naturalization requirements that the spectrum of political and demographic hopes and fears that shaped the nation's immigrant policies at the end of the eighteenth century are revealed.

The two political parties that emerged in the 1790s subscribed to different theories about the social, economic, and political development best suited for a republic and consequently disagreed on the type of foreigner and magnitude of immigration necessary to achieve those goals. Until the end of the 1790s, Jeffersonians were more skeptical about mass immigration than their political opponents. Men who became Jeffersonians believed that "the people" should play an active and meaningful role in governing. It was therefore vital that immigrants have the attributes necessary for participation in American political life. Jeffersonians believed that the ideal immigrant should have least some training in self-government and the ability to recognize and resist encroachments on his liberty by men in power; he also needed economic self-sufficiency to maintain his political independence. Jeffersonians also tended to subscribe to the cyclical theory of history, which taught that decay was an inevitable consequence of social maturity; they saw Great Britain as a prime example of a mature and decadent society that could no longer maintain liberty. Jeffersonians therefore hoped to postpone the development of the republic's young, agrarian economy into a mature manufacturing society, with its noisome cities filled with dependent wage-earners, whose livelihoods often depended on the whims of a parasitic elite. Since population growth fostered the maturation they dreaded, Jeffersonians did not encourage large-scale immigration. While most Jeffersonians worked to maintain republican America as an asylum of liberty and a sanctuary for those oppressed by tyranny, they also believed that natural increase alone would provide a population sufficient to make the American republic a strong nation of independent yeomen.[11]

In the 1790s America's Federalists worked to create a very different republican society, based on efficient government by "the better sort" and the British mercantilist model. They anticipated a limited participation of the common people in governing. Federalists believed that the role of the ordinary American citizen was to select his rulers, representatives whose judgment and motives he trusted; once elected, these representatives would implement the policies they believed most beneficial to the public welfare. The political quality the Federalists hoped to find in their ideal immigrant was not economic self-sufficiency as much as the ability to recognize and elect "the better sort" and then to defer to their judgment. The economic future envisioned by the Federalists was patterned

[11] The best description of the Jeffersonian principles that shaped Republican attitudes toward immigration and population growth is in McCoy, *The Elusive Republic.*

after that of Great Britain, a fully developed economy based on commercial credit and manufacturing. Because a manufacturing society needed an inexpensive and plentiful labor force, the Federalists were not alarmed by the prospect of large-scale immigration and recruited men with technological skills and tenants for their land, as well as men of property. Until the middle of the 1790s both Jeffersonians and Federalists assumed that most foreigners who emigrated to America would bring with them Old World political values and skills and thus promote Federalist goals.[12]

These differing demographic perspectives first appeared in the postwar debate over the readmission of American loyalists. New Yorkers, who, a decade later, became leaders of the Federalist party, advocated expanding the republic's population by allowing the return of men whose traditional principles they did not fear and whose capital and skills were needed to develop the American economy along British lines. Some radical republicans who insisted on the permanent exclusion of American tories were driven by the need for revenge. But more moderate arguments against their readmission were shaped by a distaste for the loyalists' conservative political principles by Americans who hoped to maintain and advance the revolutionary aspects of their new governments and by men who had reservations about rapid population growth and the maturation of American society.[13]

In the decade following the peace of 1783 many of the men who later became Federalists championed the immigrant while future Jeffersonians were questioning the wisdom of "The present desire of America . . . to produce rapid population by as great importations of foreigners as possible" and speculating that the American republic might be "more homogeneous, more peaceable, more durable" if it relied on natural increase rather than foreigners to expand its population.[14] Americans who were less insistent on limiting the power and scope of government than Jeffersonians also were more willing to use official power to encourage immigration. Thus in 1787 the leading supporters of a New York bill

---

[12] John Zvesper, *Political Philosophy and Rhetoric: A Study of the Origins of American Party Politics* (Cambridge: Oxford University Press, 1977); Gerald Stourz, *Alexander Hamilton and the Idea of Republican Government* (Stanford, Calif.: Stanford University Press, 1970); Manning J. Dauer, *The Adams Federalists* (Baltimore: Johns Hopkins University Press, 1953); Carl E. Prince, *The Federalists and the Origins of the U.S. Civil Service* (New York: New York University Press, 1977); David Hackett Fischer, *The Revolution of American Conservatism: The Federalist Party in the Era of Jeffersonian Democracy* (New York: Harper & Row, 1965); Linda K. Kerber, *Federalists in Dissent: Imagery and Ideology in Jeffersonian America* (Ithaca: Cornell University Press, 1970).

[13] For arguments used in the 1780s for and against the readmission of the Loyalists, see Chapter 6. Americans who urged leniency for returning tories and later became Jeffersonians tended to base their arguments on America's need to maintain its liberty and prove its humanity, rather than on the benefits to be reaped from a burgeoning population or loyalist property. See Lowell H. Harrison, *John Breckinridge: Jeffersonian Republican* (Louisville, Ky.: Filson Club, 1969), 16; "Aedanus Burke," in Allen Johnson and Dumas Malone, eds., *The Dictionary of American Biography*, 20 vols. (New York: Charles Scribner's Sons, 1928–1936), III, 280.

[14] Thomas Jefferson, *Notes on the State of Virginia*, 1782 (New York: Harper & Row, 1964), 82 (quotes); Harrison, *John Breckinridge*, 21, n.71.

"to enable the commissioners of the land office to convey to Mr. Noble, two townships of ten miles square, at a shilling per acre, for the purpose of settling Irish emigrants" were men who became leaders of the state's Federalist party. The proposal by Assemblyman William Malcom, the future Clintonian Republican "that the act should stipulate that those to whom land was conveyed by Noble be citizens and freeholders" was defeated by Alexander Hamilton and Samuel Jones, the former Tory and future Federalist. Hamilton and Jones argued that the bill should contain "no limitation or stipulation" on those Arthur Noble, a naturalized Irishman, chose to settle on his land. According to Hamilton, "Mr. Noble was a gentleman of fortune, whose ambition was to improve a great waste tract of our country, and . . . ought to have every encouragement the state could give." Hamilton also argued that "it was not within the province of the house to interfere at present, between Mr. Noble and those whom he might induce to come with him from Ireland."[15]

Three years after Hamilton denied the right of the New York Assembly to interfere in the Irish colonization project, he was urging Arthur St. Clair, governor of the Northwest Territory, to provide special protection for the French immigrants under his jurisdiction. According to Hamilton, "humanity and policy both demand our best efforts to countenance and protect them" since "it is certainly wise by kind treatment to lay hold of the affections of the settlers and attach them from the beginning to the Government of the Nation." Hamilton believed "that *various* dispositions should actuate those who people the Western Territory; which will be a consequence of emigrations from other countries." He hoped that protection by American troops and official "tenderness" might induce these foreigners to "render a favourable account of their situation to the country from which they come" that could produce untold numbers of additional immigrants.[16] These incidents clearly demonstrate that xenophobia was not inherent in the Federalist philosophy.

The Federal Debate Begins

In the 1790s Federalist leaders often expressed traditional, mercantilist beliefs on the benefits produced by a large population; many favored the adoption of traditional devices to attract the valuable subjects of rival nations. A large influx of foreign workers and capital could help men of Federalist principles achieve their

[15] *Papers of Alexander Hamilton,* ed. Syrett, IV, 66–67 (New York Assembly debate and quotes); Alfred F. Young, *The Democratic Republicans of New York: The Origins, 1763–1797* (Chapel Hill: University of North Carolina Press, 1967), 40, 50–51, 150.

[16] Hamilton to St. Clair, May 19, 1790, in *Papers of Alexander Hamilton,* ed. Syrett, VI, 421. According to Hamilton, General Henry Knox viewed "the matter in the same light with myself," whereas President Washington "has been for some time too ill to be talked to; but I have no doubt of his good will to the emigrants."

goals—whether settling the west, producing rents or profits from land sales, promoting domestic manufactures, or remaking the American economy along British lines. And, since Federalists did not fear the expansion of governmental power, they were not as reluctant to use their official power to encourage the immigrants they coveted as were future Jeffersonians. When at the end of the 1790s foreign immigrants seemed to endanger their vision of republican America, Federalist leaders also adopted traditional, Old World policies to neutralize foreign radicals. Jeffersonian Republicans, on the other hand, eschewed Old World practices throughout the decade, refusing to subsidize immigration, support measures that closed off the republic to foreign refugees, or limit the rights of aliens.

The national debate over alien policies in the 1790s also was shaped by America's wartime pledge to prepare an asylum for liberty and mankind. Americans were always aware of the dangers posed by "undesirable" foreigners and vehemently denied their obligation to receive Europe's depraved masses. However, vocal groups stoutly maintained their nation's obligation to serve as a refuge for the victims of European oppression, to prove their probity and republican principles. Even more Americans agreed that their governments could not institute policies that abridged the rights of aliens in ways that violated republican principles, because such measures could destroy their own liberty. As a result, America's political leaders were constantly forced to weigh the need to safeguard the republic from the deleterious consequences of immigration against the need to maintain the nation's republican principles and honor.

In debating what alien rights were appropriate to republican government delegates to the Constitutional Convention of 1787 balanced their fear of the political beliefs and attachments that foreigners (and returning loyalists) brought with them against America's revolutionary principles and promises. The delegates agreed that some period of acculturation was necessary before granting full political rights to foreigners, but voted down Gouverneur Morris's motion to require fourteen years of citizenship before an alien could be elected to the U.S. Senate, largely because it would impart "a tincture of illiberality to the Constitution."[17] James Madison believed that a fourteen-year probationary period would "discourage the most desireable class of people from emigrating to the United States. Should the proposed Constitution have the intended effect of giving stability and reputation to our governments, great numbers of respectable Europeans: men who love liberty and wish to partake its blessings, will be ready to transfer their fortunes hither. All such would feel the mortification of being marked with suspicious incapacitations though they should not covet the public honors." Both Benjamin Franklin and Edmund Randolph supported Madison and pointed out the many friends they had in Europe and the strangers who had served the

[17] *Notes of Debates in the Federal Convention of 1787, Reported by James Madison,* ed. Adrienne Koch (Athens: Ohio University Press, 1995), 419 (quote), 420.

republic so faithfully during the Revolution. Neither wanted "to see anything like illiberality inserted in the Constitution," although Randolph thought it "problematical whether emigrations to this country were on the whole useful or not." On the other hand, Pierce Butler, who had emigrated from Ireland to South Carolina as a British army officer in 1770, opposed "the admission of foreigners without a long residence in the country. They bring with them, not only attachments to other countries, but ideas of government so distinct from ours that in every point of view they are dangerous." And it was Gouverneur Morris's contention that "The men who can shake off their attachments to their own country can never love any other."[18]

The debate over the qualifications for U.S. representatives produced a similar spectrum of opinions. Elbridge Gerry claimed to be speaking for "A great many of the most influential men in Massts." when he urged that eligibility be confined to natives. He feared that "Foreign powers will intermeddle in our affairs and spare no expence to influence them. Persons having foreign attachments will be sent among us and insinuated into our councils, to be made instruments for their purposes. Every one knows the vast sums laid out in Europe for secret services." Hugh Williamson of North Carolina believed that "Wealthy emigrants do more harm by their luxurious examples, than good, by the money, they bring with them." Alexander Hamilton thought the immigration of "Persons in Europe of moderate fortunes" should be encouraged. And James Madison, seconded by James Wilson of Pennsylvania, reiterated his call for "foreigners of merit & republican principles." The delegates eventually settled the issue by requiring seven years' of citizenship for U.S. representatives and nine years for U.S. senators and by handing Congress the responsibility of establishing a uniform rule of naturalization.[19]

Federal naturalization debates began in February 1790 at the first session of the first Congress under the new Constitution and continued, intermittently, until the passage of the fourth Naturalization Act in 1802. During these twelve years American lawmakers tried to formulate a naturalization procedure that would resolve the basic ambiguity of their desire for a populous and prosperous country and their concern for safeguarding the new republic. Terms had to be devised that were liberal enough to attract desirable immigrants and consistent with America's republican principles and promise to serve as an asylum for liberty, yet stringent enough to winnow out unsuitable candidates for citizenship. These concerns shaped America's first four naturalization acts. Differences in the provisions for citizenship in these four statutes reflect the

[18] Samuel Eliot Morison, ed., *Sources and Documents Illustrating the American Revolution, 1764–1788, and the Formation of the Federal Constitution*, 2d ed. (London: Oxford University Press, 1965), 279–82. Of these speakers, only Gouverneur Morris became a Federalist in the 1790s.

[19] Max Farrand, ed., *The Records of the Federal Convention of 1787*, 4 vols. (New Haven: Yale University Press, 1911–1937), II, 268–69.

effect of international and domestic developments on the legislators' assessment of the ability of foreigners to uphold the republican future they envisioned for America.

Volitional Citizenship

Naturalization policy also was shaped by the new American concept of citizenship. By the end of 1783 Great Britain had been stripped of a large portion of its population, through wartime deaths and desertions and the loss of over two million colonial subjects. Determined to prevent further losses, British officials stoutly maintained the principle of citizenship based on birthright and perpetual allegiance that held that the British could not simply renounce the allegiance they owed their king. The tie between British subjects and their monarch could only be dissolved by treason. Thus only those Britons who had resided in the colonies during the Revolution and had forsworn their natural allegiance by engaging in war against their king were recognized by Great Britain as citizens of the United States. In formulating this position, Great Britain hoped not only to deter the emigration of its subjects, but also to establish the legal foundation by which England could reclaim those who defied its laws and settled in the new republic after the American Revolution.[20]

As Great Britain was clarifying its official position on subjectship through propaganda, orders in council, and parliamentary acts, a new concept of volitional citizenship was evolving in the United States that challenged traditional precepts. The American revolutionaries had rested their claim for independence on a contractual theory of allegiance, one that could be nullified or broken. During the war for independence Americans were confronted with the problem of how to deal with neighbors who denied that the contract been the colonists and George III had been abrogated. These loyalists refused to renounce their old allegiance and accept the legitimacy of the new state governments. Although wartime conditions produced some expedient compromises, Americans emerged from the Revolution with the idea that individuals had the right to choose their own loyalty, that citizenship could not be forced on anyone and subjectship was not perpetual. To be legitimate, a government had to rest on the consent of the governed. Although these ideas were not new, it was only after the American Revolution that they were implemented. England, after the Glorious Revolution, had theoretically based its government on these same principles, yet had developed a concept of citizenship based on birthright and perpetual allegiance.[21] Thus the republican concept of citizenship was an untested

---

[20] James H. Kettner, *The Development of American Citizenship, 1608–1870* (Chapel Hill: University of North Carolina Press, 1978), 183–87, 269–70.

[21] Ibid., chaps. 6–8.

theory that postwar Americans tried to implement while the Old World denied its validity.

In addition to any doubts Americans may have had about breaking with English precedent, volitional and contractual allegiance in itself embodied certain threatening implications. The right of an individual to join a community implied the reciprocal right of voluntary expatriation. As the American Revolution had been based on this claim, the new republic could hardly deny its citizens that right, although only Virginia expressly guaranteed "that natural right which all men may have of relinquishing the country in which birth or other accident may have thrown them, and seeking subsistence and happiness wheresoever they may be able, or may hope to find them." The right of expatriation gave volitional allegiance a somewhat transitory and unstable character. Once a naturalized citizen swore his allegiance to the United States, nothing could prevent him from renouncing his new loyalty and actively promoting the interests of another country. Furthermore, a citizen might escape prosecution for treason by claiming that he had previously renounced his allegiance. To counteract this possibility, Secretary of State Thomas Jefferson pointed out that "the laws do not admit that the bare commission of a crime amounts of itself to a divestment of the character of citizen, and withdraws the criminal from their coercion. They could never prescribe an illegal act among the legal modes by which a citizen must disfranchise himself; nor render treason, for instance, innocent, by giving it the force of a dissolution of the obligation of the criminal to his country."[22] But without a legal definition, the American republic had no grounds for revoking the citizenship of potential traitors. For this reason it was vitally important to establish a naturalization process that would admit only men dedicated to republican ideals and American interests.

The Naturalization Act of 1790

The 1790 Congressional debates on the nation's first naturalization act revolved around the issues that had been skirted earlier in the Constitutional Convention. Three basic positions emerged from these deliberations. Each group was a coalition of men reasoning from differing assumptions and principles. The group arguing for virtually no impediments for foreigners desiring American citizenship contained republican idealists who advocated an open American society that would serve as an asylum for the international community of people and traditionalists who simply believed that people were the wealth of a nation. At the

---

[22] Ibid., quotes on 268, 269. The proposal to add a provision to the Naturalization Act of 1795 barring American expatriates from being readmitted as citizens is evidence of America's continuing concern over the voluntary nature of republican citizenship and the right of peaceful expatriation. Gales, ed., *Annals of Congress, 5th Cong.*, 1005–6.

other extreme were those who preferred to leave American lands vacant rather than admit strangers who lacked the experience or principles necessary to uphold "true" republicanism. In the middle was a large coalition of liberals who were anxious to maintain the nation's principles and reputation and moderates who would welcome the wealth foreigners would add—both of whom felt that some period of apprenticeship was needed before immigrants could be entrusted with the full rights of citizenship.

The Constitutional Convention's decision to shift the burden of establishing a uniform naturalization code to the U.S. Congress transferred the debate over citizenship policies and alien rights from the states to the national arena. While voicing the same arguments, and building on postwar experiments in the states, national legislators faced different constraints. Ultimately, constitutional issues would lead the members of Congress to different conclusions about what naturalization procedures and alien rights were consistent with their vision of republicanism and the nation's future development.

The naturalization bill that was introduced in the First Congress followed state models quite closely. It would have granted an alien after a single year's residence "all the rights of citizenship, except being capable of holding an office under the State or General Government, which capacity they are to acquire after a residence of two years more." In proposing "citizenship by progression," this bill adopted the mechanism devised by state legislatures in the years immediately following the Revolution, when anti-tory sentiment was running high. The admission of aliens to citizenship by steps was the compromise that had allowed the states to reap the anticipated mercantilist benefits of immigration and prove their humanity and honor to the watching world while neutralizing the danger of endowing men "of tory principles" with the power to subvert republican government.[23]

A familiar mixture of arguments emerged when the members of the U.S. House of Representatives began debating the naturalization bill of 1790. John Page of Virginia, stated the case for the idealists on the opening day of debate: we shall be inconsistent with ourselves if, after boasting of having opened an asylum for the oppressed of all nations, and established a Government which is the admiration of the world, we make the terms of admission to the full enjoyment of that asylum so hard as is now proposed. It is nothing to us whether Jews or Roman Catholics settle amongst us; whether subjects of Kings, or citizens of free States wish to reside in the United States, they will find it in their interest to be good citizens, and neither their religious nor political opinions can injure us, if we have good laws well executed."

Page was supported by the mercantilist arguments of Representative John

[23] Gales, ed., *Annals of Congress, 1st Cong.*, 1109–23; quotes on: 1109 (Lawrence), 1110 (Page). For the "citizenship by progression" model in the states see ibid., 1112, 1113, and Chapter 6 of this book.

Lawrence who would become a stalwart of New York's Federalist party. Lawrence argued that "every person, rich or poor, must add to our wealth and strength, in a greater or less degree." Nonetheless, the House was almost unanimous in its opposition to becoming an asylum for all who would apply or be sent. According to James Madison, it was "very desirable that we should hold out as many inducements as possible for the worthy part of mankind to come and settle amongst us, and throw their fortunes into a common lot with ours. But why is this desirable? Not merely to swell the catalogue of people. No, sir, it is to increase the wealth and strength of the community; and those who acquire the rights of citizenship, without adding to the strength or wealth of the community are not the people we are in want of."

Representative Burke of South Carolina, an "ardent democrat" who had emigrated from Ireland in the late 1760s, thought it important "to fill the country with useful men, such as farmers, mechanics, and manufacturers" and recommended receiving this class on "liberal terms." On the other hand, he "did not care what impediments were erected to keep out European merchants and their factors who come with a view of remaining so long as will enable them to acquire a fortune." Burke also recommended making the importation of "the convicts and criminals which they pour out of British jails" a high misdemeanor.[24]

Although the arguments and concerns were similar, constitutional issues prevented the U.S. Congress from adopting the state model of "step-by step citizenship." John Lawrence raised the first problem when he asked how, in a country that had established the "principle that taxation and representation ought to go hand and hand," aliens who had "to pay taxes from the time they settle amongst us" could be denied the right to vote and hold office for a period of years. The nearly unanimous belief of the members of the House in the need for a probationary period before granting political power to aliens prevented a resolution of this anomaly.[25]

Even though it would take five years, Congress was more successful in resolving the problem introduced in 1790 by James Madison's observation that "It may be a question of some nicety, how far we can make our law to admit an alien to the right of citizenship, step by step." At first, members of the House of Representatives saw no problem in disposing of Madison's query as they cited international and historical precedent and the new Constitution to prove that they could, if they wished, limit the rights of aliens and "admit a man in the rights of citizenship by progression." According to Thomas Hartley of Pennsylvania, "ever

---

[24] Debate, Feb. 3, 1790, Gales, ed., *Annals of Congress, 1st Cong.*, quotes on 1110 (Page), 1115 (Lawrence), 1111 (Madison), 1117–18 (Burke); Johnson and Malone, eds., *The Dictionary of American Biography*, XI, 31–32 (John Laurence); III, 280 (Aedanus Burke); XIV, 137–38 (John Page); Prince, *Federalists and the Origins of the U.S. Civil Service*, 75, 83, 243, 245.

[25] Gales, ed., *Annals of Congress, 1st Cong.*, quote on 1111 (Lawrence).

since the foundation of the Roman Empire" it had been "The policy of the old nations of Europe" to draw "a line between citizens and aliens." Representatives William L. Smith of South Carolina and Hartley cited state practice, showing how the laws of "several States admit aliens to the privilege of citizenship, step by step," with South Carolina granting "citizenship for certain purposes at first, extending them afterwards as the person is fitted to receive them."[26] Several representatives used the new Constitution to justify progressive citizenship. They argued that, because the Constitution gave Congress the mandate "to create a uniform rule of naturalization," Congress could use that power to confer limited rights, or a gradual acquisition of the full rights of American citizenship.[27] Furthermore, the Constitution itself had limited the rights of naturalized foreigners by requiring "additional terms of residence . . . to [their] right of holding a seat in the House and in the Senate, and of being chosen President" and in declaring "that no other than a natural born citizen, or a citizen at the time of the adoption of this Constitution, shall be eligible to the office of President." Thus, as Representative Thomas Tucker pointed out, the Constitution "plainly infers" that a foreigner "might have been a citizen for other purposes, with a shorter residence."[28]

However, as the debate progressed, unexpected complexities cropped up. The first emerged when Representative Page pointed out "that the policy of European nations and States respecting naturalization did not apply to the situation of the United States. Bigotry and superstition, or a deep-rooted prejudice against the Government, laws, religion, or manners of neighboring nations had a weight in that policy, which cannot exist here, where a more liberal system ought to prevail." Elias Boudinot of New Jersey thought "that after a person was admitted to the rights of citizenship, he ought to have them full and complete, and not be divested of any part."[29] But the most serious roadblocks to progressive citizenship were constitutional—the belief that Congress could not exceed its enumerated powers or invade the rights of the states[30] and the comity clause that guaranteed that "The citizens of each State shall be entitled to all privileges and immunities of citizens in the several States."[31] Several representatives employed states' rights arguments to oppose progressive citizenship. For example, Thomas Tucker of South Carolina "had no doubt the Government had a right to make the admission to citizenship progressive," but he saw the bill's "interference with the State Governments," by dictating qualifications for state

---

[26] Gales, ed., Annals of Congress, quotes on 1113 (Thomas Hartley); 1112 (William Loughton Smith).

[27] Ibid., 1112 (Smith of South Carolina).

[28] Ibid., 1113 (Hartley), 1116 (Tucker).

[29] Ibid., 1110 (Page and Boudinot).

[30] These constraints became even more overt and compelling when the 10th Amendment, which expressly reserved to the States all "powers not delegated to the United States by the Constitution, nor prohibited by it to the States," was ratified in 1792.

[31] U.S. Constitution, Article IV, sec. 2.

officeholders, "improper; and hoped, therefore, that the bill would be confined solely to the objects of the General Government."[32] Alexander White of Virginia argued that, as the "Constitution had expressly said how long [aliens] should reside among us before they were admitted to seats in the [Federal] Legislature; the propriety of annexing any additional qualification is therefore much to be questioned . . . it may be doubly questioned how far Congress has the power to declare what residence shall entitle an alien to the right of a seat in the State Legislature." Representative White then used the comity clause to deliver the coup de grace to progressive citizenship by pointing out that "After a person has become a citizen, the power of Congress ceases to operate upon him" as "a citizen of one State is entitled to all the privileges and immunities of the citizens in the several States." Therefore, there could be no partial citizenship for aliens naturalized by federal statute.[33]

The Naturalization Act of 1790 evaded, rather than resolved, many of the questions raised during this session of Congress. The Act eschewed progressive naturalization by providing simply "That any alien, being a free white person" who had resided "under the jurisdiction of the United States for the term of two years, may be admitted to become a citizen thereof, on application to any common law court of record in any one of the States wherein he shall have resided for the term of one year at least," proved his "good character . . . to the satisfaction of the court," and had taken "the oath or affirmation prescribed by law, to support the Constitution of the United States." Other things the Act did not do also are significant. The Naturalization Act of 1790 scrupulously respected the rights of the states. Its final sentence provided "That no person heretofore proscribed by any State shall be admitted a citizen aforesaid except by an act of the legislature of the State in which such person was proscribed." No attempt was made to invade the right of the individual states to regulate their internal affairs—the states would continue to decide the rights and disabilities of their resident aliens and who should or should not vote or hold local office. And, there was no clause that announced that the new federal naturalization procedure was exclusive, which resulted in the naturalizing of aliens under state as well as federal statute between 1790 and 1795.[34]

The Naturalization Act of 1790 was a compromise measure that fell short of the visionary goals of American idealists. John Page in the House and Samuel Maclay in the Senate failed in their fight to expunge all residency requirements from what Maclay termed "a vile bill, illiberal and void of philanthropy." For the majority of the legislators, however, philanthropy had never been a serious consideration. Colonial experience testified to the validity of Representative Sedgwick's fears of "being overrun with the outcasts of Europe." The failed

[32] Gales, ed., *Annals of Congress, 1st Cong.*, 1116 (Tucker quotes); 1115.
[33] Ibid., 1111, 1113.
[34] "An Act to Establish a Uniform Rule of Naturalization," 1790, in ibid., 2205–6.

attempt to establish a "denizen class" mandated the adoption of a probationary period during which an immigrant's character could be observed and the alien acculturated to American values and interests before being entrusted with full political rights. While republican principles and fears generated temporary political disabilities for aliens, those principles, combined with the need to uphold America's reputation abroad and to honor her pledge to create a republican asylum for liberty led Congress to adopt a surprisingly liberal policy. These considerations resulted in a two-year residency rather than the three- to seven-year terms proposed by Representatives Tucker and Stone and the promise of full citizenship for naturalized aliens, barred only from the office of president.[35]

The French Revolution

By 1795 growing national fears about the future of republicanism led America to revise its requirements for citizenship. Disturbing international and domestic developments increased the demand for American unity and homogeneity. With the splintering of America's political leadership into two increasingly hostile parties, both sides attempted to use foreign voters and American xenophobia to annihilate their political opponents and win the support of America's "true" republicans. More and more emphasis was placed on protecting the nation from disruptive alien elements and less on a concern that men of good character and sound principles might be kept away by "illiberal" laws. In 1790 Representative Burke had asserted that "foreigners made as good citizens of Republics as the natives themselves. Frenchmen, brought up under an absolute Monarchy, evinced their love of liberty in the late arduous struggle; many of them are now worthy citizens, who esteem and venerate the principles of our Revolution."[36] But events in Europe seemed to demonstrate the fragility of republican institutions and the inability of Europeans to maintain that form of government. By absorbing neighboring states, France had involved existing European republics in its own revolution. Thus the corruption of the French Republic subverted republican government throughout Europe. The French Revolution also divided the United States into irreconcilable factions that seemed to spell disaster in a country ruled by the people.

At the beginning of the French Revolution most Americans gloried in the spectacle of their former allies following in America's footsteps. As Gouverneur Morris wrote from Paris, "The leaders here are our friends; many of them have imbibed their principles in America, and all have been fired by our example." At home, American newspapers made the same observation. The *Boston Gazette*

---

[35] *Journal of William Maclay*, 203; Gales, ed., *Annals of Congress, 1st Cong.*, 1116–18.
[36] Ibid., 1123.

proclaimed that "liberty will have another feather in her cap. The seraphic contagion was caught from Britain, it crossed the Atlantic to North America, from whence the flame has been communicated to France." But even in these early years the French Revolution was sowing seeds of doubt in America. In April 1790 John Adams was already voicing his foreboding. Adams did not know "what to make of a republic of thirty million atheists. . . . Too many Frenchmen, like too many Americans, pant for equality of persons and property. The impracticality of this God Almighty has decreed, and the advocates for liberty who attempt it will surely suffer for it."[37]

The division between Federalists and Republicans was a natural outgrowth of American experience and reflected personal, ideological differences between men with differing visions for the future of the republic and the role of the people in government. The French Revolution widened these differences and increased the stridency of each group. The execution of Louis XVI prompted John Adams to ask, "When will these savages be satiated with blood?" The *Vermont Gazette*, on the other hand, refused to judge "whether the execution of Louis XVI was politic or impolitic," but declared that "the general fact that the French people have the right to chuse whatever form of government they please admits of no doubt." And the *National Gazette* published an article entitled "Louis Capet has lost his Caput," in which the author described the incident as "no more than the execution of another malefactor."[38]

The violence of the French Revolution that divided Americans also produced war between Great Britain and republican France. This, in turn, heightened the differences between the pro-British Federalists and francophile Republicans. Americans were soon split into two warring camps, and both sides grew increasingly wary of the foreign supporters of their adversaries. As Federalists began to question the value of mass immigration, Jeffersonians witnessed the apparent confirmation of their fear of the political impact of foreigners who clung to monarchical principles. The result was the politicization of America's alien policies and increased requirements for citizenship.

"The Wild Irish"

By 1795 several events had demonstrated the political danger of adding foreigners to the nation's population. In 1793 the triumphal march of French Ambassador Edmond Genêt from South Carolina to Philadelphia produced public demonstrations by immigrants as well as native-born Americans. This outpour-

---

[37] Morris, Paris, April 29, 1789, to President Washington, in *Diary and Letters of Gouverneur Morris*, I, 68; *Boston Gazette*, in Charles Downer Hazen, *Contemporary American Opinion of the French Revolution*, 1st publ. 1897 (Gloucester, Mass.: Peter Smith, 1964), quotes on 142 (*Boston Gazette*), 153 (John Adams).

[38] Ibid., quotes on 254, 255, 257.

ing of support for French revolutionary principles disabused the Federalists of their assumption that immigrants arriving from the Old World would exhibit in America the traditional values and deference allegedly inculcated in them from birth. Federalists also were dismayed by the tumultuous welcome extended to English "Jacobins," who, driven from Great Britain for their treasonous support of the French Revolution, began seeking refuge in republican America in 1793. The democratic clubs that sprouted everywhere to support French radicalism and subvert the constituted authority that the Federalists had so carefully crafted seemed to be the work of men infected by European Jacobinism and encouraged by foreign agitators and the Federalists' domestic political opponents. In 1794 the Whiskey Rebellion in the western counties of Pennsylvania gave evidence of the subversive radicalism of at least one group of immigrants, the Irish. According to a report from Fort Pitt in August of 1794, "The wild Irish" had "assumed the reigns [*sic*], and have threatened to shoot every man who may not choose to oppose the old, in hopes to establish a new government. Brackenridge, Gallatin, and Smilie are spoken of for chiefs, and it is reported that General Simcoe is to supply arms and ammunition."[39]

The events of 1793 and 1794 gave America's Federalists valuable ammunition to use against their domestic rivals. By blaming low-born foreigners, Republican leaders, and a Jacobin fifth-column for the upheavals of the mid-1790s, the Federalists were expressing their increased doubts about the benefits of immigration. But their rhetoric also was shaped by political ambition. The Irish frontiersmen who staged the Whiskey Rebellion, led by foreign-born Republicans such as John Smilie and Albert Gallatin, did indeed seem to be governed by a "Wild ranting fury" rather than deference or a true understanding of liberty. But Harrison Gray Otis's description of Gallatin as "a vagrant foreigner . . . a foreigner who to his knowledge ten years ago came to this Country without a *second shirt to his back*," was designed to win votes, rather than define Otis's attitude toward immigrants. Unfortunately for their political future, many Federalists fell into a similar trap, succumbing to the use of xenophobic rhetoric rather than carefully defining their now more cautious position on immigration.[40]

By the beginning of 1795 less spectacular events also had convinced America's Republicans of the need to guard the republic more fully from the political principles of recent immigrants. Many Republican leaders were politically embarrassed by Genet's arrogant actions, believing them both inappropriate and

[39]Dumas Malone, *Jefferson and the Ordeal of Liberty* (Boston: Little, Brown, 1962), chaps. 6–7; Eugene Perry Link, *Democratic-Republican Societies, 1790–1800* (New York: Columbia University Press, 1942), chaps. 1 and 8; quotes from *American Minerva and the New York Evening Advertiser*, Aug. 21, 1794.

[40]Thomas P. Slaughter, *The Whiskey Rebellion: Frontier Epilogue to the American Revolution* (New York: Oxford University Press, 1986), quote on 134; Samuel Eliot Morison, *The Life and Letters of Harrison Gray Otis: Federalist, 1765–1848*, 2 vols. (Boston: Houghton Mifflin, 1913), I, quote on 56.

damaging to their political prospects. Thomas Jefferson, persisting in his belief that "a little rebellion now and then" was a good thing, could view the Whiskey Rebellion as evidence of the sound political principles of the rebels. But other Republicans were less sanguine and contended that in a government by the people, the ballot was the proper mode of protest. Under a Constitution written and ratified by the people, there was no need for recourse to extralegal associations or rebellion. Furthermore, the law and order reaction to the Whiskey rebels undermined the political position of men who opposed the Hamiltonian system of government.[41]

Although the Republicans provided less than wholehearted support for the actions of immigrants who belonged to democratic clubs or took part in the Whiskey Rebellion, they, too, had identified a group of foreigners as dangerous to the nation. The influx of French planters and their slaves following the black insurrections in St. Domingue confirmed traditional Jeffersonian doubts about introducing foreigners with monarchical principles. Stung by President Washington's condemnation of their conduct and his backing of Hamilton's "militarism" and "monocratic" schemes, Jefferson and his followers could only view the aristocratic refugees as men who would lend their support to the Federalist corruption of the American republic. To George Nicholas, a Virginia Republican, the 20,000 Americans who volunteered to put down the Whiskey Rebellion were a more ominous sign than the rebels themselves. According to Nicholas, "Men must be far advanced into that state which will make them proper objects for slavery, when they place such a blind reliance on any man's judgment or representations, as to be induced to offer their services to be the butchers of their countrymen."[42] The support French aristocrats would lend to Federalist schemes could only hasten this degeneration of American society.

Congressional Republicans also opposed, on constitutional grounds, governmental aid to the aristocratic refugees who fled from St. Domingue following the massacre at Cape François in July 1793. Alexander Hamilton, as Secretary of the Treasury, presided over the disbursement of federal funds to French refugees that Republicans had voted against as a "dangerous precedent, which might hereafter be perverted to the countenance of purposes, very different from those of charity." Southern Republicans who opposed such an expansion of the executive power also feared that blacks who had been exposed to radical ideas before fleeing from St. Domingue with their masters would infect American slaves and trigger local insurrections. In 1798 Federalists who hoped to detach Southern

---

[41] Lester J. Cappon, ed., *The Adams–Jefferson Letters: The Complete Correspondence between Thomas Jefferson and Abigail and John Adams*, 2 vols. (Chapel Hill: University of North Carolina Press, 1959), I, 173 (quote); II, 346–47; *Jefferson: Writings*, ed. Peterson, 1015–17; Malone, *Jefferson and the Ordeal of Liberty*, 188–91; *Papers of James Madison*, ed. Hutchinson, XV, 393–97.

[42] Nicholas to Madison, Nov. 29, 1794, in *Papers of James Madison*, ed. Hutchinson, XV, 393–96.

voters from their francophile Republicanism fanned those fears by reporting the imminent invasion of the American states by a French army headed by ten thousand blacks from St. Domingue.[43]

The Naturalization Act of 1795

The Naturalization Act of 1795 was shaped by this internal strife and the fear that foreigners would add to the discord that threatened to destroy the republican visions of both the Federalists and the Jeffersonians. In the 1794–1795 session of Congress, representatives of all political persuasions, while aiming at different targets, recognized the need for additional restrictions on the political power of foreigners. Debate on the Act of 1795 was opened by Samuel Dexter, the Federalist representative from Massachusetts, who expressed "his disapprobation of the facility by which, under the existing law, aliens may acquire citizenship." Dexter's Federalist colleague, Theodore Sedgwick painted especially horrifying scenarios of the "miseries" that resulted when "the subjects of all Governments, Despotic, Monarchical, and Aristocratical" were granted a "general and indiscriminate admission to the rights of citizenship." During the debate on the naturalization bill Sedgwick also gave evidence of the waning of the mercantilist argument for immigration when he challenged "what was termed our liberal policy" and the assumptions "that our country wanted commercial capital; that we had an immense tract of vacant territory; and that we ought not, with the avarice of a miser, to engross to our selves the exclusive enjoyment of our political treasures."[44]

James Madison, leader of the House Republicans, agreed on the need to revise the Naturalization Act of 1790 "which from its defects & the progress of things in Europe was exposing us to very serious inconveniences." Although John Page, the Virginia idealist of 1790, opposed proposals to adopt additional impediments to American citizenship, he now based his opposition on the fact that such devices would be ineffective. Certificates of character might be denied to good men on technicalities, "Yet bad men, associating chiefly with men like themselves, regardless of oaths, might procure the requisite certificate." Page argued that "should bad men come amongst us, they will be discountenanced by the more virtuous class of citizens, and if necessary be punished by laws." However, as an extra precaution, Page suggested that an extensive school system be created so that "good

[43] *The Writings of Thomas Jefferson*, ed. Paul Leicester Ford, 10 vols. (New York: G.P. Putnam's Sons, 1892–1899), VII, 345; *Papers of James Madison*, ed. Hutchinson, XV, 177–79, quote on 177; Winston Chandler Babb, "French Refugees from Saint Domingue to the Southern United States, 1791–1810" (Ph.D. diss., University of Virginia, 1954), chap. 5; *Papers of Alexander Hamilton*, ed. Syrett, XVII, 423–33, 444–45, 537–38; Alexander DeConde, *The Quasi-War: The Politics and Diplomacy of the Undeclared War with France, 1797–1801* (New York: Charles Scribner's Sons, 1966), 84–85.

[44] Gales, ed., *Annals of Congress, 3rd Cong.*, 1004 (Dexter), 1006, 1007 (Sedgwick).

sense and virtue will be so generally diffused among us, that emigrants will be unable to corrupt our manners."[45]

In hammering out the provisions of the new act, Congress finally fulfilled its constitutional mandate "to establish a uniform rule of naturalization." Beginning in 1795, all federal naturalization statutes would contain the clause "That any alien, being a free white person, may be admitted to become a citizen of the United States, or any of them, on the following conditions, and not *otherwise*."[46] The waning of American confidence in the ability of foreigners infected with European radicalism or untrained in self-government to uphold republican institutions combined with the institution of a single class of American citizenship also produced more rigorous prerequisites for naturalization. The Act of 1795 increased the residency requirement from two to five years, including one year in the state or territory in which the alien petitioned. Henceforth aliens also were required to declare their intention to seek American citizenship three years in advance, renounce "all allegiance and fidelity to any foreign prince, potentate, State, or sovereignty whatever," and provide proof of their "good moral character" and attachment "to the principles of the constitution of the United States, and . . . to the good order and happiness of the same." House Republicans also succeeded, over the bitter opposition of their Federalist colleagues, in requiring alien petitioners to renounce any title of nobility they may have "borne" prior to naturalization.[47] These provisions remained the nucleus of American naturalization policy throughout the nineteenth century and represented the resolution of

[45] *Papers of James Madison*, ed. Hutchinson, XV, 440 (quote), 448; Gales, ed., *Annals of Congress, 3rd Cong.*, 1004 (Page). While Madison spoke of "inconveniences," some of his Virginia constituents were more outspoken. One Virginia Republican lobbied Madison to work for the "total exclusion of the naturalized from all functions of Government," arguing that since most of the nation's immigrants were "needy & unknown adventurers, swept from every Corner of the british empire; it is a more than Common prostitution of our Safety & Dignity, to admit them into Government. Population would Surely be enough consulted, by giving foriegners [*sic*] an easy access to Marriage, to the acquisition & Security of all Species of property, to the participation of Socialities & Enjoyments, but The functions of government I would never concede to them." Walter Jones, Jan. 4, 1795, to James Madison, in *Papers of James Madison*, ed. Hutchinson, XV, 435.

[46] Quote from Naturalization Act of 1795, Gales, ed., *Annals of Congress, 3rd Cong.*, 1497 (emphasis added); the same phrase appears in the Act of 1802, *Annals of Congress, 7th Cong.*, 1329; the Act of 1798 stated that "no alien shall be admitted to become a citizen of the United States, or of any State, unless in the manner prescribed," Gales, ed., *Annals of Congress, 5th Cong.*, 3739–40.

[47] Naturalization Act of 1795, Gales, ed., *Annals of Congress, 3rd Cong.*, 1497. The debate over the renunciation of hereditary titles in the House of Representatives is peppered with accusations of inappropriate partisan behavior. Federalist Representatives who opposed the provision viewed the extended discussion, and insistence on a role call vote, "as a design to hold up certain people to public odium" by portraying them as secret monarchists. Representatives Samuel Dexter and William Smith challenged their political adversaries to extend their putative concern for equality to all aliens by forcing the renunciation of any "connexions with the Jacobin club. The one was fully as abhorrent to the Constitution as the other." Dexter, hoping to embarrass those "who call themselves Democrats," also facetiously introduced an amendment to require aliens to renounce slavery "and declare that he holds all men free and equal." In the end, the fear of being denounced by their political opponents as secret monarchists forced the Federalist Representatives to acquiesce in the clause that required naturalized aliens to renounce any hereditary title they may have held. Ibid., 1030–57; quotes on 1040, 1031, 1032.

the conflicting hopes and fears of the nation's revolutionary idealists, liberals, moderates, and conservatives.

Although fear of the increasing radicalism of the French Revolution was clearly a factor in producing the stricter provisions of the Naturalization Act of 1795, it is likely that the more onerous requirements for naturalization were dictated by the act itself, which was now designated the exclusive mode of naturalization and conferred full citizenship rights.[48] A five-year residence and a declaration of intent three years prior to naturalization provided the kind of safeguards that the states had incorporated into their progressive citizenship laws, but could no longer use. Ultimately constitutional issues prevented the members of Congress from creating even a temporary "denizen" class that would result from "step-by-step citizenship" because they were unable to find a way to do so without invading the rights of the states or exceeding the powers vested in them by the Constitution. The belief that the Constitution and republican principles required a single class of citizens would have momentous consequences in the future. It would hamper attempts to levy permanent disabilities on America's immigrants or a term of residence so long that the immigrant would, in effect, be disfranchised for life.

Although America's leaders became more and more fearful of alien principles and activities during the 1790s, the need to preserve liberty—for themselves as well as humanity—continued to shape alien policies and the American asylum throughout the decade. During the 1795 naturalization debate, in which virtually every member of Congress agreed on the need to increase residency requirements, Representative Boudinot of New Jersey "reminded the House of a late Proclamation by the PRESIDENT, wherein, among other things, it is said that this country is an asylum to the oppressed of all nations." Thomas Fitzsimons of Pennsylvania opposed a proposal to require a ten-year residence on the grounds that "Nature seems to have pointed out this country as an asylum for the people oppressed in other parts of the world. It would be wrong therefore, to . . . treat them for so long a time so hardly." Even Representative Sedgwick, ever so adamant about taking steps to prevent "a general and indiscriminate admission of aliens," stated that "he did not wish it should go to a complete exclusion." Sedgwick "considered America as in possession of a greater stock of enjoyment than any other people on earth. That it was our duty to husband it with care; yet he could not altogether exclude such virtuous individuals, as might fly here, as to an asylum against oppression. On the one hand, he would not dissipate our treasures with the thoughtless profusion of a prodigal; nor would he, on the other, hoard them, as in the unfeeling grasp of a miser." William Vans Murray of Maryland, who "was quite indifferent if not fifty emigrants came into

---

[48]Naturalized aliens continued to be subject to the disabilities established by the Constitution of 1787 (barred from the presidency and ineligible for election to the U.S. House of Representatives for seven years after naturalization or to the U.S. Senate for nine years).

this Continent in a year's time" expressed his belief that "It would be unjust to hinder them."[49]

Private individuals who questioned the benefits of immigration also expressed their acceptance of America's role as an asylum for distressed Europeans well into the 1790s. In 1795 "a number of gentlemen" in Massachusetts organized an Immigrant Society to aid the

> great numbers of people from France, Great-Britain, and their West-India islands, impelled by necessity, or prompted by a desire to avoid impending evils, [that] have taken refuge in the United States. The principles of religion and humanity require the friendly attention of Americans to these strangers many of whom arrive in circumstances of such wretchedness as to give pain to every feeling mind.... Not with design to *encourage* emigration, was our society formed; for in our opinion, the happiness of our country depends not on any *forced* increase of its population, its *natural* increase being sufficiently rapid, and more conducive to *uniformity* in principles, habits, and manners, the basis of political and social order and happiness; but solely with a view to afford comfort and relief to such as voluntarily, and from real or supposed necessity, seek an asylum among us.[50]

Partisan Politics

In 1795 Federalists and Republicans agreed that foreigners needed a longer period of acculturation and closer scrutiny before entering America's political arena. While the safeguards inaugurated by the Act of 1795 were aimed against immigrants with differing political principles, both parties had reason to hope the results would tend to their benefit. The Republicans gained some assurance that the French refugees who were more committed to aristocratic principles and hereditary rights than republicanism would be neutralized by the provision requiring aliens to renounce their hereditary titles. Federalists who hoped to confer citizenship only on responsible men of means and deferential immigrants could rely on character witnesses to keep radical foreigners out of the electorate. A declaration of intent three years prior to naturalization gave both Federalists and Republicans the opportunity to observe an alien's character and political principles and to promote the naturalization of their friends and deter those they deemed "unsuitable."

Federalist hopes that the Naturalization Act of 1795 would undermine the

---

[49] Gales, ed., *Annals of Congress, 3rd Cong.,* 1066 (Boudinot and Fitzsimons), 1007 (Sedgwick), 1023 (Murray).

[50] "Information for immigrants to the New-England States," "Published by Order of the Immigrant Society in Boston, Thomas Russell, President; Jedidiah Morse, Corresponding Secretary, Oct. 27, 1795," Houghton Library, Harvard University. By the end of the decade Jedidiah Morse was a prominent champion of religious [Congregational] and political orthodoxy in Massachusetts, referred to by "some of his contemporaries ... as a 'Pillar of Adamant in the Temple of Federalism.'" Johnson and Malone, eds., *Dictionary of American Biography,* XIII, 245–47, quote on 246.

political opposition and induce domestic tranquillity were short-lived. The arrival of Jay's Treaty, which should have removed the stigma attached to the Federalists' support for Great Britain, increased political dissension and provided the Republican opposition with a new weapon to bludgeon Hamilton and his supporters. Once again, immigrants played prominent roles in the attack on Federalist policies. In New York City immigrants were identified as members of the rock-throwing mob that jeered Federalist mayor Richard Varick and Alexander Hamilton as they tried to defend the terms of Jay's Treaty. Three days later, on July 21, 1795, a similar group of outraged New Yorkers burned a copy of the treaty and hanged John Jay in effigy. By the end of the year New York's Republicans had used this popular discontent to wrest the city's congressional seat from Federalist control. By April 1797 a Republican also represented the Southern District of New York in the U.S. Senate.[51]

The activities of the treaty's opponents in Congress reinforced the Federalist characterization of the Republican opposition as seditious Jacobins who drew their strength from foreign influence and the votes of radical immigrants and deluded Americans. In the House of Representatives the opposition party mounted repeated attacks on the Federalist interpretation of the Constitution. First the Treaty's opponents leaked the document to the press to stir up public opprobrium after the Senate had voted to keep its deliberations secret. Then, in the spring of 1796 Edward Livingston, the newly elected Republican Representative from New York, demanded that President Washington turn copies of Jay's instructions and other executive documents over to the House. Next, the Republican opposition attempted to intrude the House of Representatives into the treaty-making process by threatening to withhold the appropriations necessary to implement the agreement with Great Britain. Prominent among the leaders of the opposition was the Genevan immigrant Albert Gallatin, described by Theodore Sedgwick as "intoxicated with power." And, once again, during the presidential election of 1796, the French Ambassador intermeddled in American politics, as he tried to secure Jefferson's victory over John Adams.[52] Thus, even though the Republican party was unable to prevent the ratification of Jay's treaty, its unpopular provisions proved costly to the Federalist party—continuing the attacks on law, order, and government that the Federalists had hoped to termi-

[51] Young, *Democratic Republicans*, 445–54; Sidney I. Pomerantz, *New York: An American City, 1783–1803* (New York: Columbia University Press, 1938), 119; Jabez D. Hammond, *The History of Political Parties in the State of New-York*, 2 vols. (Syracuse, New York: Hall, Mills & Co., 1852), I, 95, 108. According to Grant Thorburn, a Scot who emigrated to New York in 1794 and became a warm admirer of Alexander Hamilton, Jay's Treaty "was burned, while Irishmen danced the 'White Boys' March' and Frenchmen sang 'Dansons La Carmagnole'." Grant Thorburn, *Fifty Years' Reminiscences of New-York* (New York: D. Fanshaw, 1845), 23–26, quote on 26.

[52] Noble E. Cunningham, Jr., *The Jeffersonian Republicans: The Formation of Party Organization, 1789–1801* (Chapel Hill: University of North Carolina Press, 1957), quote on 123; Norman K. Risjord, *Chesapeake Politics, 1781–1800* (New York: Columbia University Press, 1978), chap. 16; Young, *Democratic Republicans*, chap. 21.

nate. Stronger measures than those embodied in the Naturalization Act of 1795 were now needed to undercut the growing support of foreign-born radicals for the Jeffersonian Republicans.

By 1797 many Federalists were disillusioned with the character and principles of immigrants who supported the opposition's attack on the American Constitution and Federalist government. Developments outside the political arena also fueled Federalist doubts about America's immigrants. In 1791 Alexander Hamilton's "Report on Manufactures" had painted a glowing portrait of the benefits the nation would reap once Americans began producing their own manufactured goods. In this the nation would be aided by foreign workmen, who, "listening to the powerful invitations of a better price for their fabrics, or their labor, of greater cheapness of provisions and raw materials, of an exemption from the chief part of the taxes, burthens, and restraints, which they endure in the old world, of greater personal independence and consequence, under the operation of a more equal government, and of what is far more precious than mere religious toleration, a perfect equality of religious privileges, would probably flock from Europe to the United States, to pursue their own trades or professions, if they were once made sensible of the advantages they would enjoy."

However, by July 1796 the stockholders of the Society for the Encouragement of Manufactures, who included Hamilton in their number, were meeting to consider dissolving the corporation. According to a correspondent in the *Newark Gazette*, in June of 1796 "all attempts to establish the manufacture of woolen and cotton cloathes [*sic*] on a large scale, in these states have proved unsuccessful. The manufacture of woolens, at Hartford, is in a great measure fallen to the ground. That of cotton at Paterson, is wholly suspended, and the machinery taken to pieces. This is the state also of that at Pompton and nearly that of York Island." Although this article acknowledged that "The high price of labor, in consequence of an unforeseen war, may be considered as the . . . immediate cause of these failures," much of the blame had to be placed on immigrant employees. The proprietors of these manufacturing ventures had "employed emigrants who in most instances direct many of the most essential branches.—Many of these men have proved to be imposters: wholly ignorant of the business they professed. Others have been idle projectors, without experience or system and without integrity." A precipitous decline in the American land market occurred almost simultaneously with the failure of the country's most ambitious domestic manufacturing ventures. Indeed, because many men who invested in factories also speculated in land, failures in one area often triggered failures in the other. By 1796 many of the nation's leading Federalist investors were bankrupt or in prison for debt.[53]

[53] "Report on Manufactures," *American States Papers, Finance* (Washington, D.C.: Government Printing Office, 1832–1861), I, quote on 126; Davis, *Essays in the Earlier History of American Corporations*, I, 111–344, 349–518, quotes on 497–98; Sakolski, *Great American Land Bubble*.

The magnanimity with which early Federalists had viewed immigration was thus undermined by more than the political behavior of foreign-born radicals. The bursting of America's land bubble and the failure of the nation's manufacturing ventures reduced the need for foreign-born workers and tenants. As the Federalists began to view immigrants as a threat, rather than an enabling factor, to their vision of America's proper social, economic, and political development, they began to question their earlier assumption that demographic expansion through immigration was a positive good. In May of 1798 Robert Goodloe Harper, the Federalist Representative from South Carolina, disparaged "the folly of believing that the strength and happiness of the country would be promoted by admitting all the congregations of people from every part of the world to the rights of citizenship." According to President Adams's nephew, "The grand cause of all our present difficulties may be traced . . . to so many *hordes of Foreigners* imigrating [*sic*] to America. . . . Let us no longer pray that America may become an asylum to all nations."[54]

The Federalist Frenzy

By 1797 many Federalists had been disabused of their optimistic assessment of the economic and social benefits of immigration. But these considerations only reinforced the political factors that were the root of the Federalist party's descent into nativism. Once Great Britain rescinded its orders to detain the nation's neutral shipping and France began harassing American ships, it became politically rewarding to stir up and reap the benefits of American anger at French attacks on the nation's commerce and sovereignty—just as Jeffersonian Republicans had benefited from the outcry against similar actions by the British. So the Federalist party turned loose its most bombastic orators who became increasingly vitriolic in their denunciation of America's immigrants and the politicians who used them, while presenting themselves as the guardians of true American republicanism, unsullied by foreign principles.

In the spring of 1797 President Adams, hoping to improve the defensive posture of the United States during the Wars of the French Revolution, called a special session of Congress. During this session, presidential hopes for a stronger military establishment were dashed by Congressmen who opposed war with France, "standing armies," new taxes, and increasing the power of the federal government. A Federalist proposal to institute a twenty-dollar tax on naturalization certificates also initiated an intense debate on the nature of the American asylum.

[54] Gales, ed., *Annals of Congress, 5th Cong.*, 1566 (Harper); James Morton Smith, *Freedom's Fetters: The Alien and Sedition Laws and American Civil Liberties* (Ithaca: Cornell University Press, 1956), quote on 24.

Although it was ostensibly a revenue measure, some Federalists saw the proposed tax on naturalization certificates as a way "to foreclose" the hordes of wild Irishmen "and the turbulent and disorderly of all parts of the world," who emigrated "with a view to disturb our tranquillity, after having succeeded in the overthrow of their own Governments." The tax was opposed by legislators who saw it as a violation of America's pledge to serve as an asylum for liberty and "mankind." In the House of Representative Nathaniel Macon of North Carolina "opposed the tax altogether, as tending to injure the poor and industrious part of the immigrants to this country, which he looked upon as the most valuable." North Carolina's Robert Williams also categorically denied the propriety of such "a tax upon liberty," and John Swanwick of Pennsylvania declared it "contrary" to America's previous policy. According to Swanwick, "Since the year 1776, it had uniformly been the language of this country that we had in the Western world opened an asylum for emigrants from every country. This was our language, 'Come and join us in the blessing we enjoy in a country large and fertile, and under a Government founded upon the principles of liberty and justice.'" Representative Joseph McDowell of North Carolina agreed, stating "we had fought and bled for liberty . . . we did not mean to confine it to ourselves. . . . On the contrary, people of other countries had been invited to come, and partake with us our blessings—our laws had all gone to this." Matthew Lyon thought such a tax "injurious, cruel, and impolitic . . . because we had dealt out a different kind of language heretofore; we had told the world that there was in this country a good spring of liberty, and invited all to come and drink of it" and "did not think it was right now to turn round to them and say, you shall not be admitted as citizens unless you pay twenty dollars."[55]

Even proponents of the tax did not deny America's promise. Representative Samuel Sewall of Massachusetts stated that, "though he wished this country to be an asylum for men of every other who chose to come to it, yet he did not wish to see foreigners our governors." Robert Goodloe Harper of South Carolina conceded that "There was a moment of enthusiasm in this country, when this was thought to be right," although the Federalist leader now contended that the "experience of ten or fifteen years . . . had convinced us we were wrong."[56] The argument that a twenty-dollar "tax on liberty" violated America's wartime pledge was instrumental in securing its defeat.[57]

In the spring of 1798 President Adams's call for preparedness could no longer be dismissed by the Republican opposition as "warmongering." French diplo-

[55] Gales, ed., *Annals of Congress, 5th Cong.*, 421–31, quotes on 429–30 (Otis), 425 (Macon), 427 (Williams), 423 (Swanwick), 427 (McDowell), 425–26 (Lyon).

[56] Ibid., 426 (Sewall), 424–25 (Harper). Harper now favored the extreme measure of denying American citizenship to all but the native-born, but he "would have all foreigners freely admitted, and . . . admit their children to have a right of citizenship."

[57] The House also voted against a $10.00 tax on naturalization certificates and eventually compromised on $5.00. Ibid., 430–31.

matic blunders convinced a vocal segment of the American public that they might become the next victims of French aggression. News of the humiliating treatment of American envoys, French decrees and actions that trampled on America's rights as a neutral trader, and the publication of French dispatches that boasted of the strength of the "French party" in America generated popularity for President Adams, support for his legislative program, calls for war against France, and savage attacks on the rights of aliens and the American asylum.[58]

By 1798 any Federalist desire to reap the mercantilist benefits of immigration was overcome by the fear of aliens who had been radicalized by the Wars of the French Revolution. Convinced of the need to control the actions and writings of all potential subversives, the Federalist "friends of order" took advantage of their newfound popularity during the quasi-war with France to pass laws that they hoped would emasculate both their political rivals and foreign radicals. The Federalists seemed to feed on their success, as their predictions of the disasters awaiting an unprepared and beleaguered America escalated with each legislative triumph, along with their attacks on aliens, the political opposition, and those who denied the increasingly extravagant Federalist reading of the U.S. Constitution. By the middle of June, Federalist extremists were arguing that the national government, and Congress in particular, had the right to do virtually anything it deemed "necessary and proper" in order "to provide for the common defence and general welfare" of the United States against the nefarious schemes of aliens "who have assisted in laying other countries prostrate; whose hands are reeking with blood, and whose hearts rankle with hatred toward us."[59] As the severity of these attacks on foreigners and the political opposition mounted, Jeffersonian Republicans who had previously questioned the wisdom of large-scale immigration rallied to the defense of alien rights and the American asylum to preserve their own political future, as well as free government, the Constitution, and republican liberty.

In April 1798 the Federalist leaders in Congress, arguing that "we may very shortly be involved in war," called for a revision of the nation's naturalization laws to deal with the "immense number of French citizens in our country." On April 17th, Representative Joshua Coit of Connecticut proposed that "the

---

[58] President Adams sent reports from American envoys, telling of their humiliating treatment by the French government and special presidential messages to Congress on Apr. 3, May 4, and June 5, 18, 21, 1798. On June 18 and 19, Representative Gallatin was "twice interrupted," while speaking against the Alien Friends Act, by the reading of these communications and by the House's discussion of the number of copies of the dispatches that should be printed for public distribution. On June 21 the debate on the Alien Friends bill in the House of Representatives was again "interrupted by a Message from the President of the United States, enclosing the last letter from Mr. Gerry, with the other papers brought by General Marshall; which having been read, were ordered to be printed." The dispatches that were published included references to the "French party in America," which, combined with "The diplomatic skill of France," would be "sufficient . . . to throw the blame which will attend the rupture of the negotiations on the Federalists." Ibid., quotes on 1793, 3355, 3794; Smith, *Freedom's Fetters*, esp. 7–9, 102–3; John C. Miller, *Crisis in Freedom: The Alien and Sedition Acts* (Boston: Little, Brown, 1951), esp. 3–15.

[59] Gales, ed., *Annals of Congress, 5th Cong.*, quotes on 1965–66 (Bayard) and 1987 (Otis).

committee appointed for the protection of commerce and the defence of our country, be directed to inquire and report whether it be not expedient to suspend or to amend the act establishing an uniform rule of naturalization." On April 19th Representative Sitgreaves of Massachusetts moved that the committee also "consider and report upon the expediency of establishing by law, regulations respecting aliens arriving or residing within the United States." The House then voted to instruct the "Committee for the Protection of Commerce and the Defence of the Country . . . to inquire and report whether any and what alterations were necessary in the naturalization act, and into the expedience of establishing, by law, regulations respecting aliens arriving, or residing, within the United States."[60]

While some Federalists had a larger agenda, the call to revise the nation's naturalization code seemed reasonable to Americans who feared that the United States would share the fate of the Dutch, Swiss, and Batavian republics. Arguing that Europe's republics had been destroyed by the covert machinations of French saboteurs and their traitorous domestic henchmen, the Federalists proposed reducing the political power of America's immigrants by postponing their admission to citizenship and monitoring their movements. On May 1 Representative Sewall, chairman of the "Committee for the Protection of Commerce and the Defence of the Country," reported its recommendations to the House. During their deliberations, the committee had concluded that "a longer residence within the United States, before admission" to citizenship was "essential"; they "were also of opinion that some precautions against the promiscuous reception and residence of aliens, which may be thought at all times advisable, are, at this time, more apparently necessary and important, especially for the securing or removal of those who may be suspected of hostile intentions." Therefore the committee recommended that the new naturalization law "prolong the term of residence" required for citizenship, and make provision "for a report and registry of all aliens who shall continue residence, or shall hereafter arrive within the United States, with suitable descriptions of their places of birth and citizenship, and places of arrival and residence within the United States." The committee also recommended "That provision be made by law for the apprehending, securing, or removal, as the case may require" of all resident male aliens, "of fourteen years and upwards," whose governments "shall declare war against the United States, or shall threaten, attempt, or perpetrate any invasion or predatory incursions . . . as soon as may be after the President of the United States shall make proclamation of such event."[61]

On May 2, 1798, Samuel Sewall opened the House debate on the naturalization bill by moving "to fill the blank specifying the length of time necessary for

[60] Gales, ed., *Annals of Congress, 5th Cong.,* quotes on 1427 (Coit), 1453–54 (Sitgreaves), 1566 (instructions).

[61] Ibid., 1566–67.

an alien to give notice of his intention to become a citizen, before he can be admitted, with 'five years.'" When this passed, with no recorded opposition, Sewall moved to fill the blank, "declaring the length of time necessary for an alien to reside here before he can be admitted a citizen . . . with 'fourteen years.'" Sewall's proposal to triple the residence requirement for naturalization (from five to fourteen years) came close to denying citizenship to adult immigrants for life, which would make them permanent second-class citizens. Several Representatives, including Sewall's Federalist colleagues, argued that his proposal was too extreme and unjust. John Williams, a Federalist from the state of New York, went so far as to repeat the argument made by the New Yorker John Lawrence in 1790—that resident aliens should not be denied access to American citizenship because "They contribute their share of the expense of Government, and it was an acknowledged principle that representation and taxation ought to go together."[62] Representative Joseph Varnum of Massachusetts, believing that "the impulse of the moment led members to believe that these restrictions upon foreigners were necessary," argued that "there was no necessity for any measures being taken with respect to foreigners, except such as belong to the nation with whom we expect to be at war; yet he had no particular objection to restrictions being made with respect to such foreigners as shall hereafter come to this country; but having heretofore held out inducements to foreigners to come to this country, and when they are come, with an expectation of becoming entitled to the rights of citizens in a certain time, he would not disappoint these expectations."[63]

Representative Macon also expressed his "apprehensive that gentlemen in their zeal to get at particular persons will go too far in this business," and his Republican colleague from North Carolina, Joseph McDowell, spoke out against a fourteen-year residency, because he did "not wish to discourage an emigration to this country of respectable foreigners, by barring them from the rights of citizenship. The policy of this country had always been different, and he did not wish entirely to change it. When persons come here from foreign countries, it was our interest to attach them to us, and not always to look upon them as aliens and strangers." McDowell would, however, "not object to an increase . . . to seven years; or, if the committee thought nine better, he would not object to it." On the other hand, William Craik, a Federalist from Maryland, announced that "he was disposed to go much further than is proposed . . . in restricting aliens from becoming citizens of this country." While arguing against making the law retrospective, Craik "would have no objection to say, that no foreigner coming into this country after this time, shall ever become a citizen."[64] The vote was close, 41 to 40, but

[62] Gales, ed., *Annals of Congress, 5th Cong.*, 1776 (Sewall), 1781–82 (Williams).

[63] Ibid., 1782 (Varnum).

[64] Ibid., 1780 (Macon), 1776 (McDowell), 1779 (Craik).

the House approved Sewall's motion to increase the residency requirement to fourteen years.[65]

The arguments in the House of Representatives did little to change the provisions of the Federalist bill. Under the Naturalization Act of 1798, aliens who applied for American citizenship had to declare their intent five years prior to naturalization and reside in the United States for at least fourteen years. The Act also required all white aliens residing in the United States to register with the closest district court or an agent appointed by the President within six months of the passage of the Act; all future white immigrants were to report themselves within 48 hours of their arrival. Copies of alien reports and the papers of "cases of naturalization heretofore permitted, or which shall be permitted, under the laws of the United States" were to be forwarded to the U.S. Secretary of State. Shipmasters who failed to report their alien passengers would be subject to a $300.00 fine and their vessel detained until payment was made; fines on foreigners who did not report themselves and their alien dependents, would accumulate at the rate of $2.00 for each month of noncompliance. The new Act also provided that "no alien, who shall be a native citizen, denizen, or subject of any nation or State with whom the United States shall be at war, at the time of his application, shall be then admitted to become a citizen of the United States."[66]

Albert Gallatin, a Swiss-born naturalized citizen and leader of the House Republicans, secured a minor modification of the original bill, a clause allowing aliens who had arrived prior to the passage of the Naturalization Act of 1795 and those who had already declared their intention to become citizens, to be naturalized under the terms of the Act of 1795 if they applied within one and four years respectively after the passage of the new bill. Gallatin had been adamant about exempting aliens, who, although qualified, had "neglected to become citizens" under the Act of 1795 as well as those arriving after the passage of that Act who had begun citizenship proceedings (by making their declaration of intent), but had not been in the country long enough to complete their application. Nathaniel Macon, a Republican from North Carolina, supported Gallatin's amendment, pointing to the "persons in distant parts of the Continent" who remained unnaturalized, "perhaps from their not being in the way of going through the ceremony and because [they] had no apprehension of the privilege being taken from them. Many had also omitted to do it from an ignorance of our language." Macon also argued that if foreigners had "given notice of their intention to become citizens, they have complied in part with the laws" and therefore

---

[65] Ibid., 1776. The residency issue seems to have been even more closely contested in the Senate, where, according to Thomas Jefferson, "We were within one vote . . . of striking out 14 years and inserting 7." Smith, *Freedom's Fetters*, 33.

[66] Act of 1798, Gales, ed., *Annals of Congress, 5th Cong.*, 3739–42.

"he did not think it would be right to put it out of their power to comply with the other part."[67]

The Federalist Representatives Sewall, Sitgreaves, Bayard, and Coit had, however, little concern for immigrants who had "neglected to avail themselves of the privilege of becoming citizens," arguing that such laxity seemed evidence that they "did not place any high value upon it." Furthermore, according to James Bayard of Delaware, "Aliens cannot be considered as members of the society of the United States . . . whatever is granted to aliens is a mere matter of favor; and, if it is taken away, they have no right to complain." On more expedient grounds, it was Bayard's opinion that "there were as many Jacobins and vagabonds come into the United States during the last two years, as may come for ten years hence; so that these very persons against whom this law was intended to operate, will," if Gallatin's amendment was adopted, "become citizens, and may be chosen into the Government."[68]

On May 22, 1798, the "bill to establish a uniform rule of naturalization, and to repeal the former act for that purpose, was read the third time and passed" in the U.S. House of Representatives. On the same day, the House went into a Committee of the Whole to consider a bill "respecting alien enemies." Virtually all members of the House agreed on the need for a law to deal with the subjects of hostile powers in wartime; the opposition that emerged was nonpartisan and revolved around the "very extraordinary power" given to the President to decide when the threat of "invasion, or predatory incursion" required that "all natives, denizens, citizens, or subjects of the hostile Nation or Government, being males of the age of fourteen years and upwards" residing in the United States, "and not actually naturalized, shall be liable to be apprehended, restrained, secured and removed, as alien enemies" and, after issuing a "public proclamation of the event . . . to direct the conduct to be observed, on the part of the United States, towards the aliens who shall become liable as aforesaid."[69]

Several Representatives feared that the bill's provisions would expand the power of the president to a dangerous level and violate the principles of American "jurisprudence," the separation of powers, and the Bill of Rights. James Bayard, the Delaware Federalist, led the way in attacking the clause that required "the good people of the United States" to "be obedient" to, and assist in the implementation of, presidential proclamations concerning alien enemies and subjected American citizens "who shall harbor or conceal any alien liable as an enemy, knowing him to be such," to unspecified punishment.[70] Bayard saw these provisions as violating American legal principles by providing "punishment for a crime by a law to be passed after the fact is committed." According to the

[67]Gales, ed., *Annals of Congress, 5th Cong.*, 3740, 1779 (Macon).
[68]Ibid., 1776–82, quotes on 1778 (Sewall) and 1780 (Bayard).
[69]Ibid., 1783–97, quotes on 1783, 1786, 1785.
[70]Ibid., 1785–96, the original bill is on 1785–86.

Republican leader Albert Gallatin, "the evil did not stop here." The bill, as drafted, "was grounded upon the principle that the President of the United States shall have the power to do by proclamation what ought only to be done by law." This left "not only alien enemies, but citizens of the United States, to the will of the President." The combined objections of Federalists and Jeffersonians were successful in safeguarding the rights of citizens, as the provisions to punish Americans for "harboring or concealing alien enemies" were deleted from the bill that was passed.[71]

The Alien Enemies Act set up the machinery to control the subjects of nations at war with the United States; it did not, however, answer the Federalist urge to control aliens suspected of harboring subversive designs and their domestic lackeys prior to a declaration of war. This was the object of the next Federalist bill, the Act concerning Aliens. The heated debates that preceded and followed the passage of this Alien Act prompted Congress and the nation to stake out increasingly extreme, and antithetical, political positions. The growing fear of French aggression, fanned by presidential messages and the publication of diplomatic dispatches, destroyed the remnants of nonpartisan opposition to actions that encroached on the rights of Americans and aliens alike. These debates also demonstrate why the Jeffersonian Republicans found it necessary to rally to the defense of alien rights and the American asylum to preserve their own conception of free and uncorrupted republican government.

The "Alien Friends Act" received its name from Representative Gallatin's remark that, as the House was already debating a bill relating to alien enemies, this bill must "be considered as applying to alien friends." The primary Republican objections to the Alien Friends bill were constitutional. Albert Gallatin set the tone as he opened the debate in the House by challenging the power that the bill gave the president, for the next two years, to deport any alien "whose continuance within the United States shall be, in the opinion of the President of the United States, injurious to the public peace and safety." Gallatin pointed out that, as "whatever power Congress may have in relation to alien enemies [was] derived from its power over war and peace," that power did not encompass alien friends. Therefore the question to be resolved was "whether the Government of the United States are [*sic*] vested with any power to order alien friends to depart from this country."[72]

Gallatin and his colleagues in the House identified three areas in which the proposed bill violated the Constitution. While Representative Gallatin stated it as a truism "that every nation had a right to permit or exclude alien friends from entering within the bounds of their society," that power, he argued, "does solely belong to each individual State." The Constitution not only omitted the right to

[71] Gales, ed., *Annals of Congress, 5th Cong.,* 1786–88 (Bayard), 1788–96 (Gallatin).
[72] Debate on the Act concerning Aliens in ibid., 1954–2029, 2034–35, 2049, 2088; quotes on 1955 (Gallatin).

deport alien friends among the enumerated powers conveyed to Congress, but also the 12th Amendment expressly guaranteed "That the powers, not delegated to the United States by the Constitution, nor prohibited by it to the States, are reserved to the States respectively, or to the people." Therefore, according to Gallatin, "all the provisions in this bill are perfectly unconstitutional." Republican members of the House also argued that the alien bill violated the constitutional guarantees that "no person shall be deprived of life, liberty, or property, without due process of law" and that "The privilege of the writ of habeas corpus shall not be suspended unless when, in cases of rebellion or invasion, the public safety may require it." The third constitutional impediment to the bill identified by the Republican opposition was the clause that denied Congress the power to prohibit "The emigration or importation of such persons as any of the States now existing shall think proper to admit" prior to 1808.[73]

Federalist sponsors of the bill, incensed by opposition arguments to a measure that they deemed essential to the survival of the United States, were goaded into adopting an extremely expansive, and ultimately indefensible, position on the power of the federal government. Harrison Gray Otis of Massachusetts pronounced it "an absurd supposition that Congress has not the power to restrain and to banish persons who may have been sent into this country for the very purposes of spreading sedition and of dividing the people, whose intrigues and malpractices threaten the welfare and the very existence of the Government. If the Constitution prevented Congress from exercising these powers . . . such a Constitution" would not "be worth a farthing." In casting about for ways to refute Republican arguments, Representatives Sewall and Otis fastened on the preamble to the Constitution. Sewall, believing that "a candid examination of the subject would convince all reasonable men that Congress has, and ought to have this power" over alien friends, found that power in "the general nature of the Constitution itself." According to Sewall's reading of the preamble, the Constitution was written, and ratified by the American people, to create a government ("a more perfect union") able to "provide for the common defence, promote the general welfare, and secure the blessings of liberty to ourselves and our posterity." Therefore, he argued, the Constitution "establishes the sovereignty of the United States, and that sovereignty must reside in the [federal] Government." Because congressional power "to provide for the general welfare and internal tranquillity . . . [takes] cognizance of every thing which relates to aliens, . . . if the residence of any aliens in this country would be likely, in their opinion to endanger the public peace and tranquillity, Congress have a right to take such measures respecting them as they shall think fit."[74] Representative Bayard came up with a similar argument based on Article I, section 8 of the Constitution, which

---

[73] Gales, ed., *Annals of Congress, 5th Cong.*, quotes on 1955, 1956, 1957.
[74] Ibid., 1959–62 (Otis), 1957–58 (Sewall).

states that "Congress shall have power to lay and collect taxes . . . pay the debts and provide for the common defence and general welfare of the United States." Thus, according to Bayard,

> it is evident that the power is expressly given to Congress to provide for the common defence and general welfare, and it is not necessary to be given specifically. The concluding article of the same section also provides "that Congress shall make all laws which shall be necessary and proper for carrying into execution the foregoing powers." Hence, it is extremely clear that Congress has the power to do what is necessary for the common defence and general welfare and the only question before the committee is whether this law is necessary for these purposes. Because if it is, it comes within the express letter of the Constitution.[75]

Representatives Sewall and Otis also argued that the bill did not deny an alien's right to habeas corpus. According to Sewall, "To suspend the habeas corpus, is to commit a person to prison without law; but this bill does not propose any such thing." Since "Congress has a right to describe certain crimes, or circumstances, which lead to the suspicion of crimes, in which case a commitment ought to take place . . . Government has a right to suspend the liberty of persons in cases where they suppose there would be danger in their being at large." In addition, "the persons thus imprisoned would also have the power of demanding a trial."[76]

The Federalist defense of the Alien Friends Act and their extravagant interpretation of the powers granted to Congress by the Constitution exacerbated Republican fears and increased the need to defend both aliens and free government from the encroachments of power-hungry men who threatened to destroy the Constitution and create a despotic state. As Representatives Robert Williams and Abraham Baldwin sarcastically pointed out, "If the principle which the gentlemen from Massachusetts have drawn from the preamble of the Constitution, of providing for the common defence and welfare of the Union be correct, it appeared . . . unnecessary to have any other provision in the Constitution besides the preamble, as it may be inferred from that, that Congress has all power whatever," which left "the State Governments and people . . . possessing none."[77]

Republican members of the House quickly identified the ominous domestic consequences of condoning the use of arbitrary power over aliens and the other

---

[75] Gales, ed., *Annals of Congress, 5th Cong.,* 1965–66 (Bayard). Sewall also argued that the discretionary power to remove dangerous aliens "had to be placed in the President alone" since, if the states were to exercise that power, "an alien driven from Massachusetts or Pennsylvania, might take refuge in any of the other States." Ibid., 1971. Representatives Sewall and Otis interpreted the Constitutional ban on the restriction of emigration prior to 1808 as implying "that the Congress has the power to regulate this business respecting aliens, or why does the clause suspend the power till 1808?" Ibid., 1958–59.

[76] Ibid., 1958 (Sewall).

[77] Ibid., 1962 (Robert Williams), 1968 (Baldwin), 1975 (Gallatin).

unconstitutional features of the Alien Friends Act. Edward Livingston warned his colleagues, "let no man vainly imagine that the evil is to stop here, that a few unprotected aliens only are to be affected by this inquisitorial power." Both he and Representative Gallatin pointed out that "if this bill was passed, one of a similar nature may be brought in, in relation to citizens of the United States. This bill is called a bill concerning aliens; but in its consequences it affects citizens as much as aliens." Gallatin challenged

> the supporters of this bill to show him a single clause in the Constitution, which has been referred to in support of this bill, which would not equally justify a similar measure, against citizens of the United States. And, so far as relates to the necessity of the bill, the plea may be equally made against citizens as against aliens . . . since they might argue that seditious and turbulent citizens might be as dangerous to the peace of the country, as aliens of a similar description; and when gentlemen are disposed to treat the Constitution in this way to come at aliens, he had no doubt they would be ready to do it against citizens whenever they shall wish to do so.

The specious "legal distinctions" employed by proponents of the bill to justify the arbitrary imprisonment of aliens could also be used against Americans because, according to this "doctrine . . . Congress may give, by law, the power to the President, or any one else, to deprive a citizen of his liberty or property, and the act of giving that power by law, will be called the due process of law contemplated by the Constitution."[78]

As the new Federalist "doctrine" rested, in part, on the "necessary and proper" clause of the Constitution, Republican members of the House asked why it was that no evidence had been presented to show why such extraordinary measures were necessary. "The state of things, if we are to judge from the complexion of this bill," said Edward Livingston of New York, "must be, that a number of aliens enjoying the protection of our Government, were plotting its destruction; that they are engaged in treasonable machinations against a people who have given them an asylum and support." Yet Livingston's own observations painted a very different picture. "Most of the aliens" he had seen "were either triumphant Englishmen or Frenchmen, with dejection in their countenances and grief at their hearts, preparing to quit the country and seek another asylum." Republican members of the House also challenged the Federalist reading of the destruction of Old World republics. Representative Livingston denied that "the fate of Venice, Switzerland, and Batavia, was produced by the interference of foreigners." Those republics, he argued, had "been overcome by foreign force [armies], or divided by domestic faction, not by aliens who resided among them." Therefore, Livingston sarcastically observed, "if any instruction was to be gained

[78] Gales, ed., *Annals of Congress, 5th Cong.*, 2013 (Livingston), 1980–82 (Gallatin).

from those Republics, it would be, that we ought to banish not aliens, but all those who did not approve of the Executive acts."

Samuel Smith of Maryland cited the actions of foreigners during the American Revolution, when "foreign influence was much more to be dreaded . . . than at present." Although there were indeed traitors during the Revolution, Smith argued that "they were more frequently found among native Americans than among foreigners. He believed no instance could be found in which an alien had disgraced himself in the situation in which he was employed . . . therefore, from past experience of the faithfulness of foreigners, we ought not now, all at once, pass laws which will bear so hard on them." In any event, as Albert Gallatin pointed out, existing statutes would "reach alien friends if guilty of seditious and or treasonable practices, as well as citizens. And if the law is not at present sufficient to reach every case," it could be amended in ways that would not deny aliens the right to trial by jury or make them "subject to the arbitrary control of one man only."[79]

Because the bill's backers had presented "No facts . . . with respect to alien friends, which require these arbitrary means to be employed against them," what then was the real purpose of the Act concerning Aliens? For eighteenth-century Americans the answer to this question was clear. The history of humankind had taught them "that whenever Governments have wished to make inroads upon the liberties of the people, nothing has been more common than to institute an alarm of danger of some kind or other."[80] Citing the need for extraordinary power to fend off phantom threats, would-be despots insidiously encroached on the rights of the people with stealth and cunning. In the 1770s, vigilant patriots had identified such a plot to establish tyranny in America. Now, as then, vigilance was the key to preserving American liberty—and the Constitution that guarded it. In June of 1798 Representative Livingston urged his colleagues to "beware of the first act of violation" on the Constitution, as, "Habituated to overleap its bounds, we become familiarized to the guilt, and disregard the danger of a second offense, until, proceeding from one authorized act to another, we at length throw off all restraint which our Constitution has imposed; and very soon not even the semblance of its form will remain . . . every vestige of it will be gone, swallowed up in the gulf of despotism."[81]

Republican members of Congress vigorously rebutted claims that aliens were not protected by the same laws and Constitutional safeguards as American citizens. Representatives Gallatin and Livingston argued that the Constitution itself stipulated equal protection of the laws for "alien friends . . . residing among us." Gallatin cited the Fifth Amendment guarantee that "no person shall be deprived of his life, liberty, or property, without due process of law," pointing out that it

[79] Gales, ed., *Annals of Congress, 5th Cong.*, 2006–7 (Livingston), 2023 (S. Smith), 1980 (Gallatin).
[80] Ibid., 1980 (Gallatin), 1995 (R. Williams).
[81] Ibid., 2012–13, 2014 (Livingston).

extended these rights to all "persons," not just citizens. Edward Livingston's argument was similar as he argued that "the Constitution expressly excludes any idea of this distinction" between citizens and alien friends when it spoke of "all 'judicial power,' 'all trials for crime,' all 'criminal prosecutions,' all 'persons accused.' No distinction between citizens and alien, between high or low, friends or opposers to the Executive power, republican and royalist. All are entitled to the same equal distribution of justice, to the same humane provision to protect their innocence; all are liable to the same punishment that awaits their guilt. How comes it, too, if these Constitutional provisions were intended for the safety of the citizen only, that our courts uniformly extend them [to] all, and that we never hear it inquired whether the accused is a citizen, before we give him a public trial by jury?" Both men also argued that it was "an acknowledged principle of the common law, the authority of which is established here, that alien friends . . . residing among us, are entitled to the protection of our laws" and concluded that, "as far as relates to personal liberty, the Constitution and common law include aliens as well as citizens; and if Congress have the power to take it from one, they may also take it from the other." Therefore, the preservation of the Constitution and American liberty required maintaining the rights of the republic's immigrants. In Livingston's words, "the citizen has no other security for his personal safety than is extended to the stranger who is within his gates."[82]

As Republicans argued that maintaining the rights of aliens was essential to the preservation of American liberty, they also denied the national government the right to regulate or restrict immigration for the same reason. In the eighteenth century, it was an axiom that a separation of powers was essential to free government, as it prevented the monopolization of power by any one man or group of men, who, given human nature, would be irresistibly driven to abuse it. The events of 1798 convinced congressional Republicans that it was absolutely essential to maintain the rights of the states, to serve as a counterweight against the Federalists who seemed intent on engrossing all power into the hands of the "general Government." Republican opposition to national interference with immigration was generated as much by the fear of upsetting the balance of power established by the Constitution as by the need to preserve European access to the American asylum. Congressmen from several states had additional reasons for demanding that the right to control immigration remain with the states. The large alien populations in New York, Pennsylvania, and Maryland would make opposition to federal attempts to restrict immigration popular among naturalized voters and among Americans who still hoped to benefit from a burgeoning population, land sales to immigrants, and the skills and property foreigners brought with them. Even Federalists succumbed to such pressure. The Federalist

---

[82] Gales, ed., *Annals of Congress, 5th Cong.*, 1956 (Gallatin), 2011, 2012, 2013 (Livingston).

Representative from Maryland, William Craik, moderated his stance on alien issues to avoid offending his state's large German population, and Rufus King of New York helped to facilitate the immigration of an Irish rebel whose capital and business acumen he coveted.[83] The issue of immigration restriction was especially potent in the South. After the Revolution, the slave states continued to promote white immigration to reduce the danger of servile insurrection. Samuel Smith of Maryland warned that doing "anything which should impede emigration, would be illy received" by states that encouraged immigration; he also pointed out, "It would be recollected that it was one of our complaints against Great Britain, in our Declaration of Independence, that she had taken pains to prevent emigration to some of the States."[84] Edward Livingston of New York and Abraham Baldwin of Georgia also raised the point that, if Congress secured the power to deport noncitizens, what would prevent them, and their abolitionist friends, from deporting African slaves?[85]

And so it happened, in the spring of 1798, that the Jeffersonian Republicans became the defenders of alien rights and the American asylum—men who had previously urged restraint in adding foreigners to the American population and were wary of their political impact. In the 1780s, Thomas Jefferson had questioned "the present desire of America . . . to produce rapid population by as great importations of foreigners as possible" and urged his countrymen "to wait with patience" for natural increase to produce the "degree of population desired." While questioning the mercantilist benefits of such migrations, Jefferson's fears were primarily political. He anticipated that most of America's immigrants would come from "absolutist monarchies" and would

> bring with them the principles of the governments they leave, imbibed in their early youth; or, if able to throw them off, it will be in exchange for an unbounded licentiousness, passing, as is usual, from one extreme to another. It would be a miracle were they to stop precisely at the point of temperate liberty. These principles, with their language, they will transmit to their children. In proportion to their numbers, they will share with us in the legislation. They will infuse into it their spirit, warp and bias its direction, and render it a heterogeneous, incoherent, distracted mass.[86]

[83] Gales, ed., *Annals of Congress, 5th Cong.*, 1779 (Craik); *The Life and Correspondence of Rufus King*, ed. Charles R. King, 2 vols. (New York: G. P. Putnam's Sons, 1895), II, 646. On the other hand, championing alien rights, if not linked with the preservation of liberty and the rights of American citizens, could be risky and unpopular among voters stirred up by bellicose Federalist rhetoric and by those who resented immigrants for taking work and profits from native-born Americans.

[84] Gales, ed., *Annals of Congress, 5th Cong.*, 2022, 2023 (S. Smith).

[85] Ibid., 2019. The irony of using a law designed to protect the African slave trade and pro-slavery arguments to keep the American asylum open for white Europeans is readily apparent here. These rather tortured arguments also highlight the extent to which the American asylum was built on African slavery.

[86] "Notes on the State of Virginia," in *Thomas Jefferson: Writings*, ed. Peterson, 209–14, quotes on 210, 211.

Despite these reservations, Jefferson, James Madison and other Republicans who shared their doubts now identified Federalist attempts to restrict immigration and to deny to aliens the full protection of the Constitution as the opening wedge of tyranny.

The issues and alarms raised by the Republican opposition did not disappear with the passage of the Alien, Sedition, and Naturalization Acts of 1798. Petitions against these Acts flooded the House of Representatives when it reconvened in the winter of 1798–1799. Thousands of Americans from Pennsylvania, New York, New Jersey, and Virginia signed protests "censuring many of the measures of the General Government." Typical was the petition from the inhabitants of Amelia country, Virginia, which remonstrated Congress for following "too much the policy of the British government, and particularly prays that the alien and sedition laws, which it terms impolitic, tyrannical, and unconstitutional, may be obliterated from our statute book."[87] These petitions were referred to a "select committee" of the House, over the objections of men such as Representative Harper of South Carolina, who "could not help protesting against an atrocious libel" in several Pennsylvania petitions, "against the courts and juries of this country." The select committee, dominated by Federalists, was not moved by the petitions, which repeated the arguments made against the alien and sedition acts in Congress in the spring of 1798. In their report, the committee expressed "regret that the public councils should ever be invited to listen to other than expressions of respect," but assured the House that they had "impartially considered the questions referred to their examination, and formed their opinions on a just appreciation of their merits, with a due regard to the authority of Government, and the dispassionate judgment of the American people." After such due deliberation, the committee found the sedition and alien acts constitutional on all counts.[88]

The House's select committee began its defense of the right of Congress to pass laws for deporting alien friends by asserting that "the asylum given by a nation, to foreigners, is mere matter of favor, resumable at the public will." Although the report stated that "On this point, abundant authorities might be adduced," it cited only "the common practice of nations." The Federalist committee now grounded its argument for the constitutionality of the Alien Friends Act on Article 4, section 4 of the Constitution, by which "Congress is required to protect each State from invasion," and the "necessary and proper" clause granting Congress the "power to make all laws, which shall be proper to carry into effect all powers vested by the Constitution in the Government." Based on these sanctions, the committee concluded that "The right of removing aliens, as an incident to the power of war and peace, according to the Constitution, belongs

---

[87] Gales, ed., *Annals of Congress, 5th Cong.*, 2798, 2807, 2955, 2957–59. Quote from a summary of a petition from Amelia county, Virginia, Jan. 30, 1799, on 2798.

[88] Ibid., 2957 (Harper); 2985–93 (committee report, quotes on 2986).

to the Government of the United States . . . and to remove from the country, in times of hostility, dangerous aliens, who may be employed in preparing the way for invasion, is a measure necessary for the purpose of preventing invasion, and of course a measure that Congress is empowered to adopt." The committee's report was adopted by the House when the Representatives, after rebuttals by leading Republicans, voted 52 to 48 to endorse the committee's resolution "That it is inexpedient to repeal" the alien and sedition acts "passed the last session" of Congress.[89]

Debate in the States

With their defeat in Congress, the defense of the Republican vision of American liberty and alien rights retreated to the states. At this level, Republican arguments were more effective. In several state legislatures the Republican opposition successfully established a link not only between the survival of the American asylum and the republic itself but also between the rights of aliens and American citizens. They argued that Federalists who succeeded in trampling on the rights of foreigners would soon expand their depredations, invade the rights of citizens, and ultimately destroy free government in America.

In 1798–1799, the Federalist-controlled Massachusetts legislature circulated resolutions proposing an amendment to the Constitution that, at a minimum, would exclude "from a Seat in either branch of Congress, any persons who shall not have been actually naturalized at the time of making this amendment and have been admitted Citizens of the United States Fourteen years at least at the time of such election." Four New England states along with Delaware and Maryland endorsed these resolutions, but they were voted down by seven state legislatures. In the New York Assembly Republicans secured the rejection of the Massachusetts resolutions by arguing that the proposed amendment would violate the rights and sovereignty of the American people, subvert fundamental law, and renege on the pledge made at the end of the Revolution, when "America stood with open arms and presented an asylum to the oppressed of every nation; we invited them with a promise of enjoying equal rights with ourselves . . . shall we then so soon set our faces against principles so solemnly avowed, shall we deprive these persons of an important right derived from so sacred a source as our constitution?"[90]

The Alien Friends Act of 1798 and the power it gave the president over any

[89]Gales, ed., *Annals of Congress, 5th Cong.*, quotes on 2986, 2992.

[90]James M. Banner, *To the Hartford Convention: The Federalists and the Origins of Party Politics in Massachusetts, 1789–1815* (New York: Knopf, 1970), 97; *Political Correspondence and Public Papers of Aaron Burr*, ed. Mary-Jo Kline, 2 vols. (Princeton: Princeton University Press, 1983), I, 363–76, quote from speech by Aaron Burr on 367.

foreigner he considered dangerous came under especially severe fire in the South. On July 4, 1798, the inhabitants of Clark County, Kentucky, denounced the Bill as "unconstitutional, impolitic, unjust, and disgraceful to the American character." Governor James Garrard of Kentucky, echoed these sentiments when he told state legislators that their firm protests against all unconstitutional laws and impolitic proceedings" [the Alien and Sedition Acts] would "raise high the character of your country in the esteem of those whose good opinions you should be solicitous of acquiring, and convince the friends of liberty and of man that whatever may be the fate of their cause in other countries, Kentucky, removed from the contaminating influence of European politics, is steady in the principles of pure republicanism, and will ever be the asylum of her persecuted votaries.[91]

The Resolutions passed by Virginia's House of Delegates in December 1798 "particularly protest[ed] against the palpable and alarming infractions of the Constitution" in the Alien and Sedition Acts. Virginia legislators argued that the Alien Friends Act, "by uniting legislative and judicial powers to those of [the] executive, subverts the general principles of free government, as well as the particular organization and positive provisions of the Federal Constitution." In their "Address of the General Assembly to the People of the Commonwealth of Virginia," the delegates argued that

> If a suspicion that aliens are dangerous constitute the justification of that power exercised over them by Congress, then a similar suspicion will justify the exercise of a similar power over natives. . . . But this bill contains other features, still more alarming and dangerous. It dispenses with the trial by jury; it violates the judicial system; it confounds legislative, executive, and judicial powers; it punishes without trial; and it bestows upon the President despotic power over a numerous class of men. Are such measures consistent with our constitutional principles? And will an accumulation of power so extensive in the hands of the Executive, over aliens, secure to natives the blessings of republican liberty?[92]

James Madison, in his defense and explication of the Virginia Resolutions, went even further. After demonstrating the unconstitutional nature of the Alien Friends Act and its dangerous implications for native-born Americans, Madison addressed the issue of alien rights, arguing

> that although aliens are not parties to the constitution, it does not follow that the constitution has vested in Congress an absolute power over them. . . . But a more direct reply is, that it does not follow, because aliens are not parties to the constitution, as citizens are parties to it, that whilst they actually conform to it, they have no

[91] Ethelbert Dudley Warfield, *The Kentucky Resolutions of 1798: An Historical Study* (New York: G. P. Putnam, 1887), quotes on 41, 74–75.

[92] *The Writings of James Madison*, ed. Gaillard Hunt, 8 vols. (New York: G. P. Putnam's Sons, 1900–1908), VI, 326–31; 332–40; quotes on 327–28, 337–38.

right to its protection. Aliens are no more parties to the laws, yet it will not be disputed, that as they owe on one hand, a temporary obedience, they are entitled in return, to their protection and advantage.

If aliens had no rights under the constitution, they might not only "be banished, but even capitally punished, without a jury or the other incidents of a fair trial. But so far has a contrary principle been carried, in every part of the United States, that except on charges of treason, an alien has, besides all the common privileges, the special one of being tried by a jury, of which one half may be also aliens."[93]

The "Revolution of 1800"

The election of 1800 was a referendum on—and a repudiation of—the Federalist "doctrines" enunciated in the debates, in and out of doors, on standing armies, war with France, direct taxation, the power of the federal government, the sanctity of the Constitution, and the Alien, Sedition, and Naturalization Acts of 1798.[94] Although Thomas Jefferson after his election in 1800 announced that "We are all Republicans, We are all Federalists," he and his fellow Republicans were committed to implementing their interpretation of "the principles of 1776" and dismantling the Federalist "perversions" of America's revolutionary ideals. During the election campaign of 1800, Republicans promised to return America to a time when

> No alien law existed. Every industrious or valuable man who chose to contribute by his ingenuity or learning to your arts or manufactures, was invited to emigrate, every oppressed man was taught to believe, that here he would find an asylum from tyranny . . . that the sacred right of jury should be preserved to him—that it should not depend on the will of any individual, however important and elevated; and in whose breast was impenetrably locked the reason of this procedure, to force him from this asylum, and banish him without the intervention of a jury. . . . You had then a very small standing army—no stamp act—no direct tax, laid almost entirely on the landed and agricultural interests, not touching public bank, or insurance stock,

[93] *Papers of James Madison*, ed. Hutchinson, XVII, 307–50, quote on 320.
[94] James H. Broussard, *The Southern Federalists, 1800–1816* (Baton Rouge: Louisiana State University Press, 1978), chaps. 1–2; Risjord, *Chesapeake Politics*, chap. 20; Dauer, *Adams Federalists*, chap. 16; Daniel Sisson, *The American Revolution of 1800* (New York: Knopf, 1974), chaps. 8–9 and Epilogue; Cunningham, *Jeffersonian Republicans: The Formation of Party Organization*; Delbert Harold Gilpatrick, *Jeffersonian Democracy in North Carolina, 1789–1816* (New York: Columbia University Press, 1931), chap. 3; (Philadelphia) *The Universal Gazette*, Aug. 15, 1799 ("To the Republicans of Pennsylvania"), Sept. 15, 1799 ("To the Electors of Northumberland County"); *Raleigh Register and North-Carolina Weekly*, June 17, 1800 ("A Republican Farmer"), June 24, 1800 ("A Citizen"); (Washington, Penn.) *Herald of Liberty*, July 7, 1800 (editorial), Sept. 15, 1800 ("On the Naturalization Act of Congress"), Sept. 29, 1800 ("The COMMITTEE of Essex County [N. J.] to the PEOPLE"); (Newport, R.I.) *The Guardian of Liberty*, Nov. 8, 1800 (Timoleon, "A Solemn Address").

money at interest, or any securities in the possession of the speculators, who had robbed our officers and soldiers of the price of their blood and service in the revolutionary war—you had then no act for a provisional army, establishing the unexampled precedent of vesting in an individual, to raise, when in his opinion necessary, a very large regular force, and to appoint and commission, of his own authority, the whole of his officers. You had then no public loans, at the excessive rate of eight per cent.[95]

Subsequent Republican victories in the early nineteenth century validated their principles and vision for the future of the United States, whereas the Federalist principles and pronouncements of the late 1790s were increasingly seen as archaic holdovers or temporary aberrations induced by "wartime" hysteria.

As the victorious Republicans reformulated the nation's political principles, their electoral success also sealed the unique character and ambiguous nature of the American asylum. Continued skepticism about the benefits of large-scale migrations, combined with the Democratic-Republican insistence on limiting the power and size of government and reducing the national debt, removed any chance of federal subsidies or free land for immigrants. Republican insistence on the sovereign power of the American people and a single class of republican citizenship dictated a continuation of the five-year probationary period, alien reports, and other safeguards instituted by the Naturalization Acts of 1795 and 1798. These considerations also mandated a rejection of the regenerative role that had been imposed on Americans in their colonial past. While most Americans agreed that foreigners would benefit from the rich political and physical bounty of America, the survival of their free and self-governing republic required an official, though largely unenforced, exclusion of Europe's "dissolute dregs." The increasing nineteenth-century commitment of the Democratic-Republicans to slavery and to the theories of racial inferiority that justified that institution also continued the denial of liberty to black immigrants and created an unacknowledged second-class citizenship for America's free blacks.[96]

Yet the avowed political principles of the party of Jefferson also kept the door to the American asylum open for Europeans oppressed by tyranny and protected the rights of white aliens and naturalized citizens. At the end of the eighteenth century, the Republican opposition had identified Federalist attempts to abridge alien rights and limit access to the American land of liberty as part of a systematic and unconstitutional plot to subvert republicanism. Therefore, denying the federal government the right to restrict alien rights and immigration was the first line of defense in preserving liberty for American citizens. European governments could deport aliens without a trial

---

[95] Quotes from *Thomas Jefferson: Writings*, ed. Peterson, 493; "A Republican Farmer," *Raleigh Register and North-Carolina Daily Advertiser*, June 17, 1800.

[96] For the status of free blacks, see Kettner, *Development of American Citizenship*, chap. 10.

and deny foreigners full civil rights. However, similar actions by the United States had been identified by the triumphant Republicans as the unconstitutional precursors of tyranny.

The Federalist Dilemma

Although the nativism that shaped Federalist laws and policies at the end of the eighteenth century is readily apparent, the party's position on immigration was not monolithic. Federalist antipathy toward aliens was primarily political, aimed at the type of immigrant who would support the Republican opposition and threaten the nation's domestic tranquillity. Although most Federalists agreed that certain immigrants were undesirable—the radical, the dissolute, and, most of all, the "Wild Irish" and French "Jacobins"—many continued to covet the mercantilist benefits that accrued from the immigration of men of property and conservative political principles. Still others tried to disassociate themselves from the xenophobic extremes of their outspoken colleagues for political reasons.

On June 27, 1798, Pennsylvania's Governor Mifflin succumbed to the fear generated by Federalist rumors of an imminent French invasion of America led by St. Domingue blacks. Mifflin, acting on information provided by a passenger on board a vessel from St. Domingue, reported to President Adams that

> on the evacuation of Port au Prince by the British troops, a very great number of French white men and negroes were put on board of transports and sent to America. Some of the vessels, I understand, made an attempt to land their passengers in Charleston; two have arrived at this port [Philadelphia], and it is said, that the remainder of the fleet may be daily expected in some of our harbours. To prevent, as far as I can, the obvious danger from such importation at this crisis, I have determined to prohibit the landing of any French negroes arriving at the port of Philadelphia in vessels under the circumstances which I have stated; but, the limited jurisdiction of Pennsylvania, the facility with which our regulations may be evaded, by disembarking the negroes in any adjacent state, and, perhaps, the necessity of extending the prohibition to white men, induce me to submit the subject to your consideration; and to request such a cooperation of the Federal Authority, as your excellency may deem expedient for the general safety.

After President Adams presented this document to the Senate, William Bingham, the Federalist Senator from Pennsylvania who a few years earlier had been recruiting French settlers for his lands in Maine, sponsored a bill "to authorize the President to prevent and regulate the landing of French passengers, and other persons, who may arrive within the United States from foreign places."[97]

[97] *Philadelphia Gazette and Universal Daily Advertiser*, June 28 (Mifflin's report), 29, 30, July 2, 3, 1798; Gales, ed., *Annals of Congress, 5th Cong.*, 592–94 (Bingham), 2058, 2063–67.

The "French Passenger bill" passed in the Senate, but it died in the House on a motion by Samuel Sewall, a Federalist Representative from Massachusetts who had been instrumental in securing the passage of the Alien and Naturalization Acts of 1798. Sewall moved to quash the bill after receiving a memorial from the American merchants who owned the vessels that were being denied the right to land at Philadelphia and a statement by the French refugees on board. The merchants asked Congress to consider the losses they would endure if their "richly laden" vessels were not "speedily unladen," and the hardships facing the "masters of their vessels [who] never met with any difficulty of this kind heretofore, but had considered this country as an asylum for all who chose to come to it." The French passengers, in their address, labeled "the pretended facts" presented to Governor Mifflin "false, groundless and calumnious." Not only were they "all peaceable people and of good character" with "fortunes more or less inconsiderable, already lodged in the United States of America," but all of the 55 slaves on board ("of whom 27 are men") had "followed their owners from choice and [were] attached to their masters' interest." None of the slaves was armed, nor had any "one of them ever bore arms." With the defeat of the bill, the passengers on the vessels in the Delaware were eventually allowed to land; the French refugees turned away at Charleston were forced to find their "asylum" at St. Augustine.[98]

The Alien and Sedition Acts of 1798 generated similar constraints on immigration and similar Federalist ambivalence. During the summer of 1800 Irish immigrants arriving at New York reported "that many of the most vicious and bloody-minded of the United Irishmen were deterred from coming to this country merely by the report of the scrutinizing character of our Executive and of the severity of the Alien and Sedition Laws." In August 1800 Captain Delano of the Brig *Bellona* felt compelled to inform the public that he had unwittingly transported an infamous United Irishman to America from Sligo and to warn the residents of Philadelphia to have "a cautious eye upon him."[99]

In 1798 and 1799 Federalist officials did more than rely on such indirect deterrents to keep out undesirable immigrants. When the British government announced its willingness to spare the lives of the "Traitors" who had participated in the Irish Rebellion of 1798 "upon condition of being banished from Ireland and passing the remainder of their days in the dominion of a State in amity with his Majesty," Rufus King, the American Ambassador to Great Britain, lobbied vigorously against the inclusion of the United States on any list of refugee countries. It was King's opinion that the Irish rebellion had been fomented by the French to establish their own hegemony over Ireland. According to his report to Secretary of State Pickering, "every day supplies new proofs of the intimate

---

[98] Gales, ed., *Annals of Congress,* 5th Cong., 2067, 2058; *Philadelphia Gazette and Universal Daily Advertiser,* July 2, 17, 1798.

[99] Ibid., July 23, Aug. 6, 1800.

connection that subsists between the Chiefs of the [Irish] malcontents and the Directory" and "of a conspiracy formed by some of the Members of the [English] Corresponding Societies to assist the French in case of a descent, to set fire to London." Such men, would undoubtedly "seek an asylum in our country," carrying with them "principles and habits [that] would be pernicious to the order and industry of our people." Ambassador King simply could not convince himself "that the Malcontents of any country will ever become useful citizens of our own."[100]

After receiving the Ambassador's objections, British officials assured King that their government would not permit the deportation of Irish rebels to any nation that objected to receiving them. Indeed, added the Duke of Portland, who apparently still resented the loss of so many British subjects to republican America, "the country of the United States is the last in the World which I should wish to see become their residence." At the end of November 1798 the masters of vessels sailing from Ireland to America began publishing notices that they would take on board only those passengers who "do not come under the description of those whom the American Minister has said will not be admitted into the United States." Thus the Irish rebels to whom American revolutionaries had appealed in the 1770s were now denied their promised asylum. Instead of respite in America, hundreds of vanquished Irish freedom fighters, many of whom saw themselves as fighting the Irish equivalent of the American Revolution, were forced into the armies of European princes or were transported to Britain's penal colonies in Australia.[101] In the months following the defeat of the French Passenger bill and the passage of the Alien and Sedition Acts of 1798, the newspapers of America's port cities were filled with advertisements for vessels available to remove Frenchmen from their increasingly uncomfortable refuge in America and to return them to France or St. Domingue.[102]

Federalist policies and officials were responsible for denying sanctuary to Irish

[100] King, London, to Pickering, May 11, June 14, 1798, in *Life and Correspondence of Rufus King*, II, 637.

[101] Ibid., quotes on: II, 642 (Duke of Portland to the Lord Lieutenant of Ireland, Oct. 17, 1798), 641 (Duke of Portland to Rufus King, Sept. 22, 1798); *Belfast News-Letter*, Nov. 30, 1798 (passenger notice, Brig *Sally*); Robert Hughes, *The Fatal Shore: The Epic of Australia's Founding* (New York: Knopf, 1987), 183–94; *Felix Farley's Bristol Journal*, Mar. 2, 30, 1799; *Belfast News-Letter*, Apr. 12, May 31, June 7, 18, July 16, Oct. 29, 1799. Although the British government did not officially deport Irish rebels to the United States, little effort was made to prohibit the emigration of most United Irishmen who sought a voluntary refuge in America. In December 1798 the Lord Lieutenant of Ireland "caused intimation to be made" to all state prisoners except fifteen whom he named, "that if they do not depart from Ireland in the course of a month, they must afterwards remain in Prison and maintain themselves at their own expence." In January 1799, it was reported that "Several prisoners confined in Belfast for treason, have been liberated on giving bail to quit the kingdom, after settling their affairs, the 4th of March." *Felix Farley's Bristol Journal*, Dec. 15, 1798 (quotes), Jan. 19, 1799 (quote). Neither of these reports suggested that those posting bail could not emigrate to the United States. Notices in Irish newspapers that vessels for the United States would not embark United Irishmen were as easily evaded as notices that shipmasters would not take skilled artisans.

[102] For advertisements in French and English of cartels sailing from Philadelphia to France and St. Domingue and reports of other cartels sailing from New York and Boston see, *Philadelphia Gazette and Universal Daily Advertiser*, July 11, 17, 19, 20, Aug. 4, 16, 20, 1798.

and French refugees, but many party leaders displayed a residue of the earlier Federalist attitude toward immigrants. In 1799 Henry Jackson, an Irish rebel barred from emigrating to the United States, appealed to Ambassador Rufus King for an exception. Although King denied his ability to intervene, he did, after examining Jackson's business and character references, withdraw his personal objections and authorized the former rebel to use that fact to facilitate his entry into the United States. Rufus King summed up the Federalist dilemma in a letter to the Irish rebel:

> On the one hand we cannot object to the acquisition of Inhabitants from abroad possessing capital and skill in a branch of business, that with due caution, may without risque or difficulty, and with public as well as private advantage, be established among us; but on the other hand if the opinions of such inhabitants are likely to throw them into the class of malcontents, their fortune, skill and consequent influence would make them tenfold more dangerous and they might become a disadvantage instead of a benefit to our country.[103]

To some extent, Federalist disavowals of extreme anti-immigrant measures and rhetoric were driven by political expediency. Elected officials such as Representative William Craik of Maryland, whose district was home to a large number of unnaturalized aliens, had to make it clear that they did not despise the character and principles of all foreigners. Thus Craik, in 1798, had "no objection" to denying citizenship to future immigrants, but urged leniency for those already in the country, especially the Germans whom he characterized as "well entitled to every privilege that can be given them." Federalists who did not hold office also qualified their position and pointed out the admirable qualities of different groups of immigrants. In 1798 Alexander Hamilton, now a private citizen practicing law in New York City, urged Federalist legislators "not to be cruel or violent" when writing the new alien code. Although Hamilton believed that "the mass [of aliens] ought to be obliged to leave the country," he urged that the treaty provisions "in favor of Merchants ought to be observed" and that a few "*guarded* exceptions" be made "of characters whose situations would expose them too much if sent away and whose demeanor among us has been unexceptionable." In 1797 a New York City editorial criticized the "fugitive Irishman" who published a letter to Harrison Gray Otis "abusing him [Otis] for calling the cargoes of emigrants from Ireland, 'hordes of Wild Irishmen'." After describing the letter as "the usual ranting stile of modern *liberty boys*, who talk much more about government than they understand," the editor ended with a qualified disclaimer, writing: "There are many excellent citizens from Ireland, who have entered into business in the United States; and the Irish people of breeding are remarkable for generosity, hospitality, bravery, and other virtues. But whether Mr. Otis was

---

[103] King, London, Aug. 28, 1799, to Henry Jackson, in *Life and Correspondence of Rufus King*, II, 646.

correct in his expression or not, his ideas of the class of people brot [*sic*] from Ireland are just. The most of them are from the diseased and corrupted part of the Irish nation, and are a nuisance to this country."[104]

The Immigrant Vote

Federalist nativism also was mitigated by the support given the party by immigrants of all nationalities who shared their political fears, aspirations, and principles. The mass naturalization of Irish immigrants in the 1790s, especially in Philadelphia, has long been viewed as evidence that the foreign-born were the mainstay of the Republican opposition, providing the party with its margin of victory in 1800.[105] Prior to the passage of the Alien and Sedition Acts of 1798, there was, however, no reason for immigrant voters to shun the Federalist party. Immigration to republican America was not confined to political radicals. In the postwar years many of America's immigrants came in search of economic opportunity; in the 1790s thousands were conservative refugees, fleeing revolutionary upheavals in Europe and the West Indies. The widely heralded arrival of prominent English radicals, United Irishmen, and French Jacobins has masked the presence of less celebrated immigrants who retained traditional or conservative values.

Contemporaries were well aware of the traditional political beliefs held by many eighteenth-century immigrants. Charges that America's conservatives were benefiting from the votes of tories and British subjects surfaced even before the end of the American Revolution. In 1778 James Warren blamed the political opposition's "use of the Tories to prevent my being chosen by my town" as a representative to the General Court of Massachusetts. In 1796 a similar accusation appeared in the *Boston Chronicle*, claiming that the Federalist candidate Harrison Gray Otis had secured his election to Congress by the votes of over 400 "British residents, refugees [tories], etc."[106] Although such charges were a staple

---

[104] Gales, ed., *Annals of Congress, 5th Cong.* 1779 (Craik); Smith, *Freedom's Fetters*, 54–55 (Hamilton); (New York) *Minerva & Mercantile Evening Advertiser*, Sept. 9, 1797 (editorial). Even Representative Otis, during the same speech in which he advocated keeping out "the mass of vicious and disorganizing characters who could not live peaceably at home," expressed his respect for "honest and industrious" immigrants, "whether Germans, Irishmen, or foreigners of whatever country, who had become citizens . . . while they remained obedient to the laws and faithful to their adopted country," in Gales, ed., *Annals of Congress, Fifth Cong.*, 430.

[105] Edward C. Carter, Jr., "A 'Wild Irishman' under Every Federalist's Bed: Naturalization in Philadelphia, 1789–1806," *Pennsylvania Magazine of History & Biography*, 94 (1970), 332; Smith, *Freedom's Fetters*, 37–38; Morison, *Life and Letters of Harrison Gray Otis*, I, 107. In 1798 John Allen, the Federalist Representative from Connecticut, alluded to "the vast number of naturalizations which lately took place in this city [Philadelphia] to support a particular party [Republican] in a particular election" during the debate on the Naturalization Act of 1798. Gales, ed., *Annals of Congress, 5th Cong.*, 1579.

[106] Allan Nevins, *The American States during and after the Revolution, 1775–1789* (New York: Macmillan, 1924), Warren quoted on 211; *Boston Chronicle*, Nov. 10, 1796, quoted in Morison, *Life and Letters of*

of American politics, there is no reason to doubt that many aliens, whether disfranchised tories or foreign-born immigrants, would find conservative and Federalist principles more attractive than those of radicals or the Republican opposition. This was especially true in the years immediately following the Revolution, when conservative Americans were advocating leniency for returning loyalists, and in the mid-1790s when Federalists supported British leadership in the battle of "true liberty" against the libertine and leveling excesses of the French Revolution. Immigrants who had been recruited by Federalist landowners or manufacturers, as well as those with conservative political beliefs, also would find Federalist principles congenial before that party's descent into nativism at the end of the eighteenth century. Prior to 1798 there was simply no reason for America's immigrants to flock, *en masse*, to the Republican standard.

The biographies of prominent immigrants give dozens of examples of foreigners who became staunch Federalists. The Scottish-born Charles Williamson became a mainstay of the Federalist party in western New York; Duncan Phyfe, who emigrated from Scotland in 1792 performed a similar role in New York City. The histories of Baltimore, Maryland, reveal that immigrants from northern Ireland, such as Robert Oliver and Alexander Brown, became stalwarts of the Federalist party.[107] These immigrant supporters of the Federalist party undoubtedly represented the political proclivities of a substantial number of their less prominent countrymen. Among the memorials addressed to President Adams in the summer of 1798, lauding his firmness in dealing with the French threat, were many similar to that signed by "119 natives of Great-Britain and Ireland" who lived in Albany, New York. This address assured the President that the memorialists, knowing well "the blessings of a good energetic government to be of inestimable value" felt "with as keen resentment as any, the outrages and insults wantonly and daringly committed by the French republic against the interests, dignity and independence of the United States."[108]

It was only natural that nonradical British immigrants would share the Federalist hostility toward French revolutionaries who had declared war on friends and

---

Harrison Gray Otis, I, 58n. Some historians also have noted the tendency of different ethnic groups to support the Federalist party. See Fischer, *Revolution of American Conservatism*, 223–25. Morison, *The Life and Letters of Harrison Gray Otis*, I, 107, and Carter "'Wild Irishman,'" 343–45, also suggest that the Federalists, on occasion, promoted the naturalization of suitable immigrants and wooed naturalized voters.

[107] Helen I. Cowan, *Charles Williamson: Genesee Promoter, Friend of Anglo-American Rapprochement* (Rochester, N.Y.: Rochester Historical Society, 1941), 56–57, 81–82, 99, 164–169, 204–5; Sean Wilentz, *Chants Democratic: New York City & the Rise of the American Working Class, 1788–1850* (New York: Oxford University Press, 1984), 36, 74; Thorburn, *Fifty Years' Reminiscences*; Stuart Bruchey, *Robert Oliver, Merchant of Baltimore, 1783–1819* (Baltimore: Johns Hopkins University Press, 1956), 21–25; Frank R. Kent, *The Story of Alexander Brown & Sons* (Baltimore: Norman T. A. Munder & Company, 1925).

[108] "ADDRESS to His Excellency JOHN ADAMS, President of the United States" signed by "119 natives of Great-Britain and Ireland," *Philadelphia Gazette and Universal Daily Advertiser*, July 18, 1798.

neighbors who had remained at home. A study of Maryland's Germans has found that, until 1796, many were "strong adherents of the Federalist Party . . . but then the majority shifted within a comparatively short time to the Republican-Democratic Party." The French crisis seems to have had the opposite effect on German immigrants in North Carolina, transforming them from political apathy into active supporters of the Federalist party.[109]

Naturalization Patterns

American court records show that surprisingly few aliens petitioned for naturalization in the nation's first decade of independence; most who did were mariners and merchants, hoping to avoid American duties, impressment by the British, or capture by privateers at war with their native lands. It appears that the lack of interest in securing republican citizenship was primarily the result of the nonenforcement of America's relatively mild alien disabilities, which gave immigrants little incentive to undergo the expense of formal naturalization. Foreigners may also have wished to avoid the civic burdens associated with citizenship, such as jury duty or militia obligations.[110]

In the early years of the republic, many foreign merchants were able to evade commercial restrictions by forming trans-Atlantic partnerships or by employing American agents in republican ports. The records of New York City indicate that such subterfuge was largely unnecessary for unnaturalized artisans and laborers. Some aliens were indeed denied licenses to practice the trades reserved for New York City's freemen. But occupations were recorded for hundreds of foreigners who registered as aliens in New York City between 1795 and 1820, and these included occupations officially closed to them by the city's charter and ordinances. An example of the nonenforcement of alien disabilities can be found in the minute books of New York City's Common Council. At a meeting held on May 26, 1800, the Council adopted a committee report recommending "That No Aliens shall be employed as Watchmen." But just one week later, on June 2nd, the Common Council "Ordered that the Street Commissrs with the Aldn & Assist of the 6th Wds enquire into the Character of such Aliens as may be employed as City Watchmen and that they direct such as they may deem worthy of the Trust to be continued in service." When alien disabilities were not overlooked, American officials often facilitated their legal removal. This was especially true in states that restricted alien landownership. When aliens were not

---

[109] Dieter Cunz, *The Maryland Germans* (Princeton: Princeton University Press, 1948), quote on 178; Smith, *Freedom's Fetters*, 31; Risjord, *Chesapeake Politics*, 537.

[110] I am indebted to James Kettner for the observation that the obligations of American citizenship may have deterred some immigrants from petitioning for naturalization.

allowed to own land in New York, the state legislature routinely passed special acts that exempted or naturalized individual alien landowners.[111]

A similar pattern of unenforced political disabilities emerged in the postwar period. Most state laws denied aliens the right to hold public office and postponed that right for naturalized citizens until they had resided in their adopted state for a number of years. Nonetheless, the lax enforcement of municipal ordinances, state laws, and the provisions of the federal Constitution allowed some unnaturalized aliens to hold high public office. According to evidence assembled by the Federalists in 1794, the Swiss-born Albert Gallatin was never formally naturalized. Despite that fact, Gallatin served, unchallenged, as a member of Pennsylvania's Constitutional Convention in 1789–1790, as state assemblyman, and, in 1793, was elected to represent Pennsylvania in the U.S. Senate. The records of New York City provide other examples of aliens holding less exalted public offices that were, by law, reserved for American citizens.[112]

Charles Williamson, the Scottish-born agent of a British land company, was more successful in securing American citizenship than Albert Gallatin. But the dubious grounds on which he was naturalized show the nonchalance with which political rights were extended to aliens in the early years of the republic. Willamson landed in Virginia in November 1791 and, on January 9, 1792, transformed himself into an American citizen by taking the oaths of allegiance and abjuration in Philadelphia. This was the Scottish agent's second trip to America. In 1781 Williamson voyaged to America to offer his services to the British army. In December 1781 American rebels captured the vessel on which he was sailing and Williamson became a prisoner of war in Massachusetts. He and his new American wife returned to Scotland with the evacuation of the British army in 1782. Even counting Williamson's wartime sojourn, he was not qualified for American citizenship under the Naturalization Act of 1790, which required a two-year residence in the United States, including at least one year in the state that conferred citizenship. Yet Williamson's American citizenship went unchallenged. By 1793 he was a member of the judiciary in Ontario county, New York, and in 1796 was elected to represent that county in the state assembly.[113]

In the postwar period, American franchise requirements were diverse and

---

[111] *Philadelphia Gazette and Daily Advertiser*, July 12, 1800; alien reports in Kenneth Scott, comp., *Early New York Naturalizations: Abstracts of Naturalization Records from Federal, State, and Local Courts, 1792–1840* (Baltimore: Genealogical Publishing Co., 1981); New York City Common Council, *Minutes of the Common Council of the City of New York, 1784–1831*, 19 vols. (New York: M. B. Brown 1917), II, 630–34, quotes on 631, 633. Between 1790 and 1800 New York's Legislature passed seventeen Acts "to enable" various aliens "to purchase and hold real estate within this State." See *Laws of the State of New York Passed at the Sessions of the Legislature Held in the Years, 1789, 1790, 1791, 1792, 1793, 1794, 1795, and 1796 Inclusive* (Albany: Weed, Parsons & Company, 1887), chaps. 41 and 46 (1790); chap. 43 (1791); chaps. 54 and 68 (1792); chap. 62 (1793); chaps. 49 and 58 (1794); chaps. 63, 65, 67 (1795); chaps. 58, 59, 60 (1796).

[112] Kettner, *Development of American Citizenship*, 232–35; Raymond Walters, Jr., *Albert Gallatin: Jeffersonian Financier and Diplomat* (New York: Macmillan, 1957). For aliens in New York City who held minor municipal posts see Scott, comp., *Early New York Naturalizations*.

[113] Cowan, *Charles Williamson: Genesee Promoter*, 22, 39, 99, 164.

often ambiguous. Most state constitutions and laws regulating elections implied, rather than stated, that citizenship was a prerequisite for voting. These laws were more concerned with spelling out property and residence qualifications than with defining the nativity and citizenship of inhabitants who were allowed to vote.

New York's Constitution of 1777 allowed "all male inhabitants of full age" with a freehold valued at £20 who had resided six months in the county to vote for the county's representative to the state assembly. But the state Constitution did not define the term "inhabitant." In 1787 New York's assembly passed a law that explicitly restricted the franchise in town meetings to male *citizens*. By 1813, a voter in New York who was challenged by election judges was required to swear (or affirm) that he was "a natural born, or naturalized citizen of the state of New York, or of one of the United States." In New York City, the prohibition on aliens voters was more straightforward; only freemen could vote and only citizens could become freemen.[114] There is, however, no reason to believe that state officials were any more rigorous in examining the qualifications of foreign-born voters than the credentials of prospective officeholders. And, as with alien officeholding, if unnaturalized foreigners voted in state and local elections in the first decade of independence, they aroused little furor.

When America's immigrants finally began to seek citizenship in large numbers, their motivation seems to have been political rather than to remove alien disabilities. Interest in the foreign-born voter intensified along with the political battles between Federalists and Republicans in the 1790s. A rising interest in politics increased the proportion of free white males voting in state elections in the second half of the 1790s. The naturalization of immigrants was part of this general expansion of the American electorate.

An analysis of court records in five major states shows a dramatic increase in naturalization, by both Federalist and Republican judges, in the middle of the 1790s. Sudden spurts of naturalization petitions on the eve of important elections suggest that Federalist and Republican politicians were equally adept at making voters out of their foreign-born supporters. Increased partisanship and interest in the immigrant vote also led to a clarification and enforcement of the political disabilities of aliens and naturalized citizens. In December of 1793 Albert

[114] New York's Constitution of 1777, in Francis Newton Thorpe, ed., *The Federal and State Constitutions, Colonial Charters, and Other Organic Laws of the States, Territories, and Colonies Now or Heretofore Forming The United States of America*, 7 vols. (Washington, D.C.: Government Printing Office, 1909), V, 2630–31 (quote on 2630); Chilton Williamson, *American Suffrage: From Property to Democracy, 1760–1860* (Princeton: Princeton University Press, 1960), 124; *The Laws of the State of New York, Revised and Passed at the Thirty-Sixth Session of the Legislature*, 2 vols. (Albany: H. C. Southwick & Co., 1813), II, chap. XLI, quote on 251. There was similar confusion over the voting rights of aliens in Massachusetts, which persisted until at least 1835. J. R. Pole, "Suffrage and Representation in Massachusetts: A Statistical Note," *William and Mary Quarterly*, 3d ser., 14 (1957), 573. For franchise ambiguities in other states, see Chapter 6 at note 72.

Table 1. Number of Naturalizations in New York City, 1790–1800

Year	Court of Common Pleas	U.S. Dist. & Circuit Courts
1790	0	3
1791	0	2
1792	2	4
1793	12	0
1794	149	0
1795	16	62
1796	26	115
1797	22	66
1798	2	87
1799	1	86
1800	0	0
Total	230	425

Gallatin's eligibility for the U.S. Senate was finally challenged for partisan reasons.[115]

The first surge in naturalizations occurred in New York City in 1794 when the local Court of Common Pleas, presided over by the city's Federalist mayor Richard Varick, granted citizenship to 149 alien petitioners. The following year, the Federalist judges of New York's District and Circuit Courts also began naturalizing in record numbers (see Table 1). Between 1794 and 1799 these three courts granted citizenship to 632 aliens, most of whom resided in New York City. These 632 naturalized citizens could, if they possessed the necessary property requirements, determine the outcome of elections in a city where the Federalist challenger had in 1793 outpolled Governor George Clinton by 136 votes (739 to 603) and where the margin of victory in Congressional races ranged from 205 votes in 1794 to 550 votes in 1796.[116]

The political turbulence of the mid-1790s produced similar surges in naturalization activity in all sections of the country. The peak year in South Carolina was 1796, when 91 aliens were naturalized in courts sitting at Charleston. A total of 404 foreigners were added to Charleston's list of potential voters between 1790 and 1800, 72.8 per cent of whom were naturalized by the Federalist judges of the U.S. District and Circuit Courts of South Carolina. Once again, these numbers were significant in a city that cast a total of 607 votes in the 1793 Congressional

[115] J. R. Pole, *Political Representation in England and the Origins of the American Republic*, 1st publ. 1966 (Berkeley: University of California Press, 1971), Appendix; Kettner, *Development of American Citizenship*, 232–35.

[116] Votes cast in New York County (New York City) elections in Young, *Democratic Republicans*, 589–91. Data in table 1 from Minute Books for the U.S. District Court and the U.S. Circuit Court for the District of Southern New York and the naturalization records of New York County's Court of Common Pleas, in Scott, comp. *Early New York Naturalizations*.

election and where the winning candidate in 1796 received 784 votes. In Maryland, 675 aliens were transformed into American citizens in Baltimore during the 1790s. With over 600 of these naturalizations occurring before the Congressional election in October 1798, immigrant voters might well have tipped the balance in the bitter battle between Samuel Smith, a recently converted Republican, and the Federalist candidate, James Winchester. Smith defeated his rival by 200 votes, of 3,500 cast. To the west, the judges of Maryland's Frederick county Court of Common Pleas added 161 names to their roster of citizens during the same period.[117]

Similar evidence from Pennsylvania during the 1790s substantiates the oft-repeated charge that Philadelphia's Republicans orchestrated the naturalization of their foreign-born supporters to win elections. But an analysis of Philadelphia's naturalization records shows that Judge Richard Peters, an extreme Federalist who presided over the U.S. District and Circuit Courts, was responsible for granting almost 45 per cent of the citizenship petitions submitted in Philadelphia during that decade. In 1798 Judge Peters naturalized 158 aliens, whereas the admittedly faulty records of Philadelphia's Court of Common Pleas for that year indicate the naturalization of only 57 aliens by its judges.[118] If the surviving peti-

[117] In all of these examples, the vast majority of the aliens naturalized resided in the city or county in which the court sat and were thus potential voters in local elections. Naturalization figures for Charleston are derived from National Archives, RG 21, Microfilm M-1183, and Brent H. Holcomb, comp., *South Carolina Naturalizations, 1783–1850* (Baltimore: Genealogical Publishing Co., 1985). Election results for Charleston from Inter-university Consortium for Political and Social Research, file 7757, "Candidacy and Constituency Statistics of Elections in the United States, 1788–1984 (Hereafter ICPSR, "Election Statistics"). Maryland's data from Minute Books of Maryland's U.S. District Court and U.S. Circuit Court at the National Archives and Record Center, Philadelphia, RG 21; and Naturalization Registers and Minute Books of the Baltimore County Court at the Maryland State Archives, Annapolis, Md. According to the ICPSR, "Election Statistics," 2642 votes were cast in Baltimore's Congressional election of 1792, with Samuel Smith receiving 1615 and the runner-up 1027. In 1794 and 1796, Samuel Smith ran unopposed and received 203 and 337 votes, respectively. Election data for 1798 from Frank A. Cassell, *Merchant Congressman in the Young Republic: Samuel Smith of Maryland, 1752–1839* (Madison: University of Wisconsin Press, 1971), 89. Samuel Smith was reelected to Congress in 1801 with 1,739 votes out of a total of 1,764 (ICPRS). Although the number of naturalizations in the Massachusetts counties of Suffolk and Essex also rose steadily during the 1790s, the numbers involved averaged only 13 per year in Suffolk and 5.6 per year in Essex county. Data from the Minute Books of the U.S. District Court and U.S. Circuit Court for Massachusetts, RG 21, National Archives and Record Center, Waltham, Mass.; Suffolk County Court of Common Pleas and the Supreme Court of the State of Massachusetts at the Suffolk County Court House; Essex County Court of Common Pleas at the Essex County Court House.

[118] Minutes Books, Alien Landing Reports, and some original naturalization petitions of the U.S. District Court and U.S. Circuit Court for the Eastern District of Pennsylvania have been preserved and are housed in the National Archives and Record Center in Philadelphia. For naturalizations in Philadelphia's nonfederal courts, the only surviving sources are the original petitions filed, in alphabetical order by court, at the Archives for the City and County of Philadelphia in Philadelphia; official indexes prepared in the late 1800s; and indexes prepared by the Work Progress Administration (WPA) in the 1930s. Many original petitions have disappeared. Edward Carter, relying on the WPA index of Philadelphia's original naturalization petitions, alien reports, and declarations of intent, has calculated a much higher naturalization level in Philadelphia in the 1790s than that given here. According to Carter's figures, 1,856 aliens were naturalized in Philadelphia's courts between 1790 and 1800, most of them in 1798 ($N = 938$) and 1799 ($N = 466$), Carter, "'Wild Irishman,'" 338. The most likely explanation for the discrepancies between Carter's figures and my own is based on the fact that none of Philadelphia's indexes clearly differentiate alien reports and

tions of Philadelphia's Court of Common Pleas are close to complete, that city's politicians were matched in their naturalizing activity by their counterparts in both Baltimore and New York City. In Maryland the U.S. District and Circuit Courts and Baltimore's County Court naturalized 675 aliens between 1790 and 1800. In New York City these three courts granted 655 citizenship petitions; in Philadelphia the same three courts performed an estimated 601 naturalizations, while an additional 204 aliens took the oath of allegiance before Philadelphia's mayor. Court records thus make it clear that large-scale naturalization was not the sole preserve of Philadelphia Republicans—judges of both political parties in all parts of the country naturalized increasingly large numbers of aliens during the 1790s.[119]

The clustering of naturalizations in the months and days preceding hard-fought elections strongly suggests that political candidates promoted the transformation of aliens into voters for partisan reasons. Court records from Massachusetts to South Carolina document the pre-election surges in naturalization activity that began in the mid-1790s, in both Federalist and Republican courts. In 1794 the Federalist judges of New York City's Court of Common Pleas naturalized 59 aliens (39.6 per cent of their annual total) in the three months preceding the city's Congressional election. In 1796 the Federalist judges of New York's U.S. District Court granted naturalization to 39 foreign residents of New York City in the two months preceding that year's election; the 25 petitions granted on November 1st alone constituted 30 per cent of the year's total. In the same year, the Federalist judges of Maryland's U.S. District Court naturalized 64 per cent ($N = 103$) of the year's total in June, at the beginning of a hotly contested campaign for Baltimore's congressional seat. In 1802, after the installation of Republican judges in New York City's Court of Common Pleas, congressional elections were shifted to the spring. In that year, the court's Republican judge managed to naturalize 99 aliens in the two days preceding the city's April election. On April 29 Mayor Edward Livingston's courtroom must have been filled to capacity by the 72 immigrant petitioners who chose that day to seek citizenship, as well as the lawyers

---

declarations of intent from naturalization petitions. During 1798 and 1799, hundreds of immigrants registered as aliens and/or made declarations of intent in Philadelphia after the passage of the Naturalization and Alien Acts of 1798. Combining the number of aliens who reported or declared their intent with those who petitioned for naturalization, which would duplicate many individuals, could account for Carter's higher figures.

[119] Naturalization statistics for Pennsylvania from sources described in note 117; and John B. Linn and William H. Egle, eds., *Pennsylvania Archives, Second Series* (Harrisburg: B. F. Meyers, 1875), III, 69–97. Data for Maryland from Minute Books, Maryland's U.S. Circuit Court, National Archives, RG 21, Microfilm M-931; Minute Books, U.S. District Court for the District of Maryland, National Archives and Record Center, Philadelphia, RG 21; Baltimore County Court Minute Books and the Baltimore County Naturalization Docket, Maryland State Archives, Annapolis, Md. Data for New York City from Minute Books of the U.S. District and Circuit Courts for the Southern District of New York, National Archives, RG 21, Microfilm M-886 and M-854; New York City's Court of Common Pleas in Scott, comp., *Early New York Naturalizations*.

and character witnesses who may have accompanied them. Livingston's opponents, who failed to note the precedent set in earlier years by New York's Federalist judges, were quick to report, and exaggerate, this evidence of political naturalization. Articles in the city's *Evening Post* and *Gazette*, published on April 28 and 29, reported that the mayor and his henchmen were "arranging for the naturalization" of 200 United Irishmen for party purposes on the eve of the election.[120]

New York's Delaware county also provides strong evidence that partisan imperatives determined the level of naturalization activity in the early republic. On January 18, 1810, seventy immigrants, most of whom had emigrated from Scotland at the turn of the century, trekked from their farms, over the Catskill Mountains, to the courthouse in Delhi to petition for naturalization in the county's Court of Common Pleas. An additional fourteen immigrants chose that same winter day to declare their intent to become American citizens. Prior to January 18, 1810, not a single naturalization petition had been presented in Delaware county's thirteen-year history. As no new alien disabilities went into effect in 1810 that could explain this sudden and pervasive urge for naturalization, it is very likely that the county's immigrants were primarily concerned with becoming voters in that spring's election at the behest of one of the candidates or political parties.[121]

The fact that both Federalist and Republican judges naturalized large numbers of aliens just before election day is not, in itself, evidence that the immigrants whose petitions were granted shared the political principles of the presiding judge. Legally, judges had no choice but to grant naturalization to all who presented properly prepared petitions and met all the statutory requirements. Proceedings in Pennsylvania's federal courts make this fact especially clear. In October 1799 Pennsylvania's Judge Peters presided over the trial of William Duane, the crusading editor of Philadelphia's leading anti-Federalist newspaper, the *Aurora*, for seditious libel. It therefore must have given Judge Peters great pain, and William Duane a moment of unholy glee, when Peters granted the editor's petition for naturalization on July 13, 1802. In 1809 Judge Peters was obviously reluctant, for reasons that are not clear, to grant the naturalization petition of George Frederick Krimmel, a Philadelphia merchant who had emigrated from Württemberg. Peters initially denied Krimmel's petition "on the ground of his not having made Report as an Alien under the 2nd section of the Naturalization Law." When Krimmel reappeared in court one month later, after registering as

[120]Naturalization statistics derived from the sources in Notes 117 and 119; and the Minute Books and Naturalization Record of the Frederick County Court, Maryland State Archives, Annapolis, Md. Newspaper reports of Livingston's naturalization of United Irishmen in Pomerantz, *New York: An American City*, quotes on 208.

[121]Delaware County's naturalization history can be found in the original petitions, naturalization register, and Minute Books of Delaware County's Court of Common Pleas and Court of Oyer and Terminer, at the Court House in Delhi, New York.

an alien with the court's clerk, Judge Peters granted his petition but also observed that he "was not fully satisfied that he [Krimmel] had fully complied with the Law—not having made that Rept. at least 5 Years before his Application for Nat." Although Peters granted Krimmel's petition, he also misstated the law. The provisions of the Naturalization Act then in force required that the declaration of intent be made three years prior to naturalization; there was no stipulation on the time required for the petitioner's registration as an alien.[122]

From 1798 on, naturalization in republican America was a three-step process. An alien was required to register the date of his arrival in the United States and other personal data with the clerk of any court of record. Federal law also required an alien to declare his intention to seek American citizenship before a sitting court at least three years prior to petitioning for naturalization. The judges of the court in which the alien finally petitioned had some discretion in choosing which immigrants to naturalize since, beginning with the Act of 1790, all federal naturalization laws required an alien to prove his "good character" and residence "to the satisfaction of such court." Judges could be either lenient or demanding in deciding if a petitioner had fulfilled all the legal requirements for naturalization.[123]

Court records from all sections of the country give examples of judges who used their discretionary power or technicalities to deny citizenship. In 1811 the judges of Maryland's U.S. Circuit Court were at their nit-picking best when deciding against a Mr. Keplinger, an immigrant claiming to be a naturalized citizen. Keplinger lost his action when the judges ruled that "a Certificate of naturalization not having stated the proof of residence between the eighteenth day of June 1798 and the 14th day of April 1802, although it did state five years residence and upwards, but not a continued residence of five years to the time of the application, did not naturalize the plaintiff." By 1802 most recommenders who testified to an immigrant's character or length of residence in the United States in Philadelphia's Mayor's Court and Court of Quarter Sessions, identified themselves as "U.S. Citizens." This innovation suggests that presiding judges had denied earlier naturalizations petitions on the ground that only American citizens could testify to an applicant's good character and attachment to the principles of the Constitution. In 1816 the federal Naturalization code was revised to require this previously informal practice.[124]

---

[122] Smith, *Freedom's Fetters*, chap. 13; William Duane's naturalization petition, presented to Judge Peters in the U.S. District Court for the Eastern District of Pennsylvania on July 13, 1802, and certified on July 14, 1802, is filed with the original naturalization petitions for that court at the National Archives and Record Center, Philadelphia, RG 21; Krimmel's story appears in a notation on his original naturalization petition, which was granted on Sept. 22, 1809, in the U.S. District Court for the Eastern District of Pennsylvania at ibid.

[123] Sec. 1, "An Act to establish an uniform rule of Naturalization," 1790, *The Public Statutes at Large of the United States of America, 1789–1873*, 17 vols. (Boston: Charles C. Little and James Brown, 1850–1873), I, 103.

[124] Ruling in *Keplinger vs. Walsh* in Minute Books of Maryland's U.S. Circuit Court, Nov. term, 1811, National Archives, RG 21, Microfilm M-987; records of Philadelphia's Mayor's Court and Court of Quarter

Although Philadelphia's judges may have been acting within the legal bounds of their discretionary power in requiring testimony from U.S. citizens prior to 1816, the judge of New York's U.S. District Court clearly went beyond the law in 1799 when he cited section 1 of the Naturalization Act of 1798 as grounds for denying naturalization to ten French petitioners. Judge John Hobart undoubtedly joined fellow Federalists in expecting, and perhaps hoping for, war with France in June of 1799. However, section 1 of the Naturalization Act of 1798 stated "That no alien who shall be a native, Citizen, Denizen or subject of any Nation or State with whom the United States shall be at War at the time of his application shall be then admitted to become a Citizen."[125] The fact that the United States and France were not at war did not prevent Hobart from denying citizenship to French aliens in 1799.

American judges were required to grant citizenship to aliens who proved to the satisfaction of the court that they had complied with all the requirements established by the naturalization laws of the 1790s. However, the different ethnic profiles of immigrants naturalized in various courts across the country suggest that judges may have had discretionary power sufficient to influence both the level of naturalization and the type of alien naturalized in their courts. After 1798 naturalization in republican American was a relatively intricate and costly process.[126] Foreigners seeking citizenship were required not only to report themselves and declare their intent well in advance, but also to procure, pay for, and preserve for a number of years the validated certificates that proved their compliance with the law. Most immigrants seem to have hired attorneys to prepare and present their naturalization petitions, undoubtedly to ensure that all the legal provisions had been met and certified, leaving as little as possible to the discretion of the judge.[127] A lawyer hired to secure an immigrant's naturalization would

---

Sessions, which identify recommenders as U.S. Citizens, at Archives for the City and County of Philadelphia, Philadelphia; 1816 "Act relative to evidence in cases of Naturalization," in D. M. Dewey, comp., *The Naturalization Laws of the United States* (Rochester, N.Y.: Lee, Mann & Co., 1855).

[125] Judge John Sloss Hobart's ruling on the French petitioners in Minute Books of the U.S. District Court for the Southern District of New York, June 18, 1799, National Archives, RG 21, Microfilm M-886; Sec. 1, Naturalization Act of 1798, *Public Statutes at Large*, I, quote on 567.

[126] According to the fee schedule in the Naturalization Act of 1798, court clerks who registered aliens received 50 cents for each registration and 50 cents for each registration certificate they issued; the fee for naturalization certificates was $2.00. Notations in court records that certificates were withheld until fees were paid suggest that these costs, plus the lawyer's fee, stretched the means of at least some applicants. Provisions in all the federal Naturalization Acts between 1795 and 1816 that exempted certain long-term foreign residents from having to register as aliens or make a previous declaration of intent are evidence of both the hardships placed on immigrants seeking citizenship and the willingness of the majority of American lawmakers to facilitate the naturalization of aliens who had already undergone a long period of acculturation.

[127] Between Aug. 17 and Nov. 10, 1795, the Minute Books of the U.S. District Court for the Eastern District of Pennsylvania recorded the names of the attorneys representing aliens petitioning for naturalization. Fifteen consecutive alien petitioners were recorded as having legal representation before the practice of recording attorneys' names was discontinued. When, during the first three sessions of 1804, the clerk of the Court of Common Pleas of Suffolk County, Mass., decided to record the names of lawyers who represented aliens making their declaration of intent or petitioning for naturalization in the Court's Docket Books, all of the aliens so appearing in those three terms were represented by lawyers.

Table 2. Number of Naturalizations in the U.S. District Court for the Eastern District of Pennsylvania by Country of Origin, 1790–1799

Nativity	1795	1796	1797	1798	1799	Totals
Unknown	0	0	4	5	3	12
France[a]	19	24	11	30	16	100
Ireland	3	7	10	46	12	78
England	1	5	2	19	4	31
Scotland	1	1	2	6	2	12
GB[b]	1	4	2	25	4	36
Subj. GB[c]	0	0	2	9	4	15
Germany[d]	1	4	3	12	3	23
Switzerland	0	1	0	1	2	4
Netherlands	0	1	0	1	1	3
Greece	0	0	0	1	0	1
Spain	0	0	0	0	1	1
Sweden	0	0	0	1	0	1
Danish West Indies	0	0	1	1	0	2
Totals	26	47	37	157	52	319

[a]Includes 7 petitioners born in the French West Indies.
[b]Includes 1 petitioner born in Wales.
[c]Includes 4 petitioners born in the British West Indies, 1 in the British East Indies, and 1 in British North America.
[d]Includes 1 Prussian.

also steer his client's petition into the court where it was most likely to receive favorable treatment.

The different ethnic profiles of aliens naturalized in courts located in the same county, and thus drawing on the same pool of immigrants, suggest a relationship between the judge and those he naturalized. In most of the counties where the political stance of the judge is known, a single party dominated the bench, usually the Federalist party. The appointment of federal district judges in each of the American states by President Washington, acting on the advice of Alexander Hamilton, made the U.S. District and Circuit Court system a bastion of Federalism long after political power had shifted to the Republican party at the local level.[128] The judges of city and county courts often were minor figures whose political affiliation went unrecorded. Nonetheless, a few of the counties studied did show judges belonging to different political parties naturalizing at the same time. In these counties the different ethnic profiles of immigrants who were granted citizenship may indicate a tendency of the most-represented ethnic group to support the political party of that court's judge (see Table 2).

During the 1790s, the 100 Frenchmen who were granted citizenship by the Federalist judges of the U.S. District Court for Eastern Pennsylvania constituted 31

[128]Prince, *Federalists and the Origins of the U.S. Civil Service*, chaps. 1 and 10.

Table 3. Number of Naturalizations in Philadelphia, by Country of Origin, 1800–1804

Nativity	Philadelphia's Court of Quarter Sessions		Mayor's Court		U.S. District Court for Eastern Dist. of Pennsylvania	
Unknown	26	5.4%	1	0.4%	6	2.9%
England	35	7.3%	12	5.2%	26	12.4%
Scotland	18	3.8%	7	3.1%	4	1.9%
Wales	6	1.3%	3	1.3%	0	0.0%
Island of Great Britain	12	2.5%	21	9.2%	6	2.9%
Ireland	310	64.6%	157	68.6%	48	22.9%
British North America	1	0.2%	0	0.0%	1	0.5%
North America	1	0.2%	0	0.0%	4	1.9%
South America	0	0.0%	0	0.0%	1	0.5%
West Indies	1	0.2%	0	0.0%	17	8.1%
France	12	2.5%	9	3.9%	66	31.4%
Germany	50	10.4%	12	5.2%	18	8.6%
Switzerland	3	0.6%	0	0.0%	3	1.4%
Netherlands	1	0.2%	0	0.0%	1	0.5%
Denmark	3	0.6%	5	2.2%	1	0.5%
Norway	1	0.2%	0	0.0%	0	0.0%
Sweden	0	0.0%	1	0.4%	4	1.9%
Russia	0	0.0%	1	0.4%	0	0.0%
Italy	0	0.0%	0	0.0%	3	1.4%
Portugal	0	0.0%	0	0.0%	1	0.5%
Totals	480	100%	229	99.9%	210	100.2%

per cent of the total. Although 78 Irish applicants were also granted citizenship, they were outnumbered by petitioners who had emigrated from the Island of Great Britain ($N = 79$), as well as the French. Given the well-documented Irish predominance among Philadelphia's immigrants and in the immigrants naturalized by the city and county courts between 1800 and 1804, the ethnic profile of those naturalized in Pennsylvania's U.S. District Court, which met in Philadelphia, suggests that Judge Peters was more receptive to French petitioners than to Irish applicants.[129] This pattern continued in the early years of the nineteenth century (see Table 3).

The naturalization pattern in Baltimore, Maryland, strongly challenges both ethnic and political stereotypes. The profiles of immigrants naturalized in the different courts meeting in Baltimore contradict the accepted notion that most Irish immigrants were radicals who attached themselves almost exclusively to the Republican party. The judges who presided over the U.S. District and Circuit

[129] Original petitions for Philadelphia's Court of Quarter Sessions and Mayor's Court, Archives for the City and County of Philadelphia; Minute Books and original naturalization petitions of the U.S. District Court for the Eastern District of Pennsylvania, RG 21, National Archives and Record Center, Philadelphia.

Table 4. Number of Naturalizations in Baltimore, by Country of Origin, 1790–1800

Nativity	U. S. District Court, District of MD		Baltimore County Court	
Unknown	1	0.4%	2	0.5%
England	31	12.2%	96	23.7%
Scotland	18	7.1%	1	0.2%
Wales	0	0.0%	1	0.2%
Island of GB	18	7.1%	102	25.2%
Ireland	80	31.4%	37	9.1%
British North America	1	0.4%	0	0.0%
West Indies	0	0.0%	7	1.7%
France	65	25.5%	56	13.8%
Netherlands	1	0.4%	3	0.7%
Germany	30	11.8%	97	24.0%
Switzerland	3	1.2%	1	0.2%
Italy	3	1.2%	0	0.0%
Portugal	0	0.0%	1	0.2%
Scandinavia[a]	3	1.2%	1	0.2%
Spanish America	1	0.4%	0	0.0%
Totals	255	100.3%	405	99.7%

[a]Includes Denmark, Sweden, and Russia.

Courts that met in Baltimore between 1790 and 1800 were Federalists; the judges who presided over the Baltimore County Court during the same period, whose political party can be ascertained, were Republicans. Between 1790 and 1800 the Federalist judges of Maryland's U.S. District Court granted 255 naturalization petitions; 31.4 per cent ($N = 80$) of those naturalized were immigrants from *Ireland* (see Table 4). These Federalist judges may well have had a reputation as being more favorably inclined toward Irish petitioners than the Republican judges of Baltimore's County Court, where Irish naturalizations constituted only 9.1 per cent ($N = 37$) of all successful petitions ($N = 405$) during the same period. On the other hand, Baltimore's English and German applicants were twice as likely to present their petitions to the *Republican* judges of the Baltimore County Court.[130] These records strongly suggest the presence of significant numbers of Irish immigrants who supported the Federalist party and of large numbers of Baltimore's English and German immigrant community who lined up with the Republicans.

The different ethnic profiles of foreigners petitioning for citizenship in different courts located in the same city do not *prove* the attachment of the natural-

[130]Minute Books of the U.S. District Court for the District of Maryland, RG 21, National Archives and Record Center, Philadelphia; Baltimore County Court Minute Books and the Baltimore County Naturalization Docket, Maryland State Archives, Annapolis, Md.

ized immigrants to the political party of each court's judge. What these profiles do show is that Federalists and Republican judges, for some reason, granted citizenship to different types of immigrants. Ethnicity may not have been the factor that led certain immigrants to Federalist judges and others to Republican courts. The common denominator might have been religion, occupation, or some other socioeconomic characteristic.[131] But the propensity of judges from different political parties to select different groups of immigrants out of a common pool is strong evidence that in the 1790s not all of America's immigrants supported the principles and candidates of the Republican party. In the early 1790s there was no reason for Federalists not to back the naturalization of the immigrants they welcomed and hoped would support their fight against the Republican "Jacobins." Even at the end of the 1790s, it would be natural for conservative British immigrants to support Federalists who shared their hostility toward the French Revolution. Thus it seems reasonable to assume that some of the foreigners who were granted citizenship by Federalist judges were thereby transformed into voters for Federalist candidates.

In states ranging from Massachusetts to South Carolina a predominantly Federalist judiciary naturalized increasing numbers of foreigners at politically opportune moments in the 1790s. Many of the petitioners who were naturalized by Federalist judges may have sought citizenship at the urging of a local Republican politician who knew that even an inimicable judge would find it difficult to deny a properly prepared application. But provisions in the federal naturalization code gave judges a small measure of discretion, which could be used to facilitate or impede the naturalization of individual applicants. The different ethnic profiles of foreigners naturalized in courts sitting in the same city, and often in the same courthouse, suggest that this power, however limited, was used to encourage the naturalization of foreigners who espoused the political principles of the presiding judge. If a judge did tend to facilitate the naturalization of immigrants with political beliefs similar to his own, the naturalization records of the 1790s also indicate the political tendencies of different ethnic groups.

Naturalizations records from the beginning of the nineteenth century also suggest that the Federalist descent into political nativism at the end of the 1790s may have won them the votes of many native-born Americans, but only at the

[131] I am currently working on a socioeconomic study of immigrants who arrived in the United States between 1783 and 1820. My analysis of alien reports made by Irish immigrants in New York City between 1798 and 1804 shows regional differences between immigrants choosing to make their report in Federalist and Republican courts that may indicate a link between Irish Catholics and the Republican party and the Scots–Irish and the Federalist party in that city—but only by making the somewhat tenuous assumption that most Irish immigrants from Ulster province were Protestant and most born outside Ulster were Catholic. Further analysis of the characteristics of naturalized immigrants may confirm this preliminary finding or identify other traits shared by aliens who received citizenship from Federalist and Republican judges.

cost of the support of their former foreign-born allies. During the election of 1800, the Republican party was clearly labeled, by its friends and enemies, as the party of the immigrant and defender of alien rights. After the "Revolution of 1800" Republican judges became more adroit at transforming their immigrant friends into voters than their Federalist counterparts. In Federalist courts the number of aliens petitioning for citizenship declined, as the number of applicants in Republican courts soared. Thus Federalist charges that their opponents were reaping the foreign-born vote became a self-fulfilling prophesy. By failing to make a clear distinction in their political oratory between immigrants holding traditional values, whose vote they courted, and the "Wild Irish" and French "Jacobin," whose political influence they feared, the Federalists alienated a large segment of the immigrant community. When, after Jefferson's election, Republican judges continued and expanded the practice of naturalizing their alien supporters on the eve of important elections, they completed the transfer of foreign allegiance from the Federalist to the Republican party and thus cemented the demise of the Federalist party.

As the Federalists' political xenophobia at the end of the eighteenth century helped to destroy their party, it also had lasting consequences for America's immigrants. The laws concerning aliens that were passed in 1798 are usually seen as temporary perversions that were rectified after the election of Thomas Jefferson. But their effects were more widespread and enduring than popularly believed. Most historians contend that, because the repressive Acts of 1798 were not implemented against their ostensible, alien targets and expired or were repealed following the Republican victory of 1800, their impact on American immigration policy was negligible.[132] But this interpretation minimizes the effect of these measures on America's immigrants.

Alien reports generated by the Naturalization Act of 1798 that were sent, by the district court clerks and customs officials to the federal government have disappeared. But many of the original registries compiled by local officials have survived, as well as the cover letters that accompanied reports sent to the U.S. Secretary of State. These documents are evidence of a fairly widespread compliance with the draconian measures drafted in 1798 by immigrants and local federal officials. Thus the atmosphere in America was oppressive enough to force the registration of hundreds of immigrants, to prompt French refugees to seek asylum outside the United States, and to deny Irish rebels a haven in republican America.[133]

---

[132] Smith, *Freedom's Fetters*, 156–76; Hansen, *Atlantic Migration*, 67.

[133] See "Register of White Persons Being Aliens Who Have Come to Reside in the Territory of the United States," Oct. 1799–Jan. 1, 1800, Collector of Customs, City Point, Va., and loose reports made to the clerk of the U.S. District Court for the District of Virginia, June 1798–Sept. 1799 in U.S. District Court, District of Virginia, Ended cases, 1799, Virginia State Library, Richmond, Va.; "Records of Primary Declarations," vol. A, 1798–1845, U.S. District Court for the District of Massachusetts, RG 21, National Archives and Record Center, Waltham, Mass.—the first seven pages of this volume constitute an alien register for July 23, 1798,

The registration of immigrants and resident aliens was a dramatic expansion of the power of government to intrude into the lives of America's immigrants. As the Act concerning Aliens was in force for only two years and the 1798 Naturalization Act was repealed by its 1802 update, their extreme provisions were indeed temporary aberrations. But some of the policies these laws introduced did not die with them. The five-year residency, alien reports, and preliminary declaration of intent that were devised in the 1790s to acculturate foreigners to the principles of self-government and to restrict the political power of undesirable aliens, became permanent prerequisites for American citizenship. The provisions of the Alien Enemies Act of 1798 also became a permanent part of the federal law code, which would haunt its Federalist backers, who had hoped it would neutralize the political power of French Jacobins and the "Wild Irish." Instead, it would be the Jeffersonians who, fifteen years later, used the Act's provisions to intern and neutralize unnaturalized British immigrants during the War of 1812.

Yet the political maelstrom of the 1790s also liberalized the American asylum by extending constitutional safeguards to (white) aliens. As traditionalists and the Federalist party were being disabused of their optimistic assessment of the benefits of immigration, domestic politics and constitutional fears set the Republican opposition on a very different trajectory, prompting Jeffersonian Republicans to set aside their doubts about population growth through immigration and the political principles of foreigners and rally to the defense of the European "stranger within [their] gate."[134] According to the Republicans who gained control of the national government in 1800, maintaining the rights of aliens was essential to preserving liberty for American citizens.

---

through Oct. 1799, with a notation after a Jan. 12, 1799, entry, "Transcript sent to the Secretary of State to this date"; "Landing reports of Aliens," Book A, 1798–1807, 173 alien reports for June 25, 1798–June 17, 1800, U.S. District Court for the Eastern District of Pennsylvania, RG 21, National Archives and Record Center, Philadelphia, Penn.; "Report of Aliens Made to the Clerk of the U.S. District Court," individual certificates, Dec. 17, 1798–Jan. 10, 1799, U.S. District Court for the District of Rhode Island and "Miscellaneous papers, 1790–1798," and "Report of Aliens made to the Collector of Customs, Providence," Dec. 14, 1798–Feb. 2, 1808, U.S. District Court for the District of Rhode Island, in RG 21, "Miscellaneous Papers, 1790–1798, 1799–1802, 1803–1817," National Archives and Record Center, Waltham, Mass. For cover letters sent to the U.S. Secretary of State, with missing enclosures, see "Miscellaneous Letters of the Department of State, 1789–1906," National Archives, RG 59, Microfilm M-179.

[134] Edward Livingston, Gales, ed., *Annals of Congress, 5th Cong.*, 2013 (quote).

8 *Asylum of Liberty: The Legacy of the Eighteenth Century*

At the end of the eighteenth century the Federalists adopted increasingly extreme measures and doctrines to neutralize the radicalism spawned by the French Revolution and to preserve their own conception of republican government. Although President Adams and the Federalist program enjoyed an unprecedented popularity at the height of the French crisis, their attempts to create a standing army, increase taxes and the power of the national government, silence the political opposition, and deny America's immigrants rights guaranteed by the Constitution backfired. Republican arguments that Federalist initiatives were the work of power-hungry men who threatened to destroy both the Constitution and the liberty it guarded became even more potent when, despite the defusing of the French crisis, the Federalists refused to repudiate their "wartime" measures and the principles that justified them. Concern over the Federalists' high-handed, "aristocratic" government and their contempt for the "swinish multitude" was sufficient to propel the Jeffersonian Republicans to victory in 1800. The Republicans, in turn, viewed their electoral success as a mandate to repudiate Federalist principles and to dismantle the programs that threatened to destroy liberty in America. Continued success at the polls in the nineteenth century led to a Republican redefinition of the federal government, republican principles, and the American asylum of liberty.

Dismantling the Federalist Edifice

In his first annual message to Congress, President Jefferson outlined what he considered the most important elements of the Republican reform program. At the same time, Jefferson attempted to allay the fears of Americans who retained their Federalist beliefs by minimizing the political divisions that still divided the nation and urging conciliation. After happily announcing a general return of peace in Europe and along the American frontier and a great increase in both the American population and national revenue, Jefferson asked Congress to join him in reducing the size of the federal government, the nation's armed forces, and federal expenditures while abolishing internal taxes levied by the national government. The President ended his message by "recommending a revisal of the laws on the subject of naturalization." Jefferson pointed out that, given "the ordinary chances of human life, a denial of citizenship under a residence of fourteen years is a denial to a great proportion of those who ask it." "Shall we," he asked,

> refuse to the unhappy fugitives from distress that hospitality which savages of the wilderness extended to our fathers arriving in this land? Shall oppressed humanity find no asylum on this globe? The constitution, indeed, has wisely provided that, for admission to certain offices of important trust, a residence shall be required sufficient to develop character and design. But might not the general character and capabilities of a citizen be safely communicated to every one manifesting a *bona fide* purpose of embarking his life and fortunes permanently with us?[1]

Congressional response to Jefferson's emotional appeal on behalf of the nation's immigrants illuminates the complexity of the young Republic's position alien rights and policies.

During the 1790s Federalist lawmakers adopted traditional British devices to control resident aliens and to limit the rights of newly arrived immigrants. Even though the Federalist measures of 1798 were aimed primarily against the political opposition—Americans who seemed intent on destroying the government and economy that Federalist statesmen had so carefully crafted during the 1790s—they also were designed to neutralize the power of "the turbulent and disorderly of all parts of the world" who immigrated to America "with a view to disturb our tranquillity, after having succeeded in the overthrow of their own Governments." Many of the provisions of the Federalist legislation were consciously modeled after British statutes that had been designed by the Pitt ministry to secure the same ends. Indeed, during the debate on the Alien Enemies bill Representative Harper argued that those European nations which have escaped being overcome by the domineering spirit of France, owe their safety to a bill like this; and, unless we follow their example, and

[1] *Thomas Jefferson: Writings*, ed. Merrill D. Peterson (New York: Library of America, 1984), 501–9, quote on 508. Jefferson's reference to the census figures for 1800 illustrate his nonmercantilist attitude toward population growth. Jefferson considered "this rapid growth and the prospect it holds up to us, not with a view to the injuries it may enable us to do to others in some future day, but to the settlement of the extensive country still remaining vacant within our limits, to the multiplication's of men susceptible of happiness, educated in the love of order, habituated to self-government, and value its blessings above all price." Ibid., 503.

crush the viper in our breast, we shall not, like them, escape the scourge which awaits us.[2]

Some Federalists supported the more extreme elements of the new alien code only reluctantly, recognizing these laws as a regression from their optimism in the 1780s and early 1790s when they believed that the power and prosperity of the new republic would be increased by the influx of immigrants fleeing Old World oppression. Some expressed regret for the need to incorporate Old World measures of control into American republicanism. One "friend of government and peace" claimed that it was the "noisy demagogue who bellows against government; and the officious alien who attempts to excite warring passions in the minds of citizens" who had forced the Federalists to expand the power of government and adopt Old World restraints on the rights of aliens and citizens alike. Thus, he argued,

> Had our own citizens observed decency and moderation in their strictures on government, we should never have heard of a Sedition Law—and had foreigners been quiet subjects of our laws, and never intermeddled with the political affairs of our country, the Alien Bill would never have passed. The friends of our government and peace regret the necessity of such laws. They see, and they see with pain, the United States compelled to adopt the rigid rules of other nations, in respect to foreigners and our own presses. But they become gradually reconciled to such *increase of Executive power*, from a conviction that it is necessary to our safety.

Other Federalists regretted only the expiration of the "Act concerning Aliens" on June 25, 1800, because "During its operation not one of the numerous alien incendiaries which have infested, and now infests the United States, have suffered any of the penalties of it—and as they will attribute the forbearance of government, to fear, not clemency; we cannot but add, more's the pity."[3]

Although Republican Congressmen condemned the Naturalization Act of 1798 for its fourteen-year residency requirement, which came close to consigning aliens to a permanent, inferior class of citizenship, they were less appalled by other features of the Federalists' Alien legislation. Because the "Act concerning Aliens" was a temporary measure, which automatically expired two years after its passage, there was no new discussion of its provisions to delineate the republic's nineteenth-century position on immigration and alien rights. However, the failure of Congress to repeal the permanent statute governing the treatment of "Alien Enemies" provides some illumination. In the 1790s many Republicans conceded the need for a law dealing with immigrants from nations at war with

---

[2] Joseph Gales, ed., *Annals of the Congress of the United States*, 42 vols. (Washington, D.C.: Gales and Seaton, 1834–1856), 5th Cong., 430 (Harrison Gray Otis quote), 1992 (Harper quote); Manning J. Dauer, *The Adams Federalists* (Baltimore: Johns Hopkins University Press, 1953), chap. 10.

[3] Quotes from: *New York Commercial Advertiser*, July 30, 1798; *Philadelphia Gazette and Daily Advertiser*, July 9, 1800.

the United States. Although Jeffersonians opposed the original Alien Enemies bill because of the excessive power it gave to the president, negotiations between Federalist and opposition leaders eventually produced the 1798 statute that received the support of both political parties.[4]

The provisions of the Naturalization Act of 1802 give a clearer indication of America's attitude toward aliens at the beginning of the nineteenth century. One of the most striking features of the Naturalization Act of 1802 was the apparent lack of urgency with which the Republican-dominated Congress approached its task. Even though naturalization reform was an essential element of Jefferson's "Revolution of 1800," it was only one part of the Republican program to demolish Federalist principles and reestablish liberty on a more secure foundation. The House of Representatives first resolved to appoint a committee to "inquire into the expediency of amending" the Naturalization Act of 1798 in February 1801, but decided to postpone action until after the address of the new president the following December. By December 1801 immigrants, unhappy with the delay, were petitioning both the House and the Senate for immediate relief from the stringent provisions of the Act of 1798.[5]

The Naturalization Act that was passed on April 14, 1802, returned to many of the provisions of the Act of 1795, requiring a five-year residence and a prior declaration of an alien's intent to become a citizen. However, the Act of 1802 did not simply reinstate the requirements established in 1795. It also validated some of the innovations of 1798 and transformed them into permanent elements of America's naturalization code. In 1795 it had been sufficient for an alien to swear that he had been a resident of the United States for five years. The first section of the 1802 Naturalization Act decreed that "the oath of the applicant shall, in no case, be allowed to prove his residence." Any immigrant arriving after the passage of the Act of 1802 was now required to present a certificate issued by a court clerk declaring that he had registered as an alien prior to petitioning for naturalization. This "alien report" recorded a foreigner's name, birthplace, age, allegiance, country of origin, and intended place of settlement. Unless the alien report specified an exact arrival date, the date of an immigrant's registration would be used to establish his years of residence in the United States.[6] Thus, the 1798 provisions for the registration of all aliens arriving in the United States were continued in 1802 for those hoping to become American citizens and incorporated into the nineteenth-century naturalization code. Henceforth applicants for American citizenship would have to present notarized documents attesting to their compliance with federal statutes.

[4] For debate on the Alien Enemies Act, see Chapter 7 and James Morton Smith, *Freedom's Fetters: The Alien and Sedition Laws and American Civil Liberties* (Ithaca: Cornell University Press, 1956), chap. 3.

[5] *Thomas Jefferson: Writings*, ed. Peterson, 501–9; Gales, ed., *Annals of Congress, 6th Cong.*, 989 (quote); petitions in Gales, ed., *Annals of Congress, 7th Cong.*, I, 198–99, 315, 361, 375, 404, 602.

[6] Naturalization Act of 1802, in *The Public Statutes at Large of the United States of America*, 17 vols. (Boston: Charles C. Little and James Brown, 1850–1873), II, 153–55.

Immigrants who had been unhappy with the delays in securing a revision of the Naturalization Act of 1798 were not pleased with its replacement. By February of 1803 alien petitioners were again besieging Congress, protesting the five-year residency and declaration of intent requirements and in general praying for "a more easy admission to the rights of citizenship." The chief grievance of the petitioners of 1803 was the provision that required a declaration of their intention to seek American citizenship three years prior to naturalization. Since, "from the Summer of 1798 until the Spring of 1801," the presidency was "in the hands of a man notoriously hostile to aliens of republican principles; and the President was authorized by law to banish any alien at his pleasure, without trial, and without appeal ... an *alien resident* could have no inducement to declare his intention of becoming a citizen; for, by so doing, he placed his name on a list of proscription, and subjected himself to the arbitrary will of an individual." Thus, the section of the Act of 1802 that denied citizenship to an alien for three years after making his declaration, in essence, imposed an eight-year residency on all who had immigrated before 1798. Therefore, if Congress could not be persuaded to return to the two-year requirement of the Act of 1790, the petitioners hoped that another form of redress might be devised for aliens who had endured the rigors of the Adams administration.[7]

On February 17, 1803, a committee of the House of Representatives drew up a bill to exempt immigrants who had resided in the United States between the passage of the Naturalization Act of 1798 and that of 1802 from having to make a previous declaration of intent. But consideration of this bill was postponed until the November session by conservative congressmen who, offended by the language of the petitioners, were not disposed to spend any more time legislating for aliens, at the cost of neglecting the "pressing petitions from our own citizens."[8]

In March of 1804 Congress finally passed an act that exempted aliens residing in the United States during the tenure of the Naturalization Act of 1798 from the need to make a declaration of intent three years prior to petitioning for citizenship. But immigrant hopes that America's lawmakers would return the two-year residency requirement of 1790 were chimerical. In 1795 Congress had established national law as the only avenue to American citizenship and rejected the creation of an inferior denizen class; these actions made a return to the provisions of 1790 impossible. Lacking the ability to endow naturalized aliens with partial rights, Congress had no choice but to retain those elements of the Naturalization Acts of 1795 and 1798 that demanded proof of a commitment to America's constitutional principles and a genuine desire for republican citizen-

[7] Petitions in Gales, ed., *Annals of Congress, 7th Cong.,* II, 465–67, 474–80, 520–21, 533, 571; quotes on 465, 570.

[8] Ibid., quote on 570. For the postponed bill that was passed into law in March 1804, see D. M. Dewey, comp., *The Naturalization Laws of the United States* (Rochester, N.Y.: Lee, Mann & Co., 1855), 34–35.

ship and inhibited the ability of foreigners, untutored in the proper use of liberty, to threaten the survival of the American republic.

Alien Enemies

The Naturalization Act of 1798 was repealed by the Act of 1802; the Act concerning Aliens was a temporary measure that expired two years after its passage on June 25, 1798; the Sedition Act expired on March 3, 1801; but the "Act respecting Alien Enemies" became a permanent statute that prescribed the treatment of the unnaturalized subjects of any power at war with the United States. The Alien Enemies Act had been designed by its Federalist sponsors to control aliens infected with French radicalism. But it was not implemented until 1812, when, ironically, it was used to guard the nation against unnaturalized British immigrants after the United States declared war on Great Britain. Once again, procedures designed in the 1790s but implemented by a Republican administration early in the nineteenth century produced anguished outcries from immigrants who believed that the American government was reneging on its promise to provide an asylum for the oppressed. And once again, America's legislators were forced to defend the legitimacy of policies that they saw as vital to the republic.

After the American declaration of war on June 18, 1812, all unnaturalized British immigrants were automatically subject to the provisions of the Alien Enemies Act of 1798. This Act directed that

> whenever there shall be a declared war between the United States and any foreign nation or government, or any invasion or predatory incursion shall be perpetrated, attempted, or threatened against the territory of the United States, by any foreign nation or government, and the President of the United States shall make public proclamation of the event, all natives, citizens, denizens, or subjects of the nation or government, being males of the age of fourteen years and upwards, who shall be within the United States, and not actually naturalized, shall be liable to be apprehended, restrained, secured and removed, as alien enemies.

Moreover, it would be the duty of the wartime president to

> direct the conduct to be observed, on the part of the United States, towards the aliens who shall become liable, as aforesaid; the manner and degree of the restraint to which they shall be subject, and in what cases, and upon what security their residence shall be permitted, and to provide for the removal of those, who, not being permitted to reside within the United States, shall refuse or neglect to depart therefrom. ... Provided, that aliens ... who shall not be chargeable with actual hostility, or other crimes against the public safety, shall be allowed, for the recovery, disposal, and removal of

their goods and effects, and for their departure, the full time which is, or shall be stip-ulated by any treaty . . . between the United States, and the hostile nation . . . and where no such treaty shall have existed, the President of the United States may ascer-tain and declare such reasonable time as may be consistent with the public safety, and according to the dictates of humanity and national hospitality.[9]

On July 7, 1812, in accordance with the provisions of the Alien Enemies Act of 1798, the U.S. State Department ordered all male British aliens over the age of fourteen years to register with the U.S. Marshal for their district. Over 10,000 British aliens complied with this directive, giving name, age, length of time in the United States, current residence, family size, occupation, and date of their appli-cation for naturalization, if any. In February 1813 the State Department ordered all alien enemies living within forty miles of tidewater to apply for passports for their removal to an inland location designated by their U.S. Marshal. Relocation was mandatory only for British aliens who were engaged in commerce; all other alien enemies could petition their federal marshal for permission to remain. Exemptions could be renewed monthly, on evidence of the alien's continued good behavior.[10]

In April of 1813 British aliens were placed under the authority of John Mason, the newly appointed Commissary General for Prisoners of War, who then became responsible for implementing the policies formulated by President Madison. Since Jay's Treaty had expired, British subjects could, if necessary, be treated as prisoners of war.

As alien enemies, unnaturalized British subjects were prohibited from leaving the place designated for their residence without permission from their local federal marshal and a passport giving their physical description, legal destination, and the route to be taken. In May 1813, President Madison, "desirous of defining more particularly, the treatment of Alien Enemies, and of extending, as much indulgence to them as may be compatible with the precautions made necessary by the present state of things," instructed the Commissary General of Prisoners to "cause to be removed, if not already done, under former orders from the Department of State," all British aliens "who are not females, or under eighteen years of age; or who are not labourers, mechanicks, or manufacturers actually employed in their several vocations." Exceptions were to be made for aliens who had declared their intent to become American citizens at least six months before the war and had American-born wives, owned real property, or were engaged in

[9] Gales, ed., *Annals of Congress, 5th Cong.*, 3753–54.

[10] Herbert Heaton, "The Industrial Immigrant in the United States, 1783–1812," American Philosophical Society, *Proceedings*, 45 (1951), 519; Herbert Heaton, "Yorkshire Cloth Traders in the United States, 1770–1840," *Publications of the Thoresby Society Miscellany*, 37, part III (April 1944), 250; U.S. Marshals' Returns of Alien Enemies, "War of 1812 Papers, 1789–1815," National Archives, Department of State, RG 59, National Archives Microfilm M-588; "War of 1812—Alien Papers," National Archives, U.S. Office of Naval Records and Library, RG 45, University of Delaware Microfilm.

"such commerce, as is exclusively internal." Men qualifying for exemption would be "permitted to remain, or if removed, to return to, their usual places of residence; provided, such residence be not at, or in the immediate vicinity of, a town or port, on navigable water, where military works are maintained, or a body of Troops, are stationed."[11]

While the number of enemy aliens removed inland is unknown, many British subjects who were ordered from their homes expressed their belief that America had violated her promise to serve as an asylum for humankind. Unable to see themselves a threat, British aliens petitioned for relief and challenged the legitimacy of their treatment in the American land of liberty. Scores of petitions were sent to John Mason, the Commissary General for Prisoners, and to Secretary of State James Monroe expressing the writer's astonishment that he could be considered a dangerous alien and begging for an exemption. Typical was the memorial of George and John Laurie, two Scottish-born merchants who had settled in New York City in 1803 and 1807, respectively, asking Monroe to "interpose in their behalf" to rescind the order for their removal into the interior of the state:

> Conscious of the innocence and purity of their views in emigrating to and continuing in this Country, they are fully persuaded that although they may be embraced by the letter of the preceding requisition, yet that they cannot be comprehended within its spirit or intention. . . . And that should they be denied a residence in the city of New York or its vicinity where their business is principally situated, it must invariably lead not only to a sacrifice of their private fortunes but to an exposure of their Creditors to serious losses.

Although these two merchants had reported themselves to the clerk of the U.S. District Court for New York in 1808 and 1810, respectively, their declarations of intent were not Filed until the end of May 1812, thus disqualifying them for the exemptions outlined in May 1813. In any case, because of the strategic importance of New York City, there was little chance that they would be allowed to return to that city prior to the end of the war. Two months later George Laurie, writing from Fishkill, New York, petitioned for a passport that would allow him to visit a friend "in the *interior*" of New Jersey.[12]

Exceptions were made for British aliens with especially strong republican credentials. William Swan, a clerk in New York City, stated in his deposition that he had emigrated from Ireland "in consequence of his union with the opposition to

---

[11] Heaton, "Yorkshire Cloth Traders," 253; Madison, May 31, 1813, to Office of Commissary General of Prisoners (quotes), in "War of 1812—Alien Papers"; forms used for passports and "indulgences," in ibid.

[12] Petition of George and John Laurie, New York City, March 5, 1813, to "Sec. of State James Munro [*sic*]"; recommendations of Laurie brothers by: David Gelston, Collector of the Port of New York, March 5, 1813, to James Monroe; Richard I. Tucker, New York City to Thos. Tudor Tucker, Esqr. in Washington; Thos. T. Tucker, Washington, March 8, 1813, to James Monroe; Marshal Curtenius, New York City, April 29, 1813, to General Mason; Petition of George Laurie, Fishkill, N.Y., to General Mason, May 24, 1813, in ibid.

the British Government, who wished to trample upon the rights of his Countrymen." Because he had made his declaration of intent, owned real estate, held a commission as a Lieutenant in the Militia, had an American-born wife and children, and enclosed a letter of recommendation from Governor Daniel Tompkins of New York—all "evidence of a strong attachment to the interests of the United States"—a special "indulgence" was granted. Swan was allowed to return home from his Fishkill exile.[13] James Davies also secured an exemption. Davies was a fifty-nine-year-old resident of Savannah, Georgia, who, seventeen years earlier, had deserted from a British ship of war and "landed on the Shores of Freedom with a determination never to return to the land where a Tyrant rules and where liberty is unknown." In addition, Davies had a son, who was at that moment "in the American service, and fighting for the rights of Independent America." Consequently James Davies was allowed to return to his residence in the port of Savannah.[14]

Many alien enemies lacked the necessary proof of "attachment" to their adopted land. And those who had arrived after the declaration of war against Great Britain were categorically denied relief. Thus, Michael Bell, a Philadelphia cabinetmaker who had arrived in America with his wife and children on August 1, 1812, was given twenty-four hours to remove himself, leaving behind his sick wife and three small children and all prospect of being able to support them.[15]

The exigencies of war may indeed have required the removal of the alien partners of the mercantile firm of George & John Laurie. Even though they had "no interest whatever either directly or indirectly in any vessels either American or foreign," the Laurie brothers had channels of communication that linked them with a hostile power and had not clearly demonstrated their exclusive commitment to the American republic. Less understandable to bewildered immigrants, were the removals of people who clearly lacked the means or motives for treasonous activity. John Davis, a silversmith, had his permission to remain in New York City rescinded in July 1813, even though he had "twenty-nine near relations principally in this City, but all in this State" and none in England and Wales "unless an aged mother & a brother should yet be alive from whom I have not heard for more than three years."[16]

Some British aliens responded to their wartime treatment by requesting permission to leave the United States on the earliest available cartel. John Lambert,

[13] Petitions of William Swan, Fishkill, N.Y., to James Madison, April 1, 1813, May 12, 1813; recommendations by Cornelius Bogert, New York City, April 6, 1813, and Daniel D. Tompkins, Governor of New York, April 21, 1813, to James Monroe; Rachel Swan, New York City, wife of William, May 5, 1813, to General Mason; Commissary General of Prisoners, June 16, 1813, to Marshal Curtenius, in ibid.

[14] John Davies, Savannah, Ga., March 27, 1813, to John Eppinger, Marshal of Georgia, in ibid.

[15] Michael Bell, Philadelphia, March 19, 1813, to James Monroe; Clement Bensley, Philadelphia, March 23, 1813, to Marshal John Smith in Philadelphia, in ibid.

[16] John Davis, New York City, July 13, 1813, to General Mason, in ibid.

an agent for a manufacturing house in Leeds, was exiled from New York City to Fishkill. From there he rather desperately petitioned for permission to board a cartel bound for Liverpool "or any other place in the dominions belonging to His Britannic Majesty either in Europe or on this side the Atlantic or to Lisbon or Cadiz . . . [as] the unproductive manner in which he is spending his time in this secluded spot, is neither consonant with his disposition nor suitable to his circumstances."[17] Henry Clementson and his family from the British colony of Demerara may have been more committed to taking up permanent residence in the United States than the sales representative from Leeds. But in the end they, too, were forced to petition for permission to quit "the United States for the present" when the war interrupted their contact with Demerara, the source of the funds they needed to establish themselves in Portsmouth, New Hampshire.[18] For Mr. H. Russell, removal from New York City was merely the latest of a string of misfortunes. Only permission to sail for Liverpool would

> prevent on my part a total Ruin, as I am unacquainted with Country business, and from various unfortunate circumstances am reduced so low that I have not a Dollar for my support when I leave this City, when on the other hand, if you will grant me this request I have a *home* to go to and a means of subsistence. I have been five years in this Country but owing to my being under age when I arrived, have been unable to obtain my Citizenship which I have much wished for.[19]

The actions of the American government during the War of 1812 were not especially rigorous. The Alien Enemies Act of 1798 required the American executive "to direct the conduct to be observed, on the part of the United States, towards the aliens who shall become liable . . . the manner and degree of the restraint to which they shall be subject, and in what cases, and upon what security their residence shall be permitted." England had instituted a more severe program of registration, passports, and removals to control the influx of foreigners seeking refuge from a war-torn Europe.[20] Nevertheless, the treatment of alien enemies in the United States astounded British immigrants who believed that, by coming to America they had freed themselves from traditional Old World restraints. To immigrants with such high expectations, the actions of the American government seemed excessive and capricious. Aliens who had established businesses and families and had become integral parts of their communities were suddenly ordered to remove themselves to areas that lacked the

[17] John Lambert, Fishkill, N.Y., June 17, 1813, to General Mason, in ibid.

[18] Petitions of Henry Clementson and Ralph Lee Ashington of Portsmouth, N.H., to Danl. Webster, Esq., June 4, 1813, and to James Monroe, May 12, 1813; recommendations by T. Elwyn, Daniel Webster and John Langdon, Aug. 9, 1813, in ibid.

[19] H. Russell, New York City, June 17, 1813, to General Mason, in ibid.

[20] Gales, ed., *Annals of Congress, 5th Cong.*, 3753; Albert Goodwin, *The Friends of Liberty: The English Democratic Movement in the Age of the French Revolution* (Cambridge: Harvard University Press, 1979), 266; Dauer, *Adams Federalists*, 157–59.

facilities to employ their skills. The affluent gentleman could survive such an exile and, surrounded by his family, might find an avocation to help him while away his time. The poor man, on the other hand, was forced to leave his dependents and his only means for supporting them behind, knowing how his family would suffer for his failure to institute naturalization proceedings. And Charles Lockington learned the price to be paid for failing to comply with governmental directives when he was committed to prison for returning, without permission, to Philadelphia from Lancaster, "the place allotted for his residence" and then refusing to obey Marshal Smith's order to return to his place of exile.[21]

British aliens, taken by surprise by their new status, had no idea how to win exemptions. Petitions for relief were accompanied by memorials signed by ministers, employers, political figures, and relatives, all praying for an indulgence from the men they hoped could grant one. Sometimes these humble supplications worked; sometimes they failed. On June 17, 1813, John Mason answered William O'Brien's petition for an exemption by stating "that the Intention of the President being, not to grant passports to alien Enemies, at this time . . . the Request . . . cannot be granted.[22]

The fact that the British navy did indeed invade the United States and burned Washington in 1814 is evidence of the reality of the threat posed by Great Britain during these years, especially in areas within "forty miles of tidewater." Any fears that the American executive had that unnaturalized British aliens would abet in such a landing could only have been exacerbated by letters from informants, often anonymous, reporting the suspicious or inimical conduct of various British subjects. But the power exercised by President Madison over unnaturalized British aliens, even during wartime, seemed to many petitioners antithetical to the promises made by America.

A petition to Congress by immigrants in New York City also questioned the wisdom of America's wartime treatment of those who had "removed their families and property to the United States previous to the declaration of War agreeably to, and confiding in the Laws and the encouragement and protection held out to emigrants":

> The full time required by law to entitle them to become citizens not having elapsed and they having by their solemn oaths abjured their allegiance to the Sovereign in whose dominions they were born, and formally transferred that allegiance to the United States as the Country and Government of their choice, they now find and feel themselves in a most embarrassing situation being without a Country either to claim them, or to admit them to a participation of the rights of Citizens or of free men. But are held in durance by the Marshalls in their respective districts as if guilty

---

[21] Letters from Marshal John Smith, Philadelphia, Nov. 9, 13, 22, 1813, to General Mason, explain the legal steps taken against Lockington, in "War of 1812—Alien Papers."

[22] John Ferrer, New York City, June 23, 1813, to General Mason; Office of Commissary General, July 6, 1813, to Mr. John Ferrers; General Mason, June 17, 1813, to Timothy Pickering, in ibid.

of some crime deserving punishment, deprived of the liberty of attending to their personal concerns, as well as of the means of procuring a subsistence for their families or for themselves. . . . Your petitioners submit with the greatest humility and deference to your consideration whether the real interest of the United States would not be essentially promoted by naturalizing all who were in the Country previous to the declaration of war that are of good moral character and willing to take the oaths required or that should be prescribed by law—they most earnestly solicit that the present laws on that head be so amended or altered that those who have taken the oaths of allegiance and abjuration previous to the declaration of war be released from their present embarrassing thraldom.[23]

On July 30, 1813, Congress addressed this problem by passing "An act supplementary to the acts heretofore passed on the subject of an uniform rule of naturalization." Under this Act, all aliens resident in the United States at the time of its declaration of war against Great Britain, "who had before that day made a declaration according to law, of their intention to become citizens of the United States, or who by the existing laws of the United States were on that day entitled to become citizens, without making such declaration, may be admitted to become citizens, notwithstanding they shall be alien enemies, at the times and in the manner prescribed by the laws heretofore passed on that subject." Congress thus proved its responsiveness to America's immigrants, but it simultaneously reaffirmed national policy by adding the proviso, "That nothing herein contained shall be taken or construed to interfere with, or prevent the apprehension and removal agreeably to law, of any alien enemy at any time previous to the actual naturalization of such alien."[24]

As the War of 1812 restricted the rights of British aliens, diplomatic crises also reduced the number of immigrants arriving in the United States at the beginning of the nineteenth century. This incidental restriction began even before the declaration of war against Great Britain. The Embargo of 1807, passed in December of that year, prohibited the sailing of all vessels from American ports to foreign destinations. An exception was made for foreign ships already in American ports, which were allowed to sail with the cargoes already on board. If enforced, the embargo would have completely cut off the flow of immigrants into the United States, by barring the return of ships carrying passengers from Europe. While the number of immigrants arriving in American ports did indeed decline in 1808, the widespread evasion of the Embargo of 1807 ensured a continuing, if constricted, conduit for immigrants. And the reopening of trade with Great Britain in June 1809 triggered a surge of immigration that was halted only

---

[23] See the anonymous letter dated New York, May 25, 1813, to General Mason, denouncing "the notorious John Watts" and the letter from Jesse McCall, St. Martinsville, Louisiana, July 6, 1813, in "War of 1812—Alien Papers"; quotes from "Petition of George Cogghill of the City of New York on behalf of himself and Others" to "the Senate & Representatives of the United States in Congress Assembled," in ibid.

[24] Act of 1813, 13th Cong., Sess. I, in Dewey, comp., *Naturalization Laws of the United States*, 37.

by the declaration of war on June 18, 1812.[25] The American wartime ban, instituted on July 6, 1812, on commerce between all territories belonging to the United States and Great Britain was more effective in cutting off trade and immigration. But once again, the intent of the law was not to restrict immigration, and the end of hostilities spelled the resumption of the traditional trade patterns of vessels carrying cargoes of goods and passengers.[26]

The wartime disabilities on America's immigrants were exceptional and temporary, dictated by the exigencies of international politics. They also were a byproduct of American liberality. Most of the Republic's earliest immigrants never applied for citizenship because alien disabilities were relatively mild and easily evaded. Thousands of immigrants were naturalized between 1794 and 1810 at the behest of various political candidates during the showdown between the Federalist and Republican parties. But politically apathetic foreigners who had no desire to vote had little reason to seek citizenship. The result was the transformation of thousands of British immigrants into alien enemies during the War of 1812.

The hardships endured by British aliens during the war years did not produce fundamental changes in the pattern of naturalization in America. During the War of 1812 unnaturalized British subjects desperately sought the citizenship necessary to exempt them from the penalties placed on alien enemies. Yet, when the Peace of Ghent removed wartime disabilities and made naturalization again possible, British aliens did not flood American courts with citizenship petitions. The end of the war also ushered in an "Era of Good Feelings" and single-party government. With the end of the fierce party rivalries that had dominated American politics from the mid-1790s to the mid-1810s, there were fewer political candidates challenging voter qualifications and there were fewer candidates shepherding prospective voters through the intricacies of America's naturalization procedure. In the decade following the War of 1812, naturalization retained its political quality. The number of petitions increased just prior important elections and were still clustered in the weeks preceding elections. But lower political stakes produced relatively few applications for naturalization and the voting rights it conveyed.

America's alien and immigrant policies remained largely unarticulated and open to misinterpretation well into the nineteenth century. Part of the confusion that surrounded the republic's position on immigration was the result of the war

---

[25] Marshall Smelser, *The Democratic Republic, 1801–1815* (New York: Harper & Row, 1968), 164–69; Marcus Lee Hansen, *The Atlantic Migration, 1607–1860* (Cambridge: Harvard University Press, 1940), 69; "Passenger Lists of Vessels Arriving at Philadelphia, 1800–1882," National Archives, Records of the Bureau of Customs, RG 36, Microfilm M-360.

[26] "Passenger Lists of Vessels Arriving at Philadelphia, 1800–1882"; Hansen, *The Atlantic Migration*, 69–71.

of words waged in the decade after the American Revolution, when the republic's claim to be *the* asylum for liberty was challenged by most Old World governments and vigorously defended by American idealists. Part of it was the result of the decentralized government instituted by the independent American states, which produced a wide range of alien and naturalization policies. And a large part was the result of the different varieties of republicanism that evolved in the years following the American Revolution.

During the 1790s Americans who were equally committed to republican government had different hopes and fears for the future. The Federalists were given the first opportunity to implement their vision. Confident that the Constitution of 1787 had provided the foundation for erecting a republican form of government over a vast territory, Alexander Hamilton and his cohorts boldly charted a course to transform the Thirteen States into a rich, powerful, and populous nation. Able to put aside traditional American fears of a powerful central government, divided sovereignty, standing armies, and monied interest, Federalist leaders used British models to shape many of the programs and institutions that would allow the new nation to rival or surpass Great Britain.

In the first years of independence, America's Federalists did not fear Old World immigrants. Americans who gravitated to the Federalist party in the 1790s were those who retained traditional principles and mercantilist beliefs. Federalists largely ignored the pessimism embodied in the cyclical theory of history, which predicted the inevitable decay of a mature society; they had few doubts about the benefits to be derived from a burgeoning population and the economic and social developments it fostered. As a result, early Federalists welcomed the immigrants who increased the republic's population and stature in the 1780s and early 1790s—foreigners who brought the technology, capital, and labor needed to fulfill the Federalist vision. However, in the mid-1790s the Federalists felt that they were losing control. Most of their manufacturing projects had failed, the bottom dropped out of the American land market, and the political opposition was growing increasingly vociferous and vicious. The arrival of Irish and French "Jacobins" seemed to increase the power of their opponents who wanted to destroy everything the Federalists had achieved. The Alien, Sedition, and Naturalization Acts of 1798 were part of the Federalist program to stamp out the political opposition. But, in attacking both immigrants and Republicans, the Federalists lost their immigrant allies, earned the largely undeserved title of America's nativists, and placed Thomas Jefferson at the head of a group he had never recruited.

Although policy errors by the Federalists at the end of the 1790s attached most of immigrant vote to the political opposition, Republican measures passed after the election of 1800 reveal a continuation of their original ambivalence about immigration. Early-nineteenth-century Republicans were as concerned about avoiding even the appearance of illiberality as their predecessors had been in the

1780s. Proudly leading the fight for liberty on behalf of all "mankind", they were determined to maintain the nation as a bastion of liberty that would serve as both a model and a sanctuary for those who fought for freedom. Although the Republicans who won control of the American government in 1800 were committed to fighting encroachments on the rights of foreigners and Americans alike, they were a diverse group. The party included men such as Jefferson who refused to aid the French government in reclaiming subjects who had emigrated to America, on the grounds that denying Frenchmen the right of emigration would violate America's Bill of Rights; it also included men like DeWitt Clinton who, more pragmatist than Republican, was careful not to antagonize foreign-born voters.[27] Yet, as a party, Republicans preferred to see the American population increase slowly, through natural increase. They had no desire to hasten the maturation of American society, hoped to reserve the nation's lands for future generations of independent yeomen, and tended to distrust foreigners untrained in the ways of republicanism.

The political turbulence of the 1790s validated many Republican doubts about the ability of foreigners to uphold liberty. To some Republicans, the Whiskey Rebels were an example of the inability of immigrants to understand and employ constitutional methods to prevent encroachments on liberty. To others, the machinations of French and British agents revealed the danger of allowing foreign influence to permeate the American government. Thus, at the beginning of the nineteenth century, Republican lawmakers could see no reason to jettison the code that governed the nation's immigrants in its entirety or to return to the more optimistic policy of 1790. The liberal features of the Naturalization Act of 1790 had been produced by the collaboration of men who would become leaders of both the Federalist and Republican parties. Men like future Federalist John Lawrence who believed that immigrants increased the wealth of a nation by augmenting its population had supported the liberal naturalization policy advocated by John Page, who dreamed of making the American republic the center and sanctuary of an international brotherhood of people. Once the events of the 1790s had disillusioned both extremes of the coalition of 1790, there could be no turning back. However, although the dream of creating a nation without boundaries had proved illusory, the commitment to serving as an "asylum for mankind" became an integral part of American republicanism. By the end of the eighteenth century attempts to restrict the rights of America's white immigrants and access to the American refuge were identified not only as unrepublican, but also as threats to the survival of the republic and liberty itself.

Throughout the eighteenth century, America's claim to be a land of liberty and opportunity was challenged by disappointed immigrants and idealists as well as

[27] Peter P. Hill, *French Perceptions of the Early American Republic* (Philadelphia: American Philosophical Society, 1988), 139–40; Craig Raymond Hanyan, "DeWitt Clinton: Years of Molding, 1769–1807" (Ph.D. diss., Harvard University, 1964).

partisan rivals. The American asylum was indeed flawed. The European discovery of the continents of North and South America led to the perception of the "newfound lands" as an additional resource to be used to promote the power and aspirations of Continental rivals. The Europeans who claimed New World lands developed imperial policies that, they believed, would give them an edge in the mercantilist battle for world supremacy. Europeans also developed the perception of America as a refuge and place of new beginnings for their social misfits and dissidents. As French and Spanish strategists erected ever higher barriers against potentially subversive settlers, the mainland colonies of British North America inherited the primary responsibility for serving as an asylum and land of opportunity for Europe's persecuted minorities, economic failures, and social liabilities.

The Anglo-American asylum that was created to serve European ends was a complex amalgam constructed to promote the visions of a wide variety of British interests, from supporters of the royal prerogative, staunch parliamentarians, political economists, and imperialists to idealists who dreamed of creating New World utopias. The American asylum that emerged was, both by accident and design, a land of expanded liberty and opportunity for Europe's persecuted Protestants, "downtrodden masses," and "wretched refuse." But it was built at the expense of dispossessed natives and enslaved Africans. The promise of colonial America was not only reserved for Europeans, it was also qualified. The product of policies designed to fulfill European goals and visions, it could, and would, be rescinded when the American refuge no longer served those ends.

Although the American asylum that was defined during the early years of the republic remained Eurocentric, it was constructed on a more permanent foundation. The promise of the American rebels to create a haven for liberty and the victims of oppression became an integral element of American republicanism in the first decades of independence. Although the republican asylum built on this pledge differed qualitatively from the more pragmatic British-American refuge, it perpetuated many colonial elements. Chattel slavery remained an important component of the new republican asylum—as it continued to expand the economic opportunity and liberty enjoyed by European immigrants and refugees.[28] On the other hand, colonial policies that had expanded the rights and freedom of European settlers also became integral components of the new American edifice.

Revolutionary idealists who had dreamed of creating an international community—a republic without boundaries in a world based on the free movement of peoples and ideas—were quickly disabused. The policies of Europe's mercantilist states and the demands of less visionary Americans soon led to the adoption of some traditional Old World distinctions between aliens and natural-born

---

[28] For the ways in which slavery underwrote political liberty in America, see Edmund S. Morgan, *American Slavery, American Freedom: The Ordeal of Colonial Virginia* (New York: Norton, 1975).

citizens. Wartime problems with tories and recent immigrants produced state laws that limited the rights of foreigners and increased American naturalization requirements. Postwar rivalries over the control of America's commerce led to the exclusion of aliens from the nation's coastal trade and a schedule of customs duties that discriminated against traders whose nations had not signed reciprocal trade agreements with the United States. However, the restraints on the rights of aliens that were adopted by postwar Americans were modeled on the liberal variants of Old World policies that had evolved in colonial times. Consequently, European immigrants and refugees in America faced fewer disabilities than their Old World counterparts and found them cheaper and easier to remove.

At the end of the eighteenth century, aliens who settled in most European countries were saddled with a wide variety of disabilities. Virtually all unnaturalized aliens were excluded from the political nation—denied the right to vote or hold office. In early modern Europe most aliens also were subject to special laws and civil restrictions that diminished their ability to compete economically with native-born subjects. The disabilities placed on aliens in eighteenth-century France typify European practice.

By law, foreigners who emigrated to France during the *ancien regime* were burdened with extra taxes (especially the *droit d'aubaine*), possessed defective rights to own or inherit land, needed special permission to marry French subjects, and were "défendu de posséder aucuns Offices, Charges, Dignités, Commissions, ny Emplois, tenir Fermes, ny exercer la Banque, le Change, le Courtage, ny aucuns Métiers." Less typical was the propensity of France's mercantilist government to nullify these restrictions. By the middle of the eighteenth century French officials, eager to augment their demographic capital, had effectively negated most alien proscriptions; disabilities were routinely waived for skilled workers and other foreigners deemed valuable to France.[29]

The numerous restrictions on the rights of aliens in England were more rigorously enforced. By the seventeenth century English law had identified two types of aliens, alien enemies "who owed allegiance to a sovereign hostile to the king of England," over whom "the Crown enjoyed absolute rights," and alien friends, who, although enjoying the protection of English law, were denied the full rights of Englishmen. In eighteenth-century England, no naturalized aliens were able to vote, hold public office, or lease, own, inherit, or bequeath real estate to their heirs; they also were denied all interest in the real property of a deceased spouse, the right to serve as guardians for their minor children or to bring legal action in matters "related to real property." Under the Navigation Acts, first

---

[29] François Bayard, "Naturalization in Lyon during the Ancien Regime," *French History*, 4 (1990), 277–316, quote on 278; William Rogers Brubaker, *Citizenship and Nationhood in France and Germany* (Cambridge: Harvard University Press, 1992), chap. 2.

passed in the 1660s, aliens were unable to trade with England's colonies or own English ships.[30]

The municipal ordinances of English cities placed even greater handicaps on alien artisans and merchants. Eighteenth-century aliens found it especially difficult to become freemen of the City of London. Unlike native Englishmen, neither alien artisans nor their sons could claim freeman status after serving an apprenticeship; for them, freedom of the city was available only through "redemption"—the payment of a 46-shilling "fine" and the special approval of London's Court of Common Council. The paucity of aliens and denizens who attained freeman status in London is evidence of both the severity and the enforcement of these handicaps; so, too, was the tendency of immigrant artisans to settle in London's suburbs, such as Spitalfields, outside the jurisdiction of the Corporation of London.[31] London's traders also were effectively prevented from competing on equal terms with "natural-born" Englishmen. Under the terms of a charter first granted in 1640, the City of London was awarded the right to collect special duties on the packing and transporting of all goods imported into London by aliens and denizens; an additional duty was levied on alien-owned merchandise "exported on any vessel on the Thames, or one of its wharves, from within the City's liberties or suburbs." The revenues generated by these "package and scavage" duties is evidence of the assiduity with which they were enforced. At the end of the seventeenth century, the right to collect these duties was sold for £1,200 a year; records from the 1760s show that the revenue from London's alien duties "seldom fell below £1,000 per year."[32]

Not surprisingly, alien disabilities escalated during times of war, in both the Old World and the New. In the early years of their Revolution, French republicans followed in the footsteps of their American predecessors—inviting all people to participate, as full *citoyens*, in their republican experiment. French revolutionaries, believing the *droit d'aubaine* "contrary to the principles of fraternity that ought to unite all men, whatever their country or government" declared it "forever abolished." In this decree, delegates to France's National Assembly, like their American counterparts, opened up their newly free government to "all the peoples of the earth," proclaiming that all would enjoy "the sacred and inviolable rights of humanity" now enshrined on French soil. The French Constitution of 1791 promised that foreigners would be subject "to the same criminal and police laws as are French citizens . . . their person, their goods, their

[30] Daniel Statt, "The Birthright of an Englishman: The Practice of Naturalization and Denization of Immigrants under the Later Stuarts and Early Hanoverians," in Huguenot Society of London, *Proceedings*, 25 (1989), 62–64; quotes on 62, 63.

[31] Daniel Statt, *Foreigners and Englishmen: The Controversy over Immigration and Population, 1660–1760* (Newark: University of Delaware Press, 1995), 176–76; idem, "The City of London and the Controversy over Immigration, 1660–1722," *Historical Journal*, 33 (1990), 57–58.

[32] Statt, "The City of London," 53–61, quotes on 53 and 60.

industry . . . equally protected by law."[33] However, wartime stress and the definition of French citizenship soon produced a reign of terror that led to the arrest, incarceration, and execution of foreign-born freedom-fighters and subjected aliens to police surveillance, while banning their political activity and restricting their movements, residence, and commercial activities.[34]

During the Wars of the French Revolution, English officials also transformed foreigners into scapegoats and ran roughshod of the rights of alien friends and enemies alike. In 1793 an Act of Parliament extended the status of alien enemies to all future immigrants. This Act required the registration of all aliens arriving in England after 1792 and gave the crown the power to deny entry to foreigners "of any description" who might threaten "the safety and tranquillity of the kingdom." Those who failed to register or gave false information were liable to prosecution and faced "mandatory expulsion . . . for whatever period the court thought fit." Expelled aliens who returned prematurely were to be "transported for life."[35] In 1798 aliens who had arrived in England prior to 1792 also were required to report themselves; and, if "suspected of being a 'dangerous person' could be detained, interrogated and then either released, or detained 'for such time . . . as His Majesty shall think fit' or removed." These regulations remained in force through most of the period between 1798 and 1816 and were not completely removed until 1826.[36]

Americans were not immune to the temptation to blame domestic discord on the machinations of foreign *provocateurs*. However, republican fear of concentrated power and commitment to natural rights and the rule of law prevented the wartime transformation of all resident foreigners into alien enemies at the mercy of the state. During the Revolution, American rebels had exerted pressure on, intimidated, and confiscated the property of inveterate tories. But their primary animus was aimed not at aliens, but at Americans, who, having experienced the blessings of liberty, had joined the British plot to destroy it. American rebels who questioned the principles and motives of aliens in their midst adopted relatively mild measures to neutralize potential subversives. State laws that increased naturalization requirements and banned aliens from some forms of commercial activity were a far cry from measures adopted by Revolutionary France. England's alien program was copied in America by the fearful and newly xenophobic Federalists in 1798, but such measures were rejected as unrepublican in the election of 1800. When during the War of 1812, the American government was actually confronted with the problem of dealing with alien enemies during wartime, it contented itself with implementing the Alien Enemies Act that

---

[33] Brubaker, *Citizenship and Nationhood in France and Germany*, 44–45, quotes from the French National Assembly's Decree of August 1790 and the Constitution of 1791.

[34] Ibid., 46–47.

[35] Vaughan Bevan, *The Development of British Immigration Law* (London: Croom Helm, 1986), 58–59; 93, n. 68, quotes from Act of 1793 (33 Geo. III c. 4).

[36] Ibid., 60–61.

had been passed in 1798. Under this Act, unnaturalized British males over the age of 14 years were required to register and, if they resided in strategically sensitive areas, faced relocation into interior areas of the United States. No attempts were made by President Madison's administration to claim unlimited power over "alien enemies," increase the government's authority over "alien friends," or revive the Federalist program of 1798.

European immigrants who settled in republican America faced few legal proscriptions in times of peace or war. In the early republic, Americans continued the colonial practice of limiting the heritability of real estate purchased by aliens; they also continued to pass legislation that conveyed full titles to foreign landowners and their heirs. A similar pattern of rarely enforced legal impediments emerged in America's corporate cities, where city officials ignored occupational restrictions or facilitated their removal. In the first years of independence, Americans were just as casual about enforcing political restrictions on unnaturalized foreigners. Although the political battles of the 1790s produced a closer scrutiny of a voter's credentials, they also gave party leaders a vested interest in securing the speedy naturalization of their foreign-born supporters.

Old World governments not only saddled foreigners with far more disabilities, but also hampered their removal by making naturalization difficult, expensive, and, in some cases, impossible. In Germany, nonethnic foreigners generally remained aliens forever, as citizenship was reserved for those of German ancestry.[37] Prior to 1844, English naturalization was limited to propertied aliens who could pay the £60 to £100 it cost to shepherd a private act through Parliament and to foreigners whose religious beliefs allowed them to subscribe to the oath of abjuration.[38] England's religious test closed naturalization off to Catholic and Jewish immigrants until 1791 and 1826, respectively. Such aliens, along with those unable to pay for a private bill of naturalization, could never be more than second-class citizens.[39] Although a grant of denization was cheaper and required no religious oaths, it could convey only limited rights. As denization was an act of the royal prerogative, the king was prohibited from endowing an alien with the full rights of natural-born Englishmen, which only an Act of Parliament could do. As an exercise of the royal prerogative, English kings were not bound to

[37] Brubaker, *Citizenship and Nationhood in France and Germany*, chaps. 3, 4, and 6.

[38] In the eighteenth century aliens who petitioned Parliament for naturalization were required to pay almost £30 in fees to officials in the House of Commons and the House of Lords. Although denization could cost up to £25, these fees were often remitted. Statt, "The Practice of Naturalization and Denization," 66–67; idem, "The City of London," 46. The comparatively high cost of naturalization in England continues today. The fees charged for naturalization (in U.S. dollars) in the 1980s are: $30 in Canada, $50 in the United States, $82 in France, $272 in the United Kingdom, and for West Germany, 75 per cent of the applicant's monthly income. William Rogers Brubaker, "Citizenship and Naturalization: Policies and Politics," in idem, ed., *Immigration and the Politics of Citizenship in Europe and North America* (Lantham, Md.: University Press of America, 1989), table 2 on 126–27.

[39] Cecil Roth, A *History of the Jews in England* (Oxford: Clarendon, 1941), 245.

confer a fixed set of rights. Although an endenized alien was usually given the right to "hold and acquire land, he could not inherit: and a child of his, born before denization, could not inherit from him." Some letters patent removed an alien's obligation to pay special taxes and customs duties; others did not. Some grants were limited to the life of the applicant; others conveyed the stipulated rights to the alien and his heirs.[40]

The absence of a general naturalization statute in England, prior to its Aliens Act of 1844, also made the conferral of British subjectship by Act of Parliament somewhat capricious because there were no specified conditions to fulfill. The rights that Parliament granted were fixed, In the eighteenth century all naturalized aliens (as opposed to those who were endenized) enjoyed the full rights of British subjects, with a few exceptions. The most notable of these was the inability of naturalized subjects to vote, hold high political office, or receive royal land grants. After 1774 a naturalized alien also was unable to claim the foreign trade rights and immunities of the native-born until "he had resided in the British dominions for seven years subsequent" to his naturalization, without being "absent out of the same for a longer space than two months at any one time during the said seven years."[41] In addition, although the rights granted by naturalization were fixed by statute, Parliament was not bound to grant the petitions of all aliens who met the religious test and paid the requisite fees, but it usually did.[42]

Naturalization procedures and the rights they conveyed were much more liberal in the American republic. In the early decades of independence, Americans sorted through their colonial heritage, discarding nonrepublican elements and retaining those that seemed consistent with their revolutionary ideals and priorities. When this process was applied to the formulation of naturalization policy, Americans rejected the British practice of creating a separate and inferior class of citizens (denizens) while perpetuating the most liberal features of the naturalization procedures that had evolved under British tutelage. In doing so, American statesmen ensured that republican naturalization would be more universally accessible, on fixed terms, and remove an alien's legal handicaps more quickly, cheaply, and completely than in the Old World. During

---

[40] John Mervyn Jones, *British Nationality Law and Practice* (Oxford: Clarendon, 1947), 67 (quote); Statt, *Foreigners and Englishmen*, 33–34.

[41] Jones, *British Nationality Law and Practice*, 76 (quote, from 14 Geo. III, c. 84).

[42] In 1844 English naturalization became even more an act of grace and favor, rather than a right to be claimed by qualified applicants. Under the Aliens Act of 1844, most naturalizations were granted by England's Secretary of State, who could, when issuing the certificate, include restrictions on "the rights and capacities" of naturalized aliens. One of the most common restrictions included was the proviso that "the grantee 'should continue to reside permanently within the United Kingdom, and that, if at any time thereafter he should voluntarily be absent for a period of six months without licence in writing under the hand of one of His Majesty's Principal Secretaries, he should be deemed to have ceased to reside permanently in the United Kingdom; and then, in such case, the certificate and all the rights and capacities thereby provided shall cease.' " As Jones points out, "the effect of this condition was that . . . naturalization thus granted was limited in its practical effect to the period of the naturalized subject's residence in the United Kingdom." Ibid., 77–80.

the 1790s full American citizenship could be claimed by any free, white immigrant, regardless of his ethnicity or religious beliefs, who fulfilled the requirements established by statute. Under the Act of 1802,[43] any free, white immigrant who had resided in any of the American states for five years, registered as an alien, and had declared his intention to seek American citizenship could be naturalized by taking an oath to uphold the American Constitution and paying the necessary fees, which ranged from 50 cents for alien reports and registration to 2 dollars for a naturalization certificate. Naturalized aliens suffered only one permanent disability—that of being ineligible for election as president, or vice president, of the United States.[44]

America's revolutionary appeal to "Ye that dare oppose not only the tyranny but the tyrant" began the tradition of reserving a special space in the American asylum for vanquished freedom fighters.[45] Few Americans have denied their obligation to offer political sanctuary to the victims of tyrannical governments, but they have always been less enthusiastic about serving as a regenerative haven for the victims of social or economic oppression. Republican statesmen who were committed to creating government by the people feared the introduction of "the servile masses" who could be manipulated by demagogues and incipient tyrants. These fears generated laws that prohibited the landing of transported convicts and reduced the number of African slaves brought into republican America. Expressing similar doubts about destitute and "infirm" immigrants, the American states adopted less stringent measures that required little more than the "sponsorship" of impoverished immigrants, in the form of bonds that would prevent them from becoming public charges.

From the inception of the republic, America's preferred immigrant was the propertied, industrious, committed republican, rather then the "wretched refuse" from Europe's "teeming shores." Nonetheless, both self-interest and principle ensured that the American door, and citizenship, would remain open to Europe's "downtrodden masses." After the Revolution, many Americans still subscribed to the belief that a nation's wealth and power expanded along with its population; others had a vested interest in securing the services of indentured servants, tenants, or wage laborers. The writings of Radical Whigs that linked tyranny, poverty, emigration, and depopulation also could be used to portray impoverished immigrants as the oppressed, but uncowed, victims of despotic government. According to *Cato's Letters*, free governments were an irresistible magnet to men "who naturally run when they dare from Slavery and Wretchedness, whithersoever they can help themselves." Since submission to tyranny trans-

[43] The Act of 1802 is used for these comparisons because its basic provisions remained in force through most of the nineteenth century. Naturalization under the Acts of 1790 and 1795 was even easier, but the Naturalization Act of 1798 required a fourteen-year residence until it was repealed in 1802.

[44] Fees from Naturalization Act of 1802, *Public Statutes at Large of the United States of America*, II, 153–55.

[45] Quote from Thomas Paine, *Common Sense*, in *The Life and Major Writings of Thomas Paine*, ed. Philip S. Foner, 2 vols. (New York: Citadel Press, 1945), I, 30.

formed "Obedience to equal Laws, and Submission to just Authority ... into a servile and crouching Subjection ... , complaisant and respective Behaviour into slavish flattery, and supple homage to Power; Meekness and Humility into Dejection, [and] Poorness of Spirit," only those who refused to be overcome by tyranny would "dare" to escape its clutches and seek out liberty.[46]

As they hammered out the nation's immigration and naturalization policies, America's revolutionary generation concluded that the preservation of the American republic and liberty itself required both a single class of equal citizens and free access to the American asylum and citizenship for European victims of oppressive regimes who yearned "to breathe free." The resolution of the contradictory impulses generated by these two imperatives led to laws that established a period of tutelage for immigrants who were inexperienced in self-government and the proper exercise of liberty; excluded convicts who were banished to America by their governments, who could not be seen as refugees seeking liberty nor as possessing the qualities required for republican citizenship; and denied naturalization and citizenship to nonwhites, who were assumed to be Africans debased by slavery and consequently could not be entrusted with the power to destroy liberty and the American republic. Clearly, the "mankind" that revolutionary Americans served was selective and remained European. Yet, the principles that were adopted in the early republic would eventually allow Americans to fulfill their pledge. After the Civil War access to the American asylum and republican citizenship was no longer restricted to whites. By the terms of an Act passed on July 14, 1870, naturalization was "extended to aliens of African nativity and to persons of African descent." Following the passage of the Act of 1870 and the nation's repudiation of the racist immigration policies of the "Progressive Era," Americans were finally able to meet the challenge issued by Thomas Paine in 1776—"to prepare in time an asylum for mankind."[47]

---

[46] Quotes from David L. Jacobsen, ed., *The English Libertarian Heritage: From the Writings of John Tren-chard and Thomas Gordon in the Independent Whig and Cato's Letters* (New York: Bobbs-Merrill, 1965), 134 (Letter 62), 164 (Letter 66).

[47] Act of 1870 quoted in James Kettner, *The Development of American Citizenship, 1608–1870* (Chapel Hill: University of North Carolina Press, 1978), 345, n. 31; final quote from Thomas Paine's *Common Sense.*

Select Bibliography

MANUSCRIPTS

United States

1. National Archives, Washington, D.C.

RG 36. Bureau of the Customs.
Passenger Lists of Vessels Arriving at Philadelphia, 1800–1882. National Archives
Microfilm M-360.
RG 45. Office of Naval Records and Library.
War of 1812—Alien Papers. University of Delaware Microfilm.
RG 59. Department of State.
War of 1812 Papers. "U.S. Marshals' Returns of Alien Enemies." National Archives
Microfilm M-588.
Miscellaneous Letters to the Department of State, 1789–1906. National Archives
Microfilm M-179.
RG 360. Papers of the Continental Congress and Constitutional Convention.
Papers of the Continental Congress, 1774–1789. National Archives Microfilm M-247.

2. Library of Congress, Washington, D.C.

Adams Papers. Microfilm.
The Papers of Gouverneur Morris. Microfilm.
The Papers of Robert Morris. Microfilm.
George Washington Papers. Microfilm.

3. Computerized Data

Inter-university Consortium for Political and Social Research, "Candidacy and Constituency Statistics of Elections in the United States, 1788–1984." File 7757.

Great Britain

Public Record Office, London, England
American Papers in the House of Lords Record Office. Microfilm.
Journals of the House of Lords. Microfilm.
Foreign Office Archives, American Correspondence. Microfilm.

NATURALIZATION RECORDS

United States

Dewey, D. M., comp. *The Naturalization Laws of the United States.* Rochester, N.Y.: Lee, Mann & Co., 1855.
The Public Statutes at Large of the United States of America, 1789–1873. 17 vols. Boston: Charles C. Little and James Brown, 1850–1873.

Maryland

1. Maryland State Archives, Annapolis, Md.

Baltimore County Court.
Minute Books.
Naturalization Docket.
Frederick County Court.
Minute Books.
Naturalization Record.

2. Maryland State Library, Annapolis, Md.

Session Laws of the State of Maryland.

3. National Archives and Record Center, Philadelphia.

RG 21. Records of the District Courts of the United States.
U.S. District Court for the District of Maryland.
Minute Books.
U.S. Circuit Court for the District of Maryland.
Minute Books. National Archives Microfilm M-987.

4. Published Works

Browne, William Hand, ed. *Archives of Maryland.* 72 vols. Baltimore: Maryland Historical Society, 1883–present.
Eaker, Lorena Shell. "The Germans in North Carolina." *The Palatine Immigrant,* 6 (1980), 3–34.
Laws of the State of Maryland. Sessional volumes. Annapolis: General Assembly. Annapolis, Md: Maryland State Library.
Wyand, Jeffrey A., and Florence L. Wyand. *Colonial Maryland Naturalizations.* Baltimore: Genealogical Publishing Co., 1975.

Massachusetts

1. Massachusetts State Archives, Boston

The Great and General Court of Massachusetts.
Naturalization Petitions.

2. Essex County Court House, Salem, Mass.

Essex County Court of Common Pleas.
Record Books.
Naturalization Petitions.

3. Suffolk County Court House, Boston

Suffolk County Court of Common Pleas.
Dockets.
Minute Books.
Naturalization Petitions.
Supreme Judicial Court of Massachusetts.
Record Books.
Naturalization Petitions.

4. National Archives and Record Center, Waltham, Mass.

RG 21. Records of the District Courts of the United States.
U.S. District Court for the District of Massachusetts.
Minute Books.
Records of Primary Declarations, vol. A, 1798–1845.
Naturalization Petitions.
U.S. Circuit Court for the District of Massachusetts.
Minute Books.

5. Published Works

The Acts and Resolves, Public and Private, of the Province of Massachusetts Bay
[1692–1786]. 21 vols. Boston: Wright & Potter, 1869–1922.
"Information for Immigrants to the New-England States." Boston: 1795. In Houghton
Library, Harvard University, Cambridge, Mass.
Laws of Massachusetts, 1780 to 1800. Boston: Wright & Potter, 1886.

New York

1. Published Sources for the Colony and State of New York

Journal of the Legislative Council of the Colony of New York. 2 vols. Albany: Weed,
Parsons, 1861.
*Laws of the State of New York Passed at the Sessions of the Legislature held in the Years
1785 . . . 1800, Inclusive.* 4 vols. Albany: Weed, Parsons and Company, 1886–1887.

2. Delaware County Court House, Delhi, N.Y.

Delaware County Court of Common Pleas.
  Minute Books.
  Naturalization Register.
  Naturalization Petitions.
Delaware County Court of Oyer and Terminer.
  Minute Books.

3. New York County (New York City)

National Archives, Washington, D.C.
  RG 21 Records of the District Courts of the United States.
    U.S. District Court for the District of Southern New York.
    Minute Books. National Archives Microfilm M-886.
    U.S. Circuit Court for the District of Southern New York.
    Minute Books. National Archives Microfilm M-854.

4. Published Works.

New York City Common Council. *Minutes of the Common Council of the City of New York, 1784–1831.* 19 vols. New York: M. B. Brown, 1917.

Scott, Kenneth, comp. *Early New York Naturalizations: Abstracts of Naturalization Records from Federal, State, and Local Courts, 1792–1840.* Baltimore: Genealogical Publishing Co., 1981.

Pennsylvania

1. Federal Archives and Record Center, Philadelphia

RG 21 Records of the District Courts of the United States
  U.S. District Court for the District of Eastern Pennsylvania.
    Minute Books.
    Landing Reports of Aliens. Book A, 1798–1807.
    Naturalization Petitions.
  U.S. Circuit Court for the District of Eastern Pennsylvania.
    Minute Books.

2. Archives for the City and County of Philadelphia

Philadelphia Court of Common Pleas.
  Declarations of Intent.
  Naturalization Petitions.
  Alien Registers.
Philadelphia's Mayor's Court.
  Declarations of Intent.
  Naturalization Petitions.
  Alien Registers.
Philadelphia Court of Quarter Sessions.
  Declarations of Intent.
  Naturalization Petitions.
  Alien Registers.

3. Published Works

Linn, John B., and William H. Engle, eds. *Pennsylvania Archives, Second Series.* 19 vols. Harrisburg: B. F. Meyers, 1876–1893.

MacKinney, Gertrude, and Charles F. Hoban, eds. *Pennsylvania Archives,* 8th ser. 8 vols. Harrisburg, Penn.: 1931–1935.

Mitchell, James T., and Henry Flanders, comp. *The Statutes at Large of Pennsylvania from 1682 to 1801.* 16 vols. Harrisburg, Penn.: Clarence M. Busch, State Printer, 1896–1908.

Rhode Island

Federal Archives and Record Center, Waltham, Mass.
RG 21 Records of the District Courts of the United States.
    U.S. District Court for the District of Rhode Island.
        Miscellaneous Papers.
        Report of Aliens made to the Clerk of the U.S., 1790–1798, District Court [of Massachusetts].
        Report of Aliens made to the Collector of Customs, 1798–1808, Providence, R. I.

South Carolina

1. National Archives, Washington, D.C.

RG 21 Records of the District Courts of the United States
Record of Admissions to Citizenship, District of South Carolina, 1790–1857. National Archives Microfilm M-1183.

2. Published Works

Cooper, Thomas, ed. *The Statutes at Large of South Carolina.* 4 vols. Columbia, S.C.: A. S. Johnston, 1836–1838.

Holcomb, Brent H., comp. *South Carolina Naturalizations, 1783–1850.* Baltimore: Genealogical Publishing Co., 1985.

Virginia

1. Virginia State Library, Richmond, Va.

U.S. District Court for the District of Virginia.
    Ended Cases, 1799.
    Alien Reports made to the Clerk of the U.S. District for the District of Virginia, 1798–1799.
Collector of Customs, City Point, Va.
    "Register of White Persons Being Aliens Who Have Come to Reside in the Territory of the United States," 1799–1800.

2. Published Works

Hening, William Waller, ed. *The Statutes at Large: Being a Collection of All the Laws of Virginia from the First Session of the Legislature, in the Year 1619.* 13 vols. Richmond: George Cochran, 1809–1823.

Shepherd, Samuel, ed. *The Statutes at Large of Virginia, 1792–1806.* 3 vols. Richmond: Samuel Shepherd, 1836.

Winfree, Waverly K., comp. *The Laws of Virginia, Being a Supplement to Hening's, The Statutes at Large, 1700–1750.* Richmond: Virginia State Library, 1971.

NEWSPAPERS AND PERIODICALS

England

Bristol, *Felix Farley's Bristol Journal*, 1783–1800.
Leeds, *Leeds Mercury*, 1783–1800.
London, *Daily Universal Register*, 1785–1800.
London, *London Chronicle*, 1774–1776, 1783–1790.
Newcastle, *Newcastle Journal*, 1783–1786.

Ireland

Belfast, *Belfast News-Letter*, 1783–1800.
Belfast, *Northern Star*, 1792–1797.
Dublin, *Public Register*, 1783–1785.

United States

Alexandria, *Virginia Journal and Alexandria Advertiser*, 1784–1789.
Baltimore, *Maryland Gazette or the Baltimore General Advertiser*, 1783–1796.
Baltimore, *Maryland Journal and Baltimore Advertiser*, 1783–1797.
Charleston, *South Carolina Gazette and General Advertiser*, 1783–1785.
Charleston, *State Gazette of South Carolina*, 1784–1798.
Hartford, *Connecticut Courant and Weekly Intelligencer*, 1783–1784.
Newport, Rhode Island, *The Guardian of Liberty*, 1800.
New York City, *American Minerva and the New York Evening Advertiser* [title varies], 1793–1797.
New York City, *New York Gazette and Weekly Mercury*, 1783.
Philadelphia, *The American Museum, or, Repository of Ancient and Modern Fugitive Pieces, &c. Prose and Poetical*, Matthew Carey, ed., 1787–1795.
Philadelphia, *Independent Gazetteer* [title varies], 1783–1796.
Philadelphia, *Pennsylvania Evening Herald*, 1785.
Philadelphia, *Pennsylvania Gazette*, 1783–1784.
Philadelphia, *Pennsylvania Packet and General Advertiser*, 1784–1789.
Philadelphia, *Philadelphia Gazette* [title varies], 1794–1800.
Philadelphia, *The Universal Gazette*, 1799.
Raleigh, N.C., *Raleigh Register and North-Carolina Weekly Advertiser*, 1800.
Washington, Penn., *The Herald of Liberty*, 1800.

MAJOR COLLECTIONS AND STATUTES

American State Papers: Documents, Legislative and Executive, of the Congress of the United States. 38 vols. Washington, D.C.: Gales and Seaton, 1832–1861.

Bond, Phineas. "Letters of Phineas Bond, British Consul at Philadelphia, to the Foreign Office of Great Britain, 1787, 1788, 1789." Ed. J. Franklin Jameson. American Historical Association. *Annual Report for the Year 1896.*

——. "Letters of Phineas Bond, British Consul at Philadelphia, to the Foreign Office of Great Britain, 1790–1794." Ed. J. Franklin Jameson. American Historical Association. *Annual Report for the Year 1897.*

Brigham, Clarence S., ed. "British Royal Proclamations Relating to America, 1603–1783." American Antiquarian Society. *Transactions and Collections,* 12 (1911).

Brodhead, John Romeyn. *Documents Relative to the Colonial History of the State of New-York.* Ed. E. B. O'Callaghan. 11 vols. Albany: Weed, Parsons and Company, 1853–1861.

Bush, Bernard, comp. *Laws of the Royal Colony of New Jersey, 1703–1745.* Trenton: New Jersey State Library, Archives and History Bureau, 1977.

Calendar of State Papers, Colonial Series, America and West Indies, 1574–1733. 40 vols. London: Longman et al., 1860–1939.

Calendar of State Papers, Domestic Series, 1547–1704. 80 vols. London: His Majesty's Stationery Office, 1865–present.

Candler, Allen D., ed. *The Colonial Records of the State of Georgia.* 25 vols. Atlanta: Charles P. Byrd, 1904–1916.

Cobbett, William, and John Wright, eds. *The Parliamentary History of England from the Earliest Period to the Year 1803.* 36 vols. London: T. C. Hansard, 1806–1820.

Dallas, A. J., ed. *Reports of Cases Ruled and Adjudged in the Several Courts of the United States and of Pennsylvania Held at the Seat of the Federal Government.* 2 vols. Philadelphia: Aurora, 1798.

Davies, K. G. *Documents of the American Revolution, 1770–1783.* 21 vols. Dublin: Irish University Press, 1972–1981.

Donnan, Elizabeth, ed. *Documents Illustrative of the History of the Slave Trade to America.* 4 vols. Washington, D.C.: Carnegie Institution of Washington, 1930–1935.

Dow, George F., and Mary G. Thresher, eds. *Records and Files of the Quarterly Courts of Essex County, Massachusetts.* 9 vols. Salem, Mass.: Essex Institute, 1911–1975.

Elliot, Jonathan, ed. *Debates on the Adoption of the Federal Constitution in the Convention held at Philadelphia.* 2d ed., 5 vols. Philadelphia: J. B. Lippincott, 1836–1845.

Farrand, Max, ed. *The Records of the Federal Convention of 1787.* 4 vols. New Haven: Yale University Press, 1911–1937.

Faust, Albert Bernhardt, and Gaius Marcus Brumbaugh, eds. *Lists of Swiss Emigrants in the Eighteenth Century to the American Colonies.* 2 vols. Baltimore: Genealogical Publishing Co., 1920–1925.

Force, Peter, ed. *American Archives: A Documentary History of the English Colonies in North America.* 4th ser., 6 vols. Washington, D.C.: 1837–1846.

Gales, Joseph, ed. *Annals of the Congress of the United States.* 42 vols. Washington, D.C.: Gales and Seaton, 1834–1856.

Giuseppi, M. S., ed. *Naturalizations of Foreign Protestants in the American Colonies Pursuant to Statute 13 George II, c.7.* Huguenot Society of London, *Publications* 24 (1921).

Hansard, T. C., et al., eds. *The Parliamentary Debates.* London: His Majesty's Stationery Office, 1825–present.

Hastings, Hugh, ed. *Ecclesiastical Records of the State of New York.* 7 vols. Albany: J. B. Lyon, 1901–1916.

Hoadley, Charles J., et al., eds. *The Public Records of the State of Connecticut, 1776–1803.* 11 vols. Hartford: 1894–1967.

Jensen, Merrill, et al., eds. *The Documentary History of the Ratification of the Constitution by the States*. Madison: State Historical Society of Wisconsin, 1976–present.

Journals of the Continental Congress, 1774–1789. Ed. Worthington C. Ford et al. 34 vols. Washington, D.C.: Government Printing Office, 1904–1907.

Kingsbury, Susan Myra, ed. *The Records of the Virginia Company of London*. 4 vols. Washington, D.C.: Government Printing Office, 1906–1935.

Labaree, Leonard Woods, ed. *Royal Instructions to British Colonial Governors*. 2 vols. New York: D. Appleton-Century, 1935.

Madison, James. *Notes of Debates in the Federal Convention of 1787, Reported by James Madison*. Ed. Adrienne Koch. Athens: University of Ohio Press, 1995.

Ruffhead, Owen, ed. *Statutes at Large, from Magna Charta, to the Twenty-fifth Year of the Reign of King George the Third, Inclusive*. 10 vols. London: Charles Eyre and Andrew Straham, Printers, 1786.

Rushworth, John. *Historical Collections, The Second Part, Containing the Principal Matters Which Happened from the Dissolution of the PARLIAMENT on the 10th of March 4 Car.I 1628/9 Until the Summoning of Another Parliament . . . April 13,1640*. London: John Wright and Richard Chiswell, 1680.

Saunders, William L., and Walter Clark, eds. *The Colonial/State Records of North Carolina*. 26 vols. Goldsboro, N.C.: Nash Brothers, 1886–1907.

Shaw, William A., ed. *Letters of Denization and Acts of Naturalization for Aliens in England and Ireland, 1603–1700*. Huguenot Society of London, *Publications*, 18 (1911).

——. *Letters of Denization and Acts of Naturalization for Aliens in England and Ireland, 1701–1800*. Huguenot Society of London, *Publications*, 27 (1923).

Stock, Leo F., ed. *Proceedings and Debates of the British Parliaments Respecting North America, 1452–1754*. 5 vols. Washington, D.C.: Carnegie Institution of Washington, 1924–1941.

Thorpe, Francis Newton, ed. *The Federal and State Constitutions, Colonial Charters, and other Organic Laws of the States, Territories, and Colonies Now or Heretofore Forming the United States of America*. 7 vols. Washington, D.C.: Government Printing Office, 1909.

Index

Tories, American. *See* Loyalists
Tory party in England, 52
Trans-Atlantic crossing and white immigrants,
    abuses of, 93–94; and shipboard deaths, 95–
    98; and over-crowding, 93, 97–98; and
    passenger acts, 94–95. *See also* Immigrant
    mortality
Trans-Atlantic crossing and African slaves, and
    over-crowding, 97–98; and shipboard deaths,
    93–98. *See also* Immigrant mortality
Treaty of Paris, 1763, 123
Treaty of Paris, 1783, 202–3
Tucker, Josiah, 121, 124
Tucker, Thomas (S.C.): and progressive
    citizenship, 258; and states' rights, 258–59
Tuscarora War, 79

Ulster, settlement of, 29
United Irishmen, in America, 290–93, 301,
    308

Variable duties, 83–85
Varick, Richard (N.Y.C., mayor), 268, 298
Varnum, Joseph (Mass.), 274
Vergennes, Charles Gravier, Comte de, 141
Vermont, 183; and alien landowership, 218;
    naturalization in, 224; and progressive
    citizenship, 224; *Vermont Gazette*, 261
Virginia: alien disabilities in, 206–8, 221–22;
    and alien rights, 286–87; anti-Catholicism in,
    73n8, 83; antipathy toward British
    immigrants, 206–8; and Catholic immigrants,
    83–85, 143–44; and convicts, 73, 83–86, 164;
    demographic preferences of, 5–6; and
    denization, 65, 223; and desirable
    immigrants, 198; and free blacks, 107; and
    immigrant recruitment, 32, 58, 83–86, 216,
    226–27, 235; and indentured servants, 100–
    103; infant mortality in, 105; and Irish
    immigrants, 83; and loyalists, 201–3; and
    mercantilist beliefs, 228; naturalization in,
    180, 206–7, 224; and Port Bill of 1784, 208;
    and progressive citizenship, 206–7, 224; and
    Protestant immigrants, 83–85; religious
    freedom, 58, 226–27; religious intolerance in,
    57–58; and right of expatriation, 253;

and slave duties, 83–85; and slave natural
    increase, 235; and slave trade, 235; and
    racial fears, 83–84, 235; and undesirable
    immigrants, 83; and variable duties, 83–85
Volitional citizenship, 155, 254–55
Voltaire, François-Marie-Arouet de, 130

Wallace, Robert, on population growth, 128
Walloon refugees, in England, 43n3, 44
War of 1812, 320–22; and enemy aliens, 315–
    21
Warren, Alderman, on Irish right to emigrate,
    168
Warren, James (Mass.), 293
Washington, George, 214; and immigration,
    244; and land speculation, 246
Watson, Elkanah, 214
Wealth distribution, in British North America,
    118; and slavery, 118
West Indies, French, 124. *See also* St.
    Domingue
West Indies, and American trade, 247
Western Design, 32
Wetherell, Charles, 115
Whig party in England: and American
    grievances, 132–33; and naturalization, 51,
    62–63; and Parliamentary supremacy, 133;
    and religious toleration, 51; and the royal
    prerogative, 51. *See also* Rockingham
    Whigs
Whiskey rebellion, 262–63, 324
White, Alexander (Va.), 259
Wilkes, John, 134
William III (of England), 52; as Protestant
    Protector, 54
Williams, John (N.Y.), 274
Williams, Robert (N.C.), 271, 279
Williams, Roger, 46n11
Williamson, Charles, 294, 296
Williamson, Hugh (N.C.), 253
Wilson, James, 233, 253
Winchester, James (Md.), 299
Wokeck, Marianne, 96

Xenophobia: in America, 57, 64, 72, 260; in
    England, 43–44, 49–52